Advances in Fractional Integral Inequalities: Theory and Applications

Advances in Fractional Integral Inequalities: Theory and Applications

Guest Editors

Armando Gallegos
Jorge E. Macías Díaz

MDPI

Basel • Beijing • Wuhan • Barcelona • Belgrade • Novi Sad • Cluj • Manchester

Guest Editors

Armando Gallegos
Departamento de Ciencias
Exactas y Tecnología
Universidad de Guadalajara
Lagos de Moreno
Mexico

Jorge E. Macías Díaz
Department of Mathematics
Tallinn University
Tallinn
Estonia

Editorial Office

MDPI AG
Grosspeteranlage 5
4052 Basel, Switzerland

This is a reprint of the Special Issue, published open access by the journal *Fractal and Fractional* (ISSN 2504-3110), freely accessible at: https://www.mdpi.com/journal/fractalfract/special_issues/DE0AUFMY8C.

For citation purposes, cite each article independently as indicated on the article page online and as indicated below:

Lastname, A.A.; Lastname, B.B. Article Title. *Journal Name* **Year**, *Volume Number*, Page Range.

ISBN 978-3-7258-7883-3 (Hbk)
ISBN 978-3-7258-7884-0 (PDF)
https://doi.org/10.3390/books978-3-7258-7884-0

Contents

About the Editors

Armando Gallegos

Armando Gallegos is a full-time professor and researcher in the Department of Exact Sciences and Technology at the University Center of Los Lagos, University of Guadalajara, Mexico. He currently leads the Academic Group on Modeling and Applied Mathematics. His main research areas are fractional calculus, integrals of motion of nonlinear systems, mathematical oncology, and mathematical modeling of physical and biological systems in general.

Jorge E. Macías Díaz

Jorge E. Macías Díaz is a full-time professor in the Department of Mathematics and Physics at the Autonomous University of Aguascalientes, Mexico, and an associate professor in the Department of Mathematics and Didactics of Mathematics at Tallinn University, Estonia. He is a member of the Mexican Academy of Sciences. His areas of interest are numerical analysis, fractional calculus, mathematical modeling and partial differential equations, and their applications.

fractal and fractional

MDPI

Article

Boundedness and Sobolev-Type Estimates for the Exponentially Damped Riesz Potential with Applications to the Regularity Theory of Elliptic PDEs

Waqar Afzal [1], Mujahid Abbas [2,3], Jorge E. Macías-Díaz [4,5,*], Armando Gallegos [6] and Yahya Almalki [7]

1 Abdus Salam School of Mathematical Sciences, Government College University, 68-B, New Muslim Town, Lahore 54600, Pakistan; waqar_afzal_22@sms.edu.pk
2 Department of Mechanical Engineering Sciences, Faculty of Engineering and the Built Environment, Doornfontein Campus, University of Johannesburg, Johannesburg 2092, South Africa; mujahida@uj.ac.za
3 Department of Medical Research, China Medical University, Taichung 406040, Taiwan
4 Department of Mathematics and Didactics of Mathematics, Tallinn University, 10120 Tallinn, Estonia
5 Department of Mathematics and Physics, Autonomous University of Aguascalientes, Aguascalientes 20100, Aguascalientes, Mexico
6 Departamento de Ciencias Exactas y Tecnología, Centro Universitario de los Lagos, Universidad de Guadalajara, Enrique Díaz de León 1144, Colonia Paseos de la Montaña, Lagos de Moreno 47460, Jalisco, Mexico; armando.gallegos@academicos.udg.mx
7 Department of Mathematics, College of Sciences, King Khalid University, Abha 61413, Saudi Arabia; yalmalki@kku.edu.sa
* Correspondence: jemacias@correo.uaa.mx

Abstract: This paper investigates a new class of fractional integral operators, namely, the exponentially damped Riesz-type operators within the framework of variable exponent Lebesgue spaces $L^{\mathrm{p}(\cdot)}$. To the best of our knowledge, the boundedness of such operators has not been addressed in any existing functional setting. We establish their boundedness under appropriate log-Hölder continuity and growth conditions on the exponent function $\mathrm{p}(\cdot)$. To highlight the novelty and practical relevance of the proposed operator, we conduct a comparative analysis demonstrating its effectiveness in addressing convergence, regularity, and stability of solutions to partial differential equations. We also provide non-trivial examples that illustrate not only these properties but also show that, under this operator, a broader class of functions becomes locally integrable. The exponential decay factor notably broadens the domain of boundedness compared to classical Riesz and Bessel–Riesz potentials, making the operator more versatile and robust. Additionally, we generalize earlier results on Sobolev-type inequalities previously studied in constant exponent spaces by extending them to the variable exponent setting through our fractional operator, which reduces to the classical Riesz potential when the decay parameter $\lambda = 0$. Applications to elliptic PDEs are provided to illustrate the functional impact of our results. Furthermore, we develop several new structural properties tailored to variable exponent frameworks, reinforcing the strength and applicability of the proposed theory.

Keywords: Sobolev inequality; exponentially damped Riesz operator; Hardy–Littlewood maximal operator; variable Lebesgue spaces; boundedness of fractional operators; regularity of elliptic equations

MSC: 05A30; 26D10; 26D15

1. Introduction

In harmonic analysis, a basic idea that controls the behavior of several integral and multiplier operators in function spaces is the boundedness of operators. We investigate extensively operators including the Hardy–Littlewood maximal operator, singular integral operators (such as the Hilbert transform), and fractional integrals for their boundedness characteristics in Lebesgue and Sobolev spaces. Establishing convergence, regularity, and stability of solutions to partial differential equations [1,2] depends on an operator mapping one space into another boundedly. For instance, numerous findings in real-variable harmonic analysis rely on the boundedness of the maximal operator in the space L^{p} for $\mathrm{p} > 1$. Analogously, the Calderón–Zygmund theory offers a detailed framework to investigate the boundedness of singular integrals in L^{p} spaces [3]. The development of weighted norm inequalities has further extended the scope of these results to more general settings [4]. Furthermore, in the context of function spaces with variable exponents, such as $L^{\mathrm{p}(x)}$, the study of operator boundedness continues to evolve with new challenges and techniques [5]. It is also worth noting that different types of integral operators and their associated elliptic equations have gained recent relevance in applied harmonic analysis, particularly in the fields of image reconstruction, denoising, and encryption. For instance, operator frameworks involving convolutional structures and kernel decay have been effectively employed in machine learning and computer vision pipelines, including projectile prediction via hybrid deep models [6], and lightweight medical image encryption schemes leveraging structural transforms [7]. For further applications of such operators across various applied fields, including signal processing, computer vision, and mathematical modeling, we refer the reader to [8–12] and the references therein.

One fundamental work in this area is presented in [13], which thoroughly explores the behavior of fractional integrals. As shown in [14], the study of weighted norm inequalities for fractional operators, including sharp bounds and sparse dominance, has recently advanced significantly. In particular, with respect to the weights A_p, the fractional maximal operators are investigated in [15]. The modern development of classical harmonic analysis with an emphasis on non-integer-order operators acting on classical function spaces, including $L^{\mathrm{p}}(\mathbf{R}^{\mathrm{n}})$, Sobolev spaces, and Hardy spaces, is fractional harmonic analysis. The analysis of singular integrals and nonlocal partial differential equations has greatly benefited from these fractional operators, including those of the Riesz potential and fractional maximal function. The framework of variable exponent Lebesgue and Sobolev spaces is imperative to address more generalized growth conditions and variable integrability; refer to [16]. As demonstrated in [17], applications to nonlocal and fractional PDEs have been discussed in the context of nonlocal diffusions and non-standard Sobolev embeddings. A detailed explanation of the function of self-adjoint extensions of fractional Laplacians in harmonic analysis and operator theory can be found in [18]. In [19], recent advances in interpolation theory are discussed along with their applications to function space embeddings and fractional smoothness. An excellent source for a comprehensive and up-to-date introduction to Fourier and harmonic analysis that deals with fractional operators is presented in the monograph [20].

The evolution of harmonic analysis within the framework of variable exponent Lebesgue spaces $L^{\mathrm{p}(\cdot)}(\mathbf{R}^{\mathrm{n}})$ has given researchers a strong and adaptable framework to examine non-standard growth phenomena that occur in engineering and physics. The integrability exponent in $L^{\mathrm{p}(\cdot)}$ depends on the spatial variable, in contrast to classical Lebesgue spaces, enabling more realistic modeling of anisotropic structures and heterogeneous media [21]. The boundedness of classical operators on these spaces, such as the Hardy–Littlewood maximal operator, Calderón–Zygmund singular integrals, and fractional integrals, has been a focus of recent work. The well-established boundedness of the maximal operator under log-Hölder continuity conditions [22] serves as a fundamental tool to prove the boundedness of more complex operators. In this context, the generalized fractional integral operators and their commutators with bounded mean oscillation (BMO) functions have also been studied [23]. Furthermore, operators in variable exponent Morrey and Herz spaces have been extensively studied. For example, the fractional maximal operator and the singular integrals are bounded under appropriate structural conditions on the variable exponent function [24]. New results on multilinear operators and modular-type inequalities have significantly expanded classical theory [25]. The study of Triebel–Lizorkin and Besov spaces, with a variable exponent where the boundedness of operators is intimately related to smoothness functions and modular growth conditions, is one recent development [26]. The regularity theory of nonlinear partial differential equations with non-standard growth has found use for these findings, especially in image processing and fluid dynamics [27]. For additional related results that support the developed outcomes, we refer the reader to the works in [28–32].

A cornerstone result in geometric and functional analysis, the Sobolev inequality plays a fundamental role in the theory of partial differential equations. It provides crucial estimates linking the norms of functions to those of their derivatives. Specifically, if $u \in \mathbf{W}^{1,p}(\mathbf{R}^n)$, that is, u belongs to the first-order Sobolev space, then the following inequality holds:

$$\|u\|_{L^{p^*}(\mathbf{R}^n)} \leq C\|\nabla u\|_{L^p(\mathbf{R}^n)},$$

where $p^* = \frac{np}{n-p}$ is the critical Sobolev exponent and $C > 0$ is a constant independent of u [33].

There has been substantial progress in applying this classical inequality to more complex situations. As an example, it has been expanded to include spaces with variable or fractional smoothness, weighted Sobolev spaces, and Sobolev spaces on manifolds [34]. Fractional Sobolev spaces have further improved our understanding of nonlocal phenomena in analysis and PDEs [35]. In these settings, researchers have also developed compactness properties and improved the constants related to embeddings [36]. Furthermore, the interaction between geometry and analysis is demonstrated by studies of Sobolev inequalities on manifolds, where the functional inequalities are influenced by topology and curvature [37]. Sharp versions of the Sobolev inequality and the identification of extremal functions have been motivated by related variational problems such as the Yamabe problem [38]. New insights into the geometric structure of the Sobolev inequality have been revealed by recent contributions that have also examined connections between the mass transport method and functional inequalities [39].

Adams and Hedberg [40] made significant contributions to the study of Sobolev inequalities in the classical Lebesgue space framework through the lens of the Riesz potential operator . Let ψ be a locally integrable function on $\mathbf{R}^n$. The Riesz potential of order $\alpha \in (0, n)$ refers to a classical fractional integral operator and is formally given by

$$\mathcal{I}_\alpha \psi(\mu) = \int_{\mathbf{R}^n} \frac{\psi(\nu)}{|\mu - \nu|^{n-\alpha}} \, d\nu, \quad \mu \in \mathbf{R}^n.$$

A foundational result, commonly known as Sobolev's inequality, establishes that

$$\left(\int_{\mathbf{R}^n} |\mathcal{I}_\alpha \psi(\mu)|^q \, d\mu \right)^{1/q} \leq C \left(\int_{\mathbf{R}^n} |\psi(\mu)|^p \, d\mu \right)^{1/p},$$

whenever the exponents p, q satisfy the relation

$$\frac{1}{q} = \frac{1}{p} - \frac{\alpha}{n}, \quad \text{with } 1 < p < \frac{n}{\alpha}.$$

For some other recent results related to Sobolev inequalities, we refer the readers to [41–44].

The primary contribution of this study is the investigation of the boundedness of an exponentially damped Riesz-type fractional integral operator, defined in Definition 4, which, to the best of our knowledge, has not been addressed in the existing literature within any functional framework. In this work, we establish its boundedness in variable exponent Lebesgue spaces $L^{p(\cdot)}$, under suitable growth conditions on the exponent function $p(\cdot)$. To emphasize the significance, novelty, and practical relevance of the proposed operator, we conduct a comparative and critical analysis. We demonstrate that the exponentially damped Riesz-type fractional integral operator is particularly effective for analyzing the convergence, regularity, and stability of solutions to partial differential equations, due to the presence of an exponential decay factor that enhances these properties over broader domains. Specifically, in Example 2, we show that our operator remains bounded over a wider range compared to classical Riesz potentials [45] and Bessel–Riesz operators [46], which are typically restricted to narrower domains or limited classes of locally integrable functions. Several additional examples are presented to reinforce the robustness and broader applicability of the proposed operator. Moreover, while earlier work such as [40] explored Sobolev-type inequalities in the classical Lebesgue space setting via the Riesz potential operator, our study generalizes these results to the more flexible framework of variable exponent Lebesgue spaces $L^{p(\cdot)}$, employing a more general fractional operator that reduces to the classical case when the exponential decay parameter $\lambda = 0$. In addition, we present applications to elliptic partial differential equations (PDEs), showing that the corresponding solutions belong to appropriate Sobolev spaces. To further support the validity of our results, we develop several new structural properties under various exponent conditions.

The article is organized as follows. In Section 1, we provide an introduction and overview of the study. In Section 2, we recall essential definitions and existing results that are instrumental in establishing our main findings, including those related to the boundedness of operators and properties of variable exponent Lebesgue spaces. Section 3 presents our primary contributions, where we introduce new structural properties and establish the boundedness of the exponentially damped Riesz-type fractional integral operator on variable exponent Lebesgue spaces, together with several related estimates. In Section 4, we develop a new class of Sobolev-type inequalities, and the associated results involve our newly defined operator. In Section 5, we present key applications of our main results, specifically focusing on the regularity theory of elliptic partial differential equations (PDEs). Finally, Section 6 provides a summary of our main conclusions and highlights potential directions for future research.

2. Preliminary Framework

In this section, we recall essential definitions and preliminary results that are fundamental to the development of our main findings, particularly those related to the boundedness of operators and key properties of variable exponent Lebesgue spaces. For further details on these concepts, we refer the reader to the monograph [5]. Before proceeding further, we fix certain notations and concepts that will be frequently used throughout the article.

Notations

In the sequel, unless otherwise specified, we adopt the following notations:

- $\mathbf{R}^n$: The n-dimensional Euclidean space.
- $\mathbf{R}^+$: The set of all positive real numbers.
- $|\Omega|$: The Lebesgue measure of a measurable set $\Omega \subset \mathbf{R}^n$.
- $\mathbf{P}_0^{\log}(\Omega)$: The set of log-Hölder continuous exponent functions defined on a domain $\Omega \subset \mathbf{R}^n$.
- $\mathbf{W}^{1,p}(\mathbf{R}^n)$: The Sobolev space of functions in $L^p(\mathbf{R}^n)$ whose first weak derivatives also belong to $L^p(\mathbf{R}^n)$.
- The notation $\psi \lesssim \phi$ means that there exists a constant $c > 0$, independent of essential parameters, such that $\psi \leq c\,\phi$. Similarly, $\psi \approx \phi$ indicates $\psi \lesssim \phi \lesssim \psi$.

2.1. Semi-Modular Spaces

The variable Lebesgue spaces form a part of semi-modular spaces, which broaden the normed space framework. This framework begins by exploring essential definitions together with fundamental results pertaining to modular spaces.

Definition 1 ([5]). *Consider a vector space $\mathbf{M}$ over a field $\mathbf{K}$, which may be either real or complex numbers. A function $\rho : \mathbf{M} \to [0, \infty)$ is referred to as semi-modular on $\mathbf{M}$ if it satisfies the following conditions:*

- *Nullity : $\rho(0) = 0$.*
- *Unit Scalar Invariance: For all $\xi \in \mathbf{M}$ and $\tau \in \mathbf{S}$ with $|\tau| = 1$,*

$$\rho(\tau\xi) = \rho(\xi).$$

- *Definiteness: If $\rho(\tau\xi) = 0$ for all $\tau > 0$, then it necessarily follows that $\xi = 0$.*
- *Left-Continuity: The mapping $[0, \infty) \ni \tau \mapsto \rho(\tau\xi)$ exhibits left-continuity for every $\xi \in \mathbf{M}$.*
- *Monotonicity: The mapping $[0, \infty) \ni \tau \mapsto \rho(\tau\xi)$ is monotonically decreasing for each $\xi \in \mathbf{M}$.*

If ρ is a semi-modular on a vector space $\mathbf{M}$, then the associated modular space is defined as

$$\mathbf{M}_\rho := \{\xi \in \mathbf{M} \mid \exists\lambda > 0 \text{ such that } \rho(\lambda\xi) < +\infty\}.$$

This general form is used when ρ is not assumed to be convex. If convexity is assumed, it reduces to the simpler form

$$\{\xi \in \mathbf{M} \mid \rho(\xi) < +\infty\}.$$

On the space $\mathbf{M}_\rho$, we define the Luxemburg-type functional $\|\cdot\|_\rho : \mathbf{M}_\rho \to [0, +\infty]$ by

$$\|\xi\|_\rho := \inf\left\{\tau > 0 \mid \rho\left(\frac{\xi}{\tau}\right) \leq 1\right\}, \quad \text{for all } \xi \in \mathbf{M}_\rho.$$

This structure is central in the study of modular spaces and underpins normability, completeness, and related topological properties.

This formulation plays a crucial role in the study of normability and the geometric properties of semi-modular spaces. This functional serves as a key tool in the analysis of the structure of the semi-modular space, providing a framework for norm-like properties that emerge from the semi-modular function ρ.

Proposition 1 ([47]). *Let* $\mathbf{M}$ *be a vector space equipped with a semi-modular function* ρ. *Then, for every element* $\xi \in \mathbf{M}$, *the following equivalence holds:*

$$\rho(\xi) \leq 1 \Longleftrightarrow \|\xi\|_{\rho} \leq 1.$$

Proof. Suppose that $\rho(\xi) \leq 1$. By the definition of the semi-modular norm $\|\cdot\|_{\rho}$, it directly follows that $\|\xi\|_{\rho} \leq 1$.

Conversely, assume that $\|\xi\|_{\rho} \leq 1$. By the definition of $\|\xi\|_{\rho}$, this implies that for every $\tau > 1$, the left-continuity of the mapping $\tau \mapsto \rho(\xi/\tau)$ ensures that

$$\rho\left(\frac{\xi}{\tau}\right) \leq 1.$$

Thus, the equivalence is established. □

2.2. Variable Exponent Spaces

We recall the notion of variable exponent Lebesgue spaces. Let Ω be a Lebesgue measurable subset of $\mathbf{R}^n$, and let $p : \Omega \to (0, \infty)$ be a measurable function, called the variable exponent. Define the essential infimum and supremum of p by

$$p^{-} := \operatorname{ess\,inf}_{\sigma\in\Omega} p(\sigma) = \sup\{\alpha : p(\sigma) \geq \alpha \text{ a.e. in } \Omega\},$$

$$p^{+} := \operatorname{ess\,sup}_{\sigma\in\Omega} p(\sigma) = \inf\{\alpha : p(\sigma) \leq \alpha \text{ a.e. in } \Omega\}.$$

We also consider the following subsets of Ω:

$$\Omega_0 := \{\sigma \in \Omega : 1 < p(\sigma) < \infty\} = p^{-1}((1,\infty)),$$

$$\Omega_1 := \{\sigma \in \Omega : p(\sigma) = 1\} = p^{-1}(\{1\}),$$

$$\Omega_\infty := \{\sigma \in \Omega : p(\sigma) = \infty\} = p^{-1}(\{\infty\}).$$

The conjugate exponent $p' : \Omega \to [1, \infty]$ is defined by

$$p'(\sigma) := \begin{cases} \infty, & \sigma \in \Omega_1, \\ \dfrac{p(\sigma)}{p(\sigma) - 1}, & \sigma \in \Omega_0, \\ 1, & \sigma \in \Omega_\infty. \end{cases}$$

This definition satisfies the conjugacy relation

$$\frac{1}{p(\sigma)} + \frac{1}{p'(\sigma)} = 1,$$

for almost every $\sigma \in \Omega$.

Note that if $p(\cdot)$ is a constant function, $p(\sigma) \equiv p$, then $p'(\cdot) \equiv p'$ is the usual conjugate exponent. It is important to clarify that the notation $p'(\cdot)$ refers to the conjugate exponent associated with $p(\cdot)$, rather than representing the derivative of the function $p(\cdot)$.

Examples of variable exponent functions include

$$p(\sigma) = p \quad \text{(constant exponent)},$$

and oscillatory examples such as

$$p(\sigma) = 2 + \sin(\sigma).$$

We denote by $\mathbf{P}_0(\Omega)$ the collection of all measurable functions $p : \Omega \to (0, \infty)$ satisfying $p^- > 0$, and by $\mathbf{P}(\Omega)$ the subset of $\mathbf{P}_0(\Omega)$ with $p^- \geq 1$.
Let $\mathbf{M}$ be the vector space of all measurable functions on Ω. For $p \in \mathbf{P}_0(\Omega)$, define the semi-modular

$$\rho_{p(\cdot)}(\varphi) := \int_\Omega \Psi_{p(\tau)}(|\varphi(\tau)|)\, d\tau,$$

where

$$\Psi_p(\tau) = \begin{cases} \tau^p, & \text{if } p \in (0,\infty), \\ 0, & \text{if } p = \infty \text{ and } \tau \leq 1, \\ \infty, & \text{if } p = \infty \text{ and } \tau > 1. \end{cases}$$

Definition 2 ([5]). *The variable exponent Lebesgue space $L^{p(\cdot)}(\mathbb{R}^n)$ is defined as the collection of all measurable functions $\psi : \mathbb{R}^n \to C$ for which there exists some $\lambda > 0$ such that the modular functional*

$$\rho_{p(\cdot)}\left(\frac{\psi}{\lambda}\right) := \int_{\mathbb{R}^n} \left|\frac{\psi(\sigma)}{\lambda}\right|^{p(\sigma)} d\sigma$$

is finite.

Equipped with the Luxemburg quasi-norm

$$\|\psi\|_{p(\cdot)} := \inf\left\{\lambda > 0 : \rho_{p(\cdot)}\left(\frac{\psi}{\lambda}\right) \leqslant 1\right\},$$

the space $L^{p(\cdot)}(\mathbb{R}^n)$ is a quasi-norm space whenever the essential infimum of the exponent satisfies

$$p^- := \operatorname*{ess\,inf}_{\sigma \in \mathbb{R}^n} p(\sigma) \geq 1,$$

and becomes a Banach function space when $p^- > 1$.

Notably, the characterization of the space $L^{p(\cdot)}(\Omega)$ simplifies under the assumption that $p_+ := \operatorname{ess\,sup}_{\mu \in \Omega} p(\mu) < \infty$. In this case, a measurable function φ belongs to $L^{p(\cdot)}(\Omega)$ if and only if

$$\int_\Omega |\varphi(\mu)|^{p(\mu)}\, d\mu < \infty.$$

Example 1. *Let the variable exponent function $p : R \to [1, \infty)$ be defined by*

$$p(\sigma) = \begin{cases} 3, & \text{if } \sigma \in [-1,1], \\ \sigma^2 + 2, & \text{if } \sigma \in R \setminus [-1,1], \end{cases}$$

that is,

$$p(\sigma) = 3\chi_{[-1,1]}(\sigma) + (\sigma^2 + 2)\,\chi_{R\setminus[-1,1]}(\sigma).$$

Now, consider the function

$$\psi(\sigma) := (1 - \sigma^2)\,\chi_{[-1,1]}(\sigma),$$

which is supported only on the interval $[-1,1]$ and satisfies $\psi(\sigma) \geq 0$ on its support.

We aim to compute the modular $\rho_{p(\cdot)}(\psi/\lambda)$, defined by

$$\rho_{p(\cdot)}\left(\frac{\psi}{\lambda}\right) = \int_{R}\left|\frac{\psi(\sigma)}{\lambda}\right|^{p(\sigma)} d\sigma.$$

Since $\psi(\sigma) = 0$ *outside* $[-1,1]$, *and* $p(\sigma) = 3$ *on this interval, we get*

$$\rho_{p(\cdot)}\left(\frac{\psi}{\lambda}\right) = \int_{-1}^{1}\left|\frac{1-\sigma^2}{\lambda}\right|^{3} d\sigma = \frac{1}{\lambda^3}\int_{-1}^{1}(1-\sigma^2)^3 d\sigma.$$

Now compute the definite integral:

$$\int_{-1}^{1}(1-\sigma^2)^3 d\sigma.$$

Use the binomial expansion:

$$(1-\sigma^2)^3 = 1 - 3\sigma^2 + 3\sigma^4 - \sigma^6,$$

so,

$$\int_{-1}^{1}(1-\sigma^2)^3 d\sigma = \int_{-1}^{1}(1 - 3\sigma^2 + 3\sigma^4 - \sigma^6)d\sigma.$$

Due to symmetry and evenness,

$$= 2\int_{0}^{1}(1 - 3\sigma^2 + 3\sigma^4 - \sigma^6)d\sigma.$$

Now evaluate

$$\int_{0}^{1}(1 - 3\sigma^2 + 3\sigma^4 - \sigma^6)d\sigma = \left[\sigma - \sigma^3 + \frac{3}{5}\sigma^5 - \frac{1}{7}\sigma^7\right]_0^1 = \frac{21-5}{35} = \frac{16}{35}.$$

So the total integral is

$$\int_{-1}^{1}(1-\sigma^2)^3 d\sigma = 2\cdot\frac{16}{35} = \frac{32}{35}.$$

Hence, the modular becomes

$$\rho_{p(\cdot)}\left(\frac{\psi}{\lambda}\right) = \frac{32}{35\lambda^3}.$$

To compute the Luxemburg norm,

$$\|\psi\|_{p(\cdot)} = \inf\left\{\lambda > 0 : \frac{32}{35\lambda^3} \le 1\right\}.$$

Solving $\frac{32}{35\lambda^3} \le 1$ *gives*

$$\lambda^3 \ge \frac{32}{35} \quad\Rightarrow\quad \lambda \ge \left(\frac{32}{35}\right)^{1/3}.$$

Therefore, the Luxemburg norm is

$$\|\psi\|_{p(\cdot)} = \left(\frac{32}{35}\right)^{1/3}.$$

Thus, $\psi \in L^{p(\cdot)}(R)$ *with norm* $\left(\frac{32}{35}\right)^{1/3}$.

To establish the applicability of several pivotal findings throughout this study, it becomes imperative to impose appropriate regularity constraints on the exponent function $p : \Omega \to \mathbf{R}^+$. In particular, the function p is said to exhibit the property of *local log-Hölder continuity* on the domain Ω provided there exists a constant $c_{\log}(p) > 0$ such that, for every pair of points $\mu, \nu \in \Omega$,

$$|p(\mu) - p(\nu)| \leq \frac{c_{\log}(p)}{\log(e + 1/|\mu - \nu|)}.$$

Moreover, p is said to be *log-Hölder continuous at infinity* (or to exhibit log-decay at infinity) if there exists a constant exponent $p_\infty \in \Omega$ and a constant $c_{\log} > 0$ such that, for all $\mu \in \Omega$,

$$|p(\mu) - p_\infty| \leq \frac{c_{\log}(p)}{\log(e + |\mu|)}.$$

If p satisfies both local and asymptotic log-Hölder continuity conditions, then we say that p is *globally log-Hölder continuous*, and denote the class of such exponents by $\mathbf{C}_{\log}(p)$. Accordingly, the subclass of globally regular exponents is defined by

$$\mathbf{P}_0^{\log}(\Omega) := \left\{ p \in \mathbf{P}_0(\Omega) : \frac{1}{p} \in \mathbf{C}_{\log}(p) \right\}.$$

In the sequel, we shall formulate several classical and practically useful results concerning the semi-modular $\rho_{p(\cdot)}$ and the Luxemburg-type quasi-norm $\|\cdot\|_{L^{p(\cdot)}(\Omega)}$.

Proposition 2 ([47])**.** *Let $p \in \mathbf{P}_0(\Omega)$ be such that $p_+ < \infty$, and suppose that $\varphi \in L^{p(\cdot)}(\Omega)$. Then,*

$$\min\left\{ \left(\rho_{p(\cdot)}(\varphi)\right)^{\frac{1}{p_-}}, \left(\rho_{p(\cdot)}(\varphi)\right)^{\frac{1}{p_+}} \right\} \leq \|\varphi\|_{L^{p(\cdot)}(\Omega)} \leq \max\left\{ \left(\rho_{p(\cdot)}(\varphi)\right)^{\frac{1}{p_-}}, \left(\rho_{p(\cdot)}(\varphi)\right)^{\frac{1}{p_+}} \right\}.$$

Proposition 3 ([5])**.** *Given Ω and $p(\cdot) \in \mathbf{P}(\Omega)$:*

(1) If $p^+ < \infty$, then for all $\lambda \geq 1$,

$$\lambda^{p^-} \rho(\varphi) \leq \rho(\lambda\varphi) \leq \lambda^{p^+} \rho(\varphi).$$

When $0 < \lambda < 1$, the reverse inequalities hold.

(2) If $p^+(\Omega \setminus \Omega_\infty) < \infty$, then for all $\lambda \geq 1$,

$$\rho(\lambda\varphi) \leq \lambda^{p^+(\Omega \setminus \Omega_\infty)} \rho(\varphi).$$

Proposition 4 ([5])**.** *Let Ω be a measurable set and suppose that $p(\cdot) \in \mathbf{P}(\Omega)$. If $\varphi \in L^{p(\cdot)}(\Omega)$ and $\|\varphi\|_{L^{p(\cdot)}(\Omega)} > 0$, then the following inequality holds:*

$$\rho_{p(\cdot)}\left(\frac{\varphi}{\|\varphi\|_{L^{p(\cdot)}(\Omega)}}\right) \leq 1.$$

Moreover, if $p^+ < \infty$, then for every non-trivial function $\varphi \in L^{p(\cdot)}(\Omega)$, we have the equality

$$\rho_{p(\cdot)}\left(\frac{\varphi}{\|\varphi\|_{L^{p(\cdot)}(\Omega)}}\right) = 1.$$

Corollary 1 ([5]). *Given* Ω *and* $p(\cdot) \in \mathbf{P}(\Omega)$, *suppose* $p^+ < \infty$. *If* $\|\varphi\|_{L^{p(\cdot)}(\Omega)} > 1$, *then*

$$\rho_{p(\cdot)}(\varphi)^{1/p^+} \le \|\varphi\|_{L^{p(\cdot)}(\Omega)} \le \rho_{p(\cdot)}(\varphi)^{1/p^-}.$$

If $0 < \|\varphi\|_{L^{p(\cdot)}(\Omega)} \le 1$, *then*

$$\rho_{p(\cdot)}(\varphi)^{1/p^-} \le \|\varphi\|_{L^{p(\cdot)}(\Omega)} \le \rho_{p(\cdot)}(\varphi)^{1/p^+}.$$

Theorem 1 ([5]). *Given a measurable set* Ω *and a variable exponent function* $p(\cdot) \in \mathbf{P}(\Omega)$, *then for every function* $\varphi \in L^{p(\cdot)}(\Omega)$, *there exist functions* φ_1 *and* φ_2 *such that*

$$\varphi = \varphi_1 + \varphi_2,$$

where

$$\varphi_1 \in L^{p^+}(\Omega) \cap L^{p(\cdot)}(\Omega) \quad \text{and} \quad \varphi_2 \in L^{p^-}(\Omega) \cap L^{p(\cdot)}(\Omega).$$

Theorem 2 ([5]). *Let* Ω *be given, and let* $p(\cdot) \in \mathbf{P}(\Omega)$. *For any functions* $\psi \in L^{p(\cdot)}(\Omega)$ *and* $\phi \in L^{p'(\cdot)}(\Omega)$, *the product* $\psi\phi \in L^1(\Omega)$ *and the following inequality holds:*

$$\int_\Omega |\psi(\sigma)\phi(\sigma)|\, d\sigma \le \mathcal{K}_{p(\cdot)} \|\psi\|_{L^{p(\cdot)}(\Omega)} \|\phi\|_{L^{p'(\cdot)}(\Omega)},$$

where

$$\mathcal{K}_{p(\cdot)} = \frac{1}{p_-} - \frac{1}{p_+} + \|\chi_{\Omega_\infty}\|_\infty + \|\chi_{\Omega_1}\|_\infty + \|\chi_{\Omega_0}\|_\infty.$$

Definition 3 ([5]). *Let* $\psi \in L^1_{loc}(\mathbf{R}^n)$. *The* Hardy–Littlewood maximal function $\mathcal{M}\psi$ *of* ψ *is defined for each* $\mu \in \mathbf{R}^n$ *by*

$$\mathcal{M}\psi(\mu) := \sup_{Q \ni \mu} \frac{1}{|Q|} \int_Q |\psi(\mu)|\, d\mu,$$

where the supremum is taken over all cubes $Q \subset \mathbf{R}^n$ *containing* μ *whose sides are parallel to the coordinate axes.*

(p_1) Let $p(\mu)$ be a continuous function on $\mathbf{R}^n$ that is both locally and globally log-Hölder continuous, i.e., $p(\cdot) \in \mathbf{P}_0^{\log}(\mathbf{R}^n)$, satisfying the following conditions:

$$p_- := \inf_{\mu \in \mathbf{R}^n} p(\mu) > 1 \quad \text{and} \quad p_\infty := \lim_{|\mu| \to \infty} p(\mu) > 1. \tag{1}$$

(p_2) There exists a constant $\mathcal{C} > 0$ such that

$$|p(\mu) - p(\nu)| \le \frac{\mathcal{C}}{\log\left(e + \frac{1}{|\mu - \nu|}\right)}, \tag{2}$$

for all $\mu, \nu \in R^n$ with $|\mu - \nu| \le 1$.

The Hardy–Littlewood maximal operator $\mathcal{M}$ satisfies the following properties:

1. $\mathcal{M}$ is sublinear, that is, for all $\phi, \psi \in \mathbf{M}(\mathbf{R}^n)$ and $\eta \in \mathbf{R}$,

$$\mathcal{M}(\phi + \psi)(\mu) \le \mathcal{M}\phi(\mu) + \mathcal{M}\psi(\mu), \quad \text{and} \quad \mathcal{M}(\eta\phi)(\mu) = |\eta| \mathcal{M}\phi(\mu),$$

for almost every $\mu \in \mathbf{R}^n$.

2. If ϕ is not identically zero, then for any bounded measurable set $\Omega \subset \mathbf{R}^n$, there exists $\epsilon > 0$ such that
$$\mathcal{M}\phi(\mu) \geq \epsilon, \quad \forall \mu \in \Omega.$$
3. If ϕ is not zero almost everywhere, then
$$\mathcal{M}\phi \notin L^1(\mathbf{R}^n).$$
4. If $\phi \in L^\infty(\mathbf{R}^n)$, then $\mathcal{M}\phi \in L^\infty(\mathbf{R}^n)$ and the norms coincide:
$$\|\mathcal{M}\phi\|_\infty = \|\phi\|_\infty.$$

Theorem 3 ([5]). *Let $\psi \in L^p(\mathbf{R}^n)$ with $1 \leq p < \infty$. Then, for every $t > 0$, we have*
$$|\{\mu \in \mathbf{R}^n : \mathcal{M}\psi(\mu) > t\}| \leq \frac{3^n 4^{np}}{t^p} \int_{\mathbf{R}^n} |\psi(\mu)|^p \, d\mu.$$

Moreover, if $1 < p \leq \infty$, then
$$\|\mathcal{M}\psi\|_{L^p(\mathbf{R}^n)} \leq C(n)(p')^{\frac{1}{p}} \|\psi\|_{L^p(\mathbf{R}^n)}.$$

Theorem 4 ([5]). *Let $p(\cdot) \in \mathbf{P}(\mathbf{R}^n)$ such that $1/p(\cdot) \in \mathbf{P}_0^{\log}(\mathbf{R}^n)$, i.e., the function $1/p(\cdot)$ satisfies both local and decay log-Hölder continuity. Then, for any measurable function ψ and any $t > 0$, the Hardy–Littlewood maximal operator satisfies*
$$\left\| t\, \chi_{\{\mu : \mathcal{M}\psi(\mu) > t\}} \right\|_{L^{p(\cdot)}(\mathbf{R}^n)} \leq C \|\psi\|_{L^{p(\cdot)}(\mathbf{R}^n)},$$
and, if in addition $p_- > 1$, then
$$\|\mathcal{M}\psi\|_{L^{p(\cdot)}(\mathbf{R}^n)} \leq C \|\psi\|_{L^{p(\cdot)}(\mathbf{R}^n)}.$$

Here, the constant $C = C(n, p_-, p_+, (1/p(\cdot)))$ depends explicitly on the dimension n, the essential infimum and supremum p_-, p_+, and the log-Hölder constants of $1/p(\cdot)$.

3. Main Results

The objective of this section is to investigate the boundedness properties of a fractional integral operator characterized by a Riesz-type kernel with a damped exponential weight. Before presenting our main theorem, we establish several auxiliary results that play a crucial role in supporting and facilitating the proofs of the principal results.

Exponentially Damped Riesz-Type Fractional Integral Operator

Definition 4. *Let $0 < \eta < n$ and $\beta \geq 0$. The fractional exponential-type damped integral operator, denoted by $\mathcal{I}_{\eta,\beta}$, is defined as the convolution of a function $\psi \in L^{p(\cdot)}_{\mathrm{loc}}(\mathbf{R}^n)$ with an exponentially damped Riesz-type kernel:*
$$(\mathcal{I}_{\eta,\beta} * \psi)(\mu) := \int_{\mathbf{R}^n} \frac{\psi(\nu)}{|\mu - \nu|^{n-\eta}} e^{-\beta|\mu-\nu|} \, d\nu,$$
where η denotes the order of the fractional operator and $\beta \geq 0$ controls the exponential decay. For $\beta = 0$, the operator coincides with the classical Riesz potential.

Remark 1.

- *When* $\beta = 0$ *and* $\eta = 2$*, the operator defined in Definition 4 reduces to*

$$\mathcal{I}_2\psi(\mu) = c_n \int_{\mathbf{R}^n} \frac{\psi(\nu)}{|\mu - \nu|^{n-2}} \, d\nu,$$

where $c_n = \dfrac{1}{(n-2)\omega_n}$*, with* ω_n *being the surface measure of the unit sphere in* $\mathbf{R}^n$*. This is the classical* Newtonian potential*, which satisfies*

$$-\Delta(\mathcal{I}_2\psi)(\mu) = \psi(\mu)$$

in the distributional sense. For a detailed treatment, see Stein [48]. In portions of the paper where scaling is not central, we adopt $c_n = 1$ *for simplicity.*

- *When the exponential decay factor* $\beta = 0$*, we recover the classical Riesz potential:*

$$(\mathcal{I}_\eta * \psi)(\mu) := \int_{\mathbf{R}^n} \frac{\psi(\nu)}{|\mu - \nu|^{n-\eta}} \, d\nu,$$

as defined in [48].

The figure below (Figure 1) illustrates the hierarchical structure and the relationships among various classical potentials associated with this new operator.
Novelty and Significance of the Operator

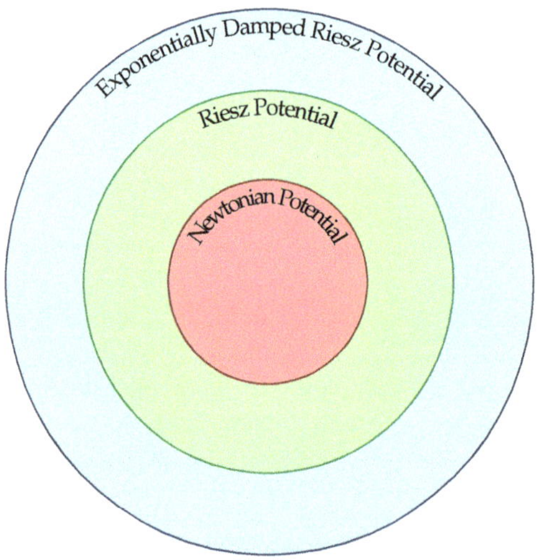

Figure 1. Hierarchical structure of potentials: from Newtonian to exponentially damped Riesz fractional operator.

A Specific Example Distinguishing the Operator $\mathcal{I}_{\eta,\beta}$:

Example 2. *Consider the fractional exponential-type damped Riesz operator defined by*

$$(\mathcal{I}_{\eta,\beta} * \psi)(\mu) := \int_{\mathbf{R}^n} \frac{\psi(\nu)}{|\mu - \nu|^{n-\eta}} e^{-\beta|\mu-\nu|} \, d\nu,$$

for $0 < \eta < n$ and $\beta > 0$. We construct a function ψ for which this operator is well-defined pointwise.

Choice of function. Let

$$\psi(\mu) := \frac{\chi_{\mathcal{B}(0,1)^c}(\mu)}{(\log(e + |\mu|))^p}, \quad p > \frac{n - \eta}{\beta}.$$

This decay condition ensures that the function ψ is sufficiently integrable at infinity for the operator to be bounded.

Boundedness under the operator $\mathcal{I}_{\eta,\beta}$. For all $\mu \in \mathbf{R}^n$, the following estimate holds:

$$|\mathcal{I}_{\eta,\beta} * \psi(\mu)| \leq \int_{\mathbf{R}^n} \frac{e^{-\beta|\mu-\nu|}}{|\mu - \nu|^{n-\eta}(\log(e + |\nu|))^p} d\nu.$$

Thanks to the imposed condition $p > \frac{n-\eta}{\beta}$, this integral converges due to the dominating exponential decay of the kernel.

Limitation of the classical Riesz and Bessel–Riesz potentials. When the exponential decay is absent (i.e., $\beta = 0$), the kernel reduces to the classical Riesz form:

$$|\mu - \nu|^{\eta-n},$$

and the associated integral

$$\int_{|\nu|>R} \frac{1}{|\nu|^{n-\eta}(\log(e + |\nu|))^p} d\nu$$

may diverge for moderate values of p. In particular, convergence typically requires $p > 1$, indicating a limitation in applying the classical Riesz potential to such slowly decaying functions.

Remark 2. *The function*

$$\psi(\mu) = \frac{\chi_{\mathcal{B}(0,1)^c}(\mu)}{(\log(e + |\mu|))^p}$$

belongs to the domain of the exponentially damped Riesz operator $\mathcal{I}_{\eta,\beta}$ provided that

$$p > \frac{n - \eta}{\beta}.$$

This ensures sufficient decay of the function at infinity to maintain integrability of the kernel. In contrast, the classical Riesz and Bessel–Riesz operators may be subject to stricter decay requirements on ψ, which limits their applicability in certain cases. This highlights the enhanced flexibility and regularizing power of the exponentially damped operator.

First of all, in order to establish the validity of this operator, we have investigated several of its structural properties, which are subsequently utilized in the derivation of the main result. In view of conditions (1) and (2), and taking into account the framework established by Diening [49], a similar type of result was obtained for the Hardy–Littlewood maximal operator.

Lemma 1. *Let ψ be a measurable function taking values in the interval $[0, 1]$ on $\mathbf{R}^n$, i.e., $\psi : \mathbf{R}^n \to [0, 1]$, satisfying the following properties:*

$$\psi = 0 \quad \textit{almost everywhere on the ball } \mathcal{B}(0, 2\kappa_0), \quad \textit{and} \quad \|\psi\|_{p(\cdot)} \leq 1,$$

where the norm is taken with respect to the variable exponent Lebesgue space $L^{p(\cdot)}(\mathbf{R}^n)$*, and the exponent function* $p(\cdot)$ *satisfies the standard log-Hölder continuity and boundedness conditions. Then the exponential-type fractional integral operator*

$$\mathcal{I}_{\eta,\lambda}\psi(\mu) := \int_{\mathbf{R}^n} \frac{\psi(\nu)}{|\mu-\nu|^{n-\eta}} e^{-\lambda|\mu-\nu|}\, d\nu$$

satisfies the inequality

$$\int_{\mathcal{B}(0,\kappa_0)} [\mathcal{I}_{\eta,\lambda}\psi(\mu)]^{p(\mu)}\, d\mu \le C,$$

where C *is a constant depending only on* $n, \eta, \lambda, p(\cdot), \kappa_0$*, and not on* ψ.

Proof. Let $\mu \in \mathcal{B}(0,\kappa_0)$. Since $\psi(\nu) = 0$ on $\mathcal{B}(0, 2\kappa_0)$, it follows that $|\nu| \ge 2\kappa_0$ wherever $\psi(\nu) \neq 0$, and hence,

$$|\mu-\nu| \ge |\nu| - |\mu| \ge 2\kappa_0 - \kappa_0 = \kappa_0.$$

Therefore,

$$\mathcal{I}_{\eta,\lambda}\psi(\mu) \le \int_{|\nu|\ge 2\kappa_0} \frac{\psi(\nu)}{|\mu-\nu|^{n-\eta}} e^{-\lambda|\mu-\nu|}\, d\nu \le C_{\kappa_0,\lambda} \int_{|\nu|\ge 2\kappa_0} \psi(\nu)\, d\nu.$$

Since $\psi(\nu) \in [0,1]$ and $\|\psi\|_{p(\cdot)} \le 1$, we use the modular inequality

$$\int_{\mathbf{R}^n} \psi(\nu)\, d\nu \le \int_{\mathbf{R}^n} \psi(\nu)^{p(\nu)}\, d\nu \le 1.$$

Thus,

$$\mathcal{I}_{\eta,\lambda}\psi(\mu) \le \mathcal{M} \quad \text{for all } \mu \in \mathcal{B}(0,\kappa_0),$$

where $\mathcal{M}$ depends only on κ_0, λ, and n.

Now we estimate

$$\int_{\mathcal{B}(0,\kappa_0)} [\mathcal{I}_{\eta,\lambda}\psi(\mu)]^{p(\mu)} d\mu \le \int_{\mathcal{B}(0,\kappa_0)} \mathcal{M}^{p(\mu)} d\mu \le C.$$

Note: Since $\psi \in [0,1] \subset L^\infty(\mathbb{R}^n) \cap L^{p(\cdot)}(\mathbb{R}^n)$, and the exponent function $p(\cdot)$ is log-Hölder continuous and essentially bounded, both the integral and modular expressions are well-defined. The change in the order of integration is justified by Fubini-type theorems adapted to variable exponent spaces (cf. Diening et al., 2011 [16]). Therefore, no issues arise concerning measurability or integrability.

This concludes the proof. □

Lemma 2. *Let* ψ *be a measurable function taking values in the interval* $[0,1]$ *on* $\mathbf{R}^n$*, that is,* $\psi : \mathbf{R}^n \to [0,1]$*, such that*

$$\psi = 0 \quad \text{on } \mathcal{B}(0,2\kappa_0), \quad \text{and} \quad \|\psi\|_{p(\cdot)} \le 1.$$

Then the exponential-type fractional integral operator

$$\mathcal{I}_{\eta,\lambda}\psi(\mu) := \int_{\mathbf{R}^n} \frac{\psi(\nu)}{|\mu-\nu|^{n-\eta}} e^{-\lambda|\mu-\nu|}\, d\nu$$

satisfies

$$\int_{\mathcal{B}(0,\kappa_0)} [\mathcal{I}_{\eta,\lambda}\psi(\mu)]^{p(\mu)} d\mu \le C,$$

where C *is a constant depending only on* $n, \eta, \lambda, p(\cdot), \kappa_0$*, but not on* ψ.

Proof. Let $\mu \in \mathcal{B}(0, \kappa_0)$. Since $\psi = 0$ on $\mathcal{B}(0, 2\kappa_0)$, it follows that if $\nu \in \operatorname{supp}(\psi)$, then $|\nu| \geq 2\kappa_0$. Here, the *support* of the function ψ, denoted by $\operatorname{supp}(\psi)$, is defined as the closure of the set where ψ is nonzero, i.e.,

$$\operatorname{supp}(\psi) := \overline{\{\nu \in \mathbf{R}^n : \psi(\nu) \neq 0\}}.$$

Thus, since $\mu \in \mathcal{B}(0, \kappa_0)$ and every point in $\operatorname{supp}(\psi)$ lies outside the ball $\mathcal{B}(0, 2\kappa_0)$, it follows that $|\mu - \nu| \geq \kappa_0$. Therefore,

$$\mathcal{I}_{\eta,\lambda}\psi(\mu) \leq \int_{\mathbf{R}^n \setminus \mathcal{B}(0,2\kappa_0)} \frac{\psi(\nu)}{\kappa_0^{n-\eta}} e^{-\lambda\kappa_0}\, d\nu = \frac{e^{-\lambda\kappa_0}}{\kappa_0^{n-\eta}} \int \psi(\nu)\, d\nu.$$

Since $\psi(\nu) \in [0,1]$ and $||\psi||_{p(\cdot)} \leq 1$, we obtain

$$\int_{\mathbf{R}^n} \psi(\nu)\, d\nu \leq \int_{\mathbf{R}^n} \psi(\nu)^{p(\nu)} d\nu \leq 1.$$

Hence,

$$\mathcal{I}_{\eta,\lambda}\psi(\mu) \leq \mathcal{M} \quad \text{for all } \mu \in \mathcal{B}(0, \kappa_0),$$

for some constant $\mathcal{M}$ depending only on the fixed parameters.

It follows that

$$\int_{\mathcal{B}(0,\kappa_0)} [\mathcal{I}_{\eta,\lambda}\psi(\mu)]^{p(\mu)} d\mu \leq \int_{\mathcal{B}(0,\kappa_0)} \mathcal{M}^{p(\mu)} d\mu \leq C,$$

which completes the proof. □

Before proving the lemma below, we define the Hardy operator, which will be used in the sequel:

$$\mathcal{M}\psi(\nu) := \frac{1}{|\mathcal{B}(0, |\nu|)|} \int_{\mathcal{B}(0,|x|)} |\psi(\mu)|\, d\mu,$$

where $\mathcal{B}(0, |\nu|)$ denotes the ball centered at the origin with radius $|\nu|$, and $|\mathcal{B}(0, |\nu|)|$ is its Lebesgue measure.

Lemma 3. *Let ψ be a measurable function on $\mathbf{R}^n$ taking values in the set of non-negative extended real numbers, i.e., $\psi : \mathbf{R}^n \to [0, \infty)$, such that $\psi = 0$ on the ball $\mathcal{B}(0, \kappa_0)$, and moreover, it satisfies the modular constraint $||\psi||_{p(\cdot)} \leq 1$. Define the exponentially damped Riesz-type operator by*

$$(\mathcal{I}_{\eta,\lambda} * \psi)(\mu) := \int_{\mathbf{R}^n} \frac{\psi(\nu)}{|\mu - \nu|^{n-\eta}} e^{-\lambda|\mu-\nu|}\, d\nu, \quad \mu \in \mathbf{R}^n,\ |\mu| > \kappa_0.$$

Then, for all $\mu \in \mathbf{R}^n$ with $|\mu| \geq \kappa_0$, it holds that

$$(\mathcal{I}_{\eta,\lambda} * \psi)(\mu) \leq C \exp\left(\left(\frac{1}{|\mathcal{B}(0, |\mu|)|} \int_{\mathcal{B}(0,|\mu|)} \psi(\nu)^{p(\nu)}\, d\nu \right)^{1/p(\mu)} \right),$$

where $C > 0$ is a constant independent of ψ and μ.

Proof. Let $\psi \in L^{p(\cdot)}(\mathbf{R}^n)$ be a measurable function taking values in the set of non-negative real numbers, i.e., $\psi(\xi) \geq 0$ for almost every $\xi \in \mathbf{R}^n$, such that $\psi = 0$ on the ball $\mathcal{B}(0, \kappa_0)$ and $||\psi||_{p(\cdot)} \leq 1$. Define

$$\mathbf{F} := \frac{1}{|\mathcal{B}(0, |\mu|)|} \int_{\mathcal{B}(0,|\mu|)} \psi(\nu)^{p(\nu)}\, d\nu.$$

Since $\psi = 0$ on $\mathcal{B}(0, \kappa_0)$, the kernel $|\mu - \nu|^{\eta - n} e^{-\lambda|\mu - \nu|}$ decays rapidly. Thus, the dominant contribution to the integral arises from $\nu \in \mathcal{B}(0, |\mu|) \setminus \mathcal{B}(0, \kappa_0)$.

We use Hölder's inequality with exponent $q(\nu) := p(\nu)$, so $q'(\nu) := \frac{p(\nu)}{p(\nu)-1}$, to estimate

$$\begin{aligned}(\mathcal{I}_{\eta,\lambda} * \psi)(\mu) &= \int_{\mathbf{R}^n} \frac{\psi(\nu)}{|\mu - \nu|^{n-\eta}} e^{-\lambda|\mu-\nu|} \, d\nu \\ &\leq \int_{\mathcal{B}(0,|\mu|)} \frac{\psi(\nu)}{|\mu - \nu|^{n-\eta}} e^{-\lambda|\mu-\nu|} \, d\nu \\ &\leq \left(\int_{\mathcal{B}(0,|\mu|)} \left[\frac{1}{|\mu - \nu|^{n-\eta}} e^{-\lambda|\mu-\nu|} \right]^{q'(\nu)} d\nu \right)^{1/q'(\mu)} \cdot \mathbf{F}^{1/p(\mu)}.\end{aligned}$$

Since the kernel is integrable over $\mathbf{R}^n$ for $0 < \eta < n$, and the exponential term ensures decay, the integral is bounded. Thus, we obtain

$$(\mathcal{I}_{\eta,\lambda} * \psi)(\mu) \leq \mathcal{C} \cdot \exp\left(\mathbf{F}^{1/p(\mu)}\right),$$

for some constant $\mathcal{C} > 0$ depending only on n, η, λ, and the modular exponent $p(\cdot)$, but not on ψ or μ. This completes the proof. □

Theorem 5. *Let $0 < \eta < n$, $0 < \gamma < \infty$ with $\eta < \gamma$, and suppose that $p(\cdot) \in \mathbf{P}_0^{\log}(\Omega)(\mathbf{R}^+)$, i.e., the exponent function satisfies the log-Hölder continuity condition. Then, the fractional integral operator with exponential-type kernel*

$$\mathcal{I}_{\eta,\beta}\psi(\mu) := \int_{\mathbf{R}^n} \frac{\psi(\nu)}{|\mu - \nu|^{n-\eta}} e^{-\beta|\mu-\nu|} \, d\nu$$

is bounded on the variable exponent Lebesgue space $L^{p(\cdot)}(\mathbf{R}^+)$, i.e.,

$$\mathcal{I}_{\eta,\beta} : L^{p(\cdot)}(\mathbf{R}^+) \to L^{p(\cdot)}(\mathbf{R}^+)$$

is a bounded operator.

Proof. Since the essential supremum $p_+ < \infty$ and the exponent function $p(\cdot)$ satisfies the log-Hölder continuity condition, i.e., $p(\cdot) \in \mathbf{P}_0^{\log}(\Omega)(\mathbf{R}^+)$, it follows that the Hardy–Littlewood maximal operator $\mathcal{M}$ is bounded on the variable exponent Lebesgue space $L^{p(\cdot)}(\mathbf{R}^+)$. More precisely, there exists a constant $c_0 > 0$ such that for every $\psi \in L^{p(\cdot)}(\mathbf{R}^+)$, we have

$$\|\mathcal{M}\psi\|_{L^{p(\cdot)}(\mathbf{R}^+)} \leq c_0 \|\psi\|_{L^{p(\cdot)}(\mathbf{R}^+)}.$$

Now, fix any $\mu \in \mathbf{R}^+$ and let $\psi \in L^{p(\cdot)}(\mathbf{R}^+)$. Consider the fractional integral operator with exponential kernel defined by

$$\mathcal{I}_{\eta,\beta}\psi(\mu) := \int_{\mathbf{R}^n} \frac{\psi(\nu)}{|\mu - \nu|^{n-\eta}} e^{-\beta|\mu-\nu|} \, d\nu.$$

To facilitate estimation, we split the integral into two parts based on the distance between μ and ν:

$$\mathcal{I}_{\eta,\beta}\psi(\mu) = \underbrace{\int_{|\mu-\nu|<1} \frac{\psi(\nu)}{|\mu - \nu|^{n-\eta}} e^{-\beta|\mu-\nu|} \, d\nu}_{:=\mathfrak{I}_1(\mu)} + \underbrace{\int_{|\mu-\nu|\geq 1} \frac{\psi(\nu)}{|\mu - \nu|^{n-\eta}} e^{-\beta|\mu-\nu|} \, d\nu}_{:=\mathfrak{I}_2(\mu)}.$$

Now, fix any $\mu \in \mathbf{R}^+$ and let $\psi \in L^{p(\cdot)}(\mathbf{R}^+)$. To estimate the *local part* of the fractional potential operator, we begin by decomposing the unit ball centered at $\mu \in \mathbf{R}^n$, defined by

$$\mathcal{B}(\mu, 1) := \{\nu \in \mathbf{R}^n : |\mu - \nu| < 1\},$$

into a countable union of *dyadic annuli*, which facilitates control over the singularity and decay behavior of the kernel.

The dyadic annuli are given by

$$\mathcal{A}_k := \left\{\nu \in \mathbf{R}^n : 2^k \le |\mu - \nu| < 2^{k+1}\right\}, \quad \text{for } k \le -1.$$

These sets are pairwise disjoint, and their union covers the unit ball:

$$\mathcal{B}(\mu, 1) = \bigcup_{k=-\infty}^{-1} \mathcal{A}_k, \quad \text{(disjoint union)}.$$

Hence, the local integral

$$\mathcal{I}_1(\mu) := \int_{|\mu-\nu|<1} \frac{|\psi(\nu)|}{|\mu - \nu|^{n-\eta}} e^{-\beta|\mu-\nu|}\, d\nu$$

can be estimated by summing over the dyadic annuli:

$$\mathcal{I}_1(\mu) \le \sum_{k=-\infty}^{-1} \int_{\mathcal{A}_k} \frac{|\psi(\nu)|}{|\mu - \nu|^{n-\eta}} e^{-\beta|\mu-\nu|}\, d\nu.$$

Since $|\mu - \nu| < 1$ for all $\nu \in \mathcal{A}_k$, we observe that $e^{-\beta|\mu-\nu|} \le 1$. Therefore,

$$\mathcal{I}_1(\mu) \le \sum_{k=-\infty}^{-1} \int_{\mathcal{A}_k} \frac{|\psi(\nu)|}{|\mu - \nu|^{n-\eta}}\, d\nu.$$

On each annulus $\mathcal{A}_k$, we have the estimate $|\mu - \nu| \sim 2^k$, so we may write

$$\int_{\mathcal{A}_k} \frac{|\psi(\nu)|}{|\mu - \nu|^{n-\eta}}\, d\nu \le \frac{1}{(2^k)^{n-\eta}} \int_{\mathcal{A}_k} |\psi(\nu)|\, d\nu.$$

Using the volume estimate for balls and the definition of the Hardy–Littlewood maximal function, we obtain

$$\int_{\mathcal{A}_k} |\psi(\nu)|\, d\nu \le |\mathcal{B}(\mu, 2^{k+1})| \cdot \mathcal{M}\psi(\mu) \le \mathcal{C}_n \cdot 2^{kn} \cdot \mathcal{M}\psi(\mu),$$

where $\mathcal{C}_n = |\mathcal{B}(0,1)| \cdot 2^n$ is a dimensional constant.

Combining the above inequalities yields

$$\int_{\mathcal{A}_k} \frac{|\psi(\nu)|}{|\mu - \nu|^{n-\eta}}\, d\nu \le \mathcal{C}_n \cdot \frac{2^{kn}}{2^{k(n-\eta)}} \cdot \mathcal{M}\psi(\mu) = \mathcal{C}_n \cdot 2^{k\eta} \cdot \mathcal{M}\psi(\mu).$$

Summing over all $k \le -1$, we obtain

$$\mathcal{I}_1(\mu) \le \mathcal{C}_n \cdot \mathcal{M}\psi(\mu) \sum_{k=-\infty}^{-1} 2^{k\eta} = \mathcal{C}_1 \cdot \mathcal{M}\psi(\mu),$$

where

$$C_1 := C_n \sum_{k=-\infty}^{-1} 2^{k\eta} = C_n \cdot \frac{2^{-\eta}}{1-2^{-\eta}},$$

since the geometric series converges for $\eta > 0$. This completes the estimate for the local term $\mathcal{I}_1(\mu)$.

Now, we consider the global component of the regularized fractional integral operator:

$$\mathcal{I}_2(\mu) = \int_{|\mu-\nu|\geq 1} \frac{\psi(\nu)}{|\mu-\nu|^{n-\eta}} e^{-\beta|\mu-\nu|}\, d\nu,$$

where $0 < \eta < n$, $\beta > 0$, and $\psi \in L^1_{\text{loc}}(\mathbf{R}^n)$. Our goal is to estimate this term in terms of the Hardy–Littlewood maximal function $\mathcal{M}\psi(\mu)$.

We decompose the domain of integration into dyadic annuli:

$$\mathcal{I}_2(\mu) \leq \sum_{k=0}^{\infty} \int_{2^k\leq|\mu-\nu|<2^{k+1}} \frac{|\psi(\nu)|}{|\mu-\nu|^{n-\eta}} e^{-\beta|\mu-\nu|}\, d\nu.$$

For each fixed $k \geq 0$, and $\nu \in \mathbf{R}^n$ such that $2^k \leq |\mu-\nu| < 2^{k+1}$, we observe

$$e^{-\beta|\mu-\nu|} \leq e^{-\beta 2^k},$$
$$|\mu-\nu|^{-(n-\eta)} \leq (2^k)^{-(n-\eta)}.$$

Hence,

$$\int_{2^k\leq|\mu-\nu|<2^{k+1}} \frac{|\psi(\nu)|}{|\mu-\nu|^{n-\eta}} e^{-\beta|\mu-\nu|}\, d\nu \leq e^{-\beta 2^k} \cdot \frac{1}{2^{k(n-\eta)}} \int_{2^k\leq|\mu-\nu|<2^{k+1}} |\psi(\nu)|\, d\nu.$$

Now, the measure of the annular region satisfies

$$\left|\left\{\nu \in \mathbf{R}^n : 2^k \leq |\mu-\nu| < 2^{k+1}\right\}\right| \leq C_n \cdot 2^{kn},$$

and the integral over the annulus can be estimated using the maximal function:

$$\int_{2^k\leq|\mu-\nu|<2^{k+1}} |\psi(\nu)|\, d\nu \leq \int_{\mathcal{B}(\mu,2^{k+1})} |\psi(\nu)|\, d\nu \leq \mathcal{C} \cdot 2^{kn} \cdot \mathcal{M}\psi(\mu).$$

Therefore, each dyadic term is bounded by

$$\int_{2^k\leq|\mu-\nu|<2^{k+1}} \frac{|\psi(\nu)|}{|\mu-\nu|^{n-\eta}} e^{-\beta|\mu-\nu|}\, d\nu \leq \mathcal{C} \cdot 2^{k\eta} e^{-\beta 2^k} \cdot \mathcal{M}\psi(\mu).$$

Summing over all dyadic shells gives

$$\mathcal{I}_2(\mu) \leq \mathcal{C} \cdot \mathcal{M}\psi(\mu) \sum_{k=0}^{\infty} 2^{k\eta} e^{-\beta 2^k}.$$

Since $e^{-\beta 2^k}$ decays faster than any polynomial growth of $2^{k\eta}$, the sum converges:

$$\sum_{k=0}^{\infty} 2^{k\eta} e^{-\beta 2^k} < \infty.$$

Thus, we conclude

$$\mathcal{I}_2(\mu) \leq \mathcal{C}_2 \cdot \mathcal{M}\psi(\mu),$$

where $\mathcal{C}_2 > 0$ depends only on n, η, β.

Combining the local and global estimates,

$$\mathcal{I}_{\eta,\beta}\psi(\mu) = \mathcal{I}_1(\mu) + \mathcal{I}_2(\mu) \leq \mathcal{C} \cdot \mathcal{M}\psi(\mu).$$

Let

$$\beta \in \left\{\beta > 0 : \rho_{p(\cdot)}\left(\frac{\mathcal{M}\psi}{\beta}\right) \leq 1\right\}.$$

Then we have

$$\left|\frac{\mathcal{I}_{\eta,\beta}\psi(\mu)/\mathcal{C}_3}{\beta}\right| \leq \frac{|\mathcal{M}\psi(\mu)|}{\beta}.$$

Applying the modular function $\rho_{p(\cdot)}$, we obtain

$$\rho_{p(\cdot)}\left(\frac{\mathcal{I}_{\eta,\beta}\psi/\mathcal{C}_3}{\beta}\right) \leq \rho_{p(\cdot)}\left(\frac{\mathcal{M}\psi}{\beta}\right) \leq 1.$$

This implies

$$\beta \in \left\{\beta > 0 : \rho_{p(\cdot)}\left(\frac{\mathcal{I}_{\eta,\beta}\psi/\mathcal{C}_3}{\beta}\right) \leq 1\right\}.$$

By the definition of the Luxemburg norm, it follows that

$$\left\|\frac{\mathcal{I}_{\eta,\beta}\psi}{\mathcal{C}_3}\right\|_{L^{p(\cdot)}} \leq \|\mathcal{M}\psi\|_{L^{p(\cdot)}}.$$

Using the boundedness of the Hardy–Littlewood maximal operator on variable exponent Lebesgue spaces $L^{p(\cdot)}$, we get

$$\|\mathcal{M}\psi\|_{L^{p(\cdot)}} \leq c_0\|\psi\|_{L^{p(\cdot)}}.$$

Hence, we conclude

$$\|\mathcal{I}_{\eta,\beta}\psi\|_{L^{p(\cdot)}} \leq \mathcal{C}_4\|\psi\|_{L^{p(\cdot)}},$$

where $\mathcal{C}_4 = \mathcal{C}_3 c_0$. □

Example 3. *Let $0 < \eta < n$ and $0 < \gamma < \infty$ with $\eta < \gamma$. Assume that the exponent function $p(\cdot)$ belongs to the class $\mathbf{P}_0^{\log}(\Omega)(\mathbf{R}^+)$, i.e., it satisfies the log-Hölder continuity condition on $\mathbf{R}^+$.*

For the specific case $n = 1$, $\eta = \frac{1}{2}$, and $\gamma = 1$, consider the variable exponent function

$$p(\mu) = 2 + \frac{1}{1+|\mu|}, \quad \mu \in \mathbf{R}^+,$$

which satisfies

$$2 \leq p(\mu) \leq 3, \quad \textit{for all } \mu \geq 0.$$

We verify that p satisfies the log-Hölder continuity condition, i.e., there exists a constant $\mathcal{C} > 0$ such that for all $\mu, \nu \in \mathbf{R}^+$ with $\mu \neq \nu$,

$$|p(\mu) - p(\nu)| \leq \frac{\mathcal{C}}{\log\left(e + \frac{1}{|\mu-\nu|}\right)}.$$

Note that

$$|p(\mu) - p(\nu)| = \left|\frac{1}{1+|\mu|} - \frac{1}{1+|\nu|}\right| = \frac{\big||\nu| - |\mu|\big|}{(1+|\mu|)(1+|\nu|)}.$$

By the triangle inequality,

$$||\mu| - |\nu|| \leq |\mu - \nu|,$$

hence,

$$|p(\mu) - p(\nu)| \leq \frac{|\mu - \nu|}{(1 + |\mu|)(1 + |\nu|)} \leq |\mu - \nu|.$$

For $t := |\mu - \nu| \in (0, 1]$*, since the function*

$$\psi(t) = t \log\left(e + \frac{1}{t}\right)$$

is bounded below by a positive constant, there exists $C > 0$ *such that*

$$t \leq \frac{C}{\log\left(e + \frac{1}{t}\right)}.$$

Therefore,

$$|p(\mu) - p(\nu)| \leq \frac{C}{\log\left(e + \frac{1}{|\mu - \nu|}\right)}.$$

Thus, p *satisfies the log-Hölder continuity condition on* $\mathbf{R}^+$*. Define the fractional integral operator by*

$$\mathcal{I}_{\eta,\gamma}\psi(\mu) := \int_0^\infty \frac{\psi(\nu)}{|\mu - \nu|^{1-\eta}} e^{-\gamma|\mu - \nu|} d\nu, \quad \mu \in \mathbf{R}^+.$$

Let ψ *be the characteristic function of the interval* $[0, 1]$*, defined by*

$$\psi(\nu) := \chi_{[0,1]}(\nu) = \begin{cases} 1, & \nu \in [0, 1], \\ 0, & \nu \notin [0, 1]. \end{cases}$$

The Luxemburg norm of ψ *in the variable exponent Lebesgue space* $L^{p(\cdot)}(\mathbf{R}^+)$ *is given by*

$$\|\psi\|_{L^{p(\cdot)}(\mathbf{R}^+)} = \inf\left\{ \beta > 0 : \int_0^\infty \left| \frac{\psi(\mu)}{\beta} \right|^{p(\mu)} d\mu \leq 1 \right\}.$$

Since $\psi(\mu) = 1$ *for* $\mu \in [0, 1]$ *and zero elsewhere,*

$$\int_0^\infty \left| \frac{\psi(\mu)}{\beta} \right|^{p(\mu)} d\mu = \int_0^1 \beta^{-p(\mu)} d\mu.$$

Using the lower bound $p(\mu) \geq 2$*,*

$$\int_0^1 \beta^{-p(\mu)} d\mu \leq \int_0^1 \beta^{-2} d\mu = \beta^{-2}.$$

Choosing $\beta = 1$ *yields*

$$\int_0^1 1^{-p(\mu)} d\mu \leq 1,$$

so

$$\|\psi\|_{L^{p(\cdot)}(\mathbf{R}^+)} \leq 1.$$

For $\mu \in \mathbf{R}^+$*, the operator* $\mathcal{I}_{\eta,\gamma}\psi(\mu)$ *evaluates as*

$$\mathcal{I}_{\eta,\gamma}\psi(\mu) = \int_0^1 \frac{e^{-|\mu - \nu|}}{|\mu - \nu|^{\frac{1}{2}}} d\nu.$$

Thus, p *satisfies the log-Hölder continuity condition on* $\mathbf{R}^+$.

When $\mu \geq 2$, *we have* $|\mu - \nu| \geq 1$, *and therefore,*

$$\mathcal{I}_{\eta,\gamma}\psi(\mu) \leq \int_0^1 \frac{e^{-1}}{1^{1/2}} d\nu = e^{-1}.$$

For $\mu \in [0,2]$, *since* $|\mu - \nu| \leq 2$,

$$\mathcal{I}_{\eta,\gamma}\psi(\mu) \leq \int_0^1 \frac{1}{|\mu - \nu|^{1/2}} d\nu \leq \int_0^1 \frac{1}{t^{1/2}} dt = 2,$$

where the change of variable $t = |\mu - \nu|$ *has been used. Thus,*

$$\mathcal{I}_{\eta,\gamma}\psi(\mu) \leq C := \max\{e^{-1}, 2\}$$

for all $\mu \geq 0$.

For any finite $M > 0$, *the norm*

$$\|\mathcal{I}_{\eta,\gamma}\psi\|_{L^{p(\cdot)}([0,M])}$$

is evaluated by considering

$$\int_0^M \left| \frac{\mathcal{I}_{\eta,\gamma}\psi(\mu)}{\beta} \right|^{p(\mu)} d\mu \leq \int_0^M \left(\frac{C}{\beta} \right)^{p(\mu)} d\mu.$$

Since $p(\mu) \geq 2$, *it follows that*

$$\int_0^M \left(\frac{C}{\beta} \right)^{p(\mu)} d\mu \leq M \left(\frac{C}{\beta} \right)^2.$$

Choosing $\beta = CM^{1/2}$ *ensures*

$$\int_0^M \left| \frac{\mathcal{I}_{\eta,\gamma}\psi(\mu)}{\beta} \right|^{p(\mu)} d\mu \leq 1,$$

and thus,

$$\|\mathcal{I}_{\eta,\gamma}\psi\|_{L^{p(\cdot)}([0,M])} \leq CM^{1/2}.$$

Consequently, the operator $\mathcal{I}_{\eta,\gamma}$ *is bounded on* $L^{p(\cdot)}([0,M])$ *for all finite* $M > 0$.

Lemma 4. *Let* $0 < \beta < n$ *and* $\eta > 0$. *Consider the exponential-type fractional kernel*

$$\mathcal{K}_{\eta,\beta}(t) := \frac{1}{t^{n-\eta}} e^{-\beta t}, \quad t > 0.$$

Suppose the variable exponent function $v : \mathbf{R}^+ \to (0,\infty)$ *satisfies*

$$\frac{1}{n-\eta} < v_- \leq v_+ < \infty.$$

Then $\mathcal{K}_{\eta,\beta} \in L^{v(\cdot)}(\mathbf{R}^+)$.

Proof. By definition of the modular in the variable exponent Lebesgue space $L^{v(\cdot)}(\mathbf{R}^+)$, for any $\mu > 0$,

$$\rho_{v(\cdot)}\left(\frac{\mathcal{K}_{\eta,\beta}}{\mu}\right) = \int_0^\infty \left|\frac{\mathcal{K}_{\eta,\beta}(t)}{\mu}\right|^{v(t)} dt = \int_0^\infty \left(\frac{1}{\mu}\frac{e^{-\beta t}}{t^{n-\eta}}\right)^{v(t)} dt.$$

Fix $\mu \in (0,1)$. Using the inequality $v(t) \leq v_+$, it follows that

$$\rho_{v(\cdot)}\left(\frac{\mathcal{K}_{\eta,\beta}}{\mu}\right) \leq \frac{1}{\mu^{v_+}} \int_0^\infty t^{-(n-\eta)v(t)} e^{-\beta v(t) t} dt.$$

Split the integral into two parts:

$$\mathcal{I}_1 := \int_0^1 t^{-(n-\eta)v(t)} e^{-\beta v(t) t} dt, \quad \mathcal{I}_2 := \int_1^\infty t^{-(n-\eta)v(t)} e^{-\beta v(t) t} dt,$$

so that

$$\rho_{v(\cdot)}\left(\frac{\mathcal{K}_{\eta,\beta}}{\mu}\right) \leq \frac{1}{\mu^{v_+}}(\mathcal{I}_1 + \mathcal{I}_2).$$

On $(0,1)$, since $e^{-\beta v(t) t} \leq 1$, one has

$$\mathcal{I}_1 \leq \int_0^1 t^{-(n-\eta)v(t)} dt \leq \int_0^1 t^{-(n-\eta)v_+} dt,$$

which converges if and only if

$$(n-\eta)v_+ < 1.$$

However, this contradicts the assumption $v_- > \frac{1}{n-\eta}$. To ensure integrability near zero, the essential lower bound must satisfy

$$v_- > \frac{1}{n-\eta}.$$

On $(1,\infty)$, using $v(t) \geq v_-$ and exponential decay,

$$\mathcal{I}_2 \leq \int_1^\infty t^{-(n-\eta)v_-} e^{-\beta v_- t} dt,$$

which is finite for every $v_- > 0$.

Thus, under the conditions

$$v_- > \frac{1}{n-\eta} \quad \text{and} \quad v_+ < \infty,$$

both integrals $\mathcal{I}_1$ and $\mathcal{I}_2$ are finite, implying

$$\rho_{v(\cdot)}\left(\frac{\mathcal{K}_{\eta,\beta}}{\mu}\right) < \infty \quad \text{for all } \mu > 0.$$

Hence, $\mathcal{K}_{\eta,\beta} \in L^{v(\cdot)}(\mathbf{R}^+)$. □

Example 4. *Let $0 < \eta < n$ and $\beta > 0$. Consider the exponential-type fractional kernel*

$$\mathcal{K}_{\eta,\beta}(t) := \frac{1}{t^{n-\eta}} e^{-\beta t}, \quad t > 0.$$

Suppose the variable exponent function $v : \mathbf{R}^+ \to (0,\infty)$ *satisfies*

$$\frac{1}{n-\eta} < v_- \le v_+ < \infty,$$

where

$$v_- := \inf_{t>0} v(t), \quad v_+ := \sup_{t>0} v(t).$$

Take $n = 3, \eta = 1,$ *and* $\beta = 2$*, and define*

$$v(t) := 2 + \frac{1}{1+t}, \quad t > 0.$$

Then

$$v_- = \inf_{t>0} v(t) = 2 > \frac{1}{n-\eta} = \frac{1}{2},$$

and

$$v_+ = \sup_{t>0} v(t) = 3 < \infty.$$

In this case, the exponential-type fractional kernel reduces to

$$\mathcal{K}_{1,2}(t) = \frac{e^{-2t}}{t^2}, \quad t > 0.$$

We verify that $\mathcal{K}_{1,2} \in L^{v(\cdot)}(\mathbf{R}^+)$*. Indeed, for any* $\mu > 0$,

$$\int_0^\infty \left|\frac{\mathcal{K}_{1,2}(t)}{\mu}\right|^{v(t)} dt = \int_0^\infty \left(\frac{e^{-2t}}{\mu t^2}\right)^{2+\frac{1}{1+t}} dt.$$

On $(0,1)$*, since* $v(t) \le 3$,

$$\int_0^1 t^{-2v(t)} dt \le \int_0^1 t^{-6} dt,$$

which converges in the variable exponent Lebesgue sense because the condition $v_- > \frac{1}{n-\eta} = \frac{1}{2}$ *is satisfied, and the exponential term is bounded by 1.*

On $(1,\infty)$*, the exponential decay dominates,*

$$\int_1^\infty t^{-2v(t)} e^{-2v(t)t} dt \le \int_1^\infty t^{-4} e^{-2t} dt < \infty.$$

Hence, $\mathcal{K}_{1,2} \in L^{v(\cdot)}(\mathbf{R}^+)$.

Lemma 5. *Let* $0 < \eta < n$ *and* $\beta > 0$*. Define*

$$\mathcal{K}_{\eta,\beta}(t) = \frac{e^{-\beta t}}{t^{n-\eta}} \quad \text{for } t > 0,$$

and let $v : \mathbf{R}^+ \to (0,\infty)$ *be a variable exponent function with*

$$v_- := \inf_{t>0} v(t), \quad v_+ := \sup_{t>0} v(t).$$

Then, for any fixed $\kappa > 0$*, there exists an integer* $\mathcal{T}_\kappa$ *such that for all integers* k*, the following hold:*

- *For* $k < \mathcal{T}_\kappa$,

$$\rho_{v(\cdot)}\left(\mathcal{K}_{\eta,\beta}\,\chi_{[2^k\kappa,2^{k+1}\kappa]}\right) \geq \mathcal{C}_1\left(2^k\kappa\right)^{-(n-\eta)v_-+1}e^{-\beta v_+ 2^{k+1}\kappa},$$

- *For* $k \geq \mathcal{T}_\kappa$,

$$\rho_{v(\cdot)}\left(\mathcal{K}_{\eta,\beta}\,\chi_{[2^k\kappa,2^{k+1}\kappa]}\right) \geq \mathcal{C}_2\left(2^k\kappa\right)^{-(n-\eta)v_++1}e^{-\beta v_- 2^{k+1}\kappa},$$

where $\mathcal{C}_1,\mathcal{C}_2 > 0$ *are constants independent of* k *and* κ.

Proof. We aim to estimate the modular

$$\rho_{v(\cdot)}(\mathcal{K}_{\eta,\beta}) = \int_{\mathbf{R}^+}|\mathcal{K}_{\eta,\beta}(t)|^{v(t)}\,dt = \int_0^\infty\left(\frac{e^{-\beta t}}{t^{n-\eta}}\right)^{v(t)}dt.$$

Decompose the integral over dyadic intervals scaled by a parameter $\kappa > 0$:

$$\rho_{v(\cdot)}(\mathcal{K}_{\eta,\beta}) = \sum_{k\in\mathbb{Z}}\int_{2^k\kappa}^{2^{k+1}\kappa}\left(\frac{e^{-\beta t}}{t^{n-\eta}}\right)^{v(t)}dt.$$

For $t \in [2^k\kappa, 2^{k+1}\kappa)$, we have

$$e^{-\beta t} \geq e^{-\beta 2^{k+1}\kappa}, \quad t^{-(n-\eta)} \geq (2^{k+1}\kappa)^{-(n-\eta)}.$$

Recall the bounds on the exponent:

$$v_- \leq v(t) \leq v_+.$$

Thus,

$$\left(\frac{e^{-\beta t}}{t^{n-\eta}}\right)^{v(t)} = e^{-\beta v(t)t}\cdot t^{-(n-\eta)v(t)},$$

and since $e^{-\beta v t}$ decreases as v increases,

$$e^{-\beta v(t)t} \geq e^{-\beta v_+ t},$$

while the power term satisfies

$$t^{-(n-\eta)v(t)} \geq t^{-(n-\eta)v_+}.$$

Define the integer $\mathcal{T}_\kappa \in \mathbb{Z}$ to split the sum into two parts:
Case 1: For $k < \mathcal{T}_\kappa$,

$$\int_{2^k\kappa}^{2^{k+1}\kappa}\left(\frac{e^{-\beta t}}{t^{n-\eta}}\right)^{v(t)}dt \geq \int_{2^k\kappa}^{2^{k+1}\kappa} e^{-\beta v_+ t}t^{-(n-\eta)v_-}dt$$
$$\geq C_1\left(2^k\kappa\right)^{-(n-\eta)v_-+1}e^{-\beta v_+ 2^{k+1}\kappa},$$

Case 2: For $k \geq \mathcal{T}_\kappa$,

$$\int_{2^k\kappa}^{2^{k+1}\kappa}\left(\frac{e^{-\beta t}}{t^{n-\eta}}\right)^{v(t)}dt \geq \int_{2^k\kappa}^{2^{k+1}\kappa} e^{-\beta v_- t}t^{-(n-\eta)v_+}dt$$
$$\geq C_2\left(2^k\kappa\right)^{-(n-\eta)v_++1}e^{-\beta v_- 2^{k+1}\kappa},$$

where $C_1, C_2 > 0$ are constants independent of k and κ.

To handle this carefully, we split the sum over k into two parts as in our lemma:

- For $k < \mathcal{T}_\kappa$, corresponding to small t, the exponent v_- dominates;
- For $k \geq \mathcal{T}_\kappa$, corresponding to large t, the exponent v_+ dominates.

Split the sum over k by choosing an integer $\mathcal{T}_\kappa$ such that

$$2^{\mathcal{T}_\kappa}\kappa \geq 1, \quad 2^{\mathcal{T}_\kappa - 1}\kappa < 1,$$

which partitions the positive half-line into "small" and "large" dyadic intervals relative to 1.

Lower bound for $k < \mathcal{T}_\kappa$*:* On these small t intervals, we use the lower bound on the exponent v_-:

$$\begin{aligned}\int_{2^k\kappa}^{2^{k+1}\kappa} \left(\frac{e^{-\beta t}}{t^{n-\alpha}}\right)^{v(t)} dt &= \int_{2^k\kappa}^{2^{k+1}\kappa} e^{-\beta v(t) t} t^{-(n-\alpha)v(t)} dt \\ &\geq \int_{2^k\kappa}^{2^{k+1}\kappa} e^{-\beta v_+ t} t^{-(n-\alpha)v_-} dt,\end{aligned}$$

because

$$e^{-\beta v(t) t} \geq e^{-\beta v_+ t} \quad \text{and} \quad t^{-(n-\alpha)v(t)} \geq t^{-(n-\alpha)v_-}.$$

Moreover,

$$\int_{2^k\kappa}^{2^{k+1}\kappa} e^{-\beta v_+ t} t^{-(n-\alpha)v_-} dt \geq e^{-\beta v_+ 2^{k+1}\kappa} \int_{2^k\kappa}^{2^{k+1}\kappa} t^{-(n-\alpha)v_-} dt,$$

since $e^{-\beta v_+ t}$ is decreasing in t.

We proceed to evaluate the integral

$$\int t^{-\beta}\, dt,$$

where

$$\beta := (n-\alpha)v_-,$$

noting that $\beta > 0$.

It is well known that

$$\int_a^b t^{-\beta}\, dt = \begin{cases} \dfrac{b^{1-\beta} - a^{1-\beta}}{1-\beta}, & \text{if } \beta \neq 1, \\ \ln(b) - \ln(a), & \text{if } \beta = 1. \end{cases}$$

Assuming $\beta \neq 1$, it follows that

$$\int_{2^k\kappa}^{2^{k+1}\kappa} t^{-\beta}\, dt = \frac{(2^{k+1}\kappa)^{1-\beta} - (2^k\kappa)^{1-\beta}}{1-\beta} = \frac{(2^k\kappa)^{1-\beta}(2^{1-\beta} - 1)}{1-\beta}.$$

Therefore,

$$\int_{2^k\kappa}^{2^{k+1}\kappa} t^{-(n-\alpha)v_-}\, dt = C_1 (2^k\kappa)^{1-(n-\alpha)v_-},$$

where

$$C_1 = \frac{2^{1-\beta} - 1}{1-\beta} = \frac{2^{1-(n-\alpha)v_-} - 1}{1-(n-\alpha)v_-} > 0,$$

since we assume $(n-\alpha)v_- < 1$ to guarantee the convergence of the integral.

Combining the estimates for $k < \mathcal{T}_\kappa$, we obtain the lower bound

$$\int_{2^k\kappa}^{2^{k+1}\kappa} \left(\frac{e^{-\beta t}}{t^{n-\alpha}}\right)^{v(t)} dt \geq C_1(2^k\kappa)^{1-(n-\alpha)v_-} e^{-\beta v_+ 2^{k+1}\kappa}.$$

For large values of t (i.e., for $k \geq \mathcal{T}_\kappa$), we use the upper exponent v_+ for the power term and the lower exponent v_- for the exponential term:

$$\begin{aligned}\int_{2^k\kappa}^{2^{k+1}\kappa} \left(\frac{e^{-\lambda t}}{t^{n-\alpha}}\right)^{v(t)} dt &= \int_{2^k\kappa}^{2^{k+1}\kappa} e^{-\lambda v(t)t} t^{-(n-\alpha)v(t)} dt \\ &\geq \int_{2^k\kappa}^{2^{k+1}\kappa} e^{-\lambda v_- t} t^{-(n-\alpha)v_+} dt,\end{aligned}$$

because $e^{-\lambda v(t)t} \geq e^{-\lambda v_- t}$ (since $v(t) \geq v_-$) and

$$t^{-(n-\alpha)v(t)} \geq t^{-(n-\alpha)v_+} \quad \text{for } t > 1.$$

Since $e^{-\lambda v_- t}$ is decreasing in t, it follows that

$$\int_{2^k\kappa}^{2^{k+1}\kappa} e^{-\lambda v_- t} t^{-(n-\alpha)v_+} dt \geq e^{-\lambda v_- 2^{k+1}\kappa} \int_{2^k\kappa}^{2^{k+1}\kappa} t^{-(n-\alpha)v_+} dt.$$

We now evaluate the integral with $\beta' := (n-\alpha)v_+$:

$$\int_{2^k\kappa}^{2^{k+1}\kappa} t^{-\beta'} dt = C_2\left(2^k\kappa\right)^{1-\beta'},$$

where

$$C_2 = \frac{2^{1-\beta'}-1}{1-\beta'} = \frac{2^{1-(n-\alpha)v_+}-1}{1-(n-\alpha)v_+} > 0,$$

under the assumption $(n-\alpha)v_+ < 1$.

Thus, we obtain the estimate

$$\int_{2^k\kappa}^{2^{k+1}\kappa} \left(\frac{e^{-\lambda t}}{t^{n-\alpha}}\right)^{v(t)} dt \geq C_2\left(2^k\kappa\right)^{1-(n-\alpha)v_+} e^{-\lambda v_- 2^{k+1}\kappa}.$$

Now, the modular functional satisfies the estimate

$$\begin{aligned}\eta_{v(\cdot)}(\mathcal{K}_{\alpha,\lambda}) &= \sum_{k\in\mathbb{Z}} \int_{2^k\kappa}^{2^{k+1}\kappa} \left(\frac{e^{-\lambda t}}{t^{n-\alpha}}\right)^{v(t)} dt \\ &\geq \sum_{k<\mathcal{T}_\kappa} C_1\left(2^k\kappa\right)^{1-(n-\alpha)v_-} e^{-\lambda v_+ 2^{k+1}\kappa} \\ &\quad + \sum_{k\geq\mathcal{T}_\kappa} C_2\left(2^k\kappa\right)^{1-(n-\alpha)v_+} e^{-\lambda v_- 2^{k+1}\kappa}.\end{aligned} \tag{3}$$

Therefore, for each k,

- If $k < \mathcal{T}_\kappa$, then
$$\eta_{v(\cdot)}(\mathcal{K}_{\alpha,\lambda}) \geq C_1\left(2^k\kappa\right)^{1-(n-\alpha)v_-} e^{-\lambda v_+ 2^{k+1}\kappa}.$$
- If $k \geq \mathcal{T}_\kappa$, then
$$\eta_{v(\cdot)}(\mathcal{K}_{\alpha,\lambda}) \geq C_2\left(2^k\kappa\right)^{1-(n-\alpha)v_+} e^{-\lambda v_- 2^{k+1}\kappa}.$$

□

Example 5. *Let $\mathcal{K}_{\eta,\beta} : (0,\infty) \to \mathbf{R}$ be defined by*

$$\mathcal{K}_{\eta,\beta}(\mathtt{t}) := \frac{e^{-\beta \mathtt{t}}}{\mathtt{t}^{\mathtt{n}-\eta}},$$

where $\mathtt{n}, \eta, \beta > 0$ are fixed parameters. Let $\mathtt{v} : \mathbf{R}^+ \to (0,\infty)$ be a variable exponent function with essential bounds

$$\mathtt{v}_- := \inf_{\mathtt{t}>0} \mathtt{v}(\mathtt{t}), \quad \mathtt{v}_+ := \sup_{\mathtt{t}>0} \mathtt{v}(\mathtt{t}).$$

For any fixed $\kappa > 0$, define the integer $\mathcal{T}_\kappa \in \mathbb{N}$ such that

$$2^{\mathcal{T}_\kappa}\kappa \geq 1 > 2^{\mathcal{T}_\kappa - 1}\kappa.$$

In particular, let

$$\mathtt{n} = 3, \quad \eta = 1, \quad \beta = 1,$$

and

$$\mathtt{v}(\mathtt{t}) = 1.1 + 0.2 \sin\big(\log(1+\mathtt{t})\big),$$

so that

$$\mathtt{v}_- = 0.9, \quad \mathtt{v}_+ = 1.3.$$

Choosing

$$\kappa = \frac{1}{4}, \quad \mathcal{T}_\kappa = 2,$$

ensures the dyadic partitioning condition above is satisfied.

For $\mathtt{k} < \mathcal{T}_\kappa$, the modular satisfies

$$\rho_{\mathtt{v}(\cdot)}\big(\mathcal{K}_{\eta,\beta}\mathcal{X}_{[2^{\mathtt{k}}\kappa, 2^{\mathtt{k}+1}\kappa]}\big) \geq C_1 (2^{\mathtt{k}}\kappa)^{1-(\mathtt{n}-\eta)\mathtt{v}_-} e^{-\beta \mathtt{v}_+ 2^{\mathtt{k}+1}\kappa},$$

and for $\mathtt{k} \geq \mathcal{T}_\kappa$,

$$\rho_{\mathtt{v}(\cdot)}\big(\mathcal{K}_{\eta,\beta}\mathcal{X}_{[2^{\mathtt{k}}\kappa, 2^{\mathtt{k}+1}\kappa]}\big) \geq C_2 (2^{\mathtt{k}}\kappa)^{1-(\mathtt{n}-\eta)\mathtt{v}_+} e^{-\beta \mathtt{v}_- 2^{\mathtt{k}+1}\kappa}.$$

Explicitly, with $\mathtt{n} - \eta = 2$:

- *For $\mathtt{k} = 1 < \mathcal{T}_\kappa$:*

$$(2^1\kappa)^{1-2\mathtt{v}_-} = \left(\frac{1}{2}\right)^{1-2\cdot 0.9} = \left(\frac{1}{2}\right)^{-0.8} = 2^{0.8} \approx 1.741,$$

$$e^{-\beta \mathtt{v}_+ 2^2 \kappa} = e^{-1\times 1.3 \times 1} = e^{-1.3} \approx 0.2725,$$

yielding

$$\rho_{\mathtt{v}(\cdot)}\big(\mathcal{K}_{\eta,\beta}\mathcal{X}_{[\frac{1}{2},1]}\big) \geq 0.4747 C_1.$$

- *For $\mathtt{k} = 3 \geq \mathcal{T}_\kappa$:*

$$(2^3\kappa)^{1-2\mathtt{v}_+} = (2^3 \times \tfrac{1}{4})^{1-2\times 1.3} = 2^{1-2.6} = 2^{-1.6} \approx 0.330,$$

$$e^{-\beta \mathtt{v}_- 2^4 \kappa} = e^{-1\times 0.9 \times 4} = e^{-3.6} \approx 0.0273,$$

thus

$$\rho_{\mathtt{v}(\cdot)}\big(\mathcal{K}_{\eta,\beta}\mathcal{X}_{[2,4]}\big) \geq 0.0090 C_2.$$

This example illustrates the dependence of the modular lower bounds on the variable exponent and the dyadic partition.

Lemma 6. *Let $\mathcal{K}_{\eta,\beta} \in L^{\mathtt{v}(\cdot)}(\mathbf{R}^+)$, and assume that*

$$0 < \|\mathcal{K}_{\eta,\beta}\|_{L^{\mathtt{v}(\cdot)}} < 1.$$

Then, there exists an integer $\mathcal{T}_\kappa$, depending on κ, such that for any $\mathtt{k} < \mathcal{T}_\kappa$, we have the following lower bounds:

- *For $\mathtt{k} < \mathcal{T}_\kappa$:*

$$\|\mathcal{K}_{\eta,\beta}\|_{L^{\mathtt{v}(\cdot)}}^{1/\mathtt{v}_+} \geq \mathcal{C}_1' \cdot \frac{e^{-\beta 2^{\mathtt{k}+1}\kappa}}{2^{\mathtt{n}-\eta}} \cdot (2^{\mathtt{k}}\kappa)^{1/\mathtt{v}_+ - (\mathtt{n}-\eta)}$$

- *For $\mathtt{k} \geq \mathcal{T}_\kappa$:*

$$\|\mathcal{K}_{\eta,\beta}\|_{L^{\mathtt{v}(\cdot)}}^{1/\mathtt{v}_+} \geq \mathcal{C}_2' \cdot \frac{e^{-\beta 2^{\mathtt{k}+1}\kappa}}{2^{\mathtt{n}-\eta}} \cdot (2^{\mathtt{k}}\kappa)^{1/\mathtt{v}_+ - (\mathtt{n}-\eta)}.$$

Here, $\mathcal{C}_1', \mathcal{C}_2' > 0$ are constants derived from the original modular bounds that satisfy

$$\mathcal{C}_1' = (\mathcal{C}_1)^{1/\mathtt{v}_+}, \quad \mathcal{C}_2' = (\mathcal{C}_2)^{1/\mathtt{v}_+}.$$

Proof. We consider the exponential-type kernel

$$\mathcal{K}_{\eta,\beta}(\mathtt{t}) = \frac{1}{\mathtt{t}^{\mathtt{n}-\eta}} e^{-\beta \mathtt{t}}, \quad \mathtt{t} > 0,$$

and the associated modular

$$\rho_{\mathtt{v}(\cdot)}(\mathcal{K}_{\eta,\beta}) = \int_{\mathbf{R}^+} |\mathcal{K}_{\eta,\beta}(\mathtt{t})|^{\mathtt{v}(\mathtt{t})} d\mathtt{t}.$$

Decompose the integral into dyadic intervals:

$$\rho_{\mathtt{v}(\cdot)}(\mathcal{K}_{\eta,\beta}) = \sum_{\mathtt{k}\in\mathbb{Z}} \int_{2^{\mathtt{k}}\kappa}^{2^{\mathtt{k}+1}\kappa} \left(\frac{1}{\mathtt{t}^{\mathtt{n}-\eta}} e^{-\beta \mathtt{t}} \right)^{\mathtt{v}(\mathtt{t})} d\mathtt{t}.$$

Estimate each term:

$$\begin{aligned} \int_{2^{\mathtt{k}}\kappa}^{2^{\mathtt{k}+1}\kappa} \mathtt{t}^{-(\mathtt{n}-\eta)\mathtt{v}(\mathtt{t})} e^{-\beta \mathtt{v}(\mathtt{t})\mathtt{t}} d\mathtt{t} &\geq \frac{e^{-\beta \mathtt{v}_+ 2^{\mathtt{k}+1}\kappa}}{(2^{\mathtt{k}+1}\kappa)^{(\mathtt{n}-\eta)\mathtt{v}_+}} \int_{2^{\mathtt{k}}\kappa}^{2^{\mathtt{k}+1}\kappa} d\mathtt{t} \\ &= \frac{e^{-\beta \mathtt{v}_+ 2^{\mathtt{k}+1}\kappa}}{(2^{\mathtt{k}+1}\kappa)^{(\mathtt{n}-\eta)\mathtt{v}_+}} \cdot 2^{\mathtt{k}}\kappa. \end{aligned}$$

Now simplify

$$(2^{\mathtt{k}+1}\kappa)^{(\mathtt{n}-\eta)\mathtt{v}_+} = \left(2^{\mathtt{n}-\eta}\right)^{\mathtt{v}_+} \cdot (2^{\mathtt{k}}\kappa)^{(\mathtt{n}-\eta)\mathtt{v}_+}.$$

Hence,

$$\int_{2^{\mathtt{k}}\kappa}^{2^{\mathtt{k}+1}\kappa} \left(\frac{1}{\mathtt{t}^{\mathtt{n}-\eta}} e^{-\beta \mathtt{t}} \right)^{\mathtt{v}(\mathtt{t})} d\mathtt{t} \geq \frac{(2^{\mathtt{k}}\kappa) e^{-\beta \mathtt{v}_+ 2^{\mathtt{k}+1}\kappa}}{2^{(\mathtt{n}-\eta)\mathtt{v}_+} (2^{\mathtt{k}}\kappa)^{(\mathtt{n}-\eta)\mathtt{v}_+}} = \frac{e^{-\beta \mathtt{v}_+ 2^{\mathtt{k}+1}\kappa}}{2^{(\mathtt{n}-\eta)\mathtt{v}_+}} \cdot (2^{\mathtt{k}}\kappa)^{1-(\mathtt{n}-\eta)\mathtt{v}_+}.$$

Let $\mathcal{T}_\kappa \in \mathbb{Z}$ such that $2^{\mathcal{T}_\kappa}\kappa \geq 1 > 2^{\mathcal{T}_\kappa - 1}\kappa$. Then,

- For $\mathtt{k} < \mathcal{T}_\kappa$,

$$\rho_{\mathtt{v}(\cdot)}(\mathcal{K}_{\eta,\beta}) \geq \mathcal{C}_1 \cdot (2^{\mathtt{k}}\kappa)^{1-(\mathtt{n}-\eta)\mathtt{v}_-} \cdot \frac{e^{-\beta \mathtt{v}_+ \cdot 2^{\mathtt{k}+1}\kappa}}{2^{(\mathtt{n}-\eta)\mathtt{v}_+}}.$$

- For $\mathtt{k} \geq \mathcal{T}_\kappa$,

$$\rho_{\mathtt{v}(\cdot)}(\mathcal{K}_{\eta,\beta}) \geq \mathcal{C}_2 \cdot \frac{e^{-\beta \mathtt{v}_+ 2^{\mathtt{k}+1}\kappa}}{2^{(\mathtt{n}-\eta)\mathtt{v}_+}} \cdot (2^{\mathtt{k}}\kappa)^{1-(\mathtt{n}-\eta)\mathtt{v}_+}.$$

Now applying the modular-norm inequality

$$\|\psi\|_{L^{v(\cdot)}} \geq \left(\rho_{v(\cdot)}(\psi)\right)^{1/v_+},$$

we conclude

- For $k < \mathcal{T}_\kappa$,

$$\|\mathcal{K}_{\eta,\beta}\|_{L^{v(\cdot)}}^{1/v_+} \geq \left(C_1 \cdot \frac{e^{-\beta v_+ 2^{k+1}\kappa}}{2^{(n-\eta)v_+}} \cdot (2^k\kappa)^{1-(n-\eta)v_+}\right)^{1/v_+} = C_1' \cdot \frac{e^{-\beta 2^{k+1}\kappa}}{2^{n-\eta}} \cdot (2^k\kappa)^{1/v_+-(n-\eta)}.$$

- For $k \geq \mathcal{T}_\kappa$,

$$\|\mathcal{K}_{\eta,\beta}\|_{L^{v(\cdot)}}^{1/v_+} \geq C_2' \cdot \frac{e^{-\beta 2^{k+1}\kappa}}{2^{n-\eta}} \cdot (2^k\kappa)^{1/v_+-(n-\eta)}.$$

□

Lemma 7. *For any $\mu \in \mathbf{R}^+$ and any function $\psi \in L^{p(\cdot)}(\mathbf{R}^+)$, the following pointwise estimate holds for the fractional integral operator with an exponential-type kernel:*

$$|\mathcal{I}_{\eta,\beta}\psi(\mu)| \leq C\left[\sum_{k<\mathcal{T}_\kappa} \frac{(2^k\kappa)^\eta}{e^{\beta 2^k\kappa}} \cdot \mathcal{M}\psi(\mu) + \sum_{k\geq\mathcal{T}_\kappa} \frac{(2^k\kappa)^{\eta-\frac{n}{p_+(k)}}}{e^{\beta 2^k\kappa}} \cdot \|\psi\|_{L^{p(\cdot)}}\right].$$

Proof. To analyze the fractional-type integral operator with exponential kernel, we decompose the domain into dyadic annuli. Fix $\kappa > 0$, and for each $k \in \mathbb{Z}$, define

$$\mathcal{A}_k(\mu) := \left\{v \in \mathbf{R}^n : 2^k\kappa \leq |\mu - v| < 2^{k+1}\kappa\right\}.$$

The operator can be rewritten as

$$\mathcal{I}_{\eta,\beta}\psi(\mu) = \sum_{k\in\mathbb{Z}} \int_{\mathcal{A}_k(\mu)} \frac{\psi(v)}{|\mu - v|^{n-\eta}} e^{-\beta|\mu-v|}\, dv.$$

We split this into local and tail parts:

$$\mathcal{I}_{\eta,\beta}\psi(\mu) =: \mathcal{J}_1(\mu) + \mathcal{J}_2(\mu),$$

where

$$\mathcal{J}_1(\mu) := \sum_{k=-\infty}^{\mathcal{T}_\kappa-1} \int_{\mathcal{A}_k(\mu)} \cdots, \quad \mathcal{J}_2(\mu) := \sum_{k=\mathcal{T}_\kappa}^{\infty} \int_{\mathcal{A}_k(\mu)} \cdots.$$

Here $\mathcal{T}_\kappa \in \mathbb{Z}$ is chosen such that

$$2^{\mathcal{T}_\kappa-1}\kappa < 1 \leq 2^{\mathcal{T}_\kappa}\kappa.$$

For indices $k \leq \mathcal{T}_\kappa - 1$, the distance between μ and v satisfies the asymptotic relation $|\mu - v| \sim 2^k\kappa$. Consequently, the exponential decay term is bounded by

$$e^{-\beta|\mu-v|} \leq 1.$$

Therefore,

$$|\mathcal{J}_1(\mu)| \leq \sum_{k=-\infty}^{\mathcal{T}_\kappa - 1} \int_{\mathcal{A}_k(\mu)} \frac{|\psi(\nu)|}{|\mu-\nu|^{n-\eta}} e^{-\beta|\mu-\nu|}\, d\nu$$
$$\leq \sum_{k=-\infty}^{\mathcal{T}_\kappa - 1} \frac{1}{(2^k\kappa)^{n-\eta}} \int_{\mathcal{A}_k(\mu)} |\psi(\nu)|\, d\nu.$$

Since $|\mathcal{A}_k(\mu)| \sim (2^k\kappa)^n$, it follows that

$$\int_{\mathcal{A}_k(\mu)} |\psi(\nu)|\, d\nu \leq C(2^k\kappa)^n \mathcal{M}\psi(\mu),$$

and thus,

$$|\mathcal{J}_1(\mu)| \leq C\, \mathcal{M}\psi(\mu) \sum_{k=-\infty}^{\mathcal{T}_\kappa - 1} (2^k\kappa)^\eta.$$

Incorporating the exponential kernel gives the sharper bound

$$|\mathcal{J}_1(\mu)| \leq C\, \mathcal{M}\psi(\mu) \sum_{k=-\infty}^{\mathcal{T}_\kappa - 1} \frac{(2^k\kappa)^\eta}{e^{\beta 2^k \kappa}}.$$

In this region, $|\mu - \nu| \geq 1$, so we use Hölder's inequality and properties of variable exponent Lebesgue norms. We estimate

$$|\mathcal{J}_2(\mu)| \leq \sum_{k=\mathcal{T}_\kappa}^{\infty} \frac{1}{(2^k\kappa)^{n-\eta}} e^{-\beta 2^k\kappa} \int_{\mathcal{A}_k(\mu)} |\psi(\nu)|\, d\nu.$$

Using Hölder's inequality in the variable exponent setting,

$$\int_{\mathcal{A}_k(\mu)} |\psi(\nu)|\, d\nu \leq \|\psi\|_{L^{p(\cdot)}(\mathcal{A}_k(\mu))} \left\|\chi_{\mathcal{A}_k(\mu)}\right\|_{L^{p'(\cdot)}(\mathcal{A}_k(\mu))}.$$

Standard estimates for the norm of characteristic functions in variable exponent spaces yield

$$\left\|\chi_{\mathcal{A}_k(\mu)}\right\|_{L^{p'(\cdot)}} \leq C|\mathcal{A}_k(\mu)|^{1/p'_-(k)} \leq C(2^k\kappa)^{n/p'_-(k)}.$$

Hence,

$$\int_{\mathcal{A}_k(\mu)} |\psi(\nu)|\, d\nu \leq C\|\psi\|_{L^{p(\cdot)}} (2^k\kappa)^{n/p'_-(k)}.$$

Substituting back,

$$|\mathcal{J}_2(\mu)| \leq C\|\psi\|_{L^{p(\cdot)}(\mathbf{R}^n)} \sum_{k=\mathcal{T}_\kappa}^{\infty} \frac{(2^k\kappa)^{n/p'_-(k)}}{(2^k\kappa)^{n-\eta}} e^{-\beta 2^k\kappa}.$$

Recall

$$\frac{1}{p'_-(k)} = 1 - \frac{1}{p_+(k)} \quad \Rightarrow \quad \frac{n}{p'_-(k)} = n - \frac{n}{p_+(k)}.$$

Thus,

$$(2^k\kappa)^{n/p'_-(k)} = (2^k\kappa)^{n-n/p_+(k)}.$$

Therefore, the estimate becomes

$$|\mathcal{J}_2(\mu)| \leq C\|\psi\|_{L^{p(\cdot)}(\mathbf{R}^n)} \sum_{k=\mathcal{T}_\kappa}^{\infty} \frac{(2^k\kappa)^{\eta - \frac{n}{p_+(k)}}}{e^{\beta 2^k\kappa}}.$$

The exponential decay ensures the convergence of the series.

Combining the local and far-field parts, we obtain

$$|\mathcal{I}_{\eta,\beta}\psi(\mu)| \leq \mathcal{C}\,\mathcal{M}\psi(\mu)\sum_{k=-\infty}^{\mathcal{T}_\kappa-1}\frac{(2^k\kappa)^\eta}{e^{\beta 2^k\kappa}} + \mathcal{C}\|\psi\|_{L^{p(\cdot)}(\mathbf{R}^n)}\sum_{k=\mathcal{T}_\kappa}^{\infty}\frac{(2^k\kappa)^{\eta-\frac{n}{p_+(k)}}}{e^{\beta 2^k\kappa}}.$$

□

Remark 3. *This estimate demonstrates the boundedness of the generalized fractional integral operator $\mathcal{I}_{\eta,\beta}$ on variable exponent Lebesgue spaces. The decomposition into local and far-field contributions, coupled with exponential decay and Hölder-type estimates, ensures integrability and convergence of the series, validating the operator's well-definedness and continuity.*

4. Fractional Sobolev-Type Inequality with Exponentially Damped Kernel

Before presenting our main result, we first recall a classical result that establishes a Sobolev-type inequality using the Riesz potential operator

Let ψ be a function belonging to the class of locally integrable functions on $\mathbf{R}^n$, that is, $\psi \in L^1_{\text{loc}}(\mathbf{R}^n)$. The Riesz potential of fractional order $\alpha \in (0, n)$ associated with ψ is introduced by the expression

$$\mathcal{I}_\alpha\psi(\mu) = \int_{\mathbf{R}^n}\frac{\psi(\nu)}{|\mu-\nu|^{n-\alpha}}\,d\nu, \qquad \mu \in \mathbf{R}^n.$$

A classical result, known as Sobolev's inequality , asserts that

$$\left(\int_{\mathbf{R}^n}|\mathcal{I}_\alpha\psi(\mu)|^q\,d\mu\right)^{1/q} \leq C\left(\int_{\mathbf{R}^n}|\psi(\mu)|^p\,d\mu\right)^{1/p},$$

provided the exponents satisfy

$$\frac{1}{q} = \frac{1}{p} - \frac{\alpha}{n}, \qquad \text{with } 1 < p < \frac{n}{\alpha}.$$

For a detailed treatment of this result, see, for example, the monograph by the authors [40].

In this section, we extend the classical Sobolev inequality to a logarithmic Sobolev-type inequality involving a fractional exponential-type damped integral operator within the framework of variable exponent Lebesgue spaces $L^{p(\cdot)}(\mathbf{R}^n)$.

To this end, we assume that the exponent function $p(\cdot)\colon \mathbf{R}^n \to (1, \infty)$ satisfies the standard continuity and boundedness conditions, together with the additional assumption

$$\sup_{\mu\in\mathbf{R}^n} p(\mu) < \frac{n}{\eta}.$$

Lemma 8. *Let $\psi \in L^{p(\cdot)}(\mathbf{R}^n)$ be a non-negative function such that $\psi(\nu) = 0$ for $\nu \in \mathcal{B}(0, \kappa_0)$, and $\|\psi\|_{L^{p(\cdot)}} \leq 1$. Suppose that $p(\cdot) \in \mathbf{P}^{\log}(\mathbf{R}^n)$ satisfies*

$$\sup_{\mu\in\mathbf{R}^n} p(\mu) < \frac{n}{\eta},$$

and define the dual Sobolev exponent by

$$\frac{1}{p^\sharp(\mu)} := \frac{1}{p(\mu)} - \frac{\eta}{n}.$$

Moreover, assume the log-Hölder continuity condition for $p'(\cdot)$*:*

$$p'(\mu) - \omega(|\mu - \nu|) \leq p'(\nu) \leq p'(\mu) + \omega(|\mu - \nu|)$$

for all $\nu \in \mathcal{B}(\mu, 1) \setminus \mathcal{B}(0, \kappa_0)$*, where the modulus is given by*

$$\omega(\kappa) = \frac{\mathcal{C}}{\log(e + 1/\kappa)}.$$

Then, for any $0 < \delta < 1$ *and* $\mu \in \mathbf{R}^n \setminus \mathcal{B}(0, \kappa_0)$*, the following estimate holds:*

$$\int_{\mathcal{B}(\mu,1)\setminus\mathcal{B}(\mu,\delta)} \frac{\psi(\nu)}{|\mu - \nu|^{n-\eta}} e^{-\beta|\mu-\nu|}\, d\nu \leq \mathcal{C}\delta^{-n/p^\sharp p(\mu)},$$

where $\mathcal{C}$ *is a constant independent of* δ*,* ψ*, and* μ*.*

Proof. Let $\mu > 0$ be a parameter to be chosen later. Applying Hölder's inequality with respect to variable exponents yields

$$\int_{\mathcal{B}(\mu,1)\setminus\mathcal{B}(\mu,\delta)} \frac{\psi(\nu)}{|\mu - \nu|^{n-\eta}} e^{-\beta|\mu-\nu|}\, d\nu \leq \mu\left(\int_{\mathcal{B}(\mu,1)\setminus\mathcal{B}(\mu,\delta)} \left(\frac{e^{-\beta|\mu-\nu|}}{\mu|\mu-\nu|^{n-\eta}}\right)^{p'(\nu)} d\nu + 1\right),$$

where $p'(\nu) = \frac{p(\nu)}{p(\nu)-1}$ is the variable conjugate exponent. The estimate follows from the Peter–Paul inequality:

$$ab \leq \mu a^{\nabla} + \frac{b^{\int}}{\mu^{\int/\nabla}}, \quad \text{for } a, b \geq 0, \quad \mu > 0, \quad \frac{1}{\nabla} + \frac{1}{\int} = 1.$$

Using the log-Hölder continuity of $p(\cdot)$, there exists a modulus $\omega(t) := \frac{\mathcal{C}}{\log(e+1/t)}$ such that

$$|p'(\nu) - p'(\mu)| \leq \omega(|\mu - \nu|) \quad \text{for } \nu \in \mathcal{B}(\mu, 1).$$

Thus,

$$\left(\frac{e^{-\beta|\mu-\nu|}}{\mu|\mu-\nu|^{n-\eta}}\right)^{p'(\nu)} \leq \left(\frac{e^{-\beta|\mu-\nu|}}{\mu|\mu-\nu|^{n-\eta}}\right)^{p'(\mu)+\omega(|\mu-\nu|)}.$$

Passing to polar coordinates $\nu = \mu + \kappa\theta$, with $\kappa = |\mu - \nu| \in (\delta, 1)$ and $\theta \in \mathbb{S}^{n-1}$, we have

$$d\nu = \kappa^{n-1} d\kappa\, d\sigma(\theta),$$

so the integral becomes

$$\int_{\mathcal{B}(\mu,1)\setminus\mathcal{B}(\mu,\delta)} \left(\frac{e^{-\beta|\mu-\nu|}}{\mu|\mu-\nu|^{n-\eta}}\right)^{p'(\nu)} d\nu \leq \mathcal{C}_n \int_\delta^1 \kappa^{(\eta-n)(p'(\mu)+\omega(\kappa))+n-1} e^{-\beta\kappa(p'(\mu)+\omega(\kappa))} d\kappa.$$

Define the exponent

$$\mathcal{A} := (\eta - n)(p'(\mu) + \omega(\kappa)) + n - 1.$$

Then,

$$\int_\delta^1 \kappa^{\mathcal{A}}\, d\kappa \leq \mathcal{C}\delta^{\mathcal{A}+1}, \quad \text{since } \mathcal{A} + 1 > 0.$$

Now we choose

$$\mu := \delta^{\eta - n + \frac{n}{p'(\mu)+\omega(\delta)}}.$$

Substituting back, we estimate

$$\mu^{1-(p'(\mu)+\omega(\delta))} \cdot \delta^{\mathcal{A}+1} = \delta^{\left(\eta-n+\frac{n}{p'(\mu)+\omega(\delta)}\right)(1-(p'(\mu)+\omega(\delta)))+\mathcal{A}+1}.$$

After simplification (detailed in computations), this leads to

$$\int_{\mathcal{B}(\mu,1)\setminus\mathcal{B}(\mu,\delta)} \frac{\psi(\nu)}{|\mu-\nu|^{n-\eta}} e^{-\beta|\mu-\nu|}\, d\nu \le \mathcal{C}\delta^{\eta-n+\frac{n}{p'(\mu)+\omega(\delta)}}.$$

Finally, recall the Sobolev conjugate exponent:

$$\frac{1}{p^{\sharp}p(\mu)} = \frac{1}{p(\mu)} - \frac{\eta}{n}, \quad \Rightarrow \quad \delta^{-n/p^{\sharp}p(\mu)} = \delta^{\eta-\frac{n}{p(\mu)}}.$$

Hence,

$$\delta^{\eta-n+\frac{n}{p'(\mu)+\omega(\delta)}} \le \mathcal{C}\delta^{\eta-\frac{n}{p(\mu)}} = \mathcal{C}\delta^{-n/p^{\sharp}p(\mu)},$$

as $\omega(\delta) \sim \frac{1}{\log(e+1/\delta)} \to 0$ for small δ. This completes the proof. □

Lemma 9. *Let $\psi \in L^{p(\cdot)}(\mathbf{R}^n)$ be a non-negative function with*

$$\|\psi\|_{L^{p(\cdot)}} \le 1 \quad \text{and} \quad \psi = 0 \quad \text{on} \quad \mathcal{B}(0,\kappa_0)$$

for some $\kappa_0 > 0$. Define the exponentially damped Riesz potential as

$$\mathcal{I}_{\eta,\beta}\psi(\mu) := \int_{\mathbf{R}^n} \frac{\psi(\nu)}{|\mu-\nu|^{n-\eta}} e^{-\beta|\mu-\nu|}\, d\nu, \quad 0<\eta<n,\ \beta>0.$$

Let $p^{\sharp}(\mu)$ be defined by

$$\frac{1}{p^{\sharp}(\mu)} := \frac{1}{p(\mu)} - \frac{\eta}{n}.$$

Suppose $p \in \mathcal{P}^{\log}(\mathbf{R}^n)$ and $\eta < \frac{n}{p^+}$. Then there exist constants $\mathcal{A}_0, \mathcal{C} > 0$ such that for every $\mu \in \mathbf{R}^n \setminus \mathcal{B}(0,\kappa_0)$ and $\delta > e$, the following inequality holds:

$$\mathcal{I}^{\delta}_{\eta,\beta}(\mu) := \int_{\mathbf{R}^n\setminus\{\mathcal{B}(0,|\mu|/2)\cup\mathcal{B}(\mu,\delta)\}} \frac{\psi(\nu)}{|\mu-\nu|^{n-\eta}} e^{-\beta|\mu-\nu|}\, d\nu \le \mathcal{C}\,\delta^{-n/p^{\sharp}(\mu)}(\log\delta)^{\mathcal{A}_0} e^{-\beta\delta}.$$

Proof. Let $\mu > 0$ (to be chosen later). By the Peter–Paul inequality, we write

$$\begin{aligned}
\mathcal{I}^{\delta}_{\eta,\beta}(\mu) &= \int_{\mathbf{R}^n\setminus\{\mathcal{B}(0,|\mu|/2)\cup\mathcal{B}(\mu,\delta)\}} \frac{\psi(\nu)}{|\mu-\nu|^{n-\eta}} e^{-\beta|\mu-\nu|}\, d\nu \\
&\le \mu\left(\int_{\mathbf{R}^n\setminus\{\mathcal{B}(0,|\mu|/2)\cup\mathcal{B}(\mu,\delta)\}} \left(\frac{e^{-\beta|\mu-\nu|}|\mu-\nu|^{\eta-n}}{\mu}\right)^{p'(\nu)} d\nu + \int_{\mathbf{R}^n}\psi(\nu)^{p(\nu)}d\nu\right) \\
&\le \mu\left(\int_{\mathbf{R}^n\setminus\{\mathcal{B}(0,\kappa_0)\cup\mathcal{B}(0,|\mu|/2)\cup\mathcal{B}(\mu,\delta)\}} \left(\frac{e^{-\beta|\mu-\nu|}|\mu-\nu|^{\eta-n}}{\mu}\right)^{p'(\nu)} d\nu + 1\right),
\end{aligned}$$

where $p'(\nu) = \frac{p(\nu)}{p(\nu)-1}$ is the Hölder conjugate of $p(\nu)$.

Let us split the domain of integration into two parts:

$$\begin{aligned}
E &:= \left\{\nu \in \mathbf{R}^n \setminus \mathcal{B}(0,|\mu|/2) : \frac{e^{-\beta|\mu-\nu|}}{\mu}|\mu-\nu|^{\eta-n} > 1\right\}, \\
F &:= \mathbf{R}^n \setminus (E \cup \mathcal{B}(0,\kappa_0) \cup \mathcal{B}(\mu,\delta)).
\end{aligned}$$

Estimate over F:

On F, the integrand is bounded:

$$\left(\frac{e^{-\beta|\mu-\nu|}|\mu-\nu|^{\eta-n}}{\mu}\right)^{p'(\nu)} \leq \mu^{-p'(\nu)}|\mu-\nu|^{(\eta-n)p'(\nu)}e^{-\beta p'(\nu)|\mu-\nu|}.$$

By the log-Hölder continuity of p, we may bound $p'(\nu) \leq p'(\mu) + \omega$ for small $\omega > 0$, yielding

$$\int_F (\cdots)d\nu \leq \mu^{-p'(\mu)+\omega} \int_{|\mu-\nu|>\delta} |\mu-\nu|^{(\eta-n)(p'(\mu)-\omega)}e^{-\beta(p'(\mu)-\omega)|\mu-\nu|}d\nu.$$

This integral converges and can be estimated by

$$C\delta^{(\eta-n)(p'(\mu)-\omega)+n}e^{-\beta(p'(\mu)-\omega)\delta}.$$

Estimate over E:

Similarly, for $\nu \in E$, we obtain

$$\int_E (\cdots)d\nu \leq \mu^{-p'(\mu)-\omega} \int_{|\mu-\nu|>\delta} |\mu-\nu|^{(\eta-n)(p'(\mu)+\omega)}e^{-\beta(p'(\mu)+\omega)|\mu-\nu|}d\nu,$$

which is bounded by

$$C\delta^{(\eta-n)(p'(\mu)+\omega)+n}e^{-\beta(p'(\mu)+\omega)\delta}.$$

Choice of μ:

Set

$$\mu := \delta^{\eta-n+\frac{n}{p'(\mu)-\omega}}e^{-\beta\delta}.$$

Then,

$$\mathcal{I}^{\delta}_{\eta,\beta}(\mu) \leq C\mu = C\delta^{-n/p^{\sharp}(\mu)}(\log\delta)^{\mathcal{A}_0}e^{-\beta\delta},$$

for some $\mathcal{A}_0 > 0$, due to the log-Hölder continuity and the behavior of the extra exponent involving ω. Thus, the proof is completed. □

For a given measurable function ϕ defined on the Euclidean space $\mathbf{R}^n$, the *Hardy-type operator* $\mathbf{H}_\eta$ of fractional order η is expressed as

$$\mathbf{H}_\eta\phi(\mu) = |\mu|^{\eta-n}\int_{\mathcal{B}(0,|\mu|)} |\phi(\nu)|\,d\nu,$$

where $\mathcal{B}(0,|\mu|)$ denotes the open ball centered at the origin with radius $|\mu|$, and the integration is taken over this region.

Lemma 10. *Let $\psi\colon \mathbf{R}^n \to [0,\infty)$ be a measurable function satisfying the norm bound $\|\psi\|_{p(\cdot)} \leq 1$. Assume further that ψ vanishes identically on the open ball $\mathcal{B}(0,\kappa_0)$ for some fixed radius $\kappa_0 > 0$. Under these conditions, we introduce the operator defined by*

$$\mathcal{I}_{\eta,\beta}\psi(\mu) := \int_{\mathbf{R}^n} \frac{\psi(\nu)}{|\mu-\nu|^{n-\eta}}e^{-\beta|\mu-\nu|}\,d\nu,$$

where $0 < \eta < n$ and $\beta > 0$. Let

$$\frac{1}{p^{\sharp}(\mu)} := \frac{1}{p(\mu)} - \frac{\eta}{n}.$$

Then the following pointwise estimate holds:

$$\mathcal{I}_{\eta,\beta}\psi(\mu) \leq C\,\mathcal{M}\psi(\mu)^{p(\mu)/p^{\sharp}(\mu)}\left(\log\left(e+\frac{1}{\mathcal{M}\psi(\mu)}\right)\right)^{a_0\eta p(\mu)/p_\infty^2} + C\,\mathbf{H}_\eta\psi(\mu),$$

where $\mathcal{M}\psi$ *denotes the maximal function,* $\mathbf{H}_\eta\psi$ *is the Hardy operator of order* η*,* $a_0 > 0$ *is a constant depending on the modular structure, and* $p_\infty := \sup_{\mu\in\mathbf{R}^n} p(\mu)$*.*

Proof. We aim to estimate $\mathcal{I}_{\eta,\beta}\psi(\mu)$ in terms of the fractional maximal type function $\mathcal{M}\psi$ and the Hardy operator $\mathbf{H}_\eta\psi$. To proceed, we split the function ψ into

$$\psi = \psi_1 + \psi_2,$$

where

$$\psi_1 := \psi\cdot\chi_{\{\nu:\psi(\nu)\geq 1\}},\quad \psi_2 := \psi\cdot\chi_{\{\nu:\psi(\nu)<1\}}.$$

To obtain a precise bound for $\mathcal{I}_{\eta,\beta}\psi_2(\mu)$, we partition the domain of integration into three mutually disjoint regions, each corresponding to a specific geometric scale relative to the point μ. This allows us to estimate the integral on each region individually and combine the contributions accordingly.

(i) $\mathcal{B}(\mu,\delta)$;
(ii) $\mathbf{R}^n \setminus [\mathcal{B}(0,|\mu|/2)\cup\mathcal{B}(\mu,\delta)]$;
(iii) $\mathcal{B}(0,|\mu|/2)$.

Region I: $\mathcal{B}(\mu,\delta)$

$$\int_{\mathcal{B}(\mu,\delta)} \frac{\psi_2(\nu)}{|\mu-\nu|^{n-\eta}} e^{-\beta|\mu-\nu|}\,d\nu \leq \delta^{\eta}\int_{\mathcal{B}(\mu,\delta)} \frac{\psi_2(\nu)}{|\mu-\nu|^{n}}\,d\nu \leq C\delta^{\eta}\mathcal{M}\psi_2(\mu).$$

Region II: $\mathbf{R}^n \setminus [\mathcal{B}(0,|\mu|/2)\cup\mathcal{B}(\mu,\delta)]$
Using the fact that $e^{-\beta|\mu-\nu|} \leq e^{-\beta\delta}$, and adapting Lemma 9, we obtain

$$\int_{\mathbf{R}^n\setminus[\mathcal{B}(0,|\mu|/2)\cup\mathcal{B}(\mu,\delta)]} \frac{\psi_2(\nu)}{|\mu-\nu|^{n-\eta}} e^{-\beta|\mu-\nu|}\,d\nu \leq Ce^{-\beta\delta}\delta^{-n/p^{\sharp}(\mu)}(\log\delta)^{A_0}.$$

Region III: $\mathcal{B}(0,|\mu|/2)$
Since $\psi = 0$ on $\mathcal{B}(0,\kappa_0)$ and $\mu \notin \mathcal{B}(0,\kappa_0)$, we have

$$\int_{\mathcal{B}(0,|\mu|/2)} \frac{\psi_2(\nu)}{|\mu-\nu|^{n-\eta}} e^{-\beta|\mu-\nu|}\,d\nu = 0.$$

Combining Regions I–III

$$\mathcal{I}_{\eta,\beta}\psi_2(\mu) \leq C\delta^{\eta}\mathcal{M}\psi_2(\mu) + Ce^{-\beta\delta}\delta^{-n/p^{\sharp}(\mu)}(\log\delta)^{A_0}.$$

Choose

$$\delta = \mathcal{M}\psi_2(\mu)^{-p(\mu)/n}\left(\log\left(e+\frac{1}{\mathcal{M}\psi_2(\mu)}\right)\right)^{a_0 p(\mu)/p_\infty^2}.$$

Then,

$$\mathcal{I}_{\eta,\beta}\psi_2(\mu) \leq C\mathcal{M}\psi_2(\mu)^{p(\mu)/p^{\sharp}(\mu)}\left(\log\left(e+\frac{1}{\mathcal{M}\psi_2(\mu)}\right)\right)^{a_0\eta p(\mu)/p_\infty^2}.$$

Estimate for $\mathcal{I}_{\eta,\beta}\psi_1(\mu)$:

Since $\psi_1(\nu) \geq 1$, we estimate using the classical Riesz potential:

$$\mathcal{I}_{\eta,\beta}\psi_1(\mu) \leq \int_{\mathbf{R}^n} \frac{\psi_1(\nu)}{|\mu-\nu|^{n-\eta}}\,d\nu = \mathcal{I}_\eta\psi_1(\mu).$$

By Lemma 8, we obtain

$$\mathcal{I}_\eta\psi_1(\mu) \leq \mathcal{C}\mathcal{M}\psi_1(\mu)^{p(\mu)/p^\sharp(\mu)}\left(\log\left(e+\frac{1}{\mathcal{M}\psi_1(\mu)}\right)\right)^{a_0\eta p(\mu)/p_\infty^2} + \mathcal{C}\mathbf{H}_\eta\psi_1(\mu).$$

Final Estimate:
Combining both parts,

$$\mathcal{I}_{\eta,\beta}\psi(\mu) \leq \mathcal{C}\mathcal{M}\psi(\mu)^{p(\mu)/p^\sharp(\mu)}\left(\log\left(e+\frac{1}{\mathcal{M}\psi(\mu)}\right)\right)^{a_0\eta p(\mu)/p_\infty^2} + \mathcal{C}\mathbf{H}_\eta\psi(\mu).$$

□

5. Applications to Elliptic Partial Differential Equation

In this section, we apply our main results concerning the boundedness of the newly defined operator and demonstrate its applications to the existence of solutions, which play a fundamental role in the regularity theory of elliptic partial differential equations. We are primarily motivated by the work of Maria Alessandra Ragusa [50], who investigated homogeneous Herz spaces and their applications to regularity results, as well as by the study of grand variable exponent Morrey spaces by Makharadze et al. [51], which provides a refined analytical framework for addressing various classes of differential and integral operators. Let $\emptyset \neq \Omega \subset \mathbf{R}^n$, with $n \geq 3$, be a bounded domain and consider the following boundary value problem:

$$\begin{cases} -\mathcal{L}\mu = \psi \in L^{p(\cdot)}(\Omega), \\ \mu \in \mathbf{W}_0^{1,2}(\Omega), \end{cases}$$

Here, $\mathcal{L}$ is a second-order elliptic partial differential operator in divergence form, defined by

$$\mathcal{L}\mu = \sum_{i,j=1}^{n} \partial_i\left(a^{ij}\,\partial_j\mu\right),$$

where the coefficient matrix $\left(a^{ij}\right)$ satisfies the following structural conditions:

$$a^{ij} \in L^\infty(\Omega) \quad \text{for all } i,j = 1,\dots,n, \text{ and a.e. } \mu \in \Omega; \tag{4}$$

$$a^{ij}(\mu) = a^{ji}(\mu) \quad \text{for all } i,j = 1,\dots,n, \text{ and a.e. } \mu \in \Omega; \tag{5}$$

$$\nu^{-1}|\xi|^2 \leq \sum_{i,j=1}^{n} a^{ij}(\mu)\,\xi_i\xi_j \leq \nu|\xi|^2, \quad \forall\xi \in \mathbf{R}^n, \text{ a.e. } \mu \in \mathcal{B}, \tag{6}$$

for some constant $\nu > 0$. These conditions guarantee that $\mathcal{L}$ is a uniformly elliptic operator with bounded, measurable, and symmetric coefficients. For almost every $\mu \in \mathcal{B}$, and for $\tau \in \mathbf{R}^n \setminus \{0\}$, we denote by $A_{ij}(\mu)$ the entries of the inverse matrix of $\left(a_{ij}(\mu)\right)_{i,j=1}^{n}$. Let us observe that if $\vec{\mathcal{B}} \subset \mathcal{B}$ is a measurable subset on which the structural conditions (4) and (5) hold pointwise, then for any fixed $\mu_0 \in \vec{\mathcal{B}}$, the function $\Gamma(\mu_0, \tau)$ defines a fundamental solution for the constant-coefficient operator

$$\mathcal{L}_0\nu(\mu) := \sum_{i,j=1}^{n} a_{ij}(\mu_0)\,\partial_{\mu_i\nu_j}\nu(\mu).$$

We define the first- and second-order partial derivatives of the fundamental solution Γ with respect to the variable τ as

$$\Gamma_i(\mu,\tau) := \frac{\partial}{\partial \tau_i}\Gamma(\mu,\tau), \quad \Gamma_{ij}(\mu,\tau) := \frac{\partial^2}{\partial \tau_i \partial \tau_j}\Gamma(\mu,\tau).$$

Furthermore, we define the uniform bound

$$M := \max_{i,j=1,\ldots,n} \max_{|\alpha|\leq 2n} \left\| \frac{\partial^{|\alpha|}\Gamma_{ij}(\mu,\tau)}{\partial \tau^{\alpha}} \right\|_{L^\infty(\Omega\times\Sigma)},$$

where α is a multi-index, and Σ denotes a compact set excluding the singularity at $\tau = 0$. It is well known that the kernels $\Gamma_{ij}(\mu,\tau)$ are Calderón–Zygmund type in the variable τ.
A particularly important instance of such an elliptic operator [52] arises in the study of the modified Helmholtz equation (also referred to as the screened Poisson equation) on the full space $\mathbf{R}^n$, given by

$$-\Delta\mu + \beta^2\mu = \psi,$$

where $\beta \in \mathbb{C}$ with $\Re(\beta) > 0$, and $\psi \in L^p(\mathbf{R}^n)$ for some $1 < p < \infty$. This equation arises in various physical contexts, including screened electrostatics, steady-state heat conduction with absorption, and wave propagation in lossy media. The operator $\mathcal{L} := -\Delta + \beta^2$ is elliptic due to the positive definiteness of the leading symbol. The zero-order term $\beta^2\mu$ introduces exponential spatial decay, with the fundamental solution exhibiting the form

$$\mathcal{G}(\mu) \sim \frac{e^{-\beta|\mu|}}{|\mu|^{n-2}}, \quad |\mu| \to \infty,$$

highlighting a significant departure from the behavior of the classical Poisson equation. Notably, exponential decay is governed by $\Re(\beta)$, and since the equation involves β^2, both β and $-\beta$ yield the same operator. Hence, requiring $\beta \neq 0$ and $\Re(\beta) > 0$ suffices; the sign of β is immaterial to ellipticity or the decay rate.

The classical Poisson equation $-\Delta\mu = \psi$ has a well-known solution given by the Newtonian potential

$$\mathcal{I}_2 = c_{n,2}\int_{\mathbf{R}^n} \frac{\psi(\nu)}{|\mu-\nu|^{n-2}}\, d\nu.$$

When the damping term $\beta^2\mu$ is included, the fundamental solution changes due to the exponential decay introduced by β. This leads to the exponentially damped Riesz potential, which describes how the influence of ψ diminishes more rapidly with distance:

$$\boxed{\mathcal{I}_2 = c_{n,2}\int_{\mathbf{R}^n} \frac{e^{-\beta|\mu-\nu|}}{|\mu-\nu|^{n-2}}\psi(\nu)\, d\nu,}$$

where $c_{n,2}$ is a normalization constant depending on the dimension n. This representation ensures integrability and decay properties necessary for solutions in unbounded domains.

To study the regularity properties of μ, we compute its gradient. Define the kernel function

$$\mathcal{K}(\mu,\nu) := \frac{e^{-\beta|\mu-\nu|}}{|\mu-\nu|^{n-2}}.$$

Then the gradient of μ is given by

$$\nabla(\mu) = \nabla_{\mu}\left(c_{n,2}\int_{\mathbf{R}^n} \mathcal{K}(\mu,\nu)\psi(\nu)\,d\nu\right) = c_{n,2}\int_{\mathbf{R}^n} \psi(\nu)\nabla_{\mu}\mathcal{K}(\mu,\nu)\,d\nu.$$

Here, we differentiate under the integral sign, which is justified by the smoothness and decay of the kernel $\mathcal{K}(\mu,\nu)$.

Letting $\kappa = |\mu - \nu|$, we apply the product and chain rules

$$\nabla_{\mu}\mathcal{K} = \nabla_{\mu}\left(e^{-\beta\kappa}\kappa^{-(n-2)}\right) = e^{-\beta\kappa}\nabla_{\mu}\left(\kappa^{-(n-2)}\right) + \kappa^{-(n-2)}\nabla_{\mu}\left(e^{-\beta\kappa}\right),$$

$$\nabla_{\mu}\kappa^{-(n-2)} = -(n-2)\kappa^{-n}(\mu-\nu), \quad \nabla_{\mu}e^{-\beta\kappa} = -\beta e^{-\beta\kappa}\frac{\mu-\nu}{\kappa}.$$

Substituting these gives

$$\nabla_{\mu}\mathcal{K} = -e^{-\beta\kappa}(\mu-\nu)\left[(n-2)\kappa^{-n} + \beta\kappa^{-(n-1)}\right].$$

Hence, the gradient of the solution is given by

$$\boxed{\nabla(\mu) = -c_{n,2}\int_{\mathbf{R}^n} \psi(\nu)e^{-\beta|\mu-\nu|}(\mu-\nu)\left[(n-2)|\mu-\nu|^{-n} + \beta|\mu-\nu|^{-(n-1)}\right]d\nu.}$$

This expression explicitly reveals the decay and singular behavior of $\nabla\mu$, demonstrating how the regularity of μ depends on the integrability properties of ψ.

To control the gradient, we estimate it by means of the Hardy–Littlewood maximal operator, a fundamental tool in harmonic analysis that provides pointwise control of singular integrals. Define the maximal operator as

$$\mathcal{M}(\psi)(\mu) := \sup_{\kappa>0}\frac{1}{|\mathcal{B}_{\kappa}(\mu)|}\int_{\mathcal{B}_{\kappa}(\mu)} |\psi(\nu)|\,d\nu,$$

where $\mathcal{B}_{\kappa}(\mu)$ denotes the ball centered at μ with radius κ. This operator captures the local average behavior of ψ and is crucial for pointwise estimates.

Let us define the kernel

$$\mathcal{L}(\mu,\nu) := e^{-\beta|\mu-\nu|}(\mu-\nu)\left[(n-2)|\mu-\nu|^{-n} + \beta|\mu-\nu|^{-(n-1)}\right].$$

We observe that the size of this kernel can be estimated as

$$|\mathcal{L}(\mu,\nu)| \lesssim e^{-\beta|\mu-\nu|}|\mu-\nu|^{-(n-1)},$$

since

$$|\mu-\nu|\cdot|\mu-\nu|^{-n} = |\mu-\nu|^{-(n-1)},$$

and the exponential factor ensures rapid decay at infinity.

This kernel satisfies the Calderón–Zygmund conditions due to its decay, size, and smoothness properties enhanced by the exponential factor. Therefore, standard singular integral theory implies the pointwise bound

$$\boxed{|\nabla(\mu)| \leq \mathcal{C}_{p(\cdot)}\mathcal{M}(\psi)(\mu),}$$

for some constant $\mathcal{C}_p$ depending only on p and n.

To see this more explicitly, we perform a dyadic decomposition of the domain into annuli

$$\mathcal{A}_k := \{\nu \in \mathbf{R}^n : 2^k \le |\mu - \nu| < 2^{k+1}\}, \quad k \in \mathbb{Z}.$$

Then,

$$|\nabla(\mu)| \lesssim \sum_{k=-\infty}^{\infty} \int_{\mathcal{A}_k} |\psi(\nu)| \frac{e^{-\beta|\mu-\nu|}}{|\mu-\nu|^{n-1}} d\nu.$$

On each annulus, using the fact that $e^{-\beta|\mu-\nu|} \le e^{-\beta 2^k}$ and $|\mu-\nu| \sim 2^k$, we obtain

$$|\nabla(\mu)| \lesssim \sum_{k=-\infty}^{\infty} e^{-\beta 2^k} (2^k)^{-(n-1)} \int_{\mathcal{A}_k} |\psi(\nu)| d\nu.$$

Since the volume of the annulus satisfies

$$|\mathcal{A}_k| \approx |\mathcal{B}_{2^{k+1}}(\mu)| \sim (2^k)^n,$$

we can bound

$$\int_{\mathcal{A}_k} |\psi(\nu)| d\nu \le \int_{\mathcal{B}_{2^{k+1}}(\mu)} |\psi(\nu)| d\nu = |\mathcal{B}_{2^{k+1}}(\mu)| \cdot \frac{1}{|\mathcal{B}_{2^{k+1}}(\mu)|} \int_{\mathcal{B}_{2^{k+1}}(\mu)} |\psi(\nu)| d\nu.$$

Applying the maximal operator yields

$$\int_{\mathcal{A}_k} |\psi(\nu)| d\nu \lesssim (2^k)^n \mathcal{M}(\psi)(\mu).$$

Substituting back, we have

$$|\nabla(\mu)| \lesssim \mathcal{M}(\psi)(\mu) \sum_{k=-\infty}^{\infty} e^{-\beta 2^k} (2^k)^{-(n-1)} (2^k)^n = \mathcal{M}(\psi)(\mu) \sum_{k=-\infty}^{\infty} e^{-\beta 2^k} 2^k.$$

The exponential decay ensures that the series converges, so we conclude

$$|\nabla(\mu)| \le \mathcal{C}\mathcal{M}(\psi)(\mu).$$

The Hardy–Littlewood maximal operator is bounded on $L^p(\mathbf{R}^n)$ for $1 < p \le \infty$, satisfying

$$\|\mathcal{M}(\psi)\|_{L^{p(\cdot)}(\mathbf{R}^n)} \le \mathcal{C}_p \|\psi\|_{L^{p(\cdot)}(\mathbf{R}^n)}.$$

This implies the gradient estimate

$$\|\nabla\mu\|_{L^{p(\cdot)}(\mathbf{R}^n)} \le \mathcal{C}_p \|\psi\|_{L^{p(\cdot)}(\mathbf{R}^n)}.$$

Consequently,

$$\mu \in \mathbf{W}_0^{1,p}(\mathbf{R}^n),$$

which shows that the solution not only exists but also inherits integrability and weak differentiability from the source term ψ. This conclusion is fundamental in the regularity theory of elliptic partial differential equations.

Theorem 6. *Under conditions* (4), (5), *and* (6), *and assuming* $p(\cdot)$ *satisfies the log-Hölder continuity as in Theorem 5, there exist constants* $\mathcal{C} = \mathcal{C}(n, p(\cdot), \eta, \beta) > 0$ *and* $\rho_0 = \rho_0(\mathcal{C}, n) > 0$ *such that for any ball* $\mathcal{B}_\sigma \subset \Omega$ *with* $\sigma < \rho_0$, *and for every* $\mu \in \mathbf{W}_0^{2,p(\cdot)}(\mathcal{B}_\sigma)$ *satisfying*

$$\mu_{x_i x_j} \in L^{p(\cdot)}(\mathcal{B}_\sigma) \quad \text{and} \quad \mathcal{L}\mu = \psi \in L^{p(\cdot)}(\mathcal{B}_\sigma),$$

the following estimate holds:

$$\left\|\mu_{x_ix_j}\right\|_{L^{p(\cdot)}(\mathcal{B}_\sigma)} \leq C\|\psi\|_{L^{p(\cdot)}(\mathcal{B}_\sigma)} \quad \textit{for all } i,j = 1,\dots,n.$$

Proof. Let $n \geq 3$ and $\mathcal{B} \subset \mathbf{R}^n$ be an open ball. Suppose $(a_{ij})_{i,j=1}^{n}$ satisfies the uniform ellipticity conditions, and let $\mu \in \mathbf{W}_0^{2,p(\cdot)}(\mathcal{B})$. Then, for almost every $\mu \in \mathcal{B}$, the following representation formula holds (see [50]):

$$\mu_{x_ix_j}(\mu) = \text{P.V.} \int_{\mathcal{B}} \Gamma_{ij}(\mu, \mu - \nu) \left[\sum_{h,k=1}^{n} (a_{hk}(\mu) - a_{hk}(\nu))\mu_{x_hx_k}(\nu) + \mathcal{L}\mu(\nu) \right] d\nu$$
$$+ \mathcal{L}\mu(\mu) \int_{|\tau|=1} \Gamma_i(\mu, \tau)\tau_j \, d\sigma_\tau,$$

where Γ_{ij} denotes the second-order derivatives of the fundamental solution associated with the frozen-coefficient operator, and the last term arises from boundary correction.

Now, using the boundedness of the exponentially damped fractional integral operator $\mathcal{I}_{\eta,\beta}$ on variable exponent spaces as shown in Theorem 5, we apply the estimate

$$\|\mathcal{I}_{\eta,\beta}(h)\|_{L^{p(\cdot)}(\mathcal{B}_\sigma)} \leq C\|h\|_{L^{p(\cdot)}(\mathcal{B}_\sigma)} \quad \text{for all } h \in L^{p(\cdot)}(\mathcal{B}_\sigma).$$

Applying the previous results to the representation formula of the second-order derivatives $\mu_{x_ix_j}$, and invoking the Calderón–Zygmund theory in the context of variable exponent spaces, we obtain the following localized estimate:

$$\left\|\mu_{x_ix_j}\right\|_{L^{p(\cdot)}(\mathcal{B}_\sigma)} \leq C\|\psi\|_{L^{p(\cdot)}(\mathcal{B}_\sigma)}.$$

To justify the above, we evaluate the norm of the second-order derivative $\mu_{x_ix_j}$ in the variable exponent Lebesgue space $L^{p(\cdot)}(\mathcal{B}_\sigma)$. Specifically, the Luxemburg norm is defined by

$$\left\|\mu_{x_ix_j}\right\|_{L^{p(\cdot)}(\mathcal{B}_\sigma)} = \inf\left\{ \lambda > 0 : \int_{\mathcal{B}_\sigma} \left| \frac{\mu_{x_ix_j}(\mu)}{\lambda} \right|^{p(\mu)} d\mu \leq 1 \right\}.$$

Based on the representation formula involving the fundamental solution $\Gamma_{ij}(\mu, \mu - \nu)$ and its derivatives, we obtain the pointwise bound

$$\mu_{x_ix_j}(\mu) \lesssim \mathcal{I}_{\eta,\beta}(\psi)(\mu),$$

where the exponentially damped fractional integral operator is given by

$$\mathcal{I}_{\eta,\beta}(\psi)(\mu) := \int_{\mathcal{B}_\sigma} \frac{\psi(\nu)}{|\mu - \nu|^{n-\eta}} e^{-\beta|\mu-\nu|} \, d\nu.$$

From Theorem 5, we know that $\mathcal{I}_{\eta,\beta}$ is a bounded operator on $L^{p(\cdot)}(\mathcal{B}_\sigma)$. Therefore,

$$\|\mathcal{I}_{\eta,\beta}(\psi)\|_{L^{p(\cdot)}(\mathcal{B}_\sigma)} \leq C\|\psi\|_{L^{p(\cdot)}(\mathcal{B}_\sigma)}.$$

Combining these results, we deduce the desired estimate

$$\boxed{\left\|\mu_{x_ix_j}\right\|_{L^{p(\cdot)}(\mathcal{B}_\sigma)} \leq C\|\psi\|_{L^{p(\cdot)}(\mathcal{B}_\sigma)},}$$

where the constant C depends on the dimension $\mathtt{n}$, the exponent function $\mathtt{p}(\cdot)$, the parameters η, β, and the ellipticity constants associated with the operator $\mathcal{L}$. □

6. Conclusions and Future Remarks

In this work, we have developed a novel and comprehensive framework for studying the exponentially damped Riesz-type fractional integral operator within the context of variable exponent Lebesgue spaces $L^{\mathtt{p}(\cdot)}$. Our primary contribution lies in establishing the boundedness of this operator under suitable conditions on the exponent function, including log-Hölder continuity and appropriate growth behavior. To support these results, we introduced several new structural properties tailored to the variable exponent setting, providing a solid functional foundation for further exploration.

Moreover, we extended classical Sobolev-type inequalities to this more general framework using our newly introduced operator, thereby offering a unified approach that encompasses both classical and exponentially modified settings. The applications to elliptic partial differential equations illustrated the practical value of our findings, especially in enhancing the understanding of regularity and integrability properties of weak solutions.

The exponential damping term not only enriches the theoretical landscape but also widens the domain of boundedness beyond that of classical Riesz and Bessel–Riesz potentials. This feature opens up new possibilities in the analysis of nonlocal operators and fractional PDEs over complex and unbounded domains.

Future Work

Several promising avenues remain open for future research. For instance,

- Investigating the compactness, weak-type estimates, and sharp bounds of the exponentially damped operator under refined modular conditions.
- Extending the current framework to more generalized function spaces such as variable exponent Morrey- or Besov-type spaces.
- Exploring connections with time-fractional and space–time nonlocal evolution equations, where the damping effect could yield improved regularity criteria.
- Developing numerical schemes or approximation theories based on this operator for solving real-world models involving anomalous diffusion or memory effects.
- Studying the boundedness and potential inequalities involving the composition of the exponentially damped operator with other integral or differential operators.

We believe that the techniques and results established in this article will serve as a foundation for further advancements in harmonic analysis, nonlinear PDE theory, and applied mathematics involving non-standard growth phenomena.

Author Contributions: Conceptualization, W.A.; validation, Y.A.; formal analysis, W.A., M.A., and A.G.; resources, J.E.M.-D.; data curation, Y.A.; writing—original draft, W.A.; writing—review and editing, M.A.; A.G., and J.E.M.-D.; supervision, M.A.; funding acquisition, J.E.M.-D. and Y.A. All authors have read and agreed to the published version of the manuscript.

Funding: This work received no external funding.

Data Availability Statement: Data are contained within the article.

Acknowledgments: The authors extend their appreciation to the Deanship of Research and Graduate Studies at King Khalid University for funding this work through Large Research Project under grant number RGP2/238/46.

Conflicts of Interest: The authors declare no conflicts of interest.

References

1. Evans, L.C. *Partial Differential Equations*; Graduate Studies in Mathematics; American Mathematical Society: Providence, RI, USA, 2010; Volume 19.
2. Zhang, Z.; Lin, M.; Li, D.; Wu, R.; Lin, R.; Yang, C. An AUV-Enabled Dockable Platform for Long-Term Dynamic and Static Monitoring of Marine Pastures. *IEEE J. Ocean. Eng.* **2024**, *50*, 276–293. [CrossRef]
3. Duoandikoetxea, J. *Fourier Analysis*; American Mathematical Society: Providence, RI, USA, 2001.
4. García-Cuerva, J.; Rubio de Francia, J.L. *Weighted Norm Inequalities and Related Topics*; Elsevier: Amsterdam, The Netherlands, 2014.
5. Cruz-Uribe, D.V.; Fiorenza, A. Variable Lebesgue spaces: Foundations and harmonic analysis. In *Lecture Notes in Mathematics*; Springer: Berlin/Heidelberg, Germany, 2003; Volume 2017.
6. Gao, Z.; Yi, W. Prediction of Projectile Interception Point and Interception Time Based on Harris Hawk Optimization–Convolutional Neural Network–Support Vector Regression Algorithm. *Mathematics* **2025**, *13*, 338. [CrossRef]
7. Alsaraireh, S.; Ahmad, A.; AbuHour, Y. New Step in Lightweight Medical Image Encryption and Authenticity. *Mathematics* **2025**, *13*, 1799. [CrossRef]
8. Zheng, D.; Cao, X. Provably efficient service function chain embedding and protection in edge networks. *IEEE/ACM Trans. Netw.* **2024**, *37*, 12345. [CrossRef]
9. Yu, Y.; Zhu, F.; Qian, J.; Fujita, H.; Yu, J.; Zeng, K.; Chen, E. CrowdFPN: Crowd counting via scale-enhanced and location-aware feature pyramid network. *Appl. Intell.* **2025**, *55*, 359. [CrossRef]
10. Zhang, D.; Li, B.; Wei, Y.; Zhang, H.; Lu, G.; Fan, L.; Xu, J. Investigation of injection and flow characteristics in an electronic injector featuring a novel control valve. *Energy Convers. Manag.* **2025**, *327*, 119609. [CrossRef]
11. Fei, R.; Wan, Y.; Hu, B.; Li, A.; Cui, Y.; Peng, H. Deep core node information embedding on networks with missing edges for community detection. *Inf. Sci.* **2025**, *707*, 122039. [CrossRef]
12. Zhang, H. H.; Yao, H. M.; Jiang, L. J. Novel time domain integral equation method hybridized with the macromodels of circuits. In Proceedings of the 2015 IEEE 24th Electrical Performance of Electronic Packaging and Systems (EPEPS), San Jose, CA, USA, 25–28 October 2015; IEEE: Piscataway, NJ, USA, 2015; pp. 135–138.
13. Afzal, W.; Cotîrlă, L.-I. New Numerical Quadrature Functional Inequalities on Hilbert Spaces in the Framework of Different Forms of Generalized Convex Mappings. *Symmetry* **2025**, *17*, 146. [CrossRef]
14. Cruz-Uribe, D.V.; Pérez, C. Sharp weighted estimates for classical operators. *Adv. Math.* **2014**, *248*, 821–847. [CrossRef]
15. Lerner, A.K. A simple proof of the A_2 conjecture. *Int. Math. Res. Not.* **2013**, *2013*, 3159–3170. [CrossRef]
16. Diening, L.; Harjulehto, P.; Hästö, P.; Růžička, M. Lebesgue and Sobolev Spaces with Variable Exponents. In *Lecture Notes in Mathematics*; Springer: Berlin/Heidelberg, Germany, 2011; Volume 2017.
17. Cazacu, C.; Dávila, J.; Valdinoci, E. Nonlocal diffusion and applications. In *Nonlocal and Nonlinear Diffusions and Interactions: New Methods and Directions*; Andreu, F., Mazón, J.M., Rossi, J.D., Toledo, J., Eds.; Springer INdAM Series; Springer: Cham, Switzerland, 2018; Volume 28, pp. 1–25.
18. Molchanov, S.; Vainberg, B. *Theory of Self-Adjoint Extensions of the Fractional Laplacian*; Memoirs of the American Mathematical Society; American Mathematical Society: Providence, RI, USA, 2020; Volume 264, No. 1278.
19. Nieraeth, B.; Cwikel, M. Interpolation methods and fractional smoothness in harmonic analysis. *Mathematics* **2022**, *10*, 120.
20. Grafakos, L. *Modern Fourier Analysis*, 3rd ed.; Springer: New York, NY, USA, 2014.
21. Kováčik, O.; Rákosník, J. Some remarks on variable exponent spaces. *Funct. Approx. Comment. Math.* **2014**, *51*, 51–68.
22. Gogatishvili, A.; Mustafayev, R.C.; Deringoz, F. Boundedness of the Hardy operator in variable exponent Lebesgue spaces. *J. Inequal. Appl.* **2016**, *2016*, 1–14.
23. Guliyev, V.S.; Deringoz, F.; Samko, S. Boundedness of the commutators of fractional maximal and integral operators in generalized Morrey spaces with variable exponents. *J. Funct. Spaces* **2018**, *2018*, 3831581.
24. Zhang, P.; Yuan, W. Boundedness of singular integrals on variable exponent Herz spaces. *Nonlinear Anal. Theory Methods Appl.* **2016**, *135*, 169–181.
25. Cleanthous, G.; Gogatishvili, A.; Růžička, M. Modular inequalities and function spaces with variable exponents. *Rev. Mat. Complut.* **2020**, *33*, 1–42.
26. Long, Y.; Yang, D.; Zhuo, C. Variable exponent function spaces on RD-spaces and applications. *Math. Nachr.* **2016**, *289*, 676–737.
27. Guan, Y.; Cui, Z.; Zhou, W. Reconstruction in off-axis digital holography based on hybrid clustering and the fractional Fourier transform. *Opt. Laser Technol.* **2025**, *186*, 112622. [CrossRef]
28. Zhang, H.H.; Xue, Z.S.; Liu, X.Y.; Li, P.; Jiang, L.; Shi, G.M. Optimization of high-speed channel for signal integrity with deep genetic algorithm. *IEEE Trans. Electromagn. Compat.* **2022**, *64*, 1270–1274. [CrossRef]
29. Chen, Z.; Zhou, W.; Kuang, H.; Chen, Z.; Yang, J.; Chen, Z.; Chen, F. Dynamic model and vibration of rack vehicle on curve line. *Veh. Syst. Dyn.* **2025**, 1–19.. [CrossRef]
30. Afzal, W.; Abbas, M.; Meetei, M.Z.; Bourazza, S. Tensorial Maclaurin Approximation Bounds and Structural Properties for Mixed-Norm Orlicz–Zygmund Spaces. *Mathematics* **2025**, *13*, 917. [CrossRef]

31. Afzal, W.; Abbas, M.; Aloraini, N.M.; Ro, J. Resolution of Open Problems via Orlicz-Zygmund Spaces and New Geometric Properties of Morrey Spaces in the Besov Sense with Non-Standard Growth. *AIMS Math.* **2025**, *10*, 13908–13940. [CrossRef]
32. Khan, Z. A.; Afzal, W. An Estimation of Different Kinds of Integral Inequalities for a Generalized Class of Godunova–Levin Convex and Preinvex Functions via Pseudo and Standard Order Relations. *J. Funct. Spaces* **2025**, *2025*, 3942793. [CrossRef]
33. Aubin, T. *Some Nonlinear Problems in Riemannian Geometry*; Springer Science & Business Media: Berlin/Heidelberg, Germany, 2007.
34. Maz'ya, V.G. *Sobolev Spaces with Applications to Elliptic Partial Differential Equations*, 2nd ed.; Springer: Berlin/Heidelberg, Germany, 2011.
35. Di Nezza, E.; Palatucci, G.; Valdinoci, E. Hitchhiker's guide to the fractional Sobolev spaces. *Bull. Sci. Math.* **2012**, *136*, 521–573. [CrossRef]
36. Palatucci, G.; Pisante, A. Improved Sobolev embeddings, profile decomposition, and concentration-compactness for fractional Sobolev spaces. *Calc. Var. Partial Differ. Equ.* **2014**, *50*, 799–829. [CrossRef]
37. Hebey, E. *Nonlinear Analysis on Manifolds: Sobolev Spaces and Inequalities*; Courant Lecture Notes; Courant Institute of Mathematical Sciences: New York, NY, USA, 2010.
38. Figalli, A.; Maggi, F. On the shape of liquid drops and crystals in the small mass regime. *Arch. Ration. Mech. Anal.* **2011**, *201*, 143–207. [CrossRef]
39. Gentil, I. The dimensional Sobolev inequality using the mass transportation method. *C. R. Math.* **2007**, *345*, 713–718.
40. Adams, D.R.; Hedberg, L.I. *Function Spaces and Potential Theory*; Springer: Berlin/Heidelberg, Germany, 1996.
41. Liu, H.; Zhao, L. Ground-state solution of a nonlinear fractional Schrödinger–Poisson system. *Math. Methods Appl. Sci.* **2022**, *45*, 1934–1958. [CrossRef]
42. Ruzhansky, M.; Suragan, D.; Yessirkegenov, N. Caffarelli–Kohn–Nirenberg and Sobolev type inequalities on stratified Lie groups. *Nonlinear Differ. Equ. Appl. NoDEA* **2017**, *24*, 56. [CrossRef]
43. Capone, C.; Fiorenza, A.; Karadzhov, G.E.; Nazeer, W. The Riesz potential operator in optimal couples of rearrangement invariant spaces. *Z. Anal. Anwend.* **2011**, *30*, 219–236. [CrossRef]
44. Afzal, W.; Abbas, M.; Alsalami, O.M. Bounds of Different Integral Operators in Tensorial Hilbert and Variable Exponent Function Spaces. *Mathematics* **2024**, *12*, 2464. [CrossRef]
45. Ohno, T.; Shimomura, T. Campanato–Morrey spaces and variable Riesz potentials. *Acta Math. Hung.* **2024**, *174*, 62–74. [CrossRef]
46. Mehmood, S.; Eridani; Fatmawati; Raza, W. Bessel–Riesz operators on Lebesgue spaces and Morrey spaces defined in measure metric spaces. *Int. J. Differ. Equ.* **2023**, *2023*, 3148049. [CrossRef]
47. Dymek, M.; Górka, P. Compactness in the spaces of variable integrability and summability. *Math. Nachr.* **2023**, *296*, 4317–4334. [CrossRef]
48. Stein, E.M. *Singular Integrals and Differentiability Properties of Functions*; Princeton University Press: Princeton, NJ, USA, 1970.
49. Diening, L. Maximal Function on Generalized Lebesgue Spaces $L^{p(\cdot)}$. *Math. Inequal. Appl.* **2004**, *7*, 245–254.
50. Ragusa, M.A. Homogeneous Herz spaces and regularity results. *Nonlinear Anal. Theory Methods Appl.* **2009**, *71*, e1909–e1914. [CrossRef]
51. Makharadze, D.; Meskhi, A.; Ragusa, M.A. Regularity results in grand variable exponent Morrey spaces and applications. *Electron. Res. Arch.* **2025**, *33*, 5. [CrossRef]
52. Boccardo, L.; Croce, G. *Elliptic Partial Differential Equations: Existence and Regularity of Distributional Solutions*; de Gruyter: Berlin, Germany, 2014.

fractal and fractional

MDPI

Article

Hermite–Hadamard-Type Inequalities for h-Godunova–Levin Convex Fuzzy Interval-Valued Functions via Riemann–Liouville Fractional q-Integrals

Muhammad Waseem Akram [1], Sajid Iqbal [1], Asfand Fahad [2] and Yuanheng Wang [3,*]

1 Department of Mathematics, University of Southern Punjab, Multan 60800, Pakistan
2 Centre for Advanced Studies in Pure and Applied Mathematics, Bahauddin Zakariya University, Multan 60800, Pakistan
3 School of Mathematical Sciences, Zhejiang Normal University, Jinhua 321004, China
* Correspondence: yhwang@zjnu.cn

Abstract

In this study, we develop new Hermite–Hadamard and Hermite–Hadamard–Fejér type inequalities for fuzzy interval-valued functions (FIVFs) that exhibit h-Godunova–Levin convexity, using the framework of the Riemann–Liouville fractional (RLF) q-integral. We introduce novel fuzzy extensions of classical inequalities and establish corresponding inclusion relations by utilizing the properties of fuzzy RLF q-integrals. Furthermore, we validate the theoretical results through illustrative numerical examples and graphical representations, demonstrating the applicability and effectiveness of the derived inequalities in the context of fuzzy and interval analysis.

Keywords: Hermite–Hadamard inequality; h-Godunova–Levin convex functions; fuzzy interval-valued functions; Riemann–Liouville fractional q-integral

1. Introduction

The concept of convexity has long played a central role in various branches of mathematical analysis, particularly in optimization, functional analysis, and inequality theory. In recent years, significant advancements have been made in the study of functions exhibiting different types of convexity, including log-convexity [1], F-convexity [2], harmonically convexity [3], h-convexity [4] and h-Godunova–Levin convexity [5]. These developments have provided powerful tools for advancing many fields within mathematical analysis. Among the classical results, the Hermite–Hadamard inequality, first introduced by Hadamard in 1893 [6], plays a central role in inequality theory. This fundamental result provides an elegant estimate of the integral mean of a convex function and has served as the foundation for countless generalizations.

Over the years, researchers have developed several extensions of the Hermite–Hadamard inequality in different frameworks. Steinerberger [7] studied the Hermite–Hadamard inequality in higher dimensions, highlighting its importance in the geometry of convex bodies. Alongside these advancements, considerable attention has also been devoted to inequalities associated with convex functions, particularly the classical Hermite–Hadamard (HH) inequality.

Theorem 1 ([8]). *Suppose $\varsigma_1 < \varsigma_2$ and $f : [\varsigma_1, \varsigma_2] \longrightarrow \mathbb{R}$ be a convex function, then*

$$f\left(\frac{\varsigma_1 + \varsigma_2}{2}\right) \le \frac{1}{\varsigma_2 - \varsigma_1}\int_{\varsigma_1}^{\varsigma_2} f(x)dx \le \frac{f(\varsigma_1) + f(\varsigma_2)}{2},$$

holds.

Fractional calculus has also seen widespread application across a broad range of fields, including mathematics, physics, and engineering. Fractional versions of these inequalities have also been established, for example, in the monograph by Wang and Fečkan [9], where fractional Hermite–Hadamard inequalities were systematically investigated. Furthermore, generalizations involving preinvexity and other convexity concepts were obtained by Awan et al. [10], who derived fractional Hermite–Hadamard–Noor type inequalities via n-polynomial preinvex functions. Recently, Du et al. [11] extended the study of Hermite–Hadamard-type inequalities to the multiplicative fractional setting by employing multiplicative Atangana–Baleanu fractional integral operators. Their results further broaden the scope of HH-type inequalities within fractional calculus, highlighting the versatility of such inequalities across different fractional frameworks. In a related work, Lakhdari et al. [12] derived new fractal–fractional Hermite–Hadamard- and Milne-type inequalities, further broadening the scope of fractional analysis. Moreover, Du and Xu [13] obtained Hermite–Hadamard- and Pachpatte-type inequalities for generalized subadditive functions in the fractal setting. These contributions highlight the richness of Hermite–Hadamard-type inequalities and their adaptability to different settings in mathematical analysis.

In particular, fractional q-calculus has emerged as a powerful tool for solving differential and difference equations, as well as in combinatorics and signal processing [14–17]. Similarly, Xu et al. [18] explored new estimates for Hermite–Hadamard inequalities in the framework of quantum calculus through (α, m)-convexity. RLF q-integral operator, introduced in [19], has served as a foundation for numerous advancements. Building upon this, Tariboon [20], introduced a modified definition of the RLF q-integral and established existence and uniqueness results for impulsive fractional q-difference equations. Further extending these ideas, the work in [21], introduced the notion of the interval-valued RLF q-integral and explored unique solutions to interval q-Abel integral equations, thereby expanding fractional q-calculus into the framework of interval analysis. Growing interest in fractional q-calculus and its applications to convexity-based inequalities. These contemporary contributions further emphasize the timeliness and wide applicability of Hermite–Hadamard-type results across multiple branches of mathematical analysis.

Interval analysis has rapidly gained attention due to its effectiveness in handling uncertain data, error analysis, nulti-attribute decision-making, inequality theory, optimization, and related fields [22–30]. Particularly in the last five years, several extensions of classical inequalities involving fractional integrals have been proposed within interval and fuzzy spaces. For instance, Budak [31] established new interval-valued RLF integrals and associated inequalities. Du and Zhou [32] proved HH-, HH–Fejér-, and Pachpatte-type inclusion relations and Khan [33], derived new fuzzy variants of HH- and HH–Fejér-type inequalities by utilizing fuzzy RLF integrals with up and down convex fuzzy interval-valued functions. Additional fuzzy HH- and HH-Fejér-type inequalities have also been investigated using fuzzy RLF integral operators with exponential kernels [34].

Motivated by the above developments, this paper aims to establish new Hermite–Hadamard- and Hermite–Hadamard–Fejér type inequalities for fuzzy interval-valued functions exhibiting h-Godunova–Levin convexity, utilizing the Riemann–Liouville fractional q-integral framework. The paper is organized as follows: Section 2 introduces preliminary concepts and fundamental results necessary for the development of the main results. Section 3 presents new inclusion relations and the main inequalities. In Section 4, we provide illustrative numerical examples to support the theoretical findings. Finally, Section 5 concludes the paper and discusses potential directions for future research.

2. Preliminaries

In this section, we provide the essential definitions and mathematical background that form the basis of our study. These include concepts from fuzzy set theory, interval analysis, generalized convexity, and fractional q-calculus. The notations and operators introduced here will be used throughout the paper.

Definition 1 ([35]). *Let $\mathbb{R}_I = \{[\varsigma_1, \varsigma_2] : \varsigma_1 \leq \varsigma_2, \varsigma_1, \varsigma_2 \in \mathbb{R}\}$. If $\varsigma_1 > 0$, then $[\varsigma_1, \varsigma_2] \in \mathbb{R}_I^+$, where $\mathbb{R}_I^+$ is the set of all real positive intervals. Given $[\varsigma_1, \varsigma_2], [v_1, v_2] \in \mathbb{R}_I$ and $\theta \in \mathbb{R}$, then $\theta[\varsigma_1, \varsigma_2]$ is defined by*

$$\theta[\varsigma_1, \varsigma_2] = \{[\theta\varsigma_1, \theta\varsigma_2] \ if \theta \geq 0, [\theta\varsigma_2, \theta\varsigma_1] \ if \theta < 0\}.$$

and the addition is given by

$$[\varsigma_1, \varsigma_2] + [v_1, v_2] = [\varsigma_1 + v_1, \varsigma_2 + v_2].$$

For $[\varsigma_1, \varsigma_2], [v_1, v_2] \in \mathbb{R}_I$, the inclusion relation "$\supseteq_I''$, also called the "up and down" ("UD") order, is defined by

$$[\varsigma_1, \varsigma_2] \supseteq_I [v_1, v_2] \Leftrightarrow \varsigma_1 \leq v_1, v_2 \leq \varsigma_2.$$

Let $\underline{f}(x), \overline{f}(x) : [\varsigma_1, \varsigma_2] \to \mathbb{R}$ be two real functions and satisfy $\underline{f}(x) \leq \overline{f}(x)$ for every $x \in [\varsigma_1, \varsigma_2]$. Then $F : [\varsigma_1, \varsigma_2] \to \mathbb{R}_I$ with $F(x) = [\underline{f}(x), \overline{f}(x)]$ is called an interval-valued function.
We employ the notation $\mathbf{C}([\varsigma_1, \varsigma_2], \mathbb{R}_I)$ to represent the set of all continuous interval-valued functions on $[\varsigma_1, \varsigma_2]$. Again, the notation $\mathbf{C}([\varsigma_1, \varsigma_2], \mathbb{R})$ characterizes the set of continuous real-valued functions.

Definition 2 ([36]). *Let $F \in \mathbf{C}([\varsigma_1, \varsigma_2], \mathbb{R}_I)$. Then the Aumann integral(AI) of F over $[\varsigma_1, \varsigma_2]$ is defined by*

$$(AI) \int_{\varsigma_1}^{\varsigma_2} F(x)dx = \left\{ \int_{\varsigma_1}^{\varsigma_2} f(x)dx : f \in S(F) \right\},$$

where $S(F) = \{f \in L^1([\varsigma_1, \varsigma_2]) : f(x) \in F(x)$ for almost all $x \in [\varsigma_1, \varsigma_2]\}$ and $L^1([\varsigma_1, \varsigma_2])$ is called the set of all mappings that are Lebesgue-integrable over $[\varsigma_1, \varsigma_2]$.

Theorem 2 ([37]). *Let $F \in \mathbf{C}([\varsigma_1, \varsigma_2], \mathbb{R}_I)$. Then F is AI-integrable over $[\varsigma_1, \varsigma_2]$ if and only if $\underline{f}, \overline{f} \in L^1([\varsigma_1, \varsigma_2])$. Furthermore, suppose F is AI-integrable over $[\varsigma_1, \varsigma_2]$, then*

$$(IA) \int_{\varsigma_1}^{\varsigma_2} F(x)dx = \left[\int_{\varsigma_1}^{\varsigma_2} \underline{f}(x)dx, \int_{\varsigma_1}^{\varsigma_2} \overline{f}(x)dx \right].$$

Definition 3 ([38]). *A fuzzy subset of $\mathbb{R}$ is a function $\widetilde{I} : \mathbb{R} \to [0, 1]$. The notation $\mathcal{F}(\mathbb{R})$ denotes the set of all fuzzy subsets of $\mathbb{R}$. A fuzzy subset $\widetilde{I}$ of $\mathbb{R}$ is regarded as a real fuzzy interval providing it satisfies the following properties:*

(i) $\widetilde{I}$ is normal.
(ii) $\widetilde{I}$ is fuzzy convex.
(iii) $\widetilde{I}$ is upper semi continuous on $\mathbb{R}$.
(iv) $\widetilde{I}$ is compactly supported.

We denote by $\mathcal{F}_C(\mathbb{R})$ the space of fuzzy intervals.

Definition 4 **([38]).** *Let $\widetilde{I} \in \mathcal{F}_C(\mathbb{R})$, the level sets of $\widetilde{I}$ are defined by $[\widetilde{I}]^\xi = \{x \in \mathbb{R} | \widetilde{I}(x) \geq \xi\}$ for every $\xi \in [0,1]$. These sets are ξ-level sets of $\widetilde{I}$. In particular, $[\widetilde{I}]^0$ is the support of $[\widetilde{I}]^1$, which is the core of $\widetilde{I}$.*
For $\widetilde{I}, \widetilde{h} \in \mathcal{F}_C(\mathbb{R})$, the UD order relation $\supseteq_{\mathbb{F}}$ is given by

$$\widetilde{I} \supseteq_{\mathbb{F}} \widetilde{h} \Leftrightarrow [\widetilde{I}]^\xi \supseteq_I [\widetilde{I}]^\xi,\ \xi \in [0,1].$$

Let $\widetilde{I}, \widetilde{h} \in \mathcal{F}_C(\mathbb{R})$, and $\theta \in [0,1]$. Then the arithmetic operations are given by

$$[\theta \odot \widetilde{I}]^\xi = \theta[\widetilde{I}]^\xi,$$

$$[\widetilde{I} \oplus \widetilde{h}]^\xi = [\widetilde{I}]^\xi + [\widetilde{h}]^\xi,$$

$$[\widetilde{I} \otimes \widetilde{h}]^\xi = [\widetilde{I}]^\xi \times [\widetilde{h}]^\xi.$$

A fuzzy interval-valued map $\widetilde{F} : [\varsigma_1, \varsigma_2] \to \mathcal{F}_C(\mathbb{R})$ is called an fuzzy interval-valued function (FIVF). For notational simplicity, we appoint $\mathbf{S}([\varsigma_1, \varsigma_2], \mathcal{F}_C(\mathbb{R}))$ and $\mathbf{SC}([\varsigma_1, \varsigma_2], \mathcal{F}_C(\mathbb{R}))$ to denote the set of all FIVFs and continuous FIVFs in $[\varsigma_1, \varsigma_2]$, respectively.

Definition 5 **([39]).** *Let $\widetilde{F} \in \mathbf{S}([\varsigma_1, \varsigma_2], \mathcal{F}_C(\mathbb{R}))$. Then the IVF $F_\xi : [\varsigma_1, \varsigma_2] \to \mathbb{R}_I$ given by $F_\xi(x) = [\widetilde{F}(x)]^\xi = [\underline{f}_\xi(x), \overline{f}_\xi(x)]$ for every $x \in [\varsigma_1, \varsigma_2]$ is said to be ξ-levels of $\widetilde{F}$ for every $\xi \in [0,1]$, where $\underline{f}_\xi(x)$ and $\overline{f}_\xi(x)$ are two real-valued functions for every $\xi \in [0,1]$.*

Definition 6 **([39]).** *Let $\widetilde{F} \in \mathbf{S}([\varsigma_1, \varsigma_2], \mathcal{F}_C(\mathbb{R}))$. Then $\widetilde{F}$ is continuous at $x \in [\varsigma_1, \varsigma_2]$ if and only if $F_\xi \in \mathbf{C}([\varsigma_1, \varsigma_2], \mathbb{R}_I)$ for all $\xi \in [0,1]$, i-e. $\underline{f}_\xi(x), \overline{f}_\xi(x) \in C([\varsigma_1, \varsigma_2], \mathbb{R})$ for all $\xi \in [0,1]$.*

Definition 7 **([37]).** *Let $\widetilde{F} \in \mathbf{S}([\varsigma_1, \varsigma_2], \mathcal{F}_C(\mathbb{R}))$. The fuzzy Aumann integral of $\widetilde{F}$ (FA-integral) over $[\varsigma_1, \varsigma_2]$, denoted by $(FA) \int_{\varsigma_1}^{\varsigma_2} \widetilde{F}(x)dx$, is defined level-wise by*

$$\left[(FA) \int_{\varsigma_1}^{\varsigma_2} \widetilde{F}(x)dx\right]^\xi = (AI) \int_{\varsigma_1}^{\varsigma_2} F_\xi(x)dx = \left\{\int_{\varsigma_1}^{\varsigma_2} f_\xi(x)dx : f_\xi \in S(F_\xi)\right\},$$

for all $\xi \in [0,1]$. If $\int_{\varsigma_1}^{\varsigma_2} \widetilde{F}(x)dx \in \mathcal{F}_C(\mathbb{R})$, then $\widetilde{F}$ is integrable over $[\varsigma_1, \varsigma_2]$.

Theorem 3 **([40]).** *Let $\widetilde{F} \in \mathbf{S}([\varsigma_1, \varsigma_2], \mathcal{F}_C(\mathbb{R}))$ and ξ-levels of $\widetilde{F}$ be given by $F_\xi(x) = [\underline{f}_\xi(x), \overline{f}_\xi(x)]$ for every $\xi \in [0,1]$ and for all $x \in [\varsigma_1, \varsigma_2]$. Then $\widetilde{F}$ is integrable over $[\varsigma_1, \varsigma_2]$ if and only if $\underline{f}_\xi(x), \overline{f}_\xi(x) \in L^1([\varsigma_1, \varsigma_2])$ for all $\xi \in [0,1]$. Moreover, suppose $\widetilde{F}$ is integrable over $[\varsigma_1, \varsigma_2]$, then*

$$\begin{aligned}\left[\int_{\varsigma_1}^{\varsigma_2} \widetilde{F}(x)dx\right]^\xi &= \left[\int_{\varsigma_1}^{\varsigma_2} \underline{f}_\xi(x), \int_{\varsigma_1}^{\varsigma_2} \overline{f}_\xi(x)\right] \\ &= \int_{\varsigma_1}^{\varsigma_2} F_\xi(x)dx.\end{aligned}$$

Definition 8 **([41]).** *Let $\widetilde{F} \in \mathbf{S}([\varsigma_1, \varsigma_2], \mathcal{F}_C(\mathbb{R}))$. Then the fuzzy left and right RLF integrals of $\widetilde{F}$ with order $\gamma > 0$ are defined by*

$$I^\gamma_{\varsigma_1^+} \widetilde{F}(x) = \frac{1}{\Gamma(\gamma)} \int_{\varsigma_1}^{x} (x-t)^{\gamma-1} \widetilde{F}(t)dt\ (x > \varsigma_1),$$

and

$$I^{\gamma}_{\varsigma_2^-}\widetilde{F}(x) = \frac{1}{\Gamma(\gamma)}\int_x^{\varsigma_2}(x-t)^{\gamma-1}\widetilde{F}(t)dt \ (\varsigma_2 < x),$$

where Γ is Euler gamma function.

Now we shall discuss the notion of convexity.

Definition 9 ([42]). *A non-negative function $f : K \to \mathbb{R}$ is known as a Godunova–Levin convex function if for all $s,t \in K$ and $v \in (0,1)$, we have*

$$f(vs + (1-v)t) \leq \frac{f(s)}{v} + \frac{f(t)}{1-v}.$$

Definition 10 ([42]). *Let $h : (0,1) \subseteq W \to \mathbb{R}$ be non-negative function. We say $f : W \to \mathbb{R}$ is known as h-Godunova–Levin convex function $f \in SGX((\frac{1}{h}), W)$ if for all $s,t \in W$ and $v \in (0,1)$, we have*

$$f(vs + (1-v)t) \leq \frac{f(s)}{h(v)} + \frac{f(t)}{h(1-v)}.$$

Definition 11 ([42]). *Let $h : (0,1) \subseteq W \to \mathbb{R}$ be non-negative function. We say $f : W \to \mathbb{R}_I^+$ is the interval valued h-Godunova–Levin convex function, or $f \in SGX((\frac{1}{h}), W, \mathbb{R}_I^+)$ if for all $s,t \in W$ and $v \in (0,1)$, we have*

$$f(vs + (1-v)t) \supseteq \frac{f(s)}{h(v)} + \frac{f(t)}{h(1-v)}.$$

Proposition 1 ([42]). *Let $f : [s,t] \to \mathbb{R}_I^+$ be h-Godunova–Levin convex interval valued function such that $f(v) = [\underline{f}(v), \overline{f}(v)]$. Then $f \in SGX((\frac{1}{h}), [s,t], \mathbb{R}_I^+)$ if and only if $\underline{f} \in SGX((\frac{1}{h}), [s,t], \mathbb{R}_I^+)$, $\overline{f} \in SGV((\frac{1}{h}), [s,t], \mathbb{R}_I^+)$.*

Proposition 2 ([42]). *Let $f : [s,t] \to \mathbb{R}_I^+$ be h-Godunova–Levin concave interval valued function such that $f(v) = [\underline{f}(v), \overline{f}(v)]$. Then $f \in SGV((\frac{1}{h}), [s,t], \mathbb{R}_I^+)$ if and only if $\underline{f} \in SGV((\frac{1}{h}), [s,t], \mathbb{R}_I^+)$, $\overline{f} \in SGX((\frac{1}{h}), [s,t], \mathbb{R}_I^+)$.*

Now we shall give details of basic concept of q-calculus.

Definition 12 ([20]). *Suppose $q \in [0,1]$ and $\varsigma_1, t, v \in \mathbb{R}$. Then the q-integral number is defined by*

$$[n]_q = 1 + q + q^2 + \ldots + q^{n-1} = \frac{1-q^n}{1-q}, n \in \mathbb{R}.$$

A q-shift operator is defined by

$${}_{\varsigma_1}\Omega_q(t) = qt + (1-q)\varsigma_1.$$

Let $m > 0$ be an integer, then we obtain

$${}_{\varsigma_1}\Omega_q^m(t) = q^m(t - \varsigma_1) + \varsigma_1.$$

Particularly,

$${}_{\varsigma_1}\Omega_q^0(t) = t.$$

Proposition 3 ([43]). *Assuming $\gamma, t, v \in \mathbb{R}$ with $v \neq \varsigma_1$, then* *(i)* $\quad {}_{\varsigma_1}(v-t)_q^{\gamma} = (v-\varsigma_1)^{\gamma} \prod_{i=0}^{\infty} \frac{1-\frac{t-\varsigma_1}{v-\varsigma_1}q^i}{1-\frac{t-\varsigma_1}{v-\varsigma_1}q^{\gamma+i}} = (v-\varsigma_1)^{\gamma} \frac{(\frac{t-\varsigma_1}{v-\varsigma_1};q)_\infty}{(\frac{t-\varsigma_1}{v-\varsigma_1}q^{\gamma};q)_\infty}.$

(ii) $\quad {}_{\varsigma_1}(v - {}_{\varsigma_1}\Omega_q^m(t))_q^{\gamma} = (v-\varsigma_1)^{\gamma} \frac{(q^m;q)_\infty}{(q^{\gamma+m};q)_\infty}.$

Choosing $\gamma \in \mathbb{R}/\{0,-1,-2,...\}$, then q-gamma function is given as

$$\Gamma_q(\gamma) = \frac{{}_0(1 - {}_0\Omega_q(1))_q^{(\gamma-1)}}{(1-q)^{\gamma-1}}.$$

Moreover, $[\gamma]_q\Gamma_q(\gamma) = \Gamma_q(\gamma+1)$.

Lemma 1 **([43]).** *let $\gamma, \chi > 0$, then we get the following relations for $x \in [\varsigma_1, \varsigma_2]$:*

$$({}_{\varsigma_1}I_q^{\gamma}(t-\varsigma_1)^{\chi})(x) = \frac{\Gamma_q(\chi+1)}{\Gamma_q(\chi+\gamma+1)}(x-\varsigma_1)^{\chi+\gamma}.$$

Definition 13 **([43]).** *Let $f \in C([\varsigma_1, \varsigma_2], \mathbb{R})$ and $\gamma \geq 0$. The RLF q-integral on $[\varsigma_1, \varsigma_2]$ is defined by $({}_{\varsigma_1}I_q^0 f(t))(x) = f(x)$ and*

$$\begin{aligned}({}_{\varsigma_1}I_q^{\gamma} f(t))(x) &= \frac{1}{\Gamma_q(\gamma)} \int_{\varsigma_1}^{x} {}_{\varsigma_1}(x - {}_{\varsigma_1}\Omega_q(t))_q^{(\gamma-1)} f(t)\, {}_{\varsigma_1}d_q t \\ &= \frac{(1-q)(x-\varsigma_1)}{\Gamma_q(\gamma)} \sum_{i=0}^{\infty} q^i\, {}_{\varsigma_1}(x - {}_{\varsigma_1}\Omega_q^{i+1}(x))_q^{(\gamma-1)} f({}_{\varsigma_1}\Omega_q^i(x)).\end{aligned}$$

Definition 14 **([44]).** *Let $F \in \mathbf{C}([\varsigma_1, \varsigma_2], \mathbb{R}_I)$ and $\gamma \geq 0$. The RLF Iq-integral on $[\varsigma_1, \varsigma_2]$ is defined by $({}_{\varsigma_1}I_q^0 F(t))(x) = F(x)$ and by*

$$({}_{\varsigma_1}I_q^{\gamma} F(t))(x) = \frac{1}{\Gamma_q(\gamma)} \int_{\varsigma_1}^{x} {}_{\varsigma_1}(x - {}_{\varsigma_1}\Omega_q(t))_q^{(\gamma-1)} F(t)\, {}_{\varsigma_1}d_q t.$$

Definition 15 **([8]).** *Let $\tilde{F} \in \mathbf{SC}([\varsigma_1, \varsigma_2], \mathcal{F}_C(\mathbb{R}))$. The fuzzy interval valued RLF q-integral on $[\varsigma_1, \varsigma_2]$ is defined as*

$$\begin{aligned}({}_{\varsigma_1}I_q^{\gamma} \tilde{F}(t))(x) &= \frac{1}{\Gamma_q(\gamma)} \int_{\varsigma_1}^{x} {}_{\varsigma_1}(x - {}_{\varsigma_1}\Omega_q(t))_q^{(\gamma-1)} \tilde{F}(t)\, {}_{\varsigma_1}d_q t \\ &= \frac{(1-q)(x-\varsigma_1)}{\Gamma_q(\gamma)} \sum_{i=0}^{\infty} q^i\, {}_{\varsigma_1}(x - {}_{\varsigma_1}\Omega_q^{i+1}(x))_q^{(\gamma-1)} \tilde{F}({}_{\varsigma_1}\Omega_q^i(x)),\end{aligned}$$

for all $\gamma > 0, x \in [\varsigma_1, \varsigma_2]$.
Moreover, it is defined level-wise by

$$\begin{aligned}[({}_{\varsigma_1}I_q^{\gamma} \tilde{F}(t))(x)]^{\xi} &= \frac{1}{\Gamma_q(\gamma)} \int_{\varsigma_1}^{x} {}_{\varsigma_1}(x - {}_{\varsigma_1}\Omega_q(t))_q^{(\gamma-1)} F_{\xi}(t)\, {}_{\varsigma_1}d_q t \\ &= \frac{1}{\Gamma_q(\gamma)} \int_{\varsigma_1}^{x} {}_{\varsigma_1}(x - {}_{\varsigma_1}\Omega_q(t))_q^{(\gamma-1)} \times [\underline{f}_{\xi}(t), \overline{f}_{\xi}(t)]_{\varsigma_1} d_q t,\end{aligned}$$

for all $\xi \in [0,1]$. If $({}_{\varsigma_1}I_q^{\gamma} \tilde{F}(t))(x) \in \mathcal{F}_C(R)$, then $\tilde{F}$ is RLF q-integrable over $[\varsigma_1, \varsigma_2]$.

Theorem 4 **([8]).** *Let $\tilde{F} \in \mathbf{S}([\varsigma_1, \varsigma_2], \mathcal{F}_C(\mathbb{R}))$. Then $\tilde{F}$ is RLF q-integrable if and only if $\underline{f}_{\xi}(x)$ and $\overline{f}_{\xi}(x)$ are RLF q-integrable over $[\varsigma_1, \varsigma_2]$. Moreover, $\tilde{F}$ is RLF q-integrable, then*

$$[({}_{\varsigma_1}I_q^{\gamma} \tilde{F}(t))(x)]^{\xi} = ({}_{\varsigma_1}I_q^{\gamma} F_{\xi}(t))(x) = [({}_{\varsigma_1}I_q^{\gamma} \underline{f}_{\xi}(t))(x), ({}_{\varsigma_1}I_q^{\gamma} \overline{f}_{\xi}(t))(x)].$$

3. The Main Results

To lay the foundation of our core results, we introduce a precise framework of notation relevant to the study of UD-*h*-Godunova–Levin convex or concave fuzzy interval-valued functions.

Definition 16. *Let $\widetilde{F} \in \mathbf{S}([\varsigma_1, \varsigma_2], \mathcal{F}_C(\mathbb{R}))$. Then $\widetilde{F}$ is a UD-h-Godunova–Levin convex function if and only if*

$$\widetilde{F}(\nu s + (1-\nu)t) \supseteq_F \frac{\widetilde{F}(s)}{h(\nu)} + \frac{\widetilde{F}(t)}{h(1-\nu)},$$

for every $\nu \in (0,1)$ and for all $s,t \in [\varsigma_1, \varsigma_2]$, where $h : (0,1) \subseteq M \to \mathbb{R}^+$ and $h \neq 0$. If is reversed, one obtains that $\widetilde{F}$ is a UD-h-Godunova–Levin concave function. The family of all UD-h-Godunova–Levin convex (UD-h-Godunova–Levin concave) FIVFs on $[\varsigma_1, \varsigma_2]$ is given by $UDSGX([\varsigma_1, \varsigma_2], F_C(\mathbb{R}), \frac{1}{h})(UDSGV([\varsigma_1, \varsigma_2], F_C(\mathbb{R}), \frac{1}{h}))$.

Remark 1. *The UD-h-Godunova–Levin convex FIVFs have some very nice properties, similar to convex FIVFs.*

1. *If $\widetilde{F}$ is a UD-h-Godunova–Levin convex FIVF, then $\Upsilon\widetilde{F}$ is also a UD-h-Godunova–Levin convex FIVF for $\Upsilon \geq 0$.*
2. *If $\widetilde{F}$ and $\widetilde{G}$ are UD-h-Godunova–Levin convex FIVFs, then $max(\widetilde{F}, \widetilde{G})$ is also a UD-h-Godunova–Levin convex FIVF.*

Next, we analyze some distinctive exceptional cases of UD-h-Godunova–Levin convex FIVFs.

1. If $h(\nu) = \nu^s$, then UD-h-Godunova–Levin convex FIVFs become UD-s-Godunova–Levin convex FIVFs, that is,

$$\widetilde{F}(\nu s + (1-\nu)t) \supseteq_F \frac{\widetilde{F}(s)}{\nu^s} + \frac{\widetilde{F}(t)}{(1-\nu)^s} \text{for all } s,t \in [\varsigma_1, \varsigma_2], \nu \in (0,1).$$

2. If $h(\nu) = 1$, then UD-h-Godunova–Levin convex FIVFs become UD-P-Godunova–Levin convex FIVFs, that is,

$$\widetilde{F}(\nu s + (1-\nu)t) \supseteq_F \widetilde{F}(s) + \widetilde{F}(t) \text{for all } s,t \in [\varsigma_1, \varsigma_2], \nu \in (0,1).$$

3. If $h(\nu) = \nu$, then UD-h-Godunova–Levin convex FIVFs become UD-Godunova–Levin convex FIVFs, that is,

$$\widetilde{F}(\nu s + (1-\nu)t) \supseteq_F \frac{\widetilde{F}(s)}{\nu} + \frac{\widetilde{F}(t)}{1-\nu} \text{for all } s,t \in [\varsigma_1, \varsigma_2], \nu \in (0,1).$$

Theorem 5. *Let $\widetilde{F} \in \mathbf{S}([\varsigma_1, \varsigma_2], \mathcal{F}_C(\mathbb{R}))$. Then*

$$\widetilde{F} \in UDSGX\left([\varsigma_1, \varsigma_2], \mathcal{F}_C(\mathbb{R}), \frac{1}{h}\right),$$

if and only if for all $\xi \in [0,1]$,

$$\underline{f}_\xi(x) \in SGX\left([\varsigma_1, \varsigma_2], \mathbb{R}^+, \frac{1}{h}\right),$$

and

$$\overline{f}_\xi(x) \in SGV\left([\varsigma_1, \varsigma_2], \mathbb{R}^+, \frac{1}{h}\right).$$

Proof. Assume $\xi \in [0,1]$, $\underline{f}_{\xi}(x)$ and $\overline{f}_{\xi}(x)$ for each h-Godunova–Levin convex and concave FIVF on $[\varsigma_1, \varsigma_2]$. Then we have

$$\underline{f}_{\xi}(\nu s+(1-\nu)t) \leq \frac{\underline{f}_{\xi}(s)}{h(\nu)} + \frac{\underline{f}_{\xi}(t)}{h(1-\nu)} \text{ for all } s,t \in [\varsigma_1,\varsigma_2], \nu \in (0,1),$$

and

$$\overline{f}_{\xi}(\nu s+(1-\nu)t) \geq \frac{\overline{f}_{\xi}(s)}{h(\nu)} + \frac{\overline{f}_{\xi}(t)}{h(1-\nu)} \text{ for all } s,t \in [\varsigma_1,\varsigma_2], \nu \in (0,1).$$

Then

$$F_{\xi}(\nu s+(1-\nu)t) = [\underline{f}_{\xi}(\nu s+(1-\nu)t), \overline{f}_{\xi}(\nu s+(1-\nu)t)]$$

$$\supseteq_I \left[\frac{\underline{f}_{\xi}(s)}{h(\nu)}, \frac{\overline{f}_{\xi}(s)}{h(\nu)}\right] + \left[\frac{\underline{f}_{\xi}(t)}{h(1-\nu)}, \frac{\overline{f}_{\xi}(t)}{h(1-\nu)}\right] \text{ for all } s,t \in [\varsigma_1,\varsigma_2], \nu \in (0,1).$$

That is,

$$\widetilde{F}(\nu s+(1-\nu)t) \supseteq_F \frac{\widetilde{F}(s)}{h(\nu)} + \frac{\widetilde{F}(t)}{h(1-\nu)}.$$

Hence,

$$\widetilde{F} \in UDSGX\left([\varsigma_1,\varsigma_2], \mathcal{F}_C(R), \frac{1}{h}\right) \text{ for all } s,t \in [\varsigma_1,\varsigma_2], \nu \in (0,1).$$

Conversely, let $\widetilde{F}$ is UD-h-Godunova–Levin convex function on $[\varsigma_1, \varsigma_2]$. Then, for all $s,t \in [\varsigma_1,\varsigma_2], \nu \in (0,1)$, we have

$$\widetilde{F}(\nu s+(1-\nu)t) \supseteq_F \frac{\widetilde{F}(s)}{h(\nu)} + \frac{\widetilde{F}(t)}{h(1-\nu)}.$$

Therefore,

$$F_{\xi}(\nu s+(1-\nu)t) = [\underline{f}_{\xi}(\nu s+(1-\nu)t), \overline{f}_{\xi}(\nu s+(1-\nu)t)].$$

This implies that

$$\frac{F_{\xi}(s)}{h(\nu)} + \frac{F_{\xi}(t)}{h(1-\nu)} = \left[\frac{\underline{f}_{\xi}(s)}{h(\nu)}, \frac{\overline{f}_{\xi}(s)}{h(\nu)}\right] + \left[\frac{\underline{f}_{\xi}(t)}{h(1-\nu)}, \frac{\overline{f}_{\xi}(t)}{h(1-\nu)}\right],$$

for all $s,t \in [\varsigma_1,\varsigma_2], \nu \in (0,1)$. Then, by the UD-h-Godunova–Levin convexity of $\widetilde{F}$, we have for all $s,t \in [\varsigma_1,\varsigma_2], \nu \in (0,1)$, such that

$$\underline{f}_{\xi}(\nu s+(1-\nu)t) \leq \frac{\underline{f}_{\xi}(s)}{h(\nu)} + \frac{\underline{f}_{\xi}(t)}{h(1-\nu)} \text{ for all } s,t \in [\varsigma_1,\varsigma_2], \nu \in (0,1),$$

and

$$\overline{f}_{\xi}(\nu s+(1-\nu)t) \geq \frac{\overline{f}_{\xi}(s)}{h(\nu)} + \frac{\overline{f}_{\xi}(t)}{h(1-\nu)} \text{ for all } s,t \in [\varsigma_1,\varsigma_2], \nu \in (0,1),$$

for each $\xi \in [0,1]$. □

The next result will be established by utilizing the UD-h-Godunova–Levin convex FIVFs to derive the RLF q-HH inequalities.

Theorem 6. *Let $\tilde{F} \in \mathbf{SC}([\varsigma_1, \varsigma_2], \mathcal{F}_C(\mathbb{R})) \bigcap UDSGX([\varsigma_1, \varsigma_2], \mathcal{F}_C(\mathcal{R}), \frac{1}{h})$ and $h(\frac{1}{2}) \neq 0$. If $\tilde{F}$ is RLF q-integrable on $[\varsigma_1, \varsigma_2]$, then*

$$\begin{aligned}
\frac{h(\frac{1}{2})}{\Gamma_q(\gamma+1)} \circ \widetilde{F}\left(\frac{\varsigma_1+\varsigma_2}{2}\right) &\supseteq_F \frac{1}{(\varsigma_2-\varsigma_1)^{\gamma}} \circ [({}_{\varsigma_1}I_q^{\gamma}\widetilde{F}(x))(\varsigma_2) \oplus ({}_{\varsigma_1}I_q^{\gamma}\widetilde{F}(\varsigma_1+\varsigma_2-x))(\varsigma_2)] \\
&\supseteq_F [\widetilde{F}(\varsigma_1) \oplus \widetilde{F}(\varsigma_2)] \circ \left({}_0I_q^{\gamma}\left[\frac{1}{h(\nu)} + \frac{1}{h(1-\nu)}\right]\right)(1).
\end{aligned}$$

Proof. By Theorem 5, it follows that

$$h\left(\frac{1}{2}\right)\underline{f}_{\xi}\left(\frac{\varsigma_1+\varsigma_2}{2}\right) = h\left(\frac{1}{2}\right)\underline{f}_{\xi}\left(\frac{(1-\nu)\varsigma_1+\nu\varsigma_2+\nu\varsigma_1+(1-\nu)\varsigma_2}{2}\right)$$

$$\leq \underline{f}_{\xi}((1-\nu)\varsigma_1+\nu\varsigma_2) + \underline{f}_{\xi}((1-\nu)\varsigma_2+\nu\varsigma_1). \tag{1}$$

Multiply (1) by $\frac{{}_0(1-{}_0\Omega_q(\nu))_q^{(\gamma-1)}}{\Gamma_q(\gamma)}$ and q-integrating over $[0,1]$. We have

$$\begin{aligned}
&\frac{h(\frac{1}{2})\underline{f}_{\xi}(\frac{\varsigma_1+\varsigma_2}{2})}{\Gamma_q(\gamma)} \times \int_0^1 {}_0(1-{}_0\Omega_q(\nu))_q^{(\gamma-1)}{}_0d\nu \\
\leq\ &\frac{1}{\Gamma_q(\gamma)}\int_0^1 {}_0(1-{}_0\Omega_q(\nu))_q^{(\gamma-1)}\underline{f}_{\xi}((1-\nu)\varsigma_1+\nu\varsigma_2)_0d\nu \\
+\ &\frac{1}{\Gamma_q(\gamma)}\int_0^1 {}_0(1-{}_0\Omega_q(\nu))_q^{(\gamma-1)}\underline{f}_{\xi}((1-\nu)\varsigma_2+\nu\varsigma_1)_0d\nu.
\end{aligned}$$

Let us say

$$I \leq I_1 + I_2. \tag{2}$$

First, we calculate I_1 by using Proposition 3, Lemma 1, Definition 12, and Definition 13; we have

$$\begin{aligned}
I_1 &= \frac{1}{\Gamma_q(\gamma)}\int_0^1 {}_0(1-{}_0\Omega_q(\nu))_q^{(\gamma-1)}\underline{f}_{\xi}((1-\nu)\varsigma_1+\nu\varsigma_2)_0d\nu \\
&= \frac{1}{\Gamma_q(\gamma)}\int_0^1 {}_0(1-{}_0\Omega_q(\nu))_q^{(\gamma-1)}\underline{f}_{\xi}({}_{\varsigma_1}\Omega_q(\varsigma_2)_0d\nu \\
&= \frac{(1-q)(1-0)}{\Gamma_q(\gamma)}\sum_{i=0}^{\infty} q^i{}_0(1-{}_0\Omega_q^{i+1}(1))_q^{(\gamma-1)}\underline{f}_{\xi}({}_{\varsigma_1}\Omega_q^i(\varsigma_2)) \\
&= \frac{(1-q)}{\Gamma_q(\gamma)}\sum_{i=0}^{\infty} q^i\frac{(q^{i+1};q)_\infty}{(q^{\gamma+i};q)_\infty}\underline{f}_{\xi}({}_{\varsigma_1}\Omega_q^i(\varsigma_2)) \\
&= \frac{(1-q)}{(\varsigma_2-\varsigma_1)^{\gamma-1}\Gamma_q(\gamma)}\sum_{i=0}^{\infty} q^i(\varsigma_2-\varsigma_1)^{\gamma-1}\frac{(q^{i+1};q)_\infty}{(q^{\gamma+i};q)_\infty}\underline{f}_{\xi}({}_{\varsigma_1}\Omega_q^i(\varsigma_2)) \\
&= \frac{(1-q)(\varsigma_2-\varsigma_1)}{(\varsigma_2-\varsigma_1)^{\gamma}\Gamma_q(\gamma)}\sum_{i=0}^{\infty} q^i(\varsigma_2-\varsigma_1)^{\gamma-1}\frac{(q^{i+1};q)_\infty}{(q^{\gamma+i};q)_\infty}\underline{f}_{\xi}({}_{\varsigma_1}\Omega_q^i(\varsigma_2)) \\
&= \frac{(1-q)(\varsigma_2-\varsigma_1)}{(\varsigma_2-\varsigma_1)^{\gamma}\Gamma_q(\gamma)}\sum_{i=0}^{\infty} q^i{}_{\varsigma_1}(\varsigma_2-{}_{\varsigma_1}\Omega_q^{i+1}(x))_q^{(\gamma-1)}\underline{f}_{\xi}({}_{\varsigma_1}\Omega_q^i(\varsigma_2) \\
&= \frac{1}{(\varsigma_2-\varsigma_1)^{\gamma}\Gamma_q(\gamma)}\int_{\varsigma_1}^{\varsigma_2} {}_{\varsigma_1}(\varsigma_2-{}_{\varsigma_1}\Omega_q(x))_q^{(\gamma-1)}\underline{f}_{\xi}(x)_{\varsigma_1}dx \\
&= \frac{1}{(\varsigma_2-\varsigma_1)^{\gamma}}({}_{\varsigma_1}I_q^{\gamma}\underline{f}_{\xi}(x))(\varsigma_2).
\end{aligned}$$

Now, similarly, we can calculate I_2, and get

$$\begin{aligned} I_2 &= \frac{1}{\Gamma_q(\gamma)} \int_0^1 {}_0(1 -_0 \Omega_q(\nu))_q^{(\gamma-1)} \underline{f}_{\xi}((1-\nu)\varsigma_2 + \nu\varsigma_1)_0 d\nu \\ &= \frac{1}{\Gamma_q(\gamma)} \int_0^1 {}_0(1 -_0 \Omega_q(\nu))_q^{(\gamma-1)} \underline{f}_{\xi}(\varsigma_1 + \varsigma_2 -_{\varsigma_1} \Omega_q(\varsigma_2))_0 d\nu \\ &= \frac{(1-q)(1-0)}{\Gamma_q(\gamma)} \sum_{i=0}^{\infty} q^i {}_0(1 -_0 \Omega_q^{i+1}(1))_q^{(\gamma-1)} \underline{f}_{\xi}(\varsigma_1 + \varsigma_2 -_{\varsigma_1} \Omega_q^i(\varsigma_2)) \\ &= \frac{(1-q)}{\Gamma_q(\gamma)} \sum_{i=0}^{\infty} q^i \frac{(q^{i+1};q)_\infty}{(q^{\gamma+i};q)_\infty} \underline{f}_{\xi}(\varsigma_1 + \varsigma_2 -_{\varsigma_1} \Omega_q^i(\varsigma_2)) \\ &= \frac{(1-q)}{(\varsigma_2-\varsigma_1)^{\gamma-1}\Gamma_q(\gamma)} \sum_{i=0}^{\infty} q^i (\varsigma_2-\varsigma_1)^{\gamma-1} \frac{(q^{i+1};q)_\infty}{(q^{\gamma+i};q)_\infty} \underline{f}_{\xi}(\varsigma_1 + \varsigma_2 -_{\varsigma_1} \Omega_q^i(\varsigma_2)) \\ &= \frac{(1-q)(\varsigma_2-\varsigma_1)}{(\varsigma_2-\varsigma_1)^{\gamma}\Gamma_q(\gamma)} \sum_{i=0}^{\infty} q^i (\varsigma_2-\varsigma_1)^{\gamma-1} \frac{(q^{i+1};q)_\infty}{(q^{\gamma+i};q)_\infty} \underline{f}_{\xi}(\varsigma_1 + \varsigma_2 -_{\varsigma_1} \Omega_q^i(\varsigma_2)) \\ &= \frac{(1-q)(\varsigma_2-\varsigma_1)}{(\varsigma_2-\varsigma_1)^{\gamma}\Gamma_q(\gamma)} \sum_{i=0}^{\infty} q^i {}_{\varsigma_1}(\varsigma_2 -_{\varsigma_1} \Omega_q^{i+1}(x))_q^{(\gamma-1)} \underline{f}_{\xi}(\varsigma_1 + \varsigma_2 -_{\varsigma_1} \Omega_q^i(\varsigma_2)) \\ &= \frac{1}{(\varsigma_2-\varsigma_1)^{\gamma}\Gamma_q(\gamma)} \int_{\varsigma_1}^{\varsigma_2} {}_{\varsigma_1}(\varsigma_2 -_{\varsigma_1} \Omega_q(x))_q^{(\gamma-1)} \underline{f}_{\xi}(\varsigma_1 + \varsigma_2 - x)_{\varsigma_1} dx \\ &= \frac{1}{(\varsigma_2-\varsigma_1)^{\gamma}} ({}_{\varsigma_1}I_q^{\gamma} \underline{f}_{\xi}(\varsigma_1 + \varsigma_2 - x))(\varsigma_2). \end{aligned}$$

Similarly, we can calculate I as

$$\begin{aligned} I &= \frac{h(\frac{1}{2})\underline{f}_{\xi}(\frac{\varsigma_1+\varsigma_2}{2})}{\Gamma_q(\gamma)} \int_0^1 {}_0(1 -_0 \Omega_q(\nu))_q^{(\gamma-1)} {}_0 d\nu = h(\frac{1}{2})\underline{f}_{\xi}(\frac{\varsigma_1+\varsigma_2}{2})({}_0I_q^{\gamma}1)(1) \\ &= \frac{h(\frac{1}{2})\underline{f}_{\xi}(\frac{\varsigma_1+\varsigma_2}{2})}{\Gamma_q(\gamma+1)}. \end{aligned}$$

Putting the values of I, I_1 and I_2 in (2), we get

$$\frac{h(\frac{1}{2})\underline{f}_{\xi}(\frac{\varsigma_1+\varsigma_2}{2})}{\Gamma_q(\gamma+1)} \leq \frac{1}{(\varsigma_2-\varsigma_1)^{\gamma}} ({}_{\varsigma_1}I_q^{\gamma} \underline{f}_{\xi}(x))(\varsigma_2) + \frac{1}{(\varsigma_2-\varsigma_1)^{\gamma}} ({}_{\varsigma_1}I_q^{\gamma} \underline{f}_{\xi}(\varsigma_1 + \varsigma_2 - x))(\varsigma_2). \quad (3)$$

Now, by the definition of the h-Godunova–Levin convex function, we have

$$\begin{aligned} & \underline{f}_{\xi}((1-\nu)\varsigma_1 + \nu\varsigma_2) + \underline{f}_{\xi}((1-\nu)\varsigma_2 + \nu\varsigma_1) \\ \leq & \frac{\underline{f}_{\xi}(\varsigma_2)}{h(\nu)} + \frac{\underline{f}_{\xi}(\varsigma_1)}{h(1-\nu)} + \frac{\underline{f}_{\xi}(\varsigma_1)}{h(\nu)} + \frac{\underline{f}_{\xi}(\varsigma_2)}{h(1-\nu)} \\ = & [\underline{f}_{\xi}(\varsigma_1) + \underline{f}_{\xi}(\varsigma_2)]\left[\frac{1}{h(\nu)} + \frac{1}{h(1-\nu)}\right]. \end{aligned} \quad (4)$$

Multiply (4) by $\frac{{}_0(1-{}_0\Omega_q(\nu))_q^{(\gamma-1)}}{\Gamma_q(\gamma)}$ and q-integrating over $[0,1]$. We have

$$\begin{aligned} & \frac{1}{\Gamma_q(\gamma)} \int_0^1 {}_0(1 -_0 \Omega_q(\nu))_q^{(\gamma-1)} \underline{f}_{\xi}((1-\nu)\varsigma_1 + \nu\varsigma_2)_0 d\nu \\ + & \frac{1}{\Gamma_q(\gamma)} \int_0^1 {}_0(1 -_0 \Omega_q(\nu))_q^{(\gamma-1)} \underline{f}_{\xi}((1-\nu)\varsigma_2 + \nu\varsigma_1)_0 d\nu \\ \leq & \frac{1}{\Gamma_q(\gamma)} (\underline{f}_{\xi}(\varsigma_1) + \underline{f}_{\xi}(\varsigma_2)) \int_0^1 {}_0(1 -_0 \Omega_q(\nu))_q^{(\gamma-1)} \left[\frac{1}{h(\nu)} + \frac{1}{h(1-\nu)}\right]_0 d\nu. \end{aligned}$$

Let us say

$$J_1 + J_2 \leq J_3, \tag{5}$$

where

$$J_1 = \frac{1}{\Gamma_q(\gamma)} \int_0^1 {}_0(1 -_0 \Omega_q(v))_q^{(\gamma-1)} \underline{f}_{\xi}((1-v)\varsigma_1 + v\varsigma_2)_0 dv,$$

$$J_2 = \frac{1}{\Gamma_q(\gamma)} \int_0^1 {}_0(1 -_0 \Omega_q(v))_q^{(\gamma-1)} \underline{f}_{\xi}((1-v)\varsigma_2 + v\varsigma_1)_0 dv,$$

and

$$J_3 = \frac{1}{\Gamma_q(\gamma)} (\underline{f}_{\xi}(\varsigma_1) + \underline{f}_{\xi}(\varsigma_2)) \int_0^1 {}_0(1 -_0 \Omega_q(v))_q^{(\gamma-1)} \left[\frac{1}{h(v)} + \frac{1}{h(1-v)}\right] {}_0dv.$$

Now we calculate, similarly, J_1, J_2, and J_3, and we get

$$\begin{aligned} J_1 &= \frac{1}{(\varsigma_2 - \varsigma_1)^\gamma} ({}_{\varsigma_1}I_q^\gamma \underline{f}_{\xi}(x))(\varsigma_2) \\ J_2 &= \frac{1}{(\varsigma_2 - \varsigma_1)^\gamma} ({}_{\varsigma_1}I_q^\gamma \underline{f}_{\xi}(\varsigma_1 + \varsigma_2 - x))(\varsigma_2) \\ J_3 &= \frac{\underline{f}_{\xi}(\varsigma_1) + \underline{f}_{\xi}(\varsigma_2)}{\Gamma_q(\gamma)} \int_0^1 {}_0(1 -_0 \Omega_q(v))_q^{(\gamma-1)} \left[\frac{1}{h(v)} + \frac{1}{h(1-v)}\right] {}_0dv \\ &= (\underline{f}_{\xi}(\varsigma_1) + \underline{f}_{\xi}(\varsigma_2)) \left({}_0I_q^\gamma \left[\frac{1}{h(v)} + \frac{1}{h(1-v)}\right]\right)(1). \end{aligned}$$

Putting the values of J_1, J_2 and J_3 in (5), we get

$$\frac{1}{(\varsigma_2 - \varsigma_1)^\gamma} ({}_{\varsigma_1}I_q^\gamma \underline{f}_{\xi}(x))(\varsigma_2) + \frac{1}{(\varsigma_2 - \varsigma_1)^\gamma} ({}_{\varsigma_1}I_q^\gamma \underline{f}_{\xi}(\varsigma_1 + \varsigma_2 - x))(\varsigma_2)$$

$$\leq (\underline{f}_{\xi}(\varsigma_1) + \underline{f}_{\xi}(\varsigma_2)) \left({}_0I_q^\gamma \left[\frac{1}{h(v)} + \frac{1}{h(1-v)}\right]\right)(1). \tag{6}$$

From (3) and (6), we can written as

$$\begin{aligned} \frac{h(\frac{1}{2}) \underline{f}_{\xi}(\frac{\varsigma_1 + \varsigma_2}{2})}{\Gamma_q(\gamma+1)} &\leq \frac{1}{(\varsigma_2 - \varsigma_1)^\gamma} ({}_{\varsigma_1}I_q^\gamma \underline{f}_{\xi}(x))(\varsigma_2) + \frac{1}{(\varsigma_2 - \varsigma_1)^\gamma} ({}_{\varsigma_1}I_q^\gamma \underline{f}_{\xi}(\varsigma_1 + \varsigma_2 - x))(\varsigma_2) \\ &\leq [\underline{f}(\varsigma_1) + \underline{f}(\varsigma_2)] \left({}_0I_q^\gamma \left[\frac{1}{h(v)} + \frac{1}{h(1-v)}\right]\right)(1). \end{aligned} \tag{7}$$

Similarly,

$$\begin{aligned} \frac{h(\frac{1}{2}) \bar{f}_{\xi}(\frac{\varsigma_1 + \varsigma_2}{2})}{\Gamma_q(\gamma+1)} &\geq \frac{1}{(\varsigma_2 - \varsigma_1)^\gamma} ({}_{\varsigma_1}I_q^\gamma \bar{f}_{\xi}(x))(\varsigma_2)) + \frac{1}{(\varsigma_2 - \varsigma_1)^\gamma} ({}_{\varsigma_1}I_q^\gamma \bar{f}_{\xi}(\varsigma_1 + \varsigma_2 - x))(\varsigma_2) \\ &\geq [\bar{f}(\varsigma_1) + \bar{f}(\varsigma_2)] \left({}_0I_q^\gamma \left[\frac{1}{h(v)} + \frac{1}{h(1-v)}\right]\right)(1). \end{aligned} \tag{8}$$

So, from (7) and (8), we have

$$\begin{aligned}
&\frac{h(\frac{1}{2})}{\Gamma_q(\gamma+1)}[\underline{f}_{\xi}(\frac{\varsigma_1+\varsigma_2}{2}),\overline{f}_{\xi}(\frac{\varsigma_1+\varsigma_2}{2})] \\
\supseteq_I\ &\frac{1}{(\varsigma_2-\varsigma_1)^{\gamma}}\times \\
&[({}_{\varsigma_1}I_q^{\gamma}\underline{f}_{\xi}(x))(\varsigma_2)+({}_{\varsigma_1}I_q^{\gamma}\underline{f}_{\xi}(\varsigma_1+\varsigma_2-x))(\varsigma_2),({}_{\varsigma_1}I_q^{\gamma}\overline{f}_{\xi}(x))(\varsigma_2)+({}_{\varsigma_1}I_q^{\gamma}\overline{f}_{\xi}(\varsigma_1+\varsigma_2-x))(\varsigma_2)] \\
\supseteq_I\ &[\underline{f}(\varsigma_1)+\underline{f}(\varsigma_2),\overline{f}(\varsigma_1)+\overline{f}(\varsigma_2)]\left({}_0I_q^{\gamma}\left[\frac{1}{h(v)}+\frac{1}{h(1-v)}\right]\right)(1)
\end{aligned}$$

Hence,

$$\begin{aligned}
\frac{h(\frac{1}{2})}{\Gamma_q(\gamma+1)}\circ\widetilde{F}(\frac{\varsigma_1+\varsigma_2}{2})\ &\supseteq_F\ \frac{1}{(\varsigma_2-\varsigma_1)^{\gamma}}\circ[({}_{\varsigma_1}I_q^{\gamma}\widetilde{F}(x))(\varsigma_2)\oplus({}_{\varsigma_1}I_q^{\gamma}\widetilde{F}(\varsigma_1+\varsigma_2-x))(\varsigma_2) \\
&\supseteq_F\ [\widetilde{F}(\varsigma_1)\oplus\widetilde{F}(\varsigma_2)]\circ\left({}_0I_q^{\gamma}\left[\frac{1}{h(v)}+\frac{1}{h(1-v)}\right]\right)(1).
\end{aligned}$$

□

Remark 2.

1. *If we replace* $h(v)$ *by* $\frac{1}{h(v)}$ *in Theorem 2, we obtain the results of in ([8], [Theorem 23]), i-e.,*

$$\begin{aligned}
\frac{1}{h(\frac{1}{2})\Gamma_q(\gamma+1)}\circ\widetilde{F}(\frac{\varsigma_1+\varsigma_2}{2})\ &\supseteq_F\ \frac{1}{(\varsigma_2-\varsigma_1)^{\gamma}}\circ[({}_{\varsigma_1}I_q^{\gamma}\widetilde{F}(x))(\varsigma_2)\oplus({}_{\varsigma_1}I_q^{\gamma}\widetilde{F}(\varsigma_1+\varsigma_2-x))(\varsigma_2) \\
&\supseteq_F\ [\widetilde{F}(\varsigma_1)\oplus\widetilde{F}(\varsigma_2)]\circ({}_0I_q^{\gamma}[h(v)+h(1-v)])(1).
\end{aligned}$$

2. *If we let* $q\to 1^-$ *and replace* $h(v)$ *by* $\frac{1}{h(v)}$ *in Theorem 2, then we get ([45], [Theorem 5]).*
3. *If we replace* $h(v)$ *by* $\frac{1}{v}$ *and* $q\to 1^-$ *in Theorem 2, then we get ([33], [Theorem 3.1]).*
4. *If we let* $q\to 1^-,\xi=1$ *and replace* $h(v)$ *by* $\frac{1}{h(v)}$ *in Theorem 2, then we get ([31], [Theorem 3.4]).*
5. *If we let* $q\to 1^-,\gamma=\xi=1$ *and replace* $h(v)$ *by* $\frac{1}{h(v)}$ *in Theorem 2, then we get ([46], [Theorem 4.1]).*

Theorem 7. *Let* $\widetilde{F},\widetilde{G}\in \mathbf{SC}([\varsigma_1,\varsigma_2],\mathcal{F}_C(\mathbb{R}))$*. If* $\widetilde{F}\otimes\widetilde{G}$ *is RLF q-integrable on* $[\varsigma_1,\varsigma_2],\widetilde{F}\in UDSGX([\varsigma_1,\varsigma_2],F_C(\mathbb{R}),\frac{1}{h_1})$ *and* $\widetilde{G}\in UDSGX([\varsigma_1,\varsigma_2],F_C(\mathbb{R}),\frac{1}{h_2})$*, then*

$$\begin{aligned}
&\frac{1}{(\varsigma_2-\varsigma_1)^{\gamma}}\circ(({}_{\varsigma_1}I_q^{\gamma}\widetilde{F}(x)\oplus\widetilde{G}(x))(\varsigma_2)\oplus({}_{\varsigma_1}I_q^{\gamma}\widetilde{F}(\varsigma_1+\varsigma_2-x)\otimes\widetilde{G}(\varsigma_1+\varsigma_2-x)(\varsigma_2)) \\
\supseteq_F\ &T(v)\odot[\widetilde{F}(\varsigma_1)\otimes\widetilde{G}(\varsigma_1)\oplus\widetilde{F}(\varsigma_2)\otimes\widetilde{G}(\varsigma_2)]\oplus R(v)[\widetilde{F}(\varsigma_1)\otimes\widetilde{G}(\varsigma_2)\oplus\widetilde{F}(\varsigma_2)\otimes\widetilde{G}(\varsigma_1)],
\end{aligned}$$

where

$$T(v)=\left({}_0I_q^{\gamma}\frac{1}{h_1(v)}\frac{1}{h_2(v)}\right)(1)+\left({}_0I_q^{\gamma}\frac{1}{h_1(1-v)}\frac{1}{h_2(1-v)}\right)(1), \tag{9}$$

and

$$R(v)=\left({}_0I_q^{\gamma}\frac{1}{h_1(v)}\frac{1}{h_2(1-v)}\right)(1)+\left({}_0I_q^{\gamma}\frac{1}{h_1(1-v)}\frac{1}{h_2(v)}\right)(1). \tag{10}$$

Proof. Derived from the stipulated conditions, one can deduce

$$\begin{aligned}
& \underline{f}_{\xi}((1-\nu)\varsigma_1+\nu\varsigma_2)\underline{g}_{\xi}((1-\nu)\varsigma_1+\nu\varsigma_2) \\
\leq & \left(\frac{\underline{f}_{\xi}(\varsigma_1)}{h_1(1-\nu)}+\frac{\underline{f}_{\xi}(\varsigma_2)}{h_1(\nu)}\right)\cdot\left(\frac{\underline{g}_{\xi}(\varsigma_1)}{h_2(1-\nu)}+\frac{\underline{g}_{\xi}(\varsigma_2)}{h_2(\nu)}\right) \\
= & \frac{\underline{f}_{\xi}(\varsigma_1)\underline{g}_{\xi}(\varsigma_1)}{h_1(1-\nu)h_2(1-\nu)}+\frac{\underline{f}_{\xi}(\varsigma_2)\underline{g}_{\xi}(\varsigma_2)}{h_1(\nu)h_2(\nu)}+\frac{\underline{f}_{\xi}(\varsigma_1)\underline{g}_{\xi}(\varsigma_2)}{h_1(1-\nu)h_2(\nu)}+\frac{\underline{f}_{\xi}(\varsigma_2)\underline{g}_{\xi}(\varsigma_1)}{h_1(\nu)h_2(1-\nu)}.
\end{aligned}$$

The remaining proof follows from Theorem 6. □

Theorem 8. *Let $\widetilde{F},\widetilde{G}\in \mathbf{SC}([\varsigma_1,\varsigma_2],\mathcal{F}_C(\mathbb{R}))$ and $h_1(\frac{1}{2})h_2(\frac{1}{2})\neq 0$. If $\widetilde{F}\otimes\widetilde{G}$ is RLF q-integrable on $[\varsigma_1,\varsigma_2]$, $\widetilde{F}\in UDSGX([\varsigma_1,\varsigma_2],F_C(\mathbb{R}),\frac{1}{h_1})$ and $\widetilde{G}\in UDSGX([\varsigma_1,\varsigma_2],F_C(\mathbb{R}),\frac{1}{h_2})$, then*

$$\begin{aligned}
& \frac{h_1(\frac{1}{2})h_2(\frac{1}{2})\widetilde{F}(\frac{\varsigma_1+\varsigma_2}{2})\otimes\widetilde{G}(\frac{\varsigma_1+\varsigma_2}{2})}{\Gamma_q(\gamma+1)} \\
\supseteq_F & \frac{1}{(\varsigma_2-\varsigma_1)^{\gamma}}\circ\left(({}_{\varsigma_1}I_q^{\gamma}\widetilde{F}(x)\otimes\widetilde{G}(x))(\varsigma_2)\oplus({}_{\varsigma_1}I_q^{\gamma}\widetilde{F}(\varsigma_1+\varsigma_2-x)\otimes\widetilde{G}(\varsigma_1+\varsigma_2-x)(\varsigma_2)\right) \\
\oplus & T(\nu)\odot[\widetilde{F}(\varsigma_1)\otimes\widetilde{G}(\varsigma_2)\oplus\widetilde{F}(\varsigma_2)\otimes\widetilde{G}(\varsigma_1)]\oplus R(\nu)[\widetilde{F}(\varsigma_1)\otimes\widetilde{G}(\varsigma_1)\oplus\widetilde{F}(\varsigma_2)\otimes\widetilde{G}(\varsigma_2)],
\end{aligned}$$

where $T(\nu)$ and $R(\nu)$ defined as in (9) and (10), respectively.

Proof. By hypothesis, we have

$$h_1\left(\frac{1}{2}\right)F_{\xi}\left(\frac{\varsigma_1+\varsigma_2}{2}\right)\supseteq_I F_{\xi}((1-\nu)\varsigma_1+\nu\varsigma_2)+F_{\xi}(\nu\varsigma_1+(1-\nu)\varsigma_2),$$

and

$$h_2\left(\frac{1}{2}\right)G_{\xi}\left(\frac{\varsigma_1+\varsigma_2}{2}\right)\supseteq_I G_{\xi}((1-\nu)\varsigma_1+\nu\varsigma_2)+G_{\xi}(\nu\varsigma_1+(1-\nu)\varsigma_2).$$

Hence,

$$\begin{aligned}
& h_1\left(\frac{1}{2}\right)h_2\left(\frac{1}{2}\right)F_{\xi}\left(\frac{\varsigma_1+\varsigma_2}{2}\right)G_{\xi}\left(\frac{\varsigma_1+\varsigma_2}{2}\right) \\
\supseteq_I & F_{\xi}((\nu)\varsigma_1+(1-\nu)\varsigma_2)G_{\xi}((\nu)\varsigma_1+(1-\nu)\varsigma_2)+F_{\xi}((\nu)\varsigma_1+(1-\nu)\varsigma_2)G_{\xi}((1-\nu)\varsigma_1+(\nu)\varsigma_2) \\
+ & F_{\xi}((1-\nu)\varsigma_1+(\nu)\varsigma_2)G_{\xi}((\nu)\varsigma_1+(1-\nu)\varsigma_2)+F_{\xi}((1-\nu)\varsigma_1+(\nu)\varsigma_2)G_{\xi}((1-\nu)\varsigma_1+(\nu)\varsigma_2) \\
\supseteq_I & F_{\xi}((\nu)\varsigma_1+(1-\nu)\varsigma_2)G_{\xi}((\nu)\varsigma_1+(1-\nu)\varsigma_2)+F_{\xi}((1-\nu)\varsigma_1+(\nu)\varsigma_2)G_{\xi}((1-\nu)\varsigma_1+(\nu)\varsigma_2) \\
+ & [F_{\xi}(\varsigma_1)G_{\xi}(\varsigma_2)+F_{\xi}(\varsigma_2)G_{\xi}(\varsigma_1)].\left[\frac{1}{h_1(\nu)h_2(\nu)}+\frac{1}{h_1(1-\nu)h_2(1-\nu)}\right] \\
+ & [F_{\xi}(\varsigma_1)G_{\xi}(\varsigma_1)+F_{\xi}(\varsigma_2)G_{\xi}(\varsigma_2)].\left[\frac{1}{h_1(\nu)h_2(1-\nu)}+\frac{1}{h_1(1-\nu)h_2(\nu)}\right].
\end{aligned}$$

Using the technique in Theorem 6 and the theorem holds true. □

Now we shall derive some known results from our general result.

Remark 3.

1. *If we replace $h_1(\nu)$ by $\frac{1}{h_1(\nu)}$ and $h_2(\nu)$ by $\frac{1}{h_2(\nu)}$, and letting $q\to 1^-$ in Theorem 3 and Theorem 4, we obtain the results of ([45], [Theorem 6 and Theorem 7]), respectively.*
2. *If we replace $h_1(\nu)$ by $\frac{1}{h_1(\nu)}$ and $h_2(\nu)$ by $\frac{1}{h_2(\nu)}$ in Theorem 3 and Theorem 4, we obtain the results of ([8], [Theorem 27 and Theorem 28]), respectively.*

3. *If we replace $h_1(\nu)$ and $h_2(\nu)$ by $\frac{1}{\nu}$ in Theorem 3 and Theorem 4, we obtain ([33], [Theorems 3.4 and Theorem 3.6]), respectively.*
4. *If we replace $h_1(\nu)$ and $h_2(\nu)$ by $\frac{1}{\nu}$, and letting $\xi = 1$ in Theorem 3 and Theorem 4, we obtain ([31], [Theorems 3.5 and Theorem 3.6]), respectively.*
5. *If we replace $h_1(\nu)$ by $\frac{1}{h_1(\nu)}$ and $h_2(\nu)$ by $\frac{1}{h_2(\nu)}$, and letting $\gamma = \xi = 1$ and $q \to 1^-$ in Theorem 3 and Theorem 4, we obtain ([46], [Theorem 4.5 and Theorem 4.6]), respectively.*

Theorem 9. *Let $\widetilde{F} \in \mathbf{SC}([\varsigma_1, \varsigma_2], \mathcal{F}_C(\mathbb{R})) \bigcap UDSGX([\varsigma_1, \varsigma_2], \mathcal{F}_C(\mathbb{R}), \frac{1}{h})$ and $\varpi \in C([\varsigma_1, \varsigma_2], \mathbb{R}_0^+)$ be symmetric with respect to $\frac{\varsigma_1+\varsigma_2}{2}$ with ${}_{\varsigma_1}I_q^{\gamma}\varpi(x))(\varsigma_2) > 0$. If $\widetilde{F}(x)\varpi(x)$ is RLF q-integrable on $[\varsigma_1, \varsigma_2]$, then*

$$\widetilde{F}(\frac{\varsigma_1+\varsigma_2}{2}) \supseteq_{\mathbb{F}} \frac{1}{h(\frac{1}{2})_{\varsigma_1}I_q^{\gamma}\varpi(x))(\varsigma_2)} \odot({}_{\varsigma_1}I_q^{\gamma}\widetilde{F}(x)\odot\varpi(x))(\varsigma_2) \oplus({}_{\varsigma_1}I_q^{\gamma}\widetilde{F}(\varsigma_1+\varsigma_2+x)\odot\varpi(\varsigma_1+\varsigma_2+x))(\varsigma_2).$$

Proof. Since $\underline{f}_{\xi}(x) \in SGX([\varsigma_1, \varsigma_2], \mathbb{R}_0^+, \frac{1}{h})$, we have

$$h(\frac{1}{2})\underline{f}_{\xi}(\frac{\varsigma_1+\varsigma_2}{2}) \leq \underline{f}_{\xi}((1-\nu)\varsigma_1+\nu\varsigma_2) + \underline{f}_{\xi}((1-\nu)\varsigma_2+\nu\varsigma_1).$$

Multiply both sides by $\frac{{}_0(1-{}_0\Omega_q(\nu))_q^{(\gamma-1)}\varpi((1-\nu)\varsigma_1+\varsigma_2)}{\Gamma_q(\gamma)}$ and q-integrating over $[0,1]$. We have

$$\begin{aligned}
&\frac{h(\frac{1}{2})\underline{f}_{\xi}(\frac{\varsigma_1+\varsigma_2}{2})}{\Gamma_q(\gamma)} \int_0^1 {}_0(1-{}_0\Omega_q(\nu))_q^{(\gamma-1)}\varpi((1-\nu)\varsigma_1+\varsigma_2)_0d_q\nu \\
\leq\ & \int_0^1 {}_0(1-{}_0\Omega_q(\nu))_q^{(\gamma-1)}\underline{f}_{\xi}((1-\nu)\varsigma_1+\nu\varsigma_2)\varpi((1-\nu)\varsigma_1+\varsigma_2)_0d_q\nu \\
+\ & \int_0^1 {}_0(1-{}_0\Omega_q(\nu))_q^{(\gamma-1)}\underline{f}_{\xi}((1-\nu)\varsigma_2+\nu\varsigma_1)\varpi((1-\nu)\varsigma_1+\varsigma_2)_0d_q\nu.
\end{aligned}$$

Let us say

$$K_1 \leq K_2 + K_3. \tag{11}$$

First, we solve K_1 by using Proposition 3, Lemma 1, Definition 12, and Definition 13. We have

$$\begin{aligned}
K_1 &= \frac{h(\frac{1}{2})\underline{f}_{\xi}(\frac{\varsigma_1+\varsigma_2}{2})}{\Gamma_q(\gamma)} \int_0^1 {}_0(1-{}_0\Omega_q(\nu))_q^{(\gamma-1)}\varpi((1-\nu)\varsigma_1+\varsigma_2)_0d_q\nu \\
&= \frac{h(\frac{1}{2})\underline{f}_{\xi}(\frac{\varsigma_1+\varsigma_2}{2})}{(\varsigma_2-\varsigma_1)^{\gamma}}({}_{\varsigma_1}I_q^{\gamma}\varpi(x))(\varsigma_2).
\end{aligned}$$

Similarly,

$$\begin{aligned}
K_2 &= \int_0^1 {}_0(1-{}_0\Omega_q(\nu))_q^{(\gamma-1)}\underline{f}_{\xi}((1-\nu)\varsigma_1+\nu\varsigma_2)\varpi((1-\nu)\varsigma_1+\varsigma_2)_0d_q\nu \\
&= \frac{1}{(\varsigma_2-\varsigma_1)^{\gamma}}({}_{\varsigma_1}I_q^{\gamma}\underline{f}_{\xi}(x)\varpi(x))(\varsigma_2),
\end{aligned}$$

and

$$K_3 = \int_0^1 {}_0(1 - {}_0\Omega_q(\nu))_q^{(\gamma-1)} \underline{f}_\xi((1-\nu)\varsigma_2 + \nu\varsigma_1)\varpi((1-\nu)\varsigma_1 + \varsigma_2)_0 d_q\nu$$
$$= \frac{1}{(\varsigma_2 - \varsigma_1)^\gamma}({}_{\varsigma_1}I_q^\gamma \underline{f}_\xi(\varsigma_1 + \varsigma_2 - x)\varpi(\varsigma_1 + \varsigma_2 - x))(\varsigma_2).$$

Putting the values of K_1, K_2, and K_3 in (11), we get

$$\frac{h(\frac{1}{2})\underline{f}_\xi(\frac{\varsigma_1+\varsigma_2}{2})}{(\varsigma_2 - \varsigma_1)^\gamma}({}_{\varsigma_1}I_q^\gamma \varpi(x))(\varsigma_2)$$
$$\leq \frac{1}{(\varsigma_2 - \varsigma_1)^\gamma}({}_{\varsigma_1}I_q^\gamma \underline{f}_\xi(x)\varpi(x))(\varsigma_2) + \frac{1}{(\varsigma_2 - \varsigma_1)^\gamma}({}_{\varsigma_1}I_q^\gamma \underline{f}_\xi(\varsigma_1 + \varsigma_2 - x)\varpi(\varsigma_1 + \varsigma_2 - x))(\varsigma_2).$$

$$h(\frac{1}{2})\underline{f}_\xi(\frac{\varsigma_1+\varsigma_2}{2})({}_{\varsigma_1}I_q^\gamma \varpi(x))(\varsigma_2) \leq ({}_{\varsigma_1}I_q^\gamma \underline{f}_\xi(x)\varpi(x))(\varsigma_2) + ({}_{\varsigma_1}I_q^\gamma \underline{f}_\xi(\varsigma_1 + \varsigma_2 - x)\varpi(\varsigma_1 + \varsigma_2 - x))(\varsigma_2).$$

Similarly,

$$h(\frac{1}{2})\overline{f}_\xi(\frac{\varsigma_1+\varsigma_2}{2})({}_{\varsigma_1}I_q^\gamma \varpi(x))(\varsigma_2) \leq ({}_{\varsigma_1}I_q^\gamma \overline{f}_\xi(x)\varpi(x))(\varsigma_2) + ({}_{\varsigma_1}I_q^\gamma \overline{f}_\xi(\varsigma_1 + \varsigma_2 - x)\varpi(\varsigma_1 + \varsigma_2 - x))(\varsigma_2).$$

So, we have

$$[\underline{f}_\xi(\frac{\varsigma_1+\varsigma_2}{2}), \overline{f}_\xi(\frac{\varsigma_1+\varsigma_2}{2})]$$
$$\supseteq_I \frac{1}{h(\frac{1}{2})({}_{\varsigma_1}I_q^\gamma \varpi(x))(\varsigma_2)}[({}_{\varsigma_1}I_q^\gamma \underline{f}_\xi(x)\varpi(x))(\varsigma_2) + ({}_{\varsigma_1}I_q^\gamma \underline{f}_\xi(\varsigma_1 + \varsigma_2 - x)\varpi(\varsigma_1 + \varsigma_2 - x))(\varsigma_2),$$
$$({}_{\varsigma_1}I_q^\gamma \overline{f}_\xi(x)\varpi(x))(\varsigma_2) + ({}_{\varsigma_1}I_q^\gamma \overline{f}_\xi(\varsigma_1 + \varsigma_2 - x)\varpi(\varsigma_1 + \varsigma_2 - x))(\varsigma_2)].$$

$$\widetilde{F}(\frac{\varsigma_1+\varsigma_2}{2}) \supseteq_{\mathbb{F}} \frac{1}{h(\frac{1}{2}){}_{\varsigma_1}I_q^\gamma \varpi(x))(\varsigma_2)} \odot({}_{\varsigma_1}I_q^\gamma \widetilde{F}(x) \odot \varpi(x))(\varsigma_2)$$
$$\oplus({}_{\varsigma_1}I_q^\gamma \widetilde{F}(\varsigma_1 + \varsigma_2 + x) \odot \varpi(\varsigma_1 + \varsigma_2 + x))(\varsigma_2).$$

□

Theorem 10. *Let* $\widetilde{F} \in \mathbf{SC}([\varsigma_1, \varsigma_2], \mathcal{F}_C(\mathbb{R})) \bigcap UDSGX([\varsigma_1, \varsigma_2], \mathcal{F}_C(\mathbb{R}), \frac{1}{h})$ *and* $\varpi \in C([\varsigma_1, \varsigma_2], \mathbb{R}_0^+)$ *be symmetric with respect to* $\frac{\varsigma_1+\varsigma_2}{2}$ *with* ${}_{\varsigma_1}I_q^\gamma \varpi(x))(\varsigma_2) > 0$. *If* $\widetilde{F}(x)\varpi(x)$ *is RLF q-integrable on* $[\varsigma_1, \varsigma_2]$, *then*

$$\frac{1}{(\varsigma_2 - \varsigma_1)^\gamma} \odot (({}_{\varsigma_1}I_q^\gamma \widetilde{F}(x) \odot \varpi(x))(\varsigma_2) \quad \oplus(({}_{\varsigma_1}I_q^\gamma \widetilde{F}(\varsigma_1 + \varsigma_2 - x) \odot \varpi(\varsigma_1 + \varsigma_2 - x))(\varsigma_2)$$
$$\supseteq_{\mathbb{F}} [\widetilde{F}(\varsigma_1) \oplus \widetilde{F}(\varsigma_2)] \odot M(\nu),$$

where $M(\nu) = ({}_0I_q^\gamma \varpi(\nu\varsigma_1 + (1-\nu)\varsigma_2)[\frac{1}{h(1-\nu)} + \frac{1}{h(\nu)}])(1)$.

Proof. According to the given condition, we have

$$\underline{f}_\xi(\nu\varsigma_1 + (1-\nu)\varsigma_2)\varpi(\nu\varsigma_1 + (1-\nu)\varsigma_2)$$
$$\leq [\frac{1}{h(\nu)}\underline{f}_\xi(\varsigma_1) + \frac{1}{h(1-\nu)}\underline{f}_\xi(\varsigma_2)]\varpi(\nu\varsigma_1 + (1-\nu)\varsigma_2), \tag{12}$$

and

$$\begin{aligned} & \underline{f}_{\xi}((1-\nu)\varsigma_1+\nu\varsigma_2)\varpi((1-\nu)\varsigma_1+\nu\varsigma_2) \\ \leq\ & [\frac{1}{h(\nu)}\underline{f}_{\xi}(\varsigma_2)+\frac{1}{h(1-\nu)}\underline{f}_{\xi}(\varsigma_1)]\varpi((1-\nu)\varsigma_1+\nu\varsigma_2). \end{aligned} \tag{13}$$

Adding (12) and (13),

$$\begin{aligned} & \underline{f}_{\xi}(\nu\varsigma_1+(1-\nu)\varsigma_2)\varpi(\nu\varsigma_1+(1-\nu)\varsigma_2)+\underline{f}_{\xi}((1-\nu)\varsigma_1+\nu\varsigma_2)\varpi((1-\nu)\varsigma_1+\nu\varsigma_2) \\ \leq\ & [\frac{1}{h(\nu)}\underline{f}_{\xi}(\varsigma_1)+\frac{1}{h(1-\nu)}\underline{f}_{\xi}(\varsigma_2)]\varpi(\nu\varsigma_1+(1-\nu)\varsigma_2) \\ +\ & [\frac{1}{h(\nu)}\underline{f}_{\xi}(\varsigma_2)+\frac{1}{h(1-\nu)}\underline{f}_{\xi}(\varsigma_1)]\varpi((1-\nu)\varsigma_1+\nu\varsigma_2). \end{aligned}$$

Multiply both sides by $\frac{{}_0(1-{}_0\Omega_q(\nu))_q^{(\gamma-1)}}{\Gamma_q(\gamma)}$; the remaining proof is similar to Theorem 5, making the result self-evident. □

Remark 4.

1. *If we replace $h(\nu)$ by $\frac{1}{h(\nu)}$ in Theorem 5 and Theorem 6, then we have ([8], [Theorem 30 and Theorem 31]), respectively.*
2. *If we replace $h(\nu)$ by $\frac{1}{h(\nu)}$, and letting $q \to 1^-$ in Theorem 5 and Theorem 6, then we have ([45], [Theorem 9 and Theorem 8]), respectively*
3. *If we replace $h(\nu)$ by $\frac{1}{\nu}$, and letting $q \to 1^-$ in Theorem 5 and Theorem 6, we have ([33], [Theorem 3.8 and Theorem 3.7]), respectively.*
4. *If we let $\xi = 1$ and replace $h(\nu)$ by $\frac{1}{h(\nu)}$ in Theorem 5 and Theorem 6, we obtain ([44], [Theorems 3.14 and Theorem 3.15]), respectively.*

4. Numerical Examples

Example 1. *Let $\widetilde{F} \in \mathbf{SC}([0,\pi], \mathcal{F}_C(\mathbb{R}))$ and ξ-levels of $\widetilde{F}$ be given by $F_{\xi}(x) = [(1-\xi)x^2 + 24\xi, (1-\xi)(25-x^2)+24\xi]$ for all $\xi \in [0,1]$ and for all $x \in [\varsigma_1, \varsigma_2]$, $h(\nu) = \frac{1}{\nu}$, for $\nu \in (0,1)$. Obviously, $\widetilde{F}(x)$ satisfies the assumptions in Theorem 2. If we let $q = \frac{1}{2}$ and $\gamma = 2$, then*

$$\begin{aligned} \frac{h(\frac{1}{2})}{\Gamma_q(\gamma+1)}\underline{f}_{\xi}(\frac{\varsigma_1+\varsigma_2}{2}) &= \frac{2}{\Gamma_{\frac{1}{2}}(3)}\underline{f}_{\xi}(\frac{0+\pi}{2}) \\ &= \frac{(1-\xi)\pi^2}{3}+32\xi. \end{aligned}$$

Secondly,

$$\begin{aligned} \frac{h(\frac{1}{2})}{\Gamma_q(\gamma+1)}\overline{f}_{\xi}(\frac{\varsigma_1+\varsigma_2}{2}) &= \frac{2}{\Gamma_{\frac{1}{2}(3)}}\overline{f}_{\xi}(\frac{0+\pi}{2}) \\ &= (1-\xi)\frac{100-\pi^2}{3}+32\xi, \end{aligned}$$

and

$$\begin{aligned}\frac{\underline{f}_{\xi}(\varsigma_1)+\underline{f}_{\xi}(\varsigma_2)}{\Gamma_q(\gamma+1)} &= \frac{\underline{f}_{\xi}(0)+\underline{f}_{\xi}(\pi)}{\Gamma_{\frac{1}{2}}(3)}\\ &= \frac{24\xi+(1-\xi)\pi^2+24\xi}{\frac{3}{2}}\\ &= \frac{2(1-\xi)\pi^2}{3}+32\xi.\end{aligned}$$

Next,

$$\begin{aligned}\frac{\overline{f}_{\xi}(\varsigma_1)+\overline{f}_{\xi}(\varsigma_2)}{\Gamma_q(\gamma+1)} &= \frac{\overline{f}_{\xi}(0)+\overline{f}_{\xi}(\pi)}{\Gamma_{\frac{1}{2}}(3)}\\ &= \frac{(1-\xi)25+24\xi+(1-\xi)(25-\pi^2)+24\xi}{\frac{3}{2}}\\ &= \frac{2(1-\xi)(50-\pi^2)}{3}+32\xi,\end{aligned}$$

and

$$\begin{aligned}&\frac{1}{(\varsigma_2-\varsigma_1)^{\gamma}}\left(({}_{\varsigma_1}I_q^{\gamma}\underline{f}_{\xi}(x))(\varsigma_2)+(({}_{\varsigma_1}I_q^{\gamma}\underline{f}_{\xi}(\varsigma_1-\varsigma_2-x))(\varsigma_2)\right)\\ &= \frac{({}_1I_{\frac{1}{2}}^{2}\underline{f}_{\xi}(x))(\pi)+({}_1I_{\frac{1}{2}}^{2}\underline{f}_{\xi}(0-\pi-x))(\pi)}{(\pi-0)^2}\\ &= \frac{54\pi^2}{105}(1-\xi)+32\xi.\end{aligned}$$

Also,

$$\begin{aligned}&\frac{1}{(\varsigma_2-\varsigma_1)^{\gamma}}\left(({}_{\varsigma_1}I_q^{\gamma}\overline{f}_{\xi}(x))(\varsigma_2)+(({}_{\varsigma_1}I_q^{\gamma}\overline{f}_{\xi}(\varsigma_1-\varsigma_2-x))(\varsigma_2)\right)\\ &= \frac{({}_1I_{\frac{1}{2}}^{2}\overline{f}_{\xi}(x))(\pi)+({}_1I_{\frac{1}{2}}^{2}\overline{f}_{\xi}(0-\pi-x))(\pi)}{(\pi-0)^2}\\ &= \frac{-54\pi^2+3500}{105}(1-\xi)+32\xi.\end{aligned}$$

Therefore,

$$\left[\frac{(1-\xi)\pi^2}{3}+32\xi,(1-\xi)\frac{100-\pi^2}{3}+32\xi\right]\supseteq_I\left[\frac{54\pi^2}{105}(1-\xi)+32\xi,\frac{-54\pi^2+3500}{105}(1-\xi)+32\xi\right]$$

$$\supseteq_I\left[\frac{2(1-\xi)\pi^2}{3}+32\xi,\frac{2(1-\xi)(50-\pi^2)}{3}+32\xi\right]. \quad (14)$$

As shown in Figure 1, the green chain line represents $F(\xi)$, where $\underline{f}(\xi)=\frac{(1-\xi)\pi^2}{3}+32\xi$, and $\overline{f}(\xi)=(1-\xi)\frac{100-\pi^2}{3}+32\xi,\xi\in[0,1]$. The dashed red line represents $G(\xi)$, where $\underline{g}(\xi)=\frac{54\pi^2}{105}(1-\xi)+32\xi$, and $\overline{g}(\xi)=\frac{-54\pi^2+3500}{105}(1-\xi)+32\xi,\xi\in[0,1]$. The solid black line represents $H(\xi)$, where $\underline{h}(\xi)=\frac{2(1-\xi)\pi^2}{3}+32\xi$, and $\overline{f}(\xi)=\frac{2(1-\xi)(50-\pi^2)}{3}+32\xi,\xi\in[0,1]$.

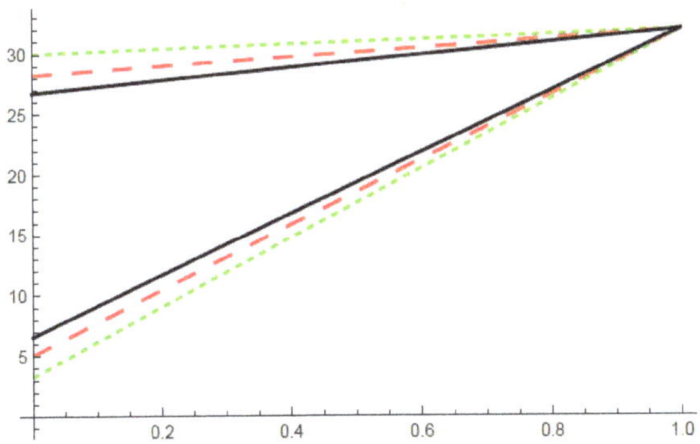

Figure 1. A visualization of the inequality (14) left, middle, and right terms.

Example 2. *Choose* $h_1(v) = h_2(v) = \frac{1}{v}$ *for* $v \in (0,1)$. *Let* $\widetilde{F}, \widetilde{G} \in \mathbf{SC}([0,2], \mathcal{F}_C(\mathbb{R}))$ *and* ξ*-levels of* $\widetilde{F}, \widetilde{G}$ *be given by* $F_\xi(x) = [(1-\xi)x^2 + 5\xi, (1-\xi)(10-x^2) + 5\xi]$ *and* $G_\xi(x) = [(1-\xi)x^2 + 5\xi, (1-\xi)(12-x^2) + 5\xi]$ *for all* $\xi \in [0,1]$ *and for all* $x \in [\varsigma_1, \varsigma_2]$, *respectively, since* $\widetilde{F}(x)$ *and* $\widetilde{G}(x)$ *satisfy the assumptions of Theorems 3 and 4. Choose* $q = \frac{1}{2}$ *and* $\gamma = 2$. *Then we have* $T(v) = \frac{18}{35}$ *and* $R(v) = \frac{16}{105}$.

$$\underline{f}_\xi(\frac{\varsigma_1+\varsigma_2}{2})\underline{g}_\xi(\frac{\varsigma_1+\varsigma_2}{2}) = (1-\xi)^2 + 10\xi(1-\xi) + 25\xi^2,$$

$$\overline{f}_\xi(\frac{\varsigma_1+\varsigma_2}{2})\overline{g}_\xi(\frac{\varsigma_1+\varsigma_2}{2}) = 99(1-\xi)^2 + 100\xi(1-\xi) + 25\xi^2,$$

$$\underline{f}_\xi(\varsigma_1)\underline{g}_\xi(\varsigma_1) + \underline{f}_\xi(\varsigma_2)\underline{g}_\xi(\varsigma_2) = 16(1-\xi)^2 + 40\xi(1-\xi) + 50\xi^2,$$

$$\underline{f}_\xi(\varsigma_1)\underline{g}_\xi(\varsigma_2) + \underline{f}_\xi(\varsigma_2)\underline{g}_\xi(\varsigma_1) = 40\xi(1-\xi) + 50\xi^2,$$

$$\overline{f}_\xi(\varsigma_1)\overline{g}_\xi(\varsigma_1) + \overline{f}_\xi(\varsigma_2)\overline{g}_\xi(\varsigma_2) = 168(1-\xi)^2 + 180\xi(1-\xi) + 50\xi^2,$$

$$\overline{f}_\xi(\varsigma_1)\overline{g}_\xi(\varsigma_2) + \overline{f}_\xi(\varsigma_2)\overline{g}_\xi(\varsigma_1) = 152(1-\xi)^2 + 180\xi(1-\xi) + 50\xi^2.$$

Since

$$\begin{aligned} &\frac{1}{(\varsigma_2-\varsigma_1)^\gamma}((_{\varsigma_1}I_q^\gamma \underline{f}_\xi(x)\underline{g}_\xi(x))(\varsigma_2) + ((_{\varsigma_1}I_q^\gamma \underline{f}_\xi(\varsigma_1-\varsigma_2-x)\underline{g}_\xi(\varsigma_1-\varsigma_2-x))(\varsigma_2)) \\ = &\frac{61664}{9765}(1-\xi)^2 + \frac{144}{7}\xi(1-\xi) + \frac{100}{3}\xi^2, \end{aligned}$$

and

$$\begin{aligned} &\frac{1}{(\varsigma_2-\varsigma_1)^\gamma}((_{\varsigma_1}I_q^\gamma \overline{f}_\xi(x)\overline{g}_\xi(x))(\varsigma_2) + ((_{\varsigma_1}I_q^\gamma \overline{f}_\xi(\varsigma_1-\varsigma_2-x)\overline{g}_\xi(\varsigma_1-\varsigma_2-x))(\varsigma_2)) \\ = &\frac{1182128}{9765}(1-\xi)^2 + \frac{2648}{21}\xi(1-\xi) + \frac{100}{3}\xi^2. \end{aligned}$$

So, we get

$$\begin{aligned} &[\frac{61664}{9765}(1-\xi)^2 + \frac{144}{7}\xi(1-\xi) + \frac{100}{3}\xi^2, \frac{1182128}{9765}(1-\xi)^2 + \frac{2648}{21}\xi(1-\xi) + \frac{100}{3}\xi^2] \\ \supseteq_I &[\frac{288}{35}(1-\xi)^2 + \frac{80}{3}\xi(1-\xi) + \frac{100}{3}\xi^2, \frac{11504}{105}(1-\xi)^2 + 120\xi(1-\xi) + \frac{100}{3}\xi^2]. \quad (15) \end{aligned}$$

As shown in Figure 2, the dashed red line represents $F(\xi)$*, where* $\underline{f}(\xi) = \frac{61664}{9765}(1-\xi)^2 + \frac{144}{7}\xi(1-\xi) + \frac{100}{3}\xi^2$ *and* $\overline{f}(\xi) = \frac{1182128}{9765}(1-\xi)^2 + \frac{2648}{21}\xi(1-\xi) + \frac{100}{3}\xi^2$*. The solid blue line represents* $G(\xi)$*, where* $\underline{g}(\xi) = \frac{288}{35}(1-\xi)^2 + \frac{80}{3}\xi(1-\xi) + \frac{100}{3}\xi^2$ *and* $\overline{g}(\xi) = \frac{11504}{105}(1-\xi)^2 + 120\xi(1-\xi) + \frac{100}{3}\xi^2$*.*

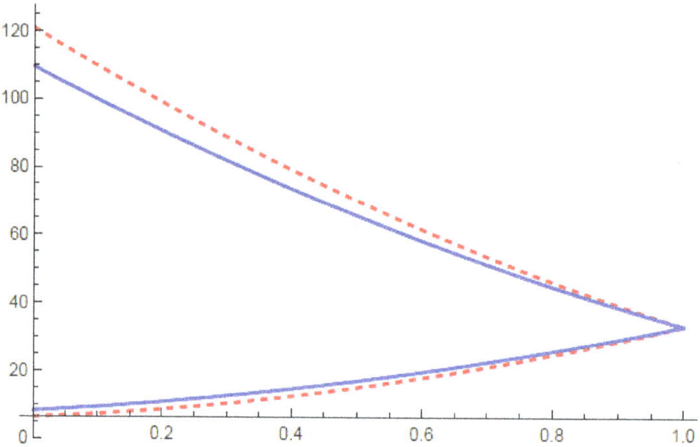

Figure 2. A visualization of the inequality (15) left and right terms.

Also,

$$[\frac{8}{3}(1-\xi)^2 + \frac{80}{3}\xi(1-\xi) + \frac{200}{3}\xi^2, 264(1-\xi)^2 + \frac{800}{3}\xi(1-\xi) + \frac{200}{3}\xi^2]$$

$$\supseteq_I [\frac{85472}{9765}(1-\xi)^2 + \frac{992}{21}\xi(1-\xi) + \frac{200}{3}\xi^2, \frac{2195456}{9765}(1-\xi)^2 + \frac{5168}{21}\xi(1-\xi) + \frac{200}{3}\xi^2]. \quad (16)$$

As shown in Figure 3, the dashed red line represents $F(\xi)$*, where* $\underline{f}(\xi) = \frac{8}{3}(1-\xi)^2 + \frac{80}{3}\xi(1-\xi) + \frac{200}{3}\xi^2$ *and* $\overline{f}(\xi) = 264(1-\xi)^2 + \frac{800}{3}\xi(1-\xi) + \frac{200}{3}\xi^2$*. The solid black line represents* $G(\xi)$*, where* $\underline{g}(\xi) = \frac{85472}{9765}(1-\xi)^2 + \frac{992}{21}\xi(1-\xi) + \frac{200}{3}\xi^2$ *and* $\overline{g}(\xi) = \frac{2195456}{9765}(1-\xi)^2 + \frac{5168}{21}\xi(1-\xi) + \frac{200}{3}\xi^2$*.*

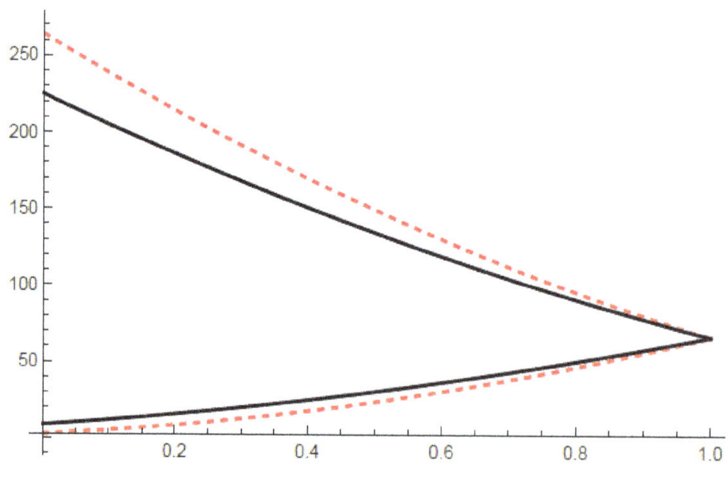

Figure 3. A visualization of the inequality (16) left and right terms.

Example 3. *Let $\widetilde{F} \in \mathbf{SC}([0,e], \mathcal{F}_C(\mathbb{R}))$ and ξ-levels of $\widetilde{F}$ be given by $F_{\xi}(x) = [(1-\xi)x^2 + 10\xi, (1-\xi)(24-x^2)+10\xi]$ for all $\xi \in [0,1]$ and for all $x \in [\varsigma_1, \varsigma_2], h(\nu) = \frac{1}{\nu}$, for $\nu \in (0,1)$. Obviously, $\widetilde{F}(x)$ satisfies the assumptions in Theorems 5 and 6. If we choose $q = \frac{1}{2}$, $\gamma = 2$ and $\varpi(x) = (x - \frac{e}{2})^2$, we have*

$$\underline{f}_{\xi}(\frac{\varsigma_1+\varsigma_2}{2}) = \frac{e^2}{4}(1-\xi) + 10\xi,$$

$$\overline{f}_{\xi}(\frac{\varsigma_1+\varsigma_2}{2}) = \frac{96-e^2}{4}(1-\xi) + 10\xi,$$

$$({}_{\varsigma_1}I_q^{\gamma}\varpi(x))(\varsigma_2) = ({}_0I_q^{\gamma}(x-\frac{e}{2})^2)(e) = \frac{19e^4}{210},$$

$$\frac{1}{h(\frac{1}{2})({}_{\varsigma_1}I_q^{\gamma}\varpi(x))(\varsigma_2)}(({}_{\varsigma_1}I_q^{\gamma}\underline{f}_{\xi}(x)\varpi(x))(\varsigma_2) + ({}_{\varsigma_1}I_q^{\gamma}\underline{f}_{\xi}(\varsigma_1+\varsigma_2-x)\varpi(\varsigma_1+\varsigma_2-x))(\varsigma_2))$$

$$= \frac{1232e^2 - 2568e + 3534}{1767}(1-\xi) + 10\xi,$$

$$\frac{1}{h(\frac{1}{2})({}_{\varsigma_1}I_q^{\gamma}\varpi(x))(\varsigma_2)}(({}_{\varsigma_1}I_q^{\gamma}\overline{f}_{\xi}(x)\varpi(x))(\varsigma_2) + ({}_{\varsigma_1}I_q^{\gamma}\overline{f}_{\xi}(\varsigma_1+\varsigma_2-x)\varpi(\varsigma_1+\varsigma_2-x))(\varsigma_2))$$

$$= \frac{38874 - 1232e^2 + 2568e}{1767}(1-\xi) + 10\xi,$$

$$[\frac{e^2}{4}(1-\xi) + 10\xi, \frac{96-e^2}{4}(1-\xi) + 10\xi]$$

$$\supseteq_I [\frac{1232e^2 - 2568e + 3534}{1767}(1-\xi) + 10\xi, \frac{38874 - 1232e^2 + 2568e}{1767}(1-\xi) + 10\xi] \quad (17)$$

As shown in Figure 4, the dashed green line represents $F(\xi)$, where $\underline{f}(\xi) = \frac{e^2}{4}(1-\xi) + 10\xi$ and $\overline{f}(\xi) = \frac{96-e^2}{4}(1-\xi) + 10\xi, \xi \in [0,1]$. The solid blue line represents $G(\xi)$, where $\underline{g}(\xi) = \frac{1232e^2-2568e+3534}{1767}(1-\xi) + 10\xi$ and $\overline{g}(\xi) = \frac{38874-1232e^2+2568e}{1767}(1-\xi) + 10\xi, \xi \in [0,1]$.

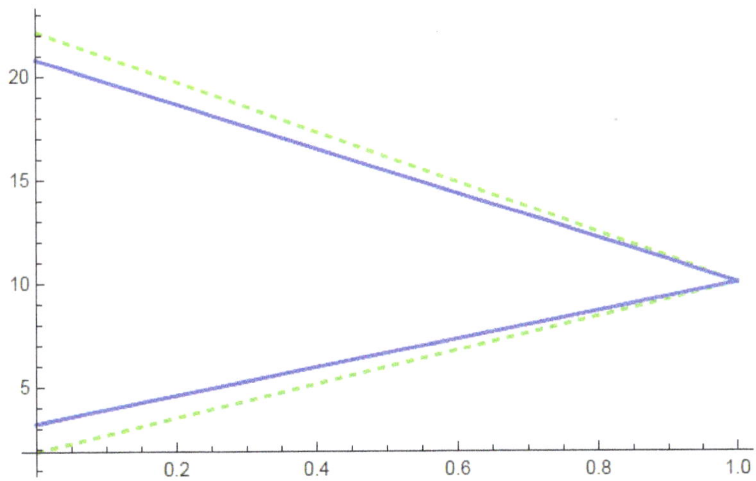

Figure 4. A visualization of the inequality (17) left and right terms.

Also,

$$\frac{1}{(\varsigma_1-\varsigma_2)^2}\big(({}_{\varsigma_1}I_q^{\gamma}\underline{f}_{\xi}(x)\varpi(x))(\varsigma_2)+({}_{\varsigma_1}I_q^{\gamma}\underline{f}_{\xi}(\varsigma_1+\varsigma_2-x)\varpi(\varsigma_1+\varsigma_2-x))(\varsigma_2)\big)$$

$$=\frac{1232e^4-2568e^3+3534e^2}{9765}(1-\xi)+\frac{38e^2}{21}\xi,$$

$$\frac{1}{(\varsigma_1-\varsigma_2)^2}\big(({}_{\varsigma_1}I_q^{\gamma}\overline{f}_{\xi}(x)\varpi(x))(\varsigma_2)+({}_{\varsigma_1}I_q^{\gamma}\overline{f}_{\xi}(\varsigma_1+\varsigma_2-x)\varpi(\varsigma_1+\varsigma_2-x))(\varsigma_2)\big)$$

$$=\frac{38874e^2-1232e^4+2568e^3}{9765}(1-\xi)+\frac{38e^2}{21}\xi,$$

$$[\underline{f}_{\xi}(\varsigma_1)+\underline{f}_{\xi}(\varsigma_2)]M(\nu)=\frac{19e^4}{210}(1-\xi)+\frac{38e^2}{21}\xi,$$

$$[\overline{f}_{\xi}(\varsigma_1)+\overline{f}_{\xi}(\varsigma_2)]M(\nu)=\frac{912e^2-19e^4}{210}(1-\xi)+\frac{38e^2}{21}\xi,$$

$$[\frac{1232e^4-2568e^3+3534e^2}{9765}(1-\xi)+\frac{38e^2}{21}\xi,\frac{38874e^2-1232e^4+2568e^3}{9765}(1-\xi)+\frac{38e^2}{21}\xi]$$

$$\supseteq_I[\frac{19e^4}{210}(1-\xi)+\frac{38e^2}{21}\xi,\frac{912e^2-19e^4}{210}(1-\xi)+\frac{38e^2}{21}\xi]. \tag{18}$$

As shown in Figure 5, the dashed red line represents $F(\xi)$, *where* $\underline{f}(\xi)=\frac{1232e^4-2568e^3+3534e^2}{9765}(1-\xi)+\frac{38e^2}{21}\xi$ *and* $\overline{f}(\xi)=\frac{38874e^2-1232e^4+2568e^3}{9765}(1-\xi)+\frac{38e^2}{21}\xi,\xi\in[0,1]$. *The solid green line represents* $G(\xi)$, *where* $\underline{g}(\xi)=\frac{19e^4}{210}(1-\xi)+\frac{38e^2}{21}\xi$ *and* $\overline{g}(\xi)=\frac{912e^2-19e^4}{210}(1-\xi)+\frac{38e^2}{21}\xi,\xi\in[0,1]$.

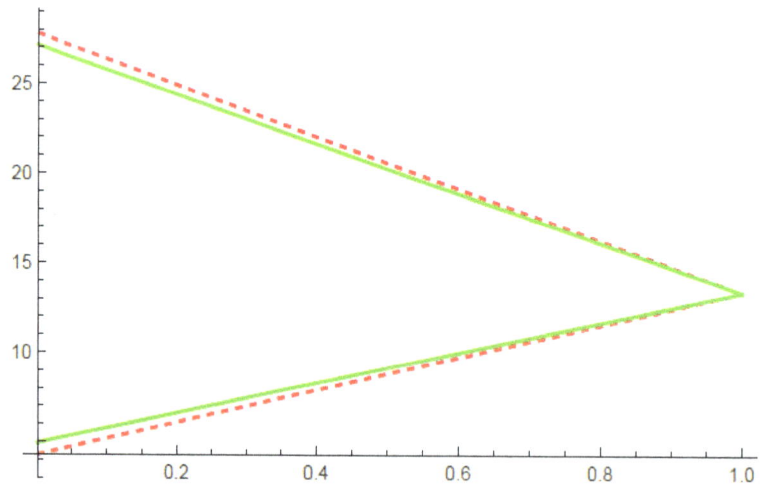

Figure 5. A visualization of the inequality (18) left and right terms.

5. Conclusions

In this paper, we successfully extended Hermite–Hadamard and Hermite–Hadamard–Fejér inequalities to the setting of fuzzy interval-valued functions possessing h-Godunova–Levin convexity by employing the Riemann–Liouville fractional q-integral operator. Through rigorous analysis, we derived new inclusion relations and demonstrated that the proposed inequalities generalize several existing results. Numerical examples and visual graphs were provided to illustrate the validity and sharpness of the obtained results. This work not only broadens the scope of convexity and integral inequalities into the fuzzy setting but also highlights the potential of fractional q-calculus in addressing problems involving uncertainty and imprecision. Future research may focus on exploring related inequalities under different fractional operators or extending these results to more generalized convex structures.

Author Contributions: Conceptualization, M.W.A. and S.I.; methodology, M.W.A.; software, A.F.; validation, S.I., A.F., and Y.W.; formal analysis, A.F.; investigation, S.I.; resources, Y.W.; data curation, S.I.; writing—original draft preparation, S.I.; writing—review and editing, M.W.A. and A.F.; visualization, Y.W.; supervision, S.I.; project administration, Y.W.; funding acquisition, Y.W. All authors have read and agreed to the published version of the manuscript.

Funding: This work was partially supported by the National Natural Science Foundation of China under Grant 12171435.

Data Availability Statement: No new data were created or analyzed in this study. Data sharing is not applicable to this article.

Acknowledgments: All authors are thankful to the reviewers for their valuable suggestions which improved the final version of the paper.

Conflicts of Interest: The authors declare no conflicts of interest.

References

1. Desvillettes, L.; Phung, K.D. Exponential decay toward equilibrium vis log convexity for a degenerate reaction-diffusion system. *J. Differ. Equ.* **2022**, *338*, 227–255. [CrossRef]
2. Razzaq, A.; Rasheed, T.; Shaokat, S. Generalized Hermite-Hadamard type inequalities for generalized F-convex function via local fractional integrals. *Chaos Solitons Fractals* **2023**, *168*, 113172. [CrossRef]
3. Butt, S.I.; Agarwal, P.; Yousaf, S.; Guirao, J.L.G. Generalized fractal Jensen and Jensen-Mercer inequalities for harmonic convex function with applications. *J. Inequal. Appl.* **2022**, *2022*, 1. [CrossRef]
4. Sun, W. Local fractional Ostrowski-type inequalities involving generalized h-convex functions and some applications for generalized moments. *Fractals* **2021**, *29*, 2150006. [CrossRef]
5. Almutairi, O.; Kiliçman, A. Some integral inequalities for h-Godunova-Levin preinvexity. *Symmetry* **2019**, *11*, 1500. [CrossRef]
6. Hadamard, J. Étude sur les propriétés des fonctions entiéres et en particulier d'une fonction considérée par Riemann. *J. Math. Pures Appl.* **1893**, *58*, 171–215.
7. Steinerberger, S. The Hermite–Hadamard Inequality in Higher Dimensions. *J. Geom. Anal.* **2020**, *30*, 466–483. [CrossRef]
8. Cheng, H.; Zhao, D.; Sarikaya, M.Z. Hermite-Hadamard type inequalities for h-convex function via fuzzy interval-valued fractional q-integral. *Fractals* **2024**, *32*, 2450042. [CrossRef]
9. Wang, J.R.; Fečkan, M. *Fractional Hermite–Hadamard Inequalities*; De Gruyter: Berlin, Germany, 2018.
10. Awan, M.U.; Ubaid Ullah, M.; Rasssisa, M.T.; Talib, S.; Noor, M.A.; Noor, K.I. Generalized Fractional Hermite–Hadamard–Noor Inequalities Via n-Polynomial Preinvex Functions. In *Mathematical Analysis, Optimization, Approximation and Applications*; Word Scientific Publising Company: Singapore, 2024; pp. 73–100.
11. Du, T.; Long, Y.; Liao, J. Multiplicative fractional HH–type inequalities via multiplicative AB–fractional integral operators. *J. Comput. Appl. Math.* **2025**, *474*, 116970. [CrossRef]
12. Lakhdari, A.; Budak, H.; Mlaiki, N.; Meftah, B.; Abdeljawad, T. New insights on fractal–fractional integral inequalities: Hermite–Hadamard and Milne estimates. *Chaos Solitons Fractals* **2025**, *193*, 116087. [CrossRef]
13. Du, T.; Xu, L. Hermite–Hadamard and Pachpatte–type integral inequalities for generalized subadditive functions in the fractal sense. *Miskolc Math. Notes* **2024**, *25*, 645–658. [CrossRef]
14. Phuong, N.D.; Etemad, S.; Rezapour, S. On two structures of the fractional q-sequential integro- differential boundary value problems. *Math. Methods Appl. Sci.* **2022**, *45*, 618–639. [CrossRef]
15. Sudsutad, W.; Ahmad, B.; Ntouyas, S.K.; Tariboon, J. Impulsively hybrid fractional quantum Langevin equation with boundary conditions involving Caputo q-k-fractional derivatives. *Chaos Solitons Fractals* **2016**, *91*, 47–62. [CrossRef]
16. Zada, A.; Alam, M.; Riaz, U. Analysis of q-fractional implicit boundary value problems having Stieltjes integral conditions. *Math. Methods Appl. Sci.* **2021**, *44*, 4381–4413. [CrossRef]
17. Zhang, T.; Tang, Y. A difference method for solving the q-fractional differential equations. *Appl. Math. Lett.* **2019**, *98*, 292–299. [CrossRef]

18. Xu, P.; Ihsan Butt, S.; Ain, Q.U.; Budak, H. New Estimates for Hermite–Hadamard Inequality in Quantum Calculus via (α, m) Convexity. *Symmetry* **2022**, *14*, 1394. [CrossRef]
19. Al–Salam, W.A. Some fractional q-integrals and q-derivatives. *Proc. Edinburgh Math. Soc.* **1966**, *15*, 135–140. [CrossRef]
20. Tariboon, J.; Ntouyas, S.K.; Agarwal, P. New concepts of fractional quantum calculus and applications to impulsive fractional q-difference equations. *Adv. Differ. Equ.* **2015**, *2015*, 18. [CrossRef]
21. Younus, A.; Asif, M.; Farhad, K. Interval-valued fractional q-calculus and applications. *Inf. Sci.* **2021**, *569*, 241–263. [CrossRef]
22. Ali, M.A.; Budak, H.; Murtaza, G.; Chu, Y.M. Post-quantum Hermite–Hadamard type inequalities for interval–valued convex functions. *J. Inequalities Appl.* **2021**, *2021*, 84. [CrossRef]
23. Costa, T.M.; Flores-Franulič, A.; Chalco-Cano, Y.; Aguirre-Cipe, I. Ostrowski-type inequalities for fuzzy-valued functions and its applications in quadrature theory. *Inf. Sci.* **2020**, *529*, 101–115. [CrossRef]
24. Guo, Y.; Ye, G.; Liu, W.; Zhao, D.; Treanţă, S. On symmetric gH-derivative: Applications to dual interval-valued optimization problems. *Chaos Solitons Fractals* **2022**, *158*, 112068. [CrossRef]
25. Guo, Y.; Ye, G.; Liu, W.; Zhao, D.; Treanţă, S. Solving nonsmooth interval optimization problems based on interval-valued symmetric invexity. *Chaos Solitons Fractals* **2023**, *174*, 113834. [CrossRef]
26. Sun, L.; Zhu, L.; Li, W.; Zhang, C.; Balezentis, T. Interval-valued functional clustering based on the Wasserstein distance with application to stock data. *Inf. Sci.* **2022**, *606*, 910–926. [CrossRef]
27. Tariboon, J.; Ali, M.A.; Budak, H.; Ntouyas, S.K. Hermite-Hadamard inclusions for co-ordinated interval-valued functions via post-quantum calculus. *Symmetry* **2021**, *13*, 1216. [CrossRef]
28. Zhao, D.; An, T.; Ye, G.; Liu, W. Chebyshev type inequalities for interval-valued functions. *Fuzzy Sets Syst.* **2020**, *396*, 82–101. [CrossRef]
29. Zhao, D.; An, T.; Ye, G.; Liu, W. Some generalizations of opial type inequalities for interval-valued functions. *Fuzzy Sets Syst.* **2022**, *436*, 128–151. [CrossRef]
30. Zhou, T.; Yuan, Z.; Du, T. On the fractional integral inclusions having exponential kernals for interval-valued convex functions. *Math. Sci.* **2023**, *17*, 107–120. [CrossRef]
31. Budak, H.; Tunc, T.; Sarikaya, M. Fractional Hermite-Hadamard-type inequalities for interval-valued functions. *Proc. Am. Math. Soc.* **2020**, *148*, 705–718. [CrossRef]
32. Du, T.; Zhou, T. On the fractional double integral inclusion relations having exponential kernels via interval-valued co-ordinate convex mappings. *Chaos Solitons Fractals* **2022**, *156*, 111846. [CrossRef]
33. Khan, M.B.; Santos-García, G.; Noor, M.A.; Soliman, M.S. Some new concepts related to fuzzy fractional calculus for up and down convex fuzzy-number valued functions and inequalities. *Chaos Solitons Fractals* **2022**, *164*, 112692. [CrossRef]
34. Khan, M.B.; Othman, H.A.; Santos-García, G.; Saeed, T.; Soliman, M.S. On fuzzy fractional integral operators having exponential kernels and related certain inequalities for exponential trigonometric convex fuzzy-number valued mappings. *Chaos Solitons Fractals* **2023**, *169*, 113274. [CrossRef]
35. Zhang, D.; Guo, C.; Chen, D.; Wang, G. Jensen's inequalities for set-valued and fuzzy set-valued functions. *Fuzzy Sets Syst.* **2021**, *404*, 178–204. [CrossRef]
36. Aumann, R.J. Integrals of set-valued functions. *J. Math. Anal. Appl.* **1965**, *12*, 1–12. [CrossRef]
37. Kaleva, O. Fuzzy differential equations. *Fuzzy Sets Syst.* **1987**, *24*, 301–317. [CrossRef]
38. Diamond, P.; Kloeden, P.E. *Metric Spaces of Fuzzy Sets: Theory and Applications*; World Scientific: Singapore, 1994; 178p.
39. Costa, T.M. Jensen's inequality type integral for fuzzy-interval-valued functions. *Fuzzy Sets Syst.* **2017**, *327*, 31–47. [CrossRef]
40. Costa, T.M.; Román-Flores, H. Some integral inequalities for fuzzy-interval-valued functions. *Inf. Sci.* **2017**, *420*, 110–125. [CrossRef]
41. Allahviranloo, T.; Salahshour, S.; Abbasbandy, S. Explicit solutions of fractional differential equations with uncertainty. *Soft Comput.* **2012**, *16*, 296–302. [CrossRef]
42. Zhang, X.; Shabbir, K.; Afzal, W.; Xiao, H.; Lin, D. Hermite-Hadamard and Jensen-Type Inequalities via Riemann Integral Operator for a Generalized Class of Godunova-Levin Functions. *J. Math.* **2022**, *12*, 3830324. [CrossRef]
43. Sudsutad, W.; Ntouyas, S.K.; Tariboon, J. Integral inequalities via fractional quantum calculus. *J. Inequalities Appl.* **2016**, *2016*, 81. [CrossRef]
44. Cheng, H.; Zhao, D.; Zhao, G. Fractional quantum Hermite-Hadamard type inequalities for interval-valued functions. *Fractals* **2023**, *31*, 2350104. [CrossRef]
45. Khan, M.B.; Zaini, H.G.; Santos-García, G.; Noor, M.A.; Soliman, M.S. New class up and down λ-convex fuzzy-number valued mappings and related fuzzy fractional inequalities. *Fractal Fract.* **2022**, *6*, 679. [CrossRef]
46. Zhao, D.; An, T.; Ye, G.; Liu, W. New Jensen and Hermite-Hadamard type inequalities for h-convex interval-valued functions. *J. Inequalities Appl.* **2018**, *2018*, 302. [CrossRef]

fractal and fractional

MDPI

Article

Hermite–Hadamard Framework for (h, m)-Convexity

Lucas Gómez [1], Juan E. Nápoles Valdés [1,2] and J. Juan Rosales [3,4,*]

[1] Facultad de Ciencias Exactas y Naturales y Agrimensura, Universidad Nacional del Nordeste, Ave. Libertad 5450, Corrientes 3400, Argentina; lucasmeinland13@gmail.com (L.G.); jnapoles@exa.unne.edu.ar (J.E.N.V.)
[2] Facultad Regional Resistencia, Universidad Tecnológica Nacional, French 414, Resistencia 3500, Argentina
[3] Centro de Investigación en Ciencias Físico Matemáticas, Facultad de Ciencias Físico Matemáticas, Universidad Autónoma de Nuevo León, Pedro de Alba s/n, San Nicolás de los Garza 66451, Nuevo León, Mexico
[4] Departamento de Ingeniería Eléctrica, División de Ingenierías, Campus Irapuato-Salamanca, Universidad de Guanajuato, Carretera Salamanca-Valle de Santiago, km. 3.5 + 1.8 km, Comunidad de Palo Blanco, Salamanca 36885, Guanajuato, Mexico
* Correspondence: rosales@ugto.mx

Abstract

This work presents generalizations and extensions of previous results by incorporating weighted integrals and a refined class of second-type (h, m)-convex functions. By utilizing classical inequalities, such as those of Hölder and Young and the Power Mean, we establish new Hermite–Hadamard-type inequalities. The findings offer a broader and more flexible analytical framework, enhancing existing results in the literature. Potential applications of the developed inequalities are also explored.

Keywords: weighted integrals; integral inequalities; Hermite–Hadamard-type inequalities; fractional derivatives

1. Introduction

Convex functions play a fundamental role in various areas of mathematical sciences today, primarily due to their properties that guarantee existence, uniqueness and the ease of finding solutions in optimization problems. For example, in optimization (Mathematical Programming), convex functions are probably most crucial. In analysis and geometry, convexity is a property that connects concepts of analysis and geometry. Epigraph: A function is convex if and only if its epigraph (the set of points on or above its graph) is a convex set. This provides a powerful geometric interpretation. Derivatives and Criteria: For doubly differentiable functions, convexity is characterized by a nonnegative second derivative (or Hessian matrix in multiple dimensions). This facilitates its identification and analytical handling. Classical Inequalities: Convex functions are the basis of important inequalities, such as Jensen's inequality, which relates the value of a function to the expectation of a random variable and is fundamental in probability and information theory. Moreover, the uses of convex functions have become widespread in interdisciplinary applications: Data Science and Machine Learning, Economics and Finance, Engineering and Signal Processing, among others, are very fertile fields where the different notions of convexity have proven their worth. In short, convexity is a structural property that, when present, transforms mathematical problems that could be intractable into well-defined and efficiently solvable problems, making it an indispensable tool in modern applied mathematics. We add to the above the Hermite–Hadamard inequality, one of the most fundamental and elegant integral inequalities in the field of analysis, since it provides an upper and lower bound on the integral mean value of a function, based solely on the property of the convexity of that function. Today, this inequality is the focus of the attention of numerous researchers, both pure and applied, for four main reasons: using new notions of convexity; using different points on the interval, not just the endpoints; using new integral operators; and defining functionals that allow establishing new bounds.

Thus, this work focuses on two of the most dynamic topics in mathematical research today: convexity and Hermite–Hadamard inequalities.

2. Preliminaries

In [1], the following definitions were introduced.

Definition 1. *Let $h : [0,1] \to [0,+\infty)$ be a non-negative function, such that $h \neq 0$, and let $g : I \subseteq [0,+\infty) \to [0,+\infty)$. The function g is called modified and (h,m)-convex of the first type on I if it satisfies*

$$g(\gamma\mu_1 + m(1-\gamma)\mu_2) \leq h^s(\gamma)g(\mu_1) + m(1-h^s(\gamma))g(\mu_2), \tag{1}$$

for all $\mu_1, \mu_2 \in I$ and $\gamma \in [0,1]$, where $m \in [0,1]$ and $s \in [-1,1]$.

Definition 2. *Let $h : [0,1] \to [0,+\infty)$ be a non-negative function, such that $h \neq 0$, and let $g : I \subseteq [0,+\infty) \to [0,+\infty)$. The function g is called modified and (h,m)-convex of the second type on I if it satisfies*

$$g(\gamma\mu_1 + m(1-\gamma)\mu_2) \leq h^s(\gamma)g(\mu_1) + m(1-h(\gamma))^s g(\mu_2), \tag{2}$$

for all $\mu_1, \mu_2 \in I$ and $\gamma \in [0,1]$, where $m \in [0,1]$ and $s \in [-1,1]$.

Remark 1. *Definitions 1 and 2 enable us to define the set $N^s_{h,m}[\mu_1,\mu_2]$, where $\mu_1, \mu_2 \in I$, as the set of modified (h,m)-convex functions. Here are some convexity classes—special cases described by the triple $(h(\gamma), m, s)$:*

1. *$(h(\gamma),0,0)$, $(\gamma,0,1)$, $(\gamma,1,1)$ and $(\gamma,0,s)$; we have, respectively, the increasing starshaped classic convex on I and s-starshaped functions [2].*
2. *$(\gamma,1,s)$ $s \in (0,1]$; then ψ is s-convex (see [3,4]), and for $s \in [-1,1]$, it is extended and s-convex on I (see [5]).*
3. *(γ^α, m, s) with $\alpha \in (0,1]$; then ψ is an s-(α,m)-convex function on I [6]. If $\alpha = 1$, we have an (s,m)-convex function on I [7], but if $m = 1$, we have an (α,s)-convex function on I [8,9], and lastly, if $s = 1$, we have an (α,m)-convex function on I [10].*
4. *$(h(\gamma), m, 1)$; then ψ is a variant of an (h,m)-convex function on I [11].*

The weighted integral operators, which underpin our analysis, are presented next [1,12].

Adding a particular weight function to the definition of an integral operator is a new and general way to define an integral operator and start the process of generalizing a known result. This may be performed as follows:

Definition 3. *Let $g \in L[\mu_1,\mu_2]$ and let $w : I \to \mathbb{R}$ be a continuous, positive function, whose first derivative is integrable in I°. The weighted fractional integral operators are introduced as follows (right and left, respectively):*

$$\mathbf{J}^{w}_{\mu_1^+} g(x) = \int_{\mu_1}^{x} w'\left(\frac{\mu_2 - z}{\mu_2 - \mu_1}\right) g(z)\,dz, \quad x > \mu_1, \tag{3}$$

$$\mathbf{J}^{w}_{\mu_2^-} g(x) = \int_{x}^{\mu_2} w'\left(\frac{z - \mu_1}{\mu_2 - \mu_1}\right) g(z)\,dz, \quad x < \mu_2. \tag{4}$$

Remark 2. *The inclusion of the first derivative of the weight function w arises from the inherent nature of the problem. Alternatively, the second derivative or a higher order derivative, can also be considered.*

Remark 3. *We examine particular examples of the weight function w' to better demonstrate the scope of Definition 3:*

(a) *Setting $w'(z) \equiv 1$ recovers the classical Riemann integral.*
(b) *Choosing $w'(z) = \frac{z^{\alpha-1}}{\Gamma(\alpha)}$ leads to the Riemann–Liouville fractional integral.*
(c) *By selecting appropriate weight functions, w', various fractional integral operators can be derived, such as the k-Riemann–Liouville integrals [13]; right-sided fractional integrals of a function, g, relative to another function, h, on $[\mu_1, \mu_2]$ [14]; and integral operators introduced in [15–18].*
(d) *Additional well-known integral operators, fractional or otherwise, can be retrieved as particular cases of the above formulation. Interested readers may consult [19,20].*

The Caputo–Fabrizio definition's main basic feature can be explained (cf. [21]) with $0 < \alpha < 1$:

$$\left({}^{CF}_{\mu_1}\mathbf{I}^{\alpha} g\right)(\chi) = \frac{1-\alpha}{M(\alpha)} g(\chi) + \frac{\alpha}{M(\alpha)} \int_{\mu_1}^{\chi} g(z)\, dz, \tag{5}$$

$$\left({}^{CF}\mathbf{I}^{\alpha}_{\mu_2} g\right)(\chi) = \frac{1-\alpha}{M(\alpha)} g(\chi) + \frac{\alpha}{M(\alpha)} \int_{\chi}^{\mu_2} g(z)\, dz, \tag{6}$$

where $M(\alpha)$ is a normalization function, such that $M(0) = M(1) = 1$.

Caputo's fractional derivative is well known, given by the following expression [22]:

$$\left({}^{C}_{0}\mathbf{D}^{\alpha}_{\chi} g\right)(\chi) = \frac{1}{\Gamma(1-\alpha)} \int_{0}^{\chi} (\chi - z)^{-\alpha} g'(z)\, dz. \tag{7}$$

The idea comes from replacing the singular kernel $(\chi - z)^{-\alpha}$ in the Caputo fractional derivative, given in Formula (7), with the kernel $\exp\left[-\frac{\alpha(\chi-z)}{1-\alpha}\right]$.

In the paper [23], the same authors proposed a more complete study of the operator (7) by presenting the definition of the adapted fractional integral operator ${}^{CF}_{0}\mathbf{I}^{\alpha}_{\chi}$, when $M(\alpha) = 1$.

$$\left({}^{CF}_{0}\mathbf{I}^{\alpha}_{\chi} g\right)(\chi) = \frac{1}{\alpha} \int_{0}^{\chi} \exp\left[-\frac{(1-\alpha)}{\alpha}(\chi - z)\right] g(z)\, dz. \tag{8}$$

As one can notice, this definition shows a significant resemblance to the classical Riemann–Liouville fractional integral, as given by

$$\left({}^{RL}_{0}\mathbf{I}^{\alpha}_{\chi} g\right)(\chi) = \frac{1}{\Gamma(\alpha)} \int_{0}^{\chi} (\chi - z)^{\alpha-1} g(z)\, dz. \tag{9}$$

In this work, we present some variants of the well-known Hermite–Hadamard inequality in the context of (h, m)-convex functions of the second kind using weighted integral operators. Our results include several well-known cases from the literature.

Definition 4. *Let $g \in L_1[\mu_1, \mu_2]$. The Riemann–Liouville integrals ${}^{RL}\mathbf{I}^{\alpha}_{\mu_1^+} g$ and ${}^{RL}\mathbf{I}^{\alpha}_{\mu_2^-} g$ of the order $\alpha > 0$ are defined as*

$${}^{RL}\mathbf{I}^{\alpha}_{\mu_1^+} g(\chi) = \frac{1}{\Gamma(\alpha)} \int_{\mu_1}^{\chi} (\chi - z)^{\alpha-1} g(z)\, dz,$$

$$^{RL}\mathbf{I}^{\alpha}_{\mu_2^-}g(\chi) = \frac{1}{\Gamma(\alpha)}\int_{\chi}^{\mu_2}(z-\chi)^{\alpha-1}g(z)\,dz,$$

where $\Gamma(\alpha)$ *is the Gamma function.*

Throughout this work, $\mathbb{N}$ will be understood as the set of natural numbers $(0,1,2,\dots)$ and $\mathbb{R}$ will denote the set of real numbers.

3. Generalizations

Theorem 1. *Let* $g: I\subset\mathbb{R}\to\mathbb{R}$ *be a differentiable mapping on* I°, $\mu_1,\mu_2\in I^\circ$ *with* $\mu_1<\mu_2$.

Let $w:[0,1]\to\mathbb{R}$ *be a continuous and positive function with first derivative integrable on* $(0,1)$. *Suppose that* g *is modified and* (h,m)*-convex of the second type and* $\frac{\mu_1}{m},\frac{\mu_2}{m}\in Dom(g)$; *then it is true that*

$$\begin{aligned}
g\left(\frac{\mu_1+\mu_2}{2}\right)(w(1)-w(0)) &\le h^s\left(\frac{1}{2}\right)\frac{r+1}{\mu_2-\mu_1}\mathbf{J}^{w}_{\mu_1^+}g\left(\frac{r\mu_1+\mu_2}{r+1}\right)\\
&\quad+m\left(1-h\left(\frac{1}{2}\right)\right)^s\frac{m(r+1)}{\mu_2-\mu_1}\mathbf{J}^{w}_{\mu_2^-}g\left(\frac{r\mu_2+\mu_1}{m(r+1)}\right)\\
&\le h^s\left(\frac{1}{2}\right)\left[g(\mu_1)\mathbf{N}_1+mg\left(\frac{\mu_2}{m}\right)\mathbf{N}_2\right]\\
&\quad+m\left(1-h\left(\frac{1}{2}\right)\right)^s\left[g(\mu_2)\mathbf{N}_3+mg\left(\frac{\mu_1}{m^2}\right)\mathbf{N}_4\right], \qquad (10)
\end{aligned}$$

where $r\in\mathbb{N}$, $\mathbf{N}_1=\int_0^1 w'(\gamma)\,h^s\left(\frac{r+\gamma}{r+1}\right)d\gamma$, $\mathbf{N}_2=\int_0^1 w'(\gamma)\left(1-h\left(\frac{r+\gamma}{r+1}\right)\right)^s d\gamma$, $\mathbf{N}_3=\int_0^1 w'(\gamma)\,h^s\left(\frac{r+\gamma}{m(r+1)}\right)d\gamma$ *and* $\mathbf{N}_4=\int_0^1 w'(\gamma)\left(1-h\left(\frac{r+\gamma}{m(r+1)}\right)\right)^s d\gamma$.

Proof. By means of the (h,m)-convexity of g with $\gamma=\frac{1}{2}$, we have

$$g\left(\frac{x+y}{2}\right)\le h^s\left(\frac{1}{2}\right)g(x)+m\left(1-h\left(\frac{1}{2}\right)\right)^s g\left(\frac{y}{m}\right), \qquad (11)$$

for $x,y\in I$.

Substituting $x=\frac{r+\gamma}{r+1}\mu_1+\frac{1-\gamma}{r+1}\mu_2$ and $y=\frac{r+\gamma}{r+1}\mu_2+\frac{1-\gamma}{r+1}\mu_1$ in (11), we get

$$\begin{aligned}
g\left(\frac{\mu_1+\mu_2}{2}\right)&\le h^s\left(\frac{1}{2}\right)g\left(\frac{r+\gamma}{r+1}\mu_1+\frac{1-\gamma}{r+1}\mu_2\right)\\
&\quad+m\left(1-h\left(\frac{1}{2}\right)\right)^s g\left(\frac{r+\gamma}{m(r+1)}\mu_2+\frac{1-\gamma}{m(r+1)}\mu_1\right). \qquad (12)
\end{aligned}$$

Multiplying both sides of (12) by $w'(\gamma)$ and integrating over $[0,1]$, we obtain

$$\begin{aligned}
g\left(\frac{\mu_1+\mu_2}{2}\right)(w(1)-w(0))&\le h^s\left(\frac{1}{2}\right)\int_0^1 w'(\gamma)g\left(\frac{r+\gamma}{r+1}\mu_1+\frac{1-\gamma}{r+1}\mu_2\right)d\gamma\\
&\quad+m\left(1-h\left(\frac{1}{2}\right)\right)^s\int_0^1 w'(\gamma)g\left(\frac{r+\gamma}{m(r+1)}\mu_2+\frac{1-\gamma}{m(r+1)}\mu_1\right)d\gamma\\
&=h^s\left(\frac{1}{2}\right)L_1+m\left(1-h\left(\frac{1}{2}\right)\right)^s L_2. \qquad (13)
\end{aligned}$$

Rewriting the integrals, we find that

$$\begin{aligned} L_1 &= -\left(\frac{r+1}{\mu_2-\mu_1}\right)\int_{\frac{r\mu_1+\mu_2}{r+1}}^{\mu_1} w'\left(\frac{\frac{r\mu_1+\mu_2}{r+1}-x}{\frac{\mu_2-\mu_1}{r+1}}\right)g(x)\,dx \\ &= \left(\frac{r+1}{\mu_2-\mu_1}\right)J^{w}_{\mu_1^+}g\left(\frac{r\mu_1+\mu_2}{r+1}\right). \end{aligned} \tag{14}$$

$$\begin{aligned} L_2 &= \left(\frac{m(r+1)}{\mu_2-\mu_1}\right)\int_{\frac{r\mu_2+\mu_1}{m(r+1)}}^{\frac{\mu_2}{m}} w'\left(\frac{y-\frac{r\mu_2+\mu_1}{m(r+1)}}{\frac{\mu_2-\mu_1}{m(r+1)}}\right)g(y)\,dy \\ &= \left(\frac{m(r+1)}{\mu_2-\mu_1}\right)J^{w}_{\frac{\mu_2}{m}^-}g\left(\frac{r\mu_2+\mu_1}{m(r+1)}\right). \end{aligned} \tag{15}$$

From (13), (14) and (15), it follows that

$$\begin{aligned} g\left(\frac{\mu_1+\mu_2}{2}\right)(w(1)-w(0)) &\le h^s\left(\frac{1}{2}\right)\frac{r+1}{\mu_2-\mu_1}\mathbf{J}^{w}_{\mu_1^+}g\left(\frac{r\mu_1+\mu_2}{r+1}\right) \\ &\quad + m\left(1-h\left(\frac{1}{2}\right)\right)^s\frac{m(r+1)}{\mu_2-\mu_1}\mathbf{J}^{w}_{\mu_2^-}g\left(\frac{r\mu_2+\mu_1}{m(r+1)}\right). \end{aligned} \tag{16}$$

Again employing the (h,m)-convexity of g, we obtain

$$\int_0^1 w'(\gamma)g\left(\frac{r+\gamma}{r+1}\mu_1+\frac{1-\gamma}{r+1}\mu_2\right)d\gamma \le g(\mu_1)\mathbf{N}_1 + mg\left(\frac{\mu_2}{m}\right)\mathbf{N}_2. \tag{17}$$

$$\int_0^1 w'(\gamma)g\left(\frac{r+\gamma}{m(r+1)}\mu_2+\frac{1-\gamma}{m(r+1)}\mu_1\right)d\gamma \le g(\mu_2)\mathbf{N}_3 + mg\left(\frac{\mu_1}{m^2}\right)\mathbf{N}_4. \tag{18}$$

By combining (13)–(18), we arrive at (10). □

Remark 4. *Setting $s = m = 1$, $r = 0$, $h(z) = z$ and $w'(z) = 1$, we recover the classical Hermite–Hadamard inequality.*

Remark 5. *Considering s, m, r and $h(z)$ as in Remark 4, but with $w'(z) = \frac{z^{\alpha-1}}{\Gamma(\alpha)}$, we obtain Theorem 2 of [24].*

Remark 6. *Letting $m = 1$, $n = 0$, $h(z) = z$ and $w'(z) = \frac{z^{\alpha-1}}{\Gamma(\alpha)}$, we have*

$$\begin{aligned} \frac{g\left(\frac{\mu_1+\mu_2}{2}\right)}{\Gamma(\alpha+1)} &\le \frac{1}{2^s(\mu_2-\mu_1)\Gamma(\alpha)}\int_{\mu_1}^{\mu_2}\left(\frac{\mu_2-z}{\mu_2-\mu_1}\right)^{\alpha-1}g(z)\,dz \\ &\quad + \frac{1}{2^s(\mu_2-\mu_1)\Gamma(\alpha)}\int_a^b\left(\frac{z-\mu_1}{\mu_2-\mu_1}\right)^{\alpha-1}g(z)\,dz \\ &\le \frac{1}{2^s}\left[\frac{g(\mu_1)}{(\alpha+s)\Gamma(\alpha)}+\frac{g(\mu_2)}{\Gamma(\alpha)}\int_0^1 z^{\alpha-1}(1-z)^s\,dz\right] \\ &\quad + \frac{1}{2^s}\left[\frac{g(\mu_2)}{(\alpha+s)\Gamma(\alpha)}+\frac{g(\mu_1)}{\Gamma(\alpha)}\int_0^1 z^{\alpha-1}(1-z)^s\,dz\right]. \end{aligned} \tag{19}$$

Utilizing Definition 4 in (19), we find

$$\frac{g\left(\frac{\mu_1+\mu_2}{2}\right)}{\Gamma(\alpha+1)} \leq \frac{1}{2^s(\mu_2-\mu_1)^\alpha}\left[{}^{RL}\mathbf{I}^\alpha_{\mu_1^+}g(\mu_2) + {}^{RL}\mathbf{I}^\alpha_{\mu_2^-}g(\mu_1)\right]$$
$$\leq \frac{\alpha}{2^{s-1}\Gamma(\alpha+1)}\left(\frac{g(\mu_1)+g(\mu_2)}{2}\right)\left[\frac{1}{\alpha+s} + \frac{2}{\alpha+s}\left(1-\frac{1}{2^{\alpha+s}}\right)\right]. \tag{20}$$

Multiplying the three terms by $2^{s-1}\Gamma(\alpha+1)$ in (20), we complete (1) of [25].

Remark 7. *Under the same assumptions as before, but with $w'(z) = 1$, we complete Theorem 2.1 of [26].*

Remark 8. *Maintaining the previous assumptions, but considering $w'(z) = \frac{z^{\alpha-1}}{\Gamma(\alpha)}$, we derive Theorem 3 of [27].*

Remark 9. *Under the conditions of Remark 4, but with $w'(z) = \frac{\exp(-\varsigma z)}{\alpha}$, where $\varsigma = \frac{1-\alpha}{\alpha}$, we retrieve Theorem 3.1 of [28].*

Remark 10. *Substituting $w(z) = \frac{z^\alpha}{\alpha}$, $r = 0$, $m = s = 1$ and $h(z) = z$ in the previous result leads to the following inequality for the Riemann–Liouville fractional integral (this refers to Theorem 2 in [24]):*

$$g\left(\frac{\mu_1+\mu_2}{2}\right) \leq \frac{\Gamma(\alpha+1)}{2(\mu_2-\mu_1)^\alpha}\left[{}^{RL}\mathbf{I}^\alpha_{\mu_2-}g(\mu_1) + {}^{RL}\mathbf{I}^\alpha_{\mu_1+}g(\mu_2)\right] \leq \frac{g(\mu_1)+g(\mu_2)}{2}.$$

Remark 11. *Theorem 5 in [29] (also see Theorem 1 in [30]), which is based on k-Riemann–Liouville fractional integrals, can be obtained from Theorem 1 by setting $w(z) = z^{\frac{\alpha}{k}}$, $r = 0$, $m = s = 1$ and $h(z) = z$.*

The above results form the foundation for deriving other inequalities by using different types of integral operators, as demonstrated in the following remark.

Remark 12. *We consider s-convex functions ($0 < \alpha < 1$; $m = 1$; $h(z) = z$); by putting $r = 0$ in (10) and choosing $w'(z) = 1$, we obtain*

$$2^{s-1}g\left(\frac{\mu_1+\mu_2}{2}\right) \leq \frac{1}{\mu_2-\mu_1}\int_{\mu_1}^{\mu_2} g(z)\,dz \leq \frac{g(\mu_1)+g(\mu_2)}{s+1},$$

taking into account

$$\frac{1}{\mu_2-\mu_1}\int_{\mu_1}^{\mu_2} g(z)\,dz = \frac{M(\alpha)}{\alpha(\mu_2-\mu_1)}\left[\frac{1-\alpha}{M(\alpha)}g(\chi) + \frac{\alpha}{M(\alpha)}\int_{\mu_1}^{\chi} g(z)\,dz\right.$$
$$\left.+\frac{1-\alpha}{M(\alpha)}g(\chi) + \frac{\alpha}{M(\alpha)}\int_{\chi}^{\mu_2} g(z)\,dz - \frac{2(1-\alpha)}{M(\alpha)}g(\chi)\right].$$

Using the last two results, we can easily derive Theorem 2.1 of [31]. If, additionally, $s = 1$, from the above we can derive Theorem 2 of [32].

Theorem 2. *Let us have g, w, r, μ_1 and μ_2 as in Theorem 1. If $g' \in L[\mu_1, \mu_2]$, then*

$$\frac{\mu_2-\mu_1}{2}\int_0^1 [w(1-\gamma)-w(\gamma)]g'\left(\frac{r+\gamma}{r+1}\mu_1+\frac{(1-\gamma)}{r+1}\mu_2\right)d\gamma$$
$$=(r+1)\left\{(w(0)-w(1))\left[g(\mu_1)+g\left(\frac{r\mu_1+\mu_2}{r+1}\right)\right]-\left[\frac{\mathbf{J}^{w}_{\mu_1^+}g\left(\frac{r\mu_1+\mu_2}{r+1}\right)+\mathbf{J}^{w}_{\left(\frac{r\mu_1+\mu_2}{r+1}\right)^-}g(\mu_1)}{2}\right]\right\}. \quad (21)$$

Proof. Let us consider

$$\int_0^1 [w(1-\gamma)-w(\gamma)]g'\left(\frac{r+\gamma}{r+1}\mu_1+\frac{(1-\gamma)}{r+1}\mu_2\right)d\gamma$$
$$=\int_0^1 w(1-\gamma)g'\left(\frac{r+\gamma}{r+1}\mu_1+\frac{(1-\gamma)}{r+1}\mu_2\right)d\gamma-\int_0^1 w(\gamma)g'\left(\frac{r+\gamma}{r+1}\mu_1+\frac{(1-\gamma)}{r+1}\mu_2\right)d\gamma$$
$$=\mathcal{I}_1-\mathcal{I}_2. \quad (22)$$

Integrating $\mathcal{I}_1$ by parts, we get

$$\mathcal{I}_1=\frac{r+1}{\mu_1-\mu_2}\left[w(0)g(\mu_1)-w(1)g\left(\frac{r\mu_1+\mu_2}{r+1}\right)\right]$$
$$-\frac{r+1}{\mu_2-\mu_1}\int_0^1 w'(1-\gamma)\,g\left(\frac{r+\gamma}{r+1}\mu_1+\frac{1-\gamma}{r+1}\mu_2\right)d\gamma. \quad (23)$$

Making a change in the variables $x=\frac{r+\gamma}{r+1}\mu_1+\frac{(1-\gamma)}{r+1}\mu_2$ in (23), we find that

$$\mathcal{I}_1=\frac{r+1}{\mu_1-\mu_2}\left[w(0)g(\mu_1)-w(1)g\left(\frac{r\mu_1+\mu_2}{r+1}\right)\right]$$
$$-\frac{r+1}{\mu_2-\mu_1}\int_{\mu_1}^{\frac{r\mu_1+\mu_2}{r+1}} w'\left(\frac{x-\mu_1}{\frac{\mu_2-\mu_1}{r+1}}\right)g\left(\frac{r+\gamma}{r+1}\mu_1+\frac{1-\gamma}{r+1}\mu_2\right)d\gamma$$
$$=\frac{r+1}{\mu_1-\mu_2}\left[w(0)g(\mu_1)-w(1)g\left(\frac{r\mu_1+\mu_2}{r+1}\right)\right]-\frac{r+1}{\mu_2-\mu_1}\mathbf{J}^{w}_{\mu_1^+}g\left(\frac{r\mu_1+\mu_2}{r+1}\right). \quad (24)$$

Analogously for $\mathcal{I}_2$, we can prove

$$\mathcal{I}_2=\frac{r+1}{\mu_1-\mu_2}\left[w(1)g(\mu_1)-w(0)g\left(\frac{r\mu_1+\mu_2}{r+1}\right)\right]-\frac{r+1}{\mu_2-\mu_1}\mathbf{J}^{w}_{\left(\frac{r\mu_1+\mu_2}{r+1}\right)^-}g(\mu_1). \quad (25)$$

From (22), (24) and (25), we have

$$\int_0^1 [w(1-\gamma)-w(\gamma)]g'\left(\frac{r+\gamma}{r+1}\mu_1+\frac{1-\gamma}{r+1}\mu_2\right)d\gamma$$
$$=\frac{2(r+1)}{\mu_1-\mu_2}\left\{(w(0)-w(1))\left[g(\mu_1)+g\left(\frac{r\mu_1+\mu_2}{r+1}\right)\right]-\left[\frac{\mathbf{J}^{w}_{\mu_1^+}g\left(\frac{r\mu_1+\mu_2}{r+1}\right)+\mathbf{J}^{w}_{\left(\frac{r\mu_1+\mu_2}{r+1}\right)^-}g(\mu_1)}{2}\right]\right\}. \quad (26)$$

By multiplying both sides of (26) by $\frac{\mu_2-\mu_1}{2}$, we obtain the desired result. □

Remark 13. *Using convex functions, $r=0$ and $w(z)=z$, in this way, Theorem 2 becomes the following lemma:*

Lemma 1. *Let g be a real-valued function defined on $[\mu_1, \mu_2]$ and differentiable on (μ_1, μ_2). If $g' \in L_1[\mu_1, \mu_2]$, then the following equality holds:*

$$\frac{g(\mu_1)+g(\mu_2)}{2} - \frac{1}{\mu_2-\mu_1}\int_a^b g(u)\,du = \frac{\mu_2-\mu_1}{2}\int_0^1 (1-2\gamma)g'(\gamma\mu_1+(1-\gamma)\mu_2)\,d\gamma,$$

which is Lemma 2.1 of [33], one of the most important results in the Theory of Integral Inequalities.

Remark 14. *Establishing $r = 0$ and $w(z) = z^{\frac{\lambda}{k}}$, Lemma 2.1 of [29] is derived for $\lambda, k > 0$.*

Theorem 3. *Let g, w, r, μ_1 and μ_2 be defined as before. Suppose that $|g'|$ is modified and (h,m)-convex of the second type; the following inequality holds:*

$$\begin{aligned}&\left|(r+1)\left\{w(1)-w(0)-\left[\frac{\mathbf{J}^{w}_{\mu_1^+}g\left(\frac{r\mu_1+\mu_2}{r+1}\right)+\mathbf{J}^{w}_{\left(\frac{r\mu_1+\mu_2}{r+1}\right)^-}g(\mu_1)}{2}\right]\right\}\right|\\&\le \frac{\mu_2-\mu_1}{2}\left[|g'(\mu_1)|\mathbf{W}_1+|g'(\mu_2)|\mathbf{W}_2\right],\end{aligned} \tag{27}$$

where

$$\mathbf{W}_1 = \int_0^1 |w(1-\gamma)-w(\gamma)|\,h^s\left(\frac{r+\gamma}{r+1}\right)d\gamma,$$

$$\mathbf{W}_2 = \int_0^1 |w(1-\gamma)-w(\gamma)|\left(1-h\left(\frac{r+\gamma}{r+1}\right)\right)^s d\gamma.$$

Proof. By using Lemma (2) and the (h,m)-convexity of g, we have

$$\begin{aligned}&\left|(r+1)\left\{w(1)-w(0)-\left[\frac{\mathbf{J}^{w}_{\mu_1^+}g\left(\frac{r\mu_1+\mu_2}{r+1}\right)+\mathbf{J}^{w}_{\left(\frac{r\mu_1+\mu_2}{r+1}\right)^-}g(\mu_1)}{2}\right]\right\}\right|\\&\le \frac{\mu_2-\mu_1}{2}\int_0^1 |w(1-\gamma)-w(\gamma)|\left|g'\left(\frac{r+\gamma}{r+1}\mu_1+\frac{1-\gamma}{r+1}\mu_2\right)\right|d\gamma\\&\le \frac{\mu_2-\mu_1}{2}\left[|g'(\mu_1)|\int_0^1 |w(1-\gamma)-w(\gamma)|h^s\left(\frac{r+\gamma}{r+1}\right)d\gamma\right.\\&\qquad\left.+|g'(\mu_2)|\int_0^1 |w(1-\gamma)-w(\gamma)|\left(1-h\left(\frac{r+\gamma}{r+1}\right)\right)^s d\gamma\right]\\&=\frac{\mu_2-\mu_1}{2}\left[|g'(\mu_1)|\mathbf{W}_1+|g'(\mu_2)|\mathbf{W}_2\right].\end{aligned}$$

The proof is finished. □

Remark 15. *Assuming the same conditions as in Remark 13 and invoking Lemma 1, we recover Theorem 2.2 of [33].*

Remark 16. *Under the same assumptions of Remark 14, we retrieve Theorem 6 of [29].*

Theorem 4. *Let g, w, n, μ_1 and μ_2 be defined as before. Suppose that g is modified and (h,m)-convex of the second type and $\frac{\mu_1}{m}, \frac{\mu_2}{m} \in Dom(g)$; then it is true that*

$$g\left(\frac{\mu_1+\mu_2}{2}\right)(w(1)-w(0)) \leq \frac{n}{\mu_2-\mu_1}\left[h^s\left(\frac{1}{2}\right)\mathbf{J}^w_{\left(\frac{n-1}{n}\mu_2+\frac{\mu_1}{n}\right)^+}g(\mu_2)\right.$$
$$\left. + m^2\left(1-h\left(\frac{1}{2}\right)\right)^s \mathbf{J}^w_{\left(\frac{n-1}{n}\mu_1+\frac{\mu_2}{n}\right)^-}g\left(\frac{\mu_1}{m}\right)\right]$$
$$\leq h^s\left(\frac{1}{2}\right)\left[g(\mu_1)\mathbf{N}_5 + mg\left(\frac{\mu_2}{m}\right)\mathbf{N}_6\right]$$
$$+ m\left(1-h\left(\frac{1}{2}\right)\right)^s\left[g(\mu_2)\mathbf{N}_7 + mg\left(\frac{\mu_1}{m^2}\right)\mathbf{N}_8\right], \tag{28}$$

where

$$\mathbf{N}_1 = \int_0^1 w'(\gamma)\,h^s\left(\frac{\gamma}{n}\right)d\gamma, \quad \mathbf{N}_2 = \int_0^1 w'(\gamma)\left(1-h\left(\frac{\gamma}{n}\right)\right)^s d\gamma,$$

$$\mathbf{N}_3 = \int_0^1 w'(\gamma)\,h^s\left(\frac{n-\gamma}{mn}\right)d\gamma, \quad \mathbf{N}_4 = \int_0^1 w'(\gamma)\left(1-h\left(\frac{n-\gamma}{mn}\right)\right)^s d\gamma.$$

Proof. By means of the (h,m)-convexity of g with $\gamma = \frac{1}{2}$, we have

$$g\left(\frac{x+y}{2}\right) \leq h^s\left(\frac{1}{2}\right)g(x) + m\left(1-h\left(\frac{1}{2}\right)\right)^s g\left(\frac{y}{m}\right), \tag{29}$$

for $x, y \in I$.

Substituting $x = \frac{\gamma}{n}\mu_1 + \frac{n-\gamma}{n}\mu_2$ and $y = \frac{\gamma}{n}\mu_2 + \frac{n-\gamma}{n}\mu_1$ in (27), we get

$$g\left(\frac{\mu_1+\mu_2}{2}\right) \leq h^s\left(\frac{1}{2}\right)g\left(\frac{\gamma}{n}\mu_1 + \frac{n-\gamma}{n}\mu_2\right)$$
$$+ m\left(1-h\left(\frac{1}{2}\right)\right)^s g\left(\frac{\gamma}{mn}\mu_2 + \frac{n-\gamma}{mn}\mu_1\right). \tag{30}$$

Multiplying both sides of (12) by $w'(\gamma)$ and integrating over $[0,1]$, we obtain

$$g\left(\frac{\mu_1+\mu_2}{2}\right)(w(1)-w(0)) \leq h^s\left(\frac{1}{2}\right)\int_0^1 w'(\gamma)\,g\left(\frac{\gamma}{n}\mu_1 + \frac{n-\gamma}{n}\mu_2\right)d\gamma$$
$$+ m\left(1-h\left(\frac{1}{2}\right)\right)^s \int_0^1 w'(\gamma)\,g\left(\frac{\gamma}{mn}\mu_2 + \frac{n-\gamma}{mn}\mu_1\right)d\gamma$$
$$= h^s\left(\frac{1}{2}\right)L_3 + m\left(1-h\left(\frac{1}{2}\right)\right)^s L_4. \tag{31}$$

Rewriting the integrals, we find

$$L_3 = -\left(\frac{n}{\mu_2-\mu_1}\right)\int_{\mu_2}^{\frac{(n-1)\mu_2+\mu_1}{n}} w'\left(\frac{x-\mu_2}{\frac{\mu_1-\mu_2}{n}}\right)g(x)\,dx$$
$$= \left(\frac{n}{\mu_2-\mu_1}\right)\int_{\frac{(n-1)\mu_2+\mu_1}{n}}^{\mu_2} w'\left(\frac{\mu_2-x}{\frac{\mu_2-\mu_1}{n}}\right)g(x)\,dx$$
$$= \left(\frac{n}{\mu_2-\mu_1}\right)\mathbf{J}^w_{\left(\frac{(n-1)\mu_2+\mu_1}{n}\right)^+}g(\mu_2), \tag{32}$$

$$L_4 = \left(\frac{mn}{\mu_2-\mu_1}\right)\int_{\frac{\mu_1}{m}}^{\frac{\mu_2+(n-1)\mu_1}{mn}} w'\left(\frac{y-\frac{\mu_1}{m}}{\frac{\mu_2-\mu_1}{mn}}\right)g(y)\,dy$$
$$= \left(\frac{mn}{\mu_2-\mu_1}\right)\mathbf{J}^{w}_{\left(\frac{\mu_2+(n-1)\mu_1}{mn}\right)^-}g\left(\frac{\mu_1}{m}\right). \tag{33}$$

From (13), (14) and (15), it follows that

$$g\left(\frac{\mu_1+\mu_2}{2}\right)(w(1)-w(0)) \le \frac{n}{\mu_2-\mu_1}\left[h^s\left(\frac{1}{2}\right)\mathbf{J}^{w}_{\left(\frac{(n-1)\mu_2+\mu_1}{n}\right)^+}g(\mu_2) + m\left(1-h\left(\frac{1}{2}\right)\right)^s\mathbf{J}^{w}_{\left(\frac{\mu_2+(n-1)\mu_1}{mn}\right)^-}g\left(\frac{\mu_1}{m}\right)\right]. \tag{34}$$

Again employing again the (h,m)-convexity of g, we get

$$\int_0^1 w'(\gamma)\,g\left(\frac{\gamma}{n}\mu_1+\frac{n-\gamma}{n}\mu_2\right)d\gamma \le g(\mu_1)\mathbf{N}_1 + m\,g\left(\frac{\mu_2}{m}\right)\mathbf{N}_2, \tag{35}$$

$$\int_0^1 w'(\gamma)\,g\left(\frac{\gamma}{mn}\mu_2+\frac{n-\gamma}{mn}\mu_1\right)d\gamma \le g\left(\frac{\mu_2}{m}\right)\mathbf{N}_3 + m\,g\left(\frac{\mu_1}{m^2}\right)\mathbf{N}_4. \tag{36}$$

By combining (29)–(36), we arrive at (28). □

Remark 17. *Specializing to the case where g is convex, $w(z)=z$ and $n=1$, we yield the celebrated Hermite–Hadamard inequality.*

Remark 18. *Considering $n=1$, we obtain a new result for modified (h,m)-convex functions of the second type.*

Remark 19. *If g is a convex function and $n=1$, by setting $w'(z)=z^{\alpha-1}$ with $\alpha>0$, we derive Expression (2.1) of Theorem 2 (see [24]).*

Indeed, applying Theorem 4, we obtain

$$\frac{1}{\alpha}g\left(\frac{\mu_1+\mu_2}{2}\right) \le \frac{1}{2(\mu_2-\mu_1)}\left[\mathbf{J}^{w}_{\mu_1^+}g(\mu_2)+\mathbf{J}^{w}_{\mu_2^-}g(\mu_1)\right] \le \frac{g(\mu_1)+g(\mu_2)}{2\alpha}.$$

According to Definition 3, we have

$$\frac{1}{\alpha}g\left(\frac{\mu_1+\mu_2}{2}\right) \le \frac{1}{2(\mu_2-\mu_1)^\alpha}\left[\int_{\mu_1}^{\mu_2}(z-\mu_1)^{\alpha-1}g(z)\,dz+\int_{\mu_1}^{\mu_2}(\mu_2-z)^{\alpha-1}g(z)\,dz\right]$$
$$\le \frac{g(\mu_1)+g(\mu_2)}{2\alpha}.$$

Given that $\Gamma(\alpha)$ is well defined for $\alpha>0$, it follows that

$$g\left(\frac{\mu_1+\mu_2}{2}\right) \le \frac{\alpha\Gamma(\alpha)}{2(\mu_2-\mu_1)^\alpha}\left[\frac{1}{\Gamma(\alpha)}\int_{\mu_1}^{\mu_2}(z-\mu_1)^{\alpha-1}g(z)\,dz+\frac{1}{\Gamma(\alpha)}\int_{\mu_1}^{\mu_2}(\mu_2-z)^{\alpha-1}g(z)\,dz\right]$$
$$\le \frac{g(\mu_1)+g(\mu_2)}{2}.$$

From Definition 4, we conclude that

$$g\left(\frac{\mu_1+\mu_2}{2}\right) \le \frac{\Gamma(\alpha+1)}{2(\mu_2-\mu_1)^\alpha}\left[{}^{RL}\mathbf{I}^{\alpha}_{\mu_2^-}g(\mu_1)+{}^{RL}\mathbf{I}^{\alpha}_{\mu_1^+}g(\mu_2)\right] \le \frac{g(\mu_1)+g(\mu_2)}{2}.$$

Remark 20. *With* $w(z) = \frac{z^\alpha}{\alpha}$, $m = s = 1$, $r = 2$ *and* $h(z) = z$, *the previous result simplifies to Theorem 4 in [34].*

For s-convex functions, using $w(z) = \frac{z^\alpha}{\alpha}$ *and* $n = 1$, *we recover Theorem 2.1 from [25]. Additionally, Theorem 3 in [27], for* $w(z) = z^\alpha$, *provides further results. In this work, Theorem 5 for m-convex functions is also established under similar conditions and can be easily derived.*

Remark 21. *By assigning* $n = m = s = 1$ *and* $h(z) = z$ *in* (28), *which corresponds to working with convex functions and choosing* $w'(z) = \frac{\alpha z^{\frac{\alpha}{k}-1}}{kB(\alpha)\Gamma_k(\alpha)}$, *the left-hand side yields*

$$g\left(\frac{\mu_1+\mu_2}{2}\right)\frac{1}{B(\alpha)\Gamma_k(\alpha)} \leq \frac{1}{2(\mu_2-\mu_1)^{\frac{\alpha}{k}}}\left[\frac{\alpha}{kB(\alpha)\Gamma_k(\alpha)}\int_{\mu_1}^{\mu_2}\frac{g(z)}{(z-\mu_1)^{1-\frac{\alpha}{k}}}dz + \frac{\alpha}{kB(\alpha)\Gamma_k(\alpha)}\int_{\mu_1}^{\mu_2}\frac{g(z)}{(\mu_2-z)^{1-\frac{\alpha}{k}}}dz\right],$$

$$g\left(\frac{\mu_1+\mu_2}{2}\right)\frac{2(\mu_2-\mu_1)^{\frac{\alpha}{k}}}{B(\alpha)\Gamma_k(\alpha)} \leq \frac{\alpha}{kB(\alpha)\Gamma_k(\alpha)}\int_{\mu_1}^{\mu_2}\frac{g(z)}{(z-\mu_1)^{1-\frac{\alpha}{k}}}dz + \frac{\alpha}{kB(\alpha)\Gamma_k(\alpha)}\int_{\mu_1}^{\mu_2}\frac{g(z)}{(\mu_2-z)^{1-\frac{\alpha}{k}}}dz. \tag{37}$$

Adding the term $\frac{1-\alpha}{B(\alpha)}(g(\mu_1)+g(\mu_2))$ *on both sides of* (37) *and considering that* $g\left(\frac{\mu_1+\mu_2}{2}\right) \leq \frac{g(\mu_1)+g(\mu_2)}{2}$, *we obtain*

$$g\left(\frac{\mu_1+\mu_2}{2}\right)\left[\frac{2(\mu_2-\mu_1)^{\frac{\alpha}{k}}}{B(\alpha)\Gamma_k(\alpha)} + \frac{(1-\alpha)}{B(\alpha)}\right] \leq {}^{AB}\,\mathbf{I}^\alpha_{\mu_1+}g(\mu_2) + {}^{AB}\,\mathbf{I}^\alpha_{\mu_2-}g(\mu_1). \tag{38}$$

A similar approach applied to the right-hand side of (28) *gives*

$$\frac{1}{2(\mu_2-\mu_1)^{\frac{\alpha}{k}}}\left[\frac{\alpha}{kB(\alpha)\Gamma_k(\alpha)}\int_{\mu_1}^{\mu_2}\frac{g(z)}{(z-\mu_1)^{1-\frac{\alpha}{k}}}dz + \frac{\alpha}{kB(\alpha)\Gamma_k(\alpha)}\int_{\mu_1}^{\mu_2}\frac{g(z)}{(\mu_2-z)^{1-\frac{\alpha}{k}}}dz\right] \leq \frac{1}{B(\alpha)\Gamma_k(\alpha)}\left(\frac{g(\mu_1)+g(\mu_2)}{2}\right).$$

Multiplying both sides by $2(\mu_2-\mu_1)^{\frac{\alpha}{k}}$, *adding* $\frac{(1-\alpha)}{B(\alpha)}(g(\mu_1)+g(\mu_2))$ *and rearranging terms, we arrive at*

$${}^{AB}\mathbf{I}^\alpha_{\mu_1+}g(\mu_2) + {}^{AB}\,\mathbf{I}^\alpha_{\mu_2-}g(\mu_1) \leq \left[\frac{2(\mu_2-\mu_1)^{\frac{\alpha}{k}}}{B(\alpha)\Gamma_k(\alpha)} + \frac{(1-\alpha)}{B(\alpha)}\right]\left(\frac{g(\mu_1)+g(\mu_2)}{2}\right). \tag{39}$$

By combining (38) *and* (39), *we obtain a relation that closely resembles Theorem 6 in [35]. Moreover, setting* $k = 1$ *in this expression yields a result comparable to Proposition 2.1 in [36].*

Remark 22. *Theorem 7 of [29] can be established by taking* $m = s = 1$, $n = 2$ *and* $w'(z) = z^{\frac{\lambda}{k}-1}$.

Lemma 2. *Let* g, w, n, μ_1 *and* μ_2 *be defined as before. If* $g' \in L[\mu_1, \mu_2]$, *then*

$$\int_0^1 w(\gamma)\left[g'\left(\frac{\gamma}{n}\mu_1+\frac{(n-\gamma)}{n}\mu_2\right)-g'\left(\frac{\gamma}{n}\mu_2+\frac{(n-\gamma)}{n}\mu_1\right)\right]d\gamma$$
$$=\frac{n}{\mu_2-\mu_1}\left[w(0)(g(\mu_1)+g(\mu_2))-w(1)\left(\left(\frac{\gamma}{n}\mu_1+\frac{(n-\gamma)}{n}\mu_2\right)+g\left(\frac{\gamma}{n}\mu_2+\frac{(n-\gamma)}{n}\mu_1\right)\right)\right]$$
$$+\left(\frac{n}{\mu_2-\mu_1}\right)^2\left[\mathbf{J}^w_{\left(\frac{\gamma}{n}\mu_1+\frac{(n-\gamma)}{n}\mu_2\right)^+}g(\mu_2)+\mathbf{J}^w_{\left(\frac{\gamma}{n}\mu_2+\frac{(n-\gamma)}{n}\mu_1\right)^-}g(\mu_1)\right]. \tag{40}$$

Proof. Let

$$\int_0^1 w(\gamma)g'\left(\frac{\gamma}{n}\mu_1+\frac{(n-\gamma)}{n}\mu_2\right)d\gamma-\int_0^1 w(\gamma)g'\left(\frac{\gamma}{n}\mu_2+\frac{(n-\gamma)}{n}\mu_1\right)d\gamma=\mathcal{I}_3-\mathcal{I}_4 \tag{41}$$

By integrating $\mathcal{I}_3$ by parts and making a change in the variables $x=\frac{\gamma}{n}\mu_1+\frac{n-\gamma}{n}\mu_2$, we have, after some computations,

$$\mathcal{I}_3=\frac{n}{\mu_2-\mu_1}\left[w(0)g(\mu_2)-w(1)g\left(\frac{\gamma}{n}\mu_1+\frac{n-\gamma}{n}\mu_2\right)\right]+\left(\frac{n}{\mu_2-\mu_1}\right)^2\mathbf{J}^w_{\left(\frac{\gamma}{n}\mu_1+\frac{n-\gamma}{n}\mu_2\right)^+}g(\mu_2). \tag{42}$$

Analogously for $\mathcal{I}_4$, we get

$$\mathcal{I}_4=\frac{n}{\mu_2-\mu_1}\left[w(1)g\left(\frac{\gamma}{n}\mu_2+\frac{n-\gamma}{n}\mu_1\right)-w(0)g(\mu_2)\right]+\left(\frac{n}{\mu_2-\mu_1}\right)^2\mathbf{J}^w_{\left(\frac{\gamma}{n}\mu_1+\frac{n-\gamma}{n}\mu_2\right)^+}g(\mu_1). \tag{43}$$

From (42) and (43), (2) follows. □

Remark 23. *By setting $n=2$ and $w(z)=z^\alpha$ with $\alpha>0$, Lemma 3 is derived from [34].*

Remark 24. *Lemma 3.1 in [29] may be derived by setting $m=s=1$, $n=2$ and $w'(z)=z^{\frac{\lambda}{k}}$.*

Remark 25. *By adopting a strategy similar to that utilized in Lemma 2, we establish a comparable result concerning the midpoint of the interval.*

Lemma 3. *Let g be a real-valued function defined on a closed real interval, $[\mu_1,\mu_2]$, differentiable on (μ_1,μ_2), and w' is an integrable function on $[\mu_1,\mu_2]$. If $g'\in L_1[\mu_1,\mu_2]$, then the following equality holds:*

$$\frac{1}{2(r+1)}\left[2w(1)g\left(\frac{\mu_1+\mu_2}{2}\right)-w(0)\left[g\left(\frac{(r+2)\mu_1+r\mu_2}{2(r+1)}\right)+g\left(\frac{r\mu_1+(r+2)\mu_2}{2(r+1)}\right)\right]\right]$$
$$-\frac{1}{\mu_2-\mu_1}\left[\mathbf{J}^w_{\left(\frac{\mu_1+\mu_2}{2}\right)^-}g\left(\frac{(r+2)\mu_1+r\mu_2}{2(r+1)}\right)+\mathbf{J}^w_{\left(\frac{\mu_1+\mu_2}{2}\right)^+}g\left(\frac{r\mu_1+(r+2)\mu_2}{2(r+1)}\right)\right]$$
$$=\frac{\mu_2-\mu_1}{4(r+1)^2}\int_0^1 w(t)\left[g'\left(\frac{r+\gamma}{r+1}\frac{\mu_1+\mu_2}{2}+\frac{1-\gamma}{r+1}\mu_1\right)-g'\left(\frac{r+\gamma}{r+1}\frac{\mu_1+\mu_2}{2}+\frac{1-\gamma}{r+1}\mu_2\right)\right]d\gamma, \tag{44}$$

for $r\in\mathbb{N}\cup\{0\}$.

Below we present some remarks that show the breadth and generality of (44).

Remark 26. *By setting $w(z)=z^\alpha$ and $r=0$, we recover Lemma 2.1 of [37]. A similar result can be obtained very easily for the k-Riemann–Liouville integral of [13].*

Remark 27. *Letting $w(z) = z$ and $r = 0$, we find a new result in the framework of the Riemann integral:*

$$g\left(\frac{\mu_1+\mu_2}{2}\right) - \frac{1}{\mu_2-\mu_1}\int_{\mu_1}^{\mu_2} g(z)\,dz$$
$$= \frac{\mu_2-\mu_1}{4}\int_0^1 w(\gamma)\left[g'\left(\gamma\frac{\mu_1+\mu_2}{2}+(1-\gamma)\mu_1\right) - g'\left(\gamma\frac{\mu_1+\mu_2}{2}+(1-\gamma)\mu_2\right)\right]d\gamma.$$

Remark 28. *Considering $w(z)$ to be a linear function, but different for $\mathbb{I}_1$ and $\mathbb{I}_2$, and $r = 0$, we get*

$$\mathbb{I} = \int_0^1 (\gamma-\lambda_1)g'\left(\gamma\frac{\mu_1+\mu_2}{2}+(1-\gamma)\mu_1\right)d\gamma - \int_0^1 (\gamma-\lambda_2)g'\left(\gamma\frac{\mu_1+\mu_2}{2}+(1-\gamma)\mu_2\right)d\gamma,$$

where

$$\lambda_1, \lambda_2 \in \mathbb{R},$$
$$\mathbb{I}_1 = \int_0^1 w(\gamma)g'\left(\frac{r+\gamma}{r+1}\frac{\mu_1+\mu_2}{2}+\frac{1-\gamma}{r+1}\mu_1\right)d\gamma,$$
$$\mathbb{I}_2 = \int_0^1 w(\gamma)g'\left(\frac{r+\gamma}{r+1}\frac{\mu_1+\mu_2}{2}+\frac{1-\gamma}{r+1}\mu_2\right)d\gamma.$$

From here we obtain

$$\frac{2-\lambda_1-\lambda_2}{2}g\left(\frac{\mu_1+\mu_2}{2}\right) + \frac{\lambda g(\mu_1)+\mu g(\mu_2)}{2} - \frac{1}{\mu_2-\mu_1}\int_{\mu_1}^{\mu_2} g(u)\,du = \frac{\mu_2-\mu_1}{4}\mathbb{I}.$$

Given that

$$\int_0^1 (\gamma-\lambda_1)g'\left(\gamma\frac{\mu_1+\mu_2}{2}+(1-\gamma)\mu_1\right)d\gamma = \int_0^1 (1-\gamma-\lambda_1)g'\left(\gamma\mu_1+(1-\gamma)\frac{\mu_1+\mu_2}{2}\right)d\gamma,$$

we retrieve Lemma 2.1 of [38].

Remark 29. *Readers will have no difficulty in proving, in a similar manner, the following result.*

Lemma 4. *Let g be a real function defined on some closed real interval $[\mu_1, \mu_2]$, differentiable on (μ_1, μ_2), and w' is an integrable function on $[\mu_1, \mu_2]$. If $g' \in L_1[\mu_1, \mu_2]$, then we find the following equality:*

$$\frac{1}{n+1}\left[-w(1)\frac{g(\mu_1)+g(\mu_2)}{2} + w(0)\frac{g\left(\frac{n\mu_1+\frac{\mu_1+\mu_2}{2}}{n+1}\right)+g\left(\frac{n\mu_2+\frac{\mu_1+\mu_2}{2}}{n+1}\right)}{2}\right]$$
$$+\frac{1}{\mu_2-\mu_1}\left[\mathbf{J}^{w}_{\mu_1+}g\left(\frac{n\mu_1+\frac{\mu_1+\mu_2}{2}}{n+1}\right)+\mathbf{J}^{w}_{\mu_2-}g\left(\frac{n\mu_2+\frac{\mu_1+\mu_2}{2}}{n+1}\right)\right]$$
$$= \frac{\mu_2-\mu_1}{4(n+1)^2}\int_0^1 w(\gamma)\left[g'\left(\frac{n+\gamma}{n+1}\frac{\mu_1+\mu_2}{2}+\frac{1-\gamma}{n+1}\mu_1\right) - g'\left(\frac{n+\gamma}{n+1}\frac{\mu_1+\mu_2}{2}+\frac{1-\gamma}{n+1}\mu_2\right)\right]d\gamma,$$

for $n \in \mathbb{N}$.

This result completes Lemma 2.1 of [37]. Of course, remarks, similar to those presented above, can be derived.

Theorem 5. *Let g, w, n, μ_1 and μ_2 be defined as before. If $|g'|$ is modified and (h,m)-convex of the second type, then it is true that*

$$|L| \leq (|g'(\mu_1)| + |g'(\mu_2)|)\mathbf{W}_3 + m\left(\left|g'\left(\frac{\mu_1}{m}\right)\right| + \left|g'\left(\frac{\mu_2}{m}\right)\right|\right)\mathbf{W}_4, \tag{45}$$

where L is the left-hand side of (2), $\mathbf{W}_3 = \int_0^1 w(\gamma)h^s\left(\frac{\gamma}{n}\right)d\gamma$ and $\mathbf{W}_4 = \int_0^1 w(\gamma)\left(1-h\left(\frac{\gamma}{n}\right)\right)^s d\gamma$.

Proof. From Lemma 2, by employing the properties of the modulus, we obtain

$$|L| \leq \int_0^1 |w(\gamma)|\left[\left|g'\left(\frac{\gamma}{n}\mu_1 + \frac{n-\gamma}{n}\mu_2\right)\right| + \left|g'\left(\frac{n-\gamma}{n}\mu_1 + \frac{\gamma}{n}\mu_2\right)\right|\right]d\gamma.$$

Utilizing the convexity property of $|g'|$, we get

$$\left|g'\left(\frac{\gamma}{n}\mu_1 + \frac{n-\gamma}{n}\mu_2\right)\right| \leq h^s\left(\frac{\gamma}{n}\right)|g'(\mu_1)| + m\left(1-h\left(\frac{\gamma}{n}\right)\right)^s\left|g'\left(\frac{\mu_2}{m}\right)\right|,$$

and

$$\left|g'\left(\frac{n-\gamma}{n}\mu_1 + \frac{\gamma}{n}\mu_2\right)\right| \leq m\left(1-h\left(\frac{\gamma}{n}\right)\right)^s\left|g'\left(\frac{\mu_1}{m}\right)\right| + h^s\left(\frac{\gamma}{n}\right)|g'(\mu_2)|.$$

Summing the last two inequalities, we have

$$\begin{aligned}&\left|g'\left(\frac{\gamma}{n}\mu_1 + \frac{n-\gamma}{n}\mu_2\right)\right| + \left|g'\left(\frac{n-\gamma}{n}\mu_1 + \frac{\gamma}{n}\mu_2\right)\right| \\ &\leq h^s\left(\frac{\gamma}{n}\right)(|g'(\mu_1)| + |g'(\mu_2)|) + m\left(1-h\left(\frac{\gamma}{n}\right)\right)^s\left(\left|g'\left(\frac{\mu_1}{m}\right)\right| + \left|g'\left(\frac{\mu_2}{m}\right)\right|\right).\end{aligned}$$

Taking into account the accepted notations, we obtain (5). The proof is completed. □

Remark 30. *If we consider the usual class of convex functions and $n = 2$, then from Theorem 5, we obtain*

$$|L| \leq (|g'(\mu_1)| + |g'(\mu_2)|)\int_0^1 w(\gamma)\,d\gamma.$$

Here, if we take $w(z) = z$, then we obtain Theorem 2.2 from [39] and Theorem 5 from [34]. If we choose $w(z) = (1-z)$, then we have Theorem 2.2 in [33], and if $w(z) = z^\alpha$, then we obtain the inequality from [40] (remark of Theorem 1, for $w(z) = (1-z)^\alpha$).

Remark 31. *By adopting a strategy similar to that utilized in Theorem 5 and by employing Lemma 3, we establish a comparable result concerning the midpoint of the interval.*

Theorem 6. *Let $g : [\mu_1, \mu_2] \to \mathbb{R}$ be a differentiable function on (μ_1, μ_2), such that $g' \in L_1[\mu_1, \mu_2]$. If $|g'|$ is modified and (h,m)-convex of the second type and $\frac{\mu_1}{m}, \frac{\mu_2}{m} \in \mathrm{Dom}(|g'|)$, then the following inequality holds:*

$$|\mathcal{L}(w,g,\mu_1,\mu_2,n)| \leq 2\left|g'\left(\frac{\mu_1+\mu_2}{2}\right)\right|\mathcal{H}_1 + m\left(\left|g'\left(\frac{\mu_1}{m}\right)\right| + \left|g'\left(\frac{\mu_2}{m}\right)\right|\right)\mathcal{H}_2,$$

where

$$
\begin{aligned}
&\mathcal{L}(w,g,\mu_1,\mu_2,r) = \\
= \ &\frac{1}{2(r+1)}\left\{2w(1)g\left(\frac{\mu_1+\mu_2}{2}\right) - w(0)\left[g\left(\frac{(r+2)\mu_1+r\mu_2}{2(r+1)}\right)+g\left(\frac{r\mu_1+(r+2)\mu_2}{2(r+1)}\right)\right]\right\} \\
- \ &\frac{1}{\mu_2-\mu_1}\left[J^w_{\left(\frac{\mu_1+\mu_2}{2}\right)^-}g\left(\frac{(r+2)\mu_1+r\mu_2}{2(r+1)}\right)+J^w_{\left(\frac{\mu_1+\mu_2}{2}\right)^+}g\left(\frac{r\mu_1+(r+2)\mu_2}{2(r+1)}\right)\right],
\end{aligned}
$$

$$
\begin{aligned}
\mathcal{H}_1 &= \int_0^1 w(\gamma)h^s\left(\frac{r+\gamma}{r+1}\right)d\gamma, \\
\mathcal{H}_2 &= \int_0^1 w(\gamma)\left[1-h\left(\frac{r+\gamma}{r+1}\right)\right]^s d\gamma.
\end{aligned}
$$

Corollary 1. *Under the assumptions of Theorem 6, we have the following:*

1. *If we choose $m=1$, then we derive the following inequality:*

$$
|\mathcal{L}(w,g,\mu_1,\mu_2,r)| \le 2\left|g'\left(\frac{\mu_1+\mu_2}{2}\right)\right|\mathcal{H}_1 + (|g'(\mu_1)|+|g'(\mu_2)|)\mathcal{H}_2,
$$

   $\mathcal{H}_1$ and $\mathcal{H}_2$ are as before.

2. *If $s=m=1$, then*

$$
|\mathcal{L}(w,g,\mu_1,\mu_2,r)| \le 2\left|g'\left(\frac{\mu_1+\mu_2}{2}\right)\right|\mathcal{H}_3(\gamma) + (|g'(\mu_1)|+|g'(\mu_2)|)\mathcal{H}_4(\gamma),
$$

   where

$$
\mathcal{H}_3 = \int_0^1 w(\gamma)h\left(\frac{r+\gamma}{r+1}\right)d\gamma, \quad \mathcal{H}_4 = \int_0^1 w(\gamma)\left[1-h\left(\frac{r+\gamma}{r+1}\right)\right]d\gamma.
$$

3. *If we take $w(z)=z$, $r=0$ and $s=m=1$, we obtain the following inequality, new for the Riemann integral:*

$$
\begin{aligned}
\left|g\left(\frac{\mu_1+\mu_2}{2}\right) - \int_{\mu_1}^{\mu_2} g(z)\,dz\right| \le 2\left|g'\left(\frac{\mu_1+\mu_2}{2}\right)\right| &\int_0^1 \gamma\,h(\gamma)\,d\gamma \\
+ (|g'(\mu_1)|+|g'(\mu_2)|) &\int_0^1 \gamma(1-h(\gamma))d\gamma.
\end{aligned}
$$

4. *Putting $w'(z) = \dfrac{z^\alpha}{\Gamma(\alpha+1)}$, $r=0$, readers will have no difficulty in obtaining a new inequality for the Riemann–Liouville integral.*

Remark 32. *The generality of this result can be easily verified since, for different notions of convexity contained in our Definition 2, with different values of r and for different kernels, w', new results can be derived under the conditions from Theorem 6.*

Theorem 7. *Let us have g, g', w, μ_1, μ_2 and n as in Theorem 9. Suppose that $|g'|^q$ is modified and (h,m)-convex of the second type and $\frac{\mu_1}{m}, \frac{\mu_2}{m} \in Dom(|g'|^q)$; then the inequality below is satisfied:*

$$
|\mathbf{U}| \le \frac{\mu_2-\mu_1}{n}\mathbf{W}_6\left[\left(|g'(\mu_1)|^q\mathbf{H}_1 + m\left|g'\left(\frac{\mu_2}{m}\right)\right|^q\mathbf{H}_2\right)^{\frac{1}{q}} + \left(|g'(\mu_2)|^q\mathbf{H}_1 + m\left|g'\left(\frac{\mu_1}{m}\right)\right|^q\mathbf{H}_2\right)^{\frac{1}{q}}\right],
$$

where $p, q > 1$, $\mathbf{U}$ is the right-hand side of Equation (2), $\mathbf{W}_5 = \left(\int_0^1 w^p(\gamma)\,d\gamma\right)^{\frac{1}{p}}$, $\mathbf{H}_1 = \int_0^1 h^s(\frac{\gamma}{n})\,d\gamma$ and $\mathbf{H}_2 = \int_0^1 (1 - h(\frac{\gamma}{n}))^s\,d\gamma$.

Proof. By adapting the approach used in Theorem 9 but by employing Hölder's inequality instead, we arrive at

$$\begin{aligned}
|\mathbf{U}| &\leq \frac{\mu_2 - \mu_1}{n}\left[\int_0^1 w(\gamma)\left|g'\left(\frac{\gamma}{n}\mu_1 + \frac{(n-\gamma)}{n}\mu_2\right)\right|d\gamma + \int_0^1 w(\gamma)\left|g'\left(\frac{\gamma}{n}\mu_2 + \frac{(n-\gamma)}{n}\mu_1\right)\right|d\gamma\right] \\
&\leq \frac{\mu_2 - \mu_1}{n}\left(\int_0^1 w^p(\gamma)\,d\gamma\right)^{\frac{1}{p}}\left[\left(\int_0^1 \left|g'\left(\frac{\gamma}{n}\mu_1 + \frac{(n-\gamma)}{n}\mu_2\right)\right|^q d\gamma\right)^{\frac{1}{q}}\right. \\
&\quad \left. + \left(\int_0^1 \left|g'\left(\frac{\gamma}{n}\mu_2 + \frac{(n-\gamma)}{n}\mu_1\right)\right|^q d\gamma\right)^{\frac{1}{q}}\right] \\
&\leq \frac{\mu_2 - \mu_1}{n}\mathbf{W}_5\left[\left(|g'(\mu_1)|^q\mathbf{H}_1 + m\left|g'\left(\frac{\mu_2}{m}\right)\right|^q\mathbf{H}_2\right)^{\frac{1}{q}} + \left(|g'(\mu_2)|^q\mathbf{H}_1 + m\left|g'\left(\frac{\mu_1}{m}\right)\right|^q\mathbf{H}_2\right)^{\frac{1}{q}}\right].
\end{aligned}$$

Therefore, the desired result has been established. □

Remark 33. *If $w(z) = z^\alpha$ and g is convex, we obtain the inequality of Theorem 6 presented in [34]:*

$$\begin{aligned}
&\left|\frac{2^{\alpha-1}\Gamma(\alpha+1)}{(\mu_2-\mu_1)^\alpha}\left[{}^{RL}\mathbf{I}^\alpha_{\left(\frac{\mu_1+\mu_2}{2}\right)^-}g(\mu_1) + {}^{RL}\mathbf{I}^\alpha_{\left(\frac{\mu_1+\mu_2}{2}\right)^+}g(\mu_2)\right] - g\left(\frac{\mu_1+\mu_2}{2}\right)\right| \\
&\leq \frac{\mu_2-\mu_1}{4}\left(\frac{1}{\alpha p+1}\right)^{\frac{1}{p}}\left[\left(\frac{|g'(\mu_1)|^q}{4} + \frac{3|g'(\mu_2)|^q}{4}\right)^{\frac{1}{q}} + \left(\frac{|g'(\mu_2)|^q}{4} + \frac{3|g'(\mu_1)|^q}{4}\right)^{\frac{1}{q}}\right] \\
&\leq \frac{\mu_2-\mu_1}{4}\left(\frac{4}{\alpha p+1}\right)^{\frac{1}{p}}\left[|g'(\mu_1)| + |g'(\mu_2)|\right].
\end{aligned}$$

Remark 34. *If $w(z) = 4z$, $q = \frac{p-1}{p}$ and g is convex, we obtain an inequality similar to Theorem 2.3 presented in [39]:*

$$\begin{aligned}
\left|\frac{1}{\mu_2-\mu_1}\int_{\mu_1}^{\mu_2} g(z)\,dz - g\left(\frac{\mu_1+\mu_2}{2}\right)\right| &\leq \frac{\mu_2-\mu_1}{16}\left(\frac{4}{p+1}\right)^{\frac{1}{p}}\left[\left(\frac{|g'(\mu_1)|^{\frac{p-1}{p}}}{4} + \frac{3|g'(\mu_2)|^{\frac{p-1}{p}}}{4}\right)^{\frac{p}{p-1}}\right. \\
&\quad \left. + \left(\frac{|g'(\mu_2)|^{\frac{p-1}{p}}}{4} + \frac{3|g'(\mu_1)|^{\frac{p-1}{p}}}{4}\right)^{\frac{p}{p-1}}\right].
\end{aligned}$$

Remark 35. *Utilizing a procedure parallel to that applied in Theorem 7 and invoking Lemma 3, we obtain an equivalent statement pertaining to the midpoint of the interval:*

Theorem 8. *Let $g : [\mu_1, \mu_2] \to \mathbb{R}$ be a differentiable function on (μ_1, μ_2) such that $g' \in L_1[\mu_1, \mu_2]$. If $|g'|^q$ is modified and (h, m)-convex of the second type and $\frac{\mu_1}{m}, \frac{\mu_2}{m} \in Dom(|g'|^q)$, then it is true that*

$$|\mathcal{L}(w,g,\mu_1,\mu_2,r)| \leq \frac{\mu_2-\mu_1}{4(r+1)^2}\mathbf{W}_5\left\{\left[\left|g'\left(\frac{\mu_1+\mu_2}{2}\right)\right|^q\mathcal{H}_5+m\left(\left|g'\left(\frac{\mu_1}{m}\right)\right|^q\right)\mathcal{H}_6\right]^{\frac{1}{q}} + \left[\left|g'\left(\frac{\mu_1+\mu_2}{2}\right)\right|^q\mathcal{H}_5+m\left(\left|g'\left(\frac{\mu_2}{m}\right)\right|^q\right)\mathcal{H}_6\right]^{\frac{1}{q}}\right\}. \tag{46}$$

with $\frac{1}{p}+\frac{1}{q}=1$, $\mathcal{H}_5=\int_0^1 h^s(\frac{r+t}{r+1})dt$, $\mathcal{H}_6=\int_0^1(1-h(\frac{r+t}{r+1}))^s dt$ *and* $\mathbf{W}_5$ *defined as before.*

Corollary 2. *Under the assumptions of Theorem 8, we have the following:*

1. *Choosing* $m=1$*, then we obtain the following inequality:*

$$|\mathcal{L}(w,g,\mu_1,\mu_2,r)| \leq \frac{\mu_2-\mu_1}{4(r+1)^2}\left(\int_0^1 w^p(t)dt\right)^{\frac{1}{p}}\left\{\left[\left|g'\left(\frac{\mu_1+\mu_2}{2}\right)\right|^q\mathcal{H}_5+\left(|g'(\mu_1)|^q\right)\mathcal{H}_6\right]^{\frac{1}{q}} + \left[\left|g'\left(\frac{\mu_1+\mu_2}{2}\right)\right|^q\mathcal{H}_5+\left(|g'(\mu_2)|^q\right)\mathcal{H}_6\right]^{\frac{1}{q}}\right\}.$$

2. *If* $s=m=1$*, then*

$$|\mathcal{L}(w,g,\mu_1,\mu_2,r)| \leq \frac{\mu_2-\mu_1}{4(r+1)^2}\left(\int_0^1 w^p(t)dt\right)^{\frac{1}{p}} \times\left\{\left[\left|g'\left(\frac{\mu_1+\mu_2}{2}\right)\right|^q\int_0^1 h\left(\frac{r+t}{r+1}\right)dt+|g'(\mu_1)|^q\int_0^1\left(1-h\left(\frac{r+t}{r+1}\right)\right)dt\right]^{\frac{1}{q}} + \left[\left|g'\left(\frac{\mu_1+\mu_2}{2}\right)\right|^q\int_0^1 h\left(\frac{r+t}{r+1}\right)dt+|g'(\mu_2)|^q\int_0^1\left(1-h\left(\frac{r+t}{r+1}\right)\right)dt\right]^{\frac{1}{q}}\right\}.$$

3. *Bearing in mind Corollary 1, items 3 and 4, we can derive new inequalities for Riemann and Riemann–Liouville integrals, respectively.*

Theorem 9. *Let* g,g',w,μ_1,μ_2,n*,* $\mathbf{W}_3$ *and* $\mathbf{W}_4$ *be as in Lemma 2. Suppose that* $|g'|^q$ *is modified and* (h,m)*-convex of the second type and* $\frac{\mu_1}{m},\frac{\mu_2}{m}\in Dom(|g'|^q)$*; then the following result emerges:*

$$|\mathbf{U}| \leq \frac{\mu_2-\mu_1}{n}\mathbf{W}_6\left[\left(|g'(\mu_1)|^q\mathbf{W}_3+m\left|g'\left(\frac{\mu_2}{m}\right)\right|^q\mathbf{W}_4\right)^{\frac{1}{q}}+\left(|g'(\mu_2)|^q\mathbf{W}_3+m\left|g'\left(\frac{\mu_1}{m}\right)\right|^q\mathbf{W}_4\right)^{\frac{1}{q}}\right],$$

where $q\geq 1$, $\mathbf{W}_6=\left(\int_0^1 w(\gamma)\,d\gamma\right)^{1-\frac{1}{q}}$ *and* $\mathbf{U}$ *is defined as before.*

Proof. Employing Lemma 2, the triangle inequality, the Power Mean inequality and Definition 2 for $|g|^q$, we obtain

$$
\begin{aligned}
|\mathbf{U}| &\leq \left| \frac{\mu_2-\mu_1}{n} \int_0^1 w(\gamma)\left[g'\left(\frac{\gamma}{n}\mu_1 + \frac{(n-\gamma)}{n}\mu_2\right) - g'\left(\frac{\gamma}{n}\mu_2 + \frac{(n-\gamma)}{n}\mu_1\right)\right] d\gamma \right| \\
&\leq \frac{\mu_2-\mu_1}{n}\left[\int_0^1 w(\gamma)\left| g'\left(\frac{\gamma}{n}\mu_1 + \frac{(n-\gamma)}{n}\mu_2\right)\right| d\gamma + \int_0^1 w(\gamma)\left| g'\left(\frac{\gamma}{n}\mu_2 + \frac{(n-\gamma)}{n}\mu_1\right)\right| d\gamma \right] \\
&\leq \frac{\mu_2-\mu_1}{n}\left(\int_0^1 w(\gamma)\, d\gamma\right)^{1-\frac{1}{q}} \left[\left(\int_0^1 w(\gamma)\left| g'\left(\frac{\gamma}{n}\mu_1 + \frac{(n-\gamma)}{n}\mu_2\right)\right|^q d\gamma\right)^{\frac{1}{q}} \right. \\
&\quad \left. + \left(\int_0^1 w(\gamma)\left| g'\left(\frac{\gamma}{n}\mu_2 + \frac{(n-\gamma)}{n}\mu_1\right)\right|^q d\gamma\right)^{\frac{1}{q}} \right] \\
&\leq \frac{\mu_2-\mu_1}{n}\mathbf{W}_6\left[\left(|g'(\mu_1)|^q \mathbf{W}_3 + m\left| g'\left(\frac{\mu_2}{m}\right)\right|^q \mathbf{W}_4 \right)^{\frac{1}{q}} + \left(|g'(\mu_2)|^q \mathbf{W}_3 + m\left| g'\left(\frac{\mu_1}{m}\right)\right|^q \mathbf{W}_4 \right)^{\frac{1}{q}} \right].
\end{aligned}
$$

Hence, the proof is finished. □

Remark 36. *Theorem 8 in [29] follows as a consequence when the parameters m, s and n and the function w' are selected as in Remark 24.*

Remark 37. *In light of Theorem 9 and Lemma 2, we similarly obtain a result for the midpoint of the interval:*

Theorem 10. *Let $g : [\mu_1, \mu_2] \to \mathbb{R}$ be a differentiable function on (μ_1, μ_2), such that $g' \in L_1[\mu_1, \mu_2]$. If $|g'|^q$ is modified and (h, m)-convex of the second type with $q \geq 1$ and $\frac{\mu_1}{m}, \frac{\mu_2}{m} \in Dom(|g'|^q)$, then it is true that*

$$
\begin{aligned}
|\mathcal{L}(w, g, \mu_1, \mu_2, r)| &\leq \frac{\mu_2-\mu_1}{4(r+1)^2}\left(\int_0^1 w(t)\, dt\right)^{1-\frac{1}{q}} \\
&\quad \times \left\{ \left[\left| g'\left(\frac{\mu_1+\mu_2}{2}\right)\right|^q \mathcal{H}_1 + m\left(\left| g'\left(\frac{\mu_1}{m}\right)\right|^q\right)\mathcal{H}_2 \right]^{\frac{1}{q}} \right. \\
&\quad \left. + \left[\left| g'\left(\frac{\mu_1+\mu_2}{2}\right)\right|^q \mathcal{H}_1 + m\left(\left| g'\left(\frac{\mu_2}{m}\right)\right|^q\right)\mathcal{H}_2 \right]^{\frac{1}{q}} \right\},
\end{aligned} \tag{47}
$$

where $\mathcal{H}_1$ and $\mathcal{H}_2$ are defined above in Theorem 6.

Theorem 11. *Let g, g', w, μ_1, μ_2, n, p, q, $\mathbf{U}$, $\mathbf{H}_1$ and $\mathbf{H}_2$ be as defined in the preceding result. Suppose that $|g'|^q$ is modified and (h, m)-convex of the second type and $\frac{\mu_1}{m}, \frac{\mu_2}{m} \in Dom(|g'|^q)$; then it is true that*

$$
|\mathbf{U}| \leq \frac{\mu_2-\mu_1}{n}\left[\mathbf{W}_7 + (|g'(\mu_1)|^q + |g'(\mu_2)|^q)\frac{\mathbf{H}_1}{q} + m\left(\left| g'\left(\frac{\mu_2}{m}\right)\right|^q + \left| g'\left(\frac{\mu_1}{m}\right)\right|^q\right)\frac{\mathbf{H}_2}{q} \right], \tag{48}
$$

where $\mathbf{W}_7 = 2\int_0^1 \frac{w(\gamma)}{p}\, d\gamma$.

Proof. Following a similar line of reasoning as in Theorem 9 but replacing the key inequality with that of Young, we get

$$
\begin{aligned}
|\mathbf{U}| &\leq \frac{\mu_2-\mu_1}{n}\left[\int_0^1 w(\gamma)\left|g'\left(\frac{\gamma}{n}\mu_1+\frac{(n-\gamma)}{n}\mu_2\right)\right|d\gamma+\int_0^1 w(\gamma)\left|g'\left(\frac{\gamma}{n}\mu_2+\frac{(n-\gamma)}{n}\mu_1\right)\right|d\gamma\right] \\
&\leq \frac{\mu_2-\mu_1}{n}\left[2\int_0^1 \frac{w^p(\gamma)}{p}\,d\gamma+\int_0^1 \frac{\left|g'\left(\frac{\gamma}{n}\mu_1+\frac{(n-\gamma)}{n}\mu_2\right)\right|^q}{q}\,d\gamma\right. \\
&\quad\left.+\int_0^1 \frac{\left|g'\left(\frac{\gamma}{n}\mu_2+\frac{(n-\gamma)}{n}\mu_1\right)\right|^q}{q}\,d\gamma\right] \\
&\leq \frac{\mu_2-\mu_1}{n}\left[\mathbf{W}_7+\left(|g'(\mu_1)|^q+|g'(\mu_2)|^q\right)\frac{\mathbf{H}_1}{q}+m\left(\left|g'\left(\frac{\mu_2}{m}\right)\right|^q+\left|g'\left(\frac{\mu_1}{m}\right)\right|^q\right)\frac{\mathbf{H}_2}{q}\right].
\end{aligned}
$$

This concludes the proof. □

Remark 38. *If we consider the usual class of convex functions and $n = 2$, then from (48), we obtain*

$$|\mathbf{U}| \leq \frac{2(\mathbf{W}_5)^p}{p}+\frac{|g'(\mu_1)|^q+|g'(\mu_2)|^q}{q}.$$

Here, if we take $w(z) = z$, then we get

$$\left|\int_{\mu_1}^{\mu_2} g(z)\,dz-g\left(\frac{\mu_1+\mu_2}{2}\right)\right| \leq \frac{2}{p(p+1)}+\frac{|g'(\mu_1)|^q+|g'(\mu_2)|^q}{q}.$$

Remark 39. *By building upon the method employed in Theorem 7 and drawing on Lemma 2, we derive a parallel result concerning the midpoint of the interval.*

Theorem 12. *Let $g : [\mu_1, \mu_2] \to \mathbb{R}$ be a differentiable function on (μ_1, μ_2) such that $g' \in L_1[\mu_1, \mu_2]$. If $|g'|^q$ is modified and (h, m)-convex of the second type with $\frac{1}{p}+\frac{1}{q} = 1$ and $\frac{\mu_1}{m}, \frac{\mu_2}{m} \in Dom(|g'|^q)$, then*

$$
\begin{aligned}
|\mathcal{L}(w,g,\mu_1,\mu_2,r)| \leq \frac{\mu_2-\mu_1}{4(r+1)^2}&\left\{\frac{2}{p}\int_0^1 w^p(t)\,dt+\frac{2}{q}\left|g'\left(\frac{\mu_1+\mu_2}{2}\right)\right|^q\mathcal{H}_5\right. \\
&\left.+\frac{m}{q}\left(\left|g'\left(\frac{\mu_1}{m}\right)\right|^q+\left|g'\left(\frac{\mu_2}{m}\right)\right|^q\right)\mathcal{H}_6\right\},
\end{aligned}
\tag{49}
$$

holds, where $\mathcal{H}_5$ and $\mathcal{H}_6$ are defined above in Theorem 8.

Remark 40. *Remark 32 remains valid in these results.*

Remark 41. *Readers will have no difficulty in formulating the corresponding corollaries to Theorems 10 and 11.*

4. Conclusions

This work focuses on the generalization and extension of existing results related to integral inequalities. The main results and contributions are Theorem 1 and Theorem 2, which establish new inequalities for (h, m)-convex functions of second type using weighted integral operators. It also provides remarks showing how these new results generalize or connect with existing theorems in the literature by establishing specific parameters for s, m, and h and the weighting function w'.

In essence, we consider this work to contribute significantly to the theory of convex functions by providing a more generalized and flexible framework for Hermite–Hadamard-type inequalities through the introduction of weighted integrals and refined classes of (h, m)-convex functions.

Author Contributions: Conceptualization, J.E.N.V., L.G. and J.J.R.; methodology, J.E.N.V., L.G. and J.J.R.; validation, J.E.N.V., L.G. and J.J.R.; formal analysis, J.E.N.V., L.G. and J.J.R.; writing original draft preparation, J.E.N.V., L.G. and J.J.R.; writing—review and editing, J.E.N.V., L.G. and J.J.R. All authors have read and agreed to the published version of the manuscript.

Funding: This research received no external funding.

Institutional Review Board Statement: Not applicable.

Informed Consent Statement: Not applicable.

Data Availability Statement: Not applicable.

Acknowledgments: J. Juan Rosales thanks CONAHCyT for its support within the framework of the Sabbatical Stays: BP-BSNAC20250411170404044-10573580.

Conflicts of Interest: The authors declare no conflicts of interest.

References

1. Bayraktar, B.; Nápoles Valdés, J.E. New generalized integral inequalities via (h, m)-convex modified functions. *Izv. Inst. Mat. Inform.* **2022**, *60*, 3–15. [CrossRef]
2. Bruckner, A.M.; Ostrow, E. Some function classes related to the class of convex functions. *Pac. J. Math.* **1962**, *12*, 1203–1215. [CrossRef]
3. Breckner, W.W. Stetigkeitsaussagen fur eine Klasse verallgemeinerter konvexer funktionen in topologischen linearen Raumen. *Publ. Inst. Math.* **1978**, *23*, 13–20.
4. Hudzik, H.; Maligranda, L. Some remarks on s-convex functions. *Aequationes Math.* **1994**, *48*, 100–111. [CrossRef]
5. Xi, B.Y.; Qi, F. Inequalities of Hermite-Hadamard type for extended s-convex functions and applications to means. *J. Nonlinear Convex. Anal.* **2015**, *16*, 873–890. [CrossRef]
6. Xi, B.Y.; Gao, D.D.; Qi, F. Integral inequalities of Hermite-Hadamard type for (α, s)-convex and (α, s, m)-convex functions. *Ital. J. Pure Appl. Math.* **2020**, *44*, 499–510.
7. Park, J. Generalization of Ostrowski-type inequalities for differentiable real (s, m)-convex mappings. *Far East J. Math. Sci.* **2011**, *49*, 157–171.
8. Bilal, M.; Imtiaz, M.; Khan, A.R.; Khan, I.U.; Zafran, M. Generalized Hermite-Hadamard inequalities for s-convex functions in the mixed kind, submitted.
9. Khan, A.R.; Khan, I.U.; Muhammad, S. Hermite-Hadamard type fractional integral inequalities for s-convex functions of mixed kind. *Trans. Math. Comput. Sci.* **2021**, *1*, 25–37.
10. Mihesan, V.G. A generalization of the convexity, Seminar on Functional Equations, Approx. *Convex Cluj-Napoca* **1993**, 1.
11. Özdemit, M.E.; Akdemri, A.O.; Set, E. On (h, m)-convexity and Hadamard-type inequalities. *Transylv. J. Math. Mech.* **2016**, *8*, 51–58.
12. Bayraktar, B.; Nápoles Valdés, J.E. Integral inequalities for mappings whose derivatives are (h, m, s)-convex modified of second type via Katugampola integrals. *Univ. Craiova Ser. Mat. Inform.* **2022**, *49*, 371–383.
13. Mubeen, S.; Habibullah, G.M. k-fractional integrals and applications. *Int. J. Contemp. Math. Sci.* **2012**, *7*, 89–94.
14. Akkurt, A.; Yildirim, M.E.; Yildirim, H. On some integral inequalities for (k, h)-RiemannLiouville fractional integral. *NTMSCI* **2016**, *4*, 138–146. [CrossRef]
15. Jarad, F.; Abdeljawad, T.; Shah, T. On the weighted fractional operators of a function with respect to another function. *Fractals* **2020**, *28*, 2040011. [CrossRef]
16. Sarikaya, M.Z.; Ertugral, F. On the generalized Hermite-Hadamard inequalities, Annals of the University of Craiova. *Math. Comput. Sci. Ser.* **2020**, *47*, 193–213.
17. Jarad, F.; Ugurlu, E.; Abdeljawad, T.; Baleanu, D. On a new class of fractional operators. *Adv. Differ. Equ.* **2017**, *2017*, 247. [CrossRef]
18. Khan, T.U.; Khan, M.A. Generalized conformable fractional integral operators. *J. Comput. Appl. Math.* **2019**, *346*, 378–389. [CrossRef]

19. Mehmood, S.; Nápoles Valdés, J.E.; Fatima, N.; Shahid, B. Some New Inequalities Using Conformable Fractional Integral of Order β. *J. Math. Ext.* **2021**, *15*, 1–22 . [CrossRef]
20. Tomar, M.; Set, E.; Sarikaya, M.Z. Hermite-Hadamard type Riemann-Liouville fractional integral inequalities for convex functions. *AIP Conf. Proc.* **2016**, *1726*, 020035. [CrossRef]
21. Caputo, M.; Fabrizio, M. A new definition of fractional derivative without singular kernel. *Prog. Fract. Differ. Appl.*, **2015**, *1*, 73–85.
22. Caputo, M. Linear Models of Dissipation whose Q is almost Frequency Independent-II. *Geophys. J. R. Astr. Soc.* **1967**, *13*, 529–539. [CrossRef]
23. Caputo, M.; Fabrizio, M. On the notion of fractional derivative and applications to the hysteresis phenomena. *Meccanica* **2017**, *52*, 3043–3052. [CrossRef]
24. Sarikaya, M.Z.; Set, E.; Yaldiz, H.; Basak, N. Hermite-Hadamard's inequalities for fractional integrals and related fractional inequalities. *Math. Comput. Model.* **2013**, *57*, 2403–2407. [CrossRef]
25. Wang, J.R.; Li, X.; Zhou, Y. Hermite-Hadamard Inequalities Involving Riemann-Liouville Fractional Integrals via s-convex Functions and Applications to Special Means. *Filomat* **2016**, *30*, 1143–1150. [CrossRef]
26. Dragomir, S.S.; Fitzpatrick, S. The Hadamard inequalities for s-convex functions in the second sense. *Demonstr. Math.* **1999**, *32*, 687–696. [CrossRef]
27. Set, E.; Sarikaya, M.Z.; Özdemir, M.E.; Yildirim, H. The Hermite-Hadamard's inequality for some convex functions via fractional integrals and related results. *JAMSI* **2014**, *10*, 69–83. [CrossRef]
28. Ahmad, B.; Alsaedi, A.; Kirane, M.; Torebek, B.T. Hermite-Hadamard, Hermite-Hadamard-Fejér, Dragomir-Agarwal and Pachpatte type inequalities for convex functions via new fractional integrals. *J. Comput. Appl. Math.* **2019**, *353*, 120–129. [CrossRef]
29. Wu, S.; Iqbal, S.; Aamir, M.; Samraiz, M.; Younus, A. On some Hermite-Hadamard inequalities involving k-fractional operators. *J. Inequalities Appl.* **2021**, *2021*, 32. [CrossRef]
30. Noor, M.A.; Noor, K.I.; Awan, M.U. Generalized fractional Hermite-Hadamard inequalities. *Miskolc Math. Notes* **2020**, *21*, 1001–1011. [CrossRef]
31. Nasir, J.; Qaisar, S.; Qayyum, A.; Budak, H. Newresults on Hermite-Hadamard type inequalities via Caputo-Fabrizio fractional integral for s-convex function. *Filomat* **2023**, *37*, 4943–4957. [CrossRef]
32. Gürbüz, M.; Akdemir, A.O.; Rashid, S.; Set, E. Hermite-Hadamard inequality for fractional integrals of Caputo-Fabrizio type and related inequalities. *J. Inequalities Appl.* **2020**, 172, 1–10. [CrossRef]
33. Dragomir, S.S.; Agarwal, R.P. Two Inequalities for Differentiable Mappings and Applications to Special Means of Real Numbers and to Trapezoidal Formula. *Appl. Math. Lett.* **1998**, *11*, 91–95. [CrossRef]
34. Sarikaya, M.Z.; Yildirim, H. On Hermite-Hadamard type inequalities for Riemann-Liouville fractional integrals. *Miskolc Math. Notes* **2017**, *17*, 1049–1059. [CrossRef]
35. Kermausuor, S.; Nwaeze, E.R. New Fractional Integral Inequalities via k-Atangana-Baleanu Fractional Integral Operators. *Fractal Fract.* **2023**, *7*, 740. [CrossRef]
36. Fernandez, A.; Mohammed, P. Hermite-Hadamard inequalities in fractional calculus defined using Mittag-Leffler kernels. *Math. Meth. Appl. Sci.* **2021**, *44*, 8414–8431. [CrossRef]
37. Matloka, M. Hermite-Hadamard type inequalities for fractional integrals. *RGMIA Res. Rep. Coll.* **2017**, *20*, 69.
38. Xi, B.Y.; Qi, F. Some Integral Inequalities of Hermite-Hadamard Type for Convex Functions with Applications to Means. *J. Funct. Spaces Appl.* **2012**, *2012*, 980438. [CrossRef]
39. Kirmaci, U. Inequalities for differentiable mappings and applications to special means of real numbers to midpoint formula. *Appl. Math. Comput.* **2004**, *147*, 137–146. [CrossRef]
40. Bayraktar, B.; Nápoles, J.E.; Florencia, R. On Generalizations of Integral Inequalities. *Probl.-Anal.—Issues Anal.* **2022**, *11*, 3–23. [CrossRef]

fractal and fractional

MDPI

Article

Local Fractional Perspective on Weddle's Inequality in Fractal Space

Yuanheng Wang [1], Usama Asif [2], Muhammad Uzair Awan [2], Muhammad Zakria Javed [2], Awais Gul Khan [2], Mona Bin-Asfour [3,*] and Kholoud Saad Albalawi [3]

[1] Department of Mathematics of Humanities College, Zhejiang Guangsha Vocational and Technical University of Construction, Jinhua 321004, China; yhwang@zjnu.cn

[2] Department of Mathematics, Government College University Faisalabad, Faisalabad 38000, Pakistan; usamaasif.mua@gmail.com (U.A.); awan.uzair@gmail.com (M.U.A.); zakriajaved071@gmail.com (M.Z.J.); awaisgulkhan@gmail.com (A.G.K.)

[3] Department of Mathematics and Statistics, College of Science, Imam Mohammad Ibn Saud Islamic University (IMSIU), Riyadh 11432, Saudi Arabia; ksalbalawi@imamu.edu.sa

* Correspondence: mibinasfour@imamu.edu.sa

Abstract

The Yang local fractional setting provides the generalized framework to explore the non-differentiable mappings considering the local properties. Due to the dominance of these concepts, mathematicians have investigated multiple problems, including mathematical modelling, optimization, and inequalities. Incorporating these useful concepts, this study aims to derive Weddle-type integral inequalities within the context of fractal space. To achieve the intended results, we establish a new local fractional identity. By using this identity, the convexity property, the bounded property of mappings, the L-Lipschitzian property of mappings, and other famous inequalities, we develop numerous upper bounds. Additionally, we provide 2D and 3D graphical representations and numerous applications, which show the significance of our main findings. To the best of our knowledge, this is the first study concerning error inequalities of Weddle's quadrature formulation within the fractal space.

Keywords: generalized convex mapping; Weddle's inequality; midpoint inequality; lipschitz mapping; applications

MSC: 26A33; 26A51; 26D07; 26D10; 26D15; 26D20

1. Introduction

Convex mappings have potential applications in many domains, which include optimization, coding hypothesis, designing, and inequality theory. But their role is unprecedented for the derivation of mathematical inequalities. Working on this benchmark class of mappings, it is not difficult to conclude the fundamental results of analysis. In the fields of applied science, mathematical inequalities are considered to be the essential structure for connecting qualitative and quantitative analysis. First, we recall the definition of convex mapping.

Definition 1 ([1]). *Any mapping $\mathcal{T} : I \subset \mathbb{R} \to \mathbb{R}$ is termed as convex, if*

$$\mathcal{T}((1-\varepsilon)\nu_1 + \varepsilon\kappa_1) \leq (1-\varepsilon)\mathcal{T}(\nu_1) + \varepsilon\mathcal{T}(\kappa_1), \tag{1}$$

for every value of $\varepsilon \in [0,1]$ *and* $\nu_1, \kappa_1 \in I$.

Many inequalities have been proposed in the literature using convex mappings and their different classes. For more details, see [2–5]. The following double inequality is commonly called Hadamard's inequality in the literature:

Theorem 1 ([1]). *Let* $\mathcal{T} : I \to \mathbb{R}$ *be a convex mapping. Then*

$$\mathcal{T}\left(\frac{\nu_1+\kappa_1}{2}\right) \leq \frac{1}{\kappa_1-\nu_1}\int_{\nu_1}^{\kappa_1} \mathcal{T}(\delta)\mathrm{d}\delta \leq \frac{\mathcal{T}(\nu_1)+\mathcal{T}(\kappa_1)}{2}, \tag{2}$$

for all $\nu_1, \kappa_1 \in I$, *and* $\nu_1 < \kappa_1$.

It was introduced by Hermite in 1881 (see [6]) and Hadamard in 1893 (see [7]). The inequality (2) also holds in reverse direction if we take $\mathcal{T}$ is a concave mapping. In scientific research, the most prominent Simpson's type of inequality is described as follows:

Theorem 2 ([8]). *Consider a four time continuously differentiable mapping* $\mathcal{T} : [\nu_1, \kappa_1] \to \mathbb{R}$. *Then,*

$$\left|\frac{1}{6}\left(\mathcal{T}(\nu_1)+4\mathcal{T}\left(\frac{\nu_1+\kappa_1}{2}\right)+\mathcal{T}(\kappa_1)\right)-\frac{1}{\kappa_1-\nu_1}\int_{\nu_1}^{\kappa_1}\mathcal{T}(\delta)\mathrm{d}\delta\right| \leq \frac{(\kappa_1-\nu_1)^4}{2880}\|\mathcal{T}^4\|_\infty,$$

where $\|\mathcal{T}^4\|_\infty = sup_{\delta\in[\nu_1,\kappa_1]}|\mathcal{T}^4(\delta)| < \infty$.

The Newton's inequality, which is based on the four-point closed formula, is described as follows:

Theorem 3 ([9]). *Let* $\mathcal{T} : [\nu_1, \kappa_1] \to \mathbb{R}$ *be four times continuously differentiable mapping. Then,*

$$\left|\frac{1}{8}\left(\mathcal{T}(\nu_1)+3\mathcal{T}\left(\frac{2\nu_1+\kappa_1}{3}\right)+3\mathcal{T}\left(\frac{\nu_1+2\kappa_1}{3}\right)+\mathcal{T}(\kappa_1)\right)-\frac{1}{\kappa_1-\nu_1}\int_{\nu_1}^{\kappa_1}\mathcal{T}(\delta)\mathrm{d}\delta\right|$$
$$\leq \frac{(\kappa_1-\nu_1)^4}{6480}\|\mathcal{T}^4\|_\infty,$$

where $\|\mathcal{T}^4\|_\infty = sup_{\delta\in[\nu_1,\kappa_1]}|\mathcal{T}^4(\delta)| < \infty$.

The Maclaurin method does not correlate with any boundary points in the quadrature method. It is utilized to alleviate the drawbacks of Simpson's approach. It is formulated as follows:

Theorem 4 ([9]). *Let* $\mathcal{T} : [\nu_1, \kappa_1] \to \mathbb{R}$ *be a four times continuously differentiable mapping on* $[\nu_1, \kappa_1]$ *and* $\|\mathcal{T}^4\|_\infty = sup_{\delta\in[\nu_1,\kappa_1]}|\mathcal{T}^4(\delta)| < \infty$. *Then,*

$$\left|\frac{1}{8}\left[3\mathcal{T}\left(\frac{5\nu_1+\kappa_1}{6}\right)+2\mathcal{T}\left(\frac{\nu_1+\kappa_1}{2}\right)+3\mathcal{T}\left(\frac{\nu_1+5\kappa_1}{6}\right)\right]-\frac{1}{\kappa_1-\nu_1}\int_{\nu_1}^{\kappa_1}\mathcal{T}(\delta)\mathrm{d}\delta\right|$$
$$\leq \frac{7(\kappa_1-\nu_1)^4}{51840}\|\mathcal{T}^4\|_\infty.$$

Now, we present Boole's formula type inequality, which is widely recognized in the literature. This formula executes a polynomial of degree four to estimate the integral over five points.

Theorem 5 ([9]). *Suppose that $\mathcal{T} : [\nu_1, \kappa_1] \to \mathbb{R}$ be a six times continuously differentiable mapping on (ν_1, κ_1). Then,*

$$\left| \frac{1}{90}\left[7(\mathcal{T}(\nu_1 + \mathcal{T}(\kappa_1))) + 32\left(\mathcal{T}\left(\frac{3\nu_1 + \kappa_1}{4}\right) + \mathcal{T}\left(\frac{\nu_1 + 3\kappa_1}{4}\right)\right) + 12\mathcal{T}\left(\frac{\nu_1 + \kappa_1}{2}\right)\right] - \frac{1}{\kappa_1 - \nu_1}\int_{\nu_1}^{\kappa_1} \mathcal{T}(\delta)\mathrm{d}\delta \right| \leq \frac{(\kappa_1 - \nu_1)^6}{1935360}\|\mathcal{T}^6\|_\infty,$$

where $\|\mathcal{T}^6\|_\infty = sup_{\delta \in [\nu_1, \kappa_1]}|\mathcal{T}^6(\delta)| < \infty$.

The exploration of non-differentiable mappings along with local attributes is a fascinating domain of mathematical sciences. Various strategies have been discussed in literature, including quantum calculus and setups within the fractal domain. Working on that problem, Yang defined λ level sets of real numbers and the operations over them. Also, he published two monographs, in which fractal calculus and local fractional functional analysis are discussed in detail. Over the years, mathematicians dealing with fractal geometries have been taking the benefit of it. Fractals are those sets whose Hausdorff dimension is greater than topological dimensions, and Hausdorff dimension measures the complexity.

Now, we recall the basics of Yang calculus.

Yang Local Fractional Calculus

In this section, we recall the basic concepts of local fractional calculus which are essential to our main findings given in [10].

- $\mathbb{Z}^\lambda := \{\pm 0^\lambda, \pm 1^\lambda, \pm 2^\lambda, \ldots\}$,
- $\mathbb{Q}^\lambda := \{v^\lambda = \left(\frac{r_1}{r_2}\right)^\lambda : r_1, r_2 \in \mathbb{Z}, r_2 \neq 0\}$,
- $\mathbb{Q}'^\lambda := \{v^\lambda \neq \left(\frac{r_1}{r_2}\right)^\lambda : r_1, r_2 \in \mathbb{Z}, r_2 \neq 0\}$,
- $\mathbb{R}^\lambda := \mathbb{Q}^\lambda \cup \mathbb{Q}'^\lambda$.

Also, the multiplication and addition are defined as

$$c^\lambda * d^\lambda = c^\lambda d^\lambda := (cd)^\lambda \quad \text{and} \quad c^\lambda + d^\lambda := (c + d)^\lambda$$

and both $c^\lambda d^\lambda, c^\lambda + d^\lambda \in \mathbb{R}^\lambda$. Clearly, $(\mathbb{R}^\lambda, +, *)$ is a field.

The local fractional continuity is defined as follows.

Definition 2 ([10]). *The local fractional derivative of $\mathcal{T}(\delta)$ of order λ at $\delta = \delta_0$ is described as*

$$\mathcal{T}^\lambda(\delta) = {}_{\delta_0}D_\delta^\lambda \mathcal{T}(\delta) = \left.\frac{\mathrm{d}^\lambda \mathcal{T}(\delta)}{(\mathrm{d}\delta)^\lambda}\right|_{\delta=\delta_0} = \lim_{\delta \to \delta_0} \frac{\Delta^\lambda(\mathcal{T}(\delta) - \mathcal{T}(\delta_0))}{(\delta - \delta_0)^\lambda}.$$

where $\Delta^\lambda(\mathcal{T}(\delta) - \mathcal{T}(\delta_0)) = \Gamma(1 + \lambda)(\mathcal{T}(\delta) - \mathcal{T}(\delta_0))$. Let $s \in \mathbb{N}$ and $\mathcal{T}^\lambda(\delta) = D_\delta^\lambda \mathcal{T}(\delta)$. If

$$\mathcal{T}^{(s+1)\lambda}(\delta) = \overbrace{D_\delta^\lambda \mathcal{T}(\delta) \cdot D_\delta^\lambda \mathcal{T}(\delta) \cdots D_\delta^\lambda \mathcal{T}(\delta)}^{(s+1)\ times} \text{ exists for any } \delta \in [\nu_1, \kappa_1],$$

then we say $\mathcal{T} \in D_{(s+1)\lambda}$.

We now present the local anti-derivative operator of $\mathcal{T}(\delta) \in C_\lambda(\nu_1, \kappa_1)$.

Definition 3 ([10]). *Let* $\triangle = \{\delta_0, \delta_1, \delta_2, \ldots, \delta_i, \delta_{i+1}, \ldots, \delta_\sigma\}$, *where* $\sigma \in \mathbb{N}$, *be a division of* $[\nu_1, \kappa_1]$ *such that* $\delta_0 < \delta_1 < \delta_2 < \ldots < \delta_\sigma$. *Then the local fractional integral of* $\mathcal{T}$ *on* $[\nu_1, \kappa_1]$ *is defined by*

$$ {}_{\nu_1}I^{\lambda}_{\kappa_1}\mathcal{T}(\delta) = \frac{1}{\Gamma(1+\lambda)} \int_{\nu_1}^{\kappa_1} \Psi(\delta)(\mathrm{d}\delta)^{\lambda} = \frac{1}{\Gamma(1+\lambda)} \lim_{\triangle\delta_i \to 0} \sum_{i=1}^{\sigma} \mathcal{T}(\delta_i)(\triangle\delta)^{\lambda}, $$

where $\triangle\delta_i = \delta_{i+1} - \delta_i$ *for* $i = 1, 2, 3 \ldots \sigma$. *The space of all local integrable mappings is represented by* $I^{\lambda}_{\delta}[\nu_1, \kappa_1]$.

From the above, one can easily conclude that ${}_{\nu_1}I^{\lambda}_{\kappa_1}\mathcal{T}(\delta) = 0$ if $\nu_1 = \kappa_1$ and ${}_{\nu_1}I^{\lambda}_{\kappa_1}\mathcal{T}(\delta) = -{}_{\kappa_1}I^{\lambda}_{\nu_1}\mathcal{T}(\delta)$ when $\nu_1 < \kappa_1$. Now, we present some significant findings about integration and local derivatives that will help us in our future work.

Lemma 1. *Consider* $0 < \lambda \leq 1$. *If* $\mathcal{T}(\delta) = r^{\lambda}(\delta) \in C_{\lambda}[\nu_1, \kappa_1]$. *Then*

$$ {}_{\nu_1}I^{\lambda}_{\kappa_1} g(\delta) = r(\kappa_1) - r(\nu_1). $$

Furthermore, we have

$$ \frac{\mathrm{d}^{\lambda}\delta^{s\lambda}}{(\mathrm{d}\delta)^{\lambda}} = \frac{\Gamma(1+s\lambda)}{\Gamma(1+(s-1)\lambda)}\delta^{(s-1)\lambda} $$

and

$$ \frac{1}{\Gamma(1+\lambda)} \int_{\nu_1}^{\kappa_1} \delta^{s\lambda}(\mathrm{d}\delta)^{\lambda} = \frac{\Gamma(1+s\lambda)}{\Gamma(1+(s+1)\lambda)} \left({\kappa_1}^{(s+1)\lambda} - {\nu_1}^{(s+1)\lambda} \right). $$

The fractal calculus has been utilized to study new mathematical inequalities. Motivated by ongoing research in this area, Mo et al. in [11] generalized the concept of convexity in fractal space as follows.

Definition 4. *A mapping* $\mathcal{T} : [\nu_1, \kappa_1] \to \mathbb{R}^{\lambda}$ *is known-as generalized convex in fractal space if*

$$ \mathcal{T}(\varepsilon\nu_1 + (1-\varepsilon)\kappa_1) \leq \varepsilon^{\lambda}\mathcal{T}(\nu_1) + (1-\varepsilon)^{\lambda}\mathcal{T}(\kappa_1) \tag{3} $$

for all $\varepsilon \in [0,1]$ *and* $0 < \lambda \leq 1$.

The trapezoidal inequality in fractal space is given next. For more details, see [11].

Theorem 6. *Let* $\mathcal{T} : [\nu_1, \kappa_1] \to \mathbb{R}^{\lambda}$ *be a generalized convex mapping, where* $0 < \lambda \leq 1$. *Then,*

$$ \mathcal{T}\left(\frac{\nu_1 + \kappa_1}{2}\right) \leq \frac{\Gamma(1+\lambda)}{(\kappa_1 - \nu_1)^{\lambda}} {}_{\nu_1}I^{\lambda}_{\kappa_1}\mathcal{T}(\delta) \leq \frac{\mathcal{T}(\nu_1) + \mathcal{T}(\kappa_1)}{2^{\lambda}}. \tag{4} $$

Sarikaya and Budak [12] utilized the generalized convexity within the framework of Yang local calculus to investigate the weighted Hadamard's type inequalities. In [13,14], the authors considered the local fractional operators along with generalized convexity to study the various error inequalities. In [15], Erden and Sarikaya explored the mean value theorem and some Pompeiu-like inequalities leveraging the concept of Yang calculus. Almutairi and Kilicman [16] investigated the trapezium-type inequalities through generalized Breckner convexity.

Lou et al. [17] discussed the fractal weighted Hadamard's inequalities through generalized convexity and also delivered the utility of results. In [18], the authors focused on the applications of Hermite–Hadamard-like inequalities in signal processing. Butt et al. [19]

proved the Jensen's type in inequalities in fractal space and developed some new counterparts of Hadamard–Mercer-like inequalities. Luo et al. [20] worked on improved Hölder's inequalities and their applications to construct some Simpson-like inequalities. Alsharari et al. [21] bridged the fractional operator and local Yang calculus to approximate the error bounds of Simpson's rule. Meftah et al. [22] looked at error analysis of Milne rules considering generalized convexity within fractal calculus. Liu et al. [23] presented upper bounds of fractional Maclaurin's inequality and presented the applications to nonlinear analysis. In [24], the authors proved some new advancements in Ostrowski's inequalities relying on Mercer inequality for fractal Breckner convexity. For more details see [25–28].

Motivation and Structure of Study: Over the years authors have tried several approaches to assess the bounds of local fractional operators, the average value of fractal mappings, and the error analysis of Newton-Cotes schemes within the context of Yang fractal calculus. It is a common fact that approximations through higher-order polynomials show minimum error. The Generalized Weddle's procedure is superior due to better accuracy and minimum error as compared to Simpson's and Newton's procedures. Here are the few questions that elaborate on the need for the study.

- How can the error terms of Weddle's rule be established for local fractional differentiable mappings? Mathematically,

$$\left|\frac{1}{(20)^{\lambda}}\left[\mathcal{T}(\nu_1)+5^{\lambda}\mathcal{T}\left(\frac{5\nu_1+\kappa_1}{6}\right)+\mathcal{T}\left(\frac{2\nu_1+\kappa_1}{3}\right)+6^{\lambda}\mathcal{T}\left(\frac{\nu_1+\kappa_1}{2}\right)\right.\right.$$
$$\left.\left.+\mathcal{T}\left(\frac{\nu_1+2\kappa_1}{3}\right)+5^{\lambda}\mathcal{T}\left(\frac{\nu_1+5\kappa_1}{6}\right)+\mathcal{T}(\kappa_1)\right]-\frac{\Gamma(1+\lambda)}{(\kappa_1-\nu_1)^{\lambda}}{}_{\nu_1}I_{\kappa_1}\mathcal{T}(\delta)\right|\leq ?$$

- How different generalized classes of mappings can be used to evaluate the bounds of the above inequality?
- What are the applications of the proposed bounds?
- How can the bounds of several local fractional integrals be found incorporated with the proposed inequalities?

To address these problems, we have organized this study into multiple steps. First, we discuss the research problem background and fundamental concepts to carry out the further proceedings. Our approach includes the generation of error bounds through identity. In the following context, we will construct a fractal identity, which will later on be helpful to estimate our main findings. At the end of each result, we provide its 2D and 3D graphical validations. Lastly, some applicable analysis will be discussed. To the extent of our knowledge, this approach is new and novel for discussing error bounds of fractal Newton–Cotes schemes.

2. Fractal Estimates of Weddle's Inequality

The space of fractal integrable mappings is denoted by $L[\nu_1,\kappa_1]$.

Lemma 2. *If $\mathcal{T}:[\nu_1,\kappa_1]\to\mathbb{R}$ is a local differentiable mapping and $\mathcal{T}^{\lambda}\in L[\nu_1,\kappa_1]$, then*

$$W(\nu_1,\kappa_1)-\frac{\Gamma(1+\lambda)}{(\kappa_1-\nu_1)^{\lambda}}{}_{\nu_1}I_{\kappa_1}\mathcal{T}(\delta)$$
$$=\left(\frac{\kappa_1-\nu_1}{2}\right)^{\lambda}\frac{1}{\Gamma(1+\lambda)}\int_0^1\triangle(\varepsilon)\left[\mathcal{T}^{\lambda}((1-\varepsilon)\nu_1+\varepsilon\kappa_1)-\mathcal{T}^{\lambda}(\varepsilon\nu_1+(1-\varepsilon)\kappa_1)\right](d\varepsilon)^{\lambda},\quad(5)$$

where

$$\triangle(\varepsilon)=\begin{cases}\left(\varepsilon-\frac{1}{20}\right)^{\lambda}, & \varepsilon\in\left[0,\frac{1}{6}\right),\\ \left(\varepsilon-\frac{6}{20}\right)^{\lambda}, & \varepsilon\in\left[\frac{1}{6},\frac{1}{3}\right),\\ \left(\varepsilon-\frac{7}{20}\right)^{\lambda}, & \varepsilon\in\left[\frac{1}{3},\frac{1}{2}\right),\\ \left(\varepsilon-\frac{13}{20}\right)^{\lambda}, & \varepsilon\in\left[\frac{1}{2},\frac{2}{3}\right),\\ \left(\varepsilon-\frac{14}{20}\right)^{\lambda}, & \varepsilon\in\left[\frac{2}{3},\frac{5}{6}\right),\\ \left(\varepsilon-\frac{19}{20}\right)^{\lambda}, & \varepsilon\in\left[\frac{5}{6},1\right],\end{cases}$$

and

$$\begin{aligned}&W(\nu_1,\kappa_1)\\ &=\frac{1}{(20)^{\lambda}}\left[\mathcal{T}(\nu_1)+5^{\lambda}\mathcal{T}\left(\frac{5\nu_1+\kappa_1}{6}\right)+\mathcal{T}\left(\frac{2\nu_1+\kappa_1}{3}\right)\right.\\ &\quad\left.+6^{\lambda}\mathcal{T}\left(\frac{\nu_1+\kappa_1}{2}\right)+\mathcal{T}\left(\frac{\nu_1+2\kappa_1}{3}\right)+5^{\lambda}\mathcal{T}\left(\frac{\nu_1+5\kappa_1}{6}\right)+\mathcal{T}(\kappa_1)\right].\end{aligned}$$

Proof. From the definition of $\triangle(\varepsilon)$, we have

$$\begin{aligned}&\frac{1}{\Gamma(1+\lambda)}\int_0^1\triangle(\varepsilon)\left[\mathcal{T}^{\lambda}((1-\varepsilon)\nu_1+\varepsilon\kappa_1)-\mathcal{T}^{\lambda}(\varepsilon\nu_1+(1-\varepsilon)\kappa_1)\right](d\varepsilon)^{\lambda}\\ &=\frac{1}{\Gamma(1+\lambda)}\int_0^{\frac{1}{6}}\left(\varepsilon-\frac{1}{20}\right)^{\lambda}\mathcal{T}^{\lambda}((1-\varepsilon)\nu_1+\varepsilon\kappa_1)(d\varepsilon)^{\lambda}\\ &\quad+\frac{1}{\Gamma(1+\lambda)}\int_{\frac{1}{6}}^{\frac{1}{3}}\left(\varepsilon-\frac{6}{20}\right)^{\lambda}\mathcal{T}^{\lambda}((1-\varepsilon)\nu_1+\varepsilon\kappa_1)(d\varepsilon)^{\lambda}\\ &\quad+\frac{1}{\Gamma(1+\lambda)}\int_{\frac{1}{3}}^{\frac{1}{2}}\left(\varepsilon-\frac{7}{20}\right)^{\lambda}\mathcal{T}^{\lambda}((1-\varepsilon)\nu_1+\varepsilon\kappa_1)(d\varepsilon)^{\lambda}\\ &\quad+\frac{1}{\Gamma(1+\lambda)}\int_{\frac{1}{2}}^{\frac{2}{3}}\left(\varepsilon-\frac{13}{20}\right)^{\lambda}\mathcal{T}^{\lambda}((1-\varepsilon)\nu_1+\varepsilon\kappa_1)(d\varepsilon)^{\lambda}\\ &\quad+\frac{1}{\Gamma(1+\lambda)}\int_{\frac{2}{3}}^{\frac{5}{6}}\left(\varepsilon-\frac{14}{20}\right)^{\lambda}\mathcal{T}^{\lambda}((1-\varepsilon)\nu_1+\varepsilon\kappa_1)(d\varepsilon)^{\lambda}\\ &\quad+\frac{1}{\Gamma(1+\lambda)}\int_{\frac{5}{6}}^{1}\left(\varepsilon-\frac{19}{20}\right)^{\lambda}\mathcal{T}^{\lambda}((1-\varepsilon)\nu_1+\varepsilon\kappa_1)(d\varepsilon)^{\lambda}\\ &\quad+\frac{1}{\Gamma(1+\lambda)}\int_0^{\frac{1}{6}}\left(\frac{1}{20}-\varepsilon\right)^{\lambda}\mathcal{T}^{\lambda}(\varepsilon\nu_1+(1-\varepsilon)\kappa_1)(d\varepsilon)^{\lambda}\\ &\quad+\frac{1}{\Gamma(1+\lambda)}\int_{\frac{1}{6}}^{\frac{1}{3}}\left(\frac{6}{20}-\varepsilon\right)^{\lambda}\mathcal{T}^{\lambda}(\varepsilon\nu_1+(1-\varepsilon)\kappa_1)(d\varepsilon)^{\lambda}\\ &\quad+\frac{1}{\Gamma(1+\lambda)}\int_{\frac{1}{3}}^{\frac{1}{2}}\left(\frac{7}{20}-\varepsilon\right)^{\lambda}\mathcal{T}^{\lambda}(\varepsilon\nu_1+(1-\varepsilon)\kappa_1)(d\varepsilon)^{\lambda}\\ &\quad+\frac{1}{\Gamma(1+\lambda)}\int_{\frac{1}{2}}^{\frac{2}{3}}\left(\frac{13}{20}-\varepsilon\right)^{\lambda}\mathcal{T}^{\lambda}(\varepsilon\nu_1+(1-\varepsilon)\kappa_1)(d\varepsilon)^{\lambda}\end{aligned}$$

$$
\begin{aligned}
&+\frac{1}{\Gamma(1+\lambda)}\int_{\frac{2}{3}}^{\frac{5}{6}}\left(\frac{14}{20}-\varepsilon\right)^{\lambda}\mathcal{T}^{\lambda}(\varepsilon\nu_1+(1-\varepsilon)\kappa_1)(d\varepsilon)^{\lambda}\\
&+\frac{1}{\Gamma(1+\lambda)}\int_{\frac{5}{6}}^{1}\left(\frac{19}{20}-\varepsilon\right)^{\lambda}\mathcal{T}^{\lambda}(\varepsilon\nu_1+(1-\varepsilon)\kappa_1)(d\varepsilon)^{\lambda}\\
&=\sum_{i=0}^{12} I_i.
\end{aligned}
$$

We can use integration by parts to solve these integrals

$$
\begin{aligned}
I_1 &= \frac{1}{\Gamma(1+\lambda)}\int_{0}^{\frac{1}{6}}\left(\varepsilon-\frac{1}{20}\right)^{\lambda}\mathcal{T}^{\lambda}((1-\varepsilon)\nu_1+\varepsilon\kappa_1)(d\varepsilon)^{\lambda}\\
&= \frac{1}{(\kappa_1-\nu_1)^{\lambda}}\left[\left(\frac{7}{60}\right)^{\lambda}\mathcal{T}\left(\frac{5\nu_1+\kappa_1}{6}\right)+\left(\frac{1}{20}\right)^{\lambda}\mathcal{T}(\nu_1)\right]-\frac{\Gamma(1+\lambda)}{(\kappa_1-\nu_1)^{2\lambda}}\,{}_{\nu_1}I_{\frac{5\nu_1+\kappa_1}{6}}\mathcal{T}(\delta),\\
I_2 &= \frac{1}{\Gamma(1+\lambda)}\int_{\frac{1}{6}}^{\frac{1}{3}}\left(\varepsilon-\frac{6}{20}\right)^{\lambda}\mathcal{T}^{\lambda}((1-\varepsilon)\nu_1+\varepsilon\kappa_1)(d\varepsilon)^{\lambda}\\
&= \frac{1}{(\kappa_1-\nu_1)^{\lambda}}\left[\left(\frac{1}{30}\right)^{\lambda}\mathcal{T}\left(\frac{2\nu_1+\kappa_1}{3}\right)+\left(\frac{2}{15}\right)^{\lambda}\mathcal{T}\left(\frac{5\nu_1+\kappa_1}{6}\right)\right]-\frac{\Gamma(1+\lambda)}{(\kappa_1-\nu_1)^{2\lambda}}\,{}_{\frac{5\nu_1+\kappa_1}{6}}I_{\frac{2\nu_1+\kappa_1}{3}}\mathcal{T}(\delta),\\
I_3 &= \frac{1}{\Gamma(1+\lambda)}\int_{\frac{1}{3}}^{\frac{1}{2}}\left(\varepsilon-\frac{7}{20}\right)^{\lambda}\mathcal{T}^{\lambda}((1-\varepsilon)\nu_1+\varepsilon\kappa_1)(d\varepsilon)^{\lambda}\\
&= \frac{1}{(\kappa_1-\nu_1)^{\lambda}}\left[\left(\frac{3}{20}\right)^{\lambda}\mathcal{T}\left(\frac{\nu_1+\kappa_1}{2}\right)+\left(\frac{1}{60}\right)^{\lambda}\mathcal{T}\left(\frac{2\nu_1+\kappa_1}{3}\right)\right]-\frac{\Gamma(1+\lambda)}{(\kappa_1-\nu_1)^{2\lambda}}\,{}_{\frac{2\nu_1+\kappa_1}{3}}I_{\frac{\nu_1+\kappa_1}{2}}\mathcal{T}(\delta),\\
I_4 &= \frac{1}{\Gamma(1+\lambda)}\int_{\frac{1}{2}}^{\frac{2}{3}}\left(\varepsilon-\frac{13}{20}\right)^{\lambda}\mathcal{T}^{\lambda}((1-\varepsilon)\nu_1+\varepsilon\kappa_1)(d\varepsilon)^{\lambda}\\
&= \frac{1}{(\kappa_1-\nu_1)^{\lambda}}\left[\left(\frac{1}{60}\right)^{\lambda}\mathcal{T}\left(\frac{\nu_1+2\kappa_1}{3}\right)+\left(\frac{3}{20}\right)^{\lambda}\mathcal{T}\left(\frac{\nu_1+\kappa_1}{2}\right)\right]-\frac{\Gamma(1+\lambda)}{(\kappa_1-\nu_1)^{2\lambda}}\,{}_{\frac{\nu_1+\kappa_1}{2}}I_{\frac{\nu_1+2\kappa_1}{3}}\mathcal{T}(\delta),\\
I_5 &= \frac{1}{\Gamma(1+\lambda)}\int_{\frac{2}{3}}^{\frac{5}{6}}\left(\varepsilon-\frac{14}{20}\right)^{\lambda}\mathcal{T}^{\lambda}((1-\varepsilon)\nu_1+\varepsilon\kappa_1)(d\varepsilon)^{\lambda}\\
&= \frac{1}{(\kappa_1-\nu_1)^{\lambda}}\left[\left(\frac{2}{15}\right)^{\lambda}\mathcal{T}\left(\frac{\nu_1+5\kappa_1}{6}\right)+\left(\frac{1}{30}\right)^{\lambda}\mathcal{T}\left(\frac{\nu_1+2\kappa_1}{3}\right)\right]-\frac{\Gamma(1+\lambda)}{(\kappa_1-\nu_1)^{2\lambda}}\,{}_{\frac{\nu_1+2\kappa_1}{3}}I_{\frac{\nu_1+5\kappa_1}{6}}\mathcal{T}(\delta),\\
I_6 &= \frac{1}{\Gamma(1+\lambda)}\int_{\frac{5}{6}}^{1}\left(\varepsilon-\frac{19}{20}\right)^{\lambda}\mathcal{T}^{\lambda}((1-\varepsilon)\nu_1+\varepsilon\kappa_1)(d\varepsilon)^{\lambda}\\
&= \frac{1}{(\kappa_1-\nu_1)^{\lambda}}\left[\left(\frac{1}{20}\right)^{\lambda}\mathcal{T}(\kappa_1)+\left(\frac{7}{60}\right)^{\lambda}\mathcal{T}\left(\frac{\nu_1+5\kappa_1}{6}\right)\right]-\frac{\Gamma(1+\lambda)}{(\kappa_1-\nu_1)^{2\lambda}}\,{}_{\frac{\nu_1+5\kappa_1}{6}}I_{\kappa_1}\mathcal{T}(\delta),\\
I_7 &= \frac{1}{\Gamma(1+\lambda)}\int_{0}^{\frac{1}{6}}\left(\frac{1}{20}-\varepsilon\right)^{\lambda}\mathcal{T}^{\lambda}(\varepsilon\nu_1+(1-\varepsilon)\kappa_1)(d\varepsilon)^{\lambda}\\
&= \frac{1}{(\kappa_1-\nu_1)^{\lambda}}\left[\left(\frac{7}{60}\right)^{\lambda}\mathcal{T}\left(\frac{\nu_1+5\kappa_1}{6}\right)+\left(\frac{1}{20}\right)^{\lambda}\mathcal{T}(\kappa_1)\right]-\frac{\Gamma(1+\lambda)}{(\kappa_1-\nu_1)^{2\lambda}}\,{}_{\frac{5\nu_1+\kappa_1}{6}}I_{\kappa_1}\mathcal{T}(\delta),\\
I_8 &= \frac{1}{\Gamma(1+\lambda)}\int_{\frac{1}{6}}^{\frac{1}{3}}\left(\frac{6}{20}-\varepsilon\right)^{\lambda}\mathcal{T}^{\lambda}(\varepsilon\nu_1+(1-\varepsilon)\kappa_1)(d\varepsilon)^{\lambda}\\
&= \frac{1}{(\kappa_1-\nu_1)^{\lambda}}\left[\left(\frac{2}{15}\right)^{\lambda}\mathcal{T}\left(\frac{\nu_1+5\kappa_1}{6}\right)+\left(\frac{1}{30}\right)^{\lambda}\mathcal{T}\left(\frac{\nu_1+2\kappa_1}{3}\right)\right]-\frac{\Gamma(1+\lambda)}{(\kappa_1-\nu_1)^{2\lambda}}\,{}_{\frac{\nu_1+2\kappa_1}{3}}I_{\frac{\nu_1+5\kappa_1}{6}}\mathcal{T}(\delta),\\
I_9 &= \frac{1}{\Gamma(1+\lambda)}\int_{\frac{1}{3}}^{\frac{1}{2}}\left(\frac{7}{20}-\varepsilon\right)^{\lambda}\mathcal{T}^{\lambda}(\varepsilon\nu_1+(1-\varepsilon)\kappa_1)(d\varepsilon)^{\lambda}\\
&= \frac{1}{(\kappa_1-\nu_1)^{\lambda}}\left[\left(\frac{1}{60}\right)^{\lambda}\mathcal{T}\left(\frac{\nu_1+2\kappa_1}{3}\right)+\left(\frac{3}{20}\right)^{\lambda}\mathcal{T}\left(\frac{\nu_1+\kappa_1}{2}\right)\right]-\frac{\Gamma(1+\lambda)}{(\kappa_1-\nu_1)^{2\lambda}}\,{}_{\frac{\nu_1+\kappa_1}{2}}I_{\frac{\nu_1+2\kappa_1}{3}}\mathcal{T}(\delta),
\end{aligned}
$$

$$I_{10} = \frac{1}{\Gamma(1+\lambda)}\int_{\frac{1}{2}}^{\frac{2}{3}}\left(\frac{13}{20}-\varepsilon\right)^{\lambda}\mathcal{T}^{\lambda}(\varepsilon\nu_1+(1-\varepsilon)\kappa_1)(d\varepsilon)^{\lambda}$$
$$= \frac{1}{(\kappa_1-\nu_1)^{\lambda}}\left[\left(\frac{3}{20}\right)^{\lambda}\mathcal{T}\left(\frac{\nu_1+\kappa_1}{2}\right)+\left(\frac{1}{60}\right)^{\lambda}\mathcal{T}\left(\frac{2\nu_1+\kappa_1}{3}\right)\right]-\frac{\Gamma(1+\lambda)}{(\kappa_1-\nu_1)^{2\lambda}}\,{}_{\frac{2\nu_1+\kappa_1}{3}}I_{\frac{\nu_1+\kappa_1}{2}}\mathcal{T}(\delta),$$
$$I_{11} = \frac{1}{\Gamma(1+\lambda)}\int_{\frac{2}{3}}^{\frac{5}{6}}\left(\frac{14}{20}-\varepsilon\right)^{\lambda}\mathcal{T}^{\lambda}(\varepsilon\nu_1+(1-\varepsilon)\kappa_1)(d\varepsilon)^{\lambda}$$
$$= \frac{1}{(\kappa_1-\nu_1)^{\lambda}}\left[\left(\frac{1}{30}\right)^{\lambda}\mathcal{T}\left(\frac{2\nu_1+\kappa_1}{3}\right)+\left(\frac{2}{15}\right)^{\lambda}\mathcal{T}\left(\frac{5\nu_1+\kappa_1}{6}\right)\right]-\frac{\Gamma(1+\lambda)}{(\kappa_1-\nu_1)^{2\lambda}}\,{}_{\frac{5\nu_1+\kappa_1}{6}}I_{\frac{2\nu_1+\kappa_1}{3}}\mathcal{T}(\delta),$$
$$I_{12} = \frac{1}{\Gamma(1+\lambda)}\int_{\frac{5}{6}}^{1}\left(\frac{19}{20}-\varepsilon\right)^{\lambda}\mathcal{T}^{\lambda}(\varepsilon\nu_1+(1-\varepsilon)\kappa_1)(d\varepsilon)^{\lambda}$$
$$= \frac{1}{(\kappa_1-\nu_1)^{\lambda}}\left[\left(\frac{1}{20}\right)^{\lambda}\mathcal{T}(\nu_1)+\left(\frac{7}{60}\right)^{\lambda}\mathcal{T}\left(\frac{5\nu_1+\kappa_1}{6}\right)\right]-\frac{\Gamma(1+\lambda)}{(\kappa_1-\nu_1)^{2\lambda}}\,{}_{\nu_1}I_{\frac{5\nu_1+\kappa_1}{6}}\mathcal{T}(\delta).$$

Now, by taking $\sum_{i=0}^{12} I_i$ and after simple computations we get (5). It ends the proof. □

Now we establish the first bound for Weddle's rule.

Theorem 7. *Suppose that all constraints of lemma 2 are fulfilled. If $|\mathcal{T}^{\lambda}|$ is a generalized convex mapping, then*

$$\left|W(\nu_1,\kappa_1)-\frac{\Gamma(1+\lambda)}{(\kappa_1-\nu_1)^{\lambda}}\,{}_{\nu_1}I_{\kappa_1}\mathcal{T}(\delta)\right|$$
$$\leq (\kappa_1-\nu_1)^{\lambda}\left\{\left[\frac{\Gamma(1+\lambda)}{\Gamma(1+2\lambda)}\left(\frac{4}{75}\right)^{\lambda}+\frac{\Gamma(1+2\lambda)}{\Gamma(1+3\lambda)}\left(\frac{1}{150}\right)^{\lambda}\right]|\mathcal{T}^{\lambda}(\nu_1)|\right.$$
$$\left.+\left[\frac{\Gamma(1+\lambda)}{\Gamma(1+2\lambda)}\left(\frac{14}{225}\right)^{\lambda}-\frac{\Gamma(1+2\lambda)}{\Gamma(1+3\lambda)}\left(\frac{1}{150}\right)^{\lambda}\right]|\mathcal{T}^{\lambda}(\kappa_1)|\right\}.$$

Proof. Through Lemma 2 and generalized convexity of $|\mathcal{T}^{\lambda}|$, we have

$$\left|W(\nu_1,\kappa_1)-\frac{\Gamma(1+\lambda)}{(\kappa_1-\nu_1)^{\lambda}}\,{}_{a}I_{\kappa_1}\mathcal{T}(\delta)\right|$$
$$\leq \left(\frac{\kappa_1-\nu_1}{2}\right)^{\lambda}\frac{1}{\Gamma(1+\lambda)}\int_0^1|\triangle(\varepsilon)|\left|\mathcal{T}^{\lambda}((1-\varepsilon)\nu_1+\varepsilon\kappa_1)-\mathcal{T}^{\lambda}(\varepsilon\nu_1+(1-\varepsilon)\kappa_1)\right|(d\varepsilon)^{\lambda}$$
$$\leq \left(\frac{\kappa_1-\nu_1}{2}\right)^{\lambda}\left[\frac{1}{\Gamma(1+\lambda)}\int_0^{\frac{1}{6}}\left|\varepsilon-\frac{1}{20}\right|^{\lambda}\left|\mathcal{T}^{\lambda}((1-\varepsilon)\nu_1+\varepsilon\kappa_1)\right|(d\varepsilon)^{\lambda}\right.$$
$$+\frac{1}{\Gamma(1+\lambda)}\int_{\frac{1}{6}}^{\frac{1}{3}}\left|\varepsilon-\frac{6}{20}\right|^{\lambda}\left|\mathcal{T}^{\lambda}((1-\varepsilon)\nu_1+\varepsilon\kappa_1)\right|(d\varepsilon)^{\lambda}$$
$$+\frac{1}{\Gamma(1+\lambda)}\int_{\frac{1}{3}}^{\frac{1}{2}}\left|\varepsilon-\frac{7}{20}\right|^{\lambda}\left|\mathcal{T}^{\lambda}((1-\varepsilon)\nu_1+\varepsilon\kappa_1)\right|(d\varepsilon)^{\lambda}$$
$$+\frac{1}{\Gamma(1+\lambda)}\int_{\frac{1}{2}}^{\frac{2}{3}}\left|\varepsilon-\frac{13}{20}\right|^{\lambda}\left|\mathcal{T}^{\lambda}((1-\varepsilon)\nu_1+\varepsilon\kappa_1)\right|(d\varepsilon)^{\lambda}$$
$$+\frac{1}{\Gamma(1+\lambda)}\int_{\frac{2}{3}}^{\frac{5}{6}}\left|\varepsilon-\frac{14}{20}\right|^{\lambda}\left|\mathcal{T}^{\lambda}((1-\varepsilon)\nu_1+\varepsilon\kappa_1)\right|(d\varepsilon)^{\lambda}$$
$$+\frac{1}{\Gamma(1+\lambda)}\int_{\frac{5}{6}}^{1}\left|\varepsilon-\frac{19}{20}\right|^{\lambda}\left|\mathcal{T}^{\lambda}((1-\varepsilon)\nu_1+\varepsilon\kappa_1)\right|(d\varepsilon)^{\lambda}$$
$$+\frac{1}{\Gamma(1+\lambda)}\int_0^{\frac{1}{6}}\left|\frac{1}{20}-\varepsilon\right|^{\lambda}\left|\mathcal{T}^{\lambda}(\varepsilon\nu_1+(1-\varepsilon)\kappa_1)\right|(d\varepsilon)^{\lambda}$$

$$+\frac{1}{\Gamma(1+\lambda)}\int_{\frac{1}{6}}^{\frac{1}{3}}\left|\frac{6}{20}-\varepsilon\right|^{\lambda}\left|\mathcal{T}^{\lambda}(\varepsilon\nu_1+(1-\varepsilon)\kappa_1)\right|(d\varepsilon)^{\lambda}$$
$$+\frac{1}{\Gamma(1+\lambda)}\int_{\frac{1}{3}}^{\frac{1}{2}}\left|\frac{7}{20}-\varepsilon\right|^{\lambda}\left|\mathcal{T}^{\lambda}(\varepsilon\nu_1+(1-\varepsilon)\kappa_1)\right|(d\varepsilon)^{\lambda}$$
$$+\frac{1}{\Gamma(1+\lambda)}\int_{\frac{1}{2}}^{\frac{2}{3}}\left|\frac{13}{20}-\varepsilon\right|^{\lambda}\left|\mathcal{T}^{\lambda}(\varepsilon\nu_1+(1-\varepsilon)\kappa_1)\right|(d\varepsilon)^{\lambda}$$
$$+\frac{1}{\Gamma(1+\lambda)}\int_{\frac{2}{3}}^{\frac{5}{6}}\left|\frac{14}{20}-\varepsilon\right|^{\lambda}\left|\mathcal{T}^{\lambda}(\varepsilon\nu_1+(1-\varepsilon)\kappa_1)\right|(d\varepsilon)^{\lambda}$$
$$+\frac{1}{\Gamma(1+\lambda)}\int_{\frac{5}{6}}^{1}\left|\frac{19}{20}-\varepsilon\right|^{\lambda}\left|\mathcal{T}^{\lambda}(\varepsilon\nu_1+(1-\varepsilon)\kappa_1)\right|(d\varepsilon)^{\lambda}\Bigg]$$
$$\leq\left(\frac{\kappa_1-\nu_1}{2}\right)^{\lambda}\Bigg[\frac{1}{\Gamma(1+\lambda)}\int_{0}^{\frac{1}{6}}\left|\varepsilon-\frac{1}{20}\right|^{\lambda}[(1-\varepsilon)^{\lambda}|\mathcal{T}^{\lambda}(\nu_1)|+\varepsilon^{\lambda}|\mathcal{T}^{\lambda}(\kappa_1)|](d\varepsilon)^{\lambda}$$
$$+\frac{1}{\Gamma(1+\lambda)}\int_{\frac{1}{6}}^{\frac{1}{3}}\left|\varepsilon-\frac{6}{20}\right|^{\lambda}[(1-\varepsilon)^{\lambda}|\mathcal{T}^{\lambda}(\nu_1)|+\varepsilon^{\lambda}|\mathcal{T}^{\lambda}(\kappa_1)|](d\varepsilon)^{\lambda}$$
$$+\frac{1}{\Gamma(1+\lambda)}\int_{\frac{1}{3}}^{\frac{1}{2}}\left|\varepsilon-\frac{7}{20}\right|^{\lambda}[(1-\varepsilon)^{\lambda}|\mathcal{T}^{\lambda}(\nu_1)|+\varepsilon^{\lambda}|\mathcal{T}^{\lambda}(\kappa_1)|](d\varepsilon)^{\lambda}$$
$$+\frac{1}{\Gamma(1+\lambda)}\int_{\frac{1}{2}}^{\frac{2}{3}}\left|\varepsilon-\frac{13}{20}\right|^{\lambda}[(1-\varepsilon)^{\lambda}|\mathcal{T}^{\lambda}(\nu_1)|+\varepsilon^{\lambda}|\mathcal{T}^{\lambda}(\kappa_1)|](d\varepsilon)^{\lambda}$$
$$+\frac{1}{\Gamma(1+\lambda)}\int_{\frac{2}{3}}^{\frac{5}{6}}\left|\varepsilon-\frac{14}{20}\right|^{\lambda}[(1-\varepsilon)^{\lambda}|\mathcal{T}^{\lambda}(\nu_1)|+\varepsilon^{\lambda}|\mathcal{T}^{\lambda}(\kappa_1)|](d\varepsilon)^{\lambda}$$
$$+\frac{1}{\Gamma(1+\lambda)}\int_{\frac{5}{6}}^{1}\left|\varepsilon-\frac{19}{20}\right|^{\lambda}[(1-\varepsilon)^{\lambda}|\mathcal{T}^{\lambda}(\nu_1)|+\varepsilon^{\lambda}|\mathcal{T}^{\lambda}(\kappa_1)|](d\varepsilon)^{\lambda}$$
$$+\frac{1}{\Gamma(1+\lambda)}\int_{0}^{\frac{1}{6}}\left|\frac{1}{20}-\varepsilon\right|^{\lambda}[\varepsilon^{\lambda}|\mathcal{T}^{\lambda}(\nu_1)|+(1-\varepsilon)^{\lambda}|\mathcal{T}^{\lambda}(\kappa_1)|](d\varepsilon)^{\lambda}$$
$$+\frac{1}{\Gamma(1+\lambda)}\int_{\frac{1}{6}}^{\frac{1}{3}}\left|\frac{6}{20}-\varepsilon\right|^{\lambda}[\varepsilon^{\lambda}|\mathcal{T}^{\lambda}(\nu_1)|+(1-\varepsilon)^{\lambda}|\mathcal{T}^{\lambda}(\kappa_1)|](d\varepsilon)^{\lambda}$$
$$+\frac{1}{\Gamma(1+\lambda)}\int_{\frac{1}{3}}^{\frac{1}{2}}\left|\frac{7}{20}-\varepsilon\right|^{\lambda}[\varepsilon^{\lambda}|\mathcal{T}^{\lambda}(\nu_1)|+(1-\varepsilon)^{\lambda}|\mathcal{T}^{\lambda}(\kappa_1)|](d\varepsilon)^{\lambda}$$
$$+\frac{1}{\Gamma(1+\lambda)}\int_{\frac{1}{2}}^{\frac{2}{3}}\left|\frac{13}{20}-\varepsilon\right|^{\lambda}[\varepsilon^{\lambda}|\mathcal{T}^{\lambda}(\nu_1)|+(1-\varepsilon)^{\lambda}|\mathcal{T}^{\lambda}(\kappa_1)|](d\varepsilon)^{\lambda}$$
$$+\frac{1}{\Gamma(1+\lambda)}\int_{\frac{2}{3}}^{\frac{5}{6}}\left|\frac{14}{20}-\varepsilon\right|^{\lambda}[\varepsilon^{\lambda}|\mathcal{T}^{\lambda}(\nu_1)|+(1-\varepsilon)^{\lambda}|\mathcal{T}^{\lambda}(\kappa_1)|](d\varepsilon)^{\lambda}$$
$$+\frac{1}{\Gamma(1+\lambda)}\int_{\frac{5}{6}}^{1}\left|\frac{19}{20}-\varepsilon\right|^{\lambda}[\varepsilon^{\lambda}|\mathcal{T}^{\lambda}(\nu_1)|+(1-\varepsilon)^{\lambda}|\mathcal{T}^{\lambda}(\kappa_1)|](d\varepsilon)^{\lambda}\Bigg]$$
$$=\left(\frac{\kappa_1-\nu_1}{2}\right)^{\lambda}\Bigg[\frac{1}{\Gamma(1+\lambda)}\int_{0}^{\frac{1}{20}}\left(\frac{1}{20}-\varepsilon\right)^{\lambda}[(1-\varepsilon)^{\lambda}|\mathcal{T}^{\lambda}(\nu_1)|+\varepsilon^{\lambda}|\mathcal{T}^{\lambda}(\kappa_1)|](d\varepsilon)^{\lambda}$$
$$+\frac{1}{\Gamma(1+\lambda)}\int_{\frac{1}{20}}^{\frac{1}{6}}\left(\varepsilon-\frac{1}{20}\right)^{\lambda}[(1-\varepsilon)^{\lambda}|\mathcal{T}^{\lambda}(\nu_1)|+\varepsilon^{\lambda}|\mathcal{T}^{\lambda}(\kappa_1)|](d\varepsilon)^{\lambda}$$
$$+\frac{1}{\Gamma(1+\lambda)}\int_{\frac{1}{6}}^{\frac{6}{20}}\left(\frac{6}{20}-\varepsilon\right)^{\lambda}[(1-\varepsilon)^{\lambda}|\mathcal{T}^{\lambda}(\nu_1)|+\varepsilon^{\lambda}|\mathcal{T}^{\lambda}(\kappa_1)|](d\varepsilon)^{\lambda}$$
$$+\frac{1}{\Gamma(1+\lambda)}\int_{\frac{6}{20}}^{\frac{1}{3}}\left(\varepsilon-\frac{6}{20}\right)^{\lambda}[(1-\varepsilon)^{\lambda}|\mathcal{T}^{\lambda}(\nu_1)|+\varepsilon^{\lambda}|\mathcal{T}^{\lambda}(\kappa_1)|](d\varepsilon)^{\lambda}$$
$$+\frac{1}{\Gamma(1+\lambda)}\int_{\frac{1}{3}}^{\frac{7}{20}}\left(\frac{7}{20}-\varepsilon\right)^{\lambda}[(1-\varepsilon)^{\lambda}|\mathcal{T}^{\lambda}(\nu_1)|+\varepsilon^{\lambda}|\mathcal{T}^{\lambda}(\kappa_1)|](d\varepsilon)^{\lambda}$$

$$
\begin{aligned}
&+\frac{1}{\Gamma(1+\lambda)}\int_{\frac{7}{20}}^{\frac{1}{2}}\left(\varepsilon-\frac{7}{20}\right)^{\lambda}[(1-\varepsilon)^{\lambda}|\mathcal{T}^{\lambda}(\nu_1)|+\varepsilon^{\lambda}|\mathcal{T}^{\lambda}(\kappa_1)|](d\varepsilon)^{\lambda}\\
&+\frac{1}{\Gamma(1+\lambda)}\int_{\frac{1}{2}}^{\frac{13}{20}}\left(\frac{13}{20}-\varepsilon\right)^{\lambda}[(1-\varepsilon)^{\lambda}|\mathcal{T}^{\lambda}(\nu_1)|+\varepsilon^{\lambda}|\mathcal{T}^{\lambda}(\kappa_1)|](d\varepsilon)^{\lambda}\\
&+\frac{1}{\Gamma(1+\lambda)}\int_{\frac{13}{20}}^{\frac{2}{3}}\left(\varepsilon-\frac{13}{20}\right)^{\lambda}[(1-\varepsilon)^{\lambda}|\mathcal{T}^{\lambda}(\nu_1)|+\varepsilon^{\lambda}|\mathcal{T}^{\lambda}(\kappa_1)|](d\varepsilon)^{\lambda}\\
&+\frac{1}{\Gamma(1+\lambda)}\int_{\frac{2}{3}}^{\frac{14}{20}}\left(\frac{14}{20}-\varepsilon\right)^{\lambda}[(1-\varepsilon)^{\lambda}|\mathcal{T}^{\lambda}(\nu_1)|+\varepsilon^{\lambda}|\mathcal{T}^{\lambda}(\kappa_1)|](d\varepsilon)^{\lambda}\\
&+\frac{1}{\Gamma(1+\lambda)}\int_{\frac{14}{20}}^{\frac{5}{6}}\left(\varepsilon-\frac{14}{20}\right)^{\lambda}[(1-\varepsilon)^{\lambda}|\mathcal{T}^{\lambda}(\nu_1)|+\varepsilon^{\lambda}|\mathcal{T}^{\lambda}(\kappa_1)|](d\varepsilon)^{\lambda}\\
&+\frac{1}{\Gamma(1+\lambda)}\int_{\frac{5}{6}}^{\frac{19}{20}}\left(\frac{19}{20}-\varepsilon\right)^{\lambda}[(1-\varepsilon)^{\lambda}|\mathcal{T}^{\lambda}(\nu_1)|+\varepsilon^{\lambda}|\mathcal{T}^{\lambda}(\kappa_1)|](d\varepsilon)^{\lambda}\\
&+\frac{1}{\Gamma(1+\lambda)}\int_{\frac{19}{20}}^{1}\left(\varepsilon-\frac{19}{20}\right)^{\lambda}[(1-\varepsilon)^{\lambda}|\mathcal{T}^{\lambda}(\nu_1)|+\varepsilon^{\lambda}|\mathcal{T}^{\lambda}(\kappa_1)|](d\varepsilon)^{\lambda}\\
&+\frac{1}{\Gamma(1+\lambda)}\int_{0}^{\frac{1}{20}}\left(\frac{1}{20}-\varepsilon\right)^{\lambda}[\varepsilon^{\lambda}|\mathcal{T}^{\lambda}(\nu_1)|+(1-\varepsilon)^{\lambda}|\mathcal{T}^{\lambda}(\kappa_1)|](d\varepsilon)^{\lambda}\\
&+\frac{1}{\Gamma(1+\lambda)}\int_{\frac{1}{20}}^{\frac{1}{6}}\left(\varepsilon-\frac{1}{20}\right)^{\lambda}[\varepsilon^{\lambda}|\mathcal{T}^{\lambda}(\nu_1)|+(1-\varepsilon)^{\lambda}|\mathcal{T}^{\lambda}(\kappa_1)|](d\varepsilon)^{\lambda}\\
&+\frac{1}{\Gamma(1+\lambda)}\int_{\frac{1}{6}}^{\frac{6}{20}}\left(\frac{6}{20}-\varepsilon\right)^{\lambda}[\varepsilon^{\lambda}|\mathcal{T}^{\lambda}(\nu_1)|+(1-\varepsilon)^{\lambda}|\mathcal{T}^{\lambda}(\kappa_1)|](d\varepsilon)^{\lambda}\\
&+\frac{1}{\Gamma(1+\lambda)}\int_{\frac{6}{20}}^{\frac{1}{3}}\left(\varepsilon-\frac{6}{20}\right)^{\lambda}[\varepsilon^{\lambda}|\mathcal{T}^{\lambda}(\nu_1)|+(1-\varepsilon)^{\lambda}|\mathcal{T}^{\lambda}(\kappa_1)|](d\varepsilon)^{\lambda}\\
&+\frac{1}{\Gamma(1+\lambda)}\int_{\frac{1}{3}}^{\frac{7}{20}}\left(\frac{7}{20}-\varepsilon\right)^{\lambda}[\varepsilon^{\lambda}|\mathcal{T}^{\lambda}(\nu_1)|+(1-\varepsilon)^{\lambda}|\mathcal{T}^{\lambda}(\kappa_1)|](d\varepsilon)^{\lambda}\\
&+\frac{1}{\Gamma(1+\lambda)}\int_{\frac{7}{20}}^{\frac{1}{2}}\left(\varepsilon-\frac{7}{20}\right)^{\lambda}[\varepsilon^{\lambda}|\mathcal{T}^{\lambda}(\nu_1)|+(1-\varepsilon)^{\lambda}|\mathcal{T}^{\lambda}(\kappa_1)|](d\varepsilon)^{\lambda}\\
&+\frac{1}{\Gamma(1+\lambda)}\int_{\frac{1}{2}}^{\frac{13}{20}}\left(\frac{13}{20}-\varepsilon\right)^{\lambda}[\varepsilon^{\lambda}|\mathcal{T}^{\lambda}(\nu_1)|+(1-\varepsilon)^{\lambda}|\mathcal{T}^{\lambda}(\kappa_1)|](d\varepsilon)^{\lambda}\\
&+\frac{1}{\Gamma(1+\lambda)}\int_{\frac{13}{20}}^{\frac{2}{3}}\left(\varepsilon-\frac{13}{20}\right)^{\lambda}[\varepsilon^{\lambda}|\mathcal{T}^{\lambda}(\nu_1)|+(1-\varepsilon)^{\lambda}|\mathcal{T}^{\lambda}(\kappa_1)|](d\varepsilon)^{\lambda}\\
&+\frac{1}{\Gamma(1+\lambda)}\int_{\frac{2}{3}}^{\frac{14}{20}}\left(\frac{14}{20}-\varepsilon\right)^{\lambda}[\varepsilon^{\lambda}|\mathcal{T}^{\lambda}(\nu_1)|+(1-\varepsilon)^{\lambda}|\mathcal{T}^{\lambda}(\kappa_1)|](d\varepsilon)^{\lambda}\\
&+\frac{1}{\Gamma(1+\lambda)}\int_{\frac{14}{20}}^{\frac{5}{6}}\left(\varepsilon-\frac{14}{20}\right)^{\lambda}[\varepsilon^{\lambda}|\mathcal{T}^{\lambda}(\nu_1)|+(1-\varepsilon)^{\lambda}|\mathcal{T}^{\lambda}(\kappa_1)|](d\varepsilon)^{\lambda}\\
&+\frac{1}{\Gamma(1+\lambda)}\int_{\frac{5}{6}}^{\frac{19}{20}}\left(\frac{19}{20}-\varepsilon\right)^{\lambda}[\varepsilon^{\lambda}|\mathcal{T}^{\lambda}(\nu_1)|+(1-\varepsilon)^{\lambda}|\mathcal{T}^{\lambda}(\kappa_1)|](d\varepsilon)^{\lambda}\\
&+\left.\frac{1}{\Gamma(1+\lambda)}\int_{\frac{19}{20}}^{1}\left(\varepsilon-\frac{19}{20}\right)^{\lambda}[\varepsilon^{\lambda}|\mathcal{T}^{\lambda}(\nu_1)|+(1-\varepsilon)^{\lambda}|\mathcal{T}^{\lambda}(\kappa_1)|](d\varepsilon)^{\lambda}\right].
\end{aligned}
$$

Finally, we get our intended inequality. □

Example 1. *If we take* $\mathcal{T}(\delta) = \delta^{\sigma\lambda}$, $\nu_1 = 0$ *and* $\kappa_1 = 3$ *in Theorem 7. Then, 2D and 3D validations of Theorem 7 are*

Figure 1a,b illustrate the comparison between sides of Theorem 7.

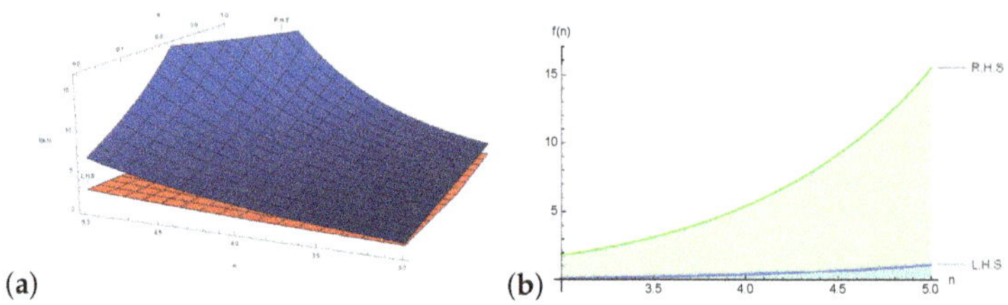

Figure 1. (**a**) Three- and (**b**) two-dimensional simulations of Theorem 7 for $\lambda \in [0.6, 1]$, $\lambda = \frac{4}{5}$ and $\sigma \in [3, 5]$, respectively.

Now we give other bounds for Weddle's rule by utilizing the well known Hölder's inequality.

Theorem 8. *Suppose that all constraints of Lemma 2 are fulfilled. If* $|\mathcal{T}^{\lambda}|^{r_2}$ *is a generalized convex mapping, then*

$$
\begin{aligned}
&\left| W(\nu_1, \kappa_1) - \frac{\Gamma(1+\lambda)}{(\kappa_1 - \nu_1)^{\lambda}} {}_{a}I_{\kappa_1} \mathcal{T}(\delta) \right| \\
&\leq (\kappa_1 - \nu_1)^{\lambda} \Bigg\{ \left(\frac{\Gamma(1+\lambda r_1)}{\Gamma(1+(r_1+1)\lambda)} \left(\left(\frac{7}{60}\right)^{(r_1+1)\lambda} + \left(\frac{1}{20}\right)^{(r_1+1)\lambda} \right) \right)^{\frac{1}{r_1}} \\
&\quad \times \left(\left[\frac{\Gamma(1+\lambda)}{\Gamma(1+2\lambda)} \left(\left(\frac{11}{36}\right)^{\lambda} |\mathcal{T}^{\lambda}(\nu_1)|^{r_2} + \left(\frac{1}{36}\right)^{\lambda} |\mathcal{T}^{\lambda}(\kappa_1)|^{r_2} \right) \right]^{\frac{1}{r_2}} \right. \\
&\quad \left. + \left[\frac{\Gamma(1+\lambda)}{\Gamma(1+2\lambda)} \left(\left(\frac{1}{36}\right)^{\lambda} |\mathcal{T}^{\lambda}(\nu_1)|^{r_2} + \left(\frac{11}{36}\right)^{\lambda} |\mathcal{T}^{\lambda}(\kappa_1)|^{r_2} \right) \right]^{\frac{1}{r_2}} \right) \\
&\quad + \left(\frac{\Gamma(1+\lambda r_1)}{\Gamma(1+(r_1+1)\lambda)} \left(\left(\frac{1}{30}\right)^{(r_1+1)\lambda} + \left(\frac{2}{15}\right)^{(r_1+1)\lambda} \right) \right)^{\frac{1}{r_1}} \\
&\quad \times \left(\left[\frac{\Gamma(1+\lambda)}{\Gamma(1+2\lambda)} \left(\left(\frac{1}{4}\right)^{\lambda} |\mathcal{T}^{\lambda}(\nu_1)|^{r_2} + \left(\frac{1}{12}\right)^{\lambda} |\mathcal{T}^{\lambda}(\kappa_1)|^{r_2} \right) \right]^{\frac{1}{r_2}} \right. \\
&\quad \left. + \left[\frac{\Gamma(1+\lambda)}{\Gamma(1+2\lambda)} \left(\left(\frac{1}{12}\right)^{\lambda} |\mathcal{T}^{\lambda}(\nu_1)|^{r_2} + \left(\frac{1}{4}\right)^{\lambda} |\mathcal{T}^{\lambda}(\kappa_1)|^{r_2} \right) \right]^{\frac{1}{r_2}} \right) \\
&\quad + \left(\frac{\Gamma(1+\lambda r_1)}{\Gamma(1+(r_1+1)\lambda)} \left(\left(\frac{3}{20}\right)^{(r_1+1)\lambda} + \left(\frac{1}{60}\right)^{(r_1+1)\lambda} \right) \right)^{\frac{1}{r_1}} \\
&\quad \times \left(\left[\frac{\Gamma(1+\lambda)}{\Gamma(1+2\lambda)} \left(\left(\frac{7}{36}\right)^{\lambda} |\mathcal{T}^{\lambda}(\nu_1)|^{r_2} + \left(\frac{5}{36}\right)^{\lambda} |\mathcal{T}^{\lambda}(\kappa_1)|^{r_2} \right) \right]^{\frac{1}{r_2}} \right. \\
&\quad \left. + \left[\frac{\Gamma(1+\lambda)}{\Gamma(1+2\lambda)} \left(\left(\frac{5}{36}\right)^{\lambda} |\mathcal{T}^{\lambda}(\nu_1)|^{r_2} + \left(\frac{7}{36}\right)^{\lambda} |\mathcal{T}^{\lambda}(\kappa_1)|^{r_2} \right) \right]^{\frac{1}{r_2}} \right) \Bigg\},
\end{aligned}
$$

where $\frac{1}{r_1} + \frac{1}{r_2} = 1$.

Proof. Through Lemma 2, Hölder's inequality and generalized convexity of $|\mathcal{T}^{\lambda}|$, we have

$$
\begin{aligned}
&\left| W(\nu_1, \kappa_1) - \frac{\Gamma(1+\lambda)}{(\kappa_1 - \nu_1)^{\lambda}} {}_{a}I_{\kappa_1} \mathcal{T}(\delta) \right| \\
&\leq \left(\frac{\kappa_1 - \nu_1}{2} \right)^{\lambda} \frac{1}{\Gamma(1+\lambda)} \int_0^1 |\triangle(\varepsilon)| \left| \mathcal{T}^{\lambda}((1-\varepsilon)\nu_1 + \varepsilon\kappa_1) - \mathcal{T}^{\lambda}(\varepsilon\nu_1 + (1-\varepsilon)\kappa_1) \right| (d\varepsilon)^{\lambda}
\end{aligned}
$$

$$
\begin{aligned}
&\leq \left(\frac{\kappa_1-\nu_1}{2}\right)^{\lambda}\left[\frac{1}{\Gamma(1+\lambda)}\int_0^{\frac{1}{6}}\left|\varepsilon-\frac{1}{20}\right|^{\lambda}\left|\mathcal{T}^{\lambda}((1-\varepsilon)\nu_1+\varepsilon\kappa_1)\right|(d\varepsilon)^{\lambda}\right.\\
&+\frac{1}{\Gamma(1+\lambda)}\int_{\frac{1}{6}}^{\frac{1}{3}}\left|\varepsilon-\frac{6}{20}\right|^{\lambda}\left|\mathcal{T}^{\lambda}((1-\varepsilon)\nu_1+\varepsilon\kappa_1)\right|(d\varepsilon)^{\lambda}\\
&+\frac{1}{\Gamma(1+\lambda)}\int_{\frac{1}{3}}^{\frac{1}{2}}\left|\varepsilon-\frac{7}{20}\right|^{\lambda}\left|\mathcal{T}^{\lambda}((1-\varepsilon)\nu_1+\varepsilon\kappa_1)\right|(d\varepsilon)^{\lambda}\\
&+\frac{1}{\Gamma(1+\lambda)}\int_{\frac{1}{2}}^{\frac{2}{3}}\left|\varepsilon-\frac{13}{20}\right|^{\lambda}\left|\mathcal{T}^{\lambda}((1-\varepsilon)\nu_1+\varepsilon\kappa_1)\right|(d\varepsilon)^{\lambda}\\
&+\frac{1}{\Gamma(1+\lambda)}\int_{\frac{2}{3}}^{\frac{5}{6}}\left|\varepsilon-\frac{14}{20}\right|^{\lambda}\left|\mathcal{T}^{\lambda}((1-\varepsilon)\nu_1+\varepsilon\kappa_1)\right|(d\varepsilon)^{\lambda}\\
&+\frac{1}{\Gamma(1+\lambda)}\int_{\frac{5}{6}}^{1}\left|\varepsilon-\frac{19}{20}\right|^{\lambda}\left|\mathcal{T}^{\lambda}((1-\varepsilon)\nu_1+\varepsilon\kappa_1)\right|(d\varepsilon)^{\lambda}\\
&+\frac{1}{\Gamma(1+\lambda)}\int_0^{\frac{1}{6}}\left|\frac{1}{20}-\varepsilon\right|^{\lambda}\left|\mathcal{T}^{\lambda}(\varepsilon\nu_1+(1-\varepsilon)\kappa_1)\right|(d\varepsilon)^{\lambda}\\
&+\frac{1}{\Gamma(1+\lambda)}\int_{\frac{1}{6}}^{\frac{1}{3}}\left|\frac{6}{20}-\varepsilon\right|^{\lambda}\left|\mathcal{T}^{\lambda}(\varepsilon\nu_1+(1-\varepsilon)\kappa_1)\right|(d\varepsilon)^{\lambda}\\
&+\frac{1}{\Gamma(1+\lambda)}\int_{\frac{1}{3}}^{\frac{1}{2}}\left|\frac{7}{20}-\varepsilon\right|^{\lambda}\left|\mathcal{T}^{\lambda}(\varepsilon\nu_1+(1-\varepsilon)\kappa_1)\right|(d\varepsilon)^{\lambda}\\
&+\frac{1}{\Gamma(1+\lambda)}\int_{\frac{1}{2}}^{\frac{2}{3}}\left|\frac{13}{20}-\varepsilon\right|^{\lambda}\left|\mathcal{T}^{\lambda}(\varepsilon\nu_1+(1-\varepsilon)\kappa_1)\right|(d\varepsilon)^{\lambda}\\
&+\frac{1}{\Gamma(1+\lambda)}\int_{\frac{2}{3}}^{\frac{5}{6}}\left|\frac{14}{20}-\varepsilon\right|^{\lambda}\left|\mathcal{T}^{\lambda}(\varepsilon\nu_1+(1-\varepsilon)\kappa_1)\right|(d\varepsilon)^{\lambda}\\
&\left.+\frac{1}{\Gamma(1+\lambda)}\int_{\frac{5}{6}}^{1}\left|\frac{19}{20}-\varepsilon\right|^{\lambda}\left|\mathcal{T}^{\lambda}(\varepsilon\nu_1+(1-\varepsilon)\kappa_1)\right|(d\varepsilon)^{\lambda}\right]\\
&\leq \left(\frac{\kappa_1-\nu_1}{2}\right)^{\lambda}\left[\left(\frac{1}{\Gamma(1+\lambda)}\int_0^{\frac{1}{6}}\left|\varepsilon-\frac{1}{20}\right|^{\lambda r_1}(d\varepsilon)^{\lambda}\right)^{\frac{1}{r_1}}\left(\frac{1}{\Gamma(1+\lambda)}\int_0^{\frac{1}{6}}|\mathcal{T}^{\lambda}((1-\varepsilon)\nu_1+\varepsilon\kappa_1)|^{r_2}(d\varepsilon)^{\lambda}\right)^{\frac{1}{r_2}}\right.\\
&+\left(\frac{1}{\Gamma(1+\lambda)}\int_{\frac{1}{6}}^{\frac{1}{3}}\left|\varepsilon-\frac{6}{20}\right|^{\lambda r_1}(d\varepsilon)^{\lambda}\right)^{\frac{1}{r_1}}\left(\frac{1}{\Gamma(1+\lambda)}\int_{\frac{1}{6}}^{\frac{1}{3}}|\mathcal{T}^{\lambda}((1-\varepsilon)\nu_1+\varepsilon\kappa_1)|^{r_2}(d\varepsilon)^{\lambda}\right)^{\frac{1}{r_2}}\\
&+\left(\frac{1}{\Gamma(1+\lambda)}\int_{\frac{1}{3}}^{\frac{1}{2}}\left|\varepsilon-\frac{7}{20}\right|^{\lambda r_1}(d\varepsilon)^{\lambda}\right)^{\frac{1}{r_1}}\left(\frac{1}{\Gamma(1+\lambda)}\int_{\frac{1}{3}}^{\frac{1}{2}}|\mathcal{T}^{\lambda}((1-\varepsilon)\nu_1+\varepsilon\kappa_1)|^{r_2}(d\varepsilon)^{\lambda}\right)^{\frac{1}{r_2}}\\
&+\left(\frac{1}{\Gamma(1+\lambda)}\int_{\frac{1}{2}}^{\frac{2}{3}}\left|\varepsilon-\frac{13}{20}\right|^{\lambda r_1}(d\varepsilon)^{\lambda}\right)^{\frac{1}{r_1}}\left(\frac{1}{\Gamma(1+\lambda)}\int_{\frac{1}{3}}^{\frac{1}{2}}|\mathcal{T}^{\lambda}((1-\varepsilon)\nu_1+\varepsilon\kappa_1)|^{r_2}(d\varepsilon)^{\lambda}\right)^{\frac{1}{r_2}}\\
&+\left(\frac{1}{\Gamma(1+\lambda)}\int_{\frac{2}{3}}^{\frac{5}{6}}\left|\varepsilon-\frac{14}{20}\right|^{\lambda r_1}(d\varepsilon)^{\lambda}\right)^{\frac{1}{r_1}}\left(\frac{1}{\Gamma(1+\lambda)}\int_{\frac{2}{3}}^{\frac{5}{6}}|\mathcal{T}^{\lambda}((1-\varepsilon)\nu_1+\varepsilon\kappa_1)|^{r_2}(d\varepsilon)^{\lambda}\right)^{\frac{1}{r_2}}\\
&+\left(\frac{1}{\Gamma(1+\lambda)}\int_{\frac{5}{6}}^{1}\left|\varepsilon-\frac{19}{20}\right|^{\lambda r_1}(d\varepsilon)^{\lambda}\right)^{\frac{1}{r_1}}\left(\frac{1}{\Gamma(1+\lambda)}\int_{\frac{5}{6}}^{1}|\mathcal{T}^{\lambda}((1-\varepsilon)\nu_1+\varepsilon\kappa_1)|^{r_2}(d\varepsilon)^{\lambda}\right)^{\frac{1}{r_2}}\\
&+\left(\frac{1}{\Gamma(1+\lambda)}\int_0^{\frac{1}{6}}\left|\varepsilon-\frac{1}{20}\right|^{\lambda r_1}(d\varepsilon)^{\lambda}\right)^{\frac{1}{r_1}}\left(\frac{1}{\Gamma(1+\lambda)}\int_0^{\frac{1}{6}}|\mathcal{T}^{\lambda}(\varepsilon\nu_1+(1-\varepsilon)\kappa_1)|^{r_2}(d\varepsilon)^{\lambda}\right)^{\frac{1}{r_2}}\\
&+\left(\frac{1}{\Gamma(1+\lambda)}\int_{\frac{1}{6}}^{\frac{1}{3}}\left|\varepsilon-\frac{6}{20}\right|^{\lambda r_1}(d\varepsilon)^{\lambda}\right)^{\frac{1}{r_1}}\left(\frac{1}{\Gamma(1+\lambda)}\int_{\frac{1}{6}}^{\frac{1}{3}}|\mathcal{T}^{\lambda}(\varepsilon\nu_1+(1-\varepsilon)\kappa_1)|^{r_2}(d\varepsilon)^{\lambda}\right)^{\frac{1}{r_2}}\\
&+\left(\frac{1}{\Gamma(1+\lambda)}\int_{\frac{1}{3}}^{\frac{1}{2}}\left|\varepsilon-\frac{7}{20}\right|^{\lambda r_1}(d\varepsilon)^{\lambda}\right)^{\frac{1}{r_1}}\left(\frac{1}{\Gamma(1+\lambda)}\int_{\frac{1}{3}}^{\frac{1}{2}}|\mathcal{T}^{\lambda}(\varepsilon\nu_1+(1-\varepsilon)\kappa_1)|^{r_2}(d\varepsilon)^{\lambda}\right)^{\frac{1}{r_2}}\\
&+\left(\frac{1}{\Gamma(1+\lambda)}\int_{\frac{1}{2}}^{\frac{2}{3}}\left|\varepsilon-\frac{13}{20}\right|^{\lambda r_1}(d\varepsilon)^{\lambda}\right)^{\frac{1}{r_1}}\left(\frac{1}{\Gamma(1+\lambda)}\int_{\frac{1}{3}}^{\frac{1}{2}}|\mathcal{T}^{\lambda}(\varepsilon\nu_1+(1-\varepsilon)\kappa_1)|^{r_2}(d\varepsilon)^{\lambda}\right)^{\frac{1}{r_2}}
\end{aligned}
$$

$$
\begin{aligned}
&+\left(\frac{1}{\Gamma(1+\lambda)}\int_{\frac{2}{3}}^{\frac{5}{6}}\left|\varepsilon-\frac{14}{20}\right|^{\lambda r_1}(\mathrm{d}\varepsilon)^{\lambda}\right)^{\frac{1}{r_1}}\left(\frac{1}{\Gamma(1+\lambda)}\int_{\frac{2}{3}}^{\frac{5}{6}}|\mathcal{T}^{\lambda}(\varepsilon\nu_1+(1-\varepsilon)\kappa_1)|^{r_2}(\mathrm{d}\varepsilon)^{\lambda}\right)^{\frac{1}{r_2}}\\
&+\left(\frac{1}{\Gamma(1+\lambda)}\int_{\frac{5}{6}}^{1}\left|\varepsilon-\frac{19}{20}\right|^{\lambda r_1}(\mathrm{d}\varepsilon)^{\lambda}\right)^{\frac{1}{r_1}}\left(\frac{1}{\Gamma(1+\lambda)}\int_{\frac{5}{6}}^{1}|\mathcal{T}^{\lambda}(\varepsilon\nu_1+(1-\varepsilon)\kappa_1)|^{r_2}(\mathrm{d}\varepsilon)^{\lambda}\right)^{\frac{1}{r_2}}\Bigg]\\
&\leq\left(\frac{\kappa_1-\nu_1}{2}\right)^{\lambda}\Bigg[\left(\frac{1}{\Gamma(1+\lambda)}\int_{0}^{\frac{1}{6}}\left|\varepsilon-\frac{1}{20}\right|^{\lambda r_1}(\mathrm{d}\varepsilon)^{\lambda}\right)^{\frac{1}{r_1}}\\
&\times\left(\frac{1}{\Gamma(1+\lambda)}\int_{0}^{\frac{1}{6}}[(1-\varepsilon)^{\lambda}|\mathcal{T}^{\lambda}(\nu_1)|^{r_2}+\varepsilon^{\lambda}|\mathcal{T}^{\lambda}(\kappa_1)|^{r_2}](\mathrm{d}\varepsilon)^{\lambda}\right)^{\frac{1}{r_2}}\\
&+\left(\frac{1}{\Gamma(1+\lambda)}\int_{\frac{1}{6}}^{\frac{1}{3}}\left|\varepsilon-\frac{6}{20}\right|^{\lambda r_1}(\mathrm{d}\varepsilon)^{\lambda}\right)^{\frac{1}{r_1}}\\
&\times\left(\frac{1}{\Gamma(1+\lambda)}\int_{\frac{1}{6}}^{\frac{1}{3}}[(1-\varepsilon)^{\lambda}|\mathcal{T}^{\lambda}(\nu_1)|^{r_2}+\varepsilon^{\lambda}|\mathcal{T}^{\lambda}(\kappa_1)|^{r_2}](\mathrm{d}\varepsilon)^{\lambda}\right)^{\frac{1}{r_2}}\\
&+\left(\frac{1}{\Gamma(1+\lambda)}\int_{\frac{1}{3}}^{\frac{1}{2}}\left|\varepsilon-\frac{7}{20}\right|^{\lambda r_1}(\mathrm{d}\varepsilon)^{\lambda}\right)^{\frac{1}{r_1}}\\
&\times\left(\frac{1}{\Gamma(1+\lambda)}\int_{\frac{1}{3}}^{\frac{1}{2}}[(1-\varepsilon)^{\lambda}|\mathcal{T}^{\lambda}(\nu_1)|^{r_2}+\varepsilon^{\lambda}|\mathcal{T}^{\lambda}(\kappa_1)|^{r_2}](\mathrm{d}\varepsilon)^{\lambda}\right)^{\frac{1}{r_2}}\\
&+\left(\frac{1}{\Gamma(1+\lambda)}\int_{\frac{1}{2}}^{\frac{2}{3}}\left|\varepsilon-\frac{13}{20}\right|^{\lambda r_1}(\mathrm{d}\varepsilon)^{\lambda}\right)^{\frac{1}{r_1}}\\
&\times\left(\frac{1}{\Gamma(1+\lambda)}\int_{\frac{1}{3}}^{\frac{1}{2}}[(1-\varepsilon)^{\lambda}|\mathcal{T}^{\lambda}(\nu_1)|^{r_2}+\varepsilon^{\lambda}|\mathcal{T}^{\lambda}(\kappa_1)|^{r_2}](\mathrm{d}\varepsilon)^{\lambda}\right)^{\frac{1}{r_2}}\\
&+\left(\frac{1}{\Gamma(1+\lambda)}\int_{\frac{2}{3}}^{\frac{5}{6}}\left|\varepsilon-\frac{14}{20}\right|^{\lambda r_1}(\mathrm{d}\varepsilon)^{\lambda}\right)^{\frac{1}{r_1}}\\
&\times\left(\frac{1}{\Gamma(1+\lambda)}\int_{\frac{2}{3}}^{\frac{5}{6}}[(1-\varepsilon)^{\lambda}|\mathcal{T}^{\lambda}(\nu_1)|^{r_2}+\varepsilon^{\lambda}|\mathcal{T}^{\lambda}(\kappa_1)|^{r_2}](\mathrm{d}\varepsilon)^{\lambda}\right)^{\frac{1}{r_2}}\\
&+\left(\frac{1}{\Gamma(1+\lambda)}\int_{\frac{5}{6}}^{1}\left|\varepsilon-\frac{19}{20}\right|^{\lambda r_1}(\mathrm{d}\varepsilon)^{\lambda}\right)^{\frac{1}{r_1}}\\
&\times\left(\frac{1}{\Gamma(1+\lambda)}\int_{\frac{5}{6}}^{1}[(1-\varepsilon)^{\lambda}|\mathcal{T}^{\lambda}(\nu_1)|^{r_2}+\varepsilon^{\lambda}|\mathcal{T}^{\lambda}(\kappa_1)|^{r_2}](\mathrm{d}\varepsilon)^{\lambda}\right)^{\frac{1}{r_2}}\\
&+\left(\frac{1}{\Gamma(1+\lambda)}\int_{0}^{\frac{1}{6}}\left|\varepsilon-\frac{1}{20}\right|^{\lambda r_1}(\mathrm{d}\varepsilon)^{\lambda}\right)^{\frac{1}{r_1}}\\
&\times\left(\frac{1}{\Gamma(1+\lambda)}\int_{0}^{\frac{1}{6}}[\varepsilon^{\lambda}|\mathcal{T}^{\lambda}(\nu_1)|^{r_2}+(1-\varepsilon)^{\lambda}|\mathcal{T}^{\lambda}(\kappa_1)|^{r_2}](\mathrm{d}\varepsilon)^{\lambda}\right)^{\frac{1}{r_2}}\\
&+\left(\frac{1}{\Gamma(1+\lambda)}\int_{\frac{1}{6}}^{\frac{1}{3}}\left|\varepsilon-\frac{6}{20}\right|^{\lambda r_1}(\mathrm{d}\varepsilon)^{\lambda}\right)^{\frac{1}{r_1}}\\
&\times\left(\frac{1}{\Gamma(1+\lambda)}\int_{\frac{1}{6}}^{\frac{1}{3}}[\varepsilon^{\lambda}|\mathcal{T}^{\lambda}(\nu_1)|^{r_2}+(1-\varepsilon)^{\lambda}|\mathcal{T}^{\lambda}(\kappa_1)|^{r_2}](\mathrm{d}\varepsilon)^{\lambda}\right)^{\frac{1}{r_2}}\\
&+\left(\frac{1}{\Gamma(1+\lambda)}\int_{\frac{1}{3}}^{\frac{1}{2}}\left|\varepsilon-\frac{7}{20}\right|^{\lambda r_1}(\mathrm{d}\varepsilon)^{\lambda}\right)^{\frac{1}{r_1}}\\
&\times\left(\frac{1}{\Gamma(1+\lambda)}\int_{\frac{1}{3}}^{\frac{1}{2}}[\varepsilon^{\lambda}|\mathcal{T}^{\lambda}(\nu_1)|^{r_2}+(1-\varepsilon)^{\lambda}|\mathcal{T}^{\lambda}(\kappa_1)|^{r_2}](\mathrm{d}\varepsilon)^{\lambda}\right)^{\frac{1}{r_2}}
\end{aligned}
$$

$$
\begin{aligned}
&+\left(\frac{1}{\Gamma(1+\lambda)}\int_{\frac{1}{2}}^{\frac{2}{3}}\left|\varepsilon-\frac{13}{20}\right|^{\lambda r_1}(\mathrm{d}\varepsilon)^{\lambda}\right)^{\frac{1}{r_1}} \\
&\times\left(\frac{1}{\Gamma(1+\lambda)}\int_{\frac{1}{3}}^{\frac{1}{2}}[\varepsilon^{\lambda}|\mathcal{T}^{\lambda}(\nu_1)|^{r_2}+(1-\varepsilon)^{\lambda}|\mathcal{T}^{\lambda}(\kappa_1)|^{r_2}](\mathrm{d}\varepsilon)^{\lambda}\right)^{\frac{1}{r_2}} \\
&+\left(\frac{1}{\Gamma(1+\lambda)}\int_{\frac{2}{3}}^{\frac{5}{6}}\left|\varepsilon-\frac{14}{20}\right|^{\lambda r_1}(\mathrm{d}\varepsilon)^{\lambda}\right)^{\frac{1}{r_1}} \\
&\times\left(\frac{1}{\Gamma(1+\lambda)}\int_{\frac{2}{3}}^{\frac{5}{6}}[\varepsilon^{\lambda}|\mathcal{T}^{\lambda}(\nu_1)|^{r_2}+(1-\varepsilon)^{\lambda}|\mathcal{T}^{\lambda}(\kappa_1)|^{r_2}](\mathrm{d}\varepsilon)^{\lambda}\right)^{\frac{1}{r_2}} \\
&+\left(\frac{1}{\Gamma(1+\lambda)}\int_{\frac{5}{6}}^{1}\left|\varepsilon-\frac{19}{20}\right|^{\lambda r_1}(\mathrm{d}\varepsilon)^{\lambda}\right)^{\frac{1}{r_1}} \\
&\times\left(\frac{1}{\Gamma(1+\lambda)}\int_{\frac{5}{6}}^{1}[\varepsilon^{\lambda}|\mathcal{T}^{\lambda}(\nu_1)|^{r_2}+(1-\varepsilon)^{\lambda}|\mathcal{T}^{\lambda}(\kappa_1)|^{r_2}](\mathrm{d}\varepsilon)^{\lambda}\right)^{\frac{1}{r_2}}\Bigg] \\
\le&\left(\frac{\kappa_1-\nu_1}{2}\right)^{\lambda}\Bigg\{\left(\frac{\Gamma(1+\lambda r_1)}{\Gamma(1+(r_1+1)\lambda)}\left(\left(\frac{7}{60}\right)^{(r_1+1)\lambda}+\left(\frac{1}{20}\right)^{(r_1+1)\lambda}\right)\right)^{\frac{1}{r_1}} \\
&\times\left(\left[\frac{\Gamma(1+\lambda)}{\Gamma(1+2\lambda)}\left(\left(\frac{11}{36}\right)^{\lambda}|\mathcal{T}^{\lambda}(\nu_1)|^{r_2}+\left(\frac{1}{36}\right)^{\lambda}|\mathcal{T}^{\lambda}(\kappa_1)|^{r_2}\right)\right]^{\frac{1}{r_2}}\right. \\
&\left.+\left[\frac{\Gamma(1+\lambda)}{\Gamma(1+2\lambda)}\left(\left(\frac{1}{36}\right)^{\lambda}|\mathcal{T}^{\lambda}(\nu_1)|^{r_2}+\left(\frac{11}{36}\right)^{\lambda}|\mathcal{T}^{\lambda}(\kappa_1)|^{r_2}\right)\right]^{\frac{1}{r_2}}\right) \\
&+\left(\frac{\Gamma(1+\lambda r_1)}{\Gamma(1+(r_1+1)\lambda)}\left(\left(\frac{1}{30}\right)^{(r_1+1)\lambda}+\left(\frac{2}{15}\right)^{(r_1+1)\lambda}\right)\right)^{\frac{1}{r_1}} \\
&\times\left(\left[\frac{\Gamma(1+\lambda)}{\Gamma(1+2\lambda)}\left(\left(\frac{1}{4}\right)^{\lambda}|\mathcal{T}^{\lambda}(\nu_1)|^{r_2}+\left(\frac{1}{12}\right)^{\lambda}|\mathcal{T}^{\lambda}(\kappa_1)|^{r_2}\right)\right]^{\frac{1}{r_2}}\right. \\
&\left.+\left[\frac{\Gamma(1+\lambda)}{\Gamma(1+2\lambda)}\left(\left(\frac{1}{12}\right)^{\lambda}|\mathcal{T}^{\lambda}(\nu_1)|^{r_2}+\left(\frac{1}{4}\right)^{\lambda}|\mathcal{T}^{\lambda}(\kappa_1)|^{r_2}\right)\right]^{\frac{1}{r_2}}\right) \\
&+\left(\frac{\Gamma(1+\lambda r_1)}{\Gamma(1+(r_1+1)\lambda)}\left(\left(\frac{3}{20}\right)^{(r_1+1)\lambda}+\left(\frac{1}{60}\right)^{(r_1+1)\lambda}\right)\right)^{\frac{1}{r_1}} \\
&\times\left(\left[\frac{\Gamma(1+\lambda)}{\Gamma(1+2\lambda)}\left(\left(\frac{7}{36}\right)^{\lambda}|\mathcal{T}^{\lambda}(\nu_1)|^{r_2}+\left(\frac{5}{36}\right)^{\lambda}|\mathcal{T}^{\lambda}(\kappa_1)|^{r_2}\right)\right]^{\frac{1}{r_2}}\right. \\
&\left.+\left[\frac{\Gamma(1+\lambda)}{\Gamma(1+2\lambda)}\left(\left(\frac{5}{36}\right)^{\lambda}|\mathcal{T}^{\lambda}(\nu_1)|^{r_2}+\left(\frac{7}{36}\right)^{\lambda}|\mathcal{T}^{\lambda}(\kappa_1)|^{r_2}\right)\right]^{\frac{1}{r_2}}\right) \\
&+\left(\frac{\Gamma(1+\lambda r_1)}{\Gamma(1+(r_1+1)\lambda)}\left(\left(\frac{1}{60}\right)^{(r_1+1)\lambda}+\left(\frac{3}{20}\right)^{(r_1+1)\lambda}\right)\right)^{\frac{1}{r_1}} \\
&\times\left(\left[\frac{\Gamma(1+\lambda)}{\Gamma(1+2\lambda)}\left(\left(\frac{5}{36}\right)^{\lambda}|\mathcal{T}^{\lambda}(\nu_1)|^{r_2}+\left(\frac{7}{36}\right)^{\lambda}|\mathcal{T}^{\lambda}(\kappa_1)|^{r_2}\right)\right]^{\frac{1}{r_2}}\right. \\
&\left.+\left[\frac{\Gamma(1+\lambda)}{\Gamma(1+2\lambda)}\left(\left(\frac{7}{36}\right)^{\lambda}|\mathcal{T}^{\lambda}(\nu_1)|^{r_2}+\left(\frac{5}{36}\right)^{\lambda}|\mathcal{T}^{\lambda}(\kappa_1)|^{r_2}\right)\right]^{\frac{1}{r_2}}\right) \\
&+\left(\frac{\Gamma(1+\lambda r_1)}{\Gamma(1+(r_1+1)\lambda)}\left(\left(\frac{2}{15}\right)^{(r_1+1)\lambda}+\left(\frac{1}{30}\right)^{(r_1+1)\lambda}\right)\right)^{\frac{1}{r_1}}
\end{aligned}
$$

$$\times\left(\left[\frac{\Gamma(1+\lambda)}{\Gamma(1+2\lambda)}\left(\left(\frac{1}{12}\right)^{\lambda}|\mathcal{T}^{\lambda}(\nu_1)|^{r_2}+\left(\frac{1}{4}\right)^{\lambda}|\mathcal{T}^{\lambda}(\kappa_1)|^{r_2}\right)\right]^{\frac{1}{r_2}}\right.$$

$$quad+\left.\left[\frac{\Gamma(1+\lambda)}{\Gamma(1+2\lambda)}\left(\left(\frac{1}{4}\right)^{\lambda}|\mathcal{T}^{\lambda}(\nu_1)|^{r_2}+\left(\frac{1}{12}\right)^{\lambda}|\mathcal{T}^{\lambda}(\kappa_1)|^{r_2}\right)\right]^{\frac{1}{r_2}}\right)$$

$$+\left(\frac{\Gamma(1+\lambda r_1)}{\Gamma(1+(r_1+1)\lambda)}\left(\left(\frac{1}{20}\right)^{(r_1+1)\lambda}+\left(\frac{7}{60}\right)^{(r_1+1)\lambda}\right)\right)^{\frac{1}{r_1}}$$

$$\times\left(\left[\frac{\Gamma(1+\lambda)}{\Gamma(1+2\lambda)}\left(\left(\frac{1}{36}\right)^{\lambda}|\mathcal{T}^{\lambda}(\nu_1)|^{r_2}+\left(\frac{11}{36}\right)^{\lambda}|\mathcal{T}^{\lambda}(\kappa_1)|^{r_2}\right)\right]^{\frac{1}{r_2}}\right.$$

$$\left.+\left[\frac{\Gamma(1+\lambda)}{\Gamma(1+2\lambda)}\left(\left(\frac{11}{36}\right)^{\lambda}|\mathcal{T}^{\lambda}(\nu_1)|^{r_2}+\left(\frac{1}{36}\right)^{\lambda}|\mathcal{T}^{\lambda}(\kappa_1)|^{r_2}\right)\right]^{\frac{1}{r_2}}\right)\Bigg\}.$$

This ends the proof. □

Example 2. *If we take $\mathcal{T}(\delta)=\delta^{\sigma\lambda}$, $\nu_1=0$ and $\kappa_1=3$ in Theorem 8. Then, 2D and 3D validations of Theorem 8 are*

Figure 2a,b illustrate the comparison between sides of Theorem 8.

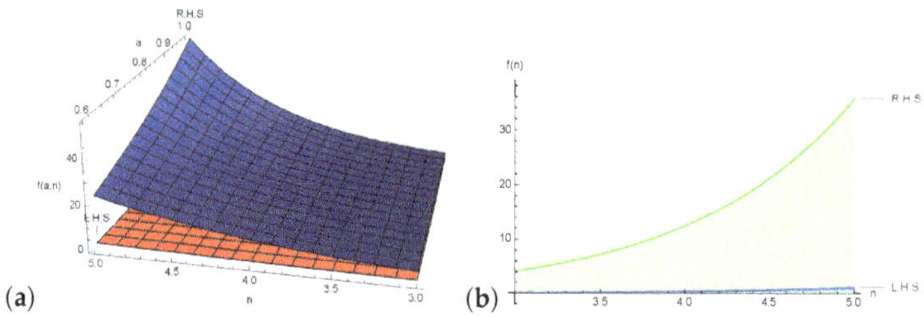

Figure 2. (**a**) Three- and (**b**) two-dimensional simulations of Theorem 8 for $\lambda\in[0.6,1]$, $\lambda=\frac{4}{5}$ and $\sigma\in[3,5]$, respectively.

Next, we construct a new estimate of Weddle's inequality.

Theorem 9. *Suppose that all constraints of lemma 2 are fulfilled. If $|\mathcal{T}^{\lambda}|^{r_2}$ is a generalized convex mapping, then*

$$\left|W(\nu_1,\kappa_1)-\frac{\Gamma(1+\lambda)}{(\kappa_1-\nu_1)^{\lambda}}{}_{a}I_{\kappa_1}\mathcal{T}(\delta)\right|$$

$$\leq\left(\frac{\kappa_1-\nu_1}{2}\right)^{\lambda}\left\{\left(\frac{\Gamma(1+\lambda)}{\Gamma(1+2\lambda)}\left(\frac{29}{1800}\right)^{\lambda}\right)^{1-\frac{1}{r_2}}\right.$$

$$\times\left[\left(A_1|\mathcal{T}^{\lambda}(\nu_1)|^{r_2}+A_2|\mathcal{T}^{\lambda}(\kappa_1)|^{r_2}\right)^{\frac{1}{r_2}}+\left(A_2|\mathcal{T}^{\lambda}(\nu_1)|^{r_2}+A_1|\mathcal{T}^{\lambda}(\kappa_1)|^{r_2}\right)^{\frac{1}{r_2}}\right]$$

$$+\left(\frac{\Gamma(1+\lambda)}{\Gamma(1+2\lambda)}\left(\frac{17}{900}\right)^{\lambda}\right)^{1-\frac{1}{r_2}}$$

$$\times\left[\left(A_3|\mathcal{T}^{\lambda}(\nu_1)|^{r_2}+A_4|\mathcal{T}^{\lambda}(\kappa_1)|^{r_2}\right)^{\frac{1}{r_2}}+\left(A_4|\mathcal{T}^{\lambda}(\nu_1)|^{r_2}+A_3|\mathcal{T}^{\lambda}(\kappa_1)|^{r_2}\right)^{\frac{1}{r_2}}\right]$$

$$+\left(\frac{\Gamma(1+\lambda)}{\Gamma(1+2\lambda)}\left(\frac{41}{1800}\right)^{\lambda}\right)^{1-\frac{1}{r_2}}$$

$$\times\left[\left(A_5|\mathcal{T}^{\lambda}(\nu_1)|^{r_2}+A_6|\mathcal{T}^{\lambda}(\kappa_1)|^{r_2}\right)^{\frac{1}{r_2}}+\left(A_6|\mathcal{T}^{\lambda}(\nu_1)|^{r_2}+A_5|\mathcal{T}^{\lambda}(\kappa_1)|^{r_2}\right)^{\frac{1}{r_2}}\right]$$
$$+\left(\frac{\Gamma(1+\lambda)}{\Gamma(1+2\lambda)}\left(\frac{41}{1800}\right)^{\lambda}\right)^{1-\frac{1}{r_2}}$$
$$\times\left[\left(A_7|\mathcal{T}^{\lambda}(\nu_1)|^{r_2}+A_8|\mathcal{T}^{\lambda}(\kappa_1)|^{r_2}\right)^{\frac{1}{r_2}}+\left(A_8|\mathcal{T}^{\lambda}(\nu_1)|^{r_2}+A_7|\mathcal{T}^{\lambda}(\kappa_1)|^{r_2}\right)^{\frac{1}{r_2}}\right]$$
$$+\left(\frac{\Gamma(1+\lambda)}{\Gamma(1+2\lambda)}\left(\frac{17}{900}\right)^{\lambda}\right)^{1-\frac{1}{r_2}}$$
$$\times\left[\left(A_9|\mathcal{T}^{\lambda}(\nu_1)|^{r_2}+A_{10}|\mathcal{T}^{\lambda}(\kappa_1)|^{r_2}\right)^{\frac{1}{r_2}}+\left(A_{10}|\mathcal{T}^{\lambda}(\nu_1)|^{r_2}+A_9|\mathcal{T}^{\lambda}(\kappa_1)|^{r_2}\right)^{\frac{1}{r_2}}\right]$$
$$+\left(\frac{\Gamma(1+\lambda)}{\Gamma(1+2\lambda)}\left(\frac{29}{1800}\right)^{\lambda}\right)^{1-\frac{1}{r_2}}$$
$$\times\left[\left(A_{11}|\mathcal{T}^{\lambda}(\nu_1)|^{r_2}+A_{12}|\mathcal{T}^{\lambda}(\kappa_1)|^{r_2}\right)^{\frac{1}{r_2}}+\left(A_{12}|\mathcal{T}^{\lambda}(\nu_1)|^{r_2}+A_{11}|\mathcal{T}^{\lambda}(\kappa_1)|^{r_2}\right)^{\frac{1}{r_2}}\right]\Bigg\},$$

$r_2 \geq 1$, *where*

- $A_1=\left(\frac{\Gamma(1+\lambda)}{\Gamma(1+2\lambda)}\left(\frac{69}{4000}\right)^{\lambda}-\frac{\Gamma(1+2\lambda)}{\Gamma(1+3\lambda)}\left(\frac{473}{108000}\right)^{\lambda}\right)$,
- $A_2=\left(\frac{\Gamma(1+2\lambda)}{\Gamma(1+3\lambda)}\left(\frac{473}{108000}\right)^{\lambda}-\frac{\Gamma(1+\lambda)}{\Gamma(1+2\lambda)}\left(\frac{41}{36000}\right)^{\lambda}\right)$,
- $A_3=\left(\frac{\Gamma(1+\lambda)}{\Gamma(1+2\lambda)}\left(\frac{59}{9000}\right)^{\lambda}+\frac{\Gamma(1+2\lambda)}{\Gamma(1+3\lambda)}\left(\frac{37}{3000}\right)^{\lambda}\right)$,
- $A_4=\left(\frac{\Gamma(1+\lambda)}{\Gamma(1+2\lambda)}\left(\frac{37}{3000}\right)^{\lambda}-\frac{\Gamma(1+2\lambda)}{\Gamma(1+3\lambda)}\left(\frac{37}{3000}\right)^{\lambda}\right)$,
- $A_5=\left(\frac{\Gamma(1+\lambda)}{\Gamma(1+2\lambda)}\left(\frac{761}{12000}\right)^{\lambda}-\frac{\Gamma(1+2\lambda)}{\Gamma(1+3\lambda)}\left(\frac{8239}{108000}\right)^{\lambda}\right)$,
- $A_6=\left(\frac{\Gamma(1+2\lambda)}{\Gamma(1+3\lambda)}\left(\frac{8239}{108000}\right)^{\lambda}-\frac{\Gamma(1+\lambda)}{\Gamma(1+2\lambda)}\left(\frac{1463}{36000}\right)^{\lambda}\right)$,
- $A_7=\left(\frac{\Gamma(1+2\lambda)}{\Gamma(1+3\lambda)}\left(\frac{13819}{108000}\right)^{\lambda}-\frac{\Gamma(1+\lambda)}{\Gamma(1+2\lambda)}\left(\frac{901}{12000}\right)^{\lambda}\right)$,
- $A_8=\left(\frac{\Gamma(1+\lambda)}{\Gamma(1+2\lambda)}\left(\frac{3523}{36000}\right)^{\lambda}-\frac{\Gamma(1+2\lambda)}{\Gamma(1+3\lambda)}\left(\frac{13819}{108000}\right)^{\lambda}\right)$,
- $A_9=\left(\frac{\Gamma(1+\lambda)}{\Gamma(1+2\lambda)}\left(\frac{1171}{9000}\right)^{\lambda}-\frac{\Gamma(1+2\lambda)}{\Gamma(1+3\lambda)}\left(\frac{189}{1000}\right)^{\lambda}\right)$,
- $A_{10}=\left(\frac{\Gamma(1+2\lambda)}{\Gamma(1+3\lambda)}\left(\frac{189}{1000}\right)^{\lambda}-\frac{\Gamma(1+\lambda)}{\Gamma(1+2\lambda)}\left(\frac{1001}{9000}\right)^{\lambda}\right)$,
- $A_{11}=\left(\frac{\Gamma(1+2\lambda)}{\Gamma(1+3\lambda)}\left(\frac{14693}{108000}\right)^{\lambda}-\frac{\Gamma(1+\lambda)}{\Gamma(1+2\lambda)}\left(\frac{1067}{12000}\right)^{\lambda}\right)$,
- $A_{12}=\left(\frac{\Gamma(1+\lambda)}{\Gamma(1+2\lambda)}\left(\frac{3781}{36000}\right)^{\lambda}-\frac{\Gamma(1+2\lambda)}{\Gamma(1+3\lambda)}\left(\frac{14693}{108000}\right)^{\lambda}\right)$.

Proof. Through Lemma 2, power mean inequality and generalized convexity of $|\mathcal{T}^{\lambda}|^{r_2}$, we have

$$\left|W(\nu_1,\kappa_1)-\frac{\Gamma(1+\lambda)}{(\kappa_1-\nu_1)^{\lambda}}{}_{a}I_{\kappa_1}\mathcal{T}(\delta)\right|$$
$$\leq\left(\frac{\kappa_1-\nu_1}{2}\right)^{\lambda}\frac{1}{\Gamma(1+\lambda)}\int_0^1|\triangle(\varepsilon)|\left|\mathcal{T}^{\lambda}((1-\varepsilon)\nu_1+\varepsilon\kappa_1)-\mathcal{T}^{\lambda}(\varepsilon\nu_1+(1-\varepsilon)\kappa_1)\right|(d\varepsilon)^{\lambda}$$
$$\leq\left(\frac{\kappa_1-\nu_1}{2}\right)^{\lambda}\left[\frac{1}{\Gamma(1+\lambda)}\int_0^{\frac{1}{6}}\left|\varepsilon-\frac{1}{20}\right|^{\lambda}\left|\mathcal{T}^{\lambda}((1-\varepsilon)\nu_1+\varepsilon\kappa_1)\right|(d\varepsilon)^{\lambda}\right.$$
$$+\frac{1}{\Gamma(1+\lambda)}\int_{\frac{1}{6}}^{\frac{1}{3}}\left|\varepsilon-\frac{6}{20}\right|^{\lambda}\left|\mathcal{T}^{\lambda}((1-\varepsilon)\nu_1+\varepsilon\kappa_1)\right|(d\varepsilon)^{\lambda}$$

$$
\begin{aligned}
&+\frac{1}{\Gamma(1+\lambda)}\int_{\frac{1}{3}}^{\frac{1}{2}}\left|\varepsilon-\frac{7}{20}\right|^{\lambda}\left|\mathcal{T}^{\lambda}((1-\varepsilon)\nu_1+\varepsilon\kappa_1)\right|(\mathrm{d}\varepsilon)^{\lambda}\\
&+\frac{1}{\Gamma(1+\lambda)}\int_{\frac{1}{2}}^{\frac{2}{3}}\left|\varepsilon-\frac{13}{20}\right|^{\lambda}\left|\mathcal{T}^{\lambda}((1-\varepsilon)\nu_1+\varepsilon\kappa_1)\right|(\mathrm{d}\varepsilon)^{\lambda}\\
&+\frac{1}{\Gamma(1+\lambda)}\int_{\frac{2}{3}}^{\frac{5}{6}}\left|\varepsilon-\frac{14}{20}\right|^{\lambda}\left|\mathcal{T}^{\lambda}((1-\varepsilon)\nu_1+\varepsilon\kappa_1)\right|(\mathrm{d}\varepsilon)^{\lambda}\\
&+\frac{1}{\Gamma(1+\lambda)}\int_{\frac{5}{6}}^{1}\left|\varepsilon-\frac{19}{20}\right|^{\lambda}\left|\mathcal{T}^{\lambda}((1-\varepsilon)\nu_1+\varepsilon\kappa_1)\right|(\mathrm{d}\varepsilon)^{\lambda}\\
&+\frac{1}{\Gamma(1+\lambda)}\int_{0}^{\frac{1}{6}}\left|\frac{1}{20}-\varepsilon\right|^{\lambda}\left|\mathcal{T}^{\lambda}(\varepsilon\nu_1+(1-\varepsilon)\kappa_1)\right|(\mathrm{d}\varepsilon)^{\lambda}\\
&+\frac{1}{\Gamma(1+\lambda)}\int_{\frac{1}{6}}^{\frac{1}{3}}\left|\frac{6}{20}-\varepsilon\right|^{\lambda}\left|\mathcal{T}^{\lambda}(\varepsilon\nu_1+(1-\varepsilon)\kappa_1)\right|(\mathrm{d}\varepsilon)^{\lambda}\\
&+\frac{1}{\Gamma(1+\lambda)}\int_{\frac{1}{3}}^{\frac{1}{2}}\left|\frac{7}{20}-\varepsilon\right|^{\lambda}\left|\mathcal{T}^{\lambda}(\varepsilon\nu_1+(1-\varepsilon)\kappa_1)\right|(\mathrm{d}\varepsilon)^{\lambda}\\
&+\frac{1}{\Gamma(1+\lambda)}\int_{\frac{1}{2}}^{\frac{2}{3}}\left|\frac{13}{20}-\varepsilon\right|^{\lambda}\left|\mathcal{T}^{\lambda}(\varepsilon\nu_1+(1-\varepsilon)\kappa_1)\right|(\mathrm{d}\varepsilon)^{\lambda}\\
&+\frac{1}{\Gamma(1+\lambda)}\int_{\frac{2}{3}}^{\frac{5}{6}}\left|\frac{14}{20}-\varepsilon\right|^{\lambda}\left|\mathcal{T}^{\lambda}(\varepsilon\nu_1+(1-\varepsilon)\kappa_1)\right|(\mathrm{d}\varepsilon)^{\lambda}\\
&+\frac{1}{\Gamma(1+\lambda)}\int_{\frac{5}{6}}^{1}\left|\frac{19}{20}-\varepsilon\right|^{\lambda}\left|\mathcal{T}^{\lambda}(\varepsilon\nu_1+(1-\varepsilon)\kappa_1)\right|(\mathrm{d}\varepsilon)^{\lambda}\Bigg]\\
\leq&\left(\frac{\kappa_1-\nu_1}{2}\right)^{\lambda}\left[\left(\frac{1}{\Gamma(1+\lambda)}\int_{0}^{\frac{1}{6}}\left|\varepsilon-\frac{1}{20}\right|^{\lambda}(\mathrm{d}\varepsilon)^{\lambda}\right)^{1-\frac{1}{r_2}}\right.\\
&\times\left(\frac{1}{\Gamma(1+\lambda)}\int_{0}^{\frac{1}{6}}\left|\varepsilon-\frac{1}{20}\right|^{\lambda}|\mathcal{T}^{\lambda}((1-\varepsilon)\nu_1+\varepsilon\kappa_1)|^{r_2}(\mathrm{d}\varepsilon)^{\lambda}\right)^{\frac{1}{r_2}}\\
&+\left(\frac{1}{\Gamma(1+\lambda)}\int_{\frac{1}{6}}^{\frac{1}{3}}\left|\varepsilon-\frac{6}{20}\right|^{\lambda}(\mathrm{d}\varepsilon)^{\lambda}\right)^{1-\frac{1}{r_2}}\\
&\times\left(\frac{1}{\Gamma(1+\lambda)}\int_{\frac{1}{6}}^{\frac{1}{3}}\left|\varepsilon-\frac{6}{20}\right|^{\lambda}|\mathcal{T}^{\lambda}((1-\varepsilon)\nu_1+\varepsilon\kappa_1)|^{r_2}(\mathrm{d}\varepsilon)^{\lambda}\right)^{\frac{1}{r_2}}\\
&+\left(\frac{1}{\Gamma(1+\lambda)}\int_{\frac{1}{3}}^{\frac{1}{2}}\left|\varepsilon-\frac{7}{20}\right|^{\lambda}(\mathrm{d}\varepsilon)^{\lambda}\right)^{1-\frac{1}{r_2}}\\
&\times\left(\frac{1}{\Gamma(1+\lambda)}\int_{\frac{1}{3}}^{\frac{1}{2}}\left|\varepsilon-\frac{7}{20}\right|^{\lambda}|\mathcal{T}^{\lambda}((1-\varepsilon)\nu_1+\varepsilon\kappa_1)|^{r_2}(\mathrm{d}\varepsilon)^{\lambda}\right)^{\frac{1}{r_2}}\\
&+\left(\frac{1}{\Gamma(1+\lambda)}\int_{\frac{1}{2}}^{\frac{2}{3}}\left|\varepsilon-\frac{13}{20}\right|^{\lambda}(\mathrm{d}\varepsilon)^{\lambda}\right)^{1-\frac{1}{r_2}}\\
&\times\left(\frac{1}{\Gamma(1+\lambda)}\int_{\frac{1}{2}}^{\frac{2}{3}}\left|\varepsilon-\frac{13}{20}\right|^{\lambda}|\mathcal{T}^{\lambda}((1-\varepsilon)\nu_1+\varepsilon\kappa_1)|^{r_2}(\mathrm{d}\varepsilon)^{\lambda}\right)^{\frac{1}{r_2}}\\
&+\left(\frac{1}{\Gamma(1+\lambda)}\int_{\frac{2}{3}}^{\frac{5}{6}}\left|\varepsilon-\frac{14}{20}\right|^{\lambda}(\mathrm{d}\varepsilon)^{\lambda}\right)^{1-\frac{1}{r_2}}\\
&\times\left(\frac{1}{\Gamma(1+\lambda)}\int_{\frac{2}{3}}^{\frac{5}{6}}\left|\varepsilon-\frac{14}{20}\right|^{\lambda}|\mathcal{T}^{\lambda}((1-\varepsilon)\nu_1+\varepsilon\kappa_1)|^{r_2}(\mathrm{d}\varepsilon)^{\lambda}\right)^{\frac{1}{r_2}}
\end{aligned}
$$

$$+\left(\frac{1}{\Gamma(1+\lambda)}\int_{\frac{5}{6}}^{1}\left|\varepsilon-\frac{19}{20}\right|^{\lambda}(\mathrm{d}\varepsilon)^{\lambda}\right)^{1-\frac{1}{r_2}}$$
$$\times\left(\frac{1}{\Gamma(1+\lambda)}\int_{\frac{5}{6}}^{1}\left|\varepsilon-\frac{19}{20}\right|^{\lambda}|\mathcal{T}^{\lambda}((1-\varepsilon)\nu_1+\varepsilon\kappa_1)|^{r_2}(\mathrm{d}\varepsilon)^{\lambda}\right)^{\frac{1}{r_2}}$$
$$+\left(\frac{1}{\Gamma(1+\lambda)}\int_{0}^{\frac{1}{6}}\left|\varepsilon-\frac{1}{20}\right|^{\lambda}(\mathrm{d}\varepsilon)^{\lambda}\right)^{1-\frac{1}{r_2}}$$
$$\times\left(\frac{1}{\Gamma(1+\lambda)}\int_{0}^{\frac{1}{6}}\left|\varepsilon-\frac{1}{20}\right|^{\lambda}|\mathcal{T}^{\lambda}(\varepsilon\nu_1+(1-\varepsilon)\kappa_1)|^{r_2}(\mathrm{d}\varepsilon)^{\lambda}\right)^{\frac{1}{r_2}}$$
$$+\left(\frac{1}{\Gamma(1+\lambda)}\int_{\frac{1}{6}}^{\frac{1}{3}}\left|\varepsilon-\frac{6}{20}\right|^{\lambda}(\mathrm{d}\varepsilon)^{\lambda}\right)^{1-\frac{1}{r_2}}$$
$$\times\left(\frac{1}{\Gamma(1+\lambda)}\int_{\frac{1}{6}}^{\frac{1}{3}}\left|\varepsilon-\frac{6}{20}\right|^{\lambda}|\mathcal{T}^{\lambda}(\varepsilon\nu_1+(1-\varepsilon)\kappa_1)|^{r_2}(\mathrm{d}\varepsilon)^{\lambda}\right)^{\frac{1}{r_2}}$$
$$+\left(\frac{1}{\Gamma(1+\lambda)}\int_{\frac{1}{3}}^{\frac{1}{2}}\left|\varepsilon-\frac{7}{20}\right|^{\lambda}(\mathrm{d}\varepsilon)^{\lambda}\right)^{1-\frac{1}{r_2}}$$
$$\times\left(\frac{1}{\Gamma(1+\lambda)}\int_{\frac{1}{3}}^{\frac{1}{2}}\left|\varepsilon-\frac{7}{20}\right|^{\lambda}|\mathcal{T}^{\lambda}(\varepsilon\nu_1+(1-\varepsilon)\kappa_1)|^{r_2}(\mathrm{d}\varepsilon)^{\lambda}\right)^{\frac{1}{r_2}}$$
$$+\left(\frac{1}{\Gamma(1+\lambda)}\int_{\frac{1}{2}}^{\frac{2}{3}}\left|\varepsilon-\frac{13}{20}\right|^{\lambda}(\mathrm{d}\varepsilon)^{\lambda}\right)^{1-\frac{1}{r_2}}$$
$$\times\left(\frac{1}{\Gamma(1+\lambda)}\int_{\frac{1}{2}}^{\frac{2}{3}}\left|\varepsilon-\frac{13}{20}\right|^{\lambda}|\mathcal{T}^{\lambda}(\varepsilon\nu_1+(1-\varepsilon)\kappa_1)|^{r_2}(\mathrm{d}\varepsilon)^{\lambda}\right)^{\frac{1}{r_2}}$$
$$+\left(\frac{1}{\Gamma(1+\lambda)}\int_{\frac{2}{3}}^{\frac{5}{6}}\left|\varepsilon-\frac{14}{20}\right|^{\lambda}(\mathrm{d}\varepsilon)^{\lambda}\right)^{1-\frac{1}{r_2}}$$
$$\times\left(\frac{1}{\Gamma(1+\lambda)}\int_{\frac{2}{3}}^{\frac{5}{6}}\left|\varepsilon-\frac{14}{20}\right|^{\lambda}|\mathcal{T}^{\lambda}(\varepsilon\nu_1+(1-\varepsilon)\kappa_1)|^{r_2}(\mathrm{d}\varepsilon)^{\lambda}\right)^{\frac{1}{r_2}}$$
$$+\left(\frac{1}{\Gamma(1+\lambda)}\int_{\frac{5}{6}}^{1}\left|\varepsilon-\frac{19}{20}\right|^{\lambda}(\mathrm{d}\varepsilon)^{\lambda}\right)^{1-\frac{1}{r_2}}$$
$$\left.\times\left(\frac{1}{\Gamma(1+\lambda)}\int_{\frac{5}{6}}^{1}\left|\varepsilon-\frac{19}{20}\right|^{\lambda}|\mathcal{T}^{\lambda}(\varepsilon\nu_1+(1-\varepsilon)\kappa_1)|^{r_2}(\mathrm{d}\varepsilon)^{\lambda}\right)^{\frac{1}{r_2}}\right]$$
$$\leq\left(\frac{\kappa_1-\nu_1}{2}\right)^{\lambda}\left[\left(\frac{1}{\Gamma(1+\lambda)}\int_{0}^{\frac{1}{6}}\left|\varepsilon-\frac{1}{20}\right|^{\lambda}(\mathrm{d}\varepsilon)^{\lambda}\right)^{1-\frac{1}{r_2}}\right.$$
$$\times\left(\frac{1}{\Gamma(1+\lambda)}\int_{0}^{\frac{1}{6}}\left|\varepsilon-\frac{1}{20}\right|^{\lambda}[(1-\varepsilon)^{\lambda}|\mathcal{T}^{\lambda}(\nu_1)|^{r_2}+\varepsilon^{\lambda}|\mathcal{T}^{\lambda}(\kappa_1)|^{r_2}](\mathrm{d}\varepsilon)^{\lambda}\right)^{\frac{1}{r_2}}$$
$$+\left(\frac{1}{\Gamma(1+\lambda)}\int_{\frac{1}{6}}^{\frac{1}{3}}\left|\varepsilon-\frac{6}{20}\right|^{\lambda}(\mathrm{d}\varepsilon)^{\lambda}\right)^{1-\frac{1}{r_2}}$$
$$\times\left(\frac{1}{\Gamma(1+\lambda)}\int_{\frac{1}{6}}^{\frac{1}{3}}\left|\varepsilon-\frac{6}{20}\right|^{\lambda}[(1-\varepsilon)^{\lambda}|\mathcal{T}^{\lambda}(\nu_1)|^{r_2}+\varepsilon^{\lambda}|\mathcal{T}^{\lambda}(\kappa_1)|^{r_2}](\mathrm{d}\varepsilon)^{\lambda}\right)^{\frac{1}{r_2}}$$

$$
\begin{aligned}
&+\left(\frac{1}{\Gamma(1+\lambda)}\int_{\frac{1}{3}}^{\frac{1}{2}}\left|\varepsilon-\frac{7}{20}\right|^{\lambda}(d\varepsilon)^{\lambda}\right)^{1-\frac{1}{r_2}}\\
&\times\left(\frac{1}{\Gamma(1+\lambda)}\int_{\frac{1}{3}}^{\frac{1}{2}}\left|\varepsilon-\frac{7}{20}\right|^{\lambda}[(1-\varepsilon)^{\lambda}|\mathcal{T}^{\lambda}(\nu_1)|^{r_2}+\varepsilon^{\lambda}|\mathcal{T}^{\lambda}(\kappa_1)|^{r_2}](d\varepsilon)^{\lambda}\right)^{\frac{1}{r_2}}\\
&+\left(\frac{1}{\Gamma(1+\lambda)}\int_{\frac{1}{2}}^{\frac{2}{3}}\left|\varepsilon-\frac{13}{20}\right|^{\lambda}(d\varepsilon)^{\lambda}\right)^{1-\frac{1}{r_2}}\\
&\times\left(\frac{1}{\Gamma(1+\lambda)}\int_{\frac{1}{2}}^{\frac{2}{3}}\left|\varepsilon-\frac{13}{20}\right|^{\lambda}[(1-\varepsilon)^{\lambda}|\mathcal{T}^{\lambda}(\nu_1)|^{r_2}+\varepsilon^{\lambda}|\mathcal{T}^{\lambda}(\kappa_1)|^{r_2}](d\varepsilon)^{\lambda}\right)^{\frac{1}{r_2}}\\
&+\left(\frac{1}{\Gamma(1+\lambda)}\int_{\frac{2}{3}}^{\frac{5}{6}}\left|\varepsilon-\frac{14}{20}\right|^{\lambda}(d\varepsilon)^{\lambda}\right)^{1-\frac{1}{r_2}}\\
&\times\left(\frac{1}{\Gamma(1+\lambda)}\int_{\frac{2}{3}}^{\frac{5}{6}}\left|\varepsilon-\frac{14}{20}\right|^{\lambda}[(1-\varepsilon)^{\lambda}|\mathcal{T}^{\lambda}(\nu_1)|^{r_2}+\varepsilon^{\lambda}|\mathcal{T}^{\lambda}(\kappa_1)|^{r_2}](d\varepsilon)^{\lambda}\right)^{\frac{1}{r_2}}\\
&+\left(\frac{1}{\Gamma(1+\lambda)}\int_{\frac{5}{6}}^{1}\left|\varepsilon-\frac{19}{20}\right|^{\lambda}(d\varepsilon)^{\lambda}\right)^{1-\frac{1}{r_2}}\\
&\times\left(\frac{1}{\Gamma(1+\lambda)}\int_{\frac{5}{6}}^{1}\left|\varepsilon-\frac{19}{20}\right|^{\lambda}[(1-\varepsilon)^{\lambda}|\mathcal{T}^{\lambda}(\nu_1)|^{r_2}+\varepsilon^{\lambda}|\mathcal{T}^{\lambda}(\kappa_1)|^{r_2}](d\varepsilon)^{\lambda}\right)^{\frac{1}{r_2}}\\
&+\left(\frac{1}{\Gamma(1+\lambda)}\int_{0}^{\frac{1}{6}}\left|\varepsilon-\frac{1}{20}\right|^{\lambda}(d\varepsilon)^{\lambda}\right)^{1-\frac{1}{r_2}}\\
&\times\left(\frac{1}{\Gamma(1+\lambda)}\int_{0}^{\frac{1}{6}}\left|\varepsilon-\frac{1}{20}\right|^{\lambda}[\varepsilon^{\lambda}|\mathcal{T}^{\lambda}(\nu_1)|^{r_2}+(1-\varepsilon)^{\lambda}|\mathcal{T}^{\lambda}(\kappa_1)|^{r_2}](d\varepsilon)^{\lambda}\right)^{\frac{1}{r_2}}\\
&+\left(\frac{1}{\Gamma(1+\lambda)}\int_{\frac{1}{6}}^{\frac{1}{3}}\left|\varepsilon-\frac{6}{20}\right|^{\lambda}(d\varepsilon)^{\lambda}\right)^{1-\frac{1}{r_2}}\\
&\times\left(\frac{1}{\Gamma(1+\lambda)}\int_{\frac{1}{6}}^{\frac{1}{3}}\left|\varepsilon-\frac{6}{20}\right|^{\lambda}[\varepsilon^{\lambda}|\mathcal{T}^{\lambda}(\nu_1)|^{r_2}+(1-\varepsilon)^{\lambda}|\mathcal{T}^{\lambda}(\kappa_1)|^{r_2}](d\varepsilon)^{\lambda}\right)^{\frac{1}{r_2}}\\
&+\left(\frac{1}{\Gamma(1+\lambda)}\int_{\frac{1}{3}}^{\frac{1}{2}}\left|\varepsilon-\frac{7}{20}\right|^{\lambda}(d\varepsilon)^{\lambda}\right)^{1-\frac{1}{r_2}}\\
&\times\left(\frac{1}{\Gamma(1+\lambda)}\int_{\frac{1}{3}}^{\frac{1}{2}}\left|\varepsilon-\frac{7}{20}\right|^{\lambda}[\varepsilon^{\lambda}|\mathcal{T}^{\lambda}(\nu_1)|^{r_2}+(1-\varepsilon)^{\lambda}|\mathcal{T}^{\lambda}(\kappa_1)|^{r_2}](d\varepsilon)^{\lambda}\right)^{\frac{1}{r_2}}\\
&+\left(\frac{1}{\Gamma(1+\lambda)}\int_{\frac{1}{2}}^{\frac{2}{3}}\left|\varepsilon-\frac{13}{20}\right|^{\lambda}(d\varepsilon)^{\lambda}\right)^{1-\frac{1}{r_2}}\\
&\times\left(\frac{1}{\Gamma(1+\lambda)}\int_{\frac{1}{2}}^{\frac{2}{3}}\left|\varepsilon-\frac{13}{20}\right|^{\lambda}[\varepsilon^{\lambda}|\mathcal{T}^{\lambda}(\nu_1)|^{r_2}+(1-\varepsilon)^{\lambda}|\mathcal{T}^{\lambda}(\kappa_1)|^{r_2}](d\varepsilon)^{\lambda}\right)^{\frac{1}{r_2}}\\
&+\left(\frac{1}{\Gamma(1+\lambda)}\int_{\frac{2}{3}}^{\frac{5}{6}}\left|\varepsilon-\frac{14}{20}\right|^{\lambda}(d\varepsilon)^{\lambda}\right)^{1-\frac{1}{r_2}}\\
&\times\left(\frac{1}{\Gamma(1+\lambda)}\int_{\frac{2}{3}}^{\frac{5}{6}}\left|\varepsilon-\frac{14}{20}\right|^{\lambda}[\varepsilon^{\lambda}|\mathcal{T}^{\lambda}(\nu_1)|^{r_2}+(1-\varepsilon)^{\lambda}|\mathcal{T}^{\lambda}(\kappa_1)|^{r_2}](d\varepsilon)^{\lambda}\right)^{\frac{1}{r_2}}
\end{aligned}
$$

$$+\left(\frac{1}{\Gamma(1+\lambda)}\int_{\frac{5}{6}}^{1}\left|\varepsilon-\frac{19}{20}\right|^{\lambda}(d\varepsilon)^{\lambda}\right)^{1-\frac{1}{r_2}}$$
$$\times\left(\frac{1}{\Gamma(1+\lambda)}\int_{\frac{5}{6}}^{1}\left|\varepsilon-\frac{19}{20}\right|^{\lambda}[\varepsilon^{\lambda}|\mathcal{T}^{\lambda}(\nu_1)|^{r_2}+(1-\varepsilon)^{\lambda}|\mathcal{T}^{\lambda}(\kappa_1)|^{r_2}](d\varepsilon)^{\lambda}\right)^{\frac{1}{r_2}}\Bigg].$$

Hence, the desired relation ia acquired. □

Example 3. *If we take $\mathcal{T}(\delta) = \delta^{\sigma\lambda}$, $\nu_1 = 0$ and $\kappa_1 = 3$ in Theorem 9. Then, 2D and 3D validations of Theorem 9 are*

Figure 3a,b demonstrate the accuracy of Theorem 9.

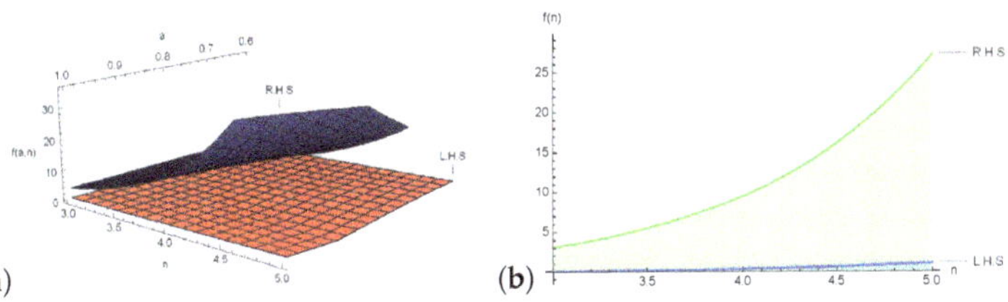

(**a**) (**b**)

Figure 3. (**a**) Three- and (**b**) two-dimensional simulations of Theorem 9 for $\lambda \in [0.6, 1]$, $\lambda = \frac{4}{5}$ and $\sigma \in [3, 5]$, respectively.

Now, we develop a new counterpart for the remainder of Weddle's quadrature rules involving Young's inequality.

Theorem 10. *Suppose that all constraints of Lemma 2 are fulfilled. If there exist $m, M \in \mathbb{R}$ such that $m \leq \mathcal{T}^{\lambda}(\varepsilon) \leq M$ for $\varepsilon \in [\nu_1, \kappa_1]$. Then*

$$\left|W(\nu_1,\kappa_1)-\frac{\Gamma(1+\lambda)}{(\kappa_1-\nu_1)^{\lambda}}{}_{a}I_{\kappa_1}\mathcal{T}(\delta)\right| \leq \frac{(M-m)(\kappa_1-\nu_1)^{\lambda}\Gamma(1+\lambda)}{2^{\lambda}\Gamma(1+2\lambda)}\left(\frac{26}{225}\right)^{\lambda},$$

$M > 0$.

Proof. From Lemma 2, we have

$$W(\nu_1,\kappa_1)-\frac{\Gamma(1+\lambda)}{(\kappa_1-\nu_1)^{\lambda}}{}_{\nu_1}I_{\kappa_1}\mathcal{T}(\delta)$$
$$=\left(\frac{\kappa_1-\nu_1}{2}\right)^{\lambda}\frac{1}{\Gamma(1+\lambda)}\int_0^1\triangle(\varepsilon)\left[\mathcal{T}^{\lambda}((1-\varepsilon)\nu_1+\varepsilon\kappa_1)-\mathcal{T}^{\lambda}(\varepsilon\nu_1+(1-\varepsilon)\kappa_1)\right](d\varepsilon)^{\lambda}$$
$$=\left(\frac{\kappa_1-\nu_1}{2}\right)^{\lambda}\Bigg[\frac{1}{\Gamma(1+\lambda)}\int_0^{\frac{1}{6}}\left(\varepsilon-\frac{1}{20}\right)^{\lambda}\left(\mathcal{T}^{\lambda}((1-\varepsilon)\nu_1+\varepsilon\kappa_1)-\frac{m+M}{2}\right)(d\varepsilon)^{\lambda}$$
$$+\frac{1}{\Gamma(1+\lambda)}\int_{\frac{1}{6}}^{\frac{1}{3}}\left(\varepsilon-\frac{6}{20}\right)^{\lambda}\left(\mathcal{T}^{\lambda}((1-\varepsilon)\nu_1+\varepsilon\kappa_1)-\frac{m+M}{2}\right)(d\varepsilon)^{\lambda}$$
$$+\frac{1}{\Gamma(1+\lambda)}\int_{\frac{1}{3}}^{\frac{1}{2}}\left(\varepsilon-\frac{7}{20}\right)^{\lambda}\left(\mathcal{T}^{\lambda}((1-\varepsilon)\nu_1+\varepsilon\kappa_1)-\frac{m+M}{2}\right)(d\varepsilon)^{\lambda}$$
$$+\frac{1}{\Gamma(1+\lambda)}\int_{\frac{1}{2}}^{\frac{2}{3}}\left(\varepsilon-\frac{13}{20}\right)^{\lambda}\left(\mathcal{T}^{\lambda}((1-\varepsilon)\nu_1+\varepsilon\kappa_1)-\frac{m+M}{2}\right)(d\varepsilon)^{\lambda}$$
$$+\frac{1}{\Gamma(1+\lambda)}\int_{\frac{2}{3}}^{\frac{5}{6}}\left(\varepsilon-\frac{14}{20}\right)^{\lambda}\left(\mathcal{T}^{\lambda}((1-\varepsilon)\nu_1+\varepsilon\kappa_1)-\frac{m+M}{2}\right)(d\varepsilon)^{\lambda}$$

$$+\frac{1}{\Gamma(1+\lambda)}\int_{\frac{5}{6}}^{1}\left(\varepsilon-\frac{19}{20}\right)^{\lambda}\left(\mathcal{T}^{\lambda}((1-\varepsilon)\nu_1+\varepsilon\kappa_1)-\frac{m+M}{2}\right)(d\varepsilon)^{\lambda}$$
$$+\frac{1}{\Gamma(1+\lambda)}\int_{0}^{\frac{1}{6}}\left(\varepsilon-\frac{1}{20}\right)^{\lambda}\left(\frac{m+M}{2}-\mathcal{T}^{\lambda}(\varepsilon\nu_1+(1-\varepsilon)\kappa_1)\right)(d\varepsilon)^{\lambda}$$
$$+\frac{1}{\Gamma(1+\lambda)}\int_{\frac{1}{6}}^{\frac{1}{3}}\left(\varepsilon-\frac{6}{20}\right)^{\lambda}\left(\frac{m+M}{2}-\mathcal{T}^{\lambda}(\varepsilon\nu_1+(1-\varepsilon)\kappa_1)\right)(d\varepsilon)^{\lambda}$$
$$+\frac{1}{\Gamma(1+\lambda)}\int_{\frac{1}{3}}^{\frac{1}{2}}\left(\varepsilon-\frac{7}{20}\right)^{\lambda}\left(\frac{m+M}{2}-\mathcal{T}^{\lambda}(\varepsilon\nu_1+(1-\varepsilon)\kappa_1)\right)(d\varepsilon)^{\lambda}$$
$$+\frac{1}{\Gamma(1+\lambda)}\int_{\frac{1}{2}}^{\frac{2}{3}}\left(\varepsilon-\frac{13}{20}\right)^{\lambda}\left(\frac{m+M}{2}-\mathcal{T}^{\lambda}(\varepsilon\nu_1+(1-\varepsilon)\kappa_1)\right)(d\varepsilon)^{\lambda}$$
$$+\frac{1}{\Gamma(1+\lambda)}\int_{\frac{2}{3}}^{\frac{5}{6}}\left(\varepsilon-\frac{14}{20}\right)^{\lambda}\left(\frac{m+M}{2}-\mathcal{T}^{\lambda}(\varepsilon\nu_1+(1-\varepsilon)\kappa_1)\right)(d\varepsilon)^{\lambda}$$
$$\left.+\frac{1}{\Gamma(1+\lambda)}\int_{\frac{5}{6}}^{1}\left(\varepsilon-\frac{19}{20}\right)^{\lambda}\left(\frac{m+M}{2}-\mathcal{T}^{\lambda}(\varepsilon\nu_1+(1-\varepsilon)\kappa_1)\right)(d\varepsilon)^{\lambda}\right].$$

By taking the modulus of the above equality, we obtain

$$\left|W(\nu_1,\kappa_1)-\frac{\Gamma(1+\lambda)}{(\kappa_1-\nu_1)^{\lambda}}{}_{\nu_1}I_{\kappa_1}\mathcal{T}(\delta)\right|$$
$$\leq\left(\frac{\kappa_1-\nu_1}{2}\right)^{\lambda}\left[\frac{1}{\Gamma(1+\lambda)}\int_{0}^{\frac{1}{6}}\left|\varepsilon-\frac{1}{20}\right|^{\lambda}\left|\mathcal{T}^{\lambda}((1-\varepsilon)\nu_1+\varepsilon\kappa_1)-\frac{m+M}{2}\right|(d\varepsilon)^{\lambda}\right.$$
$$+\frac{1}{\Gamma(1+\lambda)}\int_{\frac{1}{6}}^{\frac{1}{3}}\left|\varepsilon-\frac{6}{20}\right|^{\lambda}\left|\mathcal{T}^{\lambda}((1-\varepsilon)\nu_1+\varepsilon\kappa_1)-\frac{m+M}{2}\right|(d\varepsilon)^{\lambda}$$
$$+\frac{1}{\Gamma(1+\lambda)}\int_{\frac{1}{3}}^{\frac{1}{2}}\left|\varepsilon-\frac{7}{20}\right|^{\lambda}\left|\mathcal{T}^{\lambda}((1-\varepsilon)\nu_1+\varepsilon\kappa_1)-\frac{m+M}{2}\right|(d\varepsilon)^{\lambda}$$
$$+\frac{1}{\Gamma(1+\lambda)}\int_{\frac{1}{2}}^{\frac{2}{3}}\left|\varepsilon-\frac{13}{20}\right|^{\lambda}\left|\mathcal{T}^{\lambda}((1-\varepsilon)\nu_1+\varepsilon\kappa_1)-\frac{m+M}{2}\right|(d\varepsilon)^{\lambda}$$
$$+\frac{1}{\Gamma(1+\lambda)}\int_{\frac{2}{3}}^{\frac{5}{6}}\left|\varepsilon-\frac{14}{20}\right|^{\lambda}\left|\mathcal{T}^{\lambda}((1-\varepsilon)\nu_1+\varepsilon\kappa_1)-\frac{m+M}{2}\right|(d\varepsilon)^{\lambda}$$
$$+\frac{1}{\Gamma(1+\lambda)}\int_{\frac{5}{6}}^{1}\left|\varepsilon-\frac{19}{20}\right|^{\lambda}\left|\mathcal{T}^{\lambda}((1-\varepsilon)\nu_1+\varepsilon\kappa_1)-\frac{m+M}{2}\right|(d\varepsilon)^{\lambda}$$
$$+\frac{1}{\Gamma(1+\lambda)}\int_{0}^{\frac{1}{6}}\left|\varepsilon-\frac{1}{20}\right|^{\lambda}\left|\frac{m+M}{2}-\mathcal{T}^{\lambda}(\varepsilon\nu_1+(1-\varepsilon)\kappa_1)\right|(d\varepsilon)^{\lambda}$$
$$+\frac{1}{\Gamma(1+\lambda)}\int_{\frac{1}{6}}^{\frac{1}{3}}\left|\varepsilon-\frac{6}{20}\right|^{\lambda}\left|\frac{m+M}{2}-\mathcal{T}^{\lambda}(\varepsilon\nu_1+(1-\varepsilon)\kappa_1)\right|(d\varepsilon)^{\lambda}$$
$$+\frac{1}{\Gamma(1+\lambda)}\int_{\frac{1}{3}}^{\frac{1}{2}}\left|\varepsilon-\frac{7}{20}\right|^{\lambda}\left|\frac{m+M}{2}-\mathcal{T}^{\lambda}(\varepsilon\nu_1+(1-\varepsilon)\kappa_1)\right|(d\varepsilon)^{\lambda}$$
$$+\frac{1}{\Gamma(1+\lambda)}\int_{\frac{1}{2}}^{\frac{2}{3}}\left|\varepsilon-\frac{13}{20}\right|^{\lambda}\left|\frac{m+M}{2}-\mathcal{T}^{\lambda}(\varepsilon\nu_1+(1-\varepsilon)\kappa_1)\right|(d\varepsilon)^{\lambda}$$
$$+\frac{1}{\Gamma(1+\lambda)}\int_{\frac{2}{3}}^{\frac{5}{6}}\left|\varepsilon-\frac{14}{20}\right|^{\lambda}\left|\frac{m+M}{2}-\mathcal{T}^{\lambda}(\varepsilon\nu_1+(1-\varepsilon)\kappa_1)\right|(d\varepsilon)^{\lambda}$$
$$\left.+\frac{1}{\Gamma(1+\lambda)}\int_{\frac{5}{6}}^{1}\left|\varepsilon-\frac{19}{20}\right|^{\lambda}\left|\frac{m+M}{2}-\mathcal{T}^{\lambda}(\varepsilon\nu_1+(1-\varepsilon)\kappa_1)\right|(d\varepsilon)^{\lambda}\right].$$

As $m \leq \mathcal{T}^{\lambda}(\varepsilon) \leq M$ and $\varepsilon \in [\nu_1, \kappa_1]$, we have

$$\left|\mathcal{T}^{\lambda}(\varepsilon\nu_1 + (1-\varepsilon)\kappa_1) - \frac{m+M}{2}\right| \leq \frac{M-m}{2}, \tag{6}$$

and

$$\left|\frac{m+M}{2} - \mathcal{T}^{\lambda}(\varepsilon\nu_1 + (1-\varepsilon)\kappa_1)\right| \leq \frac{M-m}{2}. \tag{7}$$

From inequality (6) and (7), we obtain

$$\begin{aligned}
&\left|W(\nu_1,\kappa_1) - \frac{\Gamma(1+\lambda)}{(\kappa_1-\nu_1)^{\lambda}}{}_{\nu_1}I_{\kappa_1}\mathcal{T}(\delta)\right| \\
&\leq \left(\frac{\kappa_1-\nu_1}{2}\right)^{\lambda}\left[\frac{1}{\Gamma(1+\lambda)}\int_0^{\frac{1}{6}}\left|\varepsilon-\frac{1}{20}\right|^{\lambda}(d\varepsilon)^{\lambda} + \int_{\frac{1}{6}}^{\frac{1}{3}}\left|\varepsilon-\frac{6}{20}\right|^{\lambda}(d\varepsilon)^{\lambda} + \int_{\frac{1}{3}}^{\frac{1}{2}}\left|\varepsilon-\frac{7}{20}\right|^{\lambda}(d\varepsilon)^{\lambda}\right. \\
&\left.+\int_{\frac{1}{2}}^{\frac{2}{3}}\left|\varepsilon-\frac{13}{20}\right|^{\lambda}(d\varepsilon)^{\lambda} + + \int_{\frac{2}{3}}^{\frac{5}{6}}\left|\varepsilon-\frac{14}{20}\right|^{\lambda}(d\varepsilon)^{\lambda} + + \int_{\frac{5}{6}}^{1}\left|\varepsilon-\frac{19}{20}\right|^{\lambda}(d\varepsilon)^{\lambda}\right](M-m).
\end{aligned}$$

This yields the required inequality. □

Example 4. *If we take $\mathcal{T}(\delta) = \delta^{\sigma\lambda}$, $\nu_1 = 0$ and $\kappa_1 = 3$ in Theorem 10. Then, 2D and 3D validations of Theorem 10 are*

Figure 4a,b illustrate the comparison between sides of Theorem 10.

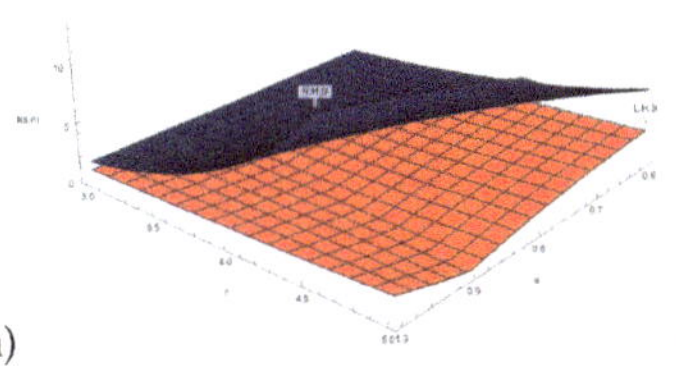

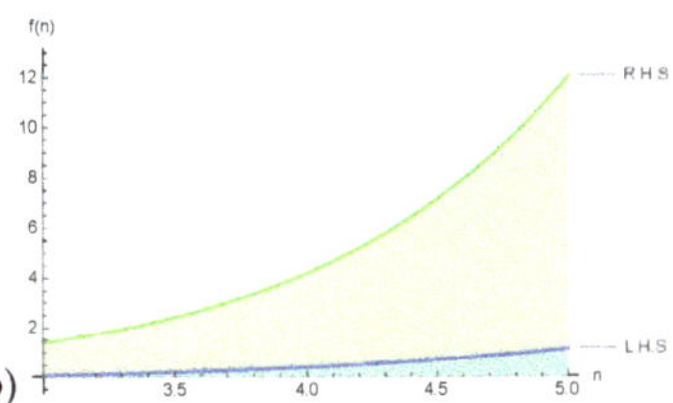

Figure 4. (**a**) Three- and (**b**) two-dimensional simulations of Theorem 10 for $\lambda \in [0.6, 1]$, $\lambda = \frac{4}{5}$ and $\sigma \in [3, 5]$, respectively.

Theorem 11. *Suppose that all constraints of lemma 2 are fulfilled and $\mathcal{T}^{\lambda}$ satisfies the L-Lipschit property. Then*

$$\left|W(\nu_1,\kappa_1) - \frac{\Gamma(1+\lambda)}{(\kappa_1-\nu_1)^{\lambda}}{}_{a}I_{\kappa_1}\mathcal{T}(\delta)\right| \leq \frac{L(\kappa_1-\nu_1)^{2\lambda}}{2^{\lambda}}\left[\frac{\Gamma(1+\lambda)}{\Gamma(1+2\lambda)}\left(\frac{109}{450}\right)^{\lambda} - \frac{\Gamma(1+2\lambda)}{\Gamma(1+3\lambda)}\left(\frac{43}{150}\right)^{\lambda}\right].$$

Proof. From Lemma 2, we have

$$\begin{aligned}
&W(\nu_1,\kappa_1) - \frac{\Gamma(1+\lambda)}{(\kappa_1-\nu_1)^{\lambda}}{}_{\nu_1}I_{\kappa_1}\mathcal{T}(\delta) \\
&= \left(\frac{\kappa_1-\nu_1}{2}\right)^{\lambda}\frac{1}{\Gamma(1+\lambda)}\int_0^1 \triangle(\varepsilon)\left[\mathcal{T}^{\lambda}((1-\varepsilon)\nu_1+\varepsilon\kappa_1) - \mathcal{T}^{\lambda}(\varepsilon\nu_1+(1-\varepsilon)\kappa_1)\right](d\varepsilon)^{\lambda} \\
&= \left(\frac{\kappa_1-\nu_1}{2}\right)^{\lambda}\left[\frac{1}{\Gamma(1+\lambda)}\int_0^{\frac{1}{6}}\left(\varepsilon-\frac{1}{20}\right)^{\lambda}\left[\mathcal{T}^{\lambda}((1-\varepsilon)\nu_1+\varepsilon\kappa_1) - \mathcal{T}^{\lambda}(\varepsilon\nu_1+(1-\varepsilon)\kappa_1)\right](d\varepsilon)^{\lambda}\right. \\
&+\frac{1}{\Gamma(1+\lambda)}\int_{\frac{1}{6}}^{\frac{1}{3}}\left(\varepsilon-\frac{6}{20}\right)^{\lambda}\left[\mathcal{T}^{\lambda}((1-\varepsilon)\nu_1+\varepsilon\kappa_1) - \mathcal{T}^{\lambda}(\varepsilon\nu_1+(1-\varepsilon)\kappa_1)\right](d\varepsilon)^{\lambda}
\end{aligned}$$

$$
\begin{aligned}
&+\frac{1}{\Gamma(1+\lambda)}\int_{\frac{1}{3}}^{\frac{1}{2}}\left(\varepsilon-\frac{7}{20}\right)^{\lambda}\Big[\mathcal{T}^{\lambda}((1-\varepsilon)\nu_1+\varepsilon\kappa_1)-\mathcal{T}^{\lambda}(\varepsilon\nu_1+(1-\varepsilon)\kappa_1)\Big](d\varepsilon)^{\lambda}\\
&+\frac{1}{\Gamma(1+\lambda)}\int_{\frac{1}{2}}^{\frac{2}{3}}\left(\varepsilon-\frac{13}{20}\right)^{\lambda}\Big[\mathcal{T}^{\lambda}((1-\varepsilon)\nu_1+\varepsilon\kappa_1)-\mathcal{T}^{\lambda}(\varepsilon\nu_1+(1-\varepsilon)\kappa_1)\Big](d\varepsilon)^{\lambda}\\
&+\frac{1}{\Gamma(1+\lambda)}\int_{\frac{2}{3}}^{\frac{5}{6}}\left(\varepsilon-\frac{14}{20}\right)^{\lambda}\Big[\mathcal{T}^{\lambda}((1-\varepsilon)\nu_1+\varepsilon\kappa_1)-\mathcal{T}^{\lambda}(\varepsilon\nu_1+(1-\varepsilon)\kappa_1)\Big](d\varepsilon)^{\lambda}\\
&+\frac{1}{\Gamma(1+\lambda)}\int_{\frac{5}{6}}^{1}\left(\varepsilon-\frac{19}{20}\right)^{\lambda}\Big[\mathcal{T}^{\lambda}((1-\varepsilon)\nu_1+\varepsilon\kappa_1)-\mathcal{T}^{\lambda}(\varepsilon\nu_1+(1-\varepsilon)\kappa_1)\Big](d\varepsilon)^{\lambda}\Bigg].
\end{aligned}
$$

Since $\mathcal{T}^{\lambda}$ is L-Lipschitzian functon, we obtain

$$
\begin{aligned}
&\left|W(\nu_1,\kappa_1)-\frac{\Gamma(1+\lambda)}{(\kappa_1-\nu_1)^{\lambda}}{}_{\nu_1}I_{\kappa_1}\mathcal{T}(\delta)\right|\\
&\leq\left(\frac{\kappa_1-\nu_1}{2}\right)^{\lambda}\Bigg[\frac{1}{\Gamma(1+\lambda)}\int_{0}^{\frac{1}{6}}\left|\varepsilon-\frac{1}{20}\right|^{\lambda}\Big|\mathcal{T}^{\lambda}((1-\varepsilon)\nu_1+\varepsilon\kappa_1)-\mathcal{T}^{\lambda}(\varepsilon\nu_1+(1-\varepsilon)\kappa_1)\Big|(d\varepsilon)^{\lambda}\\
&\quad+\frac{1}{\Gamma(1+\lambda)}\int_{\frac{1}{6}}^{\frac{1}{3}}\left|\varepsilon-\frac{6}{20}\right|^{\lambda}\Big|\mathcal{T}^{\lambda}((1-\varepsilon)\nu_1+\varepsilon\kappa_1)-\mathcal{T}^{\lambda}(\varepsilon\nu_1+(1-\varepsilon)\kappa_1)\Big|(d\varepsilon)^{\lambda}\\
&\quad+\frac{1}{\Gamma(1+\lambda)}\int_{\frac{1}{3}}^{\frac{1}{2}}\left|\varepsilon-\frac{7}{20}\right|^{\lambda}\Big|\mathcal{T}^{\lambda}((1-\varepsilon)\nu_1+\varepsilon\kappa_1)-\mathcal{T}^{\lambda}(\varepsilon\nu_1+(1-\varepsilon)\kappa_1)\Big|(d\varepsilon)^{\lambda}\\
&\quad+\frac{1}{\Gamma(1+\lambda)}\int_{\frac{1}{2}}^{\frac{2}{3}}\left|\varepsilon-\frac{13}{20}\right|^{\lambda}\Big|\mathcal{T}^{\lambda}((1-\varepsilon)\nu_1+\varepsilon\kappa_1)-\mathcal{T}^{\lambda}(\varepsilon\nu_1+(1-\varepsilon)\kappa_1)\Big|(d\varepsilon)^{\lambda}\\
&\quad+\frac{1}{\Gamma(1+\lambda)}\int_{\frac{2}{3}}^{\frac{5}{6}}\left|\varepsilon-\frac{14}{20}\right|^{\lambda}\Big|\mathcal{T}^{\lambda}((1-\varepsilon)\nu_1+\varepsilon\kappa_1)-\mathcal{T}^{\lambda}(\varepsilon\nu_1+(1-\varepsilon)\kappa_1)\Big|(d\varepsilon)^{\lambda}\\
&\quad+\frac{1}{\Gamma(1+\lambda)}\int_{\frac{5}{6}}^{1}\left|\varepsilon-\frac{19}{20}\right|^{\lambda}\Big|\mathcal{T}^{\lambda}((1-\varepsilon)\nu_1+\varepsilon\kappa_1)-\mathcal{T}^{\lambda}(\varepsilon\nu_1+(1-\varepsilon)\kappa_1)\Big|(d\varepsilon)^{\lambda}\Bigg]\\
&\leq\left(\frac{\kappa_1-\nu_1}{2}\right)^{\lambda}\Bigg[\Bigg(\frac{1}{\Gamma(1+\lambda)}\int_{0}^{\frac{1}{6}}\left|\varepsilon-\frac{1}{20}\right|^{\lambda}(d\varepsilon)^{\lambda}+\int_{\frac{1}{6}}^{\frac{1}{3}}\left|\varepsilon-\frac{6}{20}\right|^{\lambda}(d\varepsilon)^{\lambda}\\
&\quad+\int_{\frac{1}{3}}^{\frac{1}{2}}\left|\varepsilon-\frac{7}{20}\right|^{\lambda}(d\varepsilon)^{\lambda}\Bigg)L(1-2\varepsilon)^{\lambda}(\kappa_1-\nu_1)^{\lambda}+\Bigg(\int_{\frac{1}{2}}^{\frac{2}{3}}\left|\varepsilon-\frac{13}{20}\right|^{\lambda}(d\varepsilon)^{\lambda}\\
&\quad+\int_{\frac{2}{3}}^{\frac{5}{6}}\left|\varepsilon-\frac{14}{20}\right|^{\lambda}(d\varepsilon)^{\lambda}++\int_{\frac{5}{6}}^{1}\left|\varepsilon-\frac{19}{20}\right|^{\lambda}(d\varepsilon)^{\lambda}\Bigg)L(2\varepsilon-1)^{\lambda}(\kappa_1-\nu_1)^{\lambda}\Bigg].
\end{aligned}
$$

Finally, we get the required relation. □

Example 5. *If we take* $\mathcal{T}(\delta)=\delta^{\sigma\lambda}$, $\nu_1=0$ *and* $\kappa_1=3$ *in Theorem 11. Then, 2D and 3D validations of Theorem 11 are*

Figure 5a,b illustrate the comparison between sides of Theorem 11.

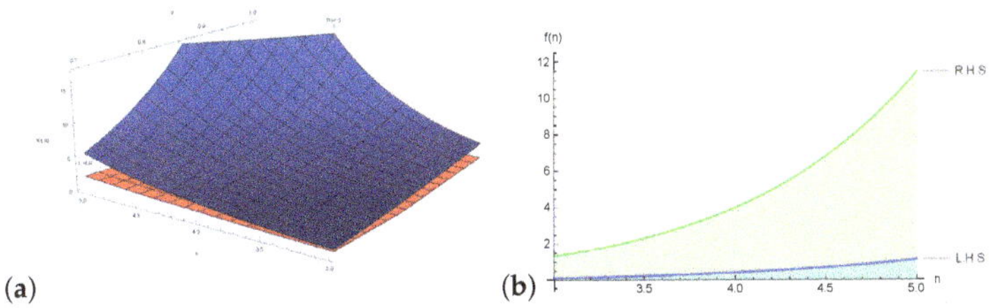

Figure 5. (**a**) Three- and (**b**) two-dimensional simulations of Theorem 11 for $\lambda \in [0.6, 1]$, $\lambda = \frac{4}{5}$ and $\sigma \in [3, 5]$, respectively.

3. Applications

3.1. Applications to Means

This subsection offers some new inequalities associated with generalized means and their differences. First, we look at binary means.

1. The generalized arithmetic mean:

$$A_\lambda(\nu_1, \kappa_1) = \frac{\nu_1{}^\lambda + \kappa_1{}^\lambda}{2^\lambda} = \left(\frac{\nu_1 + \kappa_1}{2}\right)^\lambda.$$

2. The generalized weighted arithmetic mean:

$${}_wA_\lambda(\nu_1, \kappa_1; m_1, m_2) = \frac{m_1^\lambda \nu_1{}^\lambda + m_2^\lambda \kappa_1{}^\lambda}{(\nu_1 + \kappa_1)^\lambda}.$$

3. The generalized log-r_1-mean:

$$L_{\lambda, r_1}(\nu_1, \kappa_1) = \left[\frac{\Gamma(1 + r_1\lambda)}{\Gamma(1 + (1 + r_1)\lambda)} \frac{\kappa_1{}^{(r_1+1)\lambda} - \nu_1{}^{(r_1+1)\lambda}}{(r_1 + 1)(\kappa_1 - \nu_1)^\lambda}\right]^{\frac{1}{r_1}}, r_1 \in \mathbb{R} \setminus \{-1, 0\}.$$

Proposition 1. *For $\nu_1, \kappa_1 \geq 0$, the Theorem 10 results in the following inequality,*

$$\begin{aligned}
&\left| \frac{\Gamma(1 + (\sigma - 1)\lambda)}{(90)^\lambda \Gamma(1 + \sigma\lambda)} \left[(2)^\lambda A_\lambda(\nu_1{}^\sigma, \kappa_1{}^\sigma) + 5^\lambda\, {}_wA_\lambda^\sigma\left(\nu_1, \kappa_1, \frac{5}{6}, \frac{1}{6}\right) +_w A_\lambda^\sigma\left(\nu_1, \kappa_1, \frac{1}{3}, \frac{2}{3}\right) \right.\right. \\
&\left.\left. + 6^\lambda A_\lambda^\sigma(\nu_1, \kappa_1) +_w A_\lambda^\sigma\left(\nu_1, \kappa_1, \frac{1}{3}, \frac{2}{3}\right) + 5^\lambda\, {}_wA_\lambda^\sigma\left(\nu_1, \kappa_1, \frac{1}{6}, \frac{5}{6}\right) \right] - \Gamma(1 + \lambda) L_{\lambda,\sigma}^\sigma(\nu_1, \kappa_1) \right| \\
&\leq \frac{(M - m)(\kappa_1 - \nu_1)^\lambda \Gamma(1 + \lambda)}{2^\lambda \Gamma(1 + 2\lambda)} \left(\frac{26}{225}\right)^\lambda.
\end{aligned}$$

Proof. The proof follows directly by applying $\mathcal{T}(\delta) = \frac{\Gamma(1+(\sigma-1)\lambda)}{\Gamma(1+\sigma\lambda)}(\delta)^{\sigma\lambda}, \sigma > 0$ in Theorem 10. □

3.2. Error Bounds

To conclude composite generalized Weddle's rules with the help of newly established results, we consider a partition of the interval $[\nu_1, \kappa_1]$ such as: $P : \nu_1 = \delta_0 < \delta_1 < \delta_2 < ... < \delta_\sigma = \kappa_1$, and $h_k = \frac{\delta_{i+1} - \delta_i}{6}$ $(k = 1, 2, 3 \cdots, \sigma - 1)$, where σ must be divisible by 6. Then

$$\frac{1}{\Gamma(1 + \lambda)} \int_{\nu_1}^{\kappa_1} \mathcal{T}(\delta) d\delta = \varepsilon(\lambda, \mathcal{T}) + \bar{R}(\lambda, \mathcal{T}),$$

where

$$\varepsilon(\lambda,\mathcal{T})=\sum_{i=0}^{\sigma-1}\frac{(\delta_{i+1}-\delta_i)}{(20)^\lambda}\left[\mathcal{T}(\delta_i)+5^\lambda\mathcal{T}\left(\frac{5\delta_i+\delta_{i+1}}{6}\right)+\mathcal{T}\left(\frac{2\delta_i+\delta_{i+1}}{3}\right)\right.$$
$$\left.+\mathcal{T}\left(\frac{\delta_i+\delta_{i+1}}{2}\right)+\mathcal{T}\left(\frac{\delta_i+2\delta_{i+1}}{3}\right)+5^\lambda\mathcal{T}\left(\frac{\delta_i+5\delta_{i+1}}{6}\right)+\mathcal{T}(\delta_{i+1})\right].$$

where $\bar{R}(\lambda,\mathcal{T})$ is the error term.

Proposition 2. *From Theorem 7, we have*

$$|\bar{R}(\lambda,\mathcal{T})|\leq\sum_{i=0}^{\sigma-1}(\delta_{i+1}-\delta_i)^\lambda\left\{\left[\frac{\Gamma(1+\lambda)}{\Gamma(1+2\lambda)}\left(\frac{4}{75}\right)^\lambda+\frac{\Gamma(1+2\lambda)}{\Gamma(1+3\lambda)}\left(\frac{1}{150}\right)^\lambda\right]|\mathcal{T}^\lambda(\delta_i)|\right.$$
$$\left.+\left[\frac{\Gamma(1+\lambda)}{\Gamma(1+2\lambda)}\left(\frac{14}{225}\right)^\lambda-\frac{\Gamma(1+2\lambda)}{\Gamma(1+3\lambda)}\left(\frac{1}{150}\right)^\lambda\right]|\mathcal{T}^\lambda(\delta_i)|\right\}.$$

Proof. To obtain the desired result, we apply Theorem 7 over the subinterval $[\delta_i,\delta_{i+1}]$ and take the sum from $i=0$ to $i=\sigma$. □

Proposition 3. *From Theorem 8, we have*

$$|\bar{R}(\lambda,\mathcal{T})|\leq\sum_{i=0}^{\sigma-1}(\delta_{i+1}-\delta_i)^\lambda\left\{\left(\frac{\Gamma(1+\lambda r_1)}{\Gamma(1+(r_1+1)\lambda)}\left(\left(\frac{7}{60}\right)^{(r_1+1)\lambda}+\left(\frac{1}{20}\right)^{(r_1+1)\lambda}\right)\right)^{\frac{1}{r_1}}\right.$$
$$\times\left(\left[\frac{\Gamma(1+\lambda)}{\Gamma(1+2\lambda)}\left(\left(\frac{11}{36}\right)^\lambda|\mathcal{T}^\lambda(\delta_i)|^{r_2}+\left(\frac{1}{36}\right)^\lambda|\mathcal{T}^\lambda(\delta_{i+1})|^{r_2}\right)\right]^{\frac{1}{r_2}}\right.$$
$$\left.+\left[\frac{\Gamma(1+\lambda)}{\Gamma(1+2\lambda)}\left(\left(\frac{1}{36}\right)^\lambda|\mathcal{T}^\lambda(\delta_i)|^{r_2}+\left(\frac{11}{36}\right)^\lambda|\mathcal{T}^\lambda(\delta_{i+1})|^{r_2}\right)\right]^{\frac{1}{r_2}}\right)$$
$$+\left(\frac{\Gamma(1+\lambda r_1)}{\Gamma(1+(r_1+1)\lambda)}\left(\left(\frac{1}{30}\right)^{(r_1+1)\lambda}+\left(\frac{2}{15}\right)^{(r_1+1)\lambda}\right)\right)^{\frac{1}{r_1}}$$
$$\times\left(\left[\frac{\Gamma(1+\lambda)}{\Gamma(1+2\lambda)}\left(\left(\frac{1}{4}\right)^\lambda|\mathcal{T}^\lambda(\delta_i)|^{r_2}+\left(\frac{1}{12}\right)^\lambda|\mathcal{T}^\lambda(\delta_{i+1})|^{r_2}\right)\right]^{\frac{1}{r_2}}\right.$$
$$\left.+\left[\frac{\Gamma(1+\lambda)}{\Gamma(1+2\lambda)}\left(\left(\frac{1}{12}\right)^\lambda|\mathcal{T}^\lambda(\delta_i)|^{r_2}+\left(\frac{1}{4}\right)^\lambda|\mathcal{T}^\lambda(\delta_{i+1})|^{r_2}\right)\right]^{\frac{1}{r_2}}\right)$$
$$+\left(\frac{\Gamma(1+\lambda r_1)}{\Gamma(1+(r_1+1)\lambda)}\left(\left(\frac{3}{20}\right)^{(r_1+1)\lambda}+\left(\frac{1}{60}\right)^{(r_1+1)\lambda}\right)\right)^{\frac{1}{r_1}}$$
$$\times\left(\left[\frac{\Gamma(1+\lambda)}{\Gamma(1+2\lambda)}\left(\left(\frac{7}{36}\right)^\lambda|\mathcal{T}^\lambda(\delta_i)|^{r_2}+\left(\frac{5}{36}\right)^\lambda|\mathcal{T}^\lambda(\delta_{i+1})|^{r_2}\right)\right]^{\frac{1}{r_2}}\right.$$
$$\left.\left.+\left[\frac{\Gamma(1+\lambda)}{\Gamma(1+2\lambda)}\left(\left(\frac{5}{36}\right)^\lambda|\mathcal{T}^\lambda(\delta_i)|^{r_2}+\left(\frac{7}{36}\right)^\lambda|\mathcal{T}^\lambda(\delta_{i+1})|^{r_2}\right)\right]^{\frac{1}{r_2}}\right)\right\},$$

where $\frac{1}{r_1}+\frac{1}{r_2}=1$.

Proof. To obtain the desired result, we apply Theorem 8 over the subinterval $[\delta_i,\delta_{i+1}]$ and take the sum from $i=0$ to $i=\sigma$. □

3.3. Applications to Probability

Let $p : [\nu_1, \kappa_1] \to [0,1]^\lambda$ be a probability density mapping over convex set X. Then cumulative distribution is demonstrated as

$$Pr_\lambda(X \leq \kappa_1) = F_\lambda(\kappa_1) = \frac{1}{\Gamma(1+\lambda)} \int_{\nu_1}^{\kappa_1} p(\delta)(\mathrm{d}\delta)\lambda.$$

Utilizing the fact that

$$E^\lambda(X) = \frac{1}{\Gamma(\lambda+1)} \int_{\nu_1}^{\kappa_1} \delta^\lambda p(\delta)(\mathrm{d}\delta)^\lambda$$
$$E^\lambda(X) = {\kappa_1}^\lambda - \frac{1}{\kappa_1 - \nu_1} \int_{\nu_1}^{\kappa_1} F_\lambda(\delta)(\mathrm{d}\delta)^\lambda.$$

Proposition 4. *Considering Theorem 7, we have*

$$\begin{aligned}
&\Bigg| \frac{1}{(20)^\lambda} \bigg[Pr_\lambda(\nu_1) + 5^\lambda Pr_\lambda\left(\frac{5\nu_1 + \kappa_1}{6}\right) + Pr_\lambda\left(\frac{2\nu_1 + \kappa_1}{3}\right) + 6^\lambda Pr_\lambda\left(\frac{\nu_1 + \kappa_1}{2}\right) \\
&+ Pr_\lambda\left(\frac{\nu_1 + 2\kappa_1}{3}\right) + 5^\lambda Pr_\lambda\left(\frac{\nu_1 + 5\kappa_1}{6}\right) + Pr_\lambda(\kappa_1) \bigg] - \frac{\kappa_1^\lambda - E_\lambda(X)}{(\kappa_1 - \nu_1)^\lambda} \Bigg| \\
&\leq (\kappa_1 - \nu_1)^\lambda \left\{ \left[\frac{\Gamma(1+\lambda)}{\Gamma(1+2\lambda)} \left(\frac{4}{75}\right)^\lambda + \frac{\Gamma(1+2\lambda)}{\Gamma(1+3\lambda)} \left(\frac{1}{150}\right)^\lambda \right] |p(\nu_1)| \right. \\
&\left. + \left[\frac{\Gamma(1+\lambda)}{\Gamma(1+2\lambda)} \left(\frac{14}{225}\right)^\lambda - \frac{\Gamma(1+2\lambda)}{\Gamma(1+3\lambda)} \left(\frac{1}{150}\right)^\lambda \right] |p(\kappa_1)| \right\}.
\end{aligned}$$

Proof. We conclude this result employing probability density function on Theorem 7. □

Remark 1. *By using the proposed inequalities, we can prove several bounds for generalized expected values and moments.*

- It is a known fact that various definite integrals cannot be evaluated through analytical techniques neither in classical nor in Yang local fractional calculus. They are approximated through Newton–Cotes schemes. In the aforementioned sections, we have provided the error bounds of definite integrals approximated through generalized Weddle's incorporated with various classes of mappings. Our results provide the upper bounds of error terms for first-order local differentiable mapping. Additionally, from these bounds one can compute the upper bounds of definite integrals. For this, we apply Theorem 7 for $\mathcal{T}(x) = \exp(x^{2\alpha})$ over $[0,2]$ with $\alpha = 1$. Then we get $-10.2302 < \int_0^2 \exp(x^2)\mathrm{d}x < 22.8469$. Note that this bound can be refined by increasing the order of differentiability. Through the application of our proposed inequalities, one can establish the bounds and relation between special functions like q-digamma function, modified Bessel functions and Beta functions. For further detail, consult [29–31].
- Adopting the technique of [32], several new iterative methods to solve non-linear equations can be obtained. To discuss the convergence and dynamic analysis of proposed methods will be a new challenge for researchers.
- Also by following the technique of the papers [33,34] on our proposed results and generalized Hilbert transform defined in [35], various estimates for Hilbert transform can be investigated through the utilization of diverse function classes.

4. Conclusions

In this manuscript, we have presented the error analysis of Weddle's procedure in the framework of Yang fractal calculus. Our approach involved the generation of inequalities through a local differentiable identity, generalized convexity, bounded mapping, and Lipschitz mapping. Our results unify what already exists in the literature. The confirmation of inequalities has been provided through various simulations. It is an interesting and new problem; we hope the new researchers will explore its implications across various mathematical domains. One can explore the generalized fractional calculus approach within fractal domain through other general classes of convexity especially strong convexity. In the future, we will also focus on tight bounds of fractal inequalities utilizing diverse function classes of convexity. Another interesting problem is the construction of error inequalities of general Newton–Cotes schemes up to seven points leveraging the fractal calculus.

Author Contributions: Conceptualization, U.A., M.Z.J. and M.U.A.; methodology, Y.W., U.A., M.Z.J., M.U.A., A.G.K., and M.B.-A.; software, Y.W., U.A., M.B.-A., and K.S.A.; validation, Y.W., M.Z.J., M.U.A., A.G.K., M.B.-A., and K.S.A.; formal analysis, Y.W., U.A., M.U.A., A.G.K., M.B.-A., and K.S.A.; investigation, Y.W., U.A., M.Z.J., M.U.A., A.G.K., M.B.-A., and K.S.A.; writing—original draft preparation, U.A., M.Z.J., M.U.A., A.G.K., M.B.-A., and K.S.A.; writing—review and editing, U.A., M.Z.J., M.U.A., M.B.-A., and K.S.A.; visualization, Y.W., M.Z.J., A.G.K., M.B.-A., and K.S.A.; supervision, M.U.A. All authors have read and agreed to the published version of the manuscript.

Funding: This work was supported and funded by the Deanship of Scientific Research at Imam Mohammad Ibn Saud Islamic University (IMSIU) (grant number IMSIU-DDRSP2504).

Institutional Review Board Statement: Not applicable.

Informed Consent Statement: Not applicable.

Data Availability Statement: The original contributions presented in this study are included in the article. Further inquiries can be directed to the corresponding author.

Acknowledgments: This work was supported and funded by the Deanship of Scientific Research at Imam Mohammad Ibn Saud Islamic University (IMSIU) (grant number IMSIU-DDRSP2504).

Conflicts of Interest: The authors declare no conflicts of interest.

References

1. Dwilewicz, R.J. A short history of convexity. *Differ. Geom.-Dyn. Syst.* **2009**, 112.
2. Dragomir, S.S.; Agarwal, R. Two inequalities for differentiable mappings and applications to special means of real numbers and to trapezoidal formula. *Appl. Math. Lett.* **1998**, *11*, 91–95. [CrossRef]
3. Alomari, M.; Darus, M.; Dragomir, S.S. New inequalities of Simpson's type for s–convex functions with applications. *Res. Rep. Collect.* **2009**, *12*.
4. Awan, M.U.; Noor, M.A.; Noor, K.I. Hermite-Hadamard inequalities for exponentially convex functions. *Appl. Math. Inf. Sci.* **2018**, *12*, 405–409. [CrossRef]
5. Iscan, I. Hermite-Hadamard type inequalities for r_1–convex functions. *Int. J. Anal. Appl.* **2016**, *11*, 137–145.
6. Mitrinovic, D.S.; Lackovic, I.B. Hermite and convexity. *Aequationes Math.* **1985**, *28*, 229–232. [CrossRef]
7. Beckenbach, E.F. Convex functions. *Bull. Am. Math. Soc.* **1948**, *54*, 439–460. [CrossRef]
8. Dragomir, S.S.; Agarwal, R.P.; Cerone, P. On Simpson's inequality and applications. *RGMIA Res. Rep. Collect.* **1999**, *2*. [CrossRef]
9. Davis, P.J.; Rabinowitz, P. *Methods of Numerical Integration*; Courier Corporation: New York, NY, USA, 2007.
10. Yang, X.J. *Advanced Local Fractional Calculus and Its Applications*; World Science Publisher: New York, NY, USA, 2012.
11. Mo, H.; Sui, X. Generalized s–convex functions on fractal sets. *Abstr. Appl. Anal.* **2014**, *2014*, 254737. [CrossRef]
12. Sarikaya, M.Z.; Budak, H. On Fejér type inequalities via local fractional integrals. *J. Fract. Calc. Appl.* **2017**, *8*, 59–77.
13. Sarikaya, M.Z.; Erden, S.; Budak, H. Some generalized Ostrowski type inequalities involving local fractional integrals and applications. *Adv. Inequal. Appl.* **2016**.
14. Sarikaya, M.Z.; Tunc, T.; Budak, H. On generalized some integral inequalities for local fractional integrals. *Appl. Math. Comput.* **2016**, *276*, 316–323. [CrossRef]

15. Erden, S.; Sarikaya, M.Z. Generalized Pompeiu type inequalities for local fractional integrals and its applications. *Appl. Math. Comput.* **2016**, *274*, 282–291. [CrossRef]
16. Almutairi, O.; Kilicman, A. Generalized integral inequalities for Hermite-Hadamard-type inequalities via *s*–convexity on fractal sets. *Mathematics* **2019**, *7*, 1065. [CrossRef]
17. Luo, C.; Wang, H.; Du, T. Fejér-Hermite-Hadamard type inequalities involving generalized *h*–convexity on fractal sets and their applications. *Chaos Solitons Fractals* **2020**, *131*, 109547. [CrossRef]
18. Sun, W.; He, X. Hermite–Hadamard type inequalities and convex functions in signal processing. *IEEE Access* **2024**, *12*, 92906–92918. [CrossRef]
19. Butt, S.I.; Yousaf, S.; Younas, M.; Ahmad, H.; Yao, S.W. Fractal Hadamard-Mercer-type inequalities with applications. *Fractals* **2022**, *30*, 2240055. [CrossRef]
20. Luo, C.; Yu, Y.; Du, T. An improvement of Hölder integral inequality on fractal sets and some related Simpson-like inequalities. *Fractals* **2021**, *29*, 2150126. [CrossRef]
21. Alsharari, F.; Fakhfakh, R.; Lakhdari, A. On fractal-fractional Simpson-type inequalities: New insights and refinements of classical results. *Mathematics* **2024**, *12*, 3886. [CrossRef]
22. Meftah, B.; Lakhdari, A.; Saleh, W.; Kiliçman, A. Some new fractal Milne-type integral inequalities via generalized convexity with applications. *Fractal Fract.* **2023**, *7*, 166. [CrossRef]
23. Liu, Q.; Rukhsar.; Awan, M.U.; Bin-Mohsin, B.; Javed, M.Z.; Ciurdariu, L.; Meftah, B. Bridging pre-invex mappings and fractional integrals: A pathway to iterative schemes via error boundaries of Maclaurin's rule. *Fractal Fract.* **2024**, *8*, 734. [CrossRef]
24. Vivas-Cortez, M.; Awan, M.U.; Asif, U.; Javed, M.Z.; Budak, H. Advances in Ostrowski–Mercer like inequalities within fractal space. *Fractal Fract.* **2023**, *7*, 689. [CrossRef]
25. Javed, M.Z.; Awan, M.U.; Bin-Mohsin, B.; Budak, H.; Dragomir, S.S. Some classical inequalities associated with generic identity and applications. *Axioms* **2024**, *13*, 533. [CrossRef]
26. Vivas-Cortez, M.; Asif, U.; Javed, M.Z.; Awan, M.U.; Almalki, Y.; Alsalami, O.M. A new approach to error inequalities: From Euler–Maclaurin bounds to cubically convergent algorithm. *AIMS Math.* **2024**, *9*, 35885–35909. [CrossRef]
27. Wang, Y.; Asif, U.; Javed, M.Z.; Awan, M.U.; Meftah, B.; Kashuri, A.; Noor, M.A. Numerical and visual analysis of Maclaurin type inequalities in the setting of generalized fractional calculus and applications. *J. Math. Comput. Sci.* **2025**, *38*, 281–297. [CrossRef]
28. Budak, H.; Sarikaya, M.Z.; Yildirim, H. New inequalities for local fractional integrals. *Iran. J. Sci. Technol. Trans. A Sci.* **2017**, *41*, 1039–1046. [CrossRef]
29. Tariq, M.; Ahmad, H.; Shaikh, A.A.; Ntouyas, S.K.; Hınçal, E.; Qureshi, S. Fractional Hermite–Hadamard-type inequalities for differentiable preinvex mappings and applications to modified Bessel and q-digamma functions. *Math. Comput. Appl.* **2023**, *28*, 108. [CrossRef]
30. Mohammed, P.O.; Sarikaya, M.Z.; Baleanu, D. On the generalized Hermite–Hadamard inequalities via the tempered fractional integrals. *Symmetry* **2020**, *12*, 595. [CrossRef]
31. Hwang, S.R.; Yeh, S.Y.; Tseng, K.L. On some Hermite–Hadamard inequalities for fractional integrals and their applications. *Ukr. Math. J.* **2020**, *72*, 407–424. [CrossRef]
32. Javed, M.Z.; Awan, M.U.; Bin-Mohsin, B.; Treanţă, S. Upper bounds for the remainder term in Boole's quadrature rule and applications to numerical analysis. *Mathematics* **2024**, *12*, 2920. [CrossRef]
33. Dragomir, S.S. Approximating the finite Hilbert transform via Ostrowski type inequalities for absolutely continuous functions. *Bull. Korean Math. Soc.* **2002**, *39*, 543–559. [CrossRef]
34. Liu, W.; Gao, X.; Wen, Y. Approximating the finite Hilbert transform via some companions of Ostrowski's inequalities. *Bull. Malays. Math. Sci. Soc.* **2016**, *39*, 1499–1513. [CrossRef]
35. Chen, G.S. The local fractional Hilbert transform in fractal space. *J. Appl. Eng. Sci.* **2024**.

fractal and fractional

MDPI

Article

Fractional Mean-Square Inequalities for (P, m)-Superquadratic Stochastic Processes and Their Applications to Stochastic Divergence Measures

Dawood Khan [1], Saad Ihsan Butt [2], Ghulam Jallani [2], Mohammed Alammar [3] and Youngsoo Seol [4,*]

1 Department of Mathematics, University of Balochistan, Quetta 87300, Pakistan; dawooddawood601@gmail.com
2 Department of Mathematics, COMSATS University Islamabad, Lahore Campus, Lahore 54000, Pakistan; saadihsanbutt@gmail.com (S.I.B.); fa23-pmt-002@cuilahore.edu.pk (G.J.)
3 Applied College, Shaqra University, Shaqra 11961, Saudi Arabia; alammar@su.edu.sa
4 Department of Mathematics, Dong-A University, Busan 49315, Republic of Korea
* Correspondence: prosul76@dau.ac.kr

Abstract

In this study, we introduce and rigorously formalize the notion of (P, m)-superquadratic stochastic processes, representing a novel and far-reaching generalization of classical convex stochastic processes. By exploring their intrinsic structural characteristics, we establish advanced Jensen and Hermite–Hadamard ($\mathbb{H}.\mathbb{H}$)-type inequalities within the mean-square stochastic calculus framework. Furthermore, we extend these inequalities to their fractional counterparts via stochastic Riemann–Liouville ($\mathbb{RL}$) fractional integrals, thereby enriching the analytical machinery available for fractional stochastic analysis. The theoretical findings are comprehensively validated through graphical visualizations and detailed tabular illustrations, constructed from diverse numerical examples to highlight the behavior and accuracy of the proposed results. Beyond their theoretical depth, the developed framework is applied to information theory, where we introduce new classes of stochastic divergence measures. The proposed results significantly refine the approximation of stochastic and fractional stochastic differential equations governed by convex stochastic processes, thereby enhancing the precision, stability, and applicability of existing stochastic models. To ensure reproducibility and computational transparency, all graph-generation commands, numerical procedures, and execution times are provided, offering a complete and verifiable reference for future research in stochastic and fractional inequality theory.

Keywords: mean-square stochastic $\mathbb{RL}$ fractional integrals; (P, m)-superquadratic stochastic process; Jensen's inequality; $\mathbb{H}.\mathbb{H}$'s inequality; stochastic divergence; $\mathbb{RL}$ fractional stochastic $\mathbb{H}.\mathbb{H}$-divergence

MSC: 26D15; 94A17; 26A33; 26A51; 26D10; 60G05; 94A15

1. Introduction

The mathematical notion of convexity occupies a pivotal role in engineering and mathematics, as it supports a wide range of theoretical and applied phenomena. The core of convex analysis are convex sets and convex functions that are essential tools in simplifying very complicated systems and optimizing complex mathematical models. By virtue of their well-behaved nature, especially the fact that there is a global minimum problems in convex functions become much easier to handle, and hence are central in

 https://doi.org/10.3390/fractalfract9120771

optimization. Besides its interest for its own sake as pure mathematics, convexity has deep implications in most fields like control theory, economics, and systems engineering. In control theory, for instance, convexity guarantees that the designs for systems are stable and robust over a wide range of operating conditions. In economics, convexity also plays a role in the description of consumer preferences and analysis of market behavior, hence enabling efficient decision-making and resource allocation. It is interesting to note that convexity has practical applications in addition to being a theoretical or academic idea. Convex structures are frequently encountered by engineers and practitioners who are attempting to maximise system performance in order to increase operational efficiency and dependability. Convex functions are essential to integral inequalities, which may be the most aesthetically beautiful use of convexity. In mathematical analysis, integral inequalities are essential, particularly when it comes to bounding or approximating integral values. The $\mathbb{H}.\mathbb{H}$ inequality, which gives estimates of the average value of a convex function over a specified interval, is one of the most significant of these [1–3]. The topic is a rich and potent area of current mathematics research because of the relationship between convexity and integral-type inequalities.

Fractional calculus that generalizes classical calculus to non-integer order derivatives and integrals has emerged as a hot topic in recent years due to its ability to model systems with memory and with hereditary characteristics. It emerges as a valuable tool in physics, engineering, and even perhaps surprisingly in computer science [4]. Its increasing relevance is not only restricted to practical sciences; fractional calculus has also been instrumental in the building of inequality theory. Fractional integral inequality is now a favorite and rapidly developing field of research in recent years. Sarikaya et al. [5] added an important contribution by using the $\mathbb{RL}$ fractional integrals framework to establish the generalized $\mathbb{H}.\mathbb{H}$ inequality. Their research enhanced the mathematical techniques employed in dynamic systems analysis and the theory of inequality analysis by creating tighter bounds in analytical terms and greater understanding of the behavior of convex functions. Recent studies also broadened this field with new methods for fractional integral operators and inequalities. Nápoles-Valdés and Bayraktar in 2025 [6], explored Caputo-weighted integrals and their uses, citing the potential to generalize traditional results and refine analytical procedures in fractional frameworks. Similarly, Guzmán and Nápoles-Valdés in 2025 [7], explored $\mathbb{H}.\mathbb{H}$-type fractional integral inequalities, formulating new bounds and extensions that close the gap between classic analysis and modern fractional theory. These advances in their entirety enrich the knowledge of the structural features and uses of fractional integral inequalities in mathematics analysis and applied sciences.

After the landmark discovery of the $\mathbb{H}.\mathbb{H}$ inequalities for the $\mathbb{RL}$ fractional integrals, important advances have been made in extending $\mathbb{H}.\mathbb{H}$-type inequalities to several fractional integral definitions. Researchers have explored these inequalities in the context of numerous fractional operators, including the generalized proportional fractional integrals [8], Sarikaya fractional integrals [9], Katugampola fractional integrals [10], k-fractional integrals [11], ψ-$\mathbb{RL}$-fractional integrals [12], $(k-p)$-fractional integrals [13], generalized $\mathbb{RL}$-fractional integrals [14] and conformable fractional integrals [15]. Alongside these developments, a wide array of inequalities of fractional order has also been established, reflecting the growing depth and diversity of the field. These include fractal Hadamard-Mercer-type inequalities [16], Simpson-type inequalities [17], Euler-Maclaurin-type inequalities [18], Bullen-type inequalities [19], and Ostrowski-type inequalities [20], among others. For readers seeking a comprehensive overview of recent advancements in fractional integral inequalities, several up-to-date contributions are recommended, such as those found in [21–23] and the references therein.

A collection of random variables parameterized by time or space describing the change of a system under uncertainty is referred to as a stochastic process in statistics and probability theory. They characterize the apparently random change of a system, often over different time or space separations. The term "stochastic" qualifies processes that occur at unpredictable or irregular rates. Stochastic processes can be used to simulate random change over time in systems. For instance, there are many random parameters that may result in fluctuations of bacterial growth, but long-term forecasting is not impossible. Just as thermal noise within electrical systems produces random changes in voltage or current, such apparently random behavior can be represented by simple stochastic processes, and these can offer insight into the behavior of the system.

Physicists and mathematicians have traditionally used stochastic processes as mathematical models to describe a wide range of phenomena, including changes in population in ecosystems, randomly diffusing gas molecules, and stock price fluctuation. Stochastic models, which have many uses in research and engineering, can often be used to model these processes and other elements like molecular interactions whenever there is unpredictability. They mimic population dynamics or the emergence of diseases in biology, and they depict systems based on the mobility of various molecules in physics. The importance of stochastic processes lies in their ability to systematically explain systems that behave randomly. They are vital in domains where randomness or particular results at every stage are critical, such as computer science, data transfer, cryptography, and signal processing. They are therefore essential for conducting research and resolving practical issues. Scientists and engineers are able to forecast future trends, optimize systems, and design solutions that consider environmental uncertainties by numerically simulating these processes. System state prediction, data compression algorithms, and secure communication through cryptography are other significant applications. Recent developments in fractional stochastic processes provide a strong foundation for our study. Jiang and Miao [24] examined anomalous stochastic processes via generalized fractional calculus, offering models for non-classical diffusion behavior. Sahebi Fard et al. [25] introduced a financial market model using the ψ-Caputo fractional derivative, effectively capturing memory and hereditary effects in market dynamics. Guidoum et al. [26] analyzed fractional and higher-order moments of stochastic differential equations, highlighting the behavior of moments under fractional dynamics. These works collectively illustrate the breadth and applicability of fractional stochastic modeling.

Convex stochastic processes, which generalize the concept of classical convex functions to stochastic processes systems including randomness were initially introduced by Nikodem [27] in 1980. Further, he found that such stochastic processes exhibit a number of properties similar to classical convex functions. The Jensen convex mapping, central to the theory of inequalities, is one such useful tool in this respect. A number of crucial inequalities can be obtained from this mapping, and their applicability to stochastic processes was demonstrated by Skowronski [28] in 1992. Expanding on these concepts, Kotrys [29] showed that, in particular, for convex stochastic processes, the upper and lower bounds of the $\mathbb{H}.\mathbb{H}$ inequality may be found using integral operators. Kotrys's work showed how the $\mathbb{H}.\mathbb{H}$ inequality, an important result in convex analysis, could be adapted for stochastic processes. There have been a great many papers in the literature over the last few years on all sorts of convexity for stochastic processes. Okur et al. [30] used the idea of p-convexity, which is a particular kind of convexity, to construct the $\mathbb{H}.\mathbb{H}$ inequality for stochastic processes. Erhan [31] made a further contribution by building these inequalities with the use of another version of convexity called s-convexity. Budak et al. [32] generalised the work of other academics by presenting these inequalities using the concept of h-convexity. As mentioned in the sources [33–35], there have been many research investigating different kinds of convexity for individuals who are interested in the most recent developments in stochastic processes. Further broadening the applicability of these mathematical ideas, Tunç in [36] made a substantial contribution by developing the Ostrowski-type inequality particularly for h-convex functions. Zhao et al. [37] have connected inequality to interval mathematics, putting these inequality within the context of interval analysis. Using interval analysis as a foundation, Afzal et al. [38] presented the notion of stochastic processes before the end of 2022. They also created new versions of the Jensen and $\mathbb{H}.\mathbb{H}$ inequalities that are particularly designed for stochastic processes, fusing these two mathematical ideas in an innovative way. A novel mathematical framework called the (m, h_1, h_2)-G-convex stochastic process was presented by Eliecer et al. [39]. It incorporates functions h_1 and h_2 together with a parameter m to extend classical convexity to stochastic processes. By this approach, they were able to establish some inequalities associated with stochastic analysis. By utilizing fractional operators in order to use fractional calculus on the (m, h_1, h_2)-convex stochastic process, Cortez [40] generalized this work and obtained more inequalities. These developments strengthen mathematical models in many disciplines through the power of estimating systems subject to fractional dynamics and uncertainty. Hafiz [41] discussed the applications of fractional calculus to stochastic processes, paving the way for modeling stochastic processes reliant on memory. Kotrys [42] extended classical inequalities such as Jensen, $\mathbb{H}.\mathbb{H}$, and Fejér inequalities to strongly convex stochastic processes, providing vital information regarding probabilistic convexity theory. Further advances were made by Agahi and Babakhani [43], who introduced fractional-order forms of Jensen and $\mathbb{H}.\mathbb{H}$ inequalities for convex stochastic processes to make them more effective in stochastic modeling fields. Fu et al. [44] subsequently investigated n-polynomial convex stochastic processes and presented $\mathbb{H}.\mathbb{H}$-type inequalities for such functions, which determined the domain of stochastic optimization and uncertainty modeling. The work in general stresses the importance of convexity in stochastic situations and its use in mathematical inequalities, probability theory, and optimization in practice.

Superquadraticity gives tighter and more reliable bounds than ordinary convexity, considerably enhancing integral inequality theory. This is extremely welcomed in applications of applied mathematics, where a better approximation means increased model accuracy, and for optimisation tasks, where boundary estimate quality decides the optimum solution. Thus, superquadraticity broadens the theory basis of inequality structures and enhances their applicability. It effectively presents a robust analytical foundation for the development and use of integral inequalities in a wide range of mathematical and applied problems.

The concept of superquadraticity extending the traditional convexity was first introduced by Abramovich et al. [45]. This initial work prepared the ground for a wider analytical framework that could provide tighter inequalities compared to those obtained from regular convex functions. Abramovich and co-authors [46] later introduced a formal definition for superquadratic functions together with essential theoretical observations that further enhanced the understanding of this function class. Working from this basis, Li and Chen [47] took the theory further by applying the fractional view of $\mathbb{H}.\mathbb{H}$-type inequalities through $\mathbb{RL}$ fractional integrals, representing a huge step beyond superquadraticity to the world of fractional calculus. More was done by Alomari et al. [48], who brought about the concept of h-superquadraticity, studied their structural properties and defined a new subclass within the larger family. In a valuable work in interval analysis and generalized function theory, Khan and Butt [49] introduced cr-order interval-valued superquadratic functions and their fractional counterparts, emphasizing their applicability through multiple illustrations. Following this endeavor, Khan et al. [50] introduced the (P, m)-superquadratic function, an even broader concept that includes examples, fundamental characteristics, integral inequalities, and real-world applications, thus enriching superquadraticity's functional atmosphere. Continuing their exploration of information-theoretic applications, Butt and Khan [51] developed information inequalities for superquadratic functions using the tools of interval calculus, connecting functional inequalities with measures of information. A foundational theoretical advance was made by Banić et al. [52], who refined classical inequalities and solidified the theoretical underpinnings of superquadratic functions, paving the way for future researchs in the study of superquadratic stochastic processes.

In the aforementioned, we have discussed several well-known stochastic extensions of convexity, such as convex stochastic processes, p-convex, s-convex, h-convex, (m, h_1, h_2)-G-convex, and n-polynomial convex stochastic processes, each providing generalizations within the convexity framework. However, the recently developed concept of (P, m)-superquadraticity serves as a refinement of convexity, offering significantly sharper bounds than those obtained from the classical and modern variants of convexity. Despite its strong potential, neither a stochastic formulation of (P, m)-superquadraticity nor its fractional counterpart has appeared in the literature. To fill this gap, the present work introduces the new class of (P, m)-superquadratic stochastic processes, establishes their key properties, develops Jensen-type and $\mathbb{H}.\mathbb{H}$-type inequalities of integer order, and further generalizes them to fractional $\mathbb{H}.\mathbb{H}$-type inequalities via stochastic $\mathbb{RL}$ fractional integrals. Moreover, we provide the first applications of this new class in information theory, demonstrating its analytical strength and broad applicability beyond the traditional convexity-based stochastic models.

The paragraph that follows provides an explanation of the paper's structure:

Following the review of the required background knowledge and pertinent data regarding convexity, superquadraticity, convex stochastic processes and their inequalities in Sections 1 and 2, we use 2D and 3D graphical representations to analyze the stochastic version of superquadraticity and their features. More importantly, in Section 3, we develop new Jensen's and $\mathbb{H}.\mathbb{H}$-type inequalities. Then, in Section 4, Inequalities of $\mathbb{H}.\mathbb{H}$-type are obtained in fractional form. To evaluate the effectiveness of the results, examples and graphic descriptions of the findings are also taken into account. How the findings may be used to information theory is covered in Section 5. In the final section, Section 6, a clear and concise conclusion is drawn, accompanied by an overview of potential future developments inspired by the current work.

2. Preliminaries

The terms of significance for fractional integrals, convexity, and superquadraticity are defined in this section along with the associated inequalities.

Definition 1 ([3]). *Let the function* $\Psi : [\mathcal{U}_o, \mathcal{V}_o] \subset \Re \longrightarrow \Re$ *be a convex then*

$$\Psi(\beta \mathrm{y}_1 + (1-\beta)\mathrm{y}_2) \leq \beta \Psi(\mathrm{y}_1) + (1-\beta)\Psi(\mathrm{y}_2), \tag{1}$$

is valid for every $\mathrm{y}_1, \mathrm{y}_2 \in [\mathcal{U}_o, \mathcal{V}_o]$, *and* $\beta \in [0,1]$.

The $\mathbb{H}.\mathbb{H}$'s inequality is a fundamental mathematical result that establishes both lower and upper bounds for mean values. In inequality theory, it is among the first types of inequality to use convex functions. For error calculations that use numerical integration, such as the trapezoidal and midpoint formulae, this inequality is an essential tool. This well-known finding is defined as follows.

Theorem 1 ([3]). *$\mathbb{H}.\mathbb{H}$'s inequality states that if the function $\Psi : I \subseteq \Re \longrightarrow \Re$, is convex in $\Im \subseteq \Re$, where $\mathcal{V}_o > \mathcal{U}_o$. The following statement satisfies:*

$$\Psi\left(\frac{\mathcal{U}_o + \mathcal{V}_o}{2}\right) \leq \frac{1}{\mathcal{V}_o - \mathcal{U}_o} \int_{\mathcal{U}_o}^{\mathcal{V}_o} \Psi(y)dy \leq \frac{\Psi(\mathcal{U}_o) + \Psi(\mathcal{V}_o)}{2}, \tag{2}$$

$\forall\ \mathcal{U}_o, \mathcal{V}_o \in \Im$.

Definition 2. *$\mathbb{RL}$-fractional integrals with order $\beta \geq 0$ with $\mathcal{U}_o \geq 0$ are defined as*

$$\Im^{\beta}_{\mathcal{U}_o^+}\Psi(y) = \frac{1}{\Gamma(\beta)} \int_{\mathcal{U}_o}^{y} (y - y_o)^{\beta-1}\Psi(y_o)dy_o, \quad (y > \mathcal{U}_o),$$

and

$$\Im^{\beta}_{\mathcal{V}_o^-}\Psi(y) = \frac{1}{\Gamma(\beta)} \int_{y}^{\mathcal{V}_o} (y_o - y)^{\beta-1}\Psi(y_o)dy_o, \quad (y < \mathcal{V}_o).$$

The notations $\Im^{\beta}_{\mathcal{U}_o^+}\Psi(y)$ and $\Im^{\beta}_{\mathcal{V}_o^-}\Psi(y)$ are the left and right sided operators. Where Γ is a stated as gamma function and given by $\Gamma(\beta) = \int_0^\infty {y_o}^{\beta-1}e^{-y_o}dy_o$.

Definition 3. *A function $\Psi : [0, \infty) \longrightarrow \Re$ is superquadratic, if*

$$\Psi(y_o) \geq \Psi(y) + \mathfrak{C}_y(y_o - y) + \Psi(|y_o - y|), \tag{3}$$

holds for every $y_o \geq 0$, $\mathfrak{C}_y \in \Re$, where $y \geq 0$ and $\mathfrak{C}_y$ is a constant.

Remark 1. *If the inequality* (3) *is reversed then Ψ is called subquadratic.*

As an example, we may use $\Psi(y) = y^k$. The function Ψ is superquadratic for $y \geq 0$ and $k \geq 2$, but subquadratic for $0 \leq k < 2$. Let $\mathfrak{C}_y = ky^{q_o-1}$ in this instance. At $k = 2$, equality is also preserved in (3).

More precisely, any randomly chosen superquadratic function meets the three supplementary conditions outlined in Lemma 1:

Lemma 1. *Let $\Psi : [0, \infty) \rightarrow \Re$ be a superquadratic function, then*

- *$\Psi(0) \leq 0$.*
- *Provided that Ψ is differentiable at $y > 0$ and satisfies $\Psi(0) = \Psi'(0) = 0$, it follows that $\Psi'(y) = \mathfrak{C}_y$.*
- *If Ψ is positive and $\Psi(0) = \Psi'(0) = 0$ on $(0, \infty)$, then Ψ is convex.*

Two major inequalities that contribute to the growth and development of superquadraticity are inequalities of Jensen's and $\mathbb{H}.\mathbb{H}$'s types, which are the most significant and frequently applied results.

Theorem 2 ([46]). *Let Ψ: $J \subset [0, \infty[\longrightarrow \Re$ be a superquadratic then*

$$\sum_{i=1}^{n} \beta_i \Psi(y_i) \geq \Psi(\bar{y}) + \sum_{i=1}^{n} \beta_i \Psi(|y_i - \bar{y}|), \tag{4}$$

holds for all $\beta_i \in (0, 1)$ and $y_i \geq 0$, where $\bar{y} = \sum_{i=1}^{n} \beta_i y_i$, and $\sum_{i=1}^{n} \beta_i = 1$.

Banić et al. [52] contributed to the field of superquadraticity by formulating the following $\mathbb{H}.\mathbb{H}$-type inequalities.

Theorem 3. *Let* $\Psi\colon J\subset[0,\infty[\longrightarrow\Re$ *be a superquadratic on* $J=[\mathcal{U}_o,\mathcal{V}_o]$ *then*

$$\Psi\left(\frac{\mathcal{U}_o+\mathcal{V}_o}{2}\right)+\frac{1}{\mathcal{V}_o-\mathcal{U}_o}\int_{\mathcal{U}_o}^{\mathcal{V}_o}\Psi\left(\left|y-\frac{\mathcal{U}_o+\mathcal{V}_o}{2}\right|\right)dy\leq\frac{1}{\mathcal{V}_o-\mathcal{U}_o}\int_{\mathcal{U}_o}^{\mathcal{V}_o}\Psi(y)dy$$
$$\leq\frac{\Psi(\mathcal{U}_o)+\Psi(\mathcal{V}_o)}{2}-\frac{1}{(\mathcal{V}_o-\mathcal{U}_o)^2}\int_{\mathcal{U}_o}^{\mathcal{V}_o}[(\mathcal{V}_o-y)\Psi(y-\mathcal{U}_o)+(y-\mathcal{U}_o)\Psi(\mathcal{V}_o-y)]dy. \quad (5)$$

The line of support concept of superquadraticity is defined in Definition 3. In the following, we offer an additional definition.

Definition 4 ([45]). *Let* $\Psi\colon J\subset[0,\infty[\longrightarrow\Re$ *be a superquadratic function then*

$$\Psi((1-\beta)y_1+\beta y_2)\leq(1-\beta)\Psi(y_1)+\beta\Psi(y_2)-\beta\Psi((1-\beta)|y_1-y_2|)$$
$$-(1-\beta)\Psi(\beta|y_1-y_2|), \quad (6)$$

holds for every $\beta\in(0,1)$ *and* $y_1,y_2\geq0$.

Remark 2. *Subquadraticity of the function* Ψ *corresponds to the reversal of the inequality sign in* (6).

Theorem 4 ([47]). *Let* $\Psi\colon J\subset[0,\infty[\longrightarrow\Re$ *be a superquadratic function on* $J=[\mathcal{U}_o,\mathcal{V}_o]$ *then*

$$\Psi\left(\frac{\mathcal{U}_o+\mathcal{V}_o}{2}\right)+\frac{\beta}{2(\mathcal{V}_o-\mathcal{U}_o)^\beta}\int_{\mathcal{U}_o}^{\mathcal{V}_o}\Psi\left(\left|\frac{\mathcal{U}_o+\mathcal{V}_o}{2}-x\right|\right)((\mathcal{V}_o-y)^{\beta-1}+(y-\mathcal{U}_o)^{\beta-1})dy$$
$$\leq\frac{\Gamma(1+\beta)}{2(\mathcal{V}_o-\mathcal{U}_o)^\beta}(I^\beta_{\mathcal{U}_o^+}\Psi(\mathcal{V}_o)+I^\beta_{\mathcal{V}_o^-}\Psi(\mathcal{U}_o))$$
$$\leq\frac{\Psi(\mathcal{U}_o)+\Psi(\mathcal{V}_o)}{2}-\frac{\beta}{2(\mathcal{V}_o-\mathcal{U}_o)^\beta}\int_{\mathcal{U}_o}^{\mathcal{V}_o}\left(\left(\frac{y-\mathcal{U}_o}{\mathcal{V}_o-\mathcal{U}_o}\right)\Psi(\mathcal{V}_o-y)+\left(\frac{\mathcal{V}_o-y}{\mathcal{V}_o-\mathcal{U}_o}\right)\Psi(y-\mathcal{U}_o)\right)$$
$$\times((\mathcal{V}_o-y)^{\beta-1}+(y-\mathcal{U}_o)^{\beta-1})dy, \quad (7)$$

where $I^\beta_{\mathcal{U}_o^+}$ *and* $I^\beta_{\mathcal{V}_o^-}$ *are given in Definition 2.*

Definition 5 ([50]). *A function* $\Psi:J\subseteq\Re\to\Re$ *is called (P, m)-superquadratic on* $J=[0,k]$ *for* $k>0$ *and* $m\in[0,1]$*; if*

$$\Psi(\beta\mathcal{U}_o+m(1-\beta)\mathcal{V}_o)\leq\beta[\Psi(\mathcal{U}_o)-\Psi((1-\beta)|\mathcal{U}_o-\mathcal{V}_o|)]$$
$$+m(1-\beta)[\Psi(\mathcal{V}_o)-\Psi(\beta|\mathcal{U}_o-\mathcal{V}_o|)],$$

holds for any $\mathcal{U}_o,\mathcal{V}_o\in J$ *and* $\beta\in[0,1]$. Ψ *is defined as a (P, m)-subquadratic function whenever its negation* $-\Psi$ *satisfies the (P, m)-superquadratic condition.*

Definition 6 ([27]). *A mapping* $\Psi:\prod\to\Re$ *is considered a random variable if it is* $\mathfrak{A}$*-measurable. It is defined on the probability space* $(\prod,\mathfrak{A},P)$*, where* $\prod$ *denotes the set of all possible outcomes,* $\mathfrak{A}$ *is a* σ*-algebra representing the collection of measurable events (subsets of* $\prod$*), and* P *is a probability measure that assigns probabilities to these events.*

Example 1. *Imagine a coin toss in which* $\prod=\{H=Head,T=Tail\}$*,* $\mathfrak{A}$ *includes complete subsets of* $\prod$*, and* P *assigns a probability of* $\frac{1}{2}$ *to each conceivable circumstance. So,* $\Psi(T)=1$ *and* $\Psi(H)=0$ *would be the definitions of a random variable* Ψ.

Definition 7 ([27]). *If for all* $y\in J$*,* $\Psi(y,\cdot)$ *is a random variable, then a map* $\Psi:J\times\prod\to\Re$ *is called a stochastic process.*

Example 2. *Think about taking daily readings of the temperature at noon for a week.* $\prod$ *can represent all possible weather conditions in this instance,* $J = \{1, 2, \ldots, 7\}$ *represents each day of the week, and* $\Psi(y, \omega)$ *gives the temperature on day* y*, provided that* ω *is met. As a random variable,* $\Psi(y, \cdot)$ *for each fixed day* y *shows how the temperature varies under different meteorological conditions. Temperature variation over time, as influenced by changes in* y*, is modeled by the stochastic process* $\Psi(y, \cdot)$.

Definition 8 ([27])**.** *A stochastic process* $\Psi : J \times \prod \to \Re$*, is called to be continuous on* $J \subset \Re$*, if for every* $k \in J$*, we have*

$$P - \lim_{y \to k} \Psi(y, \cdot) = \Psi(k, \cdot).$$

The notation P- lim *is used to represent convergence in probability within a probability space.*

Definition 9 ([27])**.** *A stochastic process* $\Psi : J \times \prod \to \Re$*, is called to be mean-square continuous on* $J \subset \Re$*, if for every* $k \in J$*, we have*

$$\lim_{y \to k} E\left[(\Psi(y, \cdot) - \Psi(k, \cdot))^2\right] = 0.$$

Where the random variable's expectation is represented by $E\left[\Psi(y, \cdot)\right]$.

Remark 3. *Probability continuity is obviously shown by mean-square continuity, while the contrary is not true.*

Definition 10 ([27])**.** *A stochastic process* $\Psi : J \times \prod \to \Re$ *is called to be mean-square differentiable on* $J \subset \Re$ *at* k*, if a random variable* $\Psi' : J \times \prod \to \Re$ *is given. This means that:*

$$\Psi'(k, \cdot) = P - \lim_{y \to k} \frac{\Psi(y, \cdot) - \Psi(k, \cdot)}{y - k},$$

Definition 11 ([27])**.** *A stochastic process* $\Psi : J \times \prod \to \Re$*, is called to be mean-square integrable on* $J \subset \Re$*, if for every* $y \in J$*, with* $E\left[\Psi(y, \cdot)^2\right] < \infty$*,* $[y_1, y_2] \subseteq J$*,* $y_1 = k_0 < k_1 < k_2 \ldots < k_n = y_2$*, partitions* $[y_1, y_2]$*, and* $y_i \in [k_{i-1}, k_i], \forall i = 1, \ldots, n$ *then*

$$\lim_{n \to \infty} E\left[\left(\sum_{i=1}^{n} \Psi(y_i, \cdot)(k_i - k_{i-1}) - S(\cdot)\right)^2\right] = 0.$$

It indicates that the stochastic process's mean-square integral is $S : J \times \prod \to \Re$*, and it may be expressed as*

$$S(\cdot) = \int_{y_1}^{y_2} \Psi(y, \cdot) dy. \tag{8}$$

Remark 4. *The mean-square continuity of the stochastic process* Ψ *is sufficient to ensure the existence of the mean-square integral.*

Remark 5. *It asserts that if* $\Psi(y, \cdot) \le S(y, \cdot)$ *for all* $y \in [y_1, y_2]$*, then the following holds:*

$$\int_{y_1}^{y_2} \Psi(y, \cdot) dy \le \int_{y_1}^{y_2} S(y, \cdot) dy. \tag{9}$$

Lemma 2 ([29]). *Let a stochastic process $\Psi : J \times \prod \to \Re$ be defined by $\Psi(y, \cdot) = A(\cdot)y + B(\cdot)$, where $A, B : \prod \to \Re$ are such that $E(A^2) < \infty$ and $E(B^2) < \infty$. If $[y_1, y_2] \subset J$, then the following holds:*

$$\int_{y_1}^{y_2} \Psi(y, \cdot)dy = A(\cdot)\frac{{y_2}^2 - {y_1}^2}{2} + B(\cdot)(y_2 - y_1), \tag{10}$$

where A and B denote random variables.

Definition 12 ([29]). *We define a process $\Psi : J \times \prod \to \Re$ to be convex stochastic on $J \subset \Re$ if, for every $\beta \in [0, 1]$, the following condition is satisfied:*

$$\Psi(\beta\mathcal{U}_o + (1 - \beta)\mathcal{V}_o, \cdot) \leq \beta\Psi(\mathcal{U}_o, \cdot) + (1 - \beta)\Psi(\mathcal{V}_o, \cdot), \tag{11}$$

for any $\mathcal{U}_o, \mathcal{V}_o \in J$.

If $\beta = \frac{1}{2}$ is chosen in (11)*, the process Ψ is referred to as Jensen convex. Furthermore, if Ψ exhibits convexity, then its negation $-\Psi$ is regarded as a concave stochastic process. For more interesting characteristics, the reader is referred to [28].*

Lemma 3 ([28]). *If $y_1, y_2 \in J_o$ and $y_1 < y_2$, then the following inequalities hold.*

$$\Psi'_-(y_1, \cdot) \leq \Psi'_+(y_1, \cdot) \leq \Psi'_-(y_2, \cdot) \leq \Psi'_+(y_2, \cdot). \tag{12}$$

where Ψ'_+, and Ψ'_-, are the right and left derivatives of Ψ.

Theorem 5 ([28]). *It states that if a convex stochastic process $\Psi : J \times \prod \to \Re$ is mean-square continuous and satisfies Jensen's convexity on J, then the following inequalities holds*

$$\Psi\left(\frac{y_1 + y_2}{2}, \cdot\right) \leq \frac{1}{y_2 - y_1}\int_{y_1}^{y_2} \Psi(y, \cdot)dy \leq \frac{\Psi(y_1, \cdot) + \Psi(y_2, \cdot)}{2}, \tag{13}$$

for every $y_1, y_2 \in J$

Definition 13 ([41]). *Let $\Psi : J \times \prod \to \Re$ be a stochastic process satisfying the conditions stated in Definition 11. Then, the mean-square stochastic $\mathbb{RL}$ fractional integrals of order $\alpha > 0$, denoted by $I^{\alpha}_{\mathcal{U}_o^+}$ and $I^{\alpha}_{\mathcal{V}_o^-}$, are defined for Ψ as follows.*

$$I^{\alpha}_{\mathcal{U}_o^+}[\Psi](y) = \frac{1}{\Gamma(\alpha)}\int_{\mathcal{U}_o}^{y} (y - \mathfrak{s})^{\alpha - 1}\Psi(\mathfrak{s}, \cdot)d\mathfrak{s}, \quad y > \mathcal{U}_o,$$

and

$$I^{\alpha}_{\mathcal{V}_o^-}[\Psi](y) = \frac{1}{\Gamma(\alpha)}\int_{y}^{\mathcal{V}_o} (\mathfrak{s} - y)^{\alpha - 1}\Psi(\mathfrak{s}, \cdot)d\mathfrak{s}, \quad y < \mathcal{V}_o.$$

3. Analysis of Integral Inequalities Involving (P, m)-Superquadratic Stochastic Processes

In this section, we begin by introducing the definition of an (P, m)-superquadratic stochastic process, which generalizes the concept of an (P, m)-convex stochastic process. This generalization allows for the development of more refined results. Based on this definition, we investigate its properties and establish associated integral inequalities.

Definition 14. *Let* $\Psi : J \times \prod \rightarrow \Re$ *be a (P, m)-superquadratic stochastic process over* $J = [0, \mathrm{k}]$*, Where* $\mathrm{k} > 0$ *for* $m \in [0,1]$ *then*

$$\Psi(\beta\mathcal{U}_o + m(1-\beta)\mathcal{V}_o, \cdot) \leq [\Psi(\mathcal{U}_o, \cdot) - \Psi((1-\beta)|\mathcal{V}_o - \mathcal{U}_o|, \cdot)] + m[\Psi(\mathcal{V}_o, \cdot) - \Psi(\beta|\mathcal{V}_o - \mathcal{U}_o|, .)], \tag{14}$$

holds for every $\beta \in [0,1]$ *and* $\mathcal{U}_o, \mathcal{V}_o \in J$.

If $\beta = \frac{1}{2}$ is chosen in (14), then the process Ψ is termed as Jensen-(P, m)-superquadratic. If the process Ψ is classified as (P, m)-superquadratic, then $-\Psi$ is then termed as (P, m)-subquadratic stochastic process.

Example 3. *A process* Ψ: $[2, \infty] \times \prod \rightarrow \Re$ *defined by* $\Psi(\mathrm{y}, \cdot) = \mathrm{y}^{\mathrm{k}}$ *for* $\mathrm{k} \geq 2$ *is a (P, m)-superquadratic stochastic process for every* $m \in [0,1]$*. The graphs in Figure 1 illustrate the validity of Definition 14 via the process* Ψ *considering different values of the parameters that go into it. Let R and L denote the right and left sides of the expression (14) respectively. It has been shown in the in Figure 1 that pink color represents the right term of the Definition 14 while black color represents the left term of the Definition 14. We noticed that for various values of the parameters* m, $\mathcal{U}_o$ *and* $\mathcal{V}_o$ *and* β*, the pink color always occurs above the black color. It implies that the Definition 14 holds true.*

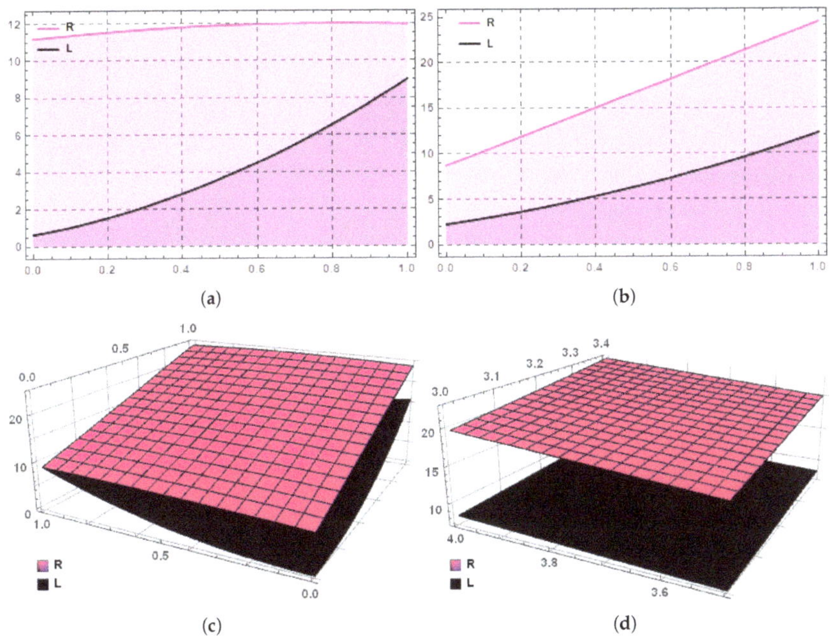

Figure 1. Graphical illustration of Definition 14. (**a**) m, $\mathcal{U}_o$ and $\mathcal{V}_o$ are fixed, while β varies such that $m = 0.2$, $\mathcal{U}_o = 3$, $\mathcal{V}_o = 4$ and $\beta \in [0,1]$. (**b**) β, $\mathcal{U}_o$ and $\mathcal{V}_o$ are fixed, while m varies such that $\beta = 0.5$, $\mathcal{U}_o = 3$, $\mathcal{V}_o = 4$ and $m \in [0,1]$. (**c**) $\mathcal{U}_o$ and $\mathcal{V}_o$ are fixed, while β and m vary such that $\mathcal{U}_o = 3$, $\mathcal{V}_o = 4$, $\beta \in [0,1]$ and $m \in [0,1]$. (**d**) $\mathcal{U}_o$ and $\mathcal{V}_o$ vary, while β and m are fixed such that $\mathcal{U}_o \in [3, 3.4]$, $\mathcal{V}_o \in [3.5, 4]$, $\beta = 0.5$ and $m = 0.7$.

Next, we investigate the core properties that define and characterize (P, m)-superquadratic stochastic processes.

Proposition 1. *If $\Psi_1, \Psi_2 : [0, k] \times \prod \to \Re$ are (P, m)-superquadratic stochastic processes, then $\Psi_1 + \Psi_2$ and $r\Psi$, where $r > 0$ are (P, m)-superquadratic stochastic processes.*

Proof. Let Ψ_1 and Ψ_2 be (P, m)-superquadratic stochastic processes, we have

$$\Psi_1(\beta\mathcal{U}_o + m(1-\beta)\mathcal{V}_o, \cdot) \leq (\Psi_1(\mathcal{U}_o, \cdot) - \Psi_1((1-\beta)|\mathcal{V}_o - \mathcal{U}_o|, \cdot)) + m(\Psi_1(\mathcal{V}_o, \cdot) - \Psi_1(\beta|\mathcal{V}_o - \mathcal{U}_o|, \cdot)),$$

and

$$\Psi_2(\beta\mathcal{U}_o + m(1-\beta)\mathcal{V}_o, \cdot) \leq (\Psi_2(\mathcal{U}_o, \cdot) - \Psi_2((1-\beta)|\mathcal{V}_o - \mathcal{U}_o|, \cdot)) + m(\Psi_2(\mathcal{V}_o, \cdot) - \Psi_2(\beta|\mathcal{V}_o - \mathcal{U}_o|, \cdot)),$$

now

$$\begin{aligned}
&(\Psi_1 + \Psi_2)(\beta\mathcal{U}_o + m(1-\beta)\mathcal{V}_o, \cdot) = \Psi_1(\beta\mathcal{U}_o + m(1-\beta)\mathcal{V}_o, \cdot) + \Psi_2(\beta\mathcal{U}_o + m(1-\beta)\mathcal{V}_o, \cdot) \\
&\leq (\Psi_1(\mathcal{U}_o, \cdot) - \Psi_1((1-\beta)|\mathcal{V}_o - \mathcal{U}_o|, \cdot)) + m(\Psi_1(\mathcal{V}_o, \cdot) - \Psi_1(\beta|\mathcal{V}_o - \mathcal{U}_o|, \cdot)) \\
&+ (\Psi_2(\mathcal{U}_o, \cdot) - \Psi_2((1-\beta)|\mathcal{V}_o - \mathcal{U}_o|, \cdot)) + m(\Psi_2(\mathcal{V}_o, \cdot) - \Psi_2(\beta|\mathcal{V}_o - \mathcal{U}_o|, \cdot)) \\
&= ((\Psi_1 + \Psi_2)(\mathcal{U}_o, \cdot) - (\Psi_1 + \Psi_2)((1-\beta)|\mathcal{V}_o - \mathcal{U}_o|, \cdot)) \\
&+ m((\Psi_1 + \Psi_2)(\mathcal{V}_o, \cdot) - (\Psi_1 + \Psi_2)(\beta|\mathcal{V}_o - \mathcal{U}_o|, \cdot)).
\end{aligned}$$

Thus we have

$$\begin{aligned}
&(\Psi_1 + \Psi_2)(\beta\mathcal{U}_o + m(1-\beta)\mathcal{V}_o, \cdot) \leq ((\Psi_1 + \Psi_2)(\mathcal{U}_o, \cdot) - (\Psi_1 + \Psi_2)((1-\beta)|\mathcal{V}_o - \mathcal{U}_o|, \cdot)) \\
&+ m((\Psi_1 + \Psi_2)(\mathcal{V}_o, \cdot) - (\Psi_1 + \Psi_2)(\beta|\mathcal{V}_o - \mathcal{U}_o|, \cdot)).
\end{aligned} \tag{15}$$

Similarly

$$\begin{aligned}
&r\Psi(\beta\mathcal{U}_o + m(1-\beta)\mathcal{V}_o, \cdot) \\
&\leq r((\Psi(\mathcal{U}_o, \cdot) - \Psi((1-\beta)|\mathcal{V}_o - \mathcal{U}_o|, \cdot)) + m(\Psi(\mathcal{V}_o, \cdot) - \Psi(\beta|\mathcal{V}_o - \mathcal{U}_o|, \cdot))) \\
&= (r\Psi(\mathcal{U}_o, \cdot) - r\Psi((1-\beta)|\mathcal{V}_o - \mathcal{U}_o|, \cdot)) + m(r\Psi(\mathcal{V}_o, \cdot) - r\Psi(\beta|\mathcal{V}_o - \mathcal{U}_o|, \cdot)).
\end{aligned}$$

Thus we have

$$\begin{aligned}
&r\Psi(\beta\mathcal{U}_o + m(1-\beta)\mathcal{V}_o, \cdot) \leq ((r\Psi(\mathcal{U}_o, \cdot) - r\Psi((1-\beta)|\mathcal{V}_o - \mathcal{U}_o|, \cdot)) \\
&+ m(r\Psi(\mathcal{V}_o, \cdot) - r\Psi(\beta|\mathcal{V}_o - \mathcal{U}_o|, \cdot)).
\end{aligned} \tag{16}$$

Therefore, (15) and (16) jointly imply that both $\Psi_1 + \Psi_2$ and $r\Psi$ satisfy the definition of m-superquadratic stochastic processes. □

Proposition 2. *Let $\Psi_1, \Psi_2 : [0, k] \times \prod \to \Re$ be the (P, m)-superquadratic stochastic processes, then $\Psi(y, \cdot) = max\{\Psi_1(y, \cdot), \Psi_2(y, \cdot)\}$ is a (P, m)-superquadratic stochastic process.*

Proof. Since one derives that

$$
\begin{aligned}
&\Psi(\beta\mathcal{U}_o+\mathrm{m}(1-\beta)\mathcal{V}_o,\cdot)\\
&=max\{\Psi_1(\beta\mathcal{U}_o+\mathrm{m}(1-\beta)\mathcal{V}_o,\cdot),\Psi_2(\beta\mathcal{U}_o+\mathrm{m}(1-\beta)\mathcal{V}_o,\cdot)\}\\
&\leq max\{[\Psi_1(\mathcal{U}_o,\cdot)-\Psi_1((1-\beta)|\mathcal{V}_o-\mathcal{U}_o|,\cdot)]+\mathrm{m}[\Psi_1(\mathcal{V}_o,\cdot)-\Psi_1(\beta|\mathcal{V}_o-\mathcal{U}_o|,\cdot)],\\
&[\Psi_2(\mathcal{U}_o,\cdot)-\Psi_2((1-\beta)|\mathcal{V}_o-\mathcal{U}_o|,\cdot)]+\mathrm{m}[\Psi_2(\mathcal{V}_o,\cdot)-\Psi_2(\beta|\mathcal{V}_o-\mathcal{U}_o|,\cdot)]\}\\
&\leq[max\{\Psi_1(\mathcal{U}_o,\cdot),\Psi_2(\mathcal{U}_o,\cdot)\}-max\{\Psi_1((1-\beta)|\mathcal{V}_o-\mathcal{U}_o|,\cdot),\Psi_2((1-\beta)|\mathcal{V}_o-\mathcal{U}_o|,\cdot)\}]\\
&+\mathrm{m}[max\{\Psi_1(\mathcal{V}_o,\cdot),\Psi_2(\mathcal{V}_o,\cdot)\}-max\{\Psi_1(\beta|\mathcal{V}_o-\mathcal{U}_o|,\cdot),\Psi_2(\beta|\mathcal{V}_o-\mathcal{U}_o|,\cdot)\}]\\
&=[\Psi(\mathcal{U}_o,\cdot)-\Psi((1-\beta)|\mathcal{V}_o-\mathcal{U}_o|,\cdot)]+\mathrm{m}[\Psi(\mathcal{V}_o.\cdot)-\Psi(\beta|\mathcal{V}_o-\mathcal{U}_o|,\cdot)].
\end{aligned}
\tag{17}
$$

Consequently, $\Psi(\mathrm{y},\cdot)$ is a (P, m)-superquadratic stochastic process. □

Theorem 6. *Let* $\Psi:[0,\mathrm{k}]\times\prod\to\Re$ *be a (P, m)-superquadratic stochastic process and* $\mathrm{y}_1<\mathrm{y}_2<\mathrm{y}_3$ *for all* $\mathrm{y}_1,\mathrm{y}_2,\mathrm{y}_3\in[0,\mathrm{k}]$*, then*

$$
\begin{vmatrix}\Psi(\mathrm{y}_2,\cdot) & 0\\ 0 & 1\end{vmatrix}\leq\begin{vmatrix}\Psi(\mathrm{y}_1,\cdot) & 1\\ \Psi\left(\left|\frac{(\mathrm{y}_2-\mathrm{y}_1)(\mathrm{y}_3-\mathrm{y}_1)}{\mathrm{my}_3-\mathrm{y}_1}\right|,\cdot\right) & 1\end{vmatrix}+\mathrm{m}\begin{vmatrix}\Psi(\mathrm{y}_3,\cdot) & 1\\ \Psi\left(\left|\frac{(\mathrm{my}_3-\mathrm{y}_2)(\mathrm{y}_3-\mathrm{y}_1)}{\mathrm{my}_3-\mathrm{y}_1}\right|,\cdot\right) & 1\end{vmatrix}
\tag{18}
$$

holds, for every $\mathrm{m}\in[0,1]$.

Proof. Let the stochastic process Ψ is a (P, m)-superquadratic, then

$$
\begin{aligned}
&\Psi(\beta\mathrm{y}+\mathrm{m}(1-\beta)\mathrm{y}_o,\cdot)\leq(\Psi(\mathrm{y},\cdot)-\Psi((1-\beta)|\mathrm{y}-\mathrm{y}_o|,\cdot))\\
&+\mathrm{m}(\Psi(\mathrm{y}_o,\cdot)-\Psi(\beta|\mathrm{y}-\mathrm{y}_o|,\cdot)).
\end{aligned}
\tag{19}
$$

Setting

$$
\mathrm{y}_2=\beta\mathrm{y}+\mathrm{m}(1-\beta)\mathrm{y}_o. \tag{20}
$$

Next putting $\mathrm{y}=\mathrm{y}_1$ and $\mathrm{y}_o=\mathrm{y}_3$ in (20), we get

$$
\begin{aligned}
&\mathrm{y}_2=\beta\mathrm{y}_1+\mathrm{m}(1-\beta)\mathrm{y}_3.\\
&\Rightarrow\beta=\frac{\mathrm{my}_3-\mathrm{y}_2}{\mathrm{my}_3-\mathrm{y}_1}.
\end{aligned}
$$

Substituting $\mathrm{y}=\mathrm{y}_1$, $\mathrm{y}_o=\mathrm{y}_3$ and $\beta=\frac{\mathrm{my}_3-\mathrm{y}_2}{\mathrm{my}_3-\mathrm{y}_1}$ in (19), we get

$$
\begin{aligned}
\Psi(\mathrm{y}_2,\cdot)\leq&\left[\Psi(\mathrm{y}_1,\cdot)-\Psi\left(\left|\frac{(\mathrm{y}_2-\mathrm{y}_1)(\mathrm{y}_3-\mathrm{y}_1)}{\mathrm{my}_3-\mathrm{y}_1}\right|,\cdot\right)\right]\\
&+m\left[\Psi(\mathrm{y}_3,\cdot)-\Psi\left(\left|\frac{(\mathrm{my}_3-\mathrm{y}_2)(\mathrm{y}_3-\mathrm{y}_1)}{\mathrm{my}_3-\mathrm{y}_1}\right|,\cdot\right)\right].
\end{aligned}
$$

It implies that

$$
\begin{aligned}
&\left[\Psi(\mathrm{y}_1,\cdot)-\Psi\left(\left|\frac{(\mathrm{y}_2-\mathrm{y}_1)(\mathrm{y}_3-\mathrm{y}_1)}{\mathrm{my}_3-\mathrm{y}_1}\right|,\cdot\right)\right]\\
&+m\left[\Psi(\mathrm{y}_3,,\cdot)-\Psi\left(\left|\frac{(\mathrm{my}_3-\mathrm{y}_2)(\mathrm{y}_3-\mathrm{y}_1)}{\mathrm{my}_3-\mathrm{y}_1}\right|,\cdot\right)\right]-\Psi(\mathrm{y}_2,\cdot)\geq 0.
\end{aligned}
\tag{21}
$$

Inequality (21) can be written as follows

$$\begin{vmatrix} \Psi(y_1,\cdot) & 1 \\ \Psi\left(\left|\frac{(y_2-y_1)(y_3-y_1)}{my_3-y_1}\right|,\cdot\right) & 1 \end{vmatrix} + m\begin{vmatrix} \Psi(y_3,\cdot) & 1 \\ \Psi\left(\left|\frac{(my_3-y_2)(y_3-y_1)}{my_3-y_1}\right|,\cdot\right) & 1 \end{vmatrix} \geq \begin{vmatrix} \Psi(y_2,\cdot) & 0 \\ 0 & 1 \end{vmatrix}. \tag{22}$$

Hence this concludes the proof. □

Next we provide the proof of an inequality of Jensen's type for (P, m)-superquadratic stochastic processes.

Theorem 7. *Let* $\Psi : [0,k] \times \prod \to \Re$ *be a (P, m)-superquadratic stochastic process then*

$$\Psi\left(\sum_{i=1}^{n} \beta_i y_i,\cdot\right) \leq \sum_{i=1}^{n} m^{n-i}\Psi\left(\frac{y_i}{m^{n-i}},\cdot\right) - \sum_{i=1}^{n} m^{n-i}\Psi\left(\left|\frac{y_i}{m^{n-i}} - \sum_{i=1}^{n}\frac{\beta_i y_i}{m^{n-i}}\right|,\cdot\right), \tag{23}$$

holds $\forall y_1,\ldots,y_n \in [0,k], \beta_1,\ldots,\beta_n > 0$, *such that* $\sum_{i=1}^{n}\beta_i = 1$, *where* $m \in [0,1]$.

Proof. We prove this result by using the principle of mathematical induction, therefore by taking $n = 2$ in (23), we have

$$\Psi(\beta_1 y_1 + \beta_2 y_2,\cdot) \leq \Psi(y_2,\cdot) - \Psi\left(\beta_1\left|y_2 - \frac{y_1}{m}\right|,\cdot\right) + m\left(\Psi\left(\frac{y_1}{m},\cdot\right) - \Psi\left(\beta_2\left|y_2 - \frac{y_1}{m}\right|,\cdot\right)\right).$$

Which reflects the Definition 14. Thus the statement (23) is true for $n = 2$.

Next we assuming the validity of (23) for $n-1$, it follows that:

$$\Psi\left(\sum_{i=1}^{n-1}\beta_i y_i,\cdot\right) \leq \sum_{i=1}^{n-1} m^{n-1-i}\Psi\left(\frac{y_i}{m^{n-1-i}},\cdot\right) - \sum_{i=1}^{n-1} m^{n-1-i}\Psi\left(\left|\frac{y_i}{m^{n-1-i}} - \sum_{i=1}^{n-1}\frac{\beta_i y_i}{m^{n-1-i}}\right|,\cdot\right), \tag{24}$$

now let us prove that (23) is valid for n.

$$\Psi\left(\sum_{i=1}^{n}\beta_i y_i,\cdot\right) = \Psi\left(\beta_n y_n + m\beta\sum_{i=1}^{n-1}\frac{\beta_i y_i}{m\beta},\cdot\right),$$

where $\beta = \sum_{i=1}^{n-1}\beta_i$, then it implies that

$$\begin{aligned}\Psi\left(\sum_{i=1}^{n}\beta_i y_i,\cdot\right) &\leq \Psi(y_n,\cdot) + m\Psi\left(\sum_{i=1}^{n-1}\left(\frac{\beta_i y_i}{m\ \beta}\right),\cdot\right) \\ &- \Psi\left(\beta\left|y_n - \sum_{i=1}^{n-1}\left(\frac{\beta_i y_i}{m\beta}\right)\right|,\cdot\right) - m\Psi\left(\beta_n\left|y_n - \sum_{i=1}^{n-1}\left(\frac{\beta_i y_i}{m\beta}\right)\right|,\cdot\right),\end{aligned} \tag{25}$$

using (24) in (25), then we obtain

$$\Psi\left(\sum_{i=1}^{n}\beta_i y_i,\cdot\right) \le \Psi(y_n,\cdot) + \sum_{i=1}^{n-1} m^{n-i}\Psi\left(\frac{y_i}{m^{n-i}},\cdot\right) - \sum_{i=1}^{n-1} m^{n-i}\Psi\left(\left|\frac{y_i}{m^{n-i}} - \sum_{i=1}^{n-1}\frac{\beta_i y_i}{m^{n-i}}\right|,\cdot\right)$$
$$-\Psi\left(\beta\left|y_n - \sum_{i=1}^{n-1}\left(\frac{\beta_i y_i}{m\beta}\right)\right|,\cdot\right) - m\Psi\left(\beta_n\left|y_n - \sum_{i=1}^{n-1}\left(\frac{\beta_i y_i}{m\beta}\right)\right|,\cdot\right)$$
$$= m^{n-n}\Psi\left(\frac{y_n}{m^{n-n}},\cdot\right) + \sum_{i=1}^{n-1} m^{n-i}\Psi\left(\frac{y_i}{m^{n-i}},\cdot\right) - \sum_{i=1}^{n-1} m^{n-i}\Psi\left(\left|\frac{y_i}{m^{n-i}} - \sum_{i=1}^{n-1}\frac{\beta_i y_i}{m^{n-i}}\right|,\cdot\right)$$
$$-\Psi\left(\beta\left|y_n - \sum_{i=1}^{n-1}\left(\frac{\beta_i y_i}{m\beta}\right)\right|,\cdot\right) - m\Psi\left(\beta_n\left|y_n - \sum_{i=1}^{n-1}\left(\frac{\beta_i y_i}{m\beta}\right)\right|,\cdot\right)$$
$$\le \sum_{i=1}^{n} m^{n-i}\Psi\left(\frac{y_i}{m^{n-i}},\cdot\right) - \sum_{i=1}^{n-1} m^{n-i}\Psi\left(\left|\frac{y_i}{m^{n-i}} - \sum_{i=1}^{n-1}\frac{\beta_i y_i}{m^{n-i}}\right|,\cdot\right) - \Psi\left(\beta\left|y_n - \sum_{i=1}^{n-1}\left(\frac{\beta_i y_i}{m^{n-i}\beta}\right)\right|,\cdot\right)$$
$$= \sum_{i=1}^{n} m^{n-i}\Psi\left(\frac{y_i}{m^{n-i}},\cdot\right) - \sum_{i=1}^{n-1} m^{n-i}\Psi\left(\left|\frac{y_i}{m^{n-i}} - \sum_{i=1}^{n-1}\frac{\beta_i y_i}{m^{n-i}}\right|,\cdot\right)$$
$$- m^{n-n}\Psi\left(\left|\frac{y_n}{m^{n-n}} - \frac{\beta_n y_n}{m^{n-n}} - \sum_{i=1}^{n-1}\left(\frac{\beta_i y_i}{m^{n-i}}\right)\right|,\cdot\right)$$
$$= \sum_{i=1}^{n} m^{n-i}\Psi\left(\frac{y_i}{m^{n-i}},\cdot\right) - \sum_{i=1}^{n-1} m^{n-i}\Psi\left(\left|\frac{y_i}{m^{n-i}} - \sum_{i=1}^{n-1}\frac{\beta_i y_i}{m^{n-i}}\right|,\cdot\right)$$
$$- m^{n-n}\Psi\left(\left|\frac{y_n}{m^{n-n}} - \frac{\beta_n y_n}{m^{n-n}} - \sum_{i=1}^{n-1}\left(\frac{\beta_i y_i}{m^{n-i}}\right)\right|,\cdot\right)$$
$$= \sum_{i=1}^{n} m^{n-i}\Psi\left(\frac{y_i}{m^{n-i}},\cdot\right) - \sum_{i=1}^{n-1} m^{n-i}\Psi\left(\left|\frac{y_i}{m^{n-i}} - \sum_{i=1}^{n-1}\frac{\beta_i y_i}{m^{n-i}}\right|,\cdot\right)$$
$$- m^{n-n}\Psi\left(\left|\frac{y_n}{m^{n-n}} - \sum_{i=1}^{n}\left(\frac{\beta_i y_i}{m^{n-i}}\right)\right|,\cdot\right)$$
$$= \sum_{i=1}^{n} m^{n-i}\Psi\left(\frac{y_i}{m^{n-i}},\cdot\right) - \sum_{i=1}^{n} m^{n-i}\Psi\left(\left|\frac{y_i}{m^{n-i}} - \sum_{i=1}^{n}\frac{\beta_i y_i}{m^{n-i}}\right|,\cdot\right).$$

Hence the proof. □

Theorem 8. *The following statements are true for* $m \in [0,1]$ *and* $\forall\ \mathcal{U}_o, \mathcal{V}_o, \mathfrak{c}_o \in [0,k]$ *and* $\beta \in [0,1]$

1. $\Psi \in S_m[0,k]$, *where* $S_m[0,k]$*=Set of (P, m)-superquadratic stochastic processes.*
2. *The process* Ψ *holds the result given below:*

$$\Psi(\beta_1\mathcal{U}_o + (1-\beta_1)\mathcal{V}_o,\cdot) \le \Psi(\mathcal{U}_o,\cdot) - \Psi\left((1-\beta_1)\left|\mathcal{U}_o - \frac{\mathcal{V}_o}{m}\right|,\cdot\right)$$
$$+ m\left(\Psi\left(\frac{\mathcal{V}_o}{m},\cdot\right) - \Psi\left(\beta_1\left|\mathcal{U}_o - \frac{\mathcal{V}_o}{m}\right|,\cdot\right)\right).$$

3. *For* $\beta_1 + \beta_2 = 1$, *the process* Ψ *holds the inequality given below:*

$$\Psi(\beta_1\mathcal{U}_o + \beta_2\mathcal{V}_o,\cdot) \le \Psi(\mathcal{U}_o,\cdot) - \Psi\left(\beta_2\left|\mathcal{U}_o - \frac{\mathcal{V}_o}{m}\right|,\cdot\right)$$
$$+ m\left(\Psi\left(\frac{\mathcal{V}_o}{m},\cdot\right) - \Psi\left(\beta_1\left|\mathcal{U}_o - \frac{\mathcal{V}_o}{m}\right|,\cdot\right)\right).$$

4. *For $\mathcal{U}_o \leq \mathfrak{c}_o \leq \mathcal{V}_o$ the inequality given below holds:*

$$\begin{vmatrix} 1 & \Psi(\mathcal{U}_o,\cdot) - \Psi((1-\beta)|\mathcal{U}_o - \frac{\mathcal{V}_o}{\mathrm{m}}|,\cdot) & 1 \\ -1 & \mathrm{m}\Big[\big(\Psi(\frac{\mathcal{V}_o}{\mathrm{m}},\cdot) - \Psi(\beta|\mathcal{U}_o - \frac{\mathcal{V}_o}{\mathrm{m}}|,\cdot)\big)\Big] & 0 \\ 0 & \Psi(\mathfrak{c}_o,\cdot) & 1 \end{vmatrix} \geq 0.$$

Proof. It is straightforward that (1) $\Leftrightarrow$ (2) $\Leftrightarrow$ (3) and (3) $\Leftrightarrow$ (4). Since $\mathcal{U}_o \leq \mathfrak{c}_o \leq \mathcal{V}_o$ there exists a scalar $\beta_1 \in [0,1]$ such that $\mathfrak{c}_o = \beta_1\mathcal{U}_o + \beta_2\mathcal{V}_o = \beta_1\mathcal{U}_o + (1-\beta_1)\mathcal{V}_o$. Consequently, the following results can be established.

$$\begin{aligned} \Psi(\mathfrak{c}_o,\cdot) &= \Psi(\beta_1\mathcal{U}_o + \beta_2\mathcal{V}_o,\cdot) = \Psi(\beta_1\mathcal{U}_o + (1-\beta_1)\mathcal{V}_o,\cdot) = \Psi\left(\beta_1\mathcal{U}_o + \mathrm{m}(1-\beta_1)\frac{\mathcal{V}_o}{\mathrm{m}},\cdot\right) \\ &\leq \left(\Psi(\mathcal{U}_o,\cdot) - \Psi\left((1-\beta_1)\left|\mathcal{U}_o - \frac{\mathcal{V}_o}{\mathrm{m}}\right|,\cdot\right)\right) + \mathrm{m}\left(\Psi\left(\frac{\mathcal{V}_o}{\mathrm{m}},\cdot\right) - \Psi\left(\beta_1\left|\mathcal{U}_o - \frac{\mathcal{V}_o}{\mathrm{m}}\right|,\cdot\right)\right). \end{aligned}$$

Since it follows that

$$\begin{aligned} &\begin{vmatrix} 1 & \Psi(\mathcal{U}_o,\cdot) - \Psi((1-\beta_1)|\mathcal{U}_o - \frac{\mathcal{V}_o}{\mathrm{m}}|,\cdot) & 1 \\ -1 & \mathrm{m}(\Psi(\frac{\mathcal{V}_o}{\mathrm{m}},\cdot) - \Psi(\beta_1|\mathcal{U}_o - \frac{\mathcal{V}_o}{\mathrm{m}}|,\cdot)) & 0 \\ 0 & \Psi(\mathfrak{c}_o,\cdot) & 1 \end{vmatrix} \\ &= \Psi(\mathcal{U}_o,\cdot) - \Psi\left((1-\beta_1)\left|\mathcal{U}_o - \frac{\mathcal{V}_o}{\mathrm{m}}\right|,\cdot\right) \\ &+\mathrm{m}\left(\Psi\left(\frac{\mathcal{V}_o}{\mathrm{m}},\cdot\right) - \Psi\left(\beta_1\left|\mathcal{U}_o - \frac{\mathcal{V}_o}{\mathrm{m}}\right|,\cdot\right)\right) - \Psi(\mathfrak{c}_o,\cdot) \geq 0. \end{aligned}$$

Hence, (4) is satisfied (4) $\Rightarrow$ (1). In view of the assumption

$$\begin{aligned} &\Psi(\mathcal{U}_o,\cdot) - \Psi\left((1-\beta_1)\left|\mathcal{U}_o - \frac{\mathcal{V}_o}{\mathrm{m}}\right|,\cdot\right) + \mathrm{m}\left(\Psi\left(\frac{\mathcal{V}_o}{\mathrm{m}},\cdot\right)\right. \\ &\left.-\Psi\left(\beta_1\left|\mathcal{U}_o - \frac{\mathcal{V}_o}{\mathrm{m}}\right|,\cdot\right)\right) - \Psi(\mathfrak{c}_o,\cdot) \leq 0, \end{aligned}$$

it can be applied to

$$\begin{aligned} &\Psi(\mathfrak{c}_o,\cdot) = \Psi(\beta_1\mathcal{U}_o + (1-\beta_1)\mathcal{V}_o,\cdot) \\ &\leq \left(\Psi(\mathcal{U}_o,\cdot) - \Psi\left((1-\beta_1)\left|\mathcal{U}_o - \frac{\mathcal{V}_o}{\mathrm{m}}\right|\right),\cdot\right) + \mathrm{m}\left(\Psi\left(\frac{\mathcal{V}_o}{\mathrm{m}},\cdot\right) - \Psi\left(\beta_1\left|\mathcal{U}_o - \frac{\mathcal{V}_o}{\mathrm{m}}\right|,\cdot\right)\right). \end{aligned}$$

Hence the proof. □

Next we offer the $\mathbb{H}.\mathbb{H}$'s inequality for (P, m)-superquadratic stochastic processes.

Theorem 9. *Let Ψ: $[\mathcal{U}_o, \frac{\mathcal{V}_o}{m}] \times \prod \to \Re$ be a mean-square integrable (P, m)-superquadratic stochastic process, then*

$$\begin{aligned}
&\Psi\left(\frac{\mathcal{U}_o + \mathcal{V}_o}{2}, \cdot\right) + \frac{1+m}{\mathcal{V}_o - \mathcal{U}_o} \int_{\mathcal{U}_o}^{\mathcal{V}_o} \Psi\left(\left|\frac{(\mathcal{U}_o + \mathcal{V}_o) - (m+1)y}{2m}\right|, \cdot\right) dy \\
&\leq \frac{1}{\mathcal{V}_o - \mathcal{U}_o} \left\{ \int_{\mathcal{U}_o}^{\mathcal{V}_o} \Psi(y, \cdot) dy + m \int_{\frac{\mathcal{U}_o}{m}}^{\frac{\mathcal{V}_o}{m}} \Psi(y, \cdot) dy \right\} \\
&\leq \Psi(\mathcal{U}_o, \cdot) + m \left\{ \Psi\left(\frac{\mathcal{V}_o}{m}, \cdot\right) + \Psi\left(\frac{\mathcal{U}_o}{m}, \cdot\right) + \Psi\left(\frac{\mathcal{V}_o}{m^2}, \cdot\right) \right\} \\
&- \frac{1}{\mathcal{V}_o - \mathcal{U}_o} \left\{ \int_{\mathcal{U}_o}^{\mathcal{V}_o} \left(\Psi\left(\left|\frac{(y - \mathcal{U}_o)(\mathcal{V}_o - m\mathcal{U}_o)}{m(\mathcal{V}_o - \mathcal{U}_o)}\right|, \cdot\right) \right.\right. \\
&+ m\Psi\left(\left|\frac{(\mathcal{V}_o - y)(\mathcal{V}_o - m\mathcal{U}_o)}{m(\mathcal{V}_o - \mathcal{U}_o)}\right|, \cdot\right) + m\Psi\left(\left|\frac{(\mathcal{V}_o - y)(\mathcal{V}_o - m\mathcal{U}_o)}{m^2(\mathcal{V}_o - \mathcal{U}_o)}\right|, \cdot\right) \\
&\left.\left. + m^2\Psi\left(\left|\frac{(y - \mathcal{U}_o)(\mathcal{V}_o - m\mathcal{U}_o)}{m^2(\mathcal{V}_o - \mathcal{U}_o)}\right|, \cdot\right) \right) dy \right\},
\end{aligned} \tag{26}$$

holds $\forall\, \mathcal{U}_o, \mathcal{V}_o > 0$ *and* $m \in (0, 1)$.

Proof. Since Ψ is a (P, m)-superquadratic stochastic process therefore we have

$$\begin{aligned}
&\Psi\left(\frac{y + y_o}{2}, \cdot\right) = \Psi\left(\frac{y}{2} + \left(\frac{m}{2}\right)\left(\frac{y_o}{m}\right), \cdot\right) \leq \left(\Psi(y, \cdot) - \Psi\left(\frac{1}{2}\left|y - \frac{y_o}{m}\right|, \cdot\right)\right) \\
&+ m\left(\Psi\left(\frac{y_o}{m}, \cdot\right) - \Psi\left(\frac{1}{2}\left|y - \frac{y_o}{m}\right|, \cdot\right)\right).
\end{aligned} \tag{27}$$

Replacing y by $\beta\mathcal{U}_o + (1-\beta)\mathcal{V}_o$ and y_o by $\beta\mathcal{V}_o + (1-\beta)\mathcal{U}_o$ in (27), we get.

$$\begin{aligned}
&\Psi\left(\frac{\mathcal{U}_o + \mathcal{V}_o}{2}, \cdot\right) \leq \Psi(\beta\mathcal{U}_o + (1-\beta)\mathcal{V}_o, \cdot) + m\Psi\left(\frac{\beta\mathcal{V}_o + (1-\beta)\mathcal{U}_o}{m}, \cdot\right) \\
&- (1+m)\Psi\left(\left|\frac{(1+m)(\mathcal{U}_o\beta + \mathcal{V}_o(1-\beta)) - (\mathcal{U}_o + \mathcal{V}_o)}{2m}\right|, \cdot\right).
\end{aligned} \tag{28}$$

After mean-square integration of (28) w.r.t β over $[0, 1]$, we have

$$\begin{aligned}
&\Psi\left(\frac{\mathcal{U}_o + \mathcal{V}_o}{2}, \cdot\right) \leq \int_0^1 \Psi(\beta\mathcal{U}_o + (1-\beta)\mathcal{V}_o, \cdot) d\beta + m \int_0^1 \Psi\left(\frac{\beta\mathcal{V}_o + (1-\beta)\mathcal{U}_o}{m}\right) d\beta \\
&- (1+m) \int_0^1 \Psi\left(\left|\frac{(1+m)(\mathcal{U}_o\beta + \mathcal{V}_o(1-\beta)) - (\mathcal{U}_o + \mathcal{V}_o)}{2m}\right|, \cdot\right) d\beta.
\end{aligned}$$

It implies after change of variables and simple calculations that

$$\begin{aligned}
&\Psi\left(\frac{\mathcal{U}_o + \mathcal{V}_o}{2}, \cdot\right) \leq \frac{1}{\mathcal{V}_o - \mathcal{U}_o} \left\{ \int_{\mathcal{U}_o}^{\mathcal{V}_o} \Psi(y, \cdot) dy + m \int_{\frac{\mathcal{U}_o}{m}}^{\frac{\mathcal{V}_o}{m}} \Psi(y, \cdot) dy \right\} \\
&- \frac{1+m}{\mathcal{V}_o - \mathcal{U}_o} \int_{\mathcal{U}_o}^{\mathcal{V}_o} \Psi\left(\left|\frac{(\mathcal{U}_o + \mathcal{V}_o) - (m+1)y}{2m}\right|, \cdot\right) dy.
\end{aligned}$$

Thus

$$\begin{aligned}
&\Psi\left(\frac{\mathcal{U}_o + \mathcal{V}_o}{2}, \cdot\right) + \frac{1+m}{\mathcal{V}_o - \mathcal{U}_o} \int_{\mathcal{U}_o}^{\mathcal{V}_o} \Psi\left(\left|\frac{(\mathcal{U}_o + \mathcal{V}_o) - (m+1)y}{2m}\right|, \cdot\right) dy \\
&\leq \frac{1}{\mathcal{V}_o - \mathcal{U}_o} \left\{ \int_{\mathcal{U}_o}^{\mathcal{V}_o} \Psi(y, \cdot) dy + m \int_{\frac{\mathcal{U}_o}{m}}^{\frac{\mathcal{V}_o}{m}} \Psi(y, \cdot) dy \right\}.
\end{aligned} \tag{29}$$

Since Ψ is an (P, m)-superquadratic stochastic process, it follows that

$$\begin{aligned}
&\Psi(\beta\mathcal{U}_o+(1-\beta)\mathcal{V}_o,\cdot)+\mathrm{m}\Psi\left(\frac{\beta\mathcal{V}_o+(1-\beta)\mathcal{U}_o}{\mathrm{m}},\cdot\right)\\
&=\Psi\left(\beta\mathcal{U}_o+\mathrm{m}(1-\beta)\left(\frac{\mathcal{V}_o}{\mathrm{m}}\right),\cdot\right)+\mathrm{m}\Psi\left((1-\beta)\frac{\mathcal{U}_o}{\mathrm{m}}+\mathrm{m}\beta\left(\frac{\mathcal{V}_o}{\mathrm{m}^2}\right),\cdot\right)\\
&\leq\left(\Psi(\mathcal{U}_o,\cdot)-\Psi\left((1-\beta)\left|\frac{\mathrm{m}\mathcal{U}_o-\mathcal{V}_o}{\mathrm{m}}\right|,\cdot\right)\right)+\mathrm{m}\left(\Psi\left(\frac{\mathcal{V}_o}{\mathrm{m}},\cdot\right)-\Psi\left(\beta\left|\frac{\mathrm{m}\mathcal{U}_o-\mathcal{V}_o}{\mathrm{m}}\right|,\cdot\right)\right)\\
&+\mathrm{m}\left(\Psi\left(\frac{\mathcal{U}_o}{\mathrm{m}},\cdot\right)-\Psi\left(\beta\left|\frac{\mathrm{m}\mathcal{U}_o-\mathcal{V}_o}{\mathrm{m}^2}\right|,\cdot\right)\right)+\mathrm{m}^2\left(\Psi\left(\frac{\mathcal{V}_o}{\mathrm{m}^2},\cdot\right)-\Psi\left((1-\beta)\left|\frac{\mathrm{m}\mathcal{U}_o-\mathcal{V}_o}{\mathrm{m}^2}\right|,\cdot\right)\right),
\end{aligned}\tag{30}$$

integrating (30) w.r.t β over $[0,1]$ and after simple calculation and change of variables we get

$$\begin{aligned}
&\frac{1}{\mathcal{V}_o-\mathcal{U}_o}\left\{\int_{\mathcal{U}_o}^{\mathcal{V}_o}\Psi(\mathrm{y},\cdot)d\mathrm{y}+\mathrm{m}\int_{\frac{\mathcal{U}_o}{\mathrm{m}}}^{\frac{\mathcal{V}_o}{\mathrm{m}}}\Psi(\mathrm{y},\cdot)d\mathrm{y}\right\}\\
&\leq\Psi(\mathcal{U}_o,\cdot)+\mathrm{m}\left\{\Psi\left(\frac{\mathcal{V}_o}{\mathrm{m}},\cdot\right)+\Psi\left(\frac{\mathcal{U}_o}{\mathrm{m}},\cdot\right)+\Psi\left(\frac{\mathcal{V}_o}{\mathrm{m}^2},\cdot\right)\right\}\\
&-\frac{1}{\mathcal{V}_o-\mathcal{U}_o}\left\{\int_{\mathcal{U}_o}^{\mathcal{V}_o}\left(\Psi\left(\left|\frac{(\mathrm{y}-\mathcal{U}_o)(\mathcal{V}_o-\mathrm{m}\mathcal{U}_o)}{\mathrm{m}(\mathcal{V}_o-\mathcal{U}_o)}\right|,\cdot\right)\right.\right.\\
&+\mathrm{m}\Psi\left(\left|\frac{(\mathcal{V}_o-\mathrm{y})(\mathcal{V}_o-\mathrm{m}\mathcal{U}_o)}{\mathrm{m}(\mathcal{V}_o-\mathcal{U}_o)}\right|,\cdot\right)+\mathrm{m}\Psi\left(\left|\frac{(\mathcal{V}_o-\mathrm{y})(\mathcal{V}_o-\mathrm{m}\mathcal{U}_o)}{\mathrm{m}^2(\mathcal{V}_o-\mathcal{U}_o)}\right|,\cdot\right)\\
&\left.\left.+\mathrm{m}^2\Psi\left(\left|\frac{(\mathrm{y}-\mathcal{U}_o)(\mathcal{V}_o-\mathrm{m}\mathcal{U}_o)}{\mathrm{m}^2(\mathcal{V}_o-\mathcal{U}_o)}\right|,\cdot\right)\right)d\mathrm{y}\right\}.
\end{aligned}\tag{31}$$

Combining (29) and (31), we get what we want. □

Corollary 1. *When the inequality in* (26) *is reversed, it gives rise to an inequality of* $\mathbb{H}.\mathbb{H}$*-type characterizing (P,m)-subquadratic stochastic processes.*

To verify Theorem 9, we present the following example involving (P,m)-superquadratic stochastic process.

Example 4. *Consider the same process as given in Example 3, then we have the Figure 2a,b given by Figure 2, depict the right, middle and left terms, which are denoted by R, M and L respectively for Theorem 9.*

m	L	M	R
0.1	2573.33	18,809.1	5.34×10^6
0.2	276.909	2372.04	169,857
0.3	72.4611	719.63	23,361.5
0.4	30.056	317.4	5984.62
0.5	17.9503	174.162	2195.01
0.6	14.0841	110.849	1022.4
0.7	12.9429	78.6475	564.916
0.8	12.7918	60.57	354.138
0.9	12.9999	49.6485	244.109
1.0	13.3151	42.6653	180.865

(**a**)

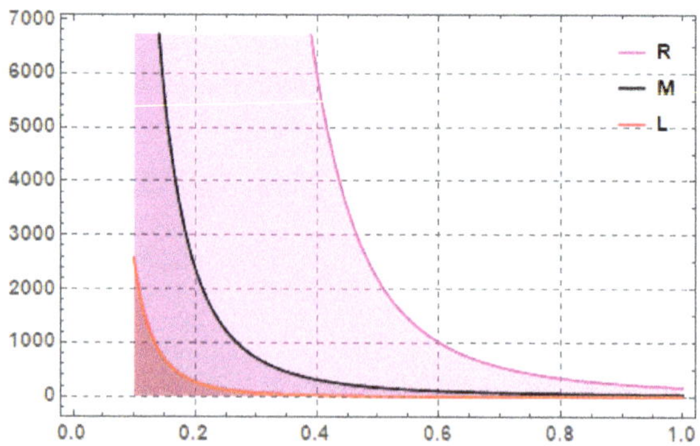

(**b**)

Figure 2. Graphical and numerical description of $\Psi = \mathrm{y}^3$ via Theorem 9 for $\mathcal{U}_o = 3, \mathcal{V}_o = 4$ and $\mathrm{m} \in (0.1, 1.0)$. (**a**) Numerical description of Theorem 9. (**b**) Graphical description of Theorem 9.

In the aforementioned Example 4, the graph consists of three colors: pink, black and red. Pink, black and red stands for the right, middle and right terms of Theorem 9, respectively. It is obvious from Theorem 9 that right term is always greater than the middle and middle term is greater than the left term, therefore the graph's pink color always occur above the black, and black always occur above the red color for various values of the parameters involved in it. This graphically confirms that the established result is true.

4. $\mathbb{H}.\mathbb{H}$ Type Inequalities for (P, m)-Superquadratic Stochastic Processes: A Fractional Calculus Approach

This section is devoted to deriving fractional analogues of the $\mathbb{H}.\mathbb{H}$ inequalities via $\mathbb{RL}$ fractional operators.

Theorem 10. *Let* Ψ: $[\mathcal{U}_o, \frac{\mathcal{V}_o}{m}] \times \prod \rightarrow \Re$ *be a mean-square integrable (P, m)-superquadratic stochastic process, then*

$$\begin{aligned}
&\Psi\left(\frac{u_o+\mathcal{V}_o}{2},\cdot\right)+\frac{2(1+m)\alpha}{(\mathcal{V}_o-\mathcal{U}_o)^\alpha}\int_{\mathcal{U}_o}^{\frac{\mathcal{U}_o+\mathcal{V}_o}{2}}(\mathcal{V}_o-y)^{\alpha-1}\Psi\left(\left|\frac{(\mathcal{U}_o+\mathcal{V}_o)-(m+1)y}{2m}\right|,\cdot\right)dy\\
&\leq\frac{\Gamma(1+\alpha)}{(\mathcal{V}_o-\mathcal{U}_o)^\alpha}\left[\mathfrak{J}^\alpha_{\mathcal{U}_o^+}\Psi(\mathcal{V}_o,\cdot)+m^\alpha\mathfrak{J}^\alpha_{\frac{\mathcal{V}_o}{m}^-}\Psi\left(\frac{\mathcal{U}_o}{m},\cdot\right)\right]\\
&\leq\Psi(\mathcal{U}_o,\cdot)+m\left\{\Psi\left(\frac{\mathcal{V}_o}{m},\cdot\right)+\Psi\left(\frac{\mathcal{U}_o}{m},\cdot\right)+\Psi\left(\frac{\mathcal{V}_o}{m^2},\cdot\right)\right\}\\
&-\frac{\alpha}{(\mathcal{V}_o-\mathcal{U}_o)^\alpha}\left\{\int_{\mathcal{U}_o}^{\mathcal{V}_o}(\mathcal{V}_o-y)^{\alpha-1}\left(\Psi\left(\left|\frac{(y-\mathcal{U}_o)(\mathcal{V}_o-m\mathcal{U}_o)}{m(\mathcal{V}_o-\mathcal{U}_o)}\right|,\cdot\right)\right.\right.\\
&+m\Psi\left(\left|\frac{(\mathcal{V}_o-y)(\mathcal{V}_o-m\mathcal{U}_o)}{m(\mathcal{V}_o-\mathcal{U}_o)}\right|,\cdot\right)+m\Psi\left(\left|\frac{(\mathcal{V}_o-y)(\mathcal{V}_o-m\mathcal{U}_o)}{m^2(\mathcal{V}_o-\mathcal{U}_o)}\right|,\cdot\right)\\
&\left.\left.+m^2\Psi\left(\left|\frac{(y-\mathcal{U}_o)(\mathcal{V}_o-m\mathcal{U}_o)}{m^2(\mathcal{V}_o-\mathcal{U}_o)}\right|,\cdot\right)\right)dy\right\},
\end{aligned}\tag{32}$$

holds for all $\mathcal{U}_o, \mathcal{V}_o \geq 0$ *and* $m \in (0,1)$.

Proof. Let the process Ψ, satisfying the conditions of (P, m)-superquadratic stochastic process, suggest that

$$\begin{aligned}
&\Psi\left(\frac{y+y_o}{2},\cdot\right)=\Psi\left(\frac{y}{2}+\left(\frac{m}{2}\right)\left(\frac{y_o}{m}\right),\cdot\right)\leq\left(\Psi(y,\cdot)-\Psi\left(\frac{1}{2}\left|y-\frac{y_o}{m}\right|,\cdot\right)\right)\\
&+m\left(\Psi\left(\frac{y_o}{m},\cdot\right)-\Psi\left(\frac{1}{2}\left|y-\frac{y_o}{m}\right|,\cdot\right)\right),
\end{aligned}\tag{33}$$

Replacing y with $\beta\mathcal{U}_o + (1-\beta)\mathcal{V}_o$ and y_o with $\beta\mathcal{V}_o + (1-\beta)\mathcal{U}_o$ in (33), we obtain the following

$$\begin{aligned}
&\Psi\left(\frac{\mathcal{U}_o+\mathcal{V}_o}{2},\cdot\right)\leq\Psi(\beta\mathcal{U}_o+(1-\beta)\mathcal{V}_o,\cdot)+m\Psi\left(\frac{\beta\mathcal{V}_o+(1-\beta)\mathcal{U}_o}{m},\cdot\right)\\
&-(1+m)\Psi\left(\left|\frac{(1+m)(\mathcal{U}_o\beta+\mathcal{V}_o(1-\beta))-(\mathcal{U}_o+\mathcal{V}_o)}{2m}\right|,\cdot\right),
\end{aligned}\tag{34}$$

Multiplying (34) by $\beta^{\alpha-1}$ and then integrating it via β over $[0,1]$, we have

$$\begin{aligned}
&\frac{1}{\alpha}\Psi\left(\frac{\mathcal{U}_o+\mathcal{V}_o}{2},\cdot\right)\leq\int_0^1\beta^{\alpha-1}\Psi(\beta\mathcal{U}_o+(1-\beta)\mathcal{V}_o,\cdot)d\beta+m\int_0^1\beta^{\alpha-1}\Psi\left(\frac{\beta\mathcal{V}_o+(1-\beta)\mathcal{U}_o}{m},\cdot\right)d\beta\\
&-(1+m)\int_0^1\beta^{\alpha-1}\Psi\left(\left|\frac{(1+m)(\mathcal{U}_o\beta+\mathcal{V}_o(1-\beta))-(\mathcal{U}_o+\mathcal{V}_o)}{2m}\right|,\cdot\right)d\beta,
\end{aligned}$$

it implies that

$$\frac{1}{\alpha}\Psi\left(\frac{\mathcal{U}_o+\mathcal{V}_o}{2},\cdot\right) \leq \frac{1}{(\mathcal{V}_o-\mathcal{U}_o)^{\alpha}}\left\{\int_{\mathcal{U}_o}^{\mathcal{V}_o}(\mathcal{V}_o-y)^{\alpha-1}\Psi(y,\cdot)dy+m^{\alpha}\int_{\frac{\mathcal{U}_o}{m}}^{\frac{\mathcal{V}_o}{m}}\left(y-\frac{\mathcal{U}_o}{m}\right)^{\alpha-1}\Psi(y,\cdot)dy\right\}$$
$$-\frac{1+m}{(\mathcal{V}_o-\mathcal{U}_o)^{\alpha}}\int_{\mathcal{U}_o}^{\mathcal{V}_o}(\mathcal{V}_o-y)^{\alpha-1}\Psi\left(\left|\frac{(\mathcal{U}_o+\mathcal{V}_o)-(m+1)y}{2m}\right|,\cdot\right)dy,$$

thus

$$\begin{aligned}&\frac{1}{\alpha}\Psi\left(\frac{\mathcal{U}_o+\mathcal{V}_o}{2},\cdot\right)+\frac{1+m}{(\mathcal{V}_o-\mathcal{U}_o)^{\alpha}}\int_{\mathcal{U}_o}^{\mathcal{V}_o}(\mathcal{V}_o-y)^{\alpha-1}\Psi\left(\left|\frac{(\mathcal{U}_o+\mathcal{V}_o)-(m+1)y}{2m}\right|,\cdot\right)dy\\&\leq\frac{\Gamma(\alpha)}{(\mathcal{V}_o-\mathcal{U}_o)^{\alpha}}\left[\mathfrak{J}^{\alpha}_{\mathcal{U}_o^+}\Psi(\mathcal{V}_o,\cdot)+m^{\alpha}\mathfrak{J}^{\alpha}_{\frac{\mathcal{V}_o}{m}^-}\Psi\left(\frac{\mathcal{U}_o}{m},\cdot\right)\right],\end{aligned}\tag{35}$$

again as Ψ is a (P, m)-superquadratic stochastic process, then we have

$$\begin{aligned}&\Psi(\beta\mathcal{U}_o+(1-\beta)\mathcal{V}_o,\cdot)+m\Psi\left(\frac{\beta\mathcal{V}_o+(1-\beta)\mathcal{U}_o}{m},\cdot\right)\\&=\Psi\left(\beta\mathcal{U}_o+m(1-\beta)\left(\frac{\mathcal{V}_o}{m}\right),\cdot\right)+m\Psi\left((1-\beta)\frac{\mathcal{U}_o}{m}+m\beta\left(\frac{\mathcal{V}_o}{m^2}\right),\cdot\right)\\&\leq\left(\Psi(\mathcal{U}_o,\cdot)-\Psi\left((1-\beta)\left|\frac{m\mathcal{U}_o-\mathcal{V}_o}{m}\right|,\cdot\right)\right)+m\left(\Psi\left(\frac{\mathcal{V}_o}{m},\cdot\right)-\Psi\left(\beta\left|\frac{m\mathcal{U}_o-\mathcal{V}_o}{m}\right|,\cdot\right)\right)\\&+m\left(\Psi\left(\frac{\mathcal{U}_o}{m},\cdot\right)-\Psi\left(\beta\left|\frac{m\mathcal{U}_o-\mathcal{V}_o}{m^2}\right|,\cdot\right)\right)\\&+m^2\left(\Psi\left(\frac{\mathcal{V}_o}{m^2},\cdot\right)-\Psi\left((1-\beta)\left|\frac{m\mathcal{U}_o-\mathcal{V}_o}{m^2}\right|,\cdot\right)\right),\end{aligned}\tag{36}$$

Multiplying (36) by $\beta^{\alpha-1}$ and then integrating it via β over $[0,1]$, we have

$$\begin{aligned}&\int_0^1\beta^{\alpha-1}\Psi(\beta\mathcal{U}_o+(1-\beta)\mathcal{V}_o,\cdot)d\beta+m\int_0^1\beta^{\alpha-1}\Psi\left(\frac{\beta\mathcal{V}_o+(1-\beta)\mathcal{U}_o}{m},\cdot\right)d\beta\\&\leq\int_0^1\beta^{\alpha-1}\left(\Psi(\mathcal{U}_o,\cdot)-\Psi\left((1-\beta)\left|\frac{m\mathcal{U}_o-\mathcal{V}_o}{m}\right|,\cdot\right)\right)d\beta\\&+m\int_0^1\beta^{\alpha-1}\left(\Psi\left(\frac{\mathcal{V}_o}{m},\cdot\right)-\Psi\left(\beta\left|\frac{m\mathcal{U}_o-\mathcal{V}_o}{m}\right|,\cdot\right)\right)d\beta\\&+m\int_0^1\beta^{\alpha-1}\left(\Psi\left(\frac{\mathcal{U}_o}{m},\cdot\right)-\Psi\left(\beta\left|\frac{m\mathcal{U}_o-\mathcal{V}_o}{m^2}\right|,\cdot\right)\right)d\beta\\&+m^2\int_0^1\beta^{\alpha-1}\left(\Psi\left(\frac{\mathcal{V}_o}{m^2},\cdot\right)-\Psi\left((1-\beta)\left|\frac{m\mathcal{U}_o-\mathcal{V}_o}{m^2}\right|,\cdot\right)\right)d\beta.\end{aligned}\tag{37}$$

It implies that

$$\begin{aligned}&\frac{1}{(\mathcal{V}_o-\mathcal{U}_o)^{\alpha}}\left\{\int_{\mathcal{U}_o}^{\mathcal{V}_o}(\mathcal{V}_o-y)^{\alpha-1}\Psi(y,\cdot)dy+m^{\alpha}\int_{\frac{\mathcal{U}_o}{m}}^{\frac{\mathcal{V}_o}{m}}\left(y-\frac{\mathcal{U}_o}{m}\right)^{\alpha-1}\Psi(y,\cdot)dy\right\}\\&\leq\frac{1}{\alpha}\Psi(\mathcal{U}_o,\cdot)+\frac{1}{\alpha}m\left\{\Psi\left(\frac{\mathcal{V}_o}{m},\cdot\right)+\Psi\left(\frac{\mathcal{U}_o}{m},\cdot\right)+\Psi\left(\frac{\mathcal{V}_o}{m^2},\cdot\right)\right\}\\&-\frac{1}{(\mathcal{V}_o-\mathcal{U}_o)^{\alpha}}\left\{\int_{\mathcal{U}_o}^{\mathcal{V}_o}(\mathcal{V}_o-y)^{\alpha-1}\left(\Psi\left(\left|\frac{(y-\mathcal{U}_o)(\mathcal{V}_o-m\mathcal{U}_o)}{m(\mathcal{V}_o-\mathcal{U}_o)}\right|,\cdot\right)\right.\right.\\&+m\Psi\left(\left|\frac{(\mathcal{V}_o-y)(\mathcal{V}_o-m\mathcal{U}_o)}{m(\mathcal{V}_o-\mathcal{U}_o)}\right|,\cdot\right)+m\Psi\left(\left|\frac{(\mathcal{V}_o-y)(\mathcal{V}_o-m\mathcal{U}_o)}{m^2(\mathcal{V}_o-\mathcal{U}_o)}\right|,\cdot\right)\\&\left.\left.+m^2\Psi\left(\left|\frac{(y-\mathcal{U}_o)(\mathcal{V}_o-m\mathcal{U}_o)}{m^2(\mathcal{V}_o-\mathcal{U}_o)}\right|,\cdot\right)\right)dy\right\},\end{aligned}\tag{38}$$

thus

$$\frac{\Gamma(\alpha)}{(\mathcal{V}_o-\mathcal{U}_o)^{\alpha}}\left[\mathfrak{I}^{\alpha}_{\mathcal{U}_o^+}\Psi(\mathcal{V}_o,\cdot)+\mathrm{m}^{\alpha}\mathfrak{I}^{\alpha}_{\frac{\mathcal{V}_o}{\mathrm{m}}^-}\Psi\left(\frac{\mathcal{U}_o}{\mathrm{m}},\cdot\right)\right]$$
$$\leq\frac{1}{\alpha}\Psi(\mathcal{U}_o,\cdot)+\frac{1}{\alpha}\mathrm{m}\left\{\Psi\left(\frac{\mathcal{V}_o}{\mathrm{m}},\cdot\right)+\Psi\left(\frac{\mathcal{U}_o}{\mathrm{m}},\cdot\right)+\Psi\left(\frac{\mathcal{V}_o}{\mathrm{m}^2},\cdot\right)\right\}$$
$$-\frac{1}{(\mathcal{V}_o-\mathcal{U}_o)^{\alpha}}\left\{\int_{\mathcal{U}_o}^{\mathcal{V}_o}(\mathcal{V}_o-\mathrm{y})^{\alpha-1}\left(\Psi\left(\left|\frac{(\mathrm{y}-\mathcal{U}_o)(\mathcal{V}_o-\mathrm{m}\mathcal{U}_o)}{\mathrm{m}(\mathcal{V}_o-\mathcal{U}_o)}\right|,\cdot\right)\right.\right.$$
$$+\mathrm{m}\Psi\left(\left|\frac{(\mathcal{V}_o-\mathrm{y})(\mathcal{V}_o-\mathrm{m}\mathcal{U}_o)}{\mathrm{m}(\mathcal{V}_o-\mathcal{U}_o)}\right|\right)+\mathrm{m}\Psi\left(\left|\frac{(\mathcal{V}_o-\mathrm{y})(\mathcal{V}_o-\mathrm{m}\mathcal{U}_o)}{\mathrm{m}^2(\mathcal{V}_o-\mathcal{U}_o)}\right|,\cdot\right)$$
$$\left.\left.+\mathrm{m}^2\Psi\left(\left|\frac{(\mathrm{y}-\mathcal{U}_o)(\mathcal{V}_o-\mathrm{m}\mathcal{U}_o)}{\mathrm{m}^2(\mathcal{V}_o-\mathcal{U}_o)}\right|,\cdot\right)\right)d\mathrm{y}\right\}. \tag{39}$$

The proof is completed by merging inequalities (35) and (39). □

Corollary 2. *The fractional inequalities of* $\mathbb{H}.\mathbb{H}$*-type for (P, m)-subquadratic stochastic processes are obtained by applying* $\mathbb{RL}$ *fractional integral operators, provided that the inequalities in* (32) *are reversed.*

Corollary 3. *The* $\mathbb{H}.\mathbb{H}$ *type inequalities for* (P,m)*-superquadratic stochastic process are obtained by taking* $\alpha=1$ *in* (32).

Theorem 11. *Let* Ψ: $[\mathcal{U}_o,\frac{\mathcal{V}_o}{\mathrm{m}}]\times\prod\to\Re$ *be a mean-square integrable (P, m)-superquadratic stochastic process, then*

$$\frac{\Gamma(1+\alpha)}{2(\mathrm{m}+1)}\left\{\frac{1}{(\mathrm{m}\mathcal{V}_o-\mathcal{U}_o)^{\alpha}}\left(\mathfrak{I}^{\alpha}_{\mathcal{U}_o^+}\Psi(\mathrm{m}\mathcal{V}_o,\cdot)+\mathfrak{I}^{\alpha}_{\mathrm{m}\mathcal{V}_o^-}\Psi(\mathcal{U}_o,\cdot)\right)\right.$$
$$\left.+\frac{1}{(\mathcal{V}_o-\mathrm{m}\mathcal{U}_o)^{\alpha}}\left(\mathfrak{I}^{\alpha}_{\mathcal{V}_o^-}\Psi(\mathrm{m}\mathcal{U}_o,\cdot)+\mathfrak{I}^{\alpha}_{\mathrm{m}\mathcal{U}_o^+}\Psi(\mathcal{V}_o,\cdot)\right)\right\}$$
$$\leq(\Psi(\mathcal{U}_o,\cdot)+\Psi(\mathcal{V}_o,\cdot))$$
$$-\frac{\alpha}{2(\mathrm{m}\mathcal{V}_o-\mathcal{U}_o)^{\alpha}}\left(\int_{\mathcal{U}_o}^{\mathrm{m}\mathcal{V}_o}(\mathrm{m}\mathcal{V}_o-\mathrm{y})^{\alpha-1}\left(\Psi\left(\left|\frac{(\mathrm{m}\mathcal{V}_o-\mathrm{y})(\mathcal{V}_o-\mathcal{U}_o)}{\mathrm{m}\mathcal{V}_o-\mathcal{U}_o}\right|,\cdot\right)\right.\right.$$
$$\left.\left.+\Psi\left(\left|\frac{(\mathrm{y}-\mathcal{U}_o)(\mathcal{V}_o-\mathcal{U}_o)}{\mathrm{m}\mathcal{V}_o-\mathcal{U}_o}\right|,\cdot\right)\right)d\beta\right)$$
$$-\frac{\alpha}{2(\mathcal{V}_o-\mathrm{m}\mathcal{U}_o)^{\alpha}}\left(\int_{\mathrm{m}\mathcal{U}_o}^{\mathcal{V}_o}(\mathrm{y}-\mathrm{m}\mathcal{U}_o)^{\alpha-1}\left(\Psi\left(\left|\frac{(\mathrm{y}-\mathrm{m}\mathcal{U}_o)(\mathcal{V}_o-\mathcal{U}_o)}{\mathcal{V}_o-\mathrm{m}\mathcal{U}_o}\right|,\cdot\right)\right.\right.$$
$$\left.\left.+\Psi\left(\left|\frac{(\mathcal{V}_o-\mathrm{y})(\mathcal{V}_o-\mathcal{U}_o)}{\mathcal{V}_o-\mathrm{m}\mathcal{U}_o}\right|,\cdot\right)\right)d\beta\right). \tag{40}$$

holds for all $\mathcal{U}_o,\mathcal{V}_o\geq 0$ *and* $m\in(0,1)$.

Proof. Suppose that the process Ψ exhibits (P,m)-superquadraticity, then

$$\Psi(\beta\mathcal{U}_o+\mathrm{m}(1-\beta)\mathcal{V}_o,\cdot)\leq\Psi(\mathcal{U}_o,\cdot)-\Psi((1-\beta)|\mathcal{V}_o-\mathcal{U}_o|,\cdot)$$
$$+\mathrm{m}(\Psi(\mathcal{V}_o,\cdot)-\Psi(\beta|\mathcal{V}_o-\mathcal{U}_o|,\cdot)), \tag{41}$$

and

$$\Psi((1-\beta)\mathcal{U}_o+\mathrm{m}\beta\mathcal{V}_o,\cdot)\leq\Psi(\mathcal{U}_o,\cdot)-\Psi(\beta|\mathcal{V}_o-\mathcal{U}_o|,\cdot)$$
$$+\mathrm{m}(\Psi(\mathcal{V}_o,\cdot)-\Psi((1-\beta)|\mathcal{V}_o-\mathcal{U}_o|,\cdot)). \tag{42}$$

Adding inequalities (41) and (42), we arrive at the following result:

$$\begin{aligned}&\Psi(\beta\mathcal{U}_o+\mathrm{m}(1-\beta)\mathcal{V}_o,\cdot)+\Psi((1-\beta)\mathcal{U}_o+\mathrm{m}\beta\mathcal{V}_o,\cdot)\\&\leq\Psi(\mathcal{U}_o,\cdot)-\Psi((1-\beta)|\mathcal{V}_o-\mathcal{U}_o|,\cdot)+\mathrm{m}\big(\Psi(\mathcal{V}_o,\cdot)-\Psi(\beta|\mathcal{V}_o-\mathcal{U}_o|,\cdot)\big)\\&+\Psi(\mathcal{U}_o,\cdot)-\Psi(\beta|\mathcal{V}_o-\mathcal{U}_o|,\cdot)+\mathrm{m}\big(\Psi(\mathcal{V}_o,\cdot)-\Psi((1-\beta)|\mathcal{V}_o-\mathcal{U}_o|,\cdot)\big)\\&=2\Psi(\mathcal{U}_o,\cdot)+2\mathrm{m}\Psi(\mathcal{V}_o,\cdot)-(1+\mathrm{m})\big(\Psi(\beta|\mathcal{V}_o-\mathcal{U}_o|,\cdot))+\Psi((1-\beta)|\mathcal{V}_o-\mathcal{U}_o|,\cdot)\big)\big).\end{aligned}\tag{43}$$

The inequality (43) is multiplied by $\beta^{\alpha-1}$ and integrating via β over [0, 1], so we then attain that

$$\begin{aligned}&\int_0^1\beta^{\alpha-1}\Psi(\beta\mathcal{U}_o+\mathrm{m}(1-\beta)\mathcal{V}_o,\cdot)d\beta+\int_0^1\beta^{\alpha-1}\Psi((1-\beta)\mathcal{U}_o+\mathrm{m}\beta\mathcal{V}_o,\cdot)d\beta\\&\leq2\int_0^1\beta^{\alpha-1}\big(\Psi(\mathcal{U}_o,\cdot)+\mathrm{m}\Psi(\mathcal{V}_o,\cdot)\big)d\beta\\&-(1+\mathrm{m})\bigg(\int_0^1\beta^{\alpha-1}\Psi(\beta|\mathcal{V}_o-\mathcal{U}_o|,\cdot)d\beta+\int_0^1\beta^{\alpha-1}\Psi((1-\beta)|\mathcal{V}_o-\mathcal{U}_o|,\cdot)d\beta\bigg),\end{aligned}\tag{44}$$

it implies that

$$\begin{aligned}&\frac{\alpha}{(\mathrm{m}\mathcal{V}_o-\mathcal{U}_o)^\alpha}\bigg\{\int_{\mathcal{U}_o}^{\mathrm{m}\mathcal{V}_o}(\mathrm{m}\mathcal{V}_o-\mathrm{y})^{\alpha-1}\Psi(\mathrm{y})d\mathrm{y}+\int_{\mathcal{U}_o}^{\mathrm{m}\mathcal{V}_o}(\mathrm{y}-\mathcal{U}_o)^{\alpha-1}\Psi(\mathrm{y},\cdot)d\mathrm{y}\bigg\}\\&\leq\big(2\Psi(\mathcal{U}_o,\cdot)+2\mathrm{m}\Psi(\mathcal{V}_o,\cdot)\big)\\&-\frac{\alpha(1+\mathrm{m})}{(\mathrm{m}\mathcal{V}_o-\mathcal{U}_o)^\alpha}\bigg(\int_{\mathcal{U}_o}^{\mathrm{m}\mathcal{V}_o}(\mathrm{m}\mathcal{V}_o-\mathrm{y})^{\alpha-1}\bigg(\Psi\bigg(\bigg|\frac{(\mathrm{m}\mathcal{V}_o-\mathrm{y})(\mathcal{V}_o-\mathcal{U}_o)}{\mathrm{m}\mathcal{V}_o-\mathcal{U}_o}\bigg|,\cdot\bigg)\\&+\Psi\bigg(\bigg|\frac{(\mathrm{y}-\mathcal{U}_o)(\mathcal{V}_o-\mathcal{U}_o)}{\mathrm{m}\mathcal{V}_o-\mathcal{U}_o}\bigg|,\cdot\bigg)\bigg)d\beta\bigg),\end{aligned}\tag{45}$$

thus

$$\begin{aligned}&\frac{\Gamma(1+\alpha)}{2(\mathrm{m}\mathcal{V}_o-\mathcal{U}_o)^\alpha}\Big\{\mathfrak{I}^\alpha_{\mathcal{U}_o^+}\Psi(\mathrm{m}\mathcal{V}_o,\cdot)+\mathfrak{I}^\alpha_{\mathrm{m}\mathcal{V}_o^-}\Psi(\mathcal{U}_o,\cdot)\Big\}\leq\big(\Psi(\mathcal{U}_o,\cdot)+\mathrm{m}\Psi(\mathcal{V}_o,\cdot)\big)\\&-\frac{\alpha(1+\mathrm{m})}{2(\mathrm{m}\mathcal{V}_o-\mathcal{U}_o)^\alpha}\bigg(\int_{\mathcal{U}_o}^{\mathrm{m}\mathcal{V}_o}(\mathrm{m}\mathcal{V}_o-\mathrm{y})^{\alpha-1}\bigg(\Psi\bigg(\bigg|\frac{(\mathrm{m}\mathcal{V}_o-\mathrm{y})(\mathcal{V}_o-\mathcal{U}_o)}{\mathrm{m}\mathcal{V}_o-\mathcal{U}_o}\bigg|,\cdot\bigg)\\&+\Psi\bigg(\bigg|\frac{(\mathrm{y}-\mathcal{U}_o)(\mathcal{V}_o-\mathcal{U}_o)}{\mathrm{m}\mathcal{V}_o-\mathcal{U}_o}\bigg|,\cdot\bigg)\bigg)d\beta\bigg),\end{aligned}\tag{46}$$

Likewise, there are

$$\begin{aligned}&\Psi(\beta\mathcal{V}_o+\mathrm{m}(1-\beta)\mathcal{U}_o,\cdot)\leq\Psi(\mathcal{V}_o,\cdot)-\Psi((1-\beta)|\mathcal{V}_o-\mathcal{U}_o|,\cdot)\\&+\mathrm{m}\big(\Psi(\mathcal{U}_o,\cdot)-\Psi(\beta|\mathcal{V}_o-\mathcal{U}_o|,\cdot)\big),\end{aligned}\tag{47}$$

and

$$\begin{aligned}&\Psi((1-\beta)\mathcal{V}_o+\mathrm{m}\beta\mathcal{U}_o,\cdot)\leq\Psi(\mathcal{V}_o,\cdot)-\Psi(\beta|\mathcal{V}_o-\mathcal{U}_o|,\cdot)\\&+\mathrm{m}\big(\Psi(\mathcal{U}_o,\cdot)-\Psi((1-\beta)|\mathcal{V}_o-\mathcal{U}_o|,\cdot)\big).\end{aligned}\tag{48}$$

Adding inequalities (47) and (48), we derive:

$$\begin{aligned}&\Psi(\beta\mathcal{V}_o+\mathrm{m}(1-\beta)\mathcal{U}_o,\cdot)+\Psi((1-\beta)\mathcal{V}_o+\mathrm{m}\beta\mathcal{U}_o,\cdot)\\&\leq2\Psi(\mathcal{V}_o,\cdot)+2\mathrm{m}\Psi(\mathcal{U}_o,\cdot)-(1+\mathrm{m})\big(\Psi(\beta|\mathcal{V}_o-\mathcal{U}_o|,\cdot)+\Psi((1-\beta)|\mathcal{V}_o-\mathcal{U}_o|,\cdot)\big)\big),\end{aligned}\tag{49}$$

the inequality (49) is multiplied by $\beta^{\alpha-1}$ and integrating via β over $[0,1]$, we then attain that

$$\begin{aligned}&\int_0^1 \beta^{\alpha-1}\Psi(\beta\mathcal{V}_o+\mathrm{m}(1-\beta)\mathcal{U}_o,\cdot)d\beta+\int_0^1 \beta^{\alpha-1}\Psi((1-\beta)\mathcal{V}_o+\mathrm{m}\beta\mathcal{U}_o,\cdot)d\beta\\&\leq 2\int_0^1 \beta^{\alpha-1}(\Psi(\mathcal{V}_o,\cdot)+\mathrm{m}\Psi(\mathcal{U}_o,\cdot))d\beta\\&-(1+\mathrm{m})\bigg(\int_0^1 \beta^{\alpha-1}\Psi(\beta|\mathcal{V}_o-\mathcal{U}_o|,\cdot)d\beta+\int_0^1 \beta^{\alpha-1}\Psi((1-\beta)|\mathcal{V}_o-\mathcal{U}_o|,\cdot)d\beta\bigg),\end{aligned}\tag{50}$$

it implies that

$$\begin{aligned}&\frac{\alpha}{(\mathcal{V}_o-\mathrm{m}\mathcal{U}_o)^{\alpha}}\bigg\{\int_{\mathrm{m}\mathcal{U}_o}^{\mathcal{V}_o}(\mathrm{y}-\mathrm{m}\mathcal{U}_o)^{\alpha-1}\Psi(\mathrm{y},\cdot)d\mathrm{y}+\int_{\mathrm{m}\mathcal{U}_o}^{\mathcal{V}_o}(\mathcal{V}_o-\mathrm{y})^{\alpha-1}\Psi(\mathrm{y},\cdot)d\mathrm{y}\bigg\}\\&\leq(2\Psi(\mathcal{V}_o,\cdot)+2\mathrm{m}\Psi(\mathcal{U}_o,\cdot))\\&-\frac{\alpha(1+\mathrm{m})}{(\mathcal{V}_o-\mathrm{m}\mathcal{U}_o)^{\alpha}}\bigg(\int_{\mathrm{m}\mathcal{U}_o}^{\mathcal{V}_o}(\mathrm{y}-\mathrm{m}\mathcal{U}_o)^{\alpha-1}\bigg(\Psi\bigg(\bigg|\frac{(\mathrm{y}-\mathrm{m}\mathcal{U}_o)(\mathcal{V}_o-\mathcal{U}_o)}{\mathcal{V}_o-\mathrm{m}\mathcal{U}_o}\bigg|,\cdot\bigg)\\&+\Psi\bigg(\bigg|\frac{(\mathcal{V}_o-\mathrm{y})(\mathcal{V}_o-\mathcal{U}_o)}{\mathcal{V}_o-\mathrm{m}\mathcal{U}_o}\bigg|,\cdot\bigg)\bigg)d\beta\bigg),\end{aligned}\tag{51}$$

thus

$$\begin{aligned}&\frac{\Gamma(1+\alpha)}{2(\mathcal{V}_o-\mathrm{m}\mathcal{U}_o)^{\alpha}}\bigg\{\mathfrak{I}^{\alpha}_{\mathcal{V}_o^-}\Psi(\mathrm{m}\mathcal{U}_o,\cdot)+\mathfrak{I}^{\alpha}_{\mathrm{m}\mathcal{U}_o^+}\Psi(\mathcal{V}_o,\cdot)\bigg\}\leq(\Psi(\mathcal{U}_o,\cdot)+\mathrm{m}\Psi(\mathcal{V}_o,\cdot))\\&-\frac{\alpha(1+\mathrm{m})}{2(\mathcal{V}_o-\mathrm{m}\mathcal{U}_o)^{\alpha}}\bigg(\int_{\mathrm{m}\mathcal{U}_o}^{\mathcal{V}_o}(\mathrm{y}-\mathrm{m}\mathcal{U}_o)^{\alpha-1}\bigg(\Psi\bigg(\bigg|\frac{(\mathrm{y}-\mathrm{m}\mathcal{U}_o)(\mathcal{V}_o-\mathcal{U}_o)}{\mathcal{V}_o-\mathrm{m}\mathcal{U}_o}\bigg|,\cdot\bigg)\\&+\Psi\bigg(\bigg|\frac{(\mathcal{V}_o-\mathrm{y})(\mathcal{V}_o-\mathcal{U}_o)}{\mathcal{V}_o-\mathrm{m}\mathcal{U}_o}\bigg|,\cdot\bigg)\bigg)d\beta\bigg).\end{aligned}\tag{52}$$

The required result is obtained by summing (46) and (52). □

Corollary 4. *Under the assumptions of Theorem 11, and by taking $\alpha = 1$, one arrives at the following inequality for (P,m)-superquadratic functions.*

$$\begin{aligned}&\frac{1}{(\mathrm{m}+1)}\bigg\{\frac{1}{\mathrm{m}\mathcal{V}_o-\mathcal{U}_o}\int_{\mathcal{U}_o}^{\mathrm{m}\mathcal{V}_o}\Psi(\mathrm{y},\cdot)d\mathrm{y}+\frac{1}{\mathcal{V}_o-\mathrm{m}\mathcal{U}_o}\int_{\mathrm{m}\mathcal{U}_o}^{\mathcal{V}_o}\Psi(\mathrm{y},\cdot)d\mathrm{y}\bigg\}\leq(\Psi(\mathcal{U}_o,\cdot)+\Psi(\mathcal{V}_o,\cdot))\\&-\frac{1}{2(\mathrm{m}\mathcal{V}_o-\mathcal{U}_o)}\bigg(\int_{\mathcal{U}_o}^{\mathrm{m}\mathcal{V}_o}\bigg(\Psi\bigg(\bigg|\frac{(\mathrm{m}\mathcal{V}_o-\mathrm{y})(\mathcal{V}_o-\mathcal{U}_o)}{\mathrm{m}\mathcal{V}_o-\mathcal{U}_o}\bigg|,\cdot\bigg)+\Psi\bigg(\bigg|\frac{(\mathrm{y}-\mathcal{U}_o)(\mathcal{V}_o-\mathcal{U}_o)}{\mathrm{m}\mathcal{V}_o-\mathcal{U}_o}\bigg|,\cdot\bigg)\bigg)d\beta\bigg)\\&-\frac{1}{2(\mathcal{V}_o-\mathrm{m}\mathcal{U}_o)}\bigg(\int_{\mathrm{m}\mathcal{U}_o}^{\mathcal{V}_o}\bigg(\Psi\bigg(\bigg|\frac{(\mathrm{y}-\mathrm{m}\mathcal{U}_o)(\mathcal{V}_o-\mathcal{U}_o)}{\mathcal{V}_o-\mathrm{m}\mathcal{U}_o}\bigg|,\cdot\bigg)+\Psi\bigg(\bigg|\frac{(\mathcal{V}_o-\mathrm{y})(\mathcal{V}_o-\mathcal{U}_o)}{\mathcal{V}_o-\mathrm{m}\mathcal{U}_o}\bigg|,\cdot\bigg)\bigg)d\beta\bigg),\end{aligned}\tag{53}$$

Example 5. *Consider the same process as given in Example 3, then we have the Figure 3a,b given by Figure 3, shows the right, middle and left terms, which are denoted by R, M and L respectively for Theorem 10.*

In the aforementioned Example 5, the graph consists of three colors: pink, black and red. Pink, black and red stand for the right, middle and right terms of Theorem 10, respectively. It is obvious from Theorem 10 that right term is always greater than the middle and middle term is greater than the left term, therefore the graph's pink color always occur above the black, and black always occur above the red color for various values of the parameters involved in it. This graphically confirms that the established result is true.

m	L	M	R
0.1	5602.88	43,793.8	5.002×10^6
0.2	606.688	5512.50	163,981
0.3	173.250	1664.12	23,032.6
0.4	83.9077	727.344	5975.39
0.5	57.7168	393.750	2204.63
0.6	48.5417	246.296	1028.33
0.7	45.0282	171.301	567.665
0.8	43.6457	129.199	355.275
0.9	43.1186	103.764	244.531
1.0	42.9375	87.5000	181.000

(**a**)

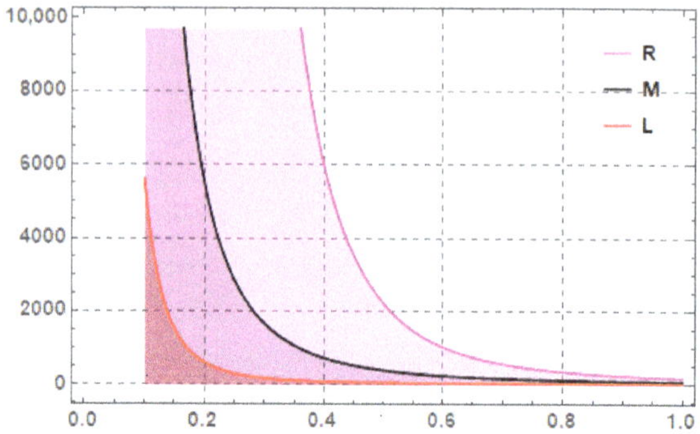

(**b**)

Figure 3. Graphical description of Theorem 10. (**a**) Numerical description of Theorem 10. (**b**) Graphical and numerical description of $\Psi = y^3$ via Theorem (10) for $\alpha = 0.6, \mathcal{U}_o = 3, \mathcal{V}_o = 4$ and $m \in [0, 1.0]$.

5. Implications for Information Theory

Distinguishing between two probability distributions is a fundamental task across various disciplines, including statistics, information theory and machine. Divergence measures serve as quantitative tools for assessing the dissimilarity between probability distributions. Lin [53], in 1991, proposed a novel class of divergence measures derived from Shannon entropy, a core principle in information theory used to quantify uncertainty and the informational content within a probability distribution. Lin's departure provided a principled, information-theoretic way of measuring distributional discrepancy. Shioya and Da-te [54] later built on Lin's contribution by bringing out the $\mathbb{H}.\mathbb{H}$ Ψ-divergence in 1995. Their development utilized the $\mathbb{H}.\mathbb{H}$ inequality, a standard mathematical finding connected with convex functions, to create an extended and more versatile basis. This breakthrough greatly extended the range of application of divergence measures, allowing deeper understanding and new applications in the comparative examination of probability distributions.

For clarity and focus, we restrict ourselves to the definitions that are directly relevant to the results that follow.

Definition 15 ([55])**.** *Csiszár Ψ-divergence is defined as follows:*

$$D_{\Psi}(\mathfrak{p}_o||\mathfrak{q}_o) = \int_{\mho} \mathfrak{q}_o(y)\Psi\left(\frac{\mathfrak{p}_o(y)}{\mathfrak{q}_o(y)}\right)d\mathcal{U}(y), \quad \mathfrak{p}_o, \mathfrak{q}_o \in \mathbf{P}.$$

In this context, $\mathbf{P}$ *represents the collection of all probability densities with respect to a σ-finite measure $\mathcal{U}$, $\mho$ is assumed to be a nonempty set, and Ψ is a convex function defined over $(0, +\infty)$.*

$$\mathbf{P} = \left\{\mathfrak{p}_o|\mathfrak{p}_o : \mho \to \Re, \mathfrak{p}_o(y) \geq 0, \int_{\mho} \mathfrak{p}_o(y)d\mathcal{U}(y) = 1\right\}.$$

Remark 6. *Taking the function Ψ as an (P, m)-superquadratic function yields the Csiszár Ψ-divergence for (P, m)-superquadratic function.*

Definition 16 ([56])**.** *$\mathbb{H}.\mathbb{H}$ Ψ-divergence is denoted and defined as follows:*

$$D^{\Psi}_{HH}(\mathfrak{p}_o||\mathfrak{q}_o) = \int_{\mho} \mathfrak{q}_o(y)\frac{\int_1^{\frac{\mathfrak{p}_o(y)}{\mathfrak{q}_o(y)}} \Psi(y)dy}{\left(\frac{\mathfrak{p}_o(y)}{\mathfrak{q}_o(y)} - 1\right)}d\mathcal{U}(y), \quad \mathfrak{p}_o, \mathfrak{q}_o \in \mathbf{P}. \tag{54}$$

Definition 17 ([57]). *$\mathbb{RL}$ fractional $\mathbb{H}.\mathbb{H}$ Ψ-divergence is denoted and defined as follows:*

$$ {}^{\alpha}D^{\Psi}_{HH}(\mathfrak{p}_o||\mathfrak{q}_o) = \int_{\mho} \mathfrak{q}_o(y) \frac{\left[(\mathfrak{J}^{\alpha}_{1^+}\Psi)\left(\frac{\mathfrak{p}_o(y)}{\mathfrak{q}_o(y)}\right) + (\mathfrak{J}^{\alpha}_{\left(\frac{\mathfrak{p}_o(y)}{\mathfrak{q}_o(y)}^-\right)}\Psi(1)) \right]}{2\left(\frac{\mathfrak{p}_o(y)}{\mathfrak{q}_o(y)} - 1\right)^{\alpha}} d\mathcal{U}(y), \quad \mathfrak{p}_o, \mathfrak{q}_o \in \mathbf{P}. \quad (55) $$

Where the Definition 2 provides the fractional operators used in (55).

Remark 7. *We obtain* (54)*, if $\alpha = 1$ is set in* (55).

Definition 18 ([58]). *Let $\Psi : J \times \prod \rightarrow \Re$ be a convex stochastic process defined on $J \subseteq (0, \infty)$, satisfying the condition $\Psi(1, \cdot) = 0$. Then, the stochastic divergence associated with $\mathfrak{p}_o, \mathfrak{q}_o \in \mathbf{P}$ is defined as follows:*

$$ SD_{\Psi}(\mathfrak{p}_o||\mathfrak{q}_o) = \int_{\mho} \mathfrak{q}_o(y)\Psi\left(\frac{\mathfrak{p}_o(y)}{\mathfrak{q}_o(y)}, .\right) d\mathcal{U}(y), \quad \mathfrak{p}_o, \mathfrak{q}_o \in \mathbf{P}. \quad (56) $$

Remark 8. *When the convex stochastic process in* (56) *is substituted with an (P, m)-superquadratic stochastic process, the resulting expression defines the stochastic divergence for (P, m)-superquadratic stochastic processes.*

Definition 19 ([58]). *The stochastic $\mathbb{H}.\mathbb{H}$-divergence for $\mathfrak{p}_o, \mathfrak{q}_o \in \mathbf{P}$ for a convex stochastic process $\Psi : J \times \prod \rightarrow \Re$ on $J \subseteq (0, \infty)$ is stated as*

$$ SD^{\Psi}_{HH}(\mathfrak{p}_o||\mathfrak{q}_o) = \int_{\mho} \mathfrak{q}_o(y) \frac{\int_1^{\frac{\mathfrak{p}_o(y)}{\mathfrak{q}_o(y)}} \Psi(y, .)dy}{\left(\frac{\mathfrak{p}_o(y)}{\mathfrak{q}_o(y)} - 1\right)} d\mathcal{U}(y), \quad \mathfrak{p}_o, \mathfrak{q}_o \in \mathbf{P}. \quad (57) $$

Remark 9. *We find stochastic $\mathbb{H}.\mathbb{H}$-divergence for P-superquadratic stochastic process when P-superquadratic stochastic process is substituted for convex stochastic process in* (57).

Definition 20 ([58]). *A convex stochastic process $\Psi : J \times \prod \rightarrow \Re$, defined on $J \subseteq (0, \infty)$ and satisfies $\Psi(1, \cdot) = 0$, provides the following definition for the stochastic divergence corresponding to $\mathfrak{p}_o, \mathfrak{q}_o \in \mathbf{P}$ and is called $\mathbb{RL}$ fractional stochastic $\mathbb{H}.\mathbb{H}$-divergence.*

$$ {}^{\alpha}SD^{\Psi}_{HH}(\mathfrak{p}_o||\mathfrak{q}_o) = \Gamma(\alpha + 1) \int_{\mho} \mathfrak{q}_o(y) \frac{\left[I^{\alpha}_{1^+}[\Psi]\left(\frac{\mathfrak{p}_o(y)}{\mathfrak{q}_o(y)}\right) + I^{\alpha}_{\frac{\mathfrak{p}_o(y)}{\mathfrak{q}_o(y)}^-}[\Psi](1) \right]}{2\left(\frac{\mathfrak{p}_o(y)}{\mathfrak{q}_o(y)} - 1\right)^{\alpha}} d\mathcal{U}(y), \quad \mathfrak{p}_o, \mathfrak{q}_o \in \mathbf{P}. \quad (58) $$

The fractional integral operators appearing in (58) *are those provided in Definition 13.*

Remark 10. *By replacing the convex stochastic process in* (58) *with an P-superquadratic stochastic process, we derive the $\mathbb{RL}$ fractional stochastic $\mathbb{H}.\mathbb{H}$ divergence corresponding to the P-superquadratic case.*

Here, we present the proofs of the results pertaining to fractional stochastic $\mathbb{H}.\mathbb{H}$-divergence and stochastic $\mathbb{H}.\mathbb{H}$-divergence for P-superquadratic stochastic processes.

Theorem 12. *Let* Ψ: $[\mathcal{U}_o, \frac{\mathcal{V}_o}{m}] \times \prod \to \Re$ *be a mean-square integrable (P, m)-superquadratic stochastic process, and* $\Psi(1,.) = 0$*, then*

$$SD_\Psi\left(\frac{1}{2}\mathfrak{q}_o + \frac{1}{2}\mathfrak{p}_o||\mathfrak{q}_o\right) + \eta_1 \le 2SD^{\Psi}_{HH}(\mathfrak{p}_o||\mathfrak{q}_o) \le 2SD_\Psi(\mathfrak{p}_o||\mathfrak{q}_o) - \eta_2. \tag{59}$$

$\forall$ $\mathfrak{p}_o, \mathfrak{q}_o \in \mathbf{P}$, *where*

$$SD^{\Psi}_{HH}(\mathfrak{p}_o||\mathfrak{q}_o) = \int_{\mho} \frac{\mathfrak{q}_o(y)}{\left(\frac{\mathfrak{p}_o(y)}{\mathfrak{q}_o(y)} - 1\right)}\left(\int_1^{\frac{\mathfrak{p}_o(y)}{\mathfrak{q}_o(y)}} \Psi(y,\cdot)dy\right)d\mathcal{U}(y),$$

$$\eta_1 = \int_{\mho} \frac{\mathfrak{q}_o(y)(2)}{\left(\frac{\mathfrak{p}_o(y)}{\mathfrak{q}_o(y)} - 1\right)}\left(\int_1^{\frac{\mathfrak{p}_o(y)}{\mathfrak{q}_o(y)}} \Psi\left(\left|\frac{\mathfrak{q}_o(y) + \mathfrak{p}_o(y)}{2\mathfrak{q}_o(y)} - y\right|,\cdot\right)dy\right)d\mathcal{U}(y),$$

and

$$\begin{aligned}\eta_2 = \Bigg\{ \int_{\mho} &\frac{\mathfrak{q}_o(y)}{\left(\frac{\mathfrak{p}_o(y)}{\mathfrak{q}_o(y)} - 1\right)}\left(\int_1^{\frac{\mathfrak{p}_o(y)}{\mathfrak{q}_o(y)}} \left(\Psi\left(\left|\frac{(y-1)(\frac{\mathfrak{p}_o(y)}{\mathfrak{q}_o(y)} - m)}{m(\frac{\mathfrak{p}_o(y)}{\mathfrak{q}_o(y)} - 1)}\right|\right)\right.\right.\\ &+ m\Psi\left(\left|\frac{(\frac{\mathfrak{p}_o(y)}{\mathfrak{q}_o(y)} - y)(\frac{\mathfrak{p}_o(y)}{\mathfrak{q}_o(y)} - m)}{m(\frac{\mathfrak{p}_o(y)}{\mathfrak{q}_o(y)} - 1)}\right|,\cdot\right) + m\Psi\left(\left|\frac{(\frac{\mathfrak{p}_o(y)}{\mathfrak{q}_o(y)} - y)(\frac{\mathfrak{p}_o(y)}{\mathfrak{q}_o(y)} - m)}{m^2(\frac{\mathfrak{p}_o(y)}{\mathfrak{q}_o(y)} - 1)}\right|,\cdot\right)\\ &\left.\left.+ m^2\Psi\left(\left|\frac{(y-1)(\frac{\mathfrak{p}_o(y)}{\mathfrak{q}_o(y)} - m)}{m^2(\frac{\mathfrak{p}_o(y)}{\mathfrak{q}_o(y)} - 1)}\right|,\cdot\right)\right)dy\right)d\mathcal{U}(y)\Bigg\}.\end{aligned}$$

holds for all $\mathcal{U}_o, \mathcal{V}_o \ge 0$ *and* $m \in (0,1)$.

Proof. Consider the $\mathbb{H}.\mathbb{H}$'s inequalities for (P, m)-superquadratic stochastic processes, from Theorem 9:

$$\begin{aligned}&\Psi\left(\frac{\mathcal{U}_o + \mathcal{V}_o}{2},\cdot\right) + \frac{1+m}{\mathcal{V}_o - \mathcal{U}_o}\int_{\mathcal{U}_o}^{\mathcal{V}_o} \Psi\left(\left|\frac{(\mathcal{U}_o + \mathcal{V}_o) - (m+1)y}{2m}\right|,\cdot\right)dy\\ &\le \frac{1}{\mathcal{V}_o - \mathcal{U}_o}\left\{\int_{\mathcal{U}_o}^{\mathcal{V}_o} \Psi(y,\cdot)dy + m\int_{\frac{\mathcal{U}_o}{m}}^{\frac{\mathcal{V}_o}{m}} \Psi(y,\cdot)dy\right\}\\ &\le \Psi(\mathcal{U}_o,\cdot) + m\left\{\Psi\left(\frac{\mathcal{V}_o}{m},\cdot\right) + \Psi\left(\frac{\mathcal{U}_o}{m},\cdot\right) + \Psi\left(\frac{\mathcal{V}_o}{m^2},\cdot\right)\right\}\\ &- \frac{1}{\mathcal{V}_o - \mathcal{U}_o}\left\{\int_{\mathcal{U}_o}^{\mathcal{V}_o}\left(\Psi\left(\left|\frac{(y - \mathcal{U}_o)(\mathcal{V}_o - m\mathcal{U}_o)}{m(\mathcal{V}_o - \mathcal{U}_o)}\right|,\cdot\right)\right.\right.\\ &+ m\Psi\left(\left|\frac{(\mathcal{V}_o - y)(\mathcal{V}_o - m\mathcal{U}_o)}{m(\mathcal{V}_o - \mathcal{U}_o)}\right|,\cdot\right) + m\Psi\left(\left|\frac{(\mathcal{V}_o - y)(\mathcal{V}_o - m\mathcal{U}_o)}{m^2(\mathcal{V}_o - \mathcal{U}_o)}\right|,\cdot\right)\\ &\left.\left.+ m^2\Psi\left(\left|\frac{(y - \mathcal{U}_o)(\mathcal{V}_o - m\mathcal{U}_o)}{m^2(\mathcal{V}_o - \mathcal{U}_o)}\right|,\cdot\right)\right)dy\right\}.\end{aligned} \tag{60}$$

Now setting $\mathcal{U}_o = 1$, and $\mathcal{V}_o = \frac{\mathfrak{p}_o(y)}{\mathfrak{q}_o(y)}$, in (60), we obtain

$$\begin{aligned}
&\Psi\left(\frac{\mathfrak{q}_o(y)+\mathfrak{p}_o(y)}{2\mathfrak{q}_o(y)},\cdot\right)+\frac{1+m}{\left(\frac{\mathfrak{p}_o(y)}{\mathfrak{q}_o(y)}-1\right)}\int_1^{\frac{\mathfrak{p}_o(y)}{\mathfrak{q}_o(y)}}\Psi\left(\left|\frac{\mathfrak{q}_o(y)+\mathfrak{p}_o(y)}{2m\mathfrak{q}_o(y)}-\frac{(m+1)y}{2m}\right|,\cdot\right)dy\\
&\leq\frac{1}{\frac{\mathfrak{p}_o(y)}{\mathfrak{q}_o(y)}-1}\left\{\int_1^{\frac{\mathfrak{p}_o(y)}{\mathfrak{q}_o(y)}}\Psi(y,\cdot)dy+m\int_{\frac{1}{m}}^{\frac{\mathfrak{p}_o(y)}{m\mathfrak{q}_o(y)}}\Psi(y,\cdot)dy\right\}\\
&\leq\Psi(1,\cdot)+m\left\{\Psi\left(\frac{\mathfrak{p}_o(y)}{m\mathfrak{q}_o(y)},\cdot\right)+\Psi\left(\frac{1}{m},\cdot\right)+\Psi\left(\frac{\mathfrak{p}_o(y)}{m^2\mathfrak{q}_o(y)},\cdot\right)\right\}\\
&-\frac{1}{\left(\frac{\mathfrak{p}_o(y)}{\mathfrak{q}_o(y)}-1\right)}\left\{\int_1^{\frac{\mathfrak{p}_o(y)}{\mathfrak{q}_o(y)}}\left(\Psi\left(\left|\frac{(y-1)\left(\frac{\mathfrak{p}_o(y)}{\mathfrak{q}_o(y)}-m\right)}{m\left(\frac{\mathfrak{p}_o(y)}{\mathfrak{q}_o(y)}-1\right)}\right|\right)\right.\right.\\
&+m\Psi\left(\left|\frac{(\frac{\mathfrak{p}_o(y)}{\mathfrak{q}_o(y)}-y)(\frac{\mathfrak{p}_o(y)}{\mathfrak{q}_o(y)}-m)}{m(\frac{\mathfrak{p}_o(y)}{\mathfrak{q}_o(y)}-1)}\right|,\cdot\right)+m\Psi\left(\left|\frac{(\frac{\mathfrak{p}_o(y)}{\mathfrak{q}_o(y)}-y)(\frac{\mathfrak{p}_o(y)}{\mathfrak{q}_o(y)}-m)}{m^2(\frac{\mathfrak{p}_o(y)}{\mathfrak{q}_o(y)}-1)}\right|,\cdot\right)\\
&\left.\left.+m^2\Psi\left(\left|\frac{(y-1)(\frac{\mathfrak{p}_o(y)}{\mathfrak{q}_o(y)}-m)}{m^2(\frac{\mathfrak{p}_o(y)}{\mathfrak{q}_o(y)}-1)}\right|,\cdot\right)\right)dy\right\}.
\end{aligned}\tag{61}$$

Since $\Psi(1,\cdot)=0$, it follows that:

$$\begin{aligned}
&\Psi\left(\frac{\mathfrak{q}_o(y)+\mathfrak{p}_o(y)}{2\mathfrak{q}_o(y)},\cdot\right)+\frac{1+m}{\left(\frac{\mathfrak{p}_o(y)}{\mathfrak{q}_o(y)}-1\right)}\int_1^{\frac{\mathfrak{p}_o(y)}{\mathfrak{q}_o(y)}}\Psi\left(\left|\frac{\mathfrak{q}_o(y)+\mathfrak{p}_o(y)}{2m\mathfrak{q}_o(y)}-\frac{(m+1)y}{2m}\right|,\cdot\right)dy\\
&\leq\frac{1}{\frac{\mathfrak{p}_o(y)}{\mathfrak{q}_o(y)}-1}\left\{\int_1^{\frac{\mathfrak{p}_o(y)}{\mathfrak{q}_o(y)}}\Psi(y,\cdot)dy+m\int_{\frac{1}{m}}^{\frac{\mathfrak{p}_o(y)}{m\mathfrak{q}_o(y)}}\Psi(y,\cdot)dy\right\}\\
&\leq m\left\{\Psi\left(\frac{\mathfrak{p}_o(y)}{m\mathfrak{q}_o(y)},\cdot\right)+\Psi\left(\frac{1}{m},\cdot\right)+\Psi\left(\frac{\mathfrak{p}_o(y)}{m^2\mathfrak{q}_o(y)},\cdot\right)\right\}\\
&-\frac{1}{\left(\frac{\mathfrak{p}_o(y)}{\mathfrak{q}_o(y)}-1\right)}\left\{\int_1^{\frac{\mathfrak{p}_o(y)}{\mathfrak{q}_o(y)}}\left(\Psi\left(\left|\frac{(y-1)\left(\frac{\mathfrak{p}_o(y)}{\mathfrak{q}_o(y)}-m\right)}{m\left(\frac{\mathfrak{p}_o(y)}{\mathfrak{q}_o(y)}-1\right)}\right|\right)\right.\right.\\
&+m\Psi\left(\left|\frac{(\frac{\mathfrak{p}_o(y)}{\mathfrak{q}_o(y)}-y)(\frac{\mathfrak{p}_o(y)}{\mathfrak{q}_o(y)}-m)}{m(\frac{\mathfrak{p}_o(y)}{\mathfrak{q}_o(y)}-1)}\right|,\cdot\right)+m\Psi\left(\left|\frac{(\frac{\mathfrak{p}_o(y)}{\mathfrak{q}_o(y)}-y)(\frac{\mathfrak{p}_o(y)}{\mathfrak{q}_o(y)}-m)}{m^2(\frac{\mathfrak{p}_o(y)}{\mathfrak{q}_o(y)}-1)}\right|,\cdot\right)\\
&\left.\left.+m^2\Psi\left(\left|\frac{(y-1)(\frac{\mathfrak{p}_o(y)}{\mathfrak{q}_o(y)}-m)}{m^2(\frac{\mathfrak{p}_o(y)}{\mathfrak{q}_o(y)}-1)}\right|,\cdot\right)\right)dy\right\}.
\end{aligned}\tag{62}$$

Multiplying both sides of (62) by $\mathfrak{q}_o(y)\geq 0$, for all $y\in\mho$, and integrating the resulting expression over $\mho$, yields:

$$\int_{\mho} \mathfrak{q}_o(y)\Psi\left(\frac{\mathfrak{q}_o(y)+\mathfrak{p}_o(y)}{2\mathfrak{q}_o(y)},\cdot\right)d\mathcal{U}(y)$$
$$+\int_{\mho} \frac{\mathfrak{q}_o(y)(1+m)}{\left(\frac{\mathfrak{p}_o(y)}{\mathfrak{q}_o(y)}-1\right)}\left(\int_1^{\frac{\mathfrak{p}_o(y)}{\mathfrak{q}_o(y)}} \Psi\left(\left|\frac{\mathfrak{q}_o(y)+\mathfrak{p}_o(y)}{2m\mathfrak{q}_o(y)}-\frac{(m+1)y}{2m}\right|,\cdot\right)dy\right)d\mathcal{U}(y)$$
$$\leq \int_{\mho} \frac{\mathfrak{q}_o(y)}{\left(\frac{\mathfrak{p}_o(y)}{\mathfrak{q}_o(y)}-1\right)}\left(\int_{\frac{1}{m}}^{\frac{\mathfrak{p}_o(y)}{\mathfrak{q}_o(y)}} \Psi(y,\cdot)dy\right)d\mathcal{U}(y)+m\int_{\mho} \frac{\mathfrak{q}_o(y)}{\left(\frac{\mathfrak{p}_o(y)}{\mathfrak{q}_o(y)}-1\right)}\left(\int_{\frac{1}{m}}^{\frac{\mathfrak{p}_o(y)}{m\mathfrak{q}_o(y)}} \Psi(y,\cdot)dy\right)d\mathcal{U}(y)$$
$$\leq m\left\{\int_{\mho} \mathfrak{q}_o(y)\Psi\left(\frac{\mathfrak{p}_o(y)}{m\mathfrak{q}_o(y)},\cdot\right)d\mathcal{U}(y)+\int_{\mho} \mathfrak{q}_o(y)\Psi\left(\frac{1}{m},\cdot\right)d\mathcal{U}(y)\right.$$
$$\left.+\int_{\mho} \mathfrak{q}_o(y)\Psi\left(\frac{\mathfrak{p}_o(y)}{m^2\mathfrak{q}_o(y)},\cdot\right)d\mathcal{U}(y)\right\}-\left\{\int_{\mho} \frac{\mathfrak{q}_o(y)}{\left(\frac{\mathfrak{p}_o(y)}{\mathfrak{q}_o(y)}-1\right)}\left(\int_1^{\frac{\mathfrak{p}_o(y)}{\mathfrak{q}_o(y)}}\left(\Psi\left(\left|\frac{(y-1)(\frac{\mathfrak{p}_o(y)}{\mathfrak{q}_o(y)}-m)}{m(\frac{\mathfrak{p}_o(y)}{\mathfrak{q}_o(y)}-1)}\right|\right)\right.\right.\right.$$
$$+m\Psi\left(\left|\frac{(\frac{\mathfrak{p}_o(y)}{\mathfrak{q}_o(y)}-y)(\frac{\mathfrak{p}_o(y)}{\mathfrak{q}_o(y)}-m)}{m(\frac{\mathfrak{p}_o(y)}{\mathfrak{q}_o(y)}-1)}\right|,\cdot\right)+m\Psi\left(\left|\frac{(\frac{\mathfrak{p}_o(y)}{\mathfrak{q}_o(y)}-y)(\frac{\mathfrak{p}_o(y)}{\mathfrak{q}_o(y)}-m)}{m^2(\frac{\mathfrak{p}_o(y)}{\mathfrak{q}_o(y)}-1)}\right|,\cdot\right)$$
$$\left.\left.\left.+m^2\Psi\left(\left|\frac{(y-1)(\frac{\mathfrak{p}_o(y)}{\mathfrak{q}_o(y)}-m)}{m^2(\frac{\mathfrak{p}_o(y)}{\mathfrak{q}_o(y)}-1)}\right|,\cdot\right)\right)dy\right)d\mathcal{U}(y)\right\}. \tag{63}$$

By applying the definitions of stochastic divergence and stochastic $\mathbb{H}.\mathbb{H}$-divergence, we arrive at the desired result. □

Theorem 13. *Let* Ψ: $[\mathcal{U}_o, \frac{\mathcal{V}_o}{m}]\times\prod \to \Re$ *be a mean-square integrable (P, m)-superquadratic stochastic process, and* $\Psi(1,.)=0$, *then*

$$\frac{SD_{\Psi}\left(\frac{1}{2}\mathfrak{q}_o+\frac{1}{2}\mathfrak{p}_o||\mathfrak{q}_o\right)}{\Gamma(1+\alpha)}+\frac{2\alpha(1+m)\tau_1}{\Gamma(1+\alpha)}\leq 2^{\alpha}SD_{mHH}^{\Psi}(\mathfrak{p}_o||\mathfrak{q}_o)$$
$$\leq \frac{m}{\Gamma(1+\alpha)}\left\{SD_{\Psi}(\mathfrak{p}_o||m\mathfrak{q}_o)+\int_{\mho}\mathfrak{q}_o(y)\Psi\left(\frac{1}{m},\cdot\right)d\mathcal{U}(y)+m\alpha SD_{\Psi}(\mathfrak{p}_o||m^2\mathfrak{q}_o)\right\}$$
$$-\frac{\alpha\tau_2}{\Gamma(1+\alpha)}.$$

$\forall$ $\mathfrak{p}_o, \mathfrak{q}_o \in \boldsymbol{P}$, *and* $\alpha>0$, *where*

$${}^{\alpha}SD_{mHH}^{\Psi}(\mathfrak{p}_o||\mathfrak{q}_o)=\int_{\mho}\frac{\mathfrak{q}_o(y)}{2\left(\frac{\mathfrak{p}_o(y)}{\mathfrak{q}_o(y)}-1\right)^{\alpha}}\left[\mathfrak{J}_{1^+}^{\alpha}\Psi\left(\frac{\mathfrak{p}_o(y)}{\mathfrak{q}_o(y)},\cdot\right)+m^{\alpha}\mathfrak{J}_{\frac{\mathfrak{p}_o(y)}{m\mathfrak{q}_o(y)}^-}^{\alpha}\Psi\left(\frac{1}{m},\cdot\right)\right]d\mathcal{U}(y),$$

$$\tau_1=\int_{\mho}\left(\frac{\mathfrak{q}_o(y)}{\left(\frac{\mathfrak{p}_o(y)}{\mathfrak{q}_o(y)}-1\right)^{\alpha}}\int_1^{\frac{\mathfrak{q}_o(y)+\mathfrak{p}_o(y)}{2\mathfrak{q}_o(y)}}\left(\frac{\mathfrak{p}_o(y)}{\mathfrak{q}_o(y)}-y\right)^{\alpha-1}\Psi\left(\left|\frac{(1+\frac{\mathfrak{p}_o(y)}{\mathfrak{q}_o(y)})-(m+1)y}{2m}\right|,\cdot\right)dy\right)d\mathcal{U}(y),$$

and

$$\tau_2 = \int_{\mho} \frac{\mathfrak{q}_o(y)}{\left(\frac{\mathfrak{p}_o(y)}{\mathfrak{q}_o(y)}-1\right)^{\alpha}} \left(\int_1^{\frac{\mathfrak{p}_o(y)}{\mathfrak{q}_o(y)}} \left(\frac{\mathfrak{p}_o(y)}{\mathfrak{q}_o(y)} - y \right)^{\alpha-1} \left(\Psi\left(\left| \frac{(y-1)(\frac{\mathfrak{p}_o(y)}{\mathfrak{q}_o(y)}-m)}{m(\frac{\mathfrak{p}_o(y)}{\mathfrak{q}_o(y)}-1)} \right|, \cdot \right) \right.\right.$$
$$+ m\Psi\left(\left| \frac{(\frac{\mathfrak{p}_o(y)}{\mathfrak{q}_o(y)}-y)(\frac{\mathfrak{p}_o(y)}{\mathfrak{q}_o(y)}-m)}{m(\frac{\mathfrak{p}_o(y)}{\mathfrak{q}_o(y)}-1)} \right|, \cdot \right) + m\Psi\left(\left| \frac{(\frac{\mathfrak{p}_o(y)}{\mathfrak{q}_o(y)}-y)(\frac{\mathfrak{p}_o(y)}{\mathfrak{q}_o(y)}-m)}{m^2(\frac{\mathfrak{p}_o(y)}{\mathfrak{q}_o(y)}-1)} \right|, \cdot \right)$$
$$\left.\left. + m^2\Psi\left(\left| \frac{(y-1)(\frac{\mathfrak{p}_o(y)}{\mathfrak{q}_o(y)}-m)}{m^2(\frac{\mathfrak{p}_o(y)}{\mathfrak{q}_o(y)}-1)} \right|, \cdot \right) \right) dy \right) d\mathcal{U}(y).$$

holds for all $\mathcal{U}_o, \mathcal{V}_o \geq 0$ *and* $m \in (0,1)$.

Proof. Consider the fractional $\mathbb{H}.\mathbb{H}$-type inequalities for (P, m)-superquadratic stochastic processes, established via $\mathbb{RL}$ integral operators of order $\alpha > 0$, as presented in Theorem 10:

$$\Psi\left(\frac{u_o+\mathcal{V}_o}{2},\cdot\right) + \frac{2(1+m)\alpha}{(\mathcal{V}_o-\mathcal{U}_o)^{\alpha}} \int_{\mathcal{U}_o}^{\frac{\mathcal{U}_o+\mathcal{V}_o}{2}} (\mathcal{V}_o-y)^{\alpha-1}\Psi\left(\left|\frac{(\mathcal{U}_o+\mathcal{V}_o)-(m+1)y}{2m}\right|,\cdot\right)dy$$
$$\leq \frac{\Gamma(1+\alpha)}{(\mathcal{V}_o-\mathcal{U}_o)^{\alpha}}\left[\mathfrak{J}^{\alpha}_{\mathcal{U}_o^+}\Psi(\mathcal{V}_o,\cdot) + m^{\alpha}\mathfrak{J}^{\alpha}_{\frac{\mathcal{V}_o}{m}^-}\Psi\left(\frac{\mathcal{U}_o}{m},\cdot\right)\right]$$
$$\leq \Psi(\mathcal{U}_o,\cdot) + m\left\{\Psi\left(\frac{\mathcal{V}_o}{m},\cdot\right) + \Psi\left(\frac{\mathcal{U}_o}{m},\cdot\right) + \Psi\left(\frac{\mathcal{V}_o}{m^2},\cdot\right)\right\}$$
$$-\frac{\alpha}{(\mathcal{V}_o-\mathcal{U}_o)^{\alpha}}\left\{\int_{\mathcal{U}_o}^{\mathcal{V}_o}(\mathcal{V}_o-y)^{\alpha-1}\left(\Psi\left(\left|\frac{(y-\mathcal{U}_o)(\mathcal{V}_o-m\mathcal{U}_o)}{m(\mathcal{V}_o-\mathcal{U}_o)}\right|,\cdot\right)\right.\right.$$
$$+m\Psi\left(\left|\frac{(\mathcal{V}_o-y)(\mathcal{V}_o-m\mathcal{U}_o)}{m(\mathcal{V}_o-\mathcal{U}_o)}\right|,\cdot\right) + m\Psi\left(\left|\frac{(\mathcal{V}_o-y)(\mathcal{V}_o-m\mathcal{U}_o)}{m^2(\mathcal{V}_o-\mathcal{U}_o)}\right|,\cdot\right)$$
$$\left.\left.+m^2\Psi\left(\left|\frac{(y-\mathcal{U}_o)(\mathcal{V}_o-m\mathcal{U}_o)}{m^2(\mathcal{V}_o-\mathcal{U}_o)}\right|,\cdot\right)\right)dy\right\}, \tag{64}$$

Now setting $\mathcal{U}_o = 1$, and $\mathcal{V}_o = \frac{\mathfrak{p}_o(y)}{\mathfrak{q}_o(y)}$, in (64), we obtain

$$\Psi\left(\frac{\mathfrak{q}_o(y)+\mathfrak{p}_o(y)}{2\mathfrak{q}_o(y)},\cdot\right) + \frac{2\alpha(1+m)}{\left(\frac{\mathfrak{p}_o(y)}{\mathfrak{q}_o(y)}-1\right)^{\alpha}}\int_1^{\frac{\mathfrak{q}_o(y)+\mathfrak{p}_o(y)}{2\mathfrak{q}_o(y)}}\left(\frac{\mathfrak{p}_o(y)}{\mathfrak{q}_o(y)}-y\right)^{\alpha-1}$$
$$\times\Psi\left(\left|\frac{(1+\frac{\mathfrak{p}_o(y)}{\mathfrak{q}_o(y)})-(m+1)y}{2m}\right|,\cdot\right)dy$$
$$\leq \frac{\Gamma(1+\alpha)}{(\frac{\mathfrak{p}_o(y)}{\mathfrak{q}_o(y)}-1)^{\alpha}}\left[\mathfrak{J}^{\alpha}_{1^+}\Psi\left(\frac{\mathfrak{p}_o(y)}{\mathfrak{q}_o(y)},\cdot\right) + m^{\alpha}\mathfrak{J}^{\alpha}_{\frac{\mathfrak{p}_o(y)}{m\mathfrak{q}_o(y)}^-}\Psi\left(\frac{1}{m},\cdot\right)\right]$$
$$\leq \Psi(1,\cdot) + m\left\{\Psi\left(\frac{\mathfrak{p}_o(y)}{m\mathfrak{q}_o(y)},\cdot\right) + \Psi\left(\frac{1}{m},\cdot\right) + \Psi\left(\frac{\mathfrak{p}_o(y)}{m^2\mathfrak{q}_o(y)},\cdot\right)\right\}$$
$$-\frac{\alpha}{\left(\frac{\mathfrak{p}_o(y)}{\mathfrak{q}_o(y)}-1\right)^{\alpha}}\left\{\int_1^{\frac{\mathfrak{p}_o(y)}{\mathfrak{q}_o(y)}}\left(\frac{\mathfrak{p}_o(y)}{\mathfrak{q}_o(y)}-y\right)^{\alpha-1}\left(\Psi\left(\left|\frac{(y-1)(\frac{\mathfrak{p}_o(y)}{\mathfrak{q}_o(y)}-m)}{m(\frac{\mathfrak{p}_o(y)}{\mathfrak{q}_o(y)}-1)}\right|,\cdot\right)\right.\right.$$
$$+m\Psi\left(\left|\frac{(\frac{\mathfrak{p}_o(y)}{\mathfrak{q}_o(y)}-y)(\frac{\mathfrak{p}_o(y)}{\mathfrak{q}_o(y)}-m)}{m(\frac{\mathfrak{p}_o(y)}{\mathfrak{q}_o(y)}-1)}\right|,\cdot\right) + m\Psi\left(\left|\frac{(\frac{\mathfrak{p}_o(y)}{\mathfrak{q}_o(y)}-y)(\frac{\mathfrak{p}_o(y)}{\mathfrak{q}_o(y)}-m)}{m^2(\frac{\mathfrak{p}_o(y)}{\mathfrak{q}_o(y)}-1)}\right|,\cdot\right)$$
$$\left.\left.+m^2\Psi\left(\left|\frac{(y-1)(\frac{\mathfrak{p}_o(y)}{\mathfrak{q}_o(y)}-m)}{m^2(\frac{\mathfrak{p}_o(y)}{\mathfrak{q}_o(y)}-1)}\right|,\cdot\right)\right)dy\right\}. \tag{65}$$

Given that $\Psi(1,\cdot)=0$, it follows that:

$$\begin{aligned}
&\Psi\left(\frac{\mathfrak{q}_o(y)+\mathfrak{p}_o(y)}{2\mathfrak{q}_o(y)},\cdot\right)+\frac{2\alpha(1+m)}{\left(\frac{\mathfrak{p}_o(y)}{\mathfrak{q}_o(y)}-1\right)^{\alpha}}\int_1^{\frac{\mathfrak{q}_o(y)+\mathfrak{p}_o(y)}{2\mathfrak{q}_o(y)}}\left(\frac{\mathfrak{p}_o(y)}{\mathfrak{q}_o(y)}-y\right)^{\alpha-1}\\
&\times\Psi\left(\left|\frac{(1+\frac{\mathfrak{p}_o(y)}{\mathfrak{q}_o(y)})-(m+1)y}{2m}\right|,\cdot\right)dy\\
&\leq\frac{\Gamma(1+\alpha)}{(\frac{\mathfrak{p}_o(y)}{\mathfrak{q}_o(y)}-1)^{\alpha}}\left[\mathfrak{J}^{\alpha}_{1^+}\Psi\left(\frac{\mathfrak{p}_o(y)}{\mathfrak{q}_o(y)},\cdot\right)+m^{\alpha}\mathfrak{J}^{\alpha}_{\frac{\mathfrak{p}_o(y)}{m\mathfrak{q}_o(y)}^-}\Psi\left(\frac{1}{m},\cdot\right)\right]\\
&\leq m\left\{\Psi\left(\frac{\mathfrak{p}_o(y)}{m\mathfrak{q}_o(y)},\cdot\right)+\Psi\left(\frac{1}{m},\cdot\right)+\Psi\left(\frac{\mathfrak{p}_o(y)}{m^2\mathfrak{q}_o(y)},\cdot\right)\right\}\\
&-\frac{\alpha}{\left(\frac{\mathfrak{p}_o(y)}{\mathfrak{q}_o(y)}-1\right)^{\alpha}}\left\{\int_1^{\frac{\mathfrak{p}_o(y)}{\mathfrak{q}_o(y)}}\left(\frac{\mathfrak{p}_o(y)}{\mathfrak{q}_o(y)}-y\right)^{\alpha-1}\left(\Psi\left(\left|\frac{(y-1)(\frac{\mathfrak{p}_o(y)}{\mathfrak{q}_o(y)}-m)}{m(\frac{\mathfrak{p}_o(y)}{\mathfrak{q}_o(y)}-1)}\right|,\cdot\right)\right.\right.\\
&+m\Psi\left(\left|\frac{(\frac{\mathfrak{p}_o(y)}{\mathfrak{q}_o(y)}-y)(\frac{\mathfrak{p}_o(y)}{\mathfrak{q}_o(y)}-m)}{m(\frac{\mathfrak{p}_o(y)}{\mathfrak{q}_o(y)}-1)}\right|,\cdot\right)+m\Psi\left(\left|\frac{(\frac{\mathfrak{p}_o(y)}{\mathfrak{q}_o(y)}-y)(\frac{\mathfrak{p}_o(y)}{\mathfrak{q}_o(y)}-m)}{m^2(\frac{\mathfrak{p}_o(y)}{\mathfrak{q}_o(y)}-1)}\right|,\cdot\right)\\
&\left.\left.+m^2\Psi\left(\left|\frac{(y-1)(\frac{\mathfrak{p}_o(y)}{\mathfrak{q}_o(y)}-m)}{m^2(\frac{\mathfrak{p}_o(y)}{\mathfrak{q}_o(y)}-1)}\right|,\cdot\right)\right)dy\right\}.
\end{aligned}\tag{66}$$

By multiplying both sides of (66) by $\mathfrak{q}_o(y)\geq 0$, where $y\in\mho$, and integrating the resulting expression over $\mho$, we derive the following:

$$\begin{aligned}
&\frac{1}{\Gamma(1+\alpha)}\int_{\mho}\mathfrak{q}_o(y)\Psi\left(\frac{\mathfrak{q}_o(y)+\mathfrak{p}_o(y)}{2\mathfrak{q}_o(y)},\cdot\right)d\mathcal{U}(y)\\
&+\frac{2\alpha(1+m)}{\Gamma(1+\alpha)}\int_{\mho}\left(\frac{\mathfrak{q}_o(y)}{\left(\frac{\mathfrak{p}_o(y)}{\mathfrak{q}_o(y)}-1\right)^{\alpha}}\int_1^{\frac{\mathfrak{q}_o(y)+\mathfrak{p}_o(y)}{2\mathfrak{q}_o(y)}}\left(\frac{\mathfrak{p}_o(y)}{\mathfrak{q}_o(y)}-y\right)^{\alpha-1}\right.\\
&\left.\times\Psi\left(\left|\frac{(1+\frac{\mathfrak{p}_o(y)}{\mathfrak{q}_o(y)})-(m+1)y}{2m}\right|,\cdot\right)dy\right)d\mathcal{U}(y)\\
&\leq\int_{\mho}\frac{\mathfrak{q}_o(y)}{\left(\frac{\mathfrak{p}_o(y)}{\mathfrak{q}_o(y)}-1\right)^{\alpha}}\left[\mathfrak{J}^{\alpha}_{1^+}\Psi\left(\frac{\mathfrak{p}_o(y)}{\mathfrak{q}_o(y)},\cdot\right)+m^{\alpha}\mathfrak{J}^{\alpha}_{\frac{\mathfrak{p}_o(y)}{m\mathfrak{q}_o(y)}^-}\Psi\left(\frac{1}{m},\cdot\right)\right]d\mathcal{U}(y)\\
&\leq\frac{m}{\Gamma(1+\alpha)}\left\{\int_{\mho}\mathfrak{q}_o(y)\Psi\left(\frac{\mathfrak{p}_o(y)}{m\mathfrak{q}_o(y)},\cdot\right)d\mathcal{U}(y)\right.\\
&\left.+\int_{\mho}\mathfrak{q}_o(y)\Psi\left(\frac{1}{m},\cdot\right)d\mathcal{U}(y)+\int_{\mho}\mathfrak{q}_o(y)\Psi\left(\frac{\mathfrak{p}_o(y)}{m^2\mathfrak{q}_o(y)},\cdot\right)d\mathcal{U}(y)\right\}\\
&-\frac{\alpha}{\Gamma(1+\alpha)}\left\{\int_{\mho}\frac{\mathfrak{q}_o(y)}{\left(\frac{\mathfrak{p}_o(y)}{\mathfrak{q}_o(y)}-1\right)^{\alpha}}\left(\int_1^{\frac{\mathfrak{p}_o(y)}{\mathfrak{q}_o(y)}}\left(\frac{\mathfrak{p}_o(y)}{\mathfrak{q}_o(y)}-y\right)^{\alpha-1}\left(\Psi\left(\left|\frac{(y-1)(\frac{\mathfrak{p}_o(y)}{\mathfrak{q}_o(y)}-m)}{m(\frac{\mathfrak{p}_o(y)}{\mathfrak{q}_o(y)}-1)}\right|,\cdot\right)\right.\right.\right.\\
&+m\Psi\left(\left|\frac{(\frac{\mathfrak{p}_o(y)}{\mathfrak{q}_o(y)}-y)(\frac{\mathfrak{p}_o(y)}{\mathfrak{q}_o(y)}-m)}{m(\frac{\mathfrak{p}_o(y)}{\mathfrak{q}_o(y)}-1)}\right|,\cdot\right)+m\Psi\left(\left|\frac{(\frac{\mathfrak{p}_o(y)}{\mathfrak{q}_o(y)}-y)(\frac{\mathfrak{p}_o(y)}{\mathfrak{q}_o(y)}-m)}{m^2(\frac{\mathfrak{p}_o(y)}{\mathfrak{q}_o(y)}-1)}\right|,\cdot\right)\\
&\left.\left.\left.+m^2\Psi\left(\left|\frac{(y-1)(\frac{\mathfrak{p}_o(y)}{\mathfrak{q}_o(y)}-m)}{m^2(\frac{\mathfrak{p}_o(y)}{\mathfrak{q}_o(y)}-1)}\right|,\cdot\right)\right)dy\right)d\mathcal{U}(y)\right\}.
\end{aligned}\tag{67}$$

Employing the definitions of stochastic divergence, stochastic $\mathbb{H}.\mathbb{H}$-divergence and $\mathbb{RL}$ fractional stochastic $\mathbb{H}.\mathbb{H}$-divergence, we obtain the required result. □

Remark 11. *By setting $\alpha = 1$ in Theorem 13, we recover the result stated in Theorem 12.*

5.1. Assumptions Underlying the Study and Their Limitations

This study is built upon a carefully designed set of assumptions that ensure both mathematical rigor and practical relevance. The new class of (P,m)-superquadratic stochastic processes is treated within the context of mean-square continuity, a general but natural assumption which ensures integrability of the stochastic $\mathbb{RL}$ fractional integrals used in our construction. The random variables and the stochastic processes are assumed to be square-integrable, thus enhancing the stability and robustness of the theoretical results. The derivation of more intricate $\mathbb{H}.\mathbb{H}$-type inequalities finds its basis in the generalized convexity through the m-superquadratic requirement, significantly broadening the range of investigation beyond the conventional techniques based on convexity. Through the use of $\mathbb{RL}$ operators within fractional extensions, the article opens new doors in stochastic fractional calculus and provides a sound basis for future investigation with other fractional operators like Caputo or Hadamard. The methodology through demonstrating its application within information theory, namely through the presentation of innovative stochastic measures of divergence, and thereby highlighting its interdisciplinary importance. To ensure the theoretical contributions are credible, the paper has informative numerical examples and accurate visualizations with the computation times specifically noted. Together, these contributions provide a solid foundation for future work and application, positioning this paper as an important contribution to the new field of stochastic analysis and applications.

5.2. Complexity and Implementation

In order to justify the theoretical results and verify the applicability of our suggested framework to (P, m)-superquadratic stochastic processes, we supply numerical benchmarks for all symbolic calculations and plot outputs. The symbolic procedures employed to create figures and numerical results for the Jensen-type and $\mathbb{H}.\mathbb{H}$ inequalities and their fractional $\mathbb{RL}$ counterparts were run using Mathematica 11.3 on a typical computing platform (Intel Core i7 processor with 16 GB RAM). For illustrative tasks, the measured wall-clock times varied between about 0.142565 and 5.36818 s, depending on the levels of symbolic integration and plotting required. In spite of the symbolic character of the procedures, these findings establish that the calculations remain within efficient and comfortably within practical limits. To allow complete reproducibility and transparency of computations, we share a publicly available GitHub repository with the entire Mathematica notebook: https://github.com/dawoodpk1947/-P-m--superquadratic-stochastic-processes.git. Further, precise timing results can be viewed through: https://github.com/dawoodpk1947/time-for-P-m--superquadratic-stochastic-processes.git (visited on 10 July 2025), enabling the users to navigate and replicate the computational steps stepwise.

6. Conclusions

In this work, we first proposed the notion of (P, m)-superquadratic stochastic processes, which provided a new and mathematically rigorous extension of traditional superquadratic theories in the context of mean-square stochastic calculus. Through rigorous analysis of their structural characteristics, we established extended forms of Jensen's inequality and $\mathbb{H}.\mathbb{H}$ inequalities, and then further extended these findings to their fractional analogues by stochastic $\mathbb{RL}$ fractional integrals. These results greatly expand the analytical arsenal available for fractional stochastic analysis.

The theoretical results were supplemented by well-conceived graphical representations and tabulated illustrations, confirming both the applicability and the generality of the inequalities suggested. The legitimacy of the framework was also demonstrated further through novel applications in information theory, specifically in constructing new classes of stochastic divergence measures.

In order to facilitate reproducibility and computational transparency, all symbolic procedures, graphical plots, and running times have been well documented and made publicly available. This work not only contributes to the theoretical development of stochastic inequalities but also opens the door for further investigation in fractional stochastic processes and their inter-disciplinary applications.

Author Contributions: Conceptualization, S.I.B. and Y.S.; methodology, D.K. and S.I.B.; software, G.J.; validation, S.I.B., D.K. and Y.S.; formal analysis, D.K.; investigation, G.J. and D.K.; writing—original draft preparation, D.K.; writing—review and editing, S.I.B. and M.A.; visualization, M.A.; supervision, Y.S.; project administration, Y.S.; funding acquisition, Y.S. All authors have read and agreed to the published version of the manuscript.

Funding: This research received no external funding.

Data Availability Statement: Data is contained within the article.

Acknowledgments: This work was supported by the Dong-A University research fund. This research was supported by the Global-Learning Academic Research Institution for Master's·PhD Students and Postdocs (LAMP) Program of the National Research Foundation of Korea (NRF) grant funded by the Ministry of Education (RS-2025-25440216).

Conflicts of Interest: The authors declare no conflicts of interest.

References

1. Agarwal, P.; Dragomir, S.S.; Jleli, M.; Samet, B. (Eds.) *Advances in Mathematical Inequalities and Applications*; Springer: Singapore, 2018. [CrossRef]
2. Qin, Y. *Integral and Discrete Inequalities and Their Applications*; Springer International Publishing: Cham, Switzerland; Birkhauser: Basel, Switzerland, 2016. [CrossRef]
3. Dragomir, S.S.; Pečarić, J.; Persson, L.E. Some inequalities of Hadamard type. *Soochow J. Math.* **1995**, *21*, 335–341.
4. Jayaraj, A.P.; Gounder, K.N.; Rajagopal, J. Optimizing signal smoothing using HERS algorithm and time fractional diffusion equation. *Expert Syst. Appl.* **2024**, *238*, 122250. [CrossRef]
5. Sarikaya, M.Z.; Set, E.; Yaldiz, H.; Başak, N. Hermite-Hadamard's inequalities for fractional integrals and related fractional inequalities. *Math. Comput. Model.* **2013**, *57*, 2403–2407. [CrossRef]
6. Nápoles Valdés, J.E.; Bayraktar, B. Some remarks on Caputo-weighted integrals and applications. In *The Fundamentals of Fractional Calculus*; Apple Academic Press: Burlington, ON, Canada , 2025; pp. 228–252.
7. Guzmán, P.M.; Nápoles Valdés, J.E. On fractional integral inequalities of Hermite-Hadamard type. In *Recent Developments in Fractional Calculus: Theory, Applications, and Numerical Simulations*; Springer Nature: Cham, Switzerland, 2025; pp. 47–84.
8. Mumcu, İ.; Set, E.; Akdemir, A.O.; Jarad, F. New extensions of Hermite-Hadamard inequalities via gener alized proportional fractional integral. *Numer. Meth. Part Differ. Equ.* **2024**, *40*, e22767. [CrossRef]
9. Han, J.F.; Mohammed, P.O.; Zeng, H.D. Generalized fractional integral inequalities of Hermite-Hadamard- type for a convex function. *Open Math.* **2020**, *18*, 794–806. [CrossRef]
10. Chen, H.; Katugampola, U.N. Hermite-Hadamard and Hermite-Hadamard-Fejér type inequalities for generalized fractional integrals. *J. Math. Anal. Appl.* **2017**, *446*, 1274–1291. [CrossRef]
11. Zafar, F.; Mehmood, S.; Asiri, A. Weighted Hermite-Hadamard inequalities for r-times differentiable prein vex functions for k-fractional integrals. *Demonstr. Math.* **2023**, *56*, 20220254 . [CrossRef]
12. Liu, K.; Wang, J.R.; O'Regan, D. On the Hermite-Hadamard type inequality for ψ-Riemann-Liouville fractional integrals via convex functions. *J. Inequal. Appl.* **2019**, *2019*, 27. [CrossRef]
13. Stojiljković, V.; Ramaswamy, R.; Alshammari, F.; Ashour, O.A.; Alghazwani, M.L.H.; Radenović, S. Hermite-Hadamard type inequalities involving $(k-p)$-fractional operator for various types of convex functions. *Fractal Fract.* **2022**, *6*, 376. [CrossRef]
14. Dragomir, S.S. Hermite-Hadamard type inequalities for generalized Riemann-Liouville fractional integrals of h-convex functions. *Math. Meth. Appl. Sci.* **2021**, *44*, 2364–2380. [CrossRef]
15. Bohner, M.; Kashuri, A.; Mohammed, P.O.; Nápoles Valdés, J.E. Hermite-Hadamard-type inequalities for conformable integrals. *Hacet. J. Math. Stat.* **2022**, *51*, 775–786. [CrossRef]

16. Butt, S.I.; Khan, A. New fractal-fractional parametric inequalities with applications. *Chaos Solitons Fractals* **2023**, *172*, 113529. [CrossRef]
17. Merad, M.; Meftah, B.; Boulares, H.; Moumen, A.; Bouye, M. Fractional Simpson-like inequalities with parameter for differential s-tgs-convex functions. *Fractal Fract.* **2023**, *7*, 772. [CrossRef]
18. Hezenci, F. Fractional inequalities of corrected Euler-Maclaurin-type for twice-differentiable functions. *Comput. Appl. Math.* **2023**, *42*, 92. [CrossRef]
19. Zhao, D.; Ali, M.A.; Budak, H.; He, Z.Y. Some Bullen-type inequalities for generalized fractional integrals. *Fractals* **2023**, *31*, 2340060. [CrossRef]
20. Rahman, G.; Vivas-Cortez, M.; Yildiz, Ç.; Samraiz, M.; Mubeen, S.; Yassen, M.F. On the generalization of Ostrowski-type integral inequalities via fractional integral operators with application to error bounds. *Fractal Fract.* **2023**, *7*, 683. [CrossRef]
21. Saleh, W.; Lakhdari, A.; Kiliçman, A.; Frioui, A.; Meftah, B. Some new fractional Hermite-Hadamard type inequalities for functions with co-ordinated extended (s, m)-prequasiinvex mixed partial derivatives. *Alex. Eng. J.* **2023**, *72*, 261–267. [CrossRef]
22. Zhou, Y.X.; Du, T.S. The Simpson-type integral inequalities involving twice local fractional differentiable generalized (s, P)-convexity and their applications. *Fractals* **2023**, *31*, 2350038. [CrossRef]
23. Atangana, A.; Baleanu, D. New fractional derivatives with non-local and non-singular kernel theory and application to heat transfer model. *Therm. Sci.* **2016**, *20*, 763–769. [CrossRef]
24. Jiang, J.; Miao, B. A study of anomalous stochastic processes via generalizing fractional calculus. *Chaos* **2025**, *35*, 023156. [CrossRef]
25. Sahebi Fard, H.; Dastranj, E.; Jajarmi, A. A Novel Fractional Stochastic Model Equipped with ψ-Caputo Fractional Derivative in a Financial Market. *Math. Methods Appl. Sci.* **2025**, *48*, 9653–9661. [CrossRef]
26. Guidoum, A.C.; Almulhim, F.A.; Bassoudi, M.; Boukhetala, K.; Alamari, M.B. Fractional and Higher Integer-Order Moments for Fractional Stochastic Differential Equations. *Symmetry* **2025**, *17*, 665. [CrossRef]
27. Nikodem, K. On convex stochastic processes. *Aequationes Math.* **1998**, *2*, 427–446. [CrossRef]
28. Skowronski, A. On some properties of j-convex stochastic processes. *Aequationes Math.* **1992**, *2*, 249–258. [CrossRef]
29. Kotrys, D. Hermite-Hadamard inequality for convex stochastic processes. *Aequationes Math.* **2012**, *83*, 143–151. [CrossRef]
30. Okur, N.; Isçan, I.; Dizdar, E.Y. Hermite-Hadamard type inequalities for p-convex stochastic processes. *Int. J. Optim. Control Theor. Appl.* **2019**, *9*, 148–153. [CrossRef]
31. Set, E.; Tomar, M.; Maden, S. Hermite-Hadamard type inequalities for s-convex stochastic processes in the second sense. *Turk. J. Anal. Number Theor.* **2014**, *2*, 202–207. [CrossRef]
32. Budak, H.; Sarikaya, M.Z. A new Hermite-Hadamard inequality for h-convex stochastic processes. *RGMIA Res. Rep. Collect.* **2019**, *19*, 30. [CrossRef]
33. Barraez, D.; Gonzalez, L.; Merentes, N. On h-convex stochastic processes. *Math. Aeterna* **2015**, *5*, 571–581.
34. Budak, H.; Sarikaya, M.Z. On generalized stochastic fractional integrals and related inequalities. *Theor. Appl.* **2018**, *5*, 471–481. [CrossRef]
35. Afzal, W.; Abbas, M.; Eldin, S.M.; Khan, Z.A. Some well known inequalities for (h_1, h_2)-convex stochastic process via interval set inclusion relation. *AIMS Math.* **2023**, *8*, 19913–19932. [CrossRef]
36. Tunç, M. Ostrowski-type inequalities via h-convex functions with applications to special means. *J. Inequalities Appl.* **2013**, *2013*, 326. [CrossRef]
37. Zhao, D.; An, T.; Ye, G.; Liu, W. New Jensen and Hermite-Hadamard type inequalities for h-convex interval-valued functions. *J. Inequalities Appl.* **2018**, *2018*, 302. [CrossRef]
38. Afzal, W.; Botmart, T. Some novel estimates of Jensen and Hermite-Hadamard inequalities for h-Godunova-Levin stochastic processes. *AIMS Math.* **2023**, *8*, 7277–7291. [CrossRef]
39. Hernandez, J.E.H. On (m, h_1, h_2)-G-convex dominated stochastic processes. *Kragujev. J. Math.* **2022**, *46*, 215–227. [CrossRef]
40. Vivas-Cortez, M.J. On (m, h_1, h_2)-convex stochastic processes using fractional integral operator. *Appl. Math. Inform. Sci.* **2018**, *12*, 45–53. [CrossRef]
41. Hafiz, F.M. The fractional calculus for some stochastic processes. *Stoch. Anal. Appl.* **2004**, *22*, 507–523. [CrossRef]
42. Kotrys, D. Remarks on Jensen, Hermite-Hadamard and Fejer inequalities for strongly convex stochastic processes. *Math. Aeterna* **2015**, *5*, 104. [CrossRef]
43. Agahi, H.; Babakhani, A. On fractional stochastic inequalities related to Hermite-Hadamard and Jensen types for convex stochastic processes. *Aequationes Math.* **2016**, *90*, 1035–1043. [CrossRef]
44. Fu, H.; Saleem, M.S.; Nazeer, W.; Ghafoor, M.; Li, P. On Hermite-Hadamard type inequalities for n-polynomial convex stochastic processes. *AIMS Math.* **2021**, *6*, 6322–6339. [CrossRef]
45. Abramovich, S.; Jameson, G.; Sinnamon, G. Refining Jensen's inequality. *Bull. Math. Sc. Math. Roum.* **2004**, *47*, 3–14. Available online: https://www.jstor.org/stable/43678937 (accessed on 10 July 2025).
46. Abramovich, S.; Jameson, G.; Sinnamon, G. Inequalities for averages of convex and superquadratic functions. *J. Inequal. Pure Appl. Math.* **2004**, *5*, 1–14.

47. Li, G.; Chen, F. Hermite-Hadamard type inequalities for superquadratic functions via fractional integrals. *Abstr. Appl. Anal.* **2014**, *2014*, 851271. [CrossRef]
48. Alomari, M.W.; Chesneau, C. On h-superquadratic functions. *Afrika Mat.* **2022**, *33*, 41. [CrossRef]
49. Khan, D.; Butt, S.I. Superquadraticity and its fractional perspective via center-radius cr-order relation. *Chaos Solitons Fractals* **2024**, *182*, 114821. [CrossRef]
50. Khan, D.; Butt, S.I.; Seol, Y. Analysis of (P, m)-superquadratic function and related fractional integral inequalities with applications. *J. Inequalities Appl.* **2024**, *2024*, 137. [CrossRef]
51. Butt, S.I.; Khan, D. Superquadratic function and its applications in information theory via interval calculus. *Chaos Solitons Fractals* **2025**, *190*, 115748. [CrossRef]
52. Banić, S.; Pečarić, J.; Varošanec, S. Superquadratic functions and refinements of some classical inequalities. *J. Korean Math. Soc.* **2008**, *45*, 513–525. [CrossRef]
53. Lin, J. Divergence measures based on the Shannon entropy. *IEEE Trans. Inf. Theory* **1991**, *37*, 145–151. [CrossRef]
54. Shioya, H.; Da-Te, T. A generalization of Lin divergence and the derivation of a new information divergence. *Electron. Commun. Jpn. (Part III Fundam. Electron. Sci.)* **1995**, *78*, 34–40. [CrossRef]
55. Csiszár, I. Information-type measures of difference of probability distributions and indirect observations. *Stud. Math. Hungar.* **1967**, *2*, 299–318. [CrossRef]
56. Basu, A.; Shioya, H.; Park, C. Statistical inference:The minimum distance approach. In *Chapman & Hall/CRC Monographs on Statistics & Applied Probability*; CRC Press: Boca Raton, FL, USA, 2011.
57. Agahi, H.; Yadollahzadeh, M. A generalization of HH f-divergence. *J. Comput. Appl. Math.* **2018**, *343*, 309–317. [CrossRef]
58. Agahi, H.; Yadollahzadeh, M. Some stochastic HH-divergences in information theory. *Aequationes Math.* **2018**, *92*, 1051–1059. [CrossRef]

fractal and fractional

MDPI

Article

New Fractional Hermite–Hadamard-Type Inequalities for Caputo Derivative and MET-(p, s)-Convex Functions with Applications

Muhammad Sajid Zahoor [1], Amjad Hussain [1] and Yuanheng Wang [2,*]

[1] Department of Mathematics, Quaid-Azam University, Islamabad 45320, Pakistan; sajidzahoor308@gmail.com (M.S.Z.); a.hussain@qau.edu.pk (A.H.)

[2] School of Mathematical Sciences, Zhejiang Normal University, Jinhua 321004, China

* Correspondence: yhwang@zjnu.cn

Abstract

This article investigates fractional Hermite–Hadamard integral inequalities through the framework of Caputo fractional derivatives and MET-(p, s)-convex functions. In particular, we introduce new modifications to two classical fractional extensions of Hermite–Hadamard-type inequalities, formulated for both MET-(p, s)-convex functions and logarithmic (p, s)-convex functions. Moreover, we obtain enhancements of inequalities like the Hermite–Hadamard, midpoint, and Fejér types for two extended convex functions by employing the Caputo fractional derivative. The research presents a numerical example with graphical representations to confirm the correctness of the obtained results.

Keywords: fractional integral inequalities; Caputo fractional derivatives; MET-(p, s) convex functions; log (p, s) convex functions; Hermite–Hadamard inequalities

MSC: 34A08; 26A33; 34A40; 34A12

1. Introduction

Convex functions play important roles in mathematical analysis, including optimization theory and numerical integration. Among the many varieties of convex functions, trigonometric convex functions have drawn a lot of interest because of their intrinsic qualities and uses in a variety of physical and mathematical issues. Refining and improving the conclusions in these disciplines has been made possible by the study of inequalities involving such functions, especially fractional integral inequalities. Fractional calculus, a generalization of classical calculus, involving derivatives and integrals of any order, has been extensively used in the analysis of convex functions. In fact, such a generalization aims to become a more general model for the problem and as such is a tool that is available for estimating and justifying the results of solving problems based on real disciplines in which the use of calculus is not possible. Therefore, it is very important to use the concept of the inequalities of fractional integrals and Hermite–Hadamard ones in particular. Inequalities of this kind play a key role in the estimation of integrals of convex functions, giving numerical estimations for different integral expressions, all of which are necessary for physics, engineering, and economic disciplines. The Hermite–Hadamard inequality is a basic result in convex analysis that provides bounds for the integral of a convex function over a certain interval. Specifically, if f is convex on $[x, y]$, the Hermite–Hadamard inequality states

$$f\left(\frac{x+y}{2}\right) \leq \frac{1}{y-x}\int_x^y f(t)\,dt \leq \frac{f(x)+f(y)}{2}.$$

The extension to fractional integrals has only recently become an attractive subject for researchers. Substantial efforts have been made by numerous authors to formulate the fractional version of Hermite–Hadamard's inequality and apply it in the context of convex functions of various types, including trigonometric ones. For instance, P. O. Mohammed et al. [1] designed a new type of discrete inequalities of the Hermite–Hadamard type for convex functions with integro-differential properties that cover trigonometric functions as special cases. However, the most significant development was the inclusion of fractional integrals in these inequalities, opening numerous new perspectives for applications in the field of fractional calculus. In a similar manner, F. X. Chen [2] approached the fractional generalization of the classical Hermite–Hadamard inequality for convex functions using fractional integrals. This approach allowed the creation of a broader field for the study of convex functions, which includes the trigonometric ones and academic methods for solving fractional calculus for integral inequalities. The importance of these new findings lies in the fact that modern applications of fractional derivatives or integrals require more precise limitation of criteria based on the behavior of various systems represented by convex functions. For the most recent discoveries related to the Hermite–Hadamard-type inequality, the interested reader is directed towards [3–5]. The application of fractional calculus to derive inequalities in relation to the behavior of convex functions includes broader fields of investigations beyond conventional Riemann–Liouville fractional integrals. T. Abdeljawad et al. [6] and G. Rahman et al. [7] have investigated the application of the Caputo fractional derivative in inequalities, providing new bounds and findings relevant to the theory behind the convex and trigonometric functions. These types of fractional derivatives provide users with more opportunities to work with real-life systems with a memory effect, such as energy consumption or material science. Furthermore, fractional calculus assisted in the development of inequalities that feature Fejer–Hadamard inequalities, which are typically associated with the Hermite–Hadamard inequalities (e.g., see [8]). G. Farid et al. [9] used these inequalities in the framework of fractional derivatives, resulting in new findings concerning convex functions. The researchers managed to include fractional integrals in the study, which helps in broadening the field of application of such inequalities and their validity over various issues associated with the study of trigonometric functions. Current researches in fractional integral inequalities allow users to formulate new strategies and approaches to study complex cases in fields involving mathematical modeling, optimization, and numerical integration. Moreover, these advanced methodologies have enormous influence on the development and enhancement of numerical quadrature of the exemplary apparatus of convex functions and other approximate techniques such as trigonometric ones. For example, M. Samraiz et al. [10] and R. S. Ali et al. [11] used fractional-type inequalities to develop various new quadrature as a new worthy estimate of the integral with convex functions.

The fractional Hermite–Hadamard-type inequality is a new area of research that has recently been attracting much attention because it describes non-local dynamics and memory-dependent processes in mathematical models. Classical convexity concepts have been developed to various generalized settings such as logarithmic and exponential convexity, but in practice, more flexible function classes are needed as well to model examples with hybrid growth and oscillatory behavior. The natural generalization which can account for both exponential and oscillatory phenomena for a wide range of its applications in engineering, physics, reliability theory and mathematical programming is the modified exponential trigonometric (p,s)-convexity. Though Caputo fractional derivatives have attracted more and more attention, to the best of our knowledge, there are no complete Hermite–Hadamard-type inequalities for MET-(p,s)-convex and log-(p,s)-convex functions in a higher-dimensional case under Caputo operators. This inspires us to consider new fractional integral inequalities which gather advanced classes of convexity with non-local fractional operators. The author overcomes this deficit by introducing new (Hermite–Hadamard-type) inequalities with the use of Caputo derivative for MET-(p,s)-convex and log-(p,s)-convex functions as well as providing motivation for their applications to engineering problems.

2. Preliminaries

This section contains the materials and basic definitions on which this paper is based. The standard definition of a convex function is stated as follows [12]:

Definition 1. *A function $f : I \subseteq \mathbb{R} \to \mathbb{R}$ is said to be convex if it fulfills the inequality*

$$f(ta_1 + (1-t)b_1) \leq tf(a_1) + (1-t)f(b_1), \tag{1}$$

where $a_1, b_1 \in I$ and $t \in [0,1]$.

Among the most significant generalizations there is s-convexity, introduced in [13] as follows:

Definition 2 (s-convex function). *For some fixed $s \in (0,1]$, a function $f : [0,\infty) \to \mathbb{R}$ is said to be s-convex in the second sense if*

$$f(ta_1 + (1-t)b_1) \leq t^s f(a_1) + (1-t)^s f(b_1), \tag{2}$$

holds for all $a_1, b_1 \in [0,\infty)$ and $t \in [0,1]$.

Definition 3 (p-convex set [14]). *If $J \subset (0,\infty)$ is a real interval and $p \in \mathbb{R} \setminus \{0\}$, then it is said to be a p-convex set if*

$$[ta_1{}^p + (1-t)b_1{}^p]^{\frac{1}{p}} \in J \quad \text{for all } a_1, b_1 \in J \text{ and } t \in [0,1]. \tag{3}$$

Definition 4 (p-convex function [14]). *Let $J \subset (0,\infty)$ be a real interval and $p \in \mathbb{R} \setminus \{0\}$. A function $f : J \to \mathbb{R}$ is said to be a p-convex function if*

$$f\left([ta_1{}^p + (1-t)b_1{}^p]^{\frac{1}{p}}\right) \leq tf(a_1) + (1-t)f(b_1), \tag{4}$$

for all $a_1, b_1 \in J$ and $t \in [0,1]$. If the inequality in (4) is reversed, then f is said to be p-concave.

Definition 5 (trigonometrically convex function [15]). *A non-negative function $f : I \subseteq \mathbb{R} \to \mathbb{R}$ is called a trigonometrically convex function on the interval I, if for each $a_1, b_1 \in I$ and $t \in [0,1]$,*

$$f(ta_1 + (1-t)b_1) \leq \sin(2\pi t)\, f(a_1) + \cos(2\pi t)\, f(b_1). \tag{5}$$

Definition 6 (exponential trigonometric convex function [16]). *A function $f : I \subseteq \mathbb{R} \to \mathbb{R}$ is defined as an exponential trigonometric convex function if*

$$f(ta_1 + (1-t)b_1) \leq \frac{\sin\left(\frac{\pi t}{2}\right)}{e^{1-t}} f(a_1) + \frac{\cos\left(\frac{\pi t}{2}\right)}{e^{t}} f(b_1), \tag{6}$$

for every $t \in [0,1]$ and $a_1, b_1 \in I$.

Definition 7 (modified exponential trigonometric convex function [17]). *Let $f : I \subseteq \mathbb{R} \to \mathbb{R}_0^+$. The function f is called a modified exponential trigonometric convex function if for every $a_1, b_1 \in I$ and $t \in [0,1]$, the following inequality holds:*

$$f(ta_1 + (1-t)b_1) \leq \sin\left(\frac{\pi t}{2}\right) e^{(1-t)} f(a_1) + \cos\left(\frac{\pi t}{2}\right) e^{t} f(b_1). \tag{7}$$

Definition 8 ([18]). *Let $p \neq 0$ and $0 < s \leq 1$. A function $f : (0,\infty) \to \mathbb{R}$ is said to be (p,s)-convex in the second sense if, for all $a_1, b_1 \in (0.\infty)$ and $t \in [0,1]$, the inequality*

$$f\left((ta_1^p + (1-t)b_1^p)^{\frac{1}{p}}\right) \leq t^s f(a_1) + (1-t)^s f(b_1), \tag{8}$$

holds.

Example 1. *Let $f : (0,\infty) \to [0,\infty)$ be defined by*

$$f(x) = x^p, \qquad p > 0,$$

and let $0 < s \leq 1$. Then, f is (p,s)-convex in the second sense.

Definition 9 ([19–21]). *Let $f \in L[a,b]$. Then, the left-sided and right-sided Riemann–Liouville fractional integrals of order $\alpha > 0$ with $a \geq 0$ and $a < x < b$ are defined as follows, respectively:*

$$I_{a+}^{\alpha} f(x) = \frac{1}{\Gamma(\alpha)} \int_a^x (x-t)^{\alpha-1} f(t)\, dt, \quad x > a, \tag{9}$$

$$I_{b-}^{\alpha} f(x) = \frac{1}{\Gamma(\alpha)} \int_x^b (t-x)^{\alpha-1} f(t)\, dt, \quad x < b, \tag{10}$$

where $\Gamma(\cdot)$ is the Gamma function.

These operators extend the classical integral to arbitrary real orders and are fundamental in fractional calculus.

Properties of Riemann–Liouville Fractional Integral

1. Linearity: [19,22] For $x, y \in \mathbb{R}$, the Riemann–Liouville fractional integral satisfies

$$I_{a+}^{\alpha}(xf + yg) = xI_{a+}^{\alpha} f + yI_{a+}^{\alpha} g,$$

and similarly for I_{b-}^{α}.

2. Reduction to the classical integral: [20,22] For $\alpha = 1$, the Riemann–Liouville fractional integral reduces to the standard first-order integral:

$$I_{a+}^{1} f(x) = \int_a^x f(t)\, dt, \qquad I_{b-}^{1} f(x) = \int_x^b f(t)\, dt.$$

3. Identity property: [19,23] In the limiting sense,

$$\lim_{\alpha\to 0^+} I^{\alpha}_{a+}f(x) = f(x), \qquad \lim_{\alpha\to 0^+} I^{\alpha}_{b-}f(x) = f(x),$$

for almost every $x \in (a,b)$.

4. Semigroup property: [19,20] For $\alpha, \beta > 0$, the following composition rule holds:

$$I^{\alpha}_{a+}\left(I^{\beta}_{a+}f\right) = I^{\alpha+\beta}_{a+}f, \qquad I^{\alpha}_{b-}\left(I^{\beta}_{b-}f\right) = I^{\alpha+\beta}_{b-}f.$$

5. Action on power functions: [19,22] For $\mu > -1$, one has

$$I^{\alpha}_{a+}(x-a)^{\mu} = \frac{\Gamma(\mu+1)}{\Gamma(\mu+\alpha+1)}(x-a)^{\mu+\alpha},$$

with an analogous expression for the right-sided operator.

6. Differentiation rule: [20,23] If the derivative exists, then

$$\frac{d}{dx}(I^{\alpha}_{a+}f(x)) = I^{\alpha-1}_{a+}f(x), \qquad \alpha > 0,$$

and

$$\frac{d}{dx}(I^{\alpha}_{b-}f(x)) = -\, I^{\alpha-1}_{b-}f(x).$$

7. Fractional integration by parts: [19,22] For suitable functions f and g, the following identity holds:

$$\int_a^b (I^{\alpha}_{a+}f)(x)\, g(x)\, dx = \int_a^b f(x)\, (I^{\alpha}_{b-}g)(x)\, dx.$$

Definition 10 ([19,21,24]). *For $\mu > 0$, $\mu \notin \mathbb{N}$, with $m = \lfloor \mu \rfloor + 1$, $m \in \mathbb{N}$, $f \in \mathbb{C}[a_1, b_1]$ and $a_1 < x < b_1$, the Caputo fractional derivatives of order μ for the left and right sides are defined as follows:*

$$^{C}D^{\mu}_{a_1^+}f(x) = \frac{1}{\Gamma(m-\mu)}\int_{a_1}^{x}(x-t)^{m-\mu-1}f^{(m)}(t)\,dt, \tag{11}$$

where $x > a_1$, and

$$^{C}D^{\mu}_{b_1^-}f(x) = \frac{1}{\Gamma(m-\mu)}\int_{x}^{b_1}(t-x)^{m-\mu-1}f^{(m)}(t)\,dt, \tag{12}$$

where $x < b_1$, respectively.

3. Main Results

Firstly, we will introduce a new class of convex functions which is a new version of the modified exponential trigonometric convex function known as the modified exponential trigonometric (p,s)-convex function (i.e., MET-(p,s)-convex function).

Definition 11 (MET-(p,s)-convex function). *A function $f : I \subseteq \mathbb{R} \to \mathbb{R}$ is called an MET-(p,s)-convex function if for every $p \in \mathbb{R} \setminus \{0\}$ and $s \in (0,1]$, then*

$$f\left(\left(ta_1{}^p + (1-t)b_1{}^p\right)^{\frac{1}{p}}\right) \le \sin\left(\frac{\pi t}{2}\right)e^{(1-t)^s}f(a_1) + \cos\left(\frac{\pi t}{2}\right)e^{t^s}f(b_1), \tag{13}$$

where $t \in [0,1]$ and $a_1, b_1 \in I$.

Graphical Validation of the MET-(p, s)-Convex Function

Example 2. *Numerical analysis of the MET-(p,s)-convex function inequality for $f(x) = e^x$ with parameters $a_1 = 1$, $b_1 \in [4, 6]$, $p = 1$, and $s = 1$ demonstrates that the inequality holds across all $t \in [0, 1]$, with equality at the boundaries $t = 0$ and $t = 1$, as evidenced by the close alignment of the left-hand side (LHS) and right-hand side (RHS) in Figure 1.*

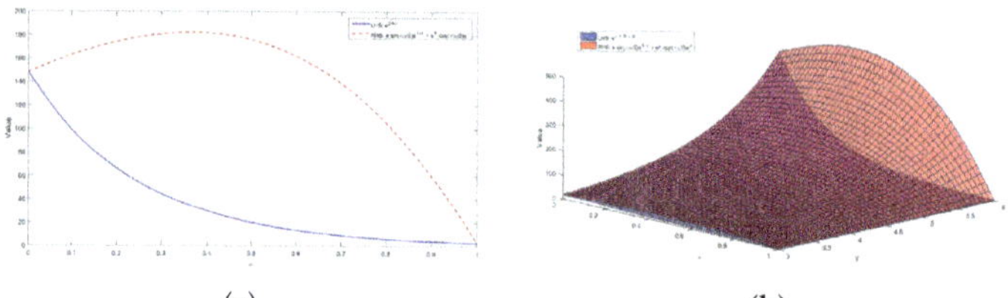

(**a**) (**b**)

Figure 1. The 2D and 3D graphs for $f(x) = e^x$ are presented in figure (**a**) and (**b**) respectively.

Two-Dimensional Visualization Insights: *The 2D plot (Figure 1a) illustrates the behavior of the LHS, e^{5-4t}, and RHS, $e \sin(\pi t/2) e^{1-t} + e^5 \cos(\pi t/2) e^t$, revealing that the RHS consistently dominates the LHS for $t \in [0, 1]$, with the largest discrepancy occurring around $t = 0.5$, confirming the robustness of the inequality for large b_1.*

Three-Dimensional Surface Analysis: *A 3D surface plot (Figure 1b) over $t \in [0, 1]$, $a_1 = 1$ and $b_1 \in [4, 6]$ highlights the exponential growth of both the LHS, $e^{t+(1-t)b_1}$, and RHS, driven by the $e^{b_1} \cos(\pi t/2) e^t$ term, with the RHS surface surpassing the LHS for $b_1 \in [4, 6]$.*

Example 3. *Let f be a mapping defined on real numbers by $f(x) = x^2$; then, f is an MET-(p, s)-convex function (see Figure 2).*

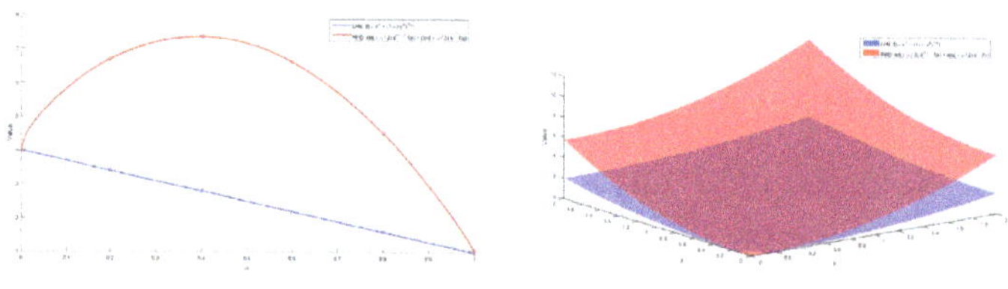

(**a**) (**b**)

Figure 2. The 2D and 3D graphs for $f(x) = x^2$ and choice of parameters $a_1 = 1, b_1 = 2, p = 2, s = 0.5$ and $t \in [0, 1]$ are presented in figure (**a**) and (**b**) respectively.

In this section, we present advancements in fractional integral inequalities involving MET-(p, s)-convex functions and Caputo fractional derivatives.

Theorem 1. *Suppose that $f : [a_1, b_1] \subset \mathbb{R} \to \mathbb{R}$ is a function such that $f^{(m)} \in \mathbb{C}[a_1, b_1]$, $m = [\mu] + 1$, $m \in \mathbb{N}$ and $0 < a_1 < b_1$. If $f^{(m)}$ is a MET- (p, s)-convex function, then with respect to the Caputo fractional derivative, the following holds for every $p \in \mathbb{R} \setminus \{0\}$ and $s \in (0, 1]$:*

$$\begin{aligned} f^{(m)}\left(\frac{a_1{}^p + b_1{}^p}{2}\right)^{\frac{1}{p}} \leq \; & \frac{p e^{\left(\frac{1}{2}\right)^s} \Gamma(m-\mu+1)}{\sqrt{2}(b_1^p - a_1^p)^{m-\mu}} \left[{}^C D^{\mu;u^p}_{b_1^-} f^{(m)}(a_1^p) \right. \\ & \left. + (-1)^m \, {}^C D^{\mu;u^p}_{a_1^+} f^{(m)}(b_1^p) \right] \leq 2 e^{2^{1-s}} \times \\ & \left[\frac{f^{(m)}(a_1) + f^{(m)}(b_1)}{2} \right], \end{aligned} \tag{14}$$

where $\mu \geq 0$.

Proof. As $f^{(m)}$ is a MET-(p,s)-convex function, then for $x_1, y_1 \in [a_1, b_1]$, we obtain

$$f^{(m)}\left(\frac{x_1^p + y_1^p}{2}\right)^{\frac{1}{p}} \leq \frac{e^{\left(\frac{1}{2}\right)^s}}{\sqrt{2}}(f^{(m)}(x_1) + f^{(m)}(y_1)), \tag{15}$$

Put $x_1^p = \alpha a_1^p + (1-\alpha)b_1^p$ and $y_1^p = (1-\alpha)a_1^p + \alpha b_1^p \quad \forall \alpha \in [0,1]$; then, Equation (15) becomes

$$f^{(m)}\left(\frac{a_1^p + b_1^p}{2}\right)^{\frac{1}{p}} \leq \frac{e^{\left(\frac{1}{2}\right)^s}}{\sqrt{2}}\left[f^{(m)}\left(\alpha a_1^p + (1-\alpha)b_1^p\right)^{\frac{1}{p}} + f^{(m)}\left((1-\alpha)a_1^p + \alpha b_1^p\right)^{\frac{1}{p}}\right].$$

Multiplying both sides by $\alpha^{m-\mu-1}$ and integrating α over $[0,1]$ yields

$$\begin{aligned} f^{(m)}\left(\frac{a_1^p + b_1^p}{2}\right)^{\frac{1}{p}} \int_0^1 \alpha^{m-\mu-1} d\alpha \quad &\leq \quad \frac{e^{\left(\frac{1}{2}\right)^s}}{\sqrt{2}}\left[\int_0^1 (f^{(m)}(\alpha a_1^p + (1-\alpha)b_1^p)^{\frac{1}{p}} \alpha^{m-\mu-1} d\alpha \right. \\ &+ \left. \int_0^1 f^{(m)}((1-\alpha)a_1^p + \alpha b_1^p)^{\frac{1}{p}})\alpha^{m-\mu-1} d\alpha\right]. \end{aligned} \tag{16}$$

After making some suitable substitutions, we obtained the following result:

$$\begin{aligned} \frac{1}{m-\mu} f^{(m)}\left(\frac{a_1^p + b_1^p}{2}\right)^{\frac{1}{p}} \quad &\leq \quad \frac{p e^{\left(\frac{1}{2}\right)^s}}{\sqrt{2}(b_1^p - a_1^p)^{m-\mu}}\left[\int_{a_1}^{b_1} f^{(m)}(u)(b_1^p - u^p)^{m-\mu-1} u^{p-1} du \right. \\ &+ \quad \left. (-1)^m \int_{a_1}^{b_1} f^{(m)}(v)(v^p - a_1^p)^{m-\mu-1} v^{p-1} dv\right]. \end{aligned}$$

This implies that

$$\begin{aligned} f^{(m)}\left(\frac{a_1^p + b_1^p}{2}\right)^{\frac{1}{p}} \quad &\leq \quad \frac{p e^{\left(\frac{1}{2}\right)^s}\Gamma(m-\mu+1)}{\sqrt{2}(b_1^p - a_1^p)^{m-\mu}}\left[{}^{C}D_{b_1^-}^{\mu;u^p} f^{(m)}(a_1^p) \right. \\ &\left. +(-1)^m \, {}^{C}D_{a_1^+}^{\mu;u^p} f^{(m)}(b_1^p)\right]. \end{aligned} \tag{17}$$

Now, for the second part of the inequality,

$$f^{(m)}(\alpha a_1^p + (1-\alpha)b_1^p)^{\frac{1}{p}} \leq \frac{\sin \pi\alpha}{2} e^{(1-\alpha)^s} f^{(m)}(a_1) + \frac{\cos \pi\alpha}{2} e^{\alpha^s} f^{(m)}(b_1), \tag{18}$$

and

$$f^{(m)}(\alpha b_1^p + (1-\alpha)a_1^p)^{\frac{1}{p}} \leq \frac{\sin \pi\alpha}{2} e^{(1-\alpha)^s} f^{(m)}(b_1) + \frac{\cos \pi\alpha}{2} e^{\alpha^s} f^{(m)}(a_1), \tag{19}$$

by adding (18) and (19), we get

$$\begin{aligned} f^{(m)}(\alpha a_1^p + (1-\alpha)b_1^p)^{\frac{1}{p}} + f^{(m)}(\alpha b_1^p + (1-\alpha)a_1^p)^{\frac{1}{p}} \quad &\leq \left[\frac{\sin \pi\alpha}{2} e^{(1-\alpha)^s} + \frac{\cos \pi\alpha}{2} e^{\alpha^s}\right] \times \\ &\left[f^{(m)}(a_1) + f^{(m)}(b_1)\right]. \end{aligned} \tag{20}$$

Since $\alpha \in [0,1]$ and $s \in (0,1]$, then $\frac{\sin \pi\alpha}{2} e^{(1-\alpha)^s} + \frac{\cos \pi\alpha}{2} e^{\alpha^s} \leq \sqrt{2} e^{(\frac{1}{2})^s}$, and Equation (20) becomes

$$f^{(m)}(\alpha a_1^p + (1-\alpha) b_1^p)^{\frac{1}{p}} + f^{(m)}(\alpha b_1^p + (1-\alpha) a_1^p)^{\frac{1}{p}} \leq \sqrt{2} e^{(\frac{1}{2})^s} \left[f^{(m)}(a_1) + f^{(m)}(b_1) \right].$$

Multiplying both sides by $\alpha^{m-\mu-1}$ and integrating α over $[0,1]$ yields

$$\begin{aligned} \int_0^1 \alpha^{m-\mu-1} f^{(m)}(\alpha a_1^p + (1-\alpha) b_1^p)^{\frac{1}{p}} d\alpha \quad &+ \quad \int_0^1 \alpha^{m-\mu-1} f^{(m)}(\alpha b_1^p + (1-\alpha) a_1^p)^{\frac{1}{p}} d\alpha \\ &\leq \sqrt{2} e^{(\frac{1}{2})^s} \int_0^1 \alpha^{m-\mu-1} d\alpha \left[f^{(m)}(a_1) + f^{(m)}(b_1) \right]. \end{aligned}$$

By using the same procedure as used in the above inequality, we get

$$\begin{aligned} \frac{p e^{(\frac{1}{2})^s} \Gamma(m-\mu+1)}{\sqrt{2}(b_1^p - a_1^p)^{m-\mu}} \left[{}^{C}D_{b_1^-}^{\mu;u^p} f^{(m)}(a_1^p) \quad + \quad (-1)^m \, {}^{C}D_{a_1^+}^{\mu;u^p} f^{(m)}(b_1^p) \right] \leq \\ 2e^{2^{1-s}} \left[\frac{f^{(m)}(a_1) + f^{(m)}(b_1)}{2} \right]. \end{aligned} \tag{21}$$

Combining (17) and (21), we get the required inequality. □

Corollary 1. *Under the assumptions of Theorem 1, if we take $p = 1$ and $s = 1$, then we obtain the fractional integral inequality for the modified exponential trigonometric convex function:*

$$\begin{aligned} f^{(m)}\left(\frac{a_1 + b_1}{2}\right) \quad &\leq \sqrt{\frac{e}{2}} \frac{\Gamma(m-\mu+1)}{(b_1 - a_1)^{m-\mu}} \left[{}^{C}D_{b_1^-}^{\mu} f^{(m)}(a_1) \right. \\ &\left. + (-1)^m \, {}^{C}D_{a_1^+}^{\mu} f^{(m)}(b_1) \right] \leq 2e \left(\frac{f^{(m)}(a_1) + f^{(m)}(b_1)}{2} \right). \end{aligned} \tag{22}$$

Theorem 2. *Suppose that $f : [a_1, b_1] \subset \mathbb{R} \to \mathbb{R}$ is a function such that $f^{(m)} \in \mathbb{C}[a_1, b_1]$, $m = [\mu] + 1$, $m \in \mathbb{N}$ and $0 < a_1 < b_1$. If $f^{(m)}$ is a MET-(p,s)-convex function, then with respect to the Caputo fractional derivative, the following holds for every $p \in \mathbb{R} \setminus \{0\}$ and $s \in (0,1]$:*

$$\begin{aligned} f^{(m)}\left(\frac{a_1^p + b_1^p}{2}\right)^{\frac{1}{p}} \quad &\leq \quad \frac{2^{m-\mu} p e^{(\frac{1}{2})^s} \Gamma(m-\mu+1)}{\sqrt{2}(b_1^p - a_1^p)^{m-\mu}} \left[{}^{C}D^{\mu;u^p}_{\left(\frac{a_1^p + b_1^p}{2}\right)^{\frac{1}{p}}+} f^{(m)}(b_1^p) \right. \\ &+ \quad \left. (-1)^m \, {}^{C}D^{\mu;u^p}_{\left(\frac{a_1^p + b_1^p}{2}\right)^{\frac{1}{p}}-} f^{(m)}(a_1^p) \right] \leq 2e^{2^{1-s}} \left[\frac{f^{(m)}(a_1) + f^{(m)}(b_1)}{2} \right], \end{aligned} \tag{23}$$

where $\mu \geq 0$.

Proof. Since f^m is a MET-(p,s)-convex function, then for $x_1, y_1 \in [a_1, b_1]$, we have

$$f^{(m)}\left(\frac{x_1^p + y_1^p}{2}\right)^{\frac{1}{p}} \leq \frac{e^{(\frac{1}{2})^s}}{\sqrt{2}} (f^{(m)}(x_1) + f^{(m)}(y_1)), \tag{24}$$

Put $x_1^p = \frac{\alpha}{2}a_1^p + \frac{2-\alpha}{2}b_1^p$ and $y_1^p = \frac{2-\alpha}{2}a_1^p + \frac{\alpha}{2}b_1^p \quad \forall \alpha \in [0,1]$,
Equation (24) becomes

$$f^{(m)}\left(\frac{a_1^p + b_1^p}{2}\right)^{\frac{1}{p}} \leq \frac{e^{\left(\frac{1}{2}\right)^s}}{\sqrt{2}}\left[f^{(m)}\left(\frac{\alpha}{2}a_1^p + \frac{2-\alpha}{2}b_1^p\right)^{\frac{1}{p}} + f^{(m)}\left(\frac{2-\alpha}{2}a_1^p + \frac{\alpha}{2}b_1^p\right)^{\frac{1}{p}}\right].$$

Multiplying both sides by $\alpha^{m-\mu-1}$ and integrating α over $[0,1]$ yields

$$\begin{aligned} f^{(m)}\left(\frac{a_1^p + b_1^p}{2}\right)^{\frac{1}{p}} \int_0^1 \alpha^{m-\mu-1} d\alpha \quad &\leq \quad \frac{e^{\left(\frac{1}{2}\right)^s}}{\sqrt{2}}\left[\int_0^1 (f^{(m)}\left(\frac{\alpha}{2}a_1^p + \frac{2-\alpha}{2}b_1^p\right)^{\frac{1}{p}} \alpha^{m-\mu-1} d\alpha \right. \\ &+ \quad \left. \int_0^1 f^{(m)}\left(\frac{2-\alpha}{2}a_1^p + \frac{\alpha}{2}b_1^p\right)^{\frac{1}{p}} \alpha^{m-\mu-1} d\alpha\right]. \end{aligned} \tag{25}$$

After making some suitable substitutions, we obtained the following result:

$$\begin{aligned} \frac{1}{m-\mu} f^{(m)}\left(\frac{a_1^p + b_1^p}{2}\right)^{\frac{1}{p}} \quad &\leq \quad \frac{2^{m-\mu} p e^{\left(\frac{1}{2}\right)^s}}{\sqrt{2}(b_1^p - a_1^p)^{m-\mu}}\left[\int_{\left(\frac{a_1^p + b_1^p}{2}\right)^{\frac{1}{p}}}^{b_1} f^{(m)}(u)(b_1^p - u^p)^{m-\mu-1} u^{p-1} du \right. \\ &+ \quad \left. (-1)^m \int_{a_1}^{\left(\frac{a_1^p + b_1^p}{2}\right)^{\frac{1}{p}}} f^{(m)}(v)(v^p - a_1^p)^{m-\mu-1} v^{p-1} dv\right]. \end{aligned}$$

This implies that

$$\begin{aligned} f^{(m)}\left(\frac{a_1^p + b_1^p}{2}\right)^{\frac{1}{p}} \quad &\leq \quad \frac{2^{m-\mu} p e^{\left(\frac{1}{2}\right)^s} \Gamma(m-\mu+1)}{\sqrt{2}(b_1^p - a_1^p)^{m-\mu}}\left[{}^{C}D^{\mu;u^p}_{\left(\frac{a_1^p + b_1^p}{2}\right)^{\frac{1}{p}}+} f^{(m)}(b_1^p) \right. \\ &+ \quad \left. (-1)^m \, {}^{C}D^{\mu;u^p}_{\left(\frac{a_1^p + b_1^p}{2}\right)^{\frac{1}{p}}-} f^{(m)}(a_1^p)\right]. \end{aligned} \tag{26}$$

Now, for the second part of the inequality,

$$f^{(m)}\left(\frac{\alpha}{2}a_1^p + \frac{2-\alpha}{2}b_1^p\right)^{\frac{1}{p}} \leq \frac{\sin \pi\alpha}{4} e^{\left(\frac{2-\alpha}{2}\right)^s} f^{(m)}(a_1) + \frac{\cos \pi\alpha}{4} e^{\left(\frac{\alpha}{2}\right)^s} f^{(m)}(b_1), \tag{27}$$

and

$$f^{(m)}\left(\frac{\alpha}{2}b_1^p + \frac{2-\alpha}{2}a_1^p\right)^{\frac{1}{p}} \leq \frac{\sin \pi\alpha}{4} e^{\left(\frac{2-\alpha}{2}\right)^s} f^{(m)}(b_1) + \frac{\cos \pi\alpha}{4} e^{\left(\frac{\alpha}{2}\right)^s} f^{(m)}(a_1), \tag{28}$$

by adding (27) and (28), we get

$$\begin{aligned} f^{(m)}\left(\frac{\alpha}{2}a_1^p + \frac{2-\alpha}{2}b_1^p\right)^{\frac{1}{p}} + f^{(m)}\left(\frac{\alpha}{2}b_1^p + \frac{2-\alpha}{2}a_1^p\right)^{\frac{1}{p}} \quad &\leq \quad \left[\frac{\sin \pi\alpha}{4} e^{\left(\frac{2-\alpha}{2}\right)^s} + \frac{\cos \pi\alpha}{4} e^{\left(\frac{\alpha}{2}\right)^s}\right] \times \\ &\quad \left[f^{(m)}(a_1) + f^{(m)}(b_1)\right]. \end{aligned} \tag{29}$$

Since $\alpha \in [0,1]$ and $s \in (0,1]$, then $\frac{\sin \pi\alpha}{4} e^{\left(\frac{2-\alpha}{2}\right)^s} + \frac{\cos \pi\alpha}{4} e^{\left(\frac{\alpha}{2}\right)^s} \leq \sqrt{2} e^{\left(\frac{1}{2}\right)^s}$ Equation (29) becomes

$$f^{(m)}\left(\frac{\alpha}{2}a_1^p + \frac{2-\alpha}{2}b_1^p\right)^{\frac{1}{p}} + f^{(m)}\left(\frac{\alpha}{2}b_1^p + \frac{2-\alpha}{2}a_1^p\right)^{\frac{1}{p}} \leq \sqrt{2}e^{\left(\frac{1}{2}\right)^s}\left[f^{(m)}(a_1) + f^{(m)}(b_1)\right].$$

Multiplying both sides by $\alpha^{m-\mu-1}$ and integrating α over $[0,1]$,

$$\int_0^1 \alpha^{m-\mu-1} f^{(m)}\left(\frac{\alpha}{2}a_1^p + \frac{2-\alpha}{2}b_1^p\right)^{\frac{1}{p}} d\alpha + \int_0^1 \alpha^{m-\mu-1} f^{(m)}\left(\frac{\alpha}{2}b_1^p + \frac{2-\alpha}{2}a_1^p\right)^{\frac{1}{p}} d\alpha \leq \sqrt{2}e^{\left(\frac{1}{2}\right)^s} \times \left[f^{(m)}(a_1) + f^{(m)}(b_1)\right]\int_0^1 \alpha^{m-\mu-1} d\alpha.$$

By using the same procedure as used in the above inequality, we get

$$\begin{aligned} &\frac{2^{m-\mu} p e^{\left(\frac{1}{2}\right)^s}\Gamma(m-\mu+1)}{\sqrt{2}(b_1^p - a_1^p)^{m-\mu}}\left[{}^{C}D^{\mu;u^p}_{\left(\frac{a_1^p+b_1^p}{2}\right)^{\frac{1}{p}}+} f^{(m)}(b_1^p) + (-1)^m\, {}^{C}D^{\mu;u^p}_{\left(\frac{a_1^p+b_1^p}{2}\right)^{\frac{1}{p}}-} f^{(m)}(a_1^p)\right] \\ &\leq 2e^{2^{1-s}}\left[\frac{f^{(m)}(a_1) + f^{(m)}(b_1)}{2}\right]. \end{aligned} \tag{30}$$

Combining (26) and (30), we get the required inequality. □

Corollary 2. *Under the assumptions of Theorem 2, if we take $p = 1$ and $s = 1$, then we obtain the Caputo fractional integral inequality for modified exponential trigonometric convex function:*

$$\begin{aligned} f^{(m)}\left(\frac{a_1+b_1}{2}\right) &\leq \sqrt{\frac{e}{2}}\frac{2^{m-\mu}\Gamma(m-\mu+1)}{(b_1-a_1)^{m-\mu}}\left[{}^{C}D^{\mu}_{\left(\frac{a_1+b_1}{2}\right)+} f^{(m)}(b_1)\right. \\ &\left. + (-1)^m\, {}^{C}D^{\mu}_{\left(\frac{a_1+b_1}{2}\right)-} f^{(m)}(a_1)\right] \leq 2e\left(\frac{f^{(m)}(a_1) + f^{(m)}(b_1)}{2}\right). \end{aligned} \tag{31}$$

Definition 12. *We assume that*

$$\|h^{(m)}\|_\infty = \sup_{x \in [a_1, b_1]} |h^{(m)}(x)|,$$

where $h : [a_1, b_1] \to \mathbb{R}$ is such that $h \in \mathbb{C}[a_1, b_1]$.

We also introduce the following convolution $f * h$ of the functions f and h, in the context of Caputo fractional derivatives:

$${}^{C}D^{\mu;t^p}_{a_1+}(f*h)(x^p) = \frac{1}{\Gamma(m-\mu)}\int_{a_1}^{x}(x^p - t^p)^{m-\mu-1} f^{(m)}(t^p) h^{(m)}(t)\, t^{p-1} dt,$$

where $x > a_1$, and

$${}^{C}D^{\mu;t^p}_{b_1-}(f*h)(x^p) = \frac{(-1)^m}{\Gamma(m-\mu)}\int_{x}^{b_1}(t^p - x^p)^{m-\mu-1} f^{(m)}(t^p) h^{(m)}(t)\, t^{p-1} dt,$$

where $x < b_1$, respectively.

Lemma 1 ([9]). *For $0 < \mu \leq 1$, we have*

$$|a_1{}^{\mu} - b_1{}^{\mu}| \leq (b_1 - a_1)^{\mu}.$$

Lemma 2 ([25]). *Let $f : [a_1, b_1] \to \mathbb{R}$, $a_1 < b_1$ be such that $f \in \mathbb{C}[a_1, b_1]$. If $f^{(m)}$ is symmetric to $\frac{a_1+b_1}{2}$; then, the inequality for fractional Caputo derivatives holds:*

$$^{C}D^{\mu}_{a_1{}^+} f(b_1) = (-1)^m \, ^{C}D^{\mu}_{b_1{}^-} f(a_1) = \tfrac{1}{2}\left[^{C}D^{\mu}_{a_1{}^+} f(b_1) + (-1)^{m\,C}D^{\mu}_{b_1{}^-} f(a_1)\right].$$

Theorem 3. *Let $f : [a_1, b_1] \to \mathbb{R}$ such that $f^{(m)} \in \mathbb{C}[a_1, b_1]$. Also let $f^{(m)}$ be a +ve and MET-(p,s)-convex function on $[a_1, b_1]$, $m = [\mu] + 1$ and $m \in \mathbb{N}$. If $h : [a_1, b_1] \to \mathbb{R}$ is a function such that $h \in \mathbb{C}[a_1, b_1]$ and h^m is non-negative integrable and symmetric to $(\frac{a_1^p+b_1^p}{2})^{\frac{1}{p}}$, then with respect to the Caputo fractional derivative, the following holds for every $p \in \mathbb{R} \setminus \{0\}$ and $s \in (0,1]$:*

$$\begin{aligned} f^{(m)}\left(\frac{a_1^p + b_1^p}{2}\right)^{\frac{1}{p}} \left[^{C}D^{\mu;u^p}_{a_1{}^+} h^m(b_1^p) + (-1)^{m\,C}D^{\mu;u^p}_{b_1{}^-} h^m(a_1^p)\right] &\leq \frac{e^{\left(\frac{1}{2}\right)^s}}{\sqrt{2}} \times \\ \left[^{C}D^{\mu;u^p}_{a_1{}^+}(f^{(m)} * h^m)(b_1^p) + (-1)^{m\,C}D^{\mu;u^p}_{b_1{}^-}(f^{(m)} * h^m)(a_1^p)\right. &\leq 2e^{2^{1-s}} \\ \left[\frac{f^{(m)}(a_1) + f^{(m)}(b_1)}{2}\right]\left[^{C}D^{\mu;u^p}_{a_1{}^+} h^m(b_1^p) + (-1)^{m\,C}D^{\mu;u^p}_{b_1{}^-} h^m(a_1^p)\right], \end{aligned} \tag{32}$$

where $\mu \geq 0$.

Proof. Since f^m is a MET-(p,s)-convex function, then for $x_1, y_1 \in [a_1, b_1]$, we have

$$f^{(m)}\left(\frac{x_1^p + y_1^p}{2}\right)^{\frac{1}{p}} \leq \frac{e^{\left(\frac{1}{2}\right)^s}}{\sqrt{2}}(f^{(m)}(x_1) + f^{(m)}(y_1)). \tag{33}$$

Put $x_1^p = \alpha a_1^p + (1-\alpha) b_1^p$ and $y_1^p = (1-\alpha) a_1^p + \alpha b_1^p \quad \forall \alpha \in [0,1]$.

Equation (33) becomes

$$f^{(m)}\left(\frac{a_1^p + b_1^p}{2}\right)^{\frac{1}{p}} \leq \frac{e^{\left(\frac{1}{2}\right)^s}}{\sqrt{2}}\left[f^{(m)}\left(\alpha a_1^p + (1-\alpha) b_1^p\right)^{\frac{1}{p}} + f^{(m)}\left((1-\alpha) a_1^p + \alpha b_1^p\right)^{\frac{1}{p}}\right].$$

Multiplying both sides by $\alpha^{m-\mu-1} h^m(\alpha b_1^p + (1-\alpha) a_1^p)$ and integrating α over $[0,1]$,

$$\begin{aligned} f^{(m)}\left(\frac{a_1^p + b_1^p}{2}\right)^{\frac{1}{p}} \int_0^1 \alpha^{m-\mu-1} h^m(\alpha b_1^p + (1-\alpha) a_1^p)^{\frac{1}{p}} d\alpha &\leq \frac{e^{\left(\frac{1}{2}\right)^s}}{\sqrt{2}} \times \\ \left[\int_0^1 \alpha^{m-\mu-1} h^m(\alpha b_1^p + (1-\alpha) a_1^p)^{\frac{1}{p}} f^{(m)}\left(\alpha a_1^p + (1-\alpha) b_1^p\right)^{\frac{1}{p}} d\alpha\right. \\ + \left. \int_0^1 \alpha^{m-\mu-1} h^m(\alpha b_1^p + (1-\alpha) a_1^p)^{\frac{1}{p}} f^{(m)}\left((1-\alpha) a_1^p + \alpha b_1^p\right)^{\frac{1}{p}} d\alpha\right]. \end{aligned}$$

After making some suitable substitutions, we obtained the following result:

$$\frac{p}{(b_1^p - a_1^p)^{m-\mu}} f^{(m)}\left(\frac{a_1^p + b_1^p}{2}\right)^{\frac{1}{p}} \int_0^1 (u^p - a_!^p)^{m-\mu-1} h^m(u) u^{p-1} du \leq \frac{pe^{\left(\frac{1}{2}\right)^s}}{\sqrt{2}(b_1^p - a_1^p)^{m-\mu}} \times \left[\int_{a_1}^{b_1} f^{(m)}(a_1^p + b_1^p - u^p)^{\frac{1}{p}})(u^p - a_1^p)^{m-\mu-1} h^m(u) u^{p-1} du + \int_{a_1}^{b_1} f^{(m)}(u)(b_1^p - u^p)^{m-\mu-1} h^m(u) u^{p-1} du\right].$$

This implies that

$$f^{(m)}\left(\frac{a_1^p + b_1^p}{2}\right)^{\frac{1}{p}} \left[{}^C D_{a_1^+}^{\mu;u^p} h^m(b_1^p) + (-1)^m \, {}^C D_{b_1^-}^{\mu;u^p} h^m(a_1^p)\right] \leq \frac{e^{\left(\frac{1}{2}\right)^s}}{\sqrt{2}} \left[{}^C D_{a_1^+}^{\mu;u^p} (f^{(m)} * h^m)(b_1^p) + (-1)^m \, {}^C D_{b_1^-}^{\mu;u^p} (f^{(m)} * h^m)(a_1^p)\right]. \tag{34}$$

Now, for the second part of the inequality,

$$f^{(m)}(\alpha a_1^p + (1-\alpha) b_1^p)^{\frac{1}{p}} \leq \frac{\sin \pi\alpha}{2} e^{(1-\alpha)^s} f^{(m)}(a_1) + \frac{\cos \pi\alpha}{2} e^{\alpha^s} f^{(m)}(b_1), \tag{35}$$

and

$$f^{(m)}(\alpha b_1^p + (1-\alpha) a_1^p)^{\frac{1}{p}} \leq \frac{\sin \pi\alpha}{2} e^{(1-\alpha)^s} f^{(m)}(b_1) + \frac{\cos \pi\alpha}{2} e^{\alpha^s} f^{(m)}(a_1), \tag{36}$$

by adding (35) and (36), we get

$$f^{(m)}(\alpha a_1^p + (1-\alpha) b_1^p)^{\frac{1}{p}} + f^{(m)}(\alpha b_1^p + (1-\alpha) a_1^p)^{\frac{1}{p}} \leq \left[\frac{\sin \pi\alpha}{2} e^{(1-\alpha)^s} + \frac{\cos \pi\alpha}{2} e^{\alpha^s}\right] \times \left[f^{(m)}(a_1) + f^{(m)}(b_1)\right]. \tag{37}$$

Since $\alpha \in [0,1]$ and $s \in (0,1]$, then $\frac{\sin \pi\alpha}{2} e^{(1-\alpha)^s} + \frac{\cos \pi\alpha}{2} e^{\alpha^s} \leq \sqrt{2} e^{(\frac{1}{2})^s}$ (37) becomes

$$f^{(m)}(\alpha a_1^p + (1-\alpha) b_1^p)^{\frac{1}{p}} + f^{(m)}(\alpha b_1^p + (1-\alpha) a_1^p)^{\frac{1}{p}} \leq \sqrt{2} e^{(\frac{1}{2})^s} \left[f^{(m)}(a_1) + f^{(m)}(b_1)\right].$$

Multiplying both sides by $\alpha^{m-\mu-1} h^m(\alpha b_1^p + (1-\alpha) a_1^p)^{\frac{1}{p}}$ and integrating α over $[0,1]$,

$$\int_0^1 \alpha^{m-\mu-1} h^m(\alpha b_1^p + (1-\alpha) a_1^p)^{\frac{1}{p}} f^{(m)}(\alpha a_1^p + (1-\alpha) b_1^p)^{\frac{1}{p}} d\alpha + \int_0^1 \alpha^{m-\mu-1} h^m(\alpha b_1^p + (1-\alpha) a_1^p)^{\frac{1}{p}} \times f^{(m)}(\alpha b_1^p + (1-\alpha) a_1^p)^{\frac{1}{p}} d\alpha \leq \sqrt{2} e^{(\frac{1}{2})^s} \left[f^{(m)}(a_1) + f^{(m)}(b_1)\right] \times \int_0^1 h^m(\alpha b_1^p + (1-\alpha) a_1^p)^{\frac{1}{p}} \alpha^{m-\mu-1} d\alpha.$$

By using the same procedure as used in the above inequality, we get

$$\frac{e\left(\frac{1}{2}\right)^s}{\sqrt{2}}\left[{}^{C}D^{\mu;u^p}_{a_1^+}(f^{(m)}*h^m)(b_1^p) + (-1)^m\,{}^{C}D^{\mu;u^p}_{b_1^-}(f^{(m)}*h^m)(a_1^p) \le 2e^{2^{1-s}}\times\right.$$
$$\left[\frac{f^{(m)}(a_1)+f^{(m)}(b_1)}{2}\right]\left[{}^{C}D^{\mu;u^p}_{a_1^+}h^m(b_1^p)\right.$$
$$\left.+(-1)^m\,{}^{C}D^{\mu;u^p}_{b_1^-}h^m(a_1^p)\right]. \tag{38}$$

Combining (34) and (38), we get the required inequality. □

Corollary 3. *Under the assumptions of Theorem 3, if we take $p=1$ and $s=1$, then we get the weighted Caputo fractional integral inequality for the modified exponential trigonometric convex function:*

$$f^{(m)}\left(\frac{a_1+b_1}{2}\right)\left[{}^{C}D^{\mu}_{a_1^+}h^m(b_1) \quad +(-1)^m\,{}^{C}D^{\mu}_{b_1^-}h^m(a_1)\right] \le \sqrt{\frac{e}{2}}\left[{}^{C}D^{\mu}_{a_1^+}(f^{(m)}*h^m)(b_1)\right.$$
$$\left.+(-1)^m\,{}^{C}D^{\mu}_{b_1^-}(f^{(m)}*h^m)(a_1)\right] \le 2e\left[\frac{f^{(m)}(a_1)+f^{(m)}(b_1)}{2}\right]\times$$
$$\left[{}^{C}D^{\mu}_{a_1^+}h^m(b_1)+(-1)^m\,{}^{C}D^{\mu}_{b_1^-}h^m(a_1)\right]. \tag{39}$$

Definition 13 (Log (p,s) convex function)**.** *A function $f: I\subseteq\mathbb{R}\to(0,\infty)$ is said to be log-convex if $\log f$ is convex, or, equivalently, has the inequality for every $p\in\mathbb{R}\setminus\{0\}$ and $s\in(0,1]$:*

$$f(\alpha a_1^p+(1-\alpha)b_1^p)^{\frac{1}{p}} \le [f(a_1)]^{\alpha^s}[f(b_1)]^{(1-\alpha)^s}, \tag{40}$$

where $\forall\, a_1,b_1\in I$ and $\alpha\in[0,1]$.

Theorem 4. *Suppose that $f:[a_1,b_1]\subseteq\mathbb{R}\to(0,\infty)$ is a positive function such that $f^{(m)}\in\mathbb{C}[a_1,b_1]$, $m=[\mu]+1$, $m\in\mathbb{N}$, and $0<a_1<b_1$. If $f^{(m)}$ is a $log-(p,s)$-convex function, then for the fractional Caputo derivative we have, for every $p\in\mathbb{R}\setminus\{0\}$ and $s\in(0,1]$,*

$$f^{(m)}\left(\frac{a_1^p+b_1^p}{2}\right)^{\frac{1}{p}} \le \left(\frac{p(m-\mu)^{\frac{1}{2s}}\Gamma(m-\mu)}{(b_1^p-a_1^p)^{m-\mu}}\right)^{2s}\left[{}^{C}D^{\mu;u^p}_{b_1^-}f^{(m)}(a_1^p)\right.$$
$$\left.\times\ (-1)^m\,{}^{C}D^{\mu;v^p}_{a_1^+}f^{(m)}(b_1^p)\right] \le \sqrt{[f^{(m)}(a_1)]^s}\sqrt{[f^{(m)}(b_1)]^s}, \tag{41}$$

where $\mu\ge 0$.

Proof. Since $f^{(m)}$ is a $log-(p,s)$-convex function, then for $x_1,y_1\in[a_1,b_1]$, we have

$$f^{(m)}\left(\frac{x_1^p+y_1^p}{2}\right)^{\frac{1}{p}} \le \sqrt{[f^{(m)}(x_1)]^s}\sqrt{[f^{(m)}(y_1)]^s}. \tag{42}$$

Put $x_1^p=\alpha a_1^p+(1-\alpha)b_1^p$ and $y_1^p=(1-\alpha)a_1^p+\alpha b_1^p$ $\forall\alpha\in[0,1]$ and $p\in(0,1]$.

Then, Equation (42) becomes

$$f^{(m)}\left(\frac{a_1^p+b_1^p}{2}\right)^{\frac{1}{p}} \le \sqrt{\left[f^{(m)}\left(\alpha a_1^p+(1-\alpha)b_1^p\right)^{\frac{1}{p}}\right]^s}\times\sqrt{\left[f^{(m)}\left((1-\alpha)a_1^p+\alpha b_1^p\right)^{\frac{1}{p}}\right]^s}.$$

Multiplying both sides by $\alpha^{m-\mu-1}$ and integrating α over $[0,1]$,

$$f^{(m)}\left(\frac{a_1^p+b_1^p}{2}\right)^{\frac{1}{p}}\int_0^1 \alpha^{m-\mu-1}d\alpha \leq \int_0^1 \alpha^{m-\mu-1}\left[\sqrt{\left[f^{(m)}\left(\alpha a_1^p+(1-\alpha)b_1^p\right)^{\frac{1}{p}}\right]^s} \times \sqrt{\left[f^{(m)}\left((1-\alpha)a_1^p+\alpha b_1^p\right)^{\frac{1}{p}}\right]^s}\right]d\alpha.$$

By using the Rogers–Holder Inequality, we get

$$\frac{1}{m-\mu}f^{(m)}\left(\frac{a_1^p+b_1^p}{2}\right)^{\frac{1}{p}} \leq \sqrt{\int_0^1 \alpha^{m-\mu-1}\left[f^{(m)}\left(\alpha a_1^p+(1-\alpha)b_1^p\right)^{\frac{1}{p}}\right]^s d\alpha} \times \sqrt{\int_0^1 \alpha^{m-\mu-1}\left[f^{(m)}\left((1-\alpha)a_1^p+\alpha b_1^p\right)^{\frac{1}{p}}\right]^s d\alpha}.$$

After making some suitable substitutions, we obtained the following result:

$$\frac{1}{m-\mu}f^{(m)}\left(\frac{a_1^p+b_1^p}{2}\right)^{\frac{1}{p}} \leq \sqrt{\left(\frac{p}{(b_1^p-a_1^p)^{m-\mu}}\int_{a_1}^{b_1} f^{(m)}(u)(b_1^p-u^p)^{m-\mu-1}u^{p-1}du\right)^s} \times \sqrt{\left(\frac{p(-1)^m}{(b_1^p-a_1^p)^{m-\mu}}\int_{a_1}^{b_1} f^{(m)}(v)(v^p-a_1^p)^{m-\mu-1}v^{p-1}dv\right)^s}.$$

This implies that

$$f^{(m)}\left(\frac{a_1^p+b_1^p}{2}\right)^{\frac{1}{p}} \leq \left(\frac{p(m-\mu)^{\frac{1}{2s}}\Gamma(m-\mu)}{(b_1^p-a_1^p)^{m-\mu}}\right)^{2s}\left[{}^{C}D^{\mu;u^p}_{b_1^-}f^{(m)}(a_1^p)\times(-1)^m\,{}^{C}D^{\mu;v^p}_{a_1^+}f^{(m)}(b_1^p)\right]. \tag{43}$$

For the second part of the inequality, we again use the definition of log-(p,s)-convex functions:

$$f^{(m)}(\alpha a_1^p+(1-\alpha)b_1^p)^{\frac{1}{p}} \leq \left[f^{(m)}(a_1)\right]^{\alpha^s}\left[f^{(m)}(b_1)\right]^{(1-\alpha)^s}, \tag{44}$$

and

$$f^{(m)}((1-\alpha)a_1^p+\alpha b_1^p)^{\frac{1}{p}} \leq \left[f^{(m)}(a_1)\right]^{(1-\alpha)^s}\left[f^{(m)}(b_1)\right]^{\alpha^s}. \tag{45}$$

Multiplying (44) and (45), we get

$$f^{(m)}(\alpha a_1^p+(1-\alpha)b_1^p)^{\frac{1}{p}}\times f^{(m)}((1-\alpha)a_1^p+\alpha b_1^p)^{\frac{1}{p}} \leq \left[f^{(m)}(a_1)\right]^{\alpha^s}\left[f^{(m)}(b_1)\right]^{(1-\alpha)^s} \times \left[f^{(m)}(a_1)\right]^{(1-\alpha)^s}\left[f^{(m)}(b_1)\right]^{\alpha^s}.$$

Since $\alpha^s+(1-\alpha)^s \geq 1$ for $s\in(0,1]$ and $\alpha\in[0,1]$, the above inequality becomes

$$f^{(m)}(\alpha a_1^p+(1-\alpha)b_1^p)^{\frac{1}{p}}\times f^{(m)}((1-\alpha)a_1^p+\alpha b_1^p)^{\frac{1}{p}} \leq \left[f^{(m)}(a_1)\right]\left[f^{(m)}(b_1)\right],$$

and taking $\frac{s}{2}$ power on both sides, we get

$$\sqrt{\left(f^{(m)}(\alpha a_1^p + (1-\alpha)b_1^p)^{\frac{1}{p}}\right)^s} \times \sqrt{\left(f^{(m)}((1-\alpha)a_1^p + \alpha b_1^p)^{\frac{1}{p}}\right)^s} \leq \sqrt{\left[f^{(m)}(a_1)\right]^s} \times \sqrt{\left[f^{(m)}(b_1)\right]^s},$$

multiplying both sides by $\alpha^{m-\mu-1}$ and integrating α over$[0,1]$, we get

$$\int_0^1 \alpha^{m-\mu-1}\sqrt{\left(f^{(m)}(\alpha a_1^p + (1-\alpha)b_1^p)^{\frac{1}{p}}\right)^s}\sqrt{\left(f^{(m)}((1-\alpha)a_1^p + \alpha b_1^p)^{\frac{1}{p}}\right)^s} d\alpha \leq \sqrt{\left[f^{(m)}(a_1)\right]^s} \times \sqrt{\left[f^{(m)}(b_1)\right]^s} \int_0^1 \alpha^{m-\mu-1} d\alpha,$$

by using the same procedure in the above inequality, we get

$$\left(\frac{p(m-\mu)^{\frac{1}{2s}}\Gamma(m-\mu)}{(b_1^p - a_1^p)^{m-\mu}}\right)^{2s}\left[{}^C D_{b_1^-}^{\mu;u^p} f^{(m)}(a_1^p) \times (-1)^m \, {}^C D_{a_1^+}^{\mu;v^p} f^{(m)}(b_1^p)\right] \leq \sqrt{\left[f^{(m)}(a_1)\right]^s} \times \sqrt{\left[f^{(m)}(b_1)\right]^s}. \tag{46}$$

Combining (43) and (46), we get (41). □

Corollary 4. *Under the assumptions of Theorem 4, if we take $p = 1$ and $s = 1$, then we obtain the Caputo fractional integral inequality for log-convex functions:*

$$\begin{aligned} f^{(m)}\left(\frac{a_1+b_1}{2}\right) &\leq \left(\frac{(m-\mu)^{1/2}\Gamma(m-\mu)}{(b_1-a_1)^{m-\mu}}\right)^2\left[{}^C D_{b_1^-}^{\mu} f^{(m)}(a_1) \cdot (-1)^m \, {}^C D_{a_1^+}^{\mu} f^{(m)}(b_1)\right] \\ &\leq \sqrt{f^{(m)}(a_1)}\sqrt{f^{(m)}(b_1)}. \end{aligned} \tag{47}$$

4. Applications

Example 4. *To authenticate the result obtained in Theorem 1, we have used Matlab, choosing $f(x) = x^2$ with $m = 2$, $p = 1$, $a_1 = 1$, $b_1 = 2$ and including a combination of values $\mu \in \{0.1, 0.3, 0.5, 0.7, 0.9\}$ and $s \in \{0.1, 0.3, 0.5, 0.7, 1.0\}$ for the graph of the Hermite–Hadmard inequality* (14) *as shown in Figure 3. In Table 1, we provide the Hermite–Hadamrd inequality* (14) *for numerical validation.*

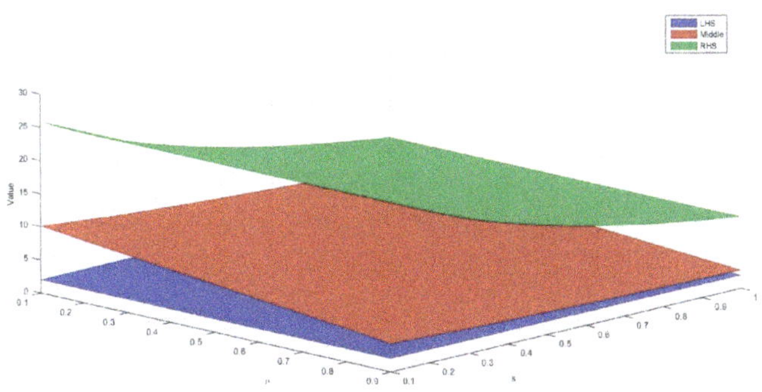

Figure 3. Three-dimensional view of the Hermite–Hadamard inequality (14).

Table 1. Numerical validation of the Hermite–Hadamard inequality.

μ	s	LHS	Middle	RHS
0.1	0.1	2.0000	10.0686	25.8260
0.1	0.3	2.0000	8.9271	20.3120
0.1	0.5	2.0000	8.0333	16.4532
0.1	0.7	2.0000	7.3307	13.6992
0.1	1.0	2.0000	6.5290	10.8732
0.3	0.1	2.0000	8.7540	25.8260
0.3	0.3	2.0000	7.7619	20.3120
0.3	0.5	2.0000	6.9858	16.4532
0.3	0.7	2.0000	6.3753	13.6992
0.3	1.0	2.0000	5.6784	10.8732
0.5	0.1	2.0000	7.1777	25.8260
0.5	0.3	2.0000	6.3665	20.3120
0.5	0.5	2.0000	5.7293	16.4532
0.5	0.7	2.0000	5.2300	13.6992
0.5	1.0	2.0000	4.6548	10.8732
0.7	0.1	2.0000	5.7453	25.8260
0.7	0.3	2.0000	5.0957	20.3120
0.7	0.5	2.0000	4.5857	16.4532
0.7	0.7	2.0000	4.1860	13.6992
0.7	1.0	2.0000	3.7261	10.8732
0.9	0.1	2.0000	4.3129	25.8260
0.9	0.3	2.0000	3.8238	20.3120
0.9	0.5	2.0000	3.4409	16.4532
0.9	0.7	2.0000	3.1409	13.6992
0.9	1.0	2.0000	2.7975	10.8732

Example 5. *To illustrate the validity of Theorem 3, we present numerical results verifying inequality* (32) *for the functions $f(x) = e^x$ and $h(x) = x^2$ over the interval $[0,1]$, setting $m = 0$, $p = 1$, and $s = 1.0$ for the graph of the Hermite–Hadamard inequality* (32)*, as shown in Figure 4. Table 2 below summarizes the values of the left, middle, and right sides of the inequality for fractional orders $\mu = 0.5, 0.75, 1.0$, and $[a_1, b_1] = [0,1]$ computed using the Caputo fractional derivatives.*

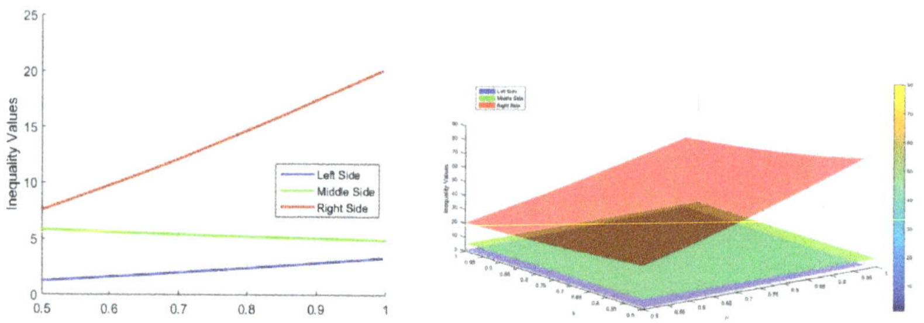

(**a**) (**b**)

Figure 4. The 2D and 3D graphs for $f(x) = e^x$ and $h(x) = x^2$; choice of parameters $a_1 = 1, b_1 = 2$ and $\alpha \in [0,1]$ are presented in figure (**a**) and (**b**) respectively.

Table 2. Numerical values verifying inequality (32) for $f(x) = e^x$, $h(x) = x^2$ on $[0, 1]$.

μ	Left Side	Middle Side	Right Side
0.5	1.240	5.858	7.596
0.75	1.128	5.324	6.917
1.0	1.042	4.917	6.387

5. Conclusions

This study successfully establishes new fractional Hermite–Hadamard integral inequalities by leveraging Caputo fractional derivatives and MET-(p, s)-convex functions. The introduced modifications to classical fractional extensions, encompassing both MET- and logarithmic (p, s)-convex functions, provide a robust framework for refining inequalities such as Hermite–Hadamard, midpoint, and Fejér types. The derived results are substantiated through a numerical example with graphical illustrations, confirming their accuracy and applicability. The results also improve and generalize fractional calculus and convex analysis, with useful implications for both theoretical and applied mathematics.

Author Contributions: M.S.Z.: Conceptualization, Investigation, Methodology, Software, Validation, Visualization, Writing—original draft, Writing—review and editing. A.H.: Conceptualization, Investigation, Methodology, Supervision, Validation, Visualization. Y.W.: Formal analysis, Funding acquisition, Investigation, Methodology, Project administration, Validation, Visualization. All authors have read and agreed to the published version of the manuscript.

Funding: This work was supported by the National Natural Science Foundation of China under Grant No. 12171435.

Data Availability Statement: No additional dataset is required to support the study.

Conflicts of Interest: The authors declare that they have no known competing financial interests or personal relationships that could have appeared to influence the work reported in this paper.

References

1. Mohammed, P.O.; Abdeljawad, T.; Alqudah, M.A.; Jarad, F. New discrete inequalities of Hermite-Hadamard type for convex functions. *Adv. Differ. Equ.* **2021**, *2021*, 122. [CrossRef]
2. Chen, F.X. Extensions of the Hermite-Hadamard inequality for convex functions via fractional integrals. *J. Math. Inequal.* **2016**, *10*, 75–81. [CrossRef]
3. Sun, W.; Wan, H. Hermite–Hadamard-type inequalities involving several kinds of fractional calculus for harmonically convex functions. *Fractals* **2023**, *31*, 2350109. [CrossRef]
4. Du, T.S.; Long, Y. The multi-parameterized integral inequalities for multiplicative Riemann–Liouville fractional integrals. *J. Math. Anal. Appl.* **2025**, *541*, 128692. [CrossRef]
5. Lakhdari, A.; Bin-Mohsin, B.; Jarad, F.; Xu, H.; Meftah, B. A parametrized approach to generalized fractional integral inequalities: Hermite–Hadamard and Maclaurin variants. *J. King Saud. Univ. Sci.* **2024**, *36*, 103523 [CrossRef]
6. Abdeljawad, T.; Ali, M.A.; Mohammed, P.O.; Kashuri, A. On inequalities of Hermite-Hadamard-Mercer type involving Riemann-Liouville fractional integrals. *AIMS Math.* **2021**, *6*, 712–725. [CrossRef]
7. Rahman, G.; Hussain, A.; Alim, A.; Nisarm, K.S.; Mohamedm, R.N. More general weighted-type fractional integral inequalities via Chebyshev functionals. *Fractal Fract.* **2021**, *5*, 232. [CrossRef]
8. Imran, M.; Mubeen, S.; Khan, A.; Abdeljawad, T. Refinements of some fractional integral inequalities involving extended convex functions and fractional Caputo derivatives. *J. Inequalities Appl.* **2025**, *2025*, 12. [CrossRef]
9. Farid, G.; Javed, A.; Naqvi, S. Hadamard and Fejer-Hadamard inequalities and related results via Caputo fractional derivatives. *Bull. Math. Anal. Appl.* **2017**, *9*, 16–30.
10. Samraiz, M.; Nawaz, F.; Abdalla, B.; Abdeljawad, T.; Rahman, G. Estimates of trapezium-type inequalities for h-convex functions with applications to quadrature formulae. *AIMS Math.* **2021**, *6*, 7625–7648. [CrossRef]
11. Ali, R.S.; Mukheimer, A.; Abdeljawad, T.; Mubeen, S.; Ali, S.; Rahman, G. Some new harmonically convex function type generalized fractional integral inequalities. *Fractal Fract.* **2021**, *5*, 54. [CrossRef]

12. Pecaric, J.; Proschan, F.; Tong, Y.L. *Convex Functions, Partial Orderings, and Statistical Applications*; Academic Press: New York, NY, USA, 1992.
13. Hudzik, H.; Maligranda, L. Some remarks on s-convex functions. *Aequ. Math.* **1994**, *48*, 100–111. [CrossRef]
14. Iscan, I. Ostrowski type inequalities for p-convex functions. *New Trends Math. Sci.* **2016**, *4*, 140–150.
15. Kadakal, H. Hermite-Hadamard type inequalities for trigonometrically convex functions. *Sci. Stud. Res. Ser. Math. Inform.* **2018**, *28*, 19–28.
16. Kadakal, M.; Iscan, I.; Agarwal, P.; Jleli, M. Exponential trigonometric convex functions and Hermite-Hadamard type inequalities. *Math. Slovaca* **2021**, *71*, 43–56. [CrossRef]
17. Budak, K.D.; Gürbüz, M.U. Modified exponential trigonometric convex functions and some integral inequalities. *Turkish J. Inequal.* **2024**, *8*, 60–72.
18. Khan, M.B.; Treanţă, S.; Budak, H. Generalized p-convex fuzzy-interval-valued functions and inequalities based upon the fuzzy-order relation. *Fractal Fract.* **2022**, *6*, 63.
19. Samko, S.G.; Kilbas, A.A.; Marichev, O.I. *Fractional Integrals and Derivatives: Theory and Applications*; Gordon and Breach Science Publishers: Yverdon, Switzerland, 1993.
20. Podlubny, I. *Fractional Differential Equations*; Arcademic Press: San Diego, CA, USA, 1999.
21. Stempin, P.; Sumelka, W. Approximation of Fractional Caputo Derivative of Variable Order and Variable Terminals with Application to Initial/Boundary Value Problems. *Fractal Fract.* **2025**, *9*, 269. [CrossRef]
22. Kilbas, A.A.; Srivastava, H.M.; Trujillo, J.J. *Theory and Applications of Fractional Differential Equations*; Elsevier: Amsterdam, The Netherlands, 2006.
23. Sarıkaya, M.Z.; Dahmani, Z.; Kırış, M.E.; Ahmad, F. (k,s)–Riemann–Liouville fractional integral and applications. *Hacet. J. Math. Stat.* **2016**, *45*, 77–89.
24. Caputo, M.; Fabrizio, M. A new definition of fractional derivative without singular kernel. *Prog. Fract. Differ. Appl.* **2015**, *1*, 73–85.
25. Khan, H.; Ahmed, S.; Alzabut, J.; Azar, A.T.; Gómez-Aguilar, J.F. Nonlinear variable order system of multi-point boundary conditions with adaptive finite-time fractional-order sliding mode control. *Int. J. Dyn. Control.* **2024**, *12*, 2597–2613. [CrossRef]

fractal and fractional

MDPI

Article

Advanced Hermite-Hadamard-Mercer Type Inequalities with Refined Error Estimates and Applications

Arslan Munir [1], Hüseyin Budak [2,3,*], Artion Kashuri [4] and Loredana Ciurdariu [5,*]

1 School of Mathematical Sciences, University of Science and Technology of China, Hefei 230026, China; munirarslan@mail.ustc.edu.cn
2 Department of Mathematics, Saveetha School of Engineering, SIMATS, Saveetha University, Chennai 602105, Tamil Nadu, India
3 Department of Mathematics, Faculty of Science and Arts, Kocaeli University, Kocaeli 41001, Türkiye
4 Department of Mathematical Engineering, Polytechnic University of Tirana, 1001 Tirana, Albania; a.kashuri@fimif.edu.al
5 Department of Mathematics, Politehnica University of Timisoara, 300006 Timisoara, Romania
* Correspondence: huseyin.budak@kocaeli.edu.tr (H.B.); loredana.ciurdariu@upt.ro (L.C.)

Abstract

The purpose of this research is to develop a set of Hermite–Hadamard–Mercer-type inequalities that involve different types of fractional integral operators such as classical Riemann–Liouville fractional integral operators. Furthermore, some fractional integral inequalities are obtained for three-times differentiable convex functions with respect to the right-hand side of the Hermite–Hadamard–Mercer-type inequality. Moreover, several new results regarding Young's inequality, bounded function and L-Lipschitzian function are deduced. The paper presents additional remarks and comments on the results to make sense of them. To illustrate the key findings, graphical representations are provided, and applications involving special means, midpoint formula, q-digamma function and modified Bessel function are presented to demonstrate the practical utility of the derived inequalities.

Keywords: Hermite–Hadamard–Mercer-type inequality; s-convex function; fractional integral operators; Hölder's inequality; power–mean inequality; Young's inequality; bounded function; L-Lipschitzian function; special means; midpoint formula; q-digamma function; modified Bessel function

MSC: 26D15; 34A08; 26A33; 26A51

1. Introduction and Preliminaries

Convex analysis, a subfield of mathematical analysis, plays a pivotal role in various fields, numerical analysis, optimization, convex programming, and statistics. Convex functions, in particular, have been extensively studied due to their significance in these domains. It is well-known that mathematical inequalities are the most useful tools in many areas such as mathematics, special functions, physics, fractals, and number theory. Consequently, this area has attracted considerable attention from researchers and continues to contribute to the advancement of different branches of mathematics. The classical Hermite–Hadamard inequality has extensive extensions and generalizations, for which it has been the subject of intensive research over the past decade. Many researchers have been working on this particular problem, as we can see in [1–5]. These investigations have led to the derivation of related inequalities, including Ostrowski, Simpson's, midpoint, and trapezoidal inequalities, as well as various Hermite–Hadamard-type inequalities [6–9]. Moreover, the literature includes studies on Hermite–Hadamard-type inequalities where the absolute value of the third derivative satisfies convexity conditions, as presented in [10,11]. In this subsection, we define and study a class of functions called convex functions.

Definition 1. *The function $\aleph_\varepsilon : I \subseteq \mathbb{R} \to \mathbb{R}$ is said to be convex on I, if*

$$\aleph_\varepsilon(\Upsilon\delta_1 + (1-\Upsilon)\delta_2) \leq \Upsilon\aleph_\varepsilon(\delta_1) + (1-\Upsilon)\aleph_\varepsilon(\delta_2),$$

holds for all $\delta_1, \delta_2 \in I$ and $\Upsilon \in [0,1]$.

Definition 2 ([12])**.** *Let $s \in (0,1]$. The function $\aleph_\varepsilon : I \subseteq \mathbb{R} \to \mathbb{R}$ is said to be s-convex in the second sense if $\aleph_\varepsilon$ is non-negative, and for any $\delta_1, \delta_2 \in I$ and $\Upsilon \in [0,1]$, the following condition holds:*

$$\aleph_\varepsilon(\Upsilon\delta_1 + (1-\Upsilon)\delta_2) \leq \Upsilon^s\aleph_\varepsilon(\delta_1) + (1-\Upsilon)^s\aleph_\varepsilon(\delta_2). \tag{1}$$

A function satisfying the reverse form of inequality (1) is referred to as s-concave in the second sense. By setting $s = 1$, the concept of an s-convex function reduces to the classical notion of convexity [13]. The required lemma was established by Benaissa and Sarikaya in [14].

Lemma 1. *Let $\Upsilon \in (0,1)$. Then,*

$$\text{for all } s \in (0,1] : (1+s)^{\frac{1}{s}} > 2. \tag{2}$$

$$\text{for all } s \in (0,1] : \left(\frac{\Upsilon}{2}\right)^s + \left(1 - \frac{\Upsilon}{2}\right)^s \leq \left(\frac{1}{2}\right)^{s-1}. \tag{3}$$

Proof. Let $\aleph_\varepsilon(s) = \ln(s+1)$ and consider the point $A(1, \ln 2)$. On the interval $[0,1]$, the graph of $\aleph_\varepsilon(s)$ lies above the line joining (OA). Consequently, for all $s \in (0,1]$,

$$\ln(1+s) \geq s\ln 2 \Leftrightarrow (1+s)^{\frac{1}{s}} \geq 2.$$

By taking $s = 0$ in (3), we obtain equality. To establish inequality (3) for $s \in (0,1]$, we proceed by contradiction. Suppose there exists $s \in (0,1]$, such that the inequality is violated:

$$\left(\frac{\Upsilon}{2}\right)^s + \left(1 - \frac{\Upsilon}{2}\right)^s > \left(\frac{1}{2}\right)^{s-1}.$$

Hence,

$$\int_0^1 \left[\left(\frac{\Upsilon}{2}\right)^s + \left(1 - \frac{\Upsilon}{2}\right)^s\right] d\Upsilon > \left(\frac{1}{2}\right)^{s-1}.$$

This gives

$$2\left(\frac{1}{s+1}\right) > \left(\frac{1}{2}\right)^{s-1} \quad \Leftrightarrow \quad s+1 < 2^s.$$

Therefore,

$$(1+s)^{\frac{1}{s}} < 2,$$

which is contrary to (2). □

The well-known Hermite–Hadamard inequality for convex functions, as established in the literature (refer to [15]), is expressed as follows:

$$\aleph_\varepsilon\left(\frac{\delta_1+\delta_2}{2}\right) \leq \frac{1}{\delta_2-\delta_1}\int_{\delta_1}^{\delta_2}\aleph_\varepsilon(u)du \leq \frac{\aleph_\varepsilon(\delta_1)+\aleph_\varepsilon(\delta_2)}{2}. \tag{4}$$

Let $\aleph_\varepsilon : [\delta_1, \delta_2] \to \mathbb{R}$ be a convex function. Additionally, if $\aleph_\varepsilon$ is concave, the inequality (4) holds in the opposite order. This inequality was originally introduced by C. Hermite in [16] and was further explored by J. Hadamard in [15].

In 2003, Mercer's presented a noteworthy variation of Jensen's inequality in [17], now commonly referred to as the Jensen–Mercer inequality. This result is outlined as follows:

For a convex function $\aleph_\varepsilon$ and any set of non-negative weights θ_i, such that $\sum_{i=1}^n \theta_i = 1$, the inequality is given by

$$\aleph_\varepsilon\left(\sum_{i=1}^n \theta_i x_i\right) \leq \sum_{i=1}^n \theta_i \aleph_\varepsilon(x_i).$$

This form generalizes the classical Jensen's inequality by considering a weighted average of points x_i.

Theorem 1. *For a convex function $\aleph_\varepsilon : [\delta_1, \delta_2] \to \mathbb{R}$, the subsequent inequality is valid for all values of $x_i \in [\delta_1, \delta_2] (i = 1, 2, \ldots, n)$:*

$$\aleph_\varepsilon\left(\delta_1+\delta_2-\sum_{i=1}^n \theta_i x_i\right) \leq \aleph_\varepsilon(\delta_1)+\aleph_\varepsilon(\delta_2)-\sum_{i=1}^n \theta_i \aleph_\varepsilon(x_i),$$

where $\theta_i \in [0,1] (i = 1, 2, \ldots, n)$ and $\sum_{i=1}^n \theta_i = 1$.

We now formulate the Jensen–Mercer inequality under Breckner's s-convex setting.

Theorem 2 ([18])**.** *Let $\theta_1, \theta_2, \ldots, \theta_n$ be positive real numbers with $n \geq 2$, satisfying $\sum_{i=1}^n \theta_i = 1$ and $\sum_{i=1}^n \theta_i^s \leq 1$. If $\aleph_\varepsilon$ is a real-valued Breckner s-convex function on $[\delta_1, \delta_2] \subset \mathbb{R}^+$, then for any finite positive increasing sequence $\{x_i\}_i^n = 1 \in [\delta_1, \delta_2]$, we have*

$$\aleph_\varepsilon\left(\delta_1+\delta_2-\sum_{i=1}^n \theta_i x_i\right) \leq \aleph_\varepsilon(\delta_1)+\aleph_\varepsilon(\delta_2)-\sum_{i=1}^n \theta_i^s \aleph_\varepsilon(x_i).$$

In [19], Moradi and Furuichi worked on extending and refining Jensen–Mercer-type inequalities. Subsequently, Adil Khan highlighted the significance of the Jensen–Mercer inequality in information theory applications in [20]. Among their contributions was the development of fresh estimates for Csiszár divergences and related measures. They also employed the Jensen–Mercer inequality to establish new bounds for Zipf–Mandelbrot entropy. Furthermore, Kian et al. [21] utilized the recently formulated Jensen inequality to propose new versions of the Hermite–Hadamard inequality, detailed as follows:

Theorem 3. *Let $\aleph_\varepsilon : [\delta_1, \delta_2] \to \mathbb{R}$ be a convex function; then, the following inequality holds for all $\Im, \beta_2 \in [\delta_1, \delta_2]$ and $\Im < \beta_2$:*

$$\begin{aligned}\aleph_\varepsilon\left(\delta_1+\delta_2-\frac{\Im+\beta_2}{2}\right) &\leq \aleph_\varepsilon(\delta_1)+\aleph_\varepsilon(\delta_2)-\frac{1}{\beta_2-\Im}\int_{\Im}^{\beta_2}\aleph_\varepsilon(u)du \\ &\leq \aleph_\varepsilon(\Im)+\aleph_\varepsilon(\beta_2)-\aleph_\varepsilon\left(\frac{\Im+\beta_2}{2}\right),\end{aligned}$$

and

$$\aleph_\varepsilon\left(\delta_1+\delta_2-\frac{\Im+\beta_2}{2}\right) \le \frac{1}{\beta_2-\Im}\int_{\delta_1+\delta_2-\Im}^{\delta_1+\delta_2-\beta_2}\aleph_\varepsilon(u)du$$

$$\le \frac{\aleph_\varepsilon(\delta_1+\delta_2-\beta_2)+\aleph_\varepsilon(\delta_1+\delta_2-\Im)}{2}$$

$$\le \aleph_\varepsilon(\delta_1)+\aleph(\delta_2)-\frac{\aleph_\varepsilon(\Im)+\aleph_\varepsilon(\beta_2)}{2}. \tag{5}$$

Remark 1. *If we put $\Im=\delta_1$ and $\beta_2=\delta_2$ in inequality (5), then we have the classical Hermite–Hadamard inequality.*

In recent years, Hermite–Hadamard–Mercer-type inequalities have been extensively refined and generalized in various directions by numerous researchers (see, for instance, [22,23]). For example, in [24,25], new forms of Hermite–Hadamard–Mercer-type inequalities were developed for Riemann–Liouville fractional integrals. In contrast, Set et al. and Ciurdariu et al. [26,27] presented Hermite–Hadamard–Mercer-type inequalities involving generalized fractional integrals, as well as fractional integrals applied to differentiable functions. Additionally, Sial et al. [28] provided new bounds for Ostrowski-type inequalities using Jensen–Mercer-type inequality, and Kara et al. [29] explored fractional Hermite–Hadamard–Mercer-type inequalities based on the concept of convexity for interval-valued functions. Furthermore, Butt et al. [30] presented several Hermite–Hadamard–Mercer-type inequalities for harmonically convex functions.

Fractional calculus has gained significant attention from researchers due to its unique properties and wide-ranging applications across various scientific disciplines, including epidemiology [31], nanotechnology [32], physics [33], and bioengineering [34]. Its importance lies in its ability to model complex phenomena and construct fractional integral inequalities, which play a crucial role in approximation theory. Utilizing the fundamental properties of fractional calculus, researchers have introduced novel fractional operators and applied them to solve numerous real-world problems.

A substantial body of work, including numerous articles and monographs, explores the use of new fractional operators to refine and extend integral inequalities such as Ostrowski inequality, Simpson's inequality, Fejér-type inequality, Hermite–Hadamard inequality, Jensen–Mercer-type inequality, among others. Among these, the well-known Hermite–Hadamard inequality, associated with convex functions, stands out as one of the most important and widely studied integral inequalities.

In recent years, an increasing number of studies have utilized new fractional operators to address integral inequalities such as Simpson's inequality, Fejér-type inequality, and the Hermite–Hadamard inequality (see [35–37]). Similarly, for the Jensen–Mercer-type inequality, relevant contributions can be found in [38,39]. Additionally, numerous Hermite–Hadamard-type inequalities have been investigated for functions whose derivatives, in absolute value, exhibit convexity within the setting of fractional calculus (see [40]).

Following the discussion on essential inequalities related to convex functions, we now proceed to recall the definitions relevant to this work. Specifically, we recall the well-known definitions of Riemann–Liouville fractional integrals, which play a central role in our analysis.

Definition 3 ([41,42])**.** *Suppose that $\aleph_\varepsilon \in L[\delta_1, \delta_2]$. The definitions of the left- and right-sided Riemann–Liouville fractional integrals of order $\rho > 0$ are as follows:*

$$\begin{aligned} J^{\rho}_{\delta_1^+}\aleph_\varepsilon(u) &= \frac{1}{\Gamma(\rho)}\int_{\delta_1}^{u}(u-\mathrm{Y})^{\rho-1}\aleph_\varepsilon(\mathrm{Y})d\mathrm{Y},\ u>\delta_1, \\ J^{\rho}_{\delta_2^-}\aleph_\varepsilon(u) &= \frac{1}{\Gamma(\rho)}\int_{u}^{\delta_2}(\mathrm{Y}-u)^{\rho-1}\aleph_\varepsilon(\mathrm{Y})d\mathrm{Y},\ u<\delta_2, \end{aligned}$$

where $\Gamma(\rho)$ represents the Gamma function, while $J^{0}_{\delta_1^+}\aleph_\varepsilon(\mathrm{Y}) = J^{0}_{\delta_2^-}\aleph_\varepsilon(\mathrm{Y}) = \aleph_\varepsilon(\mathrm{Y})$.

Recently, Pečarić [43] derived a Simpson-type inequality for L-Lipschitzian functions on $[\delta_1, \delta_2]$, under the assumption that there exists a positive constant L satisfying the following Lipschitz condition:

$$|\aleph_\varepsilon(x) - \aleph_\varepsilon(y)| \leq L|x-y| \quad \text{for all } x, y \in [\delta_1, \delta_2].$$

Theorem 4 ([43])**.** *Let $\aleph_\varepsilon : [\delta_1, \delta_2] \to \mathbb{R}$ be a L-Lipschitzian function on $[\delta_1, \delta_2]$; then, we have*

$$\begin{aligned} &\left|\frac{1}{\delta_2-\delta_1}\int_{\delta_1}^{\delta_2}\aleph_\varepsilon(u)du - \frac{\delta_2-\delta_1}{6}\left[\aleph_\varepsilon(\delta_1) + 4\aleph_\varepsilon\left(\frac{\delta_1+\delta_2}{2}\right) + \aleph_\varepsilon(\delta_2)\right]\right| \\ \leq\ & \frac{5}{36}L(\delta_2-\delta_1)^2. \end{aligned}$$

Theorem 5 (Hölder Inequality for Integrals [44])**.** *Let $p > 1$ and $\frac{1}{p} + \frac{1}{q} = 1$. Suppose that $\aleph_\varepsilon, \Phi$ are real functions defined on $[\delta_1, \delta_2]$, and if $|\aleph_\varepsilon|^p, |\Phi|^q$ are integrable on $[\delta_1, \delta_2]$, then the following inequality holds:*

$$\int_{\delta_1}^{\delta_2}|\aleph_\varepsilon(u)\Phi(u)|\,du \leq \left(\int_{\delta_1}^{\delta_2}|\aleph_\varepsilon(u)|^{p}du\right)^{\frac{1}{p}}\left(\int_{\delta_1}^{\delta_2}|\Phi(u)|^{q}\,du\right)^{\frac{1}{q}},$$

with equality holding if, and only if, $A|\aleph_\varepsilon(u)|^p = B|\Phi(u)|^q$ almost everywhere, A and B are constants.

If we get $|\aleph_\varepsilon||\Phi| = \left(|\aleph_\varepsilon|^{\frac{1}{p}}\right)\left(|\xi|^{\frac{1}{q}}|\Phi|\right)$ in the Hölder inequality, then we obtain the following power-mean integral inequality as a simple result of the Hölder inequality:

Theorem 6 (Power Mean Inequality [44])**.** *Let $q \geq 1$. Suppose that $\aleph_\varepsilon, \Phi$ are real-valued functions defined on $[\delta_1, \delta_2]$. If $|\aleph_\varepsilon|$ and $|\aleph_\varepsilon||\Phi|^q$ are integrable on $[\delta_1, \delta_2]$, then the following inequality holds:*

$$\int_{\delta_1}^{\delta_2}|\aleph_\varepsilon(u)\Phi(u)|\,du \leq \left(\int_{\delta_1}^{\delta_2}|\aleph_\varepsilon(u)|\,du\right)^{1-\frac{1}{q}}\left(\int_{\delta_1}^{\delta_2}|\aleph_\varepsilon(u)|\,|\Phi(u)|^{q}\,du\right)^{\frac{1}{q}}.$$

In the second part of this paper, we briefly recall several notions related to classical and fractional derivatives, together with their fundamental properties that will be required in the subsequent analysis. In [45], A. Khan et al. derived several results, including Theorems 7 and 8, for the particular case $\beta_2 = \delta_2$ and $\Im = \delta_1$ with $s = 1$. The primary objective of this study is to establish a comprehensive class of Hermite–Hadamard–Mercer-type inequalities involving both classical and Riemann–Liouville fractional integral operators. The obtained results provide significant generalizations of several well-known inequalities in the literature, encompassing classical Hermite–Hadamard, Mercer, and fractional forms as special cases. In particular, Theorems 13–15 generalizes the classical Mercer-type inequality, which is recovered by setting $\rho = 1$. The paper is organized into two principal sections that present the main contributions of this study. Motivated by the Hermite–Hadamard-type inequalities previously obtained for three-times differentiable convex functions, the primary objective of this work is to establish new Hermite–Hadamard–Mercer-type inequalities for differentiable functions whose powers of the absolute values of their third derivatives are convex. To achieve this objective, Section 2 introduces a new integral identity that serves as a key lemma and constitutes the main analytical tool for deriving the proposed results. Using these identities, several inequalities are established in Theorems 8 and 9 through the application of power–mean inequality and Hölder's inequality. Moreover, for the specific choices of the parameters $\beta_2 = \delta_2$ and $\Im = \delta_1$, additional midpoint-type inequalities are derived and discussed in [45]. Furthermore, some new results regarding Young's inequality, bounded function and L-Lipschitzian function will be obtained. In Section 3, we will explore some applications of our findings to special means, midpoint formula, q-digamma function and the modified Bessel function. This Section 4 also includes two illustrative examples that confirm the validity and effectiveness of the theoretical findings. All figures in this work were produced with Mathematica (version 11.2). Furthermore, the results developed in Section 2 possess a notable degree of generality, as they can be extended to a wide class of integral operators, including k-Riemann–Liouville fractional integrals, conformable fractional integrals, generalized fractional integrals, and post-quantum calculus.

This study is structured as follows: in Section 2, we will introduce two fundamental integral identities as a key lemmas, serving as the main tools for our main results. Theorems 8 and 9 leverage the power-mean and Hölder's inequalities to derive new results pertaining to the class of s-convexity functions. Additionally, for specific values of δ_1 and δ_2, several novel midpoint-type inequalities are presented. Furthermore, some new results regarding Young's inequality, bounded function and L-Lipschitzian function will be obtained. In Section 3, we will explore some applications of our findings to special means, midpoint formula, q-digamma function, and the modified Bessel function. This Section 4 also includes two illustrative examples that confirm the validity of our results. All figures in this work were produced with Mathematica (version 11.2). In Section 5, some conclusions and future research directions for interested readers will be given.

For the reader's convenience, we collect below the notation and standing assumptions used throughout the paper. Let

$$\mathbf{S} := \{\aleph_\varepsilon, I, \delta_1, \delta_2, \Im, \beta_2\},$$

where the symbols are defined as follows:

Symbol	**Description**
$\aleph_\varepsilon$	A real-valued function $\aleph_\varepsilon : I = [\delta_1, \delta_2] \subset \mathbb{R} \to \mathbb{R}$.
I	The closed interval $[\delta_1, \delta_2] \subset \mathbb{R}$.
δ_1, δ_2	Real numbers denoting the endpoints of I, with $\delta_1 < \delta_2$.
(δ_1, δ_2)	The open interval on which $\aleph_\varepsilon$ is three times differentiable.
$\aleph_\varepsilon'''$	The third derivative of $\aleph_\varepsilon$.
$\aleph_\varepsilon''' \in L[\delta_1, \delta_2]$	The third derivative of $\aleph_\varepsilon$ is Lebesgue-integrable on $[\delta_1, \delta_2]$.
$L[\delta_1, \delta_2]$	The space of all Lebesgue-integrable functions on $[\delta_1, \delta_2]$.
$\Im, \beta_2$	Arbitrary points in the interval $[\delta_1, \delta_2]$.
$\mathbb{R}$	A set of real numbers.

2. Main Results

2.1. Hermite–Hadamard–Mercer-Type Inequalities

This section aims to establish a series of Hermite–Hadamard–Mercer-type inequalities for functions where the powers of the absolute values of their third derivatives are s-convexity.

Lemma 2. *Assuming that hypothesis* **S** *is satisfied, then we obtain the following equality:*

$$\begin{aligned}&\frac{1}{\beta_2-\Im}\int_{\delta_1+\delta_2-\beta_2}^{\delta_1+\delta_2-\Im}\aleph_\varepsilon(u)du-\aleph_\varepsilon\left(\delta_1+\delta_2-\frac{\Im+\beta_2}{2}\right)-\frac{(\beta_2-\Im)^2}{24}\aleph''_\varepsilon\left(\delta_1+\delta_2-\frac{\Im+\beta_2}{2}\right) \\ =\;& \frac{(\beta_2-\Im)^3}{96}\int_0^1 \Upsilon^3\left[\aleph'''_\varepsilon\left(\delta_1+\delta_2-\left(\frac{\Upsilon}{2}\beta_2+\frac{2-\Upsilon}{2}\Im\right)\right)-\aleph'''_\varepsilon\left(\delta_1+\delta_2-\left(\frac{\Upsilon}{2}\Im+\frac{2-\Upsilon}{2}\beta_2\right)\right)\right]d\Upsilon.\end{aligned} \tag{6}$$

Proof. By using the integration by parts on the right side of equality (6), we obtain

$$\begin{aligned}
I_1 &= \int_0^1 \Upsilon^3\aleph'''_\varepsilon\left(\delta_1+\delta_2-\left(\frac{\Upsilon}{2}\Im+\frac{2-\Upsilon}{2}\beta_2\right)\right)d\Upsilon \\
&= \left.\frac{2\Upsilon^3\aleph''_\varepsilon\left(\delta_1+\delta_2-\left(\frac{\Upsilon}{2}\Im+\frac{2-\Upsilon}{2}\beta_2\right)\right)}{\beta_2-\Im}\right|_0^1-\frac{6}{\beta_2-\Im}\int_0^1 \Upsilon^2\aleph''_\varepsilon\left(\delta_1+\delta_2-\left(\frac{\Upsilon}{2}\Im+\frac{2-\Upsilon}{2}\beta_2\right)\right)d\Upsilon \\
&= \frac{2}{\beta_2-\Im}\aleph''_\varepsilon\left(\delta_1+\delta_2-\frac{\Im+\beta_2}{2}\right)-\frac{6}{\beta_2-\Im}\left[\left.\frac{2\Upsilon^2\aleph'_\varepsilon\left(\delta_1+\delta_2-\left(\frac{\Upsilon}{2}\Im+\frac{2-\Upsilon}{2}\beta_2\right)\right)}{\beta_2-\Im}\right|_0^1\right. \\
&\quad\left.-\frac{4}{\beta_2-\Im}\int_0^1 \Upsilon\aleph'_\varepsilon\left(\delta_1+\delta_2-\left(\frac{\Upsilon}{2}\Im+\frac{2-\Upsilon}{2}\beta_2\right)\right)d\Upsilon\right] \\
&= \frac{2}{\beta_2-\Im}\aleph''_\varepsilon\left(\delta_1+\delta_2-\frac{\Im+\beta_2}{2}\right)-\frac{12}{(\beta_2-\Im)^2}\aleph'_\varepsilon\left(\delta_1+\delta_2-\frac{\Im+\beta_2}{2}\right) \\
&\quad+\frac{24}{(\beta_2-\Im)^2}\int_0^1 \Upsilon\aleph'_\varepsilon\left(\delta_1+\delta_2-\left(\frac{\Upsilon}{2}\Im+\frac{2-\Upsilon}{2}\beta_2\right)\right)d\Upsilon \\
&= \frac{2}{\beta_2-\Im}\aleph''_\varepsilon\left(\delta_1+\delta_2-\frac{\Im+\beta_2}{2}\right)-\frac{12}{(\beta_2-\Im)^2}\aleph'_\varepsilon\left(\delta_1+\delta_2-\frac{\Im+\beta_2}{2}\right) \\
&\quad+\frac{24}{(\beta_2-\Im)^2}\left[\left.\frac{2\Upsilon\aleph_\varepsilon\left(\delta_1+\delta_2-\left(\frac{\Upsilon}{2}\Im+\frac{2-\Upsilon}{2}\beta_2\right)\right)}{\beta_2-\Im}\right|_0^1\right. \\
&\quad\left.-\frac{2}{(\beta_2-\Im)^2}\int_0^1 \aleph_\varepsilon\left(\delta_1+\delta_2-\left(\frac{\Upsilon}{2}\Im+\frac{2-\Upsilon}{2}\beta_2\right)\right)d\Upsilon\right] \\
&= \frac{2}{\beta_2-\Im}\aleph''_\varepsilon\left(\delta_1+\delta_2-\frac{\Im+\beta_2}{2}\right)-\frac{12}{(\beta_2-\Im)^2}\aleph'_\varepsilon\left(\delta_1+\delta_2-\frac{\Im+\beta_2}{2}\right) \\
&\quad+\frac{48}{(\beta_2-\Im)^3}\aleph_\varepsilon\left(\delta_1+\delta_2-\frac{\Im+\beta_2}{2}\right)-\frac{48}{(\beta_2-\Im)^3}\int_0^1 \aleph_\varepsilon\left(\delta_1+\delta_2-\left(\frac{\Upsilon}{2}\Im+\frac{2-\Upsilon}{2}\beta_2\right)\right)d\Upsilon.
\end{aligned}$$

Put $u=\delta_1+\delta_2-\left(\frac{\Upsilon}{2}\Im+\frac{2-\Upsilon}{2}\beta_2\right)$, then we obtain

$$I_1 = \frac{2}{\beta_2-\Im}\aleph''_\varepsilon\left(\delta_1+\delta_2-\frac{\Im+\beta_2}{2}\right)-\frac{12}{(\beta_2-\Im)^2}\aleph'_\varepsilon\left(\delta_1+\delta_2-\frac{\Im+\beta_2}{2}\right)$$

$$+\frac{48}{(\beta_2-\Im)^3}\aleph_\varepsilon\left(\delta_1+\delta_2-\frac{\Im+\beta_2}{2}\right)-\frac{96}{(\beta_2-\Im)^4}\int_{\delta_1+\delta_2-\beta_2}^{\delta_1+\delta_2-\frac{\Im+\beta_2}{2}}\aleph_\varepsilon(u)du. \quad (7)$$

Similarly, we have

$$\begin{aligned}
I_2 &= \int_0^1 Y^3\aleph_\varepsilon'''\left(\delta_1+\delta_2-\left(\frac{Y}{2}\beta_2+\frac{2-Y}{2}\Im\right)\right)dY \\
&= \left.\frac{-2Y^3\aleph_\varepsilon''\left(\delta_1+\delta_2-\left(\frac{Y}{2}\beta_2+\frac{2-Y}{2}\Im\right)\right)}{\beta_2-\Im}\right|_0^1+\frac{6}{\beta_2-\Im}\int_0^1 Y^2\aleph_\varepsilon''\left(\delta_1+\delta_2-\left(\frac{Y}{2}\beta_2+\frac{2-Y}{2}\Im\right)\right)dY \\
&= \frac{-2}{\beta_2-\Im}\aleph_\varepsilon''\left(\delta_1+\delta_2-\frac{\Im+\beta_2}{2}\right)-\frac{12}{(\beta_2-\Im)^2}\aleph_\varepsilon'\left(\delta_1+\delta_2-\frac{\Im+\beta_2}{2}\right) \\
&\quad+\frac{24}{(\beta_2-\Im)^2}\int_0^1 Y\aleph_\varepsilon'\left(\delta_1+\delta_2-\left(\frac{Y}{2}\beta_2+\frac{2-Y}{2}\Im\right)\right)dY \\
&= \frac{-2}{\beta_2-\Im}\aleph_\varepsilon''\left(\delta_1+\delta_2-\frac{\Im+\beta_2}{2}\right)-\frac{12}{(\beta_2-\Im)^2}\aleph_\varepsilon'\left(\delta_1+\delta_2-\frac{\Im+\beta_2}{2}\right) \\
&\quad-\frac{48}{(\beta_2-\Im)^3}\aleph_\varepsilon\left(\delta_1+\delta_2-\frac{\Im+\beta_2}{2}\right)+\frac{96}{(\beta_2-\Im)^4}\int_{\delta_1+\delta_2-\frac{\Im+\beta_2}{2}}^{\delta_1+\delta_2-\Im}\aleph_\varepsilon(u)du.
\end{aligned} \quad (8)$$

Subtracting the equality (8) from (7) and multiplying the equality with $\frac{(\beta_2-\Im)^3}{96}$, we obtain

$$\begin{aligned}
&\frac{1}{\beta_2-\Im}\int_{\delta_1+\delta_2-\beta_2}^{\delta_1+\delta_2-\Im}\aleph_\varepsilon(u)du-\aleph_\varepsilon\left(\delta_1+\delta_2-\frac{\Im+\beta_2}{2}\right)-\frac{(\beta_2-\Im)^2}{24}\aleph_\varepsilon''\left(\delta_1+\delta_2-\frac{\Im+\beta_2}{2}\right) \\
= &\frac{(\beta_2-\Im)^3}{96}\int_0^1 Y^3\left[\aleph_\varepsilon'''\left(\delta_1+\delta_2-\left(\frac{Y}{2}\Im+\frac{2-Y}{2}\beta_2\right)\right)-\aleph_\varepsilon'''\left(\delta_1+\delta_2-\left(\frac{Y}{2}\beta_2+\frac{2-Y}{2}\Im\right)\right)\right]dY.
\end{aligned}$$

The proof of Lemma 2 has now been established. □

Corollary 1. *Assigning $\beta_2=\delta_2$ and $\Im=\delta_1$ in Lemma 2, we obtain*

$$\begin{aligned}
&\frac{1}{\delta_2-\delta_1}\int_{\delta_1}^{\delta_2}\aleph_\varepsilon(u)du-\aleph_\varepsilon\left(\frac{\delta_1+\delta_2}{2}\right)-\frac{(\delta_2-\delta_1)^2}{24}\aleph_\varepsilon''\left(\frac{\delta_1+\delta_2}{2}\right) \\
= &\frac{(\delta_2-\delta_1)^3}{96}\left[\int_0^1 Y^3\aleph_\varepsilon'''\left(\frac{Y}{2}\delta_1+\frac{2-Y}{2}\delta_2\right)dY-\int_0^1 Y^3\aleph_\varepsilon'''\left(\frac{Y}{2}\delta_2+\frac{2-Y}{2}\delta_1\right)dY\right].
\end{aligned}$$

Corollary 2. *Assigning $\aleph_\varepsilon''\left(\frac{\delta_1+\delta_2}{2}\right)=0$ in Corollary 1, we obtain*

$$\begin{aligned}
&\frac{1}{\delta_2-\delta_1}\int_{\delta_1}^{\delta_2}\aleph_\varepsilon(u)du-\aleph_\varepsilon\left(\frac{\delta_1+\delta_2}{2}\right) \\
= &\frac{(\delta_2-\delta_1)^3}{96}\left[\int_0^1 Y^3\aleph_\varepsilon'''\left(\frac{Y}{2}\delta_1+\frac{2-Y}{2}\delta_2\right)dY-\int_0^1 Y^3\aleph_\varepsilon'''\left(\frac{Y}{2}\delta_2+\frac{2-Y}{2}\delta_1\right)dY\right].
\end{aligned}$$

Theorem 7. *Let $s\in(0,1]$. Provided that hypothesis **S** is satisfied and $|\aleph_\varepsilon'''|$ is s-convex on $[\delta_1,\delta_2]$, then the following Mercer-type inequality holds true:*

$$\begin{aligned}
&\left|\frac{1}{\beta_2-\Im}\int_{\delta_1+\delta_2-\beta_2}^{\delta_1+\delta_2-\Im}\aleph_\varepsilon(u)du-\aleph_\varepsilon\left(\delta_1+\delta_2-\frac{\Im+\beta_2}{2}\right)-\frac{(\beta_2-\Im)^2}{24}\aleph_\varepsilon''\left(\delta_1+\delta_2-\frac{\Im+\beta_2}{2}\right)\right| \\
\leq &\frac{(\beta_2-\Im)^3}{96}\left[\frac{1}{2}(|\aleph_\varepsilon'''(\delta_1)|+|\aleph_\varepsilon'''(\delta_2)|)-\left(\frac{3\times 2^{1-s}(-14+2^{4+s}-7s-s^2)}{(1+s)(2+s)(3+s)(4+s)}\right)(|\aleph_\varepsilon'''(\Im)|+|\aleph_\varepsilon'''(\beta_2)|)\right].
\end{aligned}$$

Proof. By using the Lemma 2, since $|\aleph_{\varepsilon}'''|$ is s-convex, we have

$$\left|\frac{1}{\beta_2-\Im}\int_{\delta_1+\delta_2-\beta_2}^{\delta_1+\delta_2-\Im}\aleph_{\varepsilon}(u)du-\aleph_{\varepsilon}\left(\delta_1+\delta_2-\frac{\Im+\beta_2}{2}\right)-\frac{(\beta_2-\Im)^2}{24}\aleph_{\varepsilon}''\left(\delta_1+\delta_2-\frac{\Im+\beta_2}{2}\right)\right|$$
$$\leq \frac{(\beta_2-\Im)^3}{96}\left[\int_0^1 Y^3\left|\aleph_{\varepsilon}'''\left(\delta_1+\delta_2-\left(\frac{Y}{2}\Im+\frac{2-Y}{2}\beta_2\right)\right)\right|dY\right.$$
$$\left.+\int_0^1 Y^3\left|\aleph_{\varepsilon}'''\left(\delta_1+\delta_2-\left(\frac{Y}{2}\beta_2+\frac{2-Y}{2}\Im\right)\right)\right|dY\right]$$
$$\leq \frac{(\beta_2-\Im)^3}{96}\left[\int_0^1 Y^3\left(|\aleph_{\varepsilon}'''(\delta_1)|+|\aleph_{\varepsilon}'''(\delta_2)|-\left(\left(\frac{Y}{2}\right)^s|\aleph_{\varepsilon}'''(\Im)|+\left(\frac{2-Y}{2}\right)^s|\aleph_{\varepsilon}'''(\beta_2)|\right)\right)dY\right.$$
$$\left.+\int_0^1 Y^3\left(|\aleph_{\varepsilon}'''(\delta_1)|+|\aleph_{\varepsilon}'''(\delta_2)|-\left(\left(\frac{Y}{2}\right)^s|\aleph_{\varepsilon}'''(\beta_2)|+\left(\frac{2-Y}{2}\right)^s|\aleph_{\varepsilon}'''(\Im)|\right)\right)dY\right]$$
$$=\frac{(\beta_2-\Im)^3}{96}\left[\frac{1}{2}(|\aleph_{\varepsilon}'''(\delta_1)|+|\aleph_{\varepsilon}'''(\delta_2)|)-\left(\frac{3\times 2^{1-s}(-14+2^{4+s}-7s-s^2)}{(1+s)(2+s)(3+s)(4+s)}\right)(|\aleph_{\varepsilon}'''(\Im)|+|\aleph_{\varepsilon}'''(\beta_2)|)\right].$$

Accordingly, the assertion of Theorem 7 has been verified. □

Corollary 3. *Taking $s=1$ in Theorem 7, we have*

$$\left|\frac{1}{\beta_2-\Im}\int_{\delta_1+\delta_2-\beta_2}^{\delta_1+\delta_2-\Im}\aleph_{\varepsilon}(u)du-\aleph_{\varepsilon}\left(\delta_1+\delta_2-\frac{\Im+\beta_2}{2}\right)-\frac{(\beta_2-\Im)^2}{24}\aleph_{\varepsilon}''\left(\delta_1+\delta_2-\frac{\Im+\beta_2}{2}\right)\right|$$
$$\leq \frac{(\beta_2-\Im)^3}{96}\left[\frac{1}{2}(|\aleph_{\varepsilon}'''(\delta_1)|+|\aleph_{\varepsilon}'''(\delta_2)|)-\frac{1}{4}(|\aleph_{\varepsilon}'''(\Im)|+|\aleph_{\varepsilon}'''(\beta_2)|)\right].$$

Corollary 4. *Assigning $\beta_2=\delta_2$ and $\Im=\delta_1$ in Corollary 3, we obtain*

$$\left|\frac{1}{\delta_2-\delta_1}\int_{\delta_1}^{\delta_2}\aleph_{\varepsilon}(u)du-\aleph_{\varepsilon}\left(\frac{\delta_1+\delta_2}{2}\right)-\frac{(\delta_2-\delta_1)^2}{24}\aleph_{\varepsilon}''\left(\frac{\delta_1+\delta_2}{2}\right)\right|$$
$$\leq \frac{(\delta_2-\delta_1)^3}{384}[|\aleph_{\varepsilon}'''(\delta_1)|+|\aleph_{\varepsilon}'''(\delta_2)|],$$

which was previously proved by A.Khan et al. [45].

Corollary 5. *Assigning $\aleph_{\varepsilon}''\left(\frac{\delta_1+\delta_2}{2}\right)=0$ in Corollary 4, we obtain*

$$\left|\frac{1}{\delta_2-\delta_1}\int_{\delta_1}^{\delta_2}\aleph_{\varepsilon}(u)du-\aleph_{\varepsilon}\left(\frac{\delta_1+\delta_2}{2}\right)\right|\leq \frac{(\delta_2-\delta_1)^3}{384}[|\aleph_{\varepsilon}'''(\delta_1)|+|\aleph_{\varepsilon}'''(\delta_2)|].$$

Theorem 8. *Let $s\in(0,1]$. Provided that hypothesis* **S** *is satisfied and $|\aleph_{\varepsilon}'''|^q$ is s-convex on $[\delta_1,\delta_2]$ with $\frac{1}{p}+\frac{1}{q}=1$ and $q>1$, then the following Mercer-type inequality holds true:*

$$\left|\frac{1}{\beta_2-\Im}\int_{\delta_1+\delta_2-\beta_2}^{\delta_1+\delta_2-\Im}\aleph_{\varepsilon}(u)du-\aleph_{\varepsilon}\left(\delta_1+\delta_2-\frac{\Im+\beta_2}{2}\right)-\frac{(\beta_2-\Im)^2}{24}\aleph_{\varepsilon}''\left(\delta_1+\delta_2-\frac{\Im+\beta_2}{2}\right)\right|$$
$$\leq \frac{(\beta_2-\Im)^3}{96}\left(\frac{1}{3p+1}\right)^{\frac{1}{p}}\left[\left(|\aleph_{\varepsilon}'''(\delta_1)|^q+|\aleph_{\varepsilon}'''(\delta_2)|^q-\left(\frac{1}{2^s(s+1)}|\aleph_{\varepsilon}'''(\Im)|^q+\frac{2^{s+1}-1}{2^s(s+1)}|\aleph_{\varepsilon}'''(\beta_2)|^q\right)\right)^{\frac{1}{q}}\right.$$
$$\left.+\left(|\aleph_{\varepsilon}'''(\delta_1)|^q+|\aleph_{\varepsilon}'''(\delta_2)|^q-\left(\frac{1}{2^s(s+1)}|\aleph_{\varepsilon}'''(\beta_2)|^q+\frac{2^{s+1}-1}{2^s(s+1)}|\aleph_{\varepsilon}'''(\Im)|^q\right)\right)^{\frac{1}{q}}\right].$$

Proof. Based on Lemma 2, and by employing Hölder's inequality and the s-convexity of $|\aleph_\varepsilon'''|^q$, we obtain

$$\left|\frac{1}{\beta_2-\Im}\int_{\delta_1+\delta_2-\beta_2}^{\delta_1+\delta_2-\Im}\aleph_\varepsilon(u)du-\aleph_\varepsilon\left(\delta_1+\delta_2-\frac{\Im+\beta_2}{2}\right)-\frac{(\beta_2-\Im)^2}{24}\aleph_\varepsilon''\left(\delta_1+\delta_2-\frac{\Im+\beta_2}{2}\right)\right|$$

$$\leq \frac{(\beta_2-\Im)^3}{96}\left(\int_0^1 \Upsilon^{3p}d\Upsilon\right)^{\frac{1}{p}}\left[\left(\int_0^1\left|\aleph_\varepsilon'''\left(\delta_1+\delta_2-\left(\frac{\Upsilon}{2}\Im+\frac{2-\Upsilon}{2}\beta_2\right)\right)\right|^q d\Upsilon\right)^{\frac{1}{q}}\right.$$

$$\left.+\left(\int_0^1\left|\aleph_\varepsilon'''\left(\delta_1+\delta_2-\left(\frac{\Upsilon}{2}\beta_2+\frac{2-\Upsilon}{2}\Im\right)\right)\right|^q d\Upsilon\right)^{\frac{1}{q}}\right]$$

$$\leq \frac{(\beta_2-\Im)^3}{96}\left(\int_0^1 \Upsilon^{3p}d\Upsilon\right)^{\frac{1}{p}}$$

$$\times\left[\left(\int_0^1\left(|\aleph_\varepsilon'''(\delta_1)|^q+|\aleph_\varepsilon'''(\delta_2)|^q-\left(\left(\frac{\Upsilon}{2}\right)^s|\aleph_\varepsilon'''(\Im)|^q+\left(\frac{2-\Upsilon}{2}\right)^s|\aleph_\varepsilon'''(\beta_2)|^q\right)\right)d\Upsilon\right)^{\frac{1}{q}}\right.$$

$$\left.+\left(\int_0^1\left(|\aleph_\varepsilon'''(\delta_1)|^q+|\aleph_\varepsilon'''(\delta_2)|^q-\left(\left(\frac{\Upsilon}{2}\right)^s|\aleph_\varepsilon'''(\beta_2)|^q+\left(\frac{2-\Upsilon}{2}\right)^s|\aleph_\varepsilon'''(\Im)|^q\right)\right)d\Upsilon\right)^{\frac{1}{q}}\right]$$

$$=\frac{(\beta_2-\Im)^3}{96}\left(\frac{1}{3p+1}\right)^{\frac{1}{p}}\left[\left(|\aleph_\varepsilon'''(\delta_1)|^q+|\aleph_\varepsilon'''(\delta_2)|^q-\left(\frac{1}{2^s(s+1)}|\aleph_\varepsilon'''(\Im)|^q+\frac{2^{s+1}-1}{2^s(s+1)}|\aleph_\varepsilon'''(\beta_2)|^q\right)\right)^{\frac{1}{q}}\right.$$

$$\left.+\left(|\aleph_\varepsilon'''(\delta_1)|^q+|\aleph_\varepsilon'''(\delta_2)|^q-\left(\frac{1}{2^s(s+1)}|\aleph_\varepsilon'''(\beta_2)|^q+\frac{2^{s+1}-1}{2^s(s+1)}|\aleph_\varepsilon'''(\Im)|^q\right)\right)^{\frac{1}{q}}\right].$$

Accordingly, the assertion of Theorem 8 has been verified. □

Corollary 6. *Taking $s=1$ in Theorem 8, we have*

$$\left|\frac{1}{\beta_2-\Im}\int_{\delta_1+\delta_2-\beta_2}^{\delta_1+\delta_2-\Im}\aleph_\varepsilon(u)du-\aleph_\varepsilon\left(\delta_1+\delta_2-\frac{\Im+\beta_2}{2}\right)-\frac{(\beta_2-\Im)^2}{24}\aleph_\varepsilon''\left(\delta_1+\delta_2-\frac{\Im+\beta_2}{2}\right)\right|$$

$$\leq \frac{(\beta_2-\Im)^3}{96}\left(\frac{1}{3p+1}\right)^{\frac{1}{p}}\left[\left(|\aleph_\varepsilon'''(\delta_1)|^q+|\aleph_\varepsilon'''(\delta_2)|^q-\left(\frac{1}{4}|\aleph_\varepsilon'''(\Im)|^q+\frac{3}{4}|\aleph_\varepsilon'''(\beta_2)|^q\right)\right)^{\frac{1}{q}}\right.$$

$$\left.+\left(|\aleph_\varepsilon'''(\delta_1)|^q+|\aleph_\varepsilon'''(\delta_2)|^q-\left(\frac{1}{4}|\aleph_\varepsilon'''(\beta_2)|+\frac{3}{4}|\aleph_\varepsilon'''(\Im)|\right)\right)^{\frac{1}{q}}\right].$$

Corollary 7. *Assigning $\beta_2=\delta_2$ and $\Im=\delta_1$ in Corollary 6, we obtain*

$$\left|\frac{1}{\delta_2-\delta_1}\int_{\delta_1}^{\delta_2}\aleph_\varepsilon(u)du-\aleph_\varepsilon\left(\frac{\delta_1+\delta_2}{2}\right)-\frac{(\delta_2-\delta_1)^2}{24}\aleph_\varepsilon''\left(\frac{\delta_1+\delta_2}{2}\right)\right|$$

$$\leq \frac{(\delta_2-\delta_1)^3}{384}\left(\frac{1}{3p+1}\right)^{\frac{1}{p}}\left[\left(\frac{3|\aleph_\varepsilon'''(\delta_1)|^q+|\aleph_\varepsilon'''(\delta_2)|^q}{4}\right)^{\frac{1}{q}}+\left(\frac{|\aleph_\varepsilon'''(\delta_1)|^q+3|\aleph_\varepsilon'''(\delta_2)|^q}{4}\right)^{\frac{1}{q}}\right].$$

Theorem 9. *Let $q\geq 1$ and $s\in(0,1]$. Under hypothesis* **S**, *assuming that $|\aleph_\varepsilon'''|^q$ is s-convex on $[\delta_1,\delta_2]$, then the following Mercer-type inequality holds true:*

$$\left|\frac{1}{\beta_2-\Im}\int_{\delta_1+\delta_2-\beta_2}^{\delta_1+\delta_2-\Im}\aleph_\varepsilon(u)du-\aleph_\varepsilon\left(\delta_1+\delta_2-\frac{\Im+\beta_2}{2}\right)-\frac{(\beta_2-\Im)^2}{24}\aleph_\varepsilon''\left(\delta_1+\delta_2-\frac{\Im+\beta_2}{2}\right)\right|$$

$$\leq \frac{(\beta_2-\Im)^3}{96}\left(\frac{1}{4}\right)^{1-\frac{1}{q}}\left[\left(\frac{1}{4}\left(|\aleph_\varepsilon'''(\delta_1)|^q+|\aleph_\varepsilon'''(\delta_2)|^q\right)\right.\right.$$

$$-\left(\frac{1}{2^s(s+4)}|\aleph_\varepsilon'''(\Im)|^q+\frac{2^{-s}(3\times 2^{5+s}-53s-12s^2-s^3-90)}{(s+1)(s+2)(s+3)(s+4)}|\aleph_\varepsilon'''(\beta_2)|^q\right)\Bigg)^{\frac{1}{q}}$$

$$+\Bigg(\frac{1}{4}\left(|\aleph_\varepsilon'''(\delta_1)|^q+|\aleph_\varepsilon'''(\delta_2)|^q\right)$$

$$-\left(\frac{1}{2^s(s+4)}|\aleph_\varepsilon'''(\beta_2)|^q+\frac{2^{-s}(3\times 2^{5+s}-53s-12s^2-s^3-90)}{(s+1)(s+2)(s+3)(s+4)}|\aleph_\varepsilon'''(\Im)|^q\right)\Bigg)^{\frac{1}{q}}\Bigg].$$

Proof. Based on Lemma 2, and by employing power-mean inequality and the s-convexity of $|\aleph_\varepsilon'''|^q$, we obtain

$$\left|\frac{1}{\beta_2-\Im}\int_{\delta_1+\delta_2-\beta_2}^{\delta_1+\delta_2-\Im}\aleph_\varepsilon(u)du-\aleph_\varepsilon\left(\delta_1+\delta_2-\frac{\Im+\beta_2}{2}\right)-\frac{(\beta_2-\Im)^2}{24}\aleph_\varepsilon''\left(\delta_1+\delta_2-\frac{\Im+\beta_2}{2}\right)\right|$$

$$\leq \frac{(\beta_2-\Im)^3}{96}\left(\int_0^1 Y^3dY\right)^{1-\frac{1}{q}}\Bigg[\left(\int_0^1 Y^3\left|\aleph_\varepsilon'''\left(\delta_1+\delta_2-\left(\frac{Y}{2}\Im+\frac{2-Y}{2}\beta_2\right)\right)\right|^q dY\right)^{\frac{1}{q}}$$

$$+\left(\int_0^1 Y^3\left|\aleph_\varepsilon'''\left(\delta_1+\delta_2-\left(\frac{Y}{2}\beta_2+\frac{2-Y}{2}\Im\right)\right)\right|^q dY\right)^{\frac{1}{q}}\Bigg]$$

$$\leq \frac{(\beta_2-\Im)^3}{96}\left(\int_0^1 Y^3dY\right)^{1-\frac{1}{q}}$$

$$\times\Bigg[\left(\int_0^1 Y^3\left(|\aleph_\varepsilon'''(\delta_1)|^q+|\aleph_\varepsilon'''(\delta_2)|^q-\left(\left(\frac{Y}{2}\right)^s|\aleph_\varepsilon'''(\Im)|^q+\left(\frac{2-Y}{2}\right)^s|\aleph_\varepsilon'''(\beta_2)|^q\right)\right)dY\right)^{\frac{1}{q}}$$

$$+\left(\int_0^1 Y^3\left(|\aleph_\varepsilon'''(\delta_1)|^q+|\aleph_\varepsilon'''(\delta_2)|^q-\left(\left(\frac{Y}{2}\right)^s|\aleph_\varepsilon'''(\beta_2)|^q+\left(\frac{2-Y}{2}\right)^s|\aleph_\varepsilon'''(\Im)|^q\right)\right)dY\right)^{\frac{1}{q}}\Bigg]$$

$$= \frac{(\beta_2-\Im)^3}{96}\left(\frac{1}{4}\right)^{1-\frac{1}{q}}\Bigg[\Bigg(\frac{1}{4}\left(|\aleph_\varepsilon'''(\delta_1)|^q+|\aleph_\varepsilon'''(\delta_2)|^q\right)$$

$$-\left(\frac{1}{2^s(s+4)}|\aleph_\varepsilon'''(\Im)|^q+\frac{2^{-s}(3\times 2^{5+s}-53s-12s^2-s^3-90)}{(s+1)(s+2)(s+3)(s+4)}|\aleph_\varepsilon'''(\beta_2)|^q\right)\Bigg)^{\frac{1}{q}}$$

$$+\Bigg(\frac{1}{4}\left(|\aleph_\varepsilon'''(\delta_1)|^q+|\aleph_\varepsilon'''(\delta_2)|^q\right)$$

$$-\left(\frac{1}{2^s(s+4)}|\aleph_\varepsilon'''(\beta_2)|^q+\frac{2^{-s}(3\times 2^{5+s}-53s-12s^2-s^3-90)}{(s+1)(s+2)(s+3)(s+4)}|\aleph_\varepsilon'''(\Im)|^q\right)\Bigg)^{\frac{1}{q}}\Bigg].$$

The proof of Theorem 9 has been successfully concluded. □

Corollary 8. *Taking $s=1$ in Theorem 9, we have*

$$\left|\frac{1}{\beta_2-\Im}\int_{\delta_1+\delta_2-\beta_2}^{\delta_1+\delta_2-\Im}\aleph_\varepsilon(u)du-\aleph_\varepsilon\left(\delta_1+\delta_2-\frac{\Im+\beta_2}{2}\right)-\frac{(\beta_2-\Im)^2}{24}\aleph_\varepsilon''\left(\delta_1+\delta_2-\frac{\Im+\beta_2}{2}\right)\right|$$

$$\leq \frac{(\beta_2-\Im)^3}{96}\left(\frac{1}{4}\right)^{1-\frac{1}{q}}\Bigg[\left(\frac{1}{4}\left(|\aleph_\varepsilon'''(\delta_1)|^q+|\aleph_\varepsilon'''(\delta_2)|^q\right)-\left(\frac{2|\aleph_\varepsilon'''(\Im)|^q+3|\aleph_\varepsilon'''(\beta_2)|^q}{20}\right)\right)^{\frac{1}{q}}$$

$$+\left(\frac{1}{4}\left(|\aleph_\varepsilon'''(\delta_1)|^q+|\aleph_\varepsilon'''(\delta_2)|^q\right)-\left(\frac{3|\aleph_\varepsilon'''(\Im)|^q+2|\aleph_\varepsilon'''(\beta_2)|^q}{20}\right)\right)^{\frac{1}{q}}\Bigg].$$

Corollary 9. *Assigning $\beta_2 = \delta_2$ and $\Im = \delta_1$ in Corollary 8, we obtain*

$$\begin{aligned}&\left|\frac{1}{\delta_2-\delta_1}\int_{\delta_1}^{\delta_2}\aleph_\varepsilon(u)du-\aleph_\varepsilon\left(\frac{\delta_1+\delta_2}{2}\right)-\frac{(\delta_2-\delta_1)^2}{24}\aleph_\varepsilon''\left(\frac{\delta_1+\delta_2}{2}\right)\right|\\ \le\;&\frac{(\delta_2-\delta_1)^3}{384}\left[\left(\frac{3|\aleph_\varepsilon'''(\delta_1)|^q+2|\aleph_\varepsilon'''(\delta_2)|^q}{5}\right)^{\frac{1}{q}}+\left(\frac{2|\aleph_\varepsilon'''(\delta_1)|^q+3|\aleph_\varepsilon'''(\delta_2)|^q}{5}\right)^{\frac{1}{q}}\right].\end{aligned}$$

Theorem 10. *Let $s \in (0,1]$. Provided that hypothesis **S** is satisfied and $|\aleph_\varepsilon'''|^q$ is s-convex on $[\delta_1, \delta_2]$ with $\frac{1}{p}+\frac{1}{q}=1$ and $q>1$, then the following Mercer's type inequality holds true:*

$$\begin{aligned}&\left|\frac{1}{\beta_2-\Im}\int_{\delta_1+\delta_2-\beta_2}^{\delta_1+\delta_2-\Im}\aleph_\varepsilon(u)du-\aleph_\varepsilon\left(\delta_1+\delta_2-\frac{\Im+\beta_2}{2}\right)-\frac{(\beta_2-\Im)^2}{24}\aleph_\varepsilon''\left(\delta_1+\delta_2-\frac{\Im+\beta_2}{2}\right)\right|\\ \le\;&\frac{(\beta_2-\Im)^3}{96}\left(\frac{1}{p(3p+1)}\right)\\ &\times\frac{1}{q}\left[\left(|\aleph_\varepsilon'''(\delta_1)|^q+|\aleph_\varepsilon'''(\delta_2)|^q\right)-\left(\frac{3\times 2^{1-s}(-14+2^{4+s}-7s-s^2)}{(1+s)(2+s)(3+s)(4+s)}\right)\left(|\aleph_\varepsilon'''(\Im)|^q+|\aleph_\varepsilon'''(\beta_2)|^q\right)\right].\end{aligned}$$

Proof. Using Lemma 2, s-convexity of $|\aleph_\varepsilon'''|^q$, we have

$$\begin{aligned}&\left|\frac{1}{\beta_2-\Im}\int_{\delta_1+\delta_2-\beta_2}^{\delta_1+\delta_2-\Im}\aleph_\varepsilon(u)du-\aleph_\varepsilon\left(\delta_1+\delta_2-\frac{\Im+\beta_2}{2}\right)-\frac{(\beta_2-\Im)^2}{24}\aleph_\varepsilon''\left(\delta_1+\delta_2-\frac{\Im+\beta_2}{2}\right)\right|\\ \le\;&\frac{(\beta_2-\Im)^3}{96}\left[\int_0^1 \mathrm{Y}^3\left|\aleph_\varepsilon'''\left(\delta_1+\delta_2-\left(\frac{\mathrm{Y}}{2}\Im+\frac{2-\mathrm{Y}}{2}\beta_2\right)\right)\right|d\mathrm{Y}\right.\\ &\left.+\int_0^1 \mathrm{Y}^3\left|\aleph_\varepsilon'''\left(\delta_1+\delta_2-\left(\frac{\mathrm{Y}}{2}\beta_2+\frac{2-\mathrm{Y}}{2}\Im\right)\right)\right|d\mathrm{Y}\right].\end{aligned}$$

Applying the following Young's inequality:

$$\delta_1\delta_2 \le \frac{1}{p}\delta_1^p+\frac{1}{q}\delta_2^q,$$

we derive that

$$\begin{aligned}&\left|\frac{1}{\beta_2-\Im}\int_{\delta_1+\delta_2-\beta_2}^{\delta_1+\delta_2-\Im}\aleph_\varepsilon(u)du-\aleph_\varepsilon\left(\delta_1+\delta_2-\frac{\Im+\beta_2}{2}\right)-\frac{(\beta_2-\Im)^2}{24}\aleph_\varepsilon''\left(\delta_1+\delta_2-\frac{\Im+\beta_2}{2}\right)\right|\\ \le\;&\frac{(\beta_2-\Im)^3}{96}\left[\frac{1}{p}\left(\int_0^1 \mathrm{Y}^{3p}\right)d\mathrm{Y}+\frac{1}{q}\int_0^1\left|\aleph_\varepsilon'''\left(\delta_1+\delta_2-\left(\left(\frac{\mathrm{Y}}{2}\right)^s\Im+\left(\frac{2-\mathrm{Y}}{2}\right)^s\beta_2\right)\right)\right|^q d\mathrm{Y}\right.\\ &\left.+\frac{1}{p}\left(\int_0^1 \mathrm{Y}^{3p}\right)d\mathrm{Y}+\frac{1}{q}\int_0^1\left|\aleph_\varepsilon'''\left(\delta_1+\delta_2-\left(\left(\frac{\mathrm{Y}}{2}\right)^s\beta_2+\left(\frac{2-\mathrm{Y}}{2}\right)^s\Im\right)\right)\right|^q d\mathrm{Y}\right]\\ \le\;&\frac{(\beta_2-\Im)^3}{96}\left(\frac{1}{p}\int_0^1 \mathrm{Y}^{3p}d\mathrm{Y}\right)\\ &\times\left[\left(\frac{1}{q}\int_0^1\left(|\aleph_\varepsilon'''(\delta_1)|^q+|\aleph_\varepsilon'''(\delta_2)|^q-\left(\left(\frac{\mathrm{Y}}{2}\right)^s|\aleph_\varepsilon'''(\Im)|^q+\left(\frac{2-\mathrm{Y}}{2}\right)^s|\aleph_\varepsilon'''(\beta_2)|^q\right)\right)d\mathrm{Y}\right)\right.\\ &\left.+\left(\frac{1}{q}\int_0^1\left(|\aleph_\varepsilon'''(\delta_1)|^q+|\aleph_\varepsilon'''(\delta_2)|^q-\left(\left(\frac{\mathrm{Y}}{2}\right)^s|\aleph_\varepsilon'''(\beta_2)|^q+\left(\frac{2-\mathrm{Y}}{2}\right)^s|\aleph_\varepsilon'''(\Im)|^q\right)\right)d\mathrm{Y}\right)\right]\\ =\;&\frac{(\beta_2-\Im)^3}{96}\left(\frac{1}{p(3p+1)}\right)\left[\left(\frac{1}{q}\left(|\aleph_\varepsilon'''(\delta_1)|^q+|\aleph_\varepsilon'''(\delta_2)|^q\right)\right.\right.\end{aligned}$$

$$-\frac{1}{q}\left(\frac{1}{2^s(s+4)}|\aleph_\varepsilon'''(\Im)|^q+\frac{2^{-s}(3\times 2^{5+s}-53s-12s^2-s^3-90)}{(s+1)(s+2)(s+3)(s+4)}|\aleph_\varepsilon'''(\beta_2)|^q\right)\Bigg)$$

$$+\left(\frac{1}{q}\left(|\aleph_\varepsilon'''(\delta_1)|^q+|\aleph_\varepsilon'''(\delta_2)|^q\right)\right.$$

$$\left.\left.-\frac{1}{q}\left(\frac{1}{2^s(s+4)}|\aleph_\varepsilon'''(\beta_2)|^q+\frac{2^{-s}(3\times 2^{5+s}-53s-12s^2-s^3-90)}{(s+1)(s+2)(s+3)(s+4)}|\aleph_\varepsilon'''(\Im)|^q\right)\right)\right]$$

$$=\frac{(\beta_2-\Im)^3}{96}\left(\frac{1}{p(3p+1)}\right)\frac{1}{q}\times$$

$$\left[\left(|\aleph_\varepsilon'''(\delta_1)|^q+|\aleph_\varepsilon'''(\delta_2)|^q\right)-\left(\frac{3\times 2^{1-s}(-14+2^{4+s}-7s-s^2)}{(1+s)(2+s)(3+s)(4+s)}\right)\left(|\aleph_\varepsilon'''(\Im)|^q+|\aleph_\varepsilon'''(\beta_2)|^q\right)\right].$$

The proof of Theorem 10 has been successfully concluded. □

Theorem 11. *Provided that hypothesis* **S** *is satisfied. If there exist constant $-\infty<d<D<\infty$ such that $d\le\aleph_\varepsilon'''(\Upsilon)\le D$ for all $\Upsilon\in[\delta_1,\delta_2]$, then the following Mercer-type inequality holds true:*

$$\left|\frac{1}{\beta_2-\Im}\int_{\delta_1+\delta_2-\beta_2}^{\delta_1+\delta_2-\Im}\aleph_\varepsilon(u)du-\aleph_\varepsilon\left(\delta_1+\delta_2-\frac{\Im+\beta_2}{2}\right)-\frac{(\beta_2-\Im)^2}{24}\aleph_\varepsilon''\left(\delta_1+\delta_2-\frac{\Im+\beta_2}{2}\right)\right|$$

$$\le\frac{(\beta_2-\Im)^3(D-d)}{384}.$$

Proof. Given that $\aleph_\varepsilon'''(\Upsilon)$ is a bounded function, it follows that

$$d-\frac{d+D}{2}\le\aleph_\varepsilon'''(\Upsilon)-\frac{d+D}{2}\le D-\frac{d+D}{2}.$$

Hence, we obtain

$$\left|\aleph_\varepsilon'''(\Upsilon)-\frac{d+D}{2}\right|\le\frac{D-d}{2}. \tag{9}$$

By applying the modulus property to Lemma 2 and subsequently using the observation (9), we obtain

$$\left|\frac{1}{\beta_2-\Im}\int_{\delta_1+\delta_2-\beta_2}^{\delta_1+\delta_2-\Im}\aleph_\varepsilon(u)du-\aleph_\varepsilon\left(\delta_1+\delta_2-\frac{\Im+\beta_2}{2}\right)-\frac{(\beta_2-\Im)^2}{24}\aleph_\varepsilon''\left(\delta_1+\delta_2-\frac{\Im+\beta_2}{2}\right)\right|$$

$$\le\frac{(\beta_2-\Im)^3}{96}\left[\int_0^1\Upsilon^3\left|\aleph_\varepsilon'''\left(\delta_1+\delta_2-\left(\frac{\Upsilon}{2}\Im+\frac{2-\Upsilon}{2}\beta_2\right)\right)-\frac{d+D}{2}\right|d\Upsilon\right.$$

$$\left.+\int_0^1\Upsilon^3\left|\aleph_\varepsilon'''\left(\delta_1+\delta_2-\left(\frac{\Upsilon}{2}\beta_2+\frac{2-\Upsilon}{2}\Im\right)\right)-\frac{d+D}{2}\right|d\Upsilon\right].$$

From $d\le\aleph_\varepsilon'''(\Upsilon)\le D$ for all $\Upsilon\in[\delta_1,\delta_2]$, we obtain

$$\left|\aleph_\varepsilon'''\left(\delta_1+\delta_2-\left(\frac{\Upsilon}{2}\Im+\frac{2-\Upsilon}{2}\beta_2\right)\right)-\frac{d+D}{2}\right|\le\frac{D-d}{2}, \tag{10}$$

and

$$\left|\aleph_\varepsilon'''\left(\delta_1+\delta_2-\left(\frac{\Upsilon}{2}\beta_2+\frac{2-\Upsilon}{2}\Im\right)\right)-\frac{d+D}{2}\right|\le\frac{D-d}{2}. \tag{11}$$

By combining the relations given in (10) and (11), we obtain the following result:

$$\left|\frac{1}{\beta_2-\Im}\int_{\delta_1+\delta_2-\beta_2}^{\delta_1+\delta_2-\Im}\aleph_\varepsilon(u)du-\aleph_\varepsilon\left(\delta_1+\delta_2-\frac{\Im+\beta_2}{2}\right)-\frac{(\beta_2-\Im)^2}{24}\aleph_\varepsilon''\left(\delta_1+\delta_2-\frac{\Im+\beta_2}{2}\right)\right|$$

$$\leq \frac{(\beta_2-\Im)^3(D-d)}{96}\left[\int_0^1 \Upsilon^3 d\Upsilon\right]$$
$$= \frac{(\beta_2-\Im)^3(D-d)}{384}.$$

The proof of Theorem 11 has been completed. □

Theorem 12. *Provided that hypothesis* **S** *is satisfied, and if $|\aleph_\varepsilon'''|$ is a L-Lipschitzian function on $[\delta_1,\delta_2]$, then the following Mercer's type inequality holds true:*

$$\left|\frac{1}{\beta_2-\Im}\int_{\delta_1+\delta_2-\beta_2}^{\delta_1+\delta_2-\Im}\aleph_\varepsilon(u)du-\aleph_\varepsilon\left(\delta_1+\delta_2-\frac{\Im+\beta_2}{2}\right)-\frac{(\beta_2-\Im)^2}{24}\aleph_\varepsilon''\left(\delta_1+\delta_2-\frac{\Im+\beta_2}{2}\right)\right|$$
$$\leq \frac{(\beta_2-\Im)^4L}{384}.$$

Proof. By using the Lemma 2 and the fact that $|\aleph_\varepsilon'''|$ is L-Lipschitzian function, we have

$$\left|\frac{1}{\beta_2-\Im}\int_{\delta_1+\delta_2-\beta_2}^{\delta_1+\delta_2-\Im}\aleph_\varepsilon(u)du-\aleph_\varepsilon\left(\delta_1+\delta_2-\frac{\Im+\beta_2}{2}\right)-\frac{(\beta_2-\Im)^2}{24}\aleph_\varepsilon''\left(\delta_1+\delta_2-\frac{\Im+\beta_2}{2}\right)\right|$$
$$\leq \frac{(\beta_2-\Im)^3}{96}\left[\int_0^1 \Upsilon^3\left|\aleph_\varepsilon'''\left(\delta_1+\delta_2-\left(\frac{\Upsilon}{2}\Im+\frac{2-\Upsilon}{2}\beta_2\right)\right)\right|d\Upsilon\right.$$
$$\left.+\int_0^1 \Upsilon^3\left|\aleph_\varepsilon'''\left(\delta_1+\delta_2-\left(\frac{\Upsilon}{2}\beta_2+\frac{2-\Upsilon}{2}\Im\right)\right)\right|d\Upsilon\right]$$
$$\leq \frac{(\beta_2-\Im)^3}{96}\left[\int_0^1 \Upsilon^4 L(\beta_2-\Im)d\Upsilon+\int_0^1 \Upsilon^3(1-\Upsilon)L(\beta_2-\Im)d\Upsilon\right]$$
$$= \frac{(\beta_2-\Im)^4L}{384}.$$

This completes the proof of Theorem 12. □

Corollary 10. *Assigning $\beta_2=\delta_2$ and $\Im=\delta_1$ in Theorem 12, we obtain*

$$\left|\frac{1}{\delta_2-\delta_1}\int_{\delta_1}^{\delta_2}\aleph_\varepsilon(u)du-\aleph_\varepsilon\left(\frac{\delta_1+\delta_2}{2}\right)-\frac{(\delta_2-\delta_1)^2}{24}\aleph_\varepsilon''\left(\frac{\delta_1+\delta_2}{2}\right)\right|$$
$$\leq \frac{(\delta_2-\delta_1)^4L}{384}.$$

2.2. Fractional Hermite–Hadamard–Mercer-Type Inequalities

The following is a similar integral identity involving Riemann–Liouville fractional integrals, which serves as a crucial foundation for deriving the subsequent results in the context of three-times differentiable functions.

Lemma 3. *Provided that hypothesis* **S** *is satisfied, then the following fractional equality holds true:*

$$\frac{2^{\rho-1}\Gamma(\rho+1)}{(\beta_2-\Im)^\rho}\left[J^\rho_{\left(\delta_1+\delta_2-\frac{\Im+\beta_2}{2}\right)^-}\aleph_\varepsilon(\delta_1+\delta_2-\beta_2)+J^\rho_{\left(\delta_1+\delta_2-\frac{\Im+\beta_2}{2}\right)^+}\aleph_\varepsilon(\delta_1+\delta_2-\Im)\right]$$
$$-\aleph_\varepsilon\left(\delta_1+\delta_2-\frac{\Im+\beta_2}{2}\right)-\frac{(\beta_2-\Im)^2}{4(\rho+1)(\rho+2)}\aleph_\varepsilon''\left(\delta_1+\delta_2-\frac{\Im+\beta_2}{2}\right)$$

$$= \frac{(\beta_2-\Im)^3}{16(\rho+1)(\rho+2)}\left[\int_0^1 \Upsilon^{\rho+2}\aleph_\varepsilon'''\left(\delta_1+\delta_2-\left(\frac{\Upsilon}{2}\beta_2+\frac{2-\Upsilon}{2}\Im\right)\right)d\Upsilon \right.$$
$$\left. -\int_0^1 \Upsilon^{\rho+2}\aleph_\varepsilon'''\left(\delta_1+\delta_2-\left(\frac{\Upsilon}{2}\Im+\frac{2-\Upsilon}{2}\beta_2\right)\right)d\Upsilon\right], \quad (12)$$

for all $\rho>0$ and $\Im,\beta_2\in[\delta_1,\delta_2]$, with $\Upsilon\in[0,1]$.

Proof. By using the integration by parts on the right side of equality (12), we obtain

$$\begin{aligned}
I_1 &= \int_0^1 \Upsilon^{\rho+2}\aleph_\varepsilon'''\left(\delta_1+\delta_2-\left(\frac{\Upsilon}{2}\Im+\frac{2-\Upsilon}{2}\beta_2\right)\right)d\Upsilon \\
&= \frac{2\Upsilon^{\rho+2}\aleph_\varepsilon''\left(\delta_1+\delta_2-\left(\frac{\Upsilon}{2}\Im+\frac{2-\Upsilon}{2}\beta_2\right)\right)}{\beta_2-\Im}\Bigg|_0^1 - \frac{2(\rho+2)}{\beta_2-\Im}\int_0^1 \Upsilon^{\rho+1}\aleph_\varepsilon''\left(\delta_1+\delta_2-\left(\frac{\Upsilon}{2}\Im+\frac{2-\Upsilon}{2}\beta_2\right)\right)d\Upsilon \\
&= \frac{2}{\beta_2-\Im}\aleph_\varepsilon''\left(\delta_1+\delta_2-\frac{\Im+\beta_2}{2}\right) - \frac{4(\rho+2)}{(\beta_2-\Im)^2}\aleph_\varepsilon'\left(\delta_1+\delta_2-\frac{\Im+\beta_2}{2}\right) \\
&\quad + \frac{4(\rho+1)(\rho+2)}{(\beta_2-\Im)^2}\int_0^1 \Upsilon^{\rho}\aleph_\varepsilon'\left(\delta_1+\delta_2-\left(\frac{\Upsilon}{2}\Im+\frac{2-\Upsilon}{2}\beta_2\right)\right)d\Upsilon \\
&= \frac{2}{\beta_2-\Im}\aleph_\varepsilon''\left(\delta_1+\delta_2-\frac{\Im+\beta_2}{2}\right) - \frac{4(\rho+2)}{(\beta_2-\Im)^2}\aleph_\varepsilon'\left(\delta_1+\delta_2-\frac{\Im+\beta_2}{2}\right) + \frac{8(\rho+1)(\rho+2)}{(\beta_2-\Im)^3} \\
&\quad \aleph_\varepsilon\left(\delta_1+\delta_2-\frac{\Im+\beta_2}{2}\right) - \frac{8(\rho+1)(\rho+2)}{(\beta_2-\Im)^2}\int_0^1 \Upsilon^{\rho-1}\aleph_\varepsilon'\left(\delta_1+\delta_2-\left(\frac{\Upsilon}{2}\Im+\frac{2-\Upsilon}{2}\beta_2\right)\right)d\Upsilon \\
&= \frac{2}{\beta_2-\Im}\aleph_\varepsilon''\left(\delta_1+\delta_2-\frac{\Im+\beta_2}{2}\right) - \frac{4(\rho+2)}{(\beta_2-\Im)^2}\aleph_\varepsilon'\left(\delta_1+\delta_2-\frac{\Im+\beta_2}{2}\right) \\
&\quad + \frac{8(\rho+1)(\rho+2)}{(\beta_2-\Im)^3}\aleph_\varepsilon\left(\delta_1+\delta_2-\frac{\Im+\beta_2}{2}\right) - \frac{2^{\rho+3}(\rho+1)(\rho+2)}{(\beta_2-\Im)^{\rho+3}} J^{\rho}_{\left(\delta_1+\delta_2-\frac{\Im+\beta_2}{2}\right)^-}\aleph_\varepsilon(\delta_1+\delta_2-\beta_2). \quad (13)
\end{aligned}$$

Similarly, we have

$$\begin{aligned}
I_2 &= \int_0^1 \Upsilon^{\rho+2}\aleph_\varepsilon'''\left(\delta_1+\delta_2-\left(\frac{\Upsilon}{2}\beta_2+\frac{2-\Upsilon}{2}\Im\right)\right)d\Upsilon \\
&= \frac{-2\Upsilon^{\rho+2}\aleph_\varepsilon''\left(\delta_1+\delta_2-\left(\frac{\Upsilon}{2}\beta_2+\frac{2-\Upsilon}{2}\Im\right)\right)}{\beta_2-\Im}\Bigg|_0^1 + \frac{2(\rho+2)}{\beta_2-\Im}\int_0^1 \Upsilon^{\rho+1}\aleph_\varepsilon''\left(\delta_1+\delta_2-\left(\frac{\Upsilon}{2}\beta_2+\frac{2-\Upsilon}{2}\Im\right)\right)d\Upsilon \\
&= \frac{-2}{\beta_2-\Im}\aleph_\varepsilon''\left(\delta_1+\delta_2-\frac{\Im+\beta_2}{2}\right) - \frac{4(\rho+2)}{(\beta_2-\Im)^2}\aleph_\varepsilon'\left(\delta_1+\delta_2-\frac{\Im+\beta_2}{2}\right) \\
&\quad - \frac{4(\rho+1)(\rho+2)}{(\beta_2-\Im)^2}\int_0^1 \Upsilon^{\rho}\aleph_\varepsilon'\left(\delta_1+\delta_2-\left(\frac{\Upsilon}{2}\beta_2+\frac{2-\Upsilon}{2}\Im\right)\right)d\Upsilon \\
&= \frac{-2}{\beta_2-\Im}\aleph_\varepsilon''\left(\delta_1+\delta_2-\frac{\Im+\beta_2}{2}\right) - \frac{4(\rho+2)}{(\beta_2-\Im)^2}\aleph_\varepsilon'\left(\delta_1+\delta_2-\frac{\Im+\beta_2}{2}\right) - \frac{8(\rho+1)(\rho+2)}{(\beta_2-\Im)^3} \\
&\quad \aleph_\varepsilon\left(\delta_1+\delta_2-\frac{\Im+\beta_2}{2}\right) + \frac{8(\rho+1)(\rho+2)}{(\beta_2-\Im)^2}\int_0^1 \Upsilon^{\rho-1}\aleph_\varepsilon'\left(\delta_1+\delta_2-\left(\frac{\Upsilon}{2}\Im+\frac{2-\Upsilon}{2}\beta_2\right)\right)d\Upsilon \\
&= \frac{-2}{\beta_2-\Im}\aleph_\varepsilon''\left(\delta_1+\delta_2-\frac{\Im+\beta_2}{2}\right) - \frac{4(\rho+2)}{(\beta_2-\Im)^2}\aleph_\varepsilon'\left(\delta_1+\delta_2-\frac{\Im+\beta_2}{2}\right) - \frac{8(\rho+1)(\rho+2)}{(\beta_2-\Im)^3} \\
&\quad \aleph_\varepsilon\left(\delta_1+\delta_2-\frac{\Im+\beta_2}{2}\right) + \frac{2^{\rho+3}(\rho+1)(\rho+2)}{(\beta_2-\Im)^{\rho+3}} J^{\rho}_{\left(\delta_1+\delta_2-\frac{\Im+\beta_2}{2}\right)^+}\aleph_\varepsilon(\delta_1+\delta_2-\Im). \quad (14)
\end{aligned}$$

Subtracting the equality (14) from (13) and multiplying the equality with $\frac{(\beta_2-\Im)^3}{16(\rho+1)(\rho+2)}$, we have

$$\begin{aligned}&\frac{2^{\rho-1}\Gamma(\rho+1)}{(\beta_2-\Im)^{\rho}}\left[J^{\rho}_{\left(\delta_1+\delta_2-\frac{\Im+\beta_2}{2}\right)^-}\aleph_\varepsilon(\delta_1+\delta_2-\beta_2)+J^{\rho}_{\left(\delta_1+\delta_2-\frac{\Im+\beta_2}{2}\right)^+}\aleph_\varepsilon(\delta_1+\delta_2-\Im)\right]\\&-\aleph_\varepsilon\left(\delta_1+\delta_2-\frac{\Im+\beta_2}{2}\right)-\frac{(\beta_2-\Im)^2}{4(\rho+1)(\rho+2)}\aleph''_\varepsilon\left(\delta_1+\delta_2-\frac{\Im+\beta_2}{2}\right)\\=&\frac{(\beta_2-\Im)^3}{16(\rho+1)(\rho+2)}\left[\int_0^1 \Upsilon^{\rho+2}\aleph'''_\varepsilon\left(\delta_1+\delta_2-\left(\frac{\Upsilon}{2}\beta_2+\frac{2-\Upsilon}{2}\Im\right)\right)d\Upsilon\right.\\&\left.-\int_0^1 \Upsilon^{\rho+2}\aleph'''_\varepsilon\left(\delta_1+\delta_2-\left(\frac{\Upsilon}{2}\Im+\frac{2-\Upsilon}{2}\beta_2\right)\right)d\Upsilon\right].\end{aligned}$$

Hence, Lemma 3 is proven. □

Theorem 13. *Provided that hypothesis* **S** *is satisfied, and assuming that* $|\aleph'''_\varepsilon|$ *is convex on* $[\delta_1,\delta_2]$, *then the following fractional Mercer-type inequality holds true:*

$$\begin{aligned}&\left|\frac{2^{\rho-1}\Gamma(\rho+1)}{(\beta_2-\Im)^{\rho}}\left[J^{\rho}_{\left(\delta_1+\delta_2-\frac{\Im+\beta_2}{2}\right)^-}\aleph_\varepsilon(\delta_1+\delta_2-\beta_2)+J^{\rho}_{\left(\delta_1+\delta_2-\frac{\Im+\beta_2}{2}\right)^+}\aleph_\varepsilon(\delta_1+\delta_2-\Im)\right]\right.\\&\left.-\aleph_\varepsilon\left(\delta_1+\delta_2-\frac{\Im+\beta_2}{2}\right)-\frac{(\beta_2-\Im)^2}{4(\rho+1)(\rho+2)}\aleph''_\varepsilon\left(\delta_1+\delta_2-\frac{\Im+\beta_2}{2}\right)\right|\\\leq&\frac{(\beta_2-\Im)^3}{16(\rho+1)(\rho+2)(\rho+3)}\left[2\left(|\aleph'''_\varepsilon(\delta_1)|+|\aleph'''_\varepsilon(\delta_2)|\right)-\left(|\aleph'''_\varepsilon(\Im)|+|\aleph'''_\varepsilon(\beta_2)|\right)\right].\end{aligned}$$

Proof. By using the Lemma 3, since $|\aleph'''_\varepsilon|$ is convex, we have

$$\begin{aligned}&\left|\frac{2^{\rho-1}\Gamma(\rho+1)}{(\beta_2-\Im)^{\rho}}\left[J^{\rho}_{\left(\delta_1+\delta_2-\frac{\Im+\beta_2}{2}\right)^-}\aleph_\varepsilon(\delta_1+\delta_2-\beta_2)+J^{\rho}_{\left(\delta_1+\delta_2-\frac{\Im+\beta_2}{2}\right)^+}\aleph_\varepsilon(\delta_1+\delta_2-\Im)\right]\right.\\&\left.-\aleph_\varepsilon\left(\delta_1+\delta_2-\frac{\Im+\beta_2}{2}\right)-\frac{(\beta_2-\Im)^2}{4(\rho+1)(\rho+2)}\aleph''_\varepsilon\left(\delta_1+\delta_2-\frac{\Im+\beta_2}{2}\right)\right|\\\leq&\frac{(\beta_2-\Im)^3}{16(\rho+1)(\rho+2)}\left[\int_0^1 \Upsilon^{\rho+2}\left|\aleph'''_\varepsilon\left(\delta_1+\delta_2-\left(\frac{\Upsilon}{2}\Im+\frac{2-\Upsilon}{2}\beta_2\right)\right)\right|d\Upsilon\right.\\&\left.+\int_0^1 \Upsilon^{\rho+2}\left|\aleph'''_\varepsilon\left(\delta_1+\delta_2-\left(\frac{\Upsilon}{2}\beta_2+\frac{2-\Upsilon}{2}\Im\right)\right)\right|d\Upsilon\right]\\\leq&\frac{(\beta_2-\Im)^3}{16(\rho+1)(\rho+2)}\left[\int_0^1 \Upsilon^{\rho+2}\left(|\aleph'''_\varepsilon(\delta_1)|+|\aleph'''_\varepsilon(\delta_2)|-\left(\frac{\Upsilon}{2}|\aleph'''_\varepsilon(\Im)|+\frac{2-\Upsilon}{2}|\aleph'''_\varepsilon(\beta_2)|\right)\right)d\Upsilon\right.\\&\left.+\int_0^1 \Upsilon^{\rho+2}\left(|\aleph'''_\varepsilon(\delta_1)|+|\aleph'''_\varepsilon(\delta_2)|-\left(\frac{\Upsilon}{2}|\aleph'''_\varepsilon(\beta_2)|+\frac{2-\Upsilon}{2}|\aleph'''_\varepsilon(\Im)|\right)\right)d\Upsilon\right]\\=&\frac{(\beta_2-\Im)^3}{16(\rho+1)(\rho+2)(\rho+3)}\left[2\left(|\aleph'''_\varepsilon(\delta_1)|+|\aleph'''_\varepsilon(\delta_2)|\right)-\left(|\aleph'''_\varepsilon(\Im)|+|\aleph'''_\varepsilon(\beta_2)|\right)\right].\end{aligned}$$

The proof of Theorem 13 is completed. □

Corollary 11. *Assigning* $\beta_2=\delta_2$ *and* $\Im=\delta_1$ *in Theorem 13, we have*

$$\left|\frac{2^{\rho-1}\Gamma(\rho+1)}{(\delta_2-\delta_1)^{\rho}}\left[J^{\rho}_{\left(\frac{\delta_1+\delta_2}{2}\right)^-}\aleph_\varepsilon(\delta_1)+J^{\rho}_{\left(\frac{\delta_1+\delta_2}{2}\right)^+}\aleph_\varepsilon(\delta_2)\right]-\aleph_\varepsilon\left(\frac{\delta_1+\delta_2}{2}\right)-\frac{(\delta_2-\delta_1)^2}{4(\rho+1)(\rho+2)}\aleph''_\varepsilon\left(\frac{\delta_1+\delta_2}{2}\right)\right|$$

$$\leq \frac{(\delta_2-\delta_1)^3}{16(\rho+1)(\rho+2)(\rho+3)}\left[|\aleph_\varepsilon'''(\delta_1)|+|\aleph_\varepsilon'''(\delta_2)|\right].$$

Corollary 12. *Letting $\rho=1$ in Corollary 11, we obtain*

$$\left|\frac{1}{\delta_2-\delta_1}\int_{\delta_1}^{\delta_2}\aleph_\varepsilon(u)du-\aleph_\varepsilon\left(\frac{\delta_1+\delta_2}{2}\right)-\frac{(\delta_2-\delta_1)^2}{24}\aleph_\varepsilon''\left(\frac{\delta_1+\delta_2}{2}\right)\right|$$
$$\leq \frac{(\delta_2-\delta_1)^3}{384}\left[|\aleph_\varepsilon'''(\delta_1)|+|\aleph_\varepsilon'''(\delta_2)|\right].$$

Theorem 14. *Provided that hypothesis **S** is satisfied, and assuming that $|\aleph_\varepsilon'''|^q$ is convex on $[\delta_1,\delta_2]$ with $\frac{1}{p}+\frac{1}{q}=1$ and $q>1$, then the following fractional Mercer-type inequality holds true:*

$$\left|\frac{2^{\rho-1}\Gamma(\rho+1)}{(\beta_2-\Im)^\rho}\left[J^\rho_{\left(\delta_1+\delta_2-\frac{\Im+\beta_2}{2}\right)^-}\aleph_\varepsilon(\delta_1+\delta_2-\beta_2)+J^\rho_{\left(\delta_1+\delta_2-\frac{\Im+\beta_2}{2}\right)^+}\aleph_\varepsilon(\delta_1+\delta_2-\Im)\right]\right.$$
$$\left.-\aleph_\varepsilon\left(\delta_1+\delta_2-\frac{\Im+\beta_2}{2}\right)-\frac{(\beta_2-\Im)^2}{4(\rho+1)(\rho+2)}\aleph_\varepsilon''\left(\delta_1+\delta_2-\frac{\Im+\beta_2}{2}\right)\right|$$
$$\leq \frac{(\beta_2-\Im)^3}{16(\rho+1)(\rho+2)}\left(\frac{1}{p(2+\rho)+1}\right)^{\frac{1}{p}}\left[\left(|\aleph_\varepsilon'''(\delta_1)|^q+|\aleph_\varepsilon'''(\delta_2)|^q-\left(\frac{|\aleph_\varepsilon'''(\Im)|^q+3|\aleph_\varepsilon'''(\beta_2)|^q}{4}\right)\right)^{\frac{1}{q}}\right.$$
$$\left.+\left(|\aleph_\varepsilon'''(\delta_1)|^q+|\aleph_\varepsilon'''(\delta_2)|^q-\left(\frac{3|\aleph_\varepsilon'''(\Im)|^q+|\aleph_\varepsilon'''(\beta_2)|^q}{4}\right)\right)^{\frac{1}{q}}\right].$$

Proof. Based on Lemma 3, and by employing Hölder's inequality and the convexity of $|\aleph_\varepsilon'''|^q$, we obtain

$$\left|\frac{2^{\rho-1}\Gamma(\rho+1)}{(\beta_2-\Im)^\rho}\left[J^\rho_{\left(\delta_1+\delta_2-\frac{\Im+\beta_2}{2}\right)^-}\aleph_\varepsilon(\delta_1+\delta_2-\beta_2)+J^\rho_{\left(\delta_1+\delta_2-\frac{\Im+\beta_2}{2}\right)^+}\aleph_\varepsilon(\delta_1+\delta_2-\Im)\right]\right.$$
$$\left.-\aleph_\varepsilon\left(\delta_1+\delta_2-\frac{\Im+\beta_2}{2}\right)-\frac{(\beta_2-\Im)^2}{4(\rho+1)(\rho+2)}\aleph_\varepsilon''\left(\delta_1+\delta_2-\frac{\Im+\beta_2}{2}\right)\right|$$
$$\leq \frac{(\beta_2-\Im)^3}{16(\rho+1)(\rho+2)}\left(\int_0^1 \Upsilon^{(\rho+2)p}d\Upsilon\right)^{\frac{1}{p}}\left[\left(\int_0^1\left|\aleph_\varepsilon'''\left(\delta_1+\delta_2-\left(\frac{\Upsilon}{2}\Im+\frac{2-\Upsilon}{2}\beta_2\right)\right)\right|^q d\Upsilon\right)^{\frac{1}{q}}\right.$$
$$\left.+\left(\int_0^1\left|\aleph_\varepsilon'''\left(\delta_1+\delta_2-\left(\frac{\Upsilon}{2}\beta_2+\frac{2-\Upsilon}{2}\Im\right)\right)\right|^q d\Upsilon\right)^{\frac{1}{q}}\right]$$
$$\leq \frac{(\beta_2-\Im)^3}{16(\rho+1)(\rho+2)}\left(\int_0^1 \Upsilon^{(\rho+2)p}d\Upsilon\right)^{\frac{1}{p}}$$
$$\times\left[\left(\int_0^1\left(|\aleph_\varepsilon'''(\delta_1)|^q+|\aleph_\varepsilon'''(\delta_2)|^q-\left(\frac{\Upsilon}{2}|\aleph_\varepsilon'''(\Im)|^q+\frac{2-\Upsilon}{2}|\aleph_\varepsilon'''(\beta_2)|^q\right)\right)d\Upsilon\right)^{\frac{1}{q}}\right.$$
$$\left.+\left(\int_0^1\left(|\aleph_\varepsilon'''(\delta_1)|^q+|\aleph_\varepsilon'''(\delta_2)|^q-\left(\frac{\Upsilon}{2}|\aleph_\varepsilon'''(\beta_2)|^q+\frac{2-\Upsilon}{2}|\aleph_\varepsilon'''(\Im)|^q\right)\right)d\Upsilon\right)^{\frac{1}{q}}\right]$$
$$= \frac{(\beta_2-\Im)^3}{16(\rho+1)(\rho+2)}\left(\frac{1}{p(2+\rho)+1}\right)^{\frac{1}{p}}\left[\left(|\aleph_\varepsilon'''(\delta_1)|^q+|\aleph_\varepsilon'''(\delta_2)|^q-\left(\frac{|\aleph_\varepsilon'''(\Im)|^q+3|\aleph_\varepsilon'''(\beta_2)|^q}{4}\right)\right)^{\frac{1}{q}}\right.$$
$$\left.+\left(|\aleph_\varepsilon'''(\delta_1)|^q+|\aleph_\varepsilon'''(\delta_2)|^q-\left(\frac{3|\aleph_\varepsilon'''(\Im)|^q+|\aleph_\varepsilon'''(\beta_2)|^q}{4}\right)\right)^{\frac{1}{q}}\right].$$

The proof of Theorem 14 is completed. □

Corollary 13. *Assigning $\beta_2 = \delta_2$ and $\Im = \delta_1$ in Theorem 14, we have*

$$\left|\frac{2^{\rho-1}\Gamma(\rho+1)}{(\delta_2-\delta_1)^{\rho}}\left[J^{\rho}_{\left(\frac{\delta_1+\delta_2}{2}\right)^-}\aleph_{\varepsilon}(\delta_1)+J^{\rho}_{\left(\frac{\delta_1+\delta_2}{2}\right)^+}\aleph_{\varepsilon}(\delta_2)\right]-\aleph_{\varepsilon}\left(\frac{\delta_1+\delta_2}{2}\right)-\frac{(\delta_2-\delta_1)^2}{4(\rho+1)(\rho+2)}\aleph''_{\varepsilon}\left(\frac{\delta_1+\delta_2}{2}\right)\right|$$

$$\leq \frac{(\delta_2-\delta_1)^3}{16(\rho+1)(\rho+2)}\left(\frac{1}{p(2+\rho)+1}\right)^{\frac{1}{p}}\left[\left(\frac{3|\aleph'''_{\varepsilon}(\delta_1)|^q+|\aleph'''_{\varepsilon}(\delta_2)|^q}{4}\right)^{\frac{1}{q}}+\left(\frac{|\aleph'''_{\varepsilon}(\delta_1)|^q+3|\aleph'''_{\varepsilon}(\delta_2)|^q}{4}\right)^{\frac{1}{q}}\right].$$

Theorem 15. *Provided that hypothesis **S** is satisfied, and assuming that $|\aleph'''_{\varepsilon}|^q$ is convex on $[\delta_1,\delta_2]$, with $q \geq 1$, then the following fractional Mercer-type inequality holds true:*

$$\left|\frac{2^{\rho-1}\Gamma(\rho+1)}{(\beta_2-\Im)^{\rho}}\left[J^{\rho}_{\left(\delta_1+\delta_2-\frac{\Im+\beta_2}{2}\right)^-}\aleph_{\varepsilon}(\delta_1+\delta_2-\beta_2)+J^{\rho}_{\left(\delta_1+\delta_2-\frac{\Im+\beta_2}{2}\right)^+}\aleph_{\varepsilon}(\delta_1+\delta_2-\Im)\right]\right.$$
$$\left.-\aleph_{\varepsilon}\left(\delta_1+\delta_2-\frac{\Im+\beta_2}{2}\right)-\frac{(\beta_2-\Im)^2}{4(\rho+1)(\rho+2)}\aleph''_{\varepsilon}\left(\delta_1+\delta_2-\frac{\Im+\beta_2}{2}\right)\right|$$
$$\leq \frac{(\beta_2-\Im)^3}{16(\rho+1)(\rho+2)}\left(\frac{1}{\rho+3}\right)^{1-\frac{1}{q}}$$
$$\times\left[\left(\frac{1}{\rho+3}\left(|\aleph'''_{\varepsilon}(\delta_1)|^q+|\aleph'''_{\varepsilon}(\delta_2)|^q\right)-\left(\frac{1}{2(\rho+4)}|\aleph'''_{\varepsilon}(\Im)|^q+\frac{5+\rho}{2(\rho^2+12+7\rho)}|\aleph'''_{\varepsilon}(\beta_2)|^q\right)\right)^{\frac{1}{q}}\right.$$
$$\left.+\left(\frac{1}{\rho+3}\left(|\aleph'''_{\varepsilon}(\delta_1)|^q+|\aleph'''_{\varepsilon}(\delta_2)|^q\right)-\left(\frac{1}{2(\rho+4)}|\aleph'''_{\varepsilon}(\beta_2)|^q+\frac{5+\rho}{2(\rho^2+12+7\rho)}|\aleph'''_{\varepsilon}(\Im)|^q\right)\right)^{\frac{1}{q}}\right].$$

Proof. Applying Lemma 3, along with the power–mean inequality and the convexity property of $|\aleph'''_{\varepsilon}|^q$, we obtain

$$\left|\frac{2^{\rho-1}\Gamma(\rho+1)}{(\beta_2-\Im)^{\rho}}\left[J^{\rho}_{\left(\delta_1+\delta_2-\frac{\Im+\beta_2}{2}\right)^-}\aleph_{\varepsilon}(\delta_1+\delta_2-\beta_2)+J^{\rho}_{\left(\delta_1+\delta_2-\frac{\Im+\beta_2}{2}\right)^+}\aleph_{\varepsilon}(\delta_1+\delta_2-\Im)\right]\right.$$
$$\left.-\aleph_{\varepsilon}\left(\delta_1+\delta_2-\frac{\Im+\beta_2}{2}\right)-\frac{(\beta_2-\Im)^2}{4(\rho+1)(\rho+2)}\aleph''_{\varepsilon}\left(\delta_1+\delta_2-\frac{\Im+\beta_2}{2}\right)\right|$$
$$\leq \frac{(\beta_2-\Im)^3}{16(\rho+1)(\rho+2)}\left(\int_0^1 Y^{\rho+2}dY\right)^{1-\frac{1}{q}}\left[\left(\int_0^1 Y^{\rho+2}\left|\aleph'''_{\varepsilon}\left(\delta_1+\delta_2-\left(\frac{Y}{2}\Im+\frac{2-Y}{2}\beta_2\right)\right)\right|^q dY\right)^{\frac{1}{q}}\right.$$
$$\left.+\left(\int_0^1 Y^{\rho+2}\left|\aleph'''_{\varepsilon}\left(\delta_1+\delta_2-\left(\frac{Y}{2}\beta_2+\frac{2-Y}{2}\Im\right)\right)\right|^q dY\right)^{\frac{1}{q}}\right]$$
$$\leq \frac{(\beta_2-\Im)^3}{16(\rho+1)(\rho+2)}\left(\int_0^1 Y^{\rho+2}dY\right)^{1-\frac{1}{q}}$$
$$\times\left[\left(\int_0^1 Y^{\rho+2}\left(|\aleph'''_{\varepsilon}(\delta_1)|^q+|\aleph'''_{\varepsilon}(\delta_2)|^q-\left(\frac{Y}{2}|\aleph'''_{\varepsilon}(\Im)|^q+\frac{2-Y}{2}|\aleph'''_{\varepsilon}(\beta_2)|^q\right)\right)dY\right)^{\frac{1}{q}}\right.$$
$$\left.+\left(\int_0^1 Y^{\rho+2}\left(|\aleph'''_{\varepsilon}(\delta_1)|^q+|\aleph'''_{\varepsilon}(\delta_2)|^q-\left(\frac{Y}{2}|\aleph'''_{\varepsilon}(\beta_2)|^q+\frac{2-Y}{2}|\aleph'''_{\varepsilon}(\Im)|^q\right)\right)dY\right)^{\frac{1}{q}}\right]$$
$$= \frac{(\beta_2-\Im)^3}{16(\rho+1)(\rho+2)}\left(\frac{1}{\rho+3}\right)^{1-\frac{1}{q}}$$
$$\times\left[\left(\frac{1}{\rho+3}\left(|\aleph'''_{\varepsilon}(\delta_1)|^q+|\aleph'''_{\varepsilon}(\delta_2)|^q\right)-\left(\frac{1}{2(\rho+4)}|\aleph'''_{\varepsilon}(\Im)|^q+\frac{5+\rho}{2(\rho^2+12+7\rho)}|\aleph'''_{\varepsilon}(\beta_2)|^q\right)\right)^{\frac{1}{q}}\right.$$
$$\left.+\left(\frac{1}{\rho+3}\left(|\aleph'''_{\varepsilon}(\delta_1)|^q+|\aleph'''_{\varepsilon}(\delta_2)|^q\right)-\left(\frac{1}{2(\rho+4)}|\aleph'''_{\varepsilon}(\beta_2)|^q+\frac{5+\rho}{2(\rho^2+12+7\rho)}|\aleph'''_{\varepsilon}(\Im)|^q\right)\right)^{\frac{1}{q}}\right].$$

The proof of Theorem 15 is completed. □

Corollary 14. *Assigning $\beta_2 = \delta_2$ and $\Im = \delta_1$ in Theorem 15, we have*

$$\left|\frac{2^{\rho-1}\Gamma(\rho+1)}{(\delta_2-\delta_1)^\rho}\left[J^\rho_{\left(\frac{\delta_1+\delta_2}{2}\right)^-}\aleph_\varepsilon(\delta_1)+J^\rho_{\left(\frac{\delta_1+\delta_2}{2}\right)^+}\aleph_\varepsilon(\delta_2)\right]-\aleph_\varepsilon\left(\frac{\delta_1+\delta_2}{2}\right)-\frac{(\delta_2-\delta_1)^2}{4(\rho+1)(\rho+2)}\aleph''_\varepsilon\left(\frac{\delta_1+\delta_2}{2}\right)\right|$$
$$\leq \frac{(\delta_2-\delta_1)^3}{16(\rho+1)(\rho+2)}\left(\frac{1}{\rho+3}\right)^{1-\frac{1}{q}}\left[\left(\frac{3|\aleph'''_\varepsilon(\delta_1)|^q+2|\aleph'''_\varepsilon(\delta_2)|^q}{20}\right)^{\frac{1}{q}}+\left(\frac{2|\aleph'''_\varepsilon(\delta_1)|^q+3|\aleph'''_\varepsilon(\delta_2)|^q}{20}\right)^{\frac{1}{q}}\right].$$

3. Applications

3.1. Special Means

In this section, we apply the newly derived inequalities to various special means of positive real numbers. Let δ_1 and δ_2 be arbitrary positive real numbers with $\delta_1 \neq \delta_2$. We focus on the following two special means: (a) Arithmetic mean:

$$A(\delta_1,\delta_2) := \frac{\delta_1+\delta_2}{2}.$$

(b) Generalized logarithmic mean:

$$L_n(\delta_1,\delta_2) := \left[\frac{\delta_2^{n+1}-\delta_1^{n+1}}{(n+1)(\delta_2-\delta_1)}\right]^{\frac{1}{n}}, \ \delta_1,\delta_2\in\mathbb{R},\ \delta_1<\delta_2,\ n\in\mathbb{N}.$$

Note that

$$\begin{aligned}\aleph_\varepsilon(z) &= z^{n+3}, \aleph'_\varepsilon=(n+3)z^{n+2}, \aleph''_\varepsilon=(n+3)(n+2)z^{n+1}\\ \aleph'''_\varepsilon &= (n+3)(n+2)(n+1)z^n \text{ yields the convexity of } z^n \text{ on } (0,\infty).\end{aligned}$$

$$\begin{aligned}\frac{1}{\beta_2-\Im}\int_{\delta_1+\delta_2-\beta_2}^{\delta_1+\delta_2-\Im}\aleph_\varepsilon(u)du &= L^{n+3}_{n+3}(\delta_1+\delta_2-\Im,\delta_1+\delta_2-\beta_2)\\ \aleph_\varepsilon\left(\delta_1+\delta_2-\frac{\Im+\beta_2}{2}\right) &= (2A(\delta_1,\delta_2)-A(\Im,\beta_2))^{n+3}\\ \frac{(\beta_2-\Im)^2}{24}\aleph''_\varepsilon\left(\delta_1+\delta_2-\frac{\Im+\beta_2}{2}\right) &= \frac{(n+3)(n+2)(\beta_2-\Im)^2}{24}(2A(\delta_1,\delta_2)-A(\Im,\beta_2))^{n+1}.\end{aligned}$$

Proposition 1. *Let $\delta_1,\delta_2\in\mathbb{R}$, such that $0<\delta_1<\delta_2$ and $n\in\mathbb{N}$, then we have*

$$\begin{aligned}&\Big|L^{n+3}_{n+3}(\delta_1+\delta_2-\Im,\delta_1+\delta_2-\beta_2)-(2A(\delta_1,\delta_2)-A(\Im,\beta_2))^{n+3}\\ &-\frac{(n+3)(n+2)(\beta_2-\Im)^2}{24}(2A(\delta_1,\delta_2)-A(\Im,\beta_2))^{n+1}\Big|\\ \leq\ &\frac{(n+1)(n+3)(n+2)(\beta_2-\Im)^3}{384}[2A(\delta_1^n,\delta_2^n)-A(\Im^n,\beta_2^n)].\end{aligned}$$

Proof. The outcome is obtained by applying Corollary 3 with $\aleph_\varepsilon(z)=z^{n+3},\ z>0$. □

Proposition 2. *Let $\delta_1,\delta_2\in\mathbb{R}$, such that $0<\delta_1<\delta_2$, with $n\in\mathbb{N}$ and $n\geq 4$, then we have*

$$\left|L_n(\delta_1,\delta_2)^n-A^n(\delta_1,\delta_2)-\frac{n(n-1)(\delta_2-\delta_1)^2}{24}A^{n-2}(\delta_1,\delta_2)\right|$$

$$\leq \frac{n(n-1)(n-2)(\delta_2-\delta_1)^3}{384}\left[A\left((\delta_1)^{n-3},(\delta_2)^{n-3}\right)\right].$$

Proof. The outcome is obtained by applying Corollary 12 to $\aleph_\varepsilon(z)=z^n, z>0$. □

3.2. Midpoint Formula

Let $P=\{z_0,z_1,z_2,\ldots,z_n\}$ be the partition of the points $z_i\in[\delta_1,\delta_2]$, $i=0,1,2,\ldots,n$ with $\delta_1=z_0<z_1<z_2<\ldots<z_n=\delta_2$.

For the partition P, the corresponding midpoint rule is given in [46]:

$$\Bbbk(\aleph_\varepsilon,P)=\sum_{i=0}^{n-1}\aleph_\varepsilon\left(\frac{z_i+z_{i+1}}{2}\right)(z_{i+1}-z_i).$$

It is well established that, if the function $\aleph_\varepsilon:[\delta_1,\delta_2]\to\mathbb{R}$ possesses a second derivative on the open interval (δ_1,δ_2) and

$$M = \max_{z\in(\delta_1,\delta_2)}\left|\aleph''_\varepsilon(z)\right|<\infty, \text{ then}$$

$$\int_{\delta_1}^{\delta_2}\aleph_\varepsilon(z)\,dz := \Bbbk(\aleph_\varepsilon,P)+\beta(\aleph_\varepsilon,P),$$

where $\beta(\aleph_\varepsilon,P)$ denotes the approximation error incurred when estimating the integral $\int_{\delta_1}^{\delta_2}\aleph_\varepsilon(z)dz$ via the midpoint quadrature formula $\Bbbk(\aleph_\varepsilon,P)$, and it fulfills the following condition:

$$\beta(\aleph_\varepsilon,P)=\frac{M}{24}\sum_{i=0}^{n-1}(z_{i+1}-z_i)^3.$$

Proposition 3. *Assuming the hypothesis stated in Lemma 2, if $|\aleph'''_\varepsilon|$ is convex, then we have*

$$|\beta(\aleph_\varepsilon,P)|\leq\frac{1}{384}\sum_{i=0}^{n-1}(z_{i+1}-z_i)^3\left[\left|\aleph'''_\varepsilon(z_i)\right|+\left|\aleph'''_\varepsilon(z_{i+1})\right|\right].$$

Proof. Consider the Corollary 5 on the subintervals $[z_i,z_{i+1}]$ $(i=0,1,2,\ldots,n-1)$ of the partition P, we get

$$\left|\sum_{i=0}^{n-1}\left(\frac{1}{z_{i+1}-z_i}\int_{z_i}^{z_{i+1}}\aleph_\varepsilon(z)dz\right)-\sum_{i=0}^{n-1}\aleph_\varepsilon\left(\frac{z_i+z_{i+1}}{2}\right)(z_{i+1}-z_i)\right|$$
$$\leq \frac{1}{384}\sum_{i=0}^{n-1}(z_{i+1}-z_i)^3\left[\left|\aleph'''_\varepsilon(z_i)\right|+\left|\aleph'''_\varepsilon(z_{i+1})\right|\right].$$

The result is produced, by summing the resulting inequality $(i=0,1,2,\ldots,n-1)$, and then applying the triangle inequality.

$$\left|\sum_{i=0}^{n-1}\left(\frac{1}{z_{i+1}-z_i}\int_{z_i}^{z_{i+1}}\aleph_\varepsilon(z)dz\right)-\Bbbk(\aleph_\varepsilon,P)\right|$$
$$\leq \frac{1}{384}\sum_{i=0}^{n-1}(z_{i+1}-z_i)^3\left[\left|\aleph'''_\varepsilon(z_i)\right|+\left|\aleph'''_\varepsilon(z_{i+1})\right|\right].$$

□

3.3. q-Digamma Function

Let $0 < q < 1$ and $z > 0$. The q-digamma function, $\varphi_q(z)$, is defined by

$$\begin{aligned}\varphi_q(z) &= -\ln(1-q) + \ln q \sum_{k=0}^{\infty} \frac{q^{k+z}}{1-q^{k+z}} \\ &= -\ln(1-q) + \ln q \sum_{k=1}^{\infty} \frac{q^{kz}}{1-q^{k}},\end{aligned}$$

which is well defined for all $z > 0$. It is known that for $0 < q < 1$, the q-digamma function is infinitely differentiable on $(0, \infty)$ and its higher-order derivatives admit series representations with nonnegative terms. In particular, the function $\left|\varphi_q'''(z)\right|$ is convex on $(0, \infty)$ see, for example, the monotonicity and convexity results established for q-polygamma functions in the literature [47,48]. For $q > 1$ and $z > 0$, the q-digamma function φ_q is defined as

$$\begin{aligned}\varphi_q(z) &= -\ln(q-1) + \ln q \left[z - \frac{1}{2} - \sum_{k=0}^{\infty} \frac{q^{-(k+z)}}{1-q^{-(k+z)}}\right] \\ &= -\ln(q-1) + \ln q \left[z - \frac{1}{2} - \sum_{k=1}^{\infty} \frac{q^{-kz}}{1-q^{-k}}\right].\end{aligned}$$

Proposition 4. *From Corollary 12, we acquire*

$$\begin{aligned}&\left|\frac{1}{\delta_2-\delta_1}\int_{\delta_1}^{\delta_2} \varphi_q(z)\,dz - \varphi_q\left(\frac{\delta_1+\delta_2}{2}\right) - \frac{(\delta_2-\delta_1)^2}{24}\varphi_q''\left(\frac{\delta_1+\delta_2}{2}\right)\right| \\ \leq\ & \frac{(\delta_2-\delta_1)^3}{384}\left[\left|\varphi_q'''(\delta_1)\right| + \left|\varphi_q'''(\delta_2)\right|\right].\end{aligned}$$

Proof. The outcome is obtained by applying Corollary 12 by setting $\aleph_\varepsilon(z) = \varphi_q(z)$. □

3.4. Modified Bessel Function

We assume that $\sigma > -1$ and $z \in (0, \infty)$. Under these conditions, the modified Bessel function of the first kind, I_σ, admits the series expansion [49]:

$$I_\sigma(z) = \sum_{n \geq 0} \frac{\left(\frac{z}{2}\right)^{\sigma+2n}}{n!\Gamma(\sigma+n+1)},$$

The second kind of modified Bessel function $\mathbb{C}_\sigma$ [49] is defined as

$$\mathbb{C}_\sigma(z) = \frac{\pi}{2}\frac{I_{-\sigma}(z) - I_\sigma(z)}{\sin \sigma\pi}.$$

Let the function $\Psi_\sigma(z) : \mathbb{R} \to (0, 1]$, defined by

$$\Psi_\sigma(z) = 2^\sigma \Gamma(\sigma+1) z^{-\sigma} \mathbb{C}_\sigma(z),$$

It is known [49] that $\Psi_\sigma(z)$ is positive and increasing on $(0, \infty)$ for $\sigma > -1$. Moreover, from the explicit representations of its derivatives given in

$$\Psi_\sigma'(z) = \frac{z}{2(\sigma+1)}\Psi_{\sigma+1}(z), \tag{15}$$

and second derivative can be easily obtained from Equation (15) as

$$\Psi''_{\sigma}(z) = \frac{z^2}{4(\sigma+1)(\sigma+2)}\Psi_{\sigma+2}(z) + \frac{1}{2(\sigma+1)}\Psi_{\sigma+1}(z), \tag{16}$$

and third derivative can be straightforwardly calculated from Equation (16) as

$$\Psi'''_{\sigma}(z) = \frac{z^3}{8(\sigma+1)(\sigma+2)(\sigma+3)}\Psi_{\sigma+3}(z) + \frac{3z}{4(\sigma+1)(\sigma+2)}\Psi_{\sigma+2}(z). \tag{17}$$

Proposition 5. *Let $\sigma > -1$ for any real numbers $0 < \delta_1 < \delta_2$, then we have*

$$\begin{aligned}
&\left|\frac{1}{\delta_2-\delta_1}\int_{\delta_1}^{\delta_2}\Psi_{\sigma}(z)\,dz - \Psi_{\sigma}\left(\frac{\delta_1+\delta_2}{2}\right)\right.\\
&\left.-\frac{(\delta_2-\delta_1)^2}{24}\left[\frac{(\delta_2-\delta_1)^2}{16(\sigma+1)(\sigma+2)}\Psi_{\sigma+2}\left(\frac{\delta_1+\delta_2}{2}\right) + \frac{1}{2(\sigma+1)}\Psi_{\sigma+1}\left(\frac{\delta_1+\delta_2}{2}\right)\right]\right|\\
\leq\ & \frac{(\delta_2-\delta_1)^3}{384}\left[\left\{\frac{\delta_1^3}{8(\sigma+1)(\sigma+2)(\sigma+3)}\Psi_{\sigma+3}(\delta_1) + \frac{3\delta_1}{4(\sigma+1)(\sigma+2)}\Psi_{\sigma+2}(\delta_1)\right.\right.\\
&\left.\left.+\frac{\delta_2^3}{8(\sigma+1)(\sigma+2)(\sigma+3)}\Psi_{\sigma+3}(\delta_2) + \frac{3\delta_2}{4(\sigma+1)(\sigma+2)}\Psi_{\sigma+2}(\delta_2)\right\}\right].
\end{aligned}$$

Proof. The outcome is obtained by applying Corollary 12 by setting $\aleph_{\varepsilon}(z) = \Psi_{\sigma}(z), z > 0$ along with the identities in Equations (16) and (17). □

4. Simulations

In the following section, we validate our main results through a series of graphical illustrations.

Example 1. *Suppose that all the conditions of Corollary 3 are satisfied. Let us consider the function $\aleph_{\varepsilon}(u) = (u+a)^{\alpha}$ defined on $\mathbb{R}^+$. Additionally, $\aleph'''_{\varepsilon}(u) = \alpha(\alpha-1)(\alpha-2)(u+a)^{\alpha-3}$, where $\alpha \geq 3$ and $a > 0$ are also a convex function. By fixing the values $\delta_1 = 1$, $\delta_2 = 4$, $\beta_2 = 3$ and $\Im = 2$, we proceed as follows:*

$$\begin{aligned}
&\left|\frac{(a+3)^{\alpha+1}-(a+2)^{\alpha+1}}{\alpha+1} - \left(\frac{5}{2}+a\right)^{\alpha} - \frac{\alpha(\alpha-1)}{24}\left(\frac{5}{2}+a\right)^{\alpha-2}\right| \\
\leq\ & \frac{\alpha(\alpha-1)(\alpha-2)}{384}\left[2\left\{(a+1)^{\alpha-3}+(a+4)^{\alpha-3}\right\} - \left\{(a+2)^{\alpha-3}+(a+3)^{\alpha-3}\right\}\right].
\end{aligned} \tag{18}$$

In Figure 1, we select $\alpha \in [5,6]$ and $a \in [5,6]$, as a variable to illustrate the relationship between the left-hand side and the right-hand side of inequality (18), through a graph.

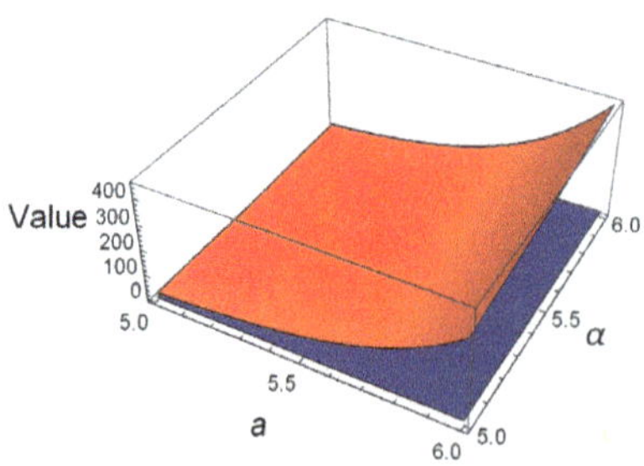

Figure 1. Verification of inequality (18) for variable α and representative a.

In Figure 2, we select $a \in [5,6]$, as a variable to illustrate the relationship between the left-hand side and the right-hand side of inequality (18), through a graph.

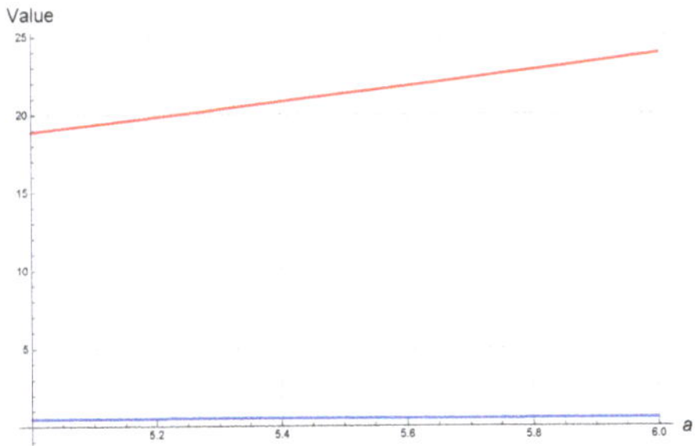

Figure 2. Left-hand side (LHS) line is shown in blue, and the right-hand side (RHS) line is shown in red as a function of $a \in [5,6]$, with fixed $\alpha = 5$.

In Figure 3, we select $\alpha \in [5,6]$, as a variable to illustrate the relationship between the left-hand side and the right-hand side of inequality (18), through a graph.

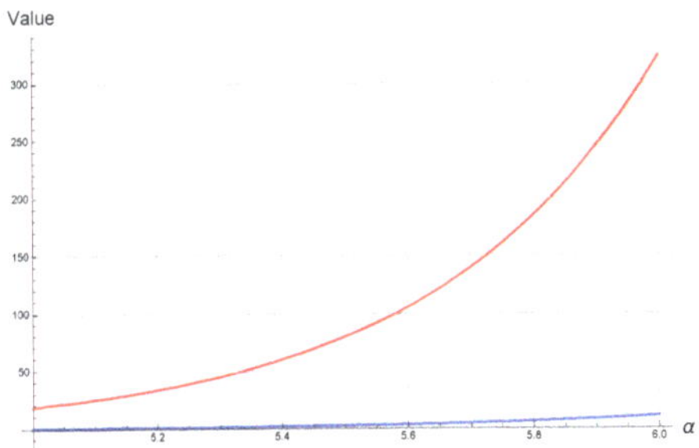

Figure 3. Left-hand side (LHS) line is shown in blue, and the right-hand side (RHS) line is shown in red as a function of $\alpha \in [5,6]$, with fixed $a = 5$.

In Table 1, we consider the parameter values $\alpha \in [3,7]$ and $a \in [1,3]$ to numerically illustrate the relationship between the left-hand side and the right-hand side of inequality (18).

Table 1. Numerical verification of inequality (18) for selected values of the parameters α and a is presented in Table 1.

α	a	Left-Hand Side	Right-Hand Side
3	1	0.0208	0.0417
4	1	0.0833	0.1667
5	2	0.3125	0.6250
6	2	0.7813	1.5625
7	3	1.9531	3.9063

Example 2. *Assume that all the conditions of Corollary 8 are satisfied. Let us consider the function* $\aleph_\varepsilon(u) = (u+a)^\alpha$ *defined on* $\mathbb{R}^+$. *Additionally,* $\aleph_\varepsilon'''(u) = \alpha(\alpha-1)(\alpha-2)(u+a)^{\alpha-3}$ *where* $\alpha \geq 3$ *and* $a > 0$, *which is also a convex function. By fixing the values* $\delta_1 = 1$, $\delta_2 = 4$, $\beta_2 = 3$ *and* $\Im = q = 2$, *we proceed as follows:*

$$\left| \frac{(a+3)^{\alpha+1} - (a+2)^{\alpha+1}}{\alpha+1} - \left(\frac{5}{2}+a\right)^{\alpha} - \frac{\alpha(\alpha-1)}{24}\left(\frac{5}{2}+a\right)^{\alpha-2} \right| \tag{19}$$

$$\leq \frac{\alpha(\alpha-1)(\alpha-2)}{192}\left[\left\{\frac{1}{4}\left(\left((a+1)^{\alpha-3}\right)^2+\left((a+4)^{\alpha-3}\right)^2\right)-\left(\frac{2\left((a+2)^{\alpha-3}\right)^2+3\left((a+3)^{\alpha-3}\right)^2}{20}\right)\right\}^{\frac{1}{2}}\right.$$
$$\left.+\left\{\frac{1}{4}\left(\left((a+1)^{\alpha-3}\right)^2+\left((a+4)^{\alpha-3}\right)^2\right)-\left(\frac{3\left((a+2)^{\alpha-3}\right)^2+2\left((a+3)^{\alpha-3}\right)^2}{20}\right)\right\}^{\frac{1}{2}}\right].$$

In Figure 4, we select $\alpha \in [5,6]$ and $a \in [5,6]$ as variables to illustrate the relationship between the left-hand side and the right-hand side of inequality (19), through a graph.

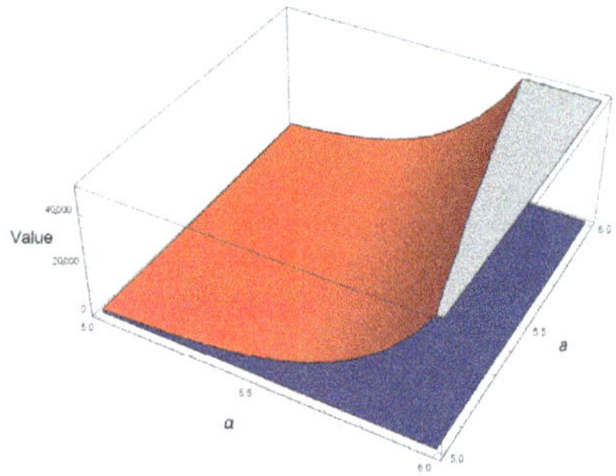

Figure 4. Verification of inequality (19) for variable α and representative a.

In Figure 5, we select $a \in [5,6]$ as a variable to illustrate the relationship between the left-hand side and the right-hand side of inequality (19), through a graph.

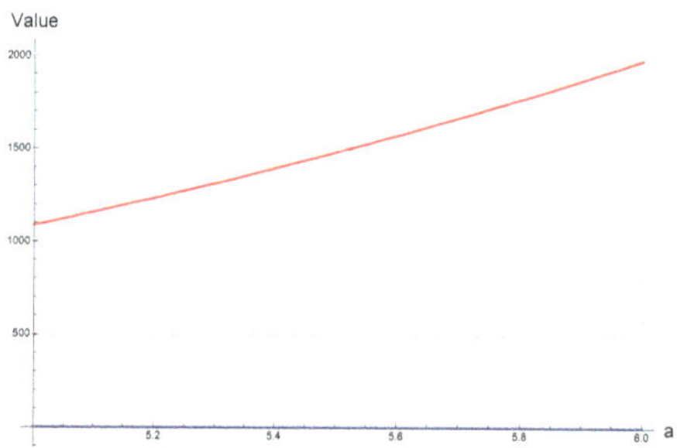

Figure 5. Left-hand side (LHS) line is shown in blue, and the right-hand side (RHS) line is shown in red as a function of $a \in [5,6]$, with fixed $\alpha = 5$.

In Figure 6, we select $\alpha \in [5,6]$ as a variable to illustrate the relationship between the left-hand side and the right-hand side of inequality (19), through a graph.

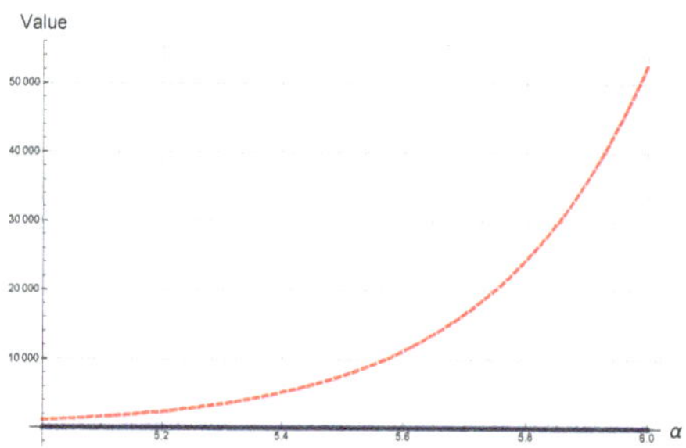

Figure 6. Left-hand side (LHS) line is shown in blue, and the right-hand side (RHS) line is shown in red as a function of $\alpha \in [5,6]$, with fixed $a = 5$.

In Table 2, we consider the parameter values $\alpha \in [5,7]$ and $a \in [5,6]$ to numerically illustrate the relationship between the left-hand side and the right-hand side of inequality (19).

Table 2. Numerical verification of inequality (19) for selected values of the parameters α and a is presented in Table 2.

α	a	**Left-Hand Side**	**Right-Hand Side**
5	5	24.3750	51.8427
5	6	29.6875	63.1042
6	5	61.3281	132.9167
6	6	74.4141	161.4583
7	5	154.7852	336.7188
7	6	187.4023	408.5938

5. Conclusions

Integral inequalities play a fundamental role in fractional calculus and mathematical analysis. Over the past forty years, this field has grown tremendously, with numerous research articles introducing fresh perspectives and innovative ideas. Convexity serves as a key tool in establishing results in this area, leading to various generalizations and extensions. To better model mathematical inequalities arising in real-world applications, researchers have turned to fractional calculus, as traditional calculus often falls short in capturing the necessary complexity. This shift has led to several unexpected and valuable discoveries, further enriching the field.

Since classical differentiation struggles to accurately model many applied problems, this work explores Hermite–Hadamard–Mercer-type inequalities using various fractional integral operators, including classical, Riemann–Liouville fractional integrals. Furthermore, we introduced several related fractional integral inequalities associated with the right side of the Hermite–Hadamard–Mercer-type inequality for three-times differentiable convex functions, providing additional insights and observations. Moreover, several new results regarding Young's inequality, bounded function, and L-Lipschitzian function are deduced. To validate our results, we presented illustrative examples with graphical visualizations. All figures in this work were produced with Mathematica (version 11.2). Notably, we compare Theorems 8 and 9 (from Khan et al. [45]) in a special case. Finally, we examined some applications related to special means, midpoint formula, q-digamma function and modified Bessel function, reinforcing the significance of our findings. We hope and believe that this work will inspire further research in fractional and quantum calculus, encouraging researchers to explore new results using different generalized convexities and fractional integral operators.

Author Contributions: Conceptualization, A.M.; funding acquisition, L.C.; investigation, A.M.; methodology, A.M. and H.B.; validation, H.B. and A.K.; visualization, A.K. and A.M.; writing—original draft, A.M.; writing—review and editing, A.M., L.C. and A.K. All authors have read and agreed to the published version of the manuscript.

Funding: This research received no external funding.

Data Availability Statement: The original contributions presented in this study are included in the article. Further inquiries can be directed to the corresponding authors.

Conflicts of Interest: The authors declare no conflicts of interest.

References

1. Alomari, M.W.; Darus, M.; Kirmaci, U.S. Some inequalities of Hermite–Hadamard type for s-convex functions. *Acta Math. Sci.* **2011**, *31*, 1643–1652. [CrossRef]
2. Sarikaya, M.Z.; Kiris, M.E. Some new inequalities of Hermite–Hadamard type for s-convex functions. *Miskolc Math. Notes* **2015**, *16*, 491–501. [CrossRef]
3. Khan, M.A.; Chu, Y.; Khan, T.U.; Khan, J. Some new inequalities of Hermite–Hadamard type for s–convex functions with applications. *Open Math.* **2017**, *15*, 1414–1430. [CrossRef]
4. Barsam, H.; Ramezani, S.M.; Sayyari, Y. On the new Hermite–Hadamard type inequalities for s-convex functions. *Afr. Mat.* **2021**, *32*, 1355–1367. [CrossRef]
5. Butt, S.I.; Nadeem, M.; Farid, G. On Caputo fractional derivatives via exponential s–convex functions. *Turk. J. Sci.* **2020**, *5*, 140–146.
6. Ramzan, S.; Awan, M.U.; Dragomir, S.S.; Bin-Mohsin, B.; Noor, M.A. Analysis and applications of some new fractional integral inequalities. *Fractal Fract.* **2023**, *7*, 797. [CrossRef]
7. Sahoo, S.K.; Kashuri, A.; Aljuaid, M.; Mishra, S.; De La Sen, M. On Ostrowski–Mercer's type fractional inequalities for convex functions and applications. *Fractal Fract.* **2023**, *7*, 215. [CrossRef]
8. Kunt, M.E.H.M.E.T.; Iscan, I. Fractional Hermite–Hadamard–Fejér type inequalities for GA-convex functions. *Turk. J. Inequal.* **2018**, *2*, 1–20.
9. Qaisar, S.; Munir, A.; Naeem, M.; Budak, H. Some Caputo-Fabrizio fractional integral inequalities with applications. *Filomat* **2024**, *38*, 5905–5923. [CrossRef]
10. Park, J. Hermite–Hadamard-Like type inequalities for s-convex functions s-Godunova–Levin functions of two kinds. *Int. Math. Forum* **2015**, *9*, 3431–3447. [CrossRef]
11. Ciurdariu, L.; Grecu, E. Several quantum Hermite–Hadamard-type integral inequalities for convex functions. *Fractal Fract.* **2023**, *7*, 463. [CrossRef]
12. Breckner, W.W. Stetigkeitsaussagen für Eine Klasse Verallgemeinerter Konvexer Funktionen in Topologischen Linearen Räumen. *Publ. Inst. Math.* **1978**, *23*, 13–20.
13. Mitrinović, D.S.; Pečarić, J.E.; Fink, A.M. *Classical and New Inequalities in Analysis*; Springer: Dordrecht, The Netherlands, 1993.
14. Benaissa, B.; Sarikaya, M.Z. Milne-Type Inequalities for h-Convex Functions. *Real Anal. Exch.* **2024**, *49*, 363–376. [CrossRef]
15. Hadamard, J. Étude sur les Propriétés des Fonctions Entières et en Particulier d'une Fonction Considérée par Riemann. *J. Math. Pures Appl.* **1893**, *9*, 171–215.
16. Hermite, C. Sur Deux Limites d'une Intégrale Définie. *Mathesis* **1883**, *3*, 182.
17. Mercer, A. A Variant of Jensen's Inequality. *J. Inequal. Pure Appl. Math.* **2003**, *4*, 73.
18. Butt, S.I.; Nasir, J.; Qaisar, S.; Abualnaja, K.M. k-Fractional variants of Hermite–Mercer-type inequalities via s-convexity with applications. *J. Funct. Spaces* **2021**, *2021*, 5566360. [CrossRef]
19. Moradi, H.R.; Furuichi, S. Improvement and generalization of some Jensen–Mercer-type inequalities. *arXiv* **2019**, arXiv:1905.01768. [CrossRef]
20. Khan, M.A.; Husain, Z.; Chu, Y.M. New estimates for Csiszár Divergence and Zipf–Mandelbrot entropy via Jensen–Mercer's inequality. *Complexity* **2020**, *2020*, 8928691.
21. Kian, M.; Moslehian, M. Refinements of the operator Jensen–Mercer inequality. *Electron. J. Linear Algebra* **2013**, *26*, 742–753. [CrossRef]
22. Zhang, Z.; Khan, M.A.; Khan, J.; Faisal, S.; Zuo, X.; Alaoui, M.K. A version of the Hermite-Hadamard-Mercer inequality and associated Results. *Ain Shams Eng. J.* **2026**, *17*, 103899. [CrossRef]
23. Abdeljawad, T.; Ali, M.A.; Mohammed, P.O.; Kashuri, A. On inequalities of Hermite–Hadamard–Mercer type involving Riemann–Liouville fractional integrals. *AIMS Math.* **2020**, *5*, 7316–7331. [CrossRef]
24. Chu, H.H.; Rashid, S.; Hammouch, Z.; Chu, Y.M. New fractional estimates for Hermite–Hadamard–Mercer's type inequalities. *Alex. Eng. J.* **2020**, *59*, 3079–3089. [CrossRef]
25. Hussain, T.; Ciurdariu, L.; Grecu, E. A new inclusion on inequalities of the Hermite–Hadamard–Mercer type for three-times differentiable functions. *Mathematics* **2024**, *12*, 3711. [CrossRef]
26. Set, E.; Çelik, B.; Özdemir, M.E.; Aslan, M. Some new results on Hermite–Hadamard–Mercer-type inequalities using a general family of fractional integral operators. *Fractal Fract.* **2021**, *5*, 68. [CrossRef]
27. Ciurdariu, L.; Grecu, E. Hermite–Hadamard–Mercer-type inequalities for three-times differentiable functions. *Axioms* **2024**, *13*, 413. [CrossRef]
28. Sial, I.B.; Patanarapeelert, N.; Ali, M.A.; Budak, H.; Sitthiwirattham, T. On Some new Ostrowski–Mercer-type inequalities for differentiable functions. *Axioms* **2022**, *11*, 132. [CrossRef]
29. Kara, H.; Ali, M.A.; Budak, H. Hermite–Hadamard–Mercer type inclusions for interval-valued functions via Riemann–Liouville fractional integrals. *Turk. J. Math.* **2022**, *46*, 2193–2207. [CrossRef]

30. Butt, S.I.; Yousaf, S.; Asghar, A.; Khan, K.A.; Moradi, H.R. New fractional Hermite–Hadamard–Mercer inequalities for Harmonically convex functions. *J. Funct. Spaces* **2021**, *2021*, 5868326. [CrossRef]
31. Atangana, A. Application of Fractional Calculus to Epidemiology. *Fract. Dyn.* **2015**, *2015*, 174–190.
32. Baleanu, D.; Güvenç, Z.B.; Machado, J.T. *New Trends in Nanotechnology and Fractional Calculus Applications*; Springer: New York, NY, USA, 2010; Volume 10.
33. Hilfer, R. *Applications of Fractional Calculus in Physics*; World Scientific: Singapore, 2000.
34. Magin, R. Fractional Calculus in Bioengineering, Part 1. *Crit. Rev. Biomed. Eng.* **2004**, *32*, 1–104. [CrossRef] [PubMed]
35. Ahmad, H.; Khokhar, R.B.; Suleman, M.; Tariq, M.; Ntouyas, S.K.; Tariboon, J. Some new notions of fractional Hermite–Hadamard-type inequalities involving applications to the physical sciences. *J. Math. Comput. Sci.* **2024**, *33*, 27–41. [CrossRef]
36. Rezaei Aderyani, S.; Saadati, R.; Li, C. Exploring stability in the Hilfer–Hadamard fractional order systems: Insights from numerical analysis and simulations. *J. Appl. Math. Comput.* **2025**, *71*, 6937–6958. [CrossRef]
37. Sahatsathatsana, C.; Nonlaopon, K. On Hermite–Hadamard and Ostrowski-type inequalities for strongly convex functions via quantum calculus with applications. *J. Math. Comput. Sci.* **2025**, *36*, 35–51. [CrossRef]
38. Ali, M.M.; Khan, A.R. Generalized integral Mercer's inequality and integral Means. *J. Inequal. Spec. Funct.* **2019**, *10*, 60–76.
39. Vivas-Cortez, M.; Javed, M.Z.; Awan, M.U.; Noor, M.A.; Dragomir, S.S. Bullen–Mercer type inequalities with applications in numerical analysis. *Alex. Eng. J.* **2024**, *96*, 15–33. [CrossRef]
40. Munir, A.; Budak, H.; Kashuri, A. Generalized error bounds for Mercer-type inequalities in fractional integrals with applications. *Univers. J. Math. Appl.* **2025**, *8*, 167–178. [CrossRef]
41. Podlubny, I. *Fractional Differential Equations: An Introduction to Fractional Derivatives, Fractional Differential Equations, Methods of Their Solution and Some of Their Applications*; Elsevier: Amsterdam, The Netherlands, 1998.
42. Gorenflo, R.; Mainardi, F. *Fractional Calculus: Integral and Differential Equations of Fractional Order*; Springer: Wien, Austria, 1997.
43. Pečarić, J.; Varošanec, S. A note on simpson's inequality for Lipschitzian functions. *Soochow J. Math.* **2001**, *27*, 53–57.
44. Iscan, I. New refinements for integral and sum forms of Hölder inequality. *J. Inequal. Appl.* **2019**, *2019*, 304. [CrossRef]
45. Khan, M.A.; Khurshid, Y.; Ali, T.; Rehman, N. Inequalities for three-times differentiable functions. *Punjab Univ. J. Math.* **2020**, *48*, 2.
46. Cerone, P.; Dragomir, S.S. Midpoint-Type Rules from an Inequalities Point of View. In *Handbook of Analytic Computational Methods in Applied Mathematics*; Chapman and Hall/CRC: Boca Raton, FL, USA, 2019; pp. 135–200.
47. Alzer, H.; Salem, A. Functional inequalities for the q-digamma function. *Acta. Math. Hung.* **2022**, *167*, 561–575. [CrossRef]
48. Alzer, H.; Grinshpan, A.Z. Inequalities for the gamma and q-gamma functions. *J. Approx. Theory* **2007**, *144*, 67–83. [CrossRef]
49. Watson, G.N. *A Treatise on the Theory of Bessel Functions*; The Cambridge University Press: Cambridge, UK, 1922.

fractal and fractional

MDPI

Article

The Hadamard and Generalized Fractional Integral Fuzzy-Number-Valued Operators for Mappings of One and Two Variables, and Their Related Fuzzy Number Inequalities

Jorge E. Macías-Díaz [1,2], Yaser Saber [3,*], Altaf Alshuhail [4], Loredana Ciurdariu [5] and Armando Gallegos [6,*]

1 Departamento de Matemáticas y Física, Universidad Autónoma de Aguascalientes, Avenida Universidad 940, Ciudad Universitaria, Aguascalientes 20131, Mexico; jemacias@correo.uaa.mx
2 Department of Mathematics, School of Digital Technologies, Tallinn University, 3 Narva Rd. 25, 10120 Tallinn, Estonia
3 Department of Mathematics, College of Science Al-Zulfi, Majmaah University, Al-Majmaah 11952, Saudi Arabia
4 Department of Mathematics, Collage of Science, University of Ha'il, Ha'il 2440, Saudi Arabia
5 Department of Mathematics, Politehnica University of Timișoara, 300006 Timisoara, Romania
6 Departamento de Ciencias Exactas y Tecnología, Centro Universitario de los Lagos, Universidad de Guadalajara, Enrique Díaz de León 1144, Lagos de Moreno 47463, Mexico
* Correspondence: y.sber@mu.edu.sa (Y.S.); gallegos@culagos.udg.mx (A.G.)

Abstract

In this study, we introduce new versions of fuzzy fractional integral operators for both one- and two-variable cases. Using these operators, several Hermite–Hadamard-type (H-type) inclusions are established for fuzzy-number-valued convex functions ($F{\cdot}N \cdot V$-functions) and $F{\cdot}N \cdot V$-coordinated convex functions. These results are obtained by employing $F{\cdot}N \cdot V$-weighted functions within the framework of the newly defined Hadamard and generalized fractional integrals in one- and two-dimensional settings. The use of generalized fractional integral operators provides a unified approach that encompasses a wide class of classical and modern fractional integrals, including the fuzzy Riemann–Liouville and Hadamard types. This unified setting enables the derivation of more comprehensive and flexible inequality results in the fuzzy-number context. The inclusions obtained in this work significantly extend and generalize several known $H \cdot H$-type inequalities previously established for real-valued and interval-valued functions ($I \cdot V$-functions). Furthermore, the proposed results yield a variety of meaningful special cases by specifying suitable kernel functions and parameters of the generalized fractional integrals. In particular, we derive new weighted $H \cdot H$-type inclusions involving logarithmic functions in the fuzzy-number framework. These findings underscore the effectiveness of generalized fractional integrals in capturing nonlocal behavior and uncertainty, and they provide new tools for further investigations in fuzzy analysis, fractional calculus, and generalized convexity.

Keywords: fuzzy convexity; Hadamard fuzzy-number-valued fractional integral operator; generalized fuzzy-number-valued fractional integral operator; Hermite–Hadamard-type inclusions

1. Introduction

One of the most fundamental results in the theory of convex functions is the $H \cdot H$-inequality, originally introduced by Charles Hermite and Jacques Hadamard; see [1,2]. This inequality has attracted considerable attention due to its elegant structure, clear geometrical interpretation, and wide range of applications in mathematical analysis, optimization, and related fields. Specifically, let $I \subset R$ be an interval and let $o, \ell \in I$ with $o < \ell$. If $\mathfrak{S} : I \subset R \to [0,1]$ is a convex function, then the $H \cdot H$-inequality states that the value of the function at the midpoint of the interval is bounded above and below by the integral mean of the function and the arithmetic mean of its endpoint values, namely,

$$\mathfrak{S}(\frac{o+\ell}{2}) \leq \frac{1}{\ell - o} \int_{o}^{\ell} \mathfrak{S}(k) dk \leq \frac{\mathfrak{S}(o) + \mathfrak{S}(\ell)}{2}. \tag{1}$$

This inequality provides a useful estimate for the integral average of a convex function and serves as a powerful analytical tool. Owing to its significance, numerous generalizations and extensions have been developed, including variants for different classes of convexity, multidimensional settings, and integral operators. These developments continue to play an important role in advancing both theoretical results and practical applications. When the function $\mathfrak{S}$ is concave, the $H \cdot H$-inequality holds with the reverse ordering of inequalities. Over the years, this classical result has motivated extensive research, and numerous authors have established various forms and extensions of $H \cdot H$-type inequalities under different assumptions. It is worth noting that the $H \cdot H$-inequality can be derived directly from Jensen's inequality, and thus may be viewed as a refined manifestation of the concept of convexity.

In recent decades, renewed interest in the $H \cdot H$-inequality for convex functions has led to a broad spectrum of refinements, improvements, and generalizations. These include extensions to different classes of convexity, alternative integral operators, and multidimensional settings, as documented in a growing body of literature (see, for example, [3,4]). Such developments highlight the continuing relevance of this inequality in modern mathematical analysis.

A significant role in these investigations is played by interval analysis, which provides a systematic framework for handling uncertainty in mathematical modeling and computer-assisted computations. Although the origins of interval-based reasoning can be traced back [5,6] to early mathematical works, such as those of Archimedes on the quadrature of the circle, interval analysis as a formal and structured theory did not gain substantial attention until the mid-twentieth century. Since then, it has become an important tool in both theoretical and applied mathematics, particularly in the study of inequalities, numerical analysis, and uncertainty quantification.

In recent years, interval analysis has become an important mathematical tool for dealing with uncertainties and rounding errors in numerical computations. It provides a reliable framework for representing imprecise quantities by intervals and for performing rigorous numerical calculations. Over the past decades, significant theoretical developments and practical applications of interval analysis have been reported in the literature. Fundamental concepts and computational techniques of interval arithmetic and interval computations were systematically studied in classical works on interval methods and their applications [7,8]. Furthermore, interval analysis has been successfully applied to global optimization problems and the reliable solution of nonlinear systems of equations [9]. Its applications have also been extended to various engineering and scientific problems, where interval methods provide guaranteed bounds for uncertain parameters and measurements [10]. In addition, interval arithmetic plays a crucial role in computer arithmetic and reliable numerical computation, ensuring accurate error control in scientific computing [11]. The development of extended interval spaces has further enriched the theoretical framework of interval analysis and opened new directions for mathematical modeling and analysis [12]. These advances have naturally led to the broader acceptance of absolute inequalities and interval-based approaches in modern mathematical analysis. As a natural

https://doi.org/10.3390/fractalfract10040228

generalization of $I \cdot V$-analysis, fuzzy-number theory provides a more flexible and expressive framework for describing uncertainty by incorporating degrees of membership rather than sharp bounds. Consequently, the study of inequalities for fuzzy-number-valued and set-valued functions has attracted growing interest. In this context, a $H \cdot H$-type inequality for set-valued functions, which generalizes $I \cdot V$-functions, was established by Sadowska, see [13]. Subsequently, several authors extended these ideas to fuzzy-number-valued functions, thereby enriching the theory and widening its range of applications.

Moreover, the introduction of generalized fractional integral operators has played a crucial role in the advancement of $H \cdot H$-type inequalities within the fuzzy setting. In particular, new $H \cdot H$-type inequalities involving fractional integrals in relation to another function were obtained by Jleli and Samet [14], providing a unified approach that encompasses several classical fractional operators. Furthermore, fractional integrals of one function in relation to another for $I \cdot V$-functions were first presented by Tunç [15], laying the groundwork for subsequent extensions to fuzzy-number-valued functions. These developments strongly motivate the present study, which focuses on establishing $H \cdot H$-type inequalities for coordinated convex fuzzy-number-valued functions involving generalized fractional integrals.

A unified framework that encompasses both the Riemann–Liouville and Hadamard fractional integrals was introduced through the novel fractional integral proposed by Katugampola. This generalization has proved to be highly effective in deriving new analytical results and has stimulated further developments in fractional inequality theory. Using generalized fractional integrals and classical integrals, Zhao et al. [16] and Budak and Agarwal [17] established $H \cdot H$-type inequalities for coordinated convex functions, thereby unifying and extending several important fractional integral operators, including the Riemann–Liouville, Hadamard, and Katugampola fractional integrals. Subsequently, $H \cdot H$-inequalities involving Riemann–Liouville fractional integrals [18] were investigated for $I \cdot V$-functions by Budak and coauthors [19], further highlighting the applicability of fractional operators in interval analysis. In a related direction, $I.V$-left- and -right-sided generalized fractional double integrals were introduced by Kara and collaborators [20], providing a broader setting for studying inequalities involving multivariable $I \cdot V$-functions. The concept of $I \cdot V$-convexity has also been extensively explored in the literature. In addition to classical $I \cdot V$-convex functions, several generalized convexity notions—such as $I \cdot V$-$L \cdot R$-convex functions—have been examined to obtain sharper and more flexible inequality results. On the other hand, the theory of fuzzy sets was first introduced by Zadeh to deal with uncertainty and vagueness in mathematical models [21]. Since then, fuzzy set theory has become an important tool in various branches of mathematics and applied sciences. In particular, the concept of metric spaces of fuzzy sets has been extensively studied, providing a fundamental framework for analyzing fuzzy-valued functions and their applications [22]. Moreover, the study of fuzzy differential equations has attracted considerable attention due to its significant role in modeling dynamic systems under uncertainty. Several researchers have contributed to the development of this field, including the pioneering work on fuzzy differential equations and their solutions [23,24]. Furthermore, the concept of fuzzy quasilinear spaces and their applications has provided a useful structure for studying fuzzy-valued mappings and related mathematical problems [25]. In addition, the theory of fuzzy integrals for set-valued and fuzzy mappings has been developed to extend classical integration concepts to fuzzy environments [26]. These developments have laid the foundation for further research in fuzzy analysis and its applications in various mathematical models. These studies form an important foundation for extending $H \cdot H$-type inequalities to fuzzy-number-valued functions—see [27]—and coordinated convexity frameworks involving fuzzy fractional integrals [28], which constitute the main focus of

 https://doi.org/10.3390/fractalfract10040228

the present work. In recent years, several researchers have introduced and investigated different notions of $L \cdot R$-convexity for $I \cdot V$-functions [29], thereby broadening the classical concept of $I \cdot V$-convexity (see, for example, [30,31]). Within this generalized framework, a variety of $H \cdot H$-type inequalities have been established for $L \cdot R$-$I \cdot V$-convex functions, demonstrating the flexibility and effectiveness of $L \cdot R$-convexity in inequality analysis.

Following the extension of the $H \cdot H$-inequality proposed by Zabandan [32] in 2020, further developments were achieved for fractional and logarithmic integral operators. These results significantly enriched the theory by incorporating nonlocal operators and logarithmic kernels. In a related direction, important $H \cdot H$-type inequalities for coordinated convex functions were derived by Sarıkaya and Kılıçer [33], highlighting the role of coordinated convexity in multivariable settings. Moreover, several authors have extended $H \cdot H$-type inequalities to the setting of Riemann–Liouville fractional integrals combined with logarithmic integral operators. These extensions have further deepened the understanding of fractional inequalities and have opened new avenues for research in $I \cdot V$ and fuzzy-number-valued analysis. Such advances provide strong motivation for the present study, which aims to develop new $H \cdot H$-type inequalities for coordinated convex fuzzy-number-valued functions involving generalized fractional integrals. The following inequality is known as fuzzy-fractional $H \cdot H$-type inequality, such that, as discussed in [34],

$$\tilde{\mathfrak{S}}\left(\frac{o+\ell}{2}\right) \leq_F \frac{\Gamma(\curlywedge+1)}{2[\ell-o]^{\curlywedge}} \odot \left\{\mathcal{J}_{o^+}^{\curlywedge}\tilde{\mathfrak{S}}(\ell) \oplus \mathcal{J}_{\ell^-}^{\curlywedge}\tilde{\mathfrak{S}}(o)\right\} \leq_F \frac{\tilde{\mathfrak{S}}(o)+\tilde{\mathfrak{S}}(\ell)}{2}. \quad (2)$$

where $\tilde{\mathfrak{S}}$ is a fuzzy-number-valued convex function over $[o, \ell]$.

The principal aim of this paper is to establish several $H \cdot H$-type inclusions for $I \cdot V$-convex functions and $I \cdot V$-coordinated convex functions by employing $I \cdot V$-weighted functions. The results obtained in this study not only unify but also extend earlier findings reported in the literature, particularly those presented in [27,28].

The paper is organized as follows. Section 2 recalls the fundamental definitions, properties, and preliminary results related to $I \cdot V$-functions that are essential for the subsequent analysis. In Section 3, we present a concise overview of fractional integrals for $I \cdot V$-functions involving one and two variables. Section 4 is devoted to the derivation of weighted $H \cdot H$-type inclusions for $I \cdot V$-convex functions, where several known results are recovered as special cases. Finally, in the context of coordinated convex functions, we establish new and significant $H \cdot H$-type inclusions, thereby further enriching the existing theory.

2. Preliminary Concepts

Let $\tilde{A}$ be a fuzzy set in a nonempty set R with the membership function

$$\eta_{\tilde{A}} : R \to [0,1] \quad (3)$$

For any $\mu \in (0,\ 1]$, the μ-cut (or μ-level set) of $\tilde{A}$ is defined as the crisp set

$$[\tilde{A}]_{\mu} = \{\hbar \in R |\ \tilde{\eta}(\hbar) \geq \mu\} \quad (4)$$

Additionally, the 0-cut of $\tilde{A}$ is defined as

$$[\tilde{A}]_0 = \overline{\{\hbar \in R |\ \tilde{\eta}(\hbar) \geq 0\}} \quad (5)$$

where the bar denotes the closure of the set.

https://doi.org/10.3390/fractalfract10040228

The family of μ-cuts $\left\{ [\tilde{A}]_{\mu} \middle| \mu \in [0,\ 1] \right\}$ provides a complete characterization of the fuzzy set $\tilde{A}$ and plays a fundamental role in fuzzy analysis, particularly in the definition of fuzzy numbers, fuzzy arithmetic, and fuzzy-valued integrals.

Note that the following four conditions are standard and essential for characterizing a fuzzy number. Normality ensures the existence of at least one element with full membership, convexity guarantees that intermediate values are represented consistently, upper semi-continuity ensures well-behaved membership functions, and compact support guarantees boundedness. Together, these conditions ensure that a fuzzy number is mathematically well-defined and suitable for analysis and applications.

Definition 1 ([21]). *A fuzzy number ($F{\cdot}N$) is a normal, convex, upper semi-continuous fuzzy set on R with compact support, whose μ-cuts are nonempty closed bounded intervals for all $\mu \in (0,\ 1]$. The set of all $F{\cdot}Ns$ is denoted by $\mathbb{F}_0$.*

Theorem 1 ([22]). *A fuzzy set is if $\tilde{\eta} : R \to [0,1]$ is a $F{\cdot}N$ if, and only if, there exist two real-valued functions.*

$$\eta_*,\ \eta^* : [0,1] \to R$$

such that, for every $\mu \in (0,\ 1]$, the μ-cut of $\tilde{\eta}$ is given by

$$[\eta_*(\mu), \eta^*(\mu)\ ].$$

Moreover, the endpoint functions $\eta_*(\mu), \eta^*(\mu)$ satisfy the following conditions:

1. $\eta_*(\mu)$ is bounded, non-decreasing, and left-continuous on $(0,\ 1]$;
2. $\eta^*(\mu)$ is bounded, non-increasing, and left-continuous on $(0,\ 1]$;
3. $\eta_*(\mu) \leq \eta^*(\mu)$ for all $\mu \in (0,\ 1]$.

Conversely, any pair of functions $(\eta_*(\mu), \eta^*(\mu)\ )$ satisfying conditions (1)–(3) uniquely determines a $F{\cdot}N$ "$\tilde{\eta}$".

Let $\tilde{\eta}, \tilde{o} \in \mathbb{F}_0$ represented parametrically $\{(\eta_*(\mu), \eta^*(\mu)) : \mu \in [0,\ 1]\}$ and $\{(o_*(\mu), o^*(\mu)) : \mu \in [0,\ 1]\}$, respectively. We say that $\tilde{\eta} \leq_{\mathbb{F}} \tilde{o}$ if for all $\mu \in (0,\ 1]$, $\eta^*(\mu) \leq o^*(\mu)$, and $\eta_*(\mu) \leq o_*(\mu)$ or $[\eta_*(\mu), \eta^*(\mu)\ ] \leq_I [o_*(\mu), o^*(\mu)]$, where $\leq_I$ is a partial-ordered relation between the intervals. If $\tilde{\eta} \leq_{\mathbb{F}} \tilde{o}$, then there exists $\mu \in (0,\ 1]$ such that $\eta^*(\mu) < o^*(\mu)$ or $\eta_*(\mu) \leq o_*(\mu)$. The fuzzy numbers $\tilde{\eta}$ and $\tilde{o}$ are said to be comparable in relation to the partial order $\leq_{\mathbb{F}}$ if either $\tilde{\eta} \leq_{\mathbb{F}} \tilde{o}$ or $\tilde{\eta} \geq_{\mathbb{F}} \tilde{o}$ holds. Otherwise, they are termed non-comparable. The set $\mathbb{F}_0$ forms a partially ordered set under the relation $\leq_{\mathbb{F}}$. In what follows, we may equivalently write $\tilde{\eta} \leq_{\mathbb{F}} \tilde{o}$ instead of $\tilde{o} \geq_{\mathbb{F}} \tilde{\eta}$ whenever convenient.

Let $\tilde{\eta}, \tilde{o} \in \mathbb{F}_0$. If there exists a fuzzy number $\tilde{\delta} \in \mathbb{F}_0$ such that

$$\tilde{\eta} = \tilde{o} \oplus \tilde{\delta}, \tag{6}$$

where $\oplus$ denotes fuzzy addition, then the generalized Hukuhara ($g\mathscr{H}$) difference between $\tilde{\eta}$ and $\tilde{o}$ is said to exist. In that sense, $\tilde{\delta}$ is called the $g\mathscr{H}$-difference of $\tilde{\eta}$ and $\tilde{o}$, and it is denoted by

$$\tilde{\eta} \ominus_{g\mathscr{H}} \tilde{o}, \tag{7}$$

as defined in ref. [25].

If the $g\mathscr{H}$-difference exists, then for each $\mu \in (0,\ 1]$ the endpoint functions satisfy

$$(\tilde{\delta})^*(\mu) = (\tilde{\eta} \ominus_{g\mathscr{H}} \tilde{o})^*(\mu) = \eta^*(\mu) - o^*(\mu), (\tilde{\delta})_*(\mu) = (\tilde{\eta} \ominus_{g\mathscr{H}} \tilde{o})_*(\mu) = \eta_*(\mu) - o_*(\mu),$$

https://doi.org/10.3390/fractalfract10040228

and

$$\tilde{\eta} \ominus_{g\mathscr{H}} \tilde{\mathrm{o}} = \tilde{\delta} \Leftrightarrow \begin{cases} \tilde{\delta} = \tilde{\eta} \ominus_{g\mathscr{H}} \tilde{\mathrm{o}} \\ or\ \tilde{\eta} = \tilde{\mathrm{o}} \oplus (-1) \odot \tilde{\delta} \end{cases} \tag{8}$$

Having established these fundamental properties of fuzzy numbers under addition and scalar multiplication, we now proceed to the case where $0 < \mathfrak{e} \in R$ and $\tilde{\eta}, \tilde{\mathrm{o}} \in \mathbb{F}_0$; then, $\mathfrak{e} \odot \tilde{\eta}$ and $\tilde{\eta} \oplus \tilde{\mathrm{o}}$ are defined as

$$\tilde{\eta} \oplus \tilde{\mathrm{o}} = \{(\eta_*(\mu) + \mathrm{o}_*(\mu), \eta^*(\mu) + \mathrm{o}^*(\mu)) : \mu \in [0,\ 1]\}, \tag{9}$$

$$\mathfrak{e} \odot \tilde{\eta} = \{(\mathfrak{e}\eta_*(\mu), \mathfrak{e}\eta^*(\mu)) : \mu \in [0,\ 1]\}. \tag{10}$$

Remark 1. *It is evident that $\mathbb{F}_0$ is closed under "$\odot$" scalar addition, and the features of $\mathbb{F}_0$ that were previously defined match those that result from the traditional extension concept. Furthermore, we obtain*

$$\tilde{\eta} \oplus \mathfrak{e} = \{(\eta_*(\mu) + \mathfrak{e}, \eta^*(\mu) + \mathfrak{e}) : \mu \in [0,\ 1]\}. \tag{11}$$

for every scalar number $\mathfrak{e} \in R$. A full metric space is generally understood to be the space $\mathbb{F}_0$ equipped with the supremum metric, which is written as $(\tilde{\eta}, \tilde{\mathrm{o}}) = \underset{0 \leq \mu \leq 1}{sup} H([\tilde{\eta}]^{\mu},\ [\tilde{\mathrm{o}}]^{\mu}))$ (see, e.g., [26]*).*

Definition 2 ([26])**.** *Let $\tilde{\mathfrak{S}} : [\sigma, \ell] \to \mathbb{F}_0$ be a F·N · V-mapping. Then, $\mathbb{D}$-continuouity of $\tilde{\mathfrak{S}}$ at a point $\hbar_0$ over fuzzy supremum metric $\mathbb{D}$ if*

$$\lim_{\hbar \to \hbar_0} \mathbb{D}(\tilde{\mathfrak{S}}(\hbar), \tilde{\mathfrak{S}}(\hbar_0)) = 0. \tag{12}$$

Equivalently, $\tilde{\mathfrak{S}}$ is D-continuous at $\hbar_0$ if, and only if, for every $\mu \in (0,\ 1]$, the endpoint functions

$$\mathfrak{S}_*(\cdot; \mu), \mathfrak{S}^*(\cdot; \mu) : [\sigma, \ell] \to R \tag{13}$$

are continuous at $\hbar_0$, uniformly in relation to μ.

The mapping $\tilde{\mathfrak{S}}$ is called $\mathbb{D}$-continuous on $[\sigma, \ell]$ if it is $\mathbb{D}$-continuous at every point of $[\sigma, \ell]$.

Remark 2. *$\mathbb{D}$-continuity in relation to the fuzzy supremum metric guarantees uniform level-wise continuity of the μ-cut endpoints and is particularly suitable for studying F·N · V-integrals, fractional operators, and H · H-type inequalities.*

Definition 3 ([27])**.** *A mapping $\tilde{\mathfrak{S}} : [\sigma, \ell] \to \mathbb{F}_0$ is called F·N · V-mapping if, for every $\hbar \in [\sigma, \ell]$, $\tilde{\mathfrak{S}}(\hbar)$ is a F·N. Equivalently, for every $\hbar \in [\sigma, \ell]$ and $\mu \in [0,\ 1]$, the μ-cut of $\tilde{\mathfrak{S}}(\hbar)$ is a closed and bounded interval given by*

$$[\tilde{\mathfrak{S}}(\hbar)]^{\mu} = \mathfrak{S}_{\mu}(\hbar) = [\mathfrak{S}_*(\hbar;\ \mu),\ \mathfrak{S}^*(\hbar;\ \mu)], \tag{14}$$

where $\mathfrak{S}_*(\hbar;\ \mu) \leq \mathfrak{S}^*(\hbar;\ \mu)$.

Definition 4 ([27])**.** *Let $\tilde{\mathfrak{S}} : [\sigma, \ell] \subset R \to \mathbb{F}_0$ be a F·N · V mapping such that, for each $\mu \in (0,\ 1]$, the endpoints mapping*

$$\mathfrak{S}_*(\cdot;\ \mu), \mathfrak{S}^*(\cdot;\ \mu) : [\sigma, \ell] \to R,$$

https://doi.org/10.3390/fractalfract10040228

are integrable on $[\mathscr{o},\ell]$.

The $F{\cdot}N\cdot V$ Aumann integral of $\tilde{\mathfrak{S}}$ over $[\mathscr{o},\ell]$ is defined as the $F{\cdot}N$:

$$(FA)\int_{\mathscr{o}}^{\ell}\tilde{\mathfrak{S}}(\hbar)d\hbar, \tag{15}$$

whose μ-cut is given by

$$\left[(FA)\int_{\mathscr{o}}^{\ell}\tilde{\mathfrak{S}}(\hbar)d\hbar\right]^{\mu}=(IA)\int_{\mathscr{o}}^{\ell}\mathfrak{S}_{\mu}(\hbar)d\hbar=\left[\int_{\mathscr{o}}^{\ell}\mathfrak{S}_{*}(\hbar;\mu)d\hbar,\int_{\mathscr{o}}^{\ell}\mathfrak{S}^{*}(\hbar;\mu)d\hbar\right]. \tag{16}$$

where FA and IA represent $F{\cdot}N\cdot V$-Aumann and interval Aumann integrals, respectively.

The $F{\cdot}N\cdot V$-Aumann integral preserves the $F{\cdot}N\cdot V$-structure and plays a fundamental role in fuzzy analysis, particularly in the study of f $F{\cdot}N\cdot V$-inequalities, $F{\cdot}N\cdot V$-fractional integrals, and $F{\cdot}N\cdot V$ $H\cdot H$-type results.

3. Fuzzy-Number-Valued Generalized Fractional Integral and Convexity

This section consists of the classical definition of fuzzy convex function and newly defined $\boldsymbol{F{\cdot}N}\cdot V$-generalized fractional integrals. Additionally, some extended versions of $\boldsymbol{H}\cdot\boldsymbol{H}$-type inequality are also obtained.

Definition 5. *A mapping* $\tilde{\mathfrak{S}}:\Delta=[\mathscr{o},\ell]\to\mathbb{F}_0^{+}$ *is said to be a* $F{\cdot}N\cdot V$*-convex mapping if the following inequality holds:*

$$\tilde{\mathfrak{S}}(v\hbar+(1-v)\jmath)\leq_F v\odot\tilde{\mathfrak{S}}(\hbar)\oplus(1-v)\odot\tilde{\mathfrak{S}}(\jmath)$$

for all $(\hbar,\jmath)\in[\mathscr{o},\ell]$, *and* $v\in[0,\,1]$.

Definition 6. *Let* $\mathfrak{g}:[\mathscr{o},\ell]\to\mathbb{R}$ *be an increasing and positive monotone mapping on* $(\mathscr{o},\ell)$ *having a continuous derivative* $\mathfrak{g}'(\hbar)$ *on* $(\mathscr{o},\ell)$ *and* $\tilde{\mathfrak{S}}\in IR_{([\mathscr{o},\ell])}$. *The* $F{\cdot}N\cdot V$*-left-sided* $(\mathbb{J}^{\curlywedge}_{\mathscr{o}^{+};\mathfrak{g}}\tilde{\mathfrak{S}}(\hbar))$ *and right-sided* $(\mathbb{J}^{\curlywedge}_{\ell^{-};\mathfrak{g}}\tilde{\mathfrak{S}}(\hbar))$ *fractional integrals of* $\tilde{\mathfrak{S}}$ *in relation to the mapping* $\mathfrak{g}$ *on* $[\mathscr{o},\ell]$ *of order* $\curlywedge>0$ *are described by:*

$$\mathbb{J}^{\curlywedge}_{\mathscr{o}^{+};\mathfrak{g}}\tilde{\mathfrak{S}}(\hbar)=\frac{1}{\Gamma(\curlywedge)}(FA)\int_{\mathscr{o}}^{\hbar}\frac{\mathfrak{g}'(v)}{[\mathfrak{g}(\hbar)-\mathfrak{g}(v)]^{1-\curlywedge}}\tilde{\mathfrak{S}}(v)dv,\hbar>\mathscr{o} \tag{17}$$

and

$$\mathbb{J}^{\curlywedge}_{\ell^{-};\mathfrak{g}}\tilde{\mathfrak{S}}(\hbar)=\frac{1}{\Gamma(\curlywedge)}(FA)\int_{\hbar}^{\ell}\frac{\mathfrak{g}'(v)}{[\mathfrak{g}(v)-\mathfrak{g}(\hbar)]^{1-\curlywedge}}\tilde{\mathfrak{S}}(v)dv,\hbar<\ell, \tag{18}$$

respectively.

Corollary 1. *If* $\tilde{\mathfrak{S}}:[\mathscr{o},\ell]\to\mathbb{F}_0$ *is an* $F{\cdot}N\cdot V$*-mapping such that from* μ*-cuts, here, we produce the collection of* $I\cdot V$*-mappings* $\mathfrak{S}_{\mu}:[\mathscr{o},\ell]\to\mathbb{R}_{\mathscr{J}}$ *such that* $[\tilde{\mathfrak{S}}(v)]^{\mu}=\mathfrak{S}_{\mu}(v)=[\underline{\mathfrak{S}}(v;\mu),\overline{\mathfrak{S}}(v;\mu)]$, *for all* $\mu\in[0,1]$ *and* $\mathfrak{g}:[\mathscr{o},\ell]\to\mathbb{R}$ *be an increasing and positive function on* $(\mathscr{o},\ell]$, *having a continuous derivative* $\mathfrak{g}'(\hbar)$ *on* $(\mathscr{o},\ell)$, *then we obtain the following relation*

$$\mathscr{I}^{\curlywedge}_{\mathscr{o}+;\mathfrak{g}}[\tilde{\mathfrak{S}}(\hbar)]^{\mu}=\mathscr{I}^{\curlywedge}_{\mathscr{o}+;\mathfrak{g}}\mathfrak{S}_{\mu}(\hbar)=\left[\mathscr{I}^{\curlywedge}_{\mathscr{o}+;\mathfrak{g}}\underline{\mathfrak{S}}(\hbar;\mu),\mathscr{I}^{\curlywedge}_{\mathscr{o}+;\mathfrak{g}}\overline{\mathfrak{S}}(\hbar;\mu)\right] \tag{19}$$

and

$$\mathscr{I}^{\curlywedge}_{\ell-;\mathfrak{g}}[\tilde{\mathfrak{S}}(\hbar)]^{\mu}=\mathscr{I}^{\curlywedge}_{\ell-;\mathfrak{g}}\mathfrak{S}_{\mu}(\hbar)=\left[\mathscr{I}^{\curlywedge}_{\ell-;\mathfrak{g}}\underline{\mathfrak{S}}(\hbar;\mu),\mathscr{I}^{\curlywedge}_{\ell-;\mathfrak{g}}\overline{\mathfrak{S}}(\hbar;\mu)\right]. \tag{20}$$

https://doi.org/10.3390/fractalfract10040228

Proof. The result follows directly from Theorem 1 together with the stated properties of the function $\mathfrak{g}$. □

We now proceed to the proof of the first theorem. Throughout the subsequent analysis, the following notation will be used:

$$\begin{gathered}\tilde{\mathscr{T}}(\hbar) = \tilde{\mathfrak{S}}(o+\ell-\hbar), \hbar \in [o,\ell] \\ \tilde{\Phi}(\hbar) = \tilde{\mathfrak{S}}(\hbar) \oplus \tilde{\mathscr{T}}(\hbar).\end{gathered} \tag{21}$$

Theorem 2. *Let $\mathfrak{g} : [o,\ell] \to \mathbb{R}$ be positive increasing mappings on $(o,\ell]$ with continuous derivatives such that $\mathfrak{g}'(\hbar)$ on (o,ℓ). If $\tilde{\mathfrak{S}} : [o,\ell] \to \mathbb{F}_0^+$ is a $F\cdot N\cdot V$-coordinated convex mapping on $[o,\ell]$ such that from μ-cuts here, we produce the collection of $I\cdot V$-mappings $\mathfrak{S}_\mu : [o,\ell] \to \mathbb{R}_I^+$ such that $[\tilde{\mathfrak{S}}(v)]^\mu = \mathfrak{S}_\mu(v) = [\underline{\mathfrak{S}}(v;\mu), \overline{\mathfrak{S}}(v;\mu)]$, for all $\mu \in [0,1]$, then for $\curlywedge > 0$, the following $H\cdot H$-type inequality holds in relation to $\mathfrak{g}$:*

$$\tilde{\mathfrak{S}}(\tfrac{o+\ell}{2}) \leq_F \frac{\Gamma(\curlywedge+1)}{4[\mathfrak{g}(\ell)-\mathfrak{g}(o)]^\curlywedge} \odot \left\{ \mathscr{I}^{\curlywedge}_{o^+;\mathfrak{g}} \tilde{\Phi}(\ell) \oplus \mathscr{I}^{\curlywedge}_{\ell^-;\mathfrak{g}} \tilde{\Phi}(o) \right\} \leq_F \frac{\tilde{\mathfrak{S}}(o)+\tilde{\mathfrak{S}}(\ell)}{2}. \tag{22}$$

Proof. Let $u = or + (1-r)\ell$ and $v = (1-r)o + r\ell$ for $r \in [0,1]$. Convexity of $\tilde{\mathfrak{S}}$ allows us to write

$$\tilde{\mathfrak{S}}(\frac{o+\ell}{2}) = \tilde{\mathfrak{S}}(\frac{u+v}{2}) \leq_F \frac{1}{2} \odot \tilde{\mathfrak{S}}(u) + \frac{1}{2} \odot \tilde{\mathfrak{S}}(v).$$

That is, for all μ-cuts,

$$\mathfrak{S}_\mu(\tfrac{o+\ell}{2}) \leq_I \tfrac{1}{2}\mathfrak{S}_\mu(or + (1-r)\ell) + \tfrac{1}{2}\mathfrak{S}_\mu((1-r)o + r\ell) \tag{23}$$

Both sides of (23) are multiplied by

$$\frac{(\ell-o)}{\Gamma(\curlywedge)} \frac{\mathfrak{g}'(r\ell+(1-r)o)}{[\mathfrak{g}(\ell)-\mathfrak{g}(r\ell+(1-r)o)]^{1-\curlywedge}}$$

and then integrating over $[0,1]$ in relation to r, we have

$$\begin{aligned}\mathfrak{S}_\mu(\tfrac{o+\ell}{2})\frac{[\mathfrak{g}(\ell)-\mathfrak{g}(o)]^\curlywedge}{\Gamma(\curlywedge+1)} &\leq_I \tfrac{1}{2}\mathscr{I}_{o+;\mathfrak{g}}\mathscr{T}(\ell) + \tfrac{1}{2}\mathscr{I}^{\curlywedge}_{o^+;\mathfrak{g}}\mathfrak{S}_\mu(\ell) \\ &= \tfrac{1}{2}\mathscr{I}^{\curlywedge}_{o^+;\mathfrak{g}}\Phi_\mu(\ell) \\ \frac{(\ell-o)}{\Gamma(\curlywedge)} &\frac{\mathfrak{g}'(r\ell+(1-r)o)}{[\mathfrak{g}(r\ell+(1-r)o)-\mathfrak{g}(o)]^{1-\curlywedge}}\end{aligned} \tag{24}$$

and then integrating over $[0,1]$ in relation to r, we get

$$\begin{aligned}\mathfrak{S}_\mu(\tfrac{o+\ell}{2})\frac{[\mathfrak{g}(\ell)-\mathfrak{g}(o)]^\curlywedge}{\Gamma(\curlywedge+1)} &\leq_I \tfrac{1}{2}\mathscr{I}^{\curlywedge}_{\ell^-;\mathfrak{g}}\mathscr{T}(o) + \tfrac{1}{2}\mathscr{I}^{\curlywedge}_{\ell^-;\mathfrak{g}}\mathfrak{S}_\mu(o) \\ &= \tfrac{1}{2}\mathscr{I}^{\curlywedge}_{\ell^-;\mathfrak{g}}\Phi_\mu(o)\end{aligned} \tag{25}$$

The inequalities (24) and (25) are added side by side to get

$$\mathfrak{S}_\mu(\frac{o+\ell}{2}) \leq_I \frac{\Gamma(\curlywedge+1)}{4[\mathfrak{g}(\ell)-\mathfrak{g}(o)]^\curlywedge}\left\{\mathscr{I}^{\curlywedge}_{o^+;\mathfrak{g}}\Phi_\mu(\ell) + \mathscr{I}^{\curlywedge}_{\ell^-;\mathfrak{g}}\Phi_\mu(o)\right\}$$

As a result, relation (22)'s first section is finished.

Nevertheless, due to $\mathfrak{S}_\mu$'s convexity, we may write

$$\mathfrak{S}_\mu(or + (1-r)\ell) + \mathfrak{S}_\mu((1-r)o + r\ell) \leq_I \mathfrak{S}_\mu(o) + \mathfrak{S}_\mu(\ell) \tag{26}$$

 https://doi.org/10.3390/fractalfract10040228

Both sides of (26) are multiplied by

$$\frac{(\ell - o)}{\Gamma(\lambda)} \frac{\mathfrak{g}'(r\ell + (1-r)o)}{[\mathfrak{g}(\ell) - \mathfrak{g}(r\ell + (1-r)o)]^{1-\lambda}}$$

and then integrating over $[0,1]$ in relation to r, we get

$$\mathcal{J}^{\lambda}_{o^+;\mathfrak{g}}\mathcal{T}(\ell) + \mathcal{J}^{\lambda}_{o^+;\mathfrak{g}}\mathfrak{S}_\mu(\ell) = \mathcal{J}^{\lambda}_{o^+;\mathfrak{g}}\Phi_\mu(\ell) \leq_I \frac{[\mathfrak{g}(\ell)-\mathfrak{g}(o)]^{\lambda}}{\Gamma(\lambda+1)}\{\mathfrak{S}_\mu(o) + \mathfrak{S}_\mu(\ell)\} \tag{27}$$

Similarly, both sides of (27) are multiplied by

$$\frac{(\ell - o)}{\Gamma(\lambda)} \frac{\mathfrak{g}'(r\ell + (1-r)o)}{[\mathfrak{g}(r\ell + (1-r)o) - \mathfrak{g}(o)]^{1-\lambda}}$$

and then integrating over $[0,1]$ in relation to r, we have

$$\mathcal{J}^{\lambda}_{\ell^-;\mathfrak{g}}\mathcal{T}(o) + \mathcal{J}^{\lambda}_{\ell^-;\mathfrak{g}}\mathfrak{S}_\mu(o) = \mathcal{J}^{\lambda}_{\ell^-;\mathfrak{g}}\Phi_\mu(o) \leq_I \frac{[\mathfrak{g}(\ell)-\mathfrak{g}(o)]^{\lambda}}{\Gamma(\lambda+1)}\{\mathfrak{S}_\mu(o) + \mathfrak{S}_\mu(\ell)\} \tag{28}$$

Summing the relations (27) and (28),

$$\mathcal{J}^{\lambda}_{\ell^-;\mathfrak{g}}\Phi_\mu(o) + \mathcal{J}^{\lambda}_{o^+;\mathfrak{g}}\Phi_\mu(\ell) \leq_I \frac{2[\mathfrak{g}(\ell) - \mathfrak{g}(o)]^{\lambda}}{\Gamma(\lambda+1)}\{\mathfrak{S}_\mu(o) + \mathfrak{S}_\mu(\ell)\}$$

The proof is finished in this manner. □

Remark 3. *(i) The inequality (2) is obtained by taking $\mathfrak{g}(v) = v$ in (22). (ii) The F·N · V-left-sided and right-sided Riemann–Liouville fractional integrals are obtained by taking $\mathfrak{g}(v) = v$ in (17) and (18), respectively. (iii) We obtain the FA-integral (15) of the $\tilde{\mathfrak{S}}$ function if we take $\mathfrak{g}(v) = v$ and $\lambda = 1$ in (17) and (18).*

Theorem 3. *Let $\mathfrak{g} : [o,\ell] \to \mathbb{R}$ be positive increasing mappings on $(o,\ell]$ with continuous derivatives such that $\mathfrak{g}'(k)$ on (o,ℓ). If $\tilde{\mathfrak{S}} : [o,\ell] \to \mathbb{F}_0^+$ is a F·N · V-coordinated convex mapping on $[o,\ell]$ such that from μ-cuts here, we produce the collection of I · V-mappings $\mathfrak{S}_\mu : [o,\ell] \to \mathbb{R}_I^+$ such that $[\tilde{\mathfrak{S}}(v)]^\mu = \mathfrak{S}_\mu(v) = [\underline{\mathfrak{S}}(v;\mu), \overline{\mathfrak{S}}(v;\mu)]$, for all $\mu \in [0,1]$, then for $\lambda > 0$, the following H · H-type inequality holds in relation to $\mathfrak{g}$:*

$$\begin{aligned} &\frac{\check{K}^{\lambda}_{\mathfrak{g}}}{\Gamma(\lambda+1)} \odot \tilde{\mathfrak{S}}\left(\frac{o+\ell}{2}\right) \\ \leq_F\ & \frac{1}{2} \odot \left\{ \mathcal{J}^{\lambda}_{\left(\frac{o+\ell}{2}\right)^-;\mathfrak{g}} \tilde{\Phi}(o) \oplus \mathcal{J}^{\lambda}_{\left(\frac{o+\ell}{2}\right)^+;\mathfrak{g}} \tilde{\Phi}(\ell) \right\} \\ \leq_F\ & \frac{\check{K}^{\lambda}_{\mathfrak{g}}}{\Gamma(\lambda+1)} \odot \left(\frac{\tilde{\mathfrak{S}}(o) \oplus \tilde{\mathfrak{S}}(\ell)}{2}\right) \end{aligned} \tag{29}$$

where

$$\check{K}^{\lambda}_{\mathfrak{g}} = \left[\mathfrak{g}(\ell) - \mathfrak{g}\left(\frac{o+\ell}{2}\right)\right]^{\lambda} \oplus \left[\mathfrak{g}\left(\frac{o+\ell}{2}\right) - \mathfrak{g}(o)\right]^{\lambda}$$

Proof. Convexity of $\tilde{\mathfrak{S}}$ allows us to write

$$\tilde{\mathfrak{S}}\left(\frac{k+s}{2}\right) \leq_F \frac{\tilde{\mathfrak{S}}(k) \oplus \tilde{\mathfrak{S}}(s)}{2}$$

for $k, s \in [o,\ell]$. If we take $k = \frac{r}{2}o + \frac{2-r}{2}\ell$ and $s = \frac{2-r}{2}o + \frac{r}{2}\ell$ for $r \in [0,1]$, we obtain

$$\mathfrak{S}_\mu\left(\frac{o+\ell}{2}\right) \leq_I \frac{1}{2}\mathfrak{S}_\mu\left(\frac{r}{2}o + \frac{2-r}{2}\ell\right) + \frac{1}{2}\mathfrak{S}_\mu\left(\frac{2-r}{2}o + \frac{r}{2}\ell\right) \leq_I \frac{\mathfrak{S}_\mu(o)+\mathfrak{S}_\mu(\ell)}{2}. \tag{30}$$

 https://doi.org/10.3390/fractalfract10040228

Both sides of (30) are multiplied by

$$\frac{(\ell-o)}{2\Gamma(\lambda)}\frac{\mathfrak{g}'(\frac{r}{2}o+\frac{2-r}{2}\ell)}{\left[\mathfrak{g}(\ell)-\mathfrak{g}(\frac{r}{2}o+\frac{2-r}{2}\ell)\right]^{1-\lambda}}$$

and then integrating over $[0,1]$ in relation to r, we get

$$\begin{aligned}
&\left\{\frac{(\ell-o)}{2\Gamma(\lambda)}\int_0^1 \frac{\mathfrak{g}'(\frac{r}{2}o+\frac{2-r}{2}\ell)}{\left[\mathfrak{g}(\ell)-\mathfrak{g}(\frac{r}{2}o+\frac{2-r}{2}\ell)\right]^{1-\lambda}}dr\right\}\mathfrak{S}_\mu(\frac{o+\ell}{2})\\
\leq_I\ &\frac{(\ell-o)}{4\Gamma(\lambda)}(IA)\int_0^1 \frac{\mathfrak{g}'(\frac{r}{2}o+\frac{2-r}{2}\ell)}{\left[\mathfrak{g}(\ell)-\mathfrak{g}(\frac{r}{2}o+\frac{2-r}{2}\ell)\right]^{1-\lambda}}\left[\mathfrak{S}_\mu(\frac{r}{2}o+\frac{2-r}{2}\ell)+\mathfrak{S}_\mu(\frac{2-r}{2}o+\frac{r}{2}\ell)\right]dr\\
\leq_I\ &\left\{\frac{(\ell-o)}{\Gamma(\lambda)}\int_0^1 \frac{\mathfrak{g}'(\frac{r}{2}o+\frac{2-r}{2}\ell)}{\left[\mathfrak{g}(\ell)-\mathfrak{g}(\frac{r}{2}o+\frac{2-r}{2}\ell)\right]^{1-\lambda}}dr\right\}\frac{\mathfrak{S}_\mu(o)+\mathfrak{S}_\mu(\ell)}{4}
\end{aligned}$$

By change in variable $v=\frac{r}{2}o+\frac{2-r}{2}\ell$, we have

$$\begin{aligned}
&\left\{\frac{1}{\Gamma(\lambda)}\int_{\frac{o+\ell}{2}}^{\ell} \frac{\mathfrak{g}'(v)}{[\mathfrak{g}(\ell)-\mathfrak{g}(v)]^{1-\lambda}}dv\right\}\mathfrak{S}_\mu(\frac{o+\ell}{2})\\
\leq_I\ &\frac{1}{2\Gamma(\lambda)}(IA)\int_{\frac{o+\ell}{2}}^{\ell} \frac{\mathfrak{g}'(v)}{[\mathfrak{g}(\ell)-\mathfrak{g}(v)]^{1-\lambda}}[\mathfrak{S}_\mu(v)+T(v)]dv\\
\leq_I\ &\left\{\frac{1}{\Gamma(\lambda)}\int_{\frac{o+\ell}{2}}^{\ell} \frac{\mathfrak{g}'(v)}{[\mathfrak{g}(\ell)-\mathfrak{g}(v)]^{1-\lambda}}dv\right\}\frac{\mathfrak{S}_\mu(o)+\mathfrak{S}_\mu(\ell)}{2}
\end{aligned} \tag{31}$$

It is clear that

$$\int_{\frac{o+\ell}{2}}^{\ell} \frac{\mathfrak{g}'(v)}{[\mathfrak{g}(\ell)-\mathfrak{g}(v)]^{1-\lambda}}dv=\frac{\left[\mathfrak{g}(\ell)-\mathfrak{g}(\frac{o+\ell}{2})\right]^{\lambda}}{\lambda} \tag{32}$$

Inequality (32) and Definition 6 are used to get

$$\begin{aligned}
&\tfrac{1}{\Gamma(\lambda+1)}\left[\mathfrak{g}(\ell)-\mathfrak{g}(\tfrac{o+\ell}{2})\right]^{\lambda}\mathfrak{S}_\mu(\tfrac{o+\ell}{2})\\
&\leq_I \tfrac{1}{2}\mathcal{I}^{\lambda}_{(\frac{o+\ell}{2})+;\mathfrak{g}}\Phi_\mu(\ell)\\
&\leq_I \tfrac{\left[\mathfrak{g}(\ell)-\mathfrak{g}(\frac{o+\ell}{2})\right]^{\lambda}}{\Gamma(\lambda+1)}\tfrac{\mathfrak{S}_\mu(o)+\mathfrak{S}_\mu(\ell)}{2}
\end{aligned} \tag{33}$$

Similarly, if we perform the operations that multiply (30)'s two sides by

$$\frac{(\ell-o)}{2\Gamma(\lambda)}\frac{\mathfrak{g}'(\frac{2-r}{2}o+\frac{r}{2}\ell)}{\left[\mathfrak{g}(\frac{2-r}{2}o+\frac{r}{2}\ell)-\mathfrak{g}(o)\right]^{1-\lambda}}$$

https://doi.org/10.3390/fractalfract10040228

When we change the variable $\upsilon = \frac{2-r}{2}o + \frac{r}{2}\ell$ and integrate over $[0,1]$ with respect to r, respectively, we get

$$\begin{aligned}
&\left\{\frac{1}{\Gamma(\lambda)}\int_{o}^{\frac{o+\ell}{2}} \frac{g'(\upsilon)}{[g(\upsilon)-g(o)]^{1-\lambda}}d\upsilon\right\}\mathfrak{S}_{\mu}\left(\frac{o+\ell}{2}\right) \\
\leq_I\ & \frac{1}{2\Gamma(\lambda)}(IA)\int_{o}^{\frac{o+\ell}{2}} \frac{g'(\upsilon)}{[g(\upsilon)-g(o)]^{1-\lambda}}[\mathfrak{S}_{\mu}(\upsilon)+\mathscr{T}(\upsilon)]d\upsilon \\
\leq_I\ & \left\{\frac{1}{\Gamma(\lambda)}\int_{o}^{\frac{o+\ell}{2}} \frac{g'(\upsilon)}{[g(\upsilon)-g(o)]^{1-\lambda}}d\upsilon\right\}\frac{\mathfrak{S}_{\mu}(o)+\mathfrak{S}_{\mu}(\ell)}{2}
\end{aligned} \tag{34}$$

In relation (34), if we apply the following:

$$\int_{o}^{\frac{o+\ell}{2}} \frac{g'(\upsilon)}{[g(\upsilon)-g(o)]^{1-\lambda}}d\upsilon = \frac{\left[g\left(\frac{o+\ell}{2}\right)-g(o)\right]^{\lambda}}{\lambda}$$

we obtain

$$\begin{aligned}
&\tfrac{1}{\Gamma(\lambda+1)}\left[g\left(\tfrac{o+\ell}{2}\right)-g(o)\right]^{\lambda}\mathfrak{S}_{\mu}\left(\tfrac{o+\ell}{2}\right) \\
&\leq_I \tfrac{1}{2}\mathcal{J}^{\lambda}_{\left(\frac{o+\ell}{2}\right)^{-};g}\Phi_{\mu}(o) \\
&\leq_I \tfrac{\left[g\left(\frac{o+\ell}{2}\right)-g(o)\right]^{\lambda}}{\Gamma(\lambda+1)}\tfrac{\mathfrak{S}_{\mu}(o)+\mathfrak{S}_{\mu}(\ell)}{2}
\end{aligned} \tag{35}$$

Summing the relations (33) and (35),

$$\begin{aligned}
\tfrac{\breve{K}_g^{\lambda}}{\Gamma(\lambda+1)}\mathfrak{S}_{\mu}\left(\tfrac{o+\ell}{2}\right) &\leq_I \tfrac{1}{2}\left\{\mathcal{J}^{\lambda}_{\left(\frac{o+\ell}{2}\right)^{-};g}\Phi_{\mu}(o)+\mathcal{J}^{\lambda}_{\left(\frac{o+\ell}{2}\right)^{+};g}\Phi_{\mu}(\ell)\right\} \\
&\leq_I \tfrac{\breve{K}_g^{\lambda}}{\Gamma(\lambda+1)}\tfrac{\mathfrak{S}_{\mu}(o)+\mathfrak{S}_{\mu}(\ell)}{2}
\end{aligned}$$

Thus, the proof is finished. □

Corollary 2. *Taking $g(\upsilon) = \upsilon$ from (29) gives us*

$$\tilde{\mathfrak{S}}\left(\tfrac{o+\ell}{2}\right) \leq_F \tfrac{2^{\lambda-1}\Gamma(\lambda+1)}{(\ell-o)^{\lambda}} \odot \left\{\mathcal{J}^{\lambda}_{\left(\frac{o+\ell}{2}\right)^{-}}\tilde{\mathfrak{S}}(o) \oplus \mathcal{J}^{\lambda}_{\left(\frac{o+\ell}{2}\right)^{+}}\tilde{\mathfrak{S}}(\ell)\right\} \leq_F \tfrac{\tilde{\mathfrak{S}}(o)\oplus\tilde{\mathfrak{S}}(\ell)}{2} \tag{36}$$

4. Fuzzy-Number-Valued Double Integral, and Coordinated Convexity

Firstly, we recall the concept of $F{\cdot}N \cdot V$-double integral given by Khan et al. [27] in a previous study.

Definition 7 ([27]). *Let $\Delta = [o,\ell] \times [\iota, \jmath] \subset R^2$ and let $\tilde{\mathfrak{S}} : [o,\ell] \to \mathbb{F}_0$ be a $F{\cdot}N \cdot V$-mapping. Assume that, for every $\mu \in (0, 1]$, the endpoint functions*

$$\mathfrak{S}_*((\cdot,\cdot);\ \mu), \mathfrak{S}^*((\cdot,\cdot);\ \mu) : [o,\ell] \times [\iota, \jmath] \to R,$$

are integrable over Δ.

*The $F{\cdot}N \cdot$ **V**-double integral of $\tilde{\mathfrak{S}}$ over Δ, in the sense of $F{\cdot}N \cdot$ **V**-Aumann, is defined as the $F{\cdot}N$:*

$$(FD)\iint_{\Delta}\tilde{\mathfrak{S}}(r,\upsilon)dr d\upsilon, \tag{37}$$

https://doi.org/10.3390/fractalfract10040228

whose μ-cut is given by

$$\left[(FD)\iint_{\Delta}\tilde{\mathfrak{S}}(r,v)drdv\right]^{\mu}=(ID)\iint_{\Delta}\mathfrak{S}_{\mu}(r,v)drdv$$

$$=\left[\iint_{\Delta}\mathfrak{S}_{*}((r,v);\,\mu)drdv,\iint_{\Delta}\mathfrak{S}^{*}((r,v);\,\mu)drdv\right].$$

The F·N · V-double integral preserves the F·N-structure and generalizes the classical double integral to F·N · V-mappings. It plays a fundamental role in the study of fuzzy partial differential equations, F·N · V-fractional integrals, and H · H-type inequalities for coordinated convex F·N · V-mappings.

Definition 8. *Let $\tilde{\mathfrak{S}}\in FA_{([o,\ell]\times[\imath,\jmath])}$. The Hadamard F·N · V-fractional integrals $\mathfrak{J}^{\lambda,\rtimes}_{o+,\imath+}\tilde{\mathfrak{S}}$, $\mathfrak{J}^{\lambda,\rtimes}_{o+,\jmath-}\tilde{\mathfrak{S}}$, $\mathfrak{J}^{\lambda,\rtimes}_{\ell-,\imath+}\tilde{\mathfrak{S}}$, and $\mathfrak{J}^{\lambda,\rtimes}_{\ell-,\jmath-}\tilde{\mathfrak{S}}$ of order $\lambda,\ \rtimes\ >\ 0$ with $o,\imath\ \geq\ 0$ are described by*

$$\mathfrak{J}^{\lambda,\rtimes}_{o+,\imath+}\tilde{\mathfrak{S}}(k,s):=\frac{1}{\Gamma(\lambda)\Gamma(\rtimes)}(FA)\int_{o}^{k}\int_{\imath}^{s}(ln\frac{k}{v})^{\lambda-1}(ln\frac{s}{r})^{\rtimes-1}\frac{\tilde{\mathfrak{S}}(v,r)}{vr}drdv,\ k>o,s>\imath, \tag{38}$$

$$\mathfrak{J}^{\lambda,\rtimes}_{o+,\jmath-}\tilde{\mathfrak{S}}(k,s):=\frac{1}{\Gamma(\lambda)\Gamma(\rtimes)}(FA)\int_{o}^{k}\int_{s}^{\jmath}(ln\frac{k}{v})^{\lambda-1}(ln\frac{s}{r})^{\rtimes-1}\frac{\tilde{\mathfrak{S}}(v,r)}{vr}drdv,\ k>o,s<\jmath, \tag{39}$$

$$\mathfrak{J}^{\lambda,\rtimes}_{\ell-,\imath+}\tilde{\mathfrak{S}}(k,s):=\frac{1}{\Gamma(\lambda)\Gamma(\rtimes)}(FA)\int_{k}^{\ell}\int_{\imath}^{s}(ln\frac{v}{k})^{\lambda-1}(ln\frac{s}{r})^{\rtimes-1}\frac{\tilde{\mathfrak{S}}(v,r)}{vr}drdv,\ k<\ell,s>\imath, \tag{40}$$

and

$$\mathfrak{J}^{\lambda,\rtimes}_{\ell-,\jmath-}\tilde{\mathfrak{S}}(k,s):=\frac{1}{\Gamma(\lambda)\Gamma(\rtimes)}(FA)\int_{k}^{\ell}\int_{s}^{\jmath}(ln\frac{k}{v})^{\lambda-1}(ln\frac{s}{r})^{\rtimes-1}\frac{\tilde{\mathfrak{S}}(v,r)}{vr}drdv,\ k<\ell,s<\jmath, \tag{41}$$

respectively.

Now, we give the following generalized F·N · V-fractional integral operators.

Definition 9. *Let $\mathfrak{g}:[o,\ell]\to\mathbb{R}$ be an increasing and positive monotone mapping on $(o,\ell]$, having a continuous derivative $\mathfrak{g}'(k)$ on (o,ℓ), and let $\ltimes:[\imath,\jmath]\to\mathbb{R}$ be an increasing and positive monotone mapping on $(\imath,\jmath]$, having a continuous derivative $\ltimes'(s)$on $(\imath,\jmath)$ and $\tilde{\mathfrak{S}}\in FA_{([o,\ell]\times[\imath,\jmath])}$. The F· N · V-left-sided and right-sided fractional integral operators for mappings of two variables are described by*

$$\mathbb{J}^{\lambda,\rtimes}_{o+,\imath+;\mathfrak{g},\ltimes}\tilde{\mathfrak{S}}(k,s):=\frac{1}{\Gamma(\lambda)\Gamma(\rtimes)}(FA)\int_{o}^{k}\int_{\imath}^{s}\frac{\mathfrak{g}'(v)}{[\mathfrak{g}(k)-\mathfrak{g}(v)]^{1-\lambda}}\frac{\ltimes'(r)}{[\ltimes(s)-\ltimes(r)]^{1-\rtimes}}\tilde{\mathfrak{S}}(v,r)drdv,\ k>o,s>\imath, \tag{42}$$

$$\mathbb{J}^{\lambda,\rtimes}_{o+,\jmath-;\mathfrak{g},\ltimes}\tilde{\mathfrak{S}}(k,s):=\frac{1}{\Gamma(\lambda)\Gamma(\rtimes)}(FA)\int_{o}^{k}\int_{s}^{\jmath}\frac{\mathfrak{g}'(v)}{[\mathfrak{g}(k)-\mathfrak{g}(v)]^{1-\lambda}}\frac{\ltimes'(r)}{[\ltimes(s)-\ltimes(r)]^{1-\rtimes}}\tilde{\mathfrak{S}}(v,r)drdv,\ k>o,s<\jmath, \tag{43}$$

$$\mathbb{J}^{\lambda,\rtimes}_{\ell-,\imath+;\mathfrak{g},\ltimes}\tilde{\mathfrak{S}}(k,s):=\frac{1}{\Gamma(\lambda)\Gamma(\rtimes)}(FA)\int_{k}^{\ell}\int_{\imath}^{s}\frac{\mathfrak{g}'(v)}{[\mathfrak{g}(k)-\mathfrak{g}(v)]^{1-\lambda}}\frac{\ltimes'(r)}{[\ltimes(s)-\ltimes(r)]^{1-\rtimes}}\tilde{\mathfrak{S}}(v,r)drdv,\ k<\ell,s>\imath, \tag{44}$$

and

$$\mathbb{J}^{\lambda,\rtimes}_{\ell-,\jmath-;\mathfrak{g},\ltimes}\tilde{\mathfrak{S}}(k,s):=\frac{1}{\Gamma(\lambda)\Gamma(\rtimes)}(FA)\int_{k}^{\ell}\int_{s}^{\jmath}\frac{\mathfrak{g}'(v)}{[\mathfrak{g}(k)-\mathfrak{g}(v)]^{1-\lambda}}\frac{\ltimes'(r)}{[\ltimes(s)-\ltimes(r)]^{1-\rtimes}}\tilde{\mathfrak{S}}(v,r)drdv,\ k<\ell,s<\jmath, \tag{45}$$

 https://doi.org/10.3390/fractalfract10040228

for $\measuredangle, \rtimes > 0$.

Based on the definitions given above, we may provide the $F{\cdot}N \cdot V$*-integrals as follows:*

$$\mathbb{J}^{\measuredangle}_{o^+;\mathfrak{g}}\, \tilde{\mathfrak{S}}(k, \frac{\imath+\jmath}{2}) := \frac{1}{\Gamma(\measuredangle)}(FA)\int_{o}^{k} \frac{\mathfrak{g}'(v)}{[\mathfrak{g}(k)-\mathfrak{g}(v)]^{1-\measuredangle}}\tilde{\mathfrak{S}}(v, \frac{\imath+\jmath}{2})dv, k > o \tag{46}$$

$$\mathbb{J}^{\measuredangle}_{\ell^-;\mathfrak{g}}\, \tilde{\mathfrak{S}}(k, \frac{\imath+\jmath}{2}) := \frac{1}{\Gamma(\measuredangle)}(FA)\int_{k}^{\ell} \frac{\mathfrak{g}'(v)}{[\mathfrak{g}(v)-\mathfrak{g}(k)]^{1-\measuredangle}}\tilde{\mathfrak{S}}(v, \frac{\imath+\jmath}{2})dv, k < \ell \tag{47}$$

$$\mathbb{J}^{\rtimes}_{\imath^+;\ltimes}\, \tilde{\mathfrak{S}}(\frac{o+\ell}{2}, s) := \frac{1}{\Gamma(\rtimes)}(FA)\int_{\imath}^{s} \frac{\ltimes'(v)}{[\ltimes(s)-\ltimes(r)]^{1-\rtimes}}\tilde{\mathfrak{S}}(\frac{o+\ell}{2}, r)dr, s > \imath, \tag{48}$$

and

$$\mathbb{J}^{\rtimes}_{\jmath^-;\ltimes}\, \tilde{\mathfrak{S}}(\frac{o+\ell}{2}, s) := \frac{1}{\Gamma(\rtimes)}(FA)\int_{\imath}^{s} \frac{\ltimes'(v)}{[\ltimes(r)-\ltimes(s)]^{1-\rtimes}}\tilde{\mathfrak{S}}(\frac{o+\ell}{2}, r)dr, s < \jmath. \tag{49}$$

If we decide to $\mathfrak{g}(v) = \frac{v^{\rho}}{\rho}$ *and* $\ltimes(r) = \frac{r^{\sigma}}{\sigma}$, $\rho, \sigma > 0$, *the definition that follows is found in Definition 9.*

Definition 10. *Let* $\tilde{\mathfrak{S}} \in FA_{([o,\ell]\times[\imath,\jmath])}$. *The Katugampola fractional integrals for* $F{\cdot}N \cdot V$*-mapping with two variables are described by*

$${}^{\rho,\sigma}\mathbb{I}^{\measuredangle,\rtimes}_{o^+,\imath^+}\tilde{\mathfrak{S}}(k, s) := \frac{\rho^{1-\measuredangle}\sigma^{1-\rtimes}}{\Gamma(\measuredangle)\Gamma(\rtimes)}(FA)\int_{o}^{k}\int_{\imath}^{s} \frac{v^{\rho-1}}{[k^{\rho}-v^{\rho}]^{1-\measuredangle}}\,\frac{r^{\sigma-1}}{[s^{\sigma}-r^{\sigma}]^{1-\rtimes}}\,\tilde{\mathfrak{S}}(v, r)dr dv, k > o, s > \imath, \tag{50}$$

$${}^{\rho,\sigma}\mathbb{I}^{\measuredangle,\rtimes}_{o^+,\jmath^-}\tilde{\mathfrak{S}}(k, s) := \frac{\rho^{1-\measuredangle}\sigma^{1-\rtimes}}{\Gamma(\measuredangle)\Gamma(\rtimes)}(FA)\int_{o}^{k}\int_{s}^{\jmath} \frac{v^{\rho-1}}{[k^{\rho}-v^{\rho}]^{1-\measuredangle}}\,\frac{r^{\sigma-1}}{[r^{\sigma}-s^{\sigma}]^{1-\rtimes}}\,\tilde{\mathfrak{S}}(v, r)dr dv, k > o, s < \jmath, \tag{51}$$

$${}^{\rho,\sigma}\mathbb{I}^{\measuredangle,\rtimes}_{\ell^-,\imath^+}\tilde{\mathfrak{S}}(k, s) := \frac{\rho^{1-\measuredangle}\sigma^{1-\rtimes}}{\Gamma(\measuredangle)\Gamma(\rtimes)}(FA)\int_{k}^{\ell}\int_{\imath}^{s} \frac{v^{\rho-1}}{[v^{\rho}-k^{\rho}]^{1-\measuredangle}}\,\frac{r^{\sigma-1}}{[s^{\sigma}-r^{\sigma}]^{1-\rtimes}}\,\tilde{\mathfrak{S}}(v, r)dr dv, k < \ell, s < \imath, \tag{52}$$

and

$${}^{\rho,\sigma}\mathbb{I}^{\measuredangle,\rtimes}_{\ell^-,\jmath^-}\tilde{\mathfrak{S}}(k, s) := \frac{\rho^{1-\measuredangle}\sigma^{1-\rtimes}}{\Gamma(\measuredangle)\Gamma(\rtimes)}(FA)\int_{k}^{\ell}\int_{s}^{\jmath} \frac{v^{\rho-1}}{[v^{\rho}-k^{\rho}]^{1-\measuredangle}}\,\frac{r^{\sigma-1}}{[r^{\sigma}-s^{\sigma}]^{1-\rtimes}}\,\tilde{\mathfrak{S}}(v, r)dr dv, k < \ell, s < \jmath. \tag{53}$$

Now, we recall the concept of $F{\cdot}N \cdot V$*-coordinated convex mappings that is given by Khan et al.* [27,28] *in a previous study as follows.*

Definition 11. *A mapping* $\tilde{\mathfrak{S}} : \Delta = [o, \ell] \times [\imath, \jmath] \to \mathbb{F}_0^+$ *is said to be a* $F{\cdot}N \cdot V$*-coordinated convex mapping if the following inequality holds:*

$$\begin{gathered}\tilde{\mathfrak{S}}(vk + (1-v)s, ru + (1-r)\ltimes)\\ \leq_F vr \odot \tilde{\mathfrak{S}}(k, u) \oplus v(1-r) \odot \tilde{\mathfrak{S}}(k, \ltimes) \oplus r(1-v) \odot \tilde{\mathfrak{S}}(s, u) \oplus (1-r)(1-v) \odot \tilde{\mathfrak{S}}(s, \ltimes)\end{gathered}$$

for all (k, u), $(s, \ltimes) \in \Delta$, *and* $r, v \in [0, 1]$.

Lemma 1. *A mapping* $\tilde{\mathfrak{S}} : \Delta = [o, \ell] \times [\imath, \jmath] \to \mathbb{F}_0^+$ *is* $F{\cdot}N \cdot V$*-convex on coordinates if and only if there exist two mappings* $\tilde{\mathfrak{S}}_k : [\imath, \jmath] \to \mathbb{F}_0^+$, $\tilde{\mathfrak{S}}_k(\ltimes) = \tilde{\mathfrak{S}}(k, \ltimes)$ *and* $\tilde{\mathfrak{S}}_s : [o, \ell] \to \mathbb{F}_0^+$, $\tilde{\mathfrak{S}}_s(u) = \tilde{\mathfrak{S}}(s, u)$ *that are* $F{\cdot}N \cdot V$*-convex.*

Proof. The proof of this lemma is followed immediately by the definition of $F{\cdot}N \cdot V$-coordinated convex mapping. □

https://doi.org/10.3390/fractalfract10040228

It is easy to prove that a $F\cdot N\cdot V$-convex mapping is $F\cdot N\cdot V$-coordinated convex, but the converse may not be true. For this, we can see the following example:

Example 1. *A $F\cdot N\cdot V$-mapping $\tilde{\mathfrak{S}} : [0,\ 1]^2 \to \mathbb{F}_0^+$ defined as $\tilde{\mathfrak{S}}(\hbar, \mathscr{s}) = \left[\hbar\mathscr{s},\ (6\ -\ e^{\hbar})(6\ -\ e^{\mathscr{s}})\right]$ is $F\cdot N\cdot V$-convex on coordinates, but it is not $F\cdot N\cdot V$-convex on $[0,\ 1]^2$.*

Note that the results obtained in the next section generalize and unify several existing $H\cdot H$-type inequalities. In the following section, we illustrate the applicability of our main theorems through special cases and related consequences.

Related Inequalities

In this section, the derived inequalities extend classical $H\cdot H$-results to the setting of $F\cdot N\cdot V$-coordinated convex functions involving generalized fractional integrals, thereby providing a broader and more flexible analytical framework. Several important corollaries and special cases of the main results are discussed in the subsequent section.

Theorem 4. *Let $\mathfrak{g} : [\mathscr{o}, \ell] \to \mathbb{R}$ and $\ltimes\ :\ [\imath,\ \jmath] \to \mathbb{R}$ be positive increasing mappings on $(\mathscr{o}, \ell]$ and $(\imath,\ \jmath]$ with continuous derivatives such that $\mathfrak{g}'(\hbar)$ on $(\mathscr{o}, \ell)$ and $\ltimes'(\mathscr{s})$ on $(\imath,\ \jmath)$, respectively. Let $\Delta = [\mathscr{o}, \ell] \times [\imath,\ \jmath]$. If $\tilde{\mathfrak{S}} : \Delta \to \mathbb{F}_0^+$ is a $F\cdot N\cdot V$-coordinated convex mapping on Δ such that from μ-cuts here, we produce the collection of $I\cdot V$-mappings $\mathfrak{S}_\mu : \Delta \to \mathbb{R}_I^+$ described by $\left[\tilde{\mathfrak{S}}(\hbar, \mathscr{s})\right]^\mu = \mathfrak{S}_\mu((\hbar, \mathscr{s})) = \left[\underline{\mathfrak{S}}((\hbar, \mathscr{s});\ \mu), \overline{\mathfrak{S}}((\hbar, \mathscr{s});\ \mu)\right]$, for all $\mu \in [0,1]$ and $(\hbar, \mathscr{s}) \in \Delta$, then for $\leftthreetimes,\ \rtimes > 0$, the following $H\cdot H$-type inequality holds:*

$$\begin{aligned}\tilde{\mathfrak{S}}\left(\frac{\mathscr{o}+\ell}{2}, \frac{\imath+\jmath}{2}\right) &\leq_F \frac{\Gamma(\leftthreetimes+1)\Gamma(\rtimes+1)}{16[\mathfrak{g}(\ell)-\mathfrak{g}(\mathscr{o})]^{\leftthreetimes}\ [\ltimes(\jmath)-\ltimes(\imath)]^{\rtimes}} \odot \left[\mathbb{J}^{\leftthreetimes,\rtimes}_{\mathscr{o}+,\imath+;\mathfrak{g},\ltimes}\tilde{\mathfrak{X}}(\ell,\jmath) \oplus \mathbb{J}^{\leftthreetimes,\rtimes}_{\mathscr{o}+,\jmath-;\mathfrak{g},\ltimes}\tilde{\mathfrak{X}}(\ell,\imath) \oplus \mathbb{J}^{\leftthreetimes,\rtimes}_{\ell-,\imath+;\mathfrak{g},\ltimes}\tilde{\mathfrak{X}}(\mathscr{o},\jmath) \oplus \mathbb{J}^{\leftthreetimes,\rtimes}_{\ell-,\jmath-;\mathfrak{g},\ltimes}\tilde{\mathfrak{X}}(\mathscr{o},\imath)\right] \\ &\leq_F \frac{\tilde{\mathfrak{S}}(\mathscr{o},\imath)\oplus\tilde{\mathfrak{S}}(\mathscr{o},\jmath)\oplus\tilde{\mathfrak{S}}(\ell,\imath)\oplus\tilde{\mathfrak{S}}(\ell,\jmath)}{4},\end{aligned} \tag{54}$$

where

$$\tilde{\mathfrak{X}}1(\hbar, \mathscr{s}) = \tilde{\mathfrak{S}}(\mathscr{o} + \ell - \hbar, \mathscr{s}),$$

$$\tilde{\mathfrak{X}}2(\hbar, \mathscr{s}) = \tilde{\mathfrak{S}}(\hbar, \imath + \jmath - \mathscr{s}),$$

$$\tilde{\mathfrak{X}}3(\hbar, \mathscr{s}) = \tilde{\mathfrak{S}}(\mathscr{o} + \ell - \hbar, \imath + \jmath - \mathscr{s}),$$

$$\tilde{\mathfrak{D}}(\hbar, \mathscr{s}) = \tilde{\mathfrak{S}}(\hbar, \mathscr{s}) \oplus \tilde{\mathfrak{X}}2(\hbar, \mathscr{s})$$

$$\tilde{\mathscr{H}}(\hbar, \mathscr{s}) = \tilde{\mathfrak{S}}(\hbar, \mathscr{s}) \oplus \tilde{\mathfrak{X}}1(\hbar, \mathscr{s})$$

$$\tilde{\mathfrak{K}}(\hbar, \mathscr{s}) = \tilde{\mathfrak{X}}1(\hbar, \mathscr{s}) \oplus \tilde{\mathfrak{X}}3(\hbar, \mathscr{s})$$

$$\tilde{\mathscr{L}}(\hbar, \mathscr{s}) = \tilde{\mathfrak{X}}2(\hbar, \mathscr{s}) \oplus \tilde{\mathfrak{X}}3(\hbar, \mathscr{s})$$

$$\begin{aligned}\tilde{\mathfrak{X}}(\hbar, \mathscr{s}) &= \tilde{\mathfrak{X}}1(\hbar, \mathscr{s}) \oplus \tilde{\mathfrak{X}}2(\hbar, \mathscr{s}) \oplus \tilde{\mathfrak{X}}3(\hbar, \mathscr{s}) \oplus \tilde{\mathfrak{S}}(\hbar, \mathscr{s}) \\ &= \frac{\tilde{\mathfrak{D}}(\hbar, \mathscr{s}) \oplus \tilde{\mathscr{H}}(\hbar, \mathscr{s}) \oplus \tilde{\mathfrak{K}}(\hbar, \mathscr{s}) \oplus \tilde{\mathscr{L}}(\hbar, \mathscr{s})}{2}\end{aligned}$$

https://doi.org/10.3390/fractalfract10040228

for $(\hbar, s) \in [o, \ell] \times [\imath, \jmath]$, *where for all* μ*-cuts* $\in [0,1]$, *we have* $\left[\tilde{\Sigma}1(\hbar, s)\right]^{\mu} = \Sigma_{1\mu}(\hbar, s)$, $\left[\tilde{\Sigma}2(\hbar, s)\right]^{\mu} = \Sigma_{2\mu}(\hbar, s)$, $\left[\tilde{\Sigma}3(\hbar, s)\right]^{\mu} = \Sigma_{3\mu}(\hbar, s)$, $[\tilde{\mathfrak{D}}(\hbar, s)]^{\mu} = \mathfrak{D}_{\mu}(\hbar, s)$, $[\tilde{\mathscr{H}}(\hbar, s)]^{\mu} = \mathscr{H}_{\mu}(\hbar, s)$, $\left[\tilde{\mathfrak{K}}(\hbar, s)\right]^{\mu} = \mathfrak{K}_{\mu}(\hbar, s)$, $[\tilde{\mathscr{L}}(\hbar, s)]^{\mu} = \mathscr{L}_{\mu}(\hbar, s)$ *and* $\left[\tilde{\Sigma}(\hbar, s)\right]^{\mu} = \Sigma_{\mu}(\hbar, s)$.

Proof. Since F is a $F{\cdot}N \cdot V$-coordinated convex mapping on Δ, we have

$$\tilde{\mathfrak{S}}(\frac{u+v}{2}, \frac{p+q}{2}) \leq_F \frac{\tilde{\mathfrak{S}}(u, p) \oplus \tilde{\mathfrak{S}}(u, q) \oplus \tilde{\mathfrak{S}}(v, p) \oplus \tilde{\mathfrak{S}}(v, q)}{4} \tag{55}$$

for $(u, p), (v, q) \in \Delta$. Now, for $\upsilon, \varkappa \in [0, 1]$, let $u = \upsilon o + (1 - \upsilon)\ell, v = (1 - \upsilon)o + \upsilon\ell, p = \imath\varkappa + (1 - \varkappa)\jmath$, and $q = (1 - \varkappa)\imath + \varkappa\jmath$. Then, for all μ-cuts $\in [0,1]$, we have

$$\begin{aligned} \mathfrak{D}_{\mu}(\tfrac{o+\ell}{2}, \tfrac{\imath+\jmath}{2}) \leq_I\ & \tfrac{1}{4}\, \mathfrak{D}_{\mu}(\upsilon o + (1-\upsilon)\ell, \imath\varkappa + (1-\varkappa)\jmath) \\ & + \tfrac{1}{4}\, \mathfrak{S}_{\mu}(\upsilon o + (1-\upsilon)\ell, (1-\varkappa)\imath + \varkappa\jmath) \\ & + \tfrac{1}{4}\mathfrak{S}_{\mu}((1-\upsilon)o + \upsilon\ell, \imath\varkappa + (1-\varkappa)\jmath) + \tfrac{1}{4}\mathfrak{S}_{\mu}((1-\upsilon)o + \upsilon\ell, (1-\varkappa)\imath + \varkappa\jmath). \end{aligned} \tag{56}$$

Both sides of (56) are multiplied by

$$\frac{(\ell - o)(\jmath - \imath)}{\Gamma(\curlywedge)\Gamma(\rtimes)} \frac{\mathfrak{g}'((1-\upsilon)o + \upsilon\ell)}{[\mathfrak{g}(\ell) - \mathfrak{g}\,((1-\upsilon)o + \upsilon\ell)]^{1-\curlywedge}} \frac{\ltimes'((1-\varkappa)\imath + \varkappa\jmath)}{[\ltimes(\jmath) - \ltimes((1-\varkappa)\imath + \varkappa\jmath)]^{1-\beta}}$$

and integrating the resulting inequality in relation to $\upsilon, \varkappa$ over $[0, 1] \times [0, 1]$, we get

$$\begin{aligned} &\tfrac{(\ell-o)(\jmath-\imath)}{\Gamma(\curlywedge)\Gamma(\rtimes)}\, \mathfrak{S}_{\mu}(\tfrac{o+\ell}{2}, \tfrac{\imath+\jmath}{2})\, (IA)\int_0^1 \int_0^1 \left[\tfrac{\mathfrak{g}'((1-\upsilon)o+\upsilon\ell)}{[\mathfrak{g}(\ell)-\mathfrak{g}\,((1-\upsilon)o+\upsilon\ell)]^{1-\curlywedge}}\, \tfrac{\ltimes'((1-\varkappa)\imath+\varkappa\jmath)}{[\ltimes(\jmath)-\ltimes((1-\varkappa)\imath+\varkappa\jmath)]^{1-\beta}}\right] d\varkappa d\upsilon \\ \leq_I\ & \tfrac{(\ell-o)(\jmath-\imath)}{4\Gamma(\curlywedge)\Gamma(\rtimes)}(IA)\int_0^1 \int_0^1 \left[\tfrac{\mathfrak{g}'((1-\upsilon)o+\upsilon\ell)}{[\mathfrak{g}(\ell)-\mathfrak{g}\,((1-\upsilon)o+\upsilon\ell)]^{1-\curlywedge}}\, \tfrac{\ltimes'((1-\varkappa)\imath+\varkappa\jmath)}{[\ltimes(\jmath)-\ltimes((1-\varkappa)\imath+\varkappa\jmath)]^{1-\beta}} \mathfrak{S}_{\mu}(\upsilon o + (1-\upsilon)\ell, \imath\varkappa + (1-\varkappa)\jmath)\right] d\varkappa d\upsilon \\ & + \tfrac{(\ell-o)(\jmath-\imath)}{4\Gamma(\curlywedge)\Gamma(\rtimes)}(IA)\int_0^1 \int_0^1 \left[\tfrac{\mathfrak{g}'((1-\upsilon)o+\upsilon\ell)}{[\mathfrak{g}(\ell)-\mathfrak{g}\,((1-\upsilon)o+\upsilon\ell)]^{1-\curlywedge}}\, \tfrac{\ltimes'((1-\varkappa)\imath+\varkappa\jmath)}{[\ltimes(\jmath)-\ltimes((1-\varkappa)\imath+\varkappa\jmath)]^{1-\beta}} \mathfrak{S}_{\mu}(\upsilon o + (1-\upsilon)\ell, (1-\varkappa)\imath + \varkappa\jmath)\right] d\varkappa d\upsilon \\ & + \tfrac{(\ell-o)(\jmath-\imath)}{4\Gamma(\curlywedge)\Gamma(\rtimes)}(IA)\int_0^1 \int_0^1 \left[\tfrac{\mathfrak{g}'((1-\upsilon)o+\upsilon\ell)}{[\mathfrak{g}(\ell)-\mathfrak{g}\,((1-\upsilon)o+\upsilon\ell)]^{1-\curlywedge}}\, \tfrac{\ltimes'((1-\varkappa)\imath+\varkappa\jmath)}{[\ltimes(\jmath)-\ltimes((1-\varkappa)\imath+\varkappa\jmath)]^{1-\beta}} \mathfrak{S}_{\mu}((1-\upsilon)o + \upsilon\ell, \imath\varkappa + (1-\varkappa)\jmath)\right] d\varkappa d\upsilon \\ & + \tfrac{(\ell-o)(\jmath-\imath)}{4\Gamma(\curlywedge)\Gamma(\rtimes)}(IA)\int_0^1 \int_0^1 \left[\tfrac{\mathfrak{g}'((1-\upsilon)o+\upsilon\ell)}{[\mathfrak{g}(\ell)-\mathfrak{g}\,((1-\upsilon)o+\upsilon\ell)]^{1-\curlywedge}}\, \tfrac{\ltimes'((1-\varkappa)\imath+\varkappa\jmath)}{[\ltimes(\jmath)-\ltimes((1-\varkappa)\imath+\varkappa\jmath)]^{1-\beta}} \mathfrak{S}_{\mu}((1-\upsilon)o + \upsilon\ell, (1-\varkappa)\imath + \varkappa\jmath)\right] d\varkappa d\upsilon \end{aligned}$$

By a simple calculation, we have

$$(IA)\int_0^1 \int_0^1 \left[\frac{\mathfrak{g}'((1-\upsilon)o + \upsilon\ell)}{[\mathfrak{g}(\ell) - \mathfrak{g}\,((1-\upsilon)o + \upsilon\ell)]^{1-\curlywedge}} \frac{\ltimes'((1-\varkappa)\imath + \varkappa\jmath)}{[\ltimes(\jmath) - \ltimes((1-\varkappa)\imath + \varkappa\jmath)]^{1-\beta}}\right] d\varkappa d\upsilon = \frac{[\mathfrak{g}(\ell) - \mathfrak{g}(o)]^{\curlywedge}[\ltimes(\jmath) - \ltimes(\imath)]^{\rtimes}}{\curlywedge \rtimes (\ell - o)(\jmath - \imath)}$$

Using the change in variables $\tau = (1 - \upsilon)o + \upsilon\ell$ *and* $\eta = (1 - \varkappa)\imath + \varkappa\jmath$, we obtain

$$\begin{aligned} \tfrac{[\mathfrak{g}(\ell)-\mathfrak{g}(o)]^{\curlywedge}[\ltimes(\jmath)-\ltimes(\imath)]^{\rtimes}}{\Gamma(\curlywedge+1)\Gamma(\rtimes+1)}\ \mathfrak{S}_{\mu}(\tfrac{o+\ell}{2}, \tfrac{\imath+\jmath}{2}) \leq_I\ & \tfrac{1}{4\Gamma(\curlywedge)\Gamma(\rtimes)}(IA)\int_o^{\ell}\int_{\imath}^{\jmath} \tfrac{\mathfrak{g}'(\tau)}{[\mathfrak{g}(\ell)-\mathfrak{g}\,(\tau)]^{1-\curlywedge}}\, \tfrac{\ltimes'(\eta)}{[\ltimes(\jmath)-\ltimes(\eta)]^{1-\beta}} \mathfrak{S}_{\mu}(o+\ell-\tau,\ \imath+\jmath-\eta) d\eta d\tau \\ & + \tfrac{1}{4\Gamma(\curlywedge)\Gamma(\rtimes)}(IA)\int_o^{\ell}\int_{\imath}^{\jmath} \tfrac{\mathfrak{g}'(\tau)}{[\mathfrak{g}(\ell)-\mathfrak{g}\,(\tau)]^{1-\curlywedge}}\, \tfrac{\ltimes'(\eta)}{[\ltimes(\jmath)-\ltimes(\eta)]^{1-\beta}} \mathfrak{S}_{\mu}(o+\ell-\tau,\ \eta) d\eta d\tau \\ & + \tfrac{1}{4\Gamma(\curlywedge)\Gamma(\rtimes)}(IA)\int_o^{\ell}\int_{\imath}^{\jmath} \tfrac{\mathfrak{g}'(\tau)}{[\mathfrak{g}(\ell)-\mathfrak{g}\,(\tau)]^{1-\curlywedge}}\, \tfrac{\ltimes'(\eta)}{[\ltimes(\jmath)-\ltimes(\eta)]^{1-\beta}} \mathfrak{S}_{\mu}(\tau,\ \imath+\jmath-\eta) d\eta d\tau \\ & + \tfrac{1}{4\Gamma(\curlywedge)\Gamma(\rtimes)}(IA)\int_o^{\ell}\int_{\imath}^{\jmath} \tfrac{\mathfrak{g}'(\tau)}{[\mathfrak{g}(\ell)-\mathfrak{g}\,(\tau)]^{1-\curlywedge}}\, \tfrac{\ltimes'(\eta)}{[\ltimes(\jmath)-\ltimes(\eta)]^{1-\beta}} \mathfrak{S}_{\mu}(\tau,\ \eta) d\eta d\tau \\ = \tfrac{1}{4}\Big[& \mathbb{J}^{\curlywedge,\rtimes}_{o+,\imath+;\mathfrak{g},\ltimes}\Sigma_{3\mu}(\ell,\jmath) + \mathbb{J}^{\curlywedge,\rtimes}_{o+,\imath+;\mathfrak{g},\ltimes}\Sigma_{1\mu}(\ell,\jmath) + \mathbb{J}^{\curlywedge,\rtimes}_{o+,\imath+;\mathfrak{g},\ltimes}\Sigma_{2\mu}(\ell,\jmath) + \mathbb{J}^{\curlywedge,\rtimes}_{o+,\imath+;\mathfrak{g},\ltimes}\mathfrak{S}_{\mu}(\ell,\jmath)\Big] \\ = & \tfrac{1}{4}\mathbb{J}^{\curlywedge,\rtimes}_{o+,\imath+;\mathfrak{g},\ltimes}\Sigma_{\mu}(\ell,\jmath) \end{aligned}$$

https://doi.org/10.3390/fractalfract10040228

That is, we have

$$\frac{[\mathfrak{g}(\ell)-\mathfrak{g}(\mathscr{o})]^{\leftthreetimes}[\ltimes(\jmath)-\ltimes(\iota)]^{\rtimes}}{\Gamma(\leftthreetimes+1)\Gamma(\rtimes+1)}\mathfrak{S}_{\mu}(\frac{\mathscr{o}+\ell}{2},\frac{\iota+\jmath}{2})\leq_{I}\frac{1}{4}\mathbb{J}^{\leftthreetimes,\rtimes}_{\mathscr{o}+,\iota+;\mathfrak{g},\ltimes}\mathfrak{X}_{\mu}(\ell,\jmath) \tag{57}$$

Similarly, both sides of (56) are multiplied by

$$\frac{(\ell-\mathscr{o})(\jmath-\iota)}{\Gamma(\leftthreetimes)\Gamma(\rtimes)}\frac{\mathfrak{g}'((1-\upsilon)\mathscr{o}+\upsilon\ell)}{[\mathfrak{g}(\mathrm{b})-\mathfrak{g}\left((1-\upsilon)\mathscr{o}+\upsilon\ell\right)]^{1-\leftthreetimes}}\frac{\ltimes'((1-\mathscr{r})\iota+\mathscr{r}\jmath)}{[\ltimes((1-\mathscr{r})\iota+\mathscr{r}\jmath)-\ltimes(\iota)]^{1-\beta}}$$

and integrating the obtained inequality in relation to $\upsilon,\mathscr{r}$ *over* $[0,\ 1]\ \times\ [0,\ 1]$, we obtain

$$\frac{[\mathfrak{g}(\ell)-\mathfrak{g}(\mathscr{o})]^{\leftthreetimes}[\ltimes(\jmath)-\ltimes(\iota)]^{\rtimes}}{\Gamma(\leftthreetimes+1)\Gamma(\rtimes+1)}\odot\tilde{\mathfrak{S}}(\frac{\mathscr{o}+\ell}{2},\frac{\iota+\jmath}{2})\leq_{F}\frac{1}{4}\odot\mathbb{J}^{\leftthreetimes,\rtimes}_{\mathscr{o}+,\jmath-;\mathfrak{g},\ltimes}\tilde{\mathfrak{X}}(\ell,\iota) \tag{58}$$

Moreover, both sides of (56) are multiplied by

$$\frac{(\ell-\mathscr{o})(\jmath-\iota)}{\Gamma(\leftthreetimes)\Gamma(\rtimes)}\frac{\mathfrak{g}'((1-\upsilon)\mathscr{o}+\upsilon\ell)}{[\mathfrak{g}\left((1-\upsilon)\mathscr{o}+\upsilon\ell\right)-\mathfrak{g}(\mathscr{o})]^{1-\leftthreetimes}}\frac{\ltimes'((1-\mathscr{r})\iota+\mathscr{r}\jmath)}{[\ltimes(\jmath)-\ltimes((1-\mathscr{r})\iota+\mathscr{r}\jmath)]^{1-\beta}}$$

and

$$\frac{(\ell-\mathscr{o})(\jmath-\iota)}{\Gamma(\leftthreetimes)\Gamma(\rtimes)}\frac{\mathfrak{g}'((1-\upsilon)\mathscr{o}+\upsilon\ell)}{[\mathfrak{g}\left((1-\upsilon)\mathscr{o}+\upsilon\ell\right)-\mathfrak{g}(\mathscr{o})]^{1-\leftthreetimes}}\frac{\ltimes'((1-\mathscr{r})\iota+\mathscr{r}\jmath)}{[\ltimes((1-\mathscr{r})\iota+\mathscr{r}\jmath)-\ltimes(\iota)]^{1-\beta}}$$

Then, integrating the established inequalities in relation to $\upsilon,\mathscr{r}$ over $[0,\ 1]\times[0,\ 1]$ and for all μ-cuts $\in[0,1]$, we have the following inequalities:

$$\frac{[\mathfrak{g}(\ell)-\mathfrak{g}(\mathscr{o})]^{\leftthreetimes}[\ltimes(\jmath)-\ltimes(\iota)]^{\rtimes}}{\Gamma(\leftthreetimes+1)\Gamma(\rtimes+1)}\mathfrak{S}_{\mu}(\frac{\mathscr{o}+\ell}{2},\frac{\iota+\jmath}{2})\leq_{I}\frac{1}{4}\mathbb{J}^{\leftthreetimes,\rtimes}_{\ell-,\iota+;\mathfrak{g},\ltimes}\mathfrak{X}_{\mu}(\mathscr{o},\jmath) \tag{59}$$

and

$$\frac{[\mathfrak{g}(\ell)-\mathfrak{g}(\mathscr{o})]^{\leftthreetimes}[\ltimes(\jmath)-\ltimes(\iota)]^{\rtimes}}{\Gamma(\leftthreetimes+1)\Gamma(\rtimes+1)}\mathfrak{S}_{\mu}(\frac{\mathscr{o}+\ell}{2},\frac{\iota+\jmath}{2})\leq_{I}\frac{1}{4}\mathbb{J}^{\leftthreetimes,\rtimes}_{\ell-,\jmath-;\mathfrak{g},\ltimes}\mathfrak{X}_{\mu}(\mathscr{o},\iota) \tag{60}$$

respectively.

Summing the inequalities (57) to (60), we get

$$\mathfrak{S}_{\mu}(\tfrac{\mathscr{o}+\ell}{2},\tfrac{\iota+\jmath}{2})\leq_{I}\frac{\Gamma(\leftthreetimes+1)\Gamma(\rtimes+1)}{16\,[\mathfrak{g}(\ell)-\mathfrak{g}(\mathscr{o})]^{\leftthreetimes}[\ltimes(\jmath)-\ltimes(\iota)]^{\rtimes}}$$
$$\times\Big[\mathbb{J}^{\leftthreetimes,\rtimes}_{\mathscr{o}+,\iota+;\mathfrak{g},\ltimes}\mathfrak{X}_{\mu}(\ell,\jmath)+\mathbb{J}^{\leftthreetimes,\rtimes}_{\mathscr{o}+,\jmath-;\mathfrak{g},\ltimes}\mathfrak{X}_{\mu}(\ell,\iota)+\mathbb{J}^{\leftthreetimes,\rtimes}_{\ell-,\iota+;\mathfrak{g},\ltimes}\mathfrak{X}_{\mu}(\mathscr{o},\jmath)+\mathbb{J}^{\leftthreetimes,\rtimes}_{\ell-,\jmath-;\mathfrak{g},\ltimes}\mathfrak{X}_{\mu}(\mathscr{o},\iota)\Big].$$

This completes the proof of the first inequality in (54).

For the proof of the second inequality in (54), since F is a coordinated convex, we have

$$\begin{aligned}&\mathfrak{S}_{\mu}(\upsilon\mathscr{o}+(1-\upsilon)\ell,\iota\mathscr{r}+(1-\mathscr{r})\jmath)+\mathfrak{S}_{\mu}(\upsilon\mathscr{o}+(1-\upsilon)\ell,(1-\mathscr{r})\iota+\mathscr{r}\jmath)\\&+\mathfrak{S}_{\mu}((1-\upsilon)\mathscr{o}+\upsilon\ell,\iota\mathscr{r}+(1-\mathscr{r})\jmath)+\mathfrak{S}_{\mu}((1-\upsilon)\mathscr{o}+\upsilon\ell,(1-\mathscr{r})\iota+\mathscr{r}\jmath)\\&\leq_{I}\ \mathfrak{S}_{\mu}(\mathscr{o},\iota)+\mathfrak{S}_{\mu}(\mathscr{o},\jmath)+\mathfrak{S}_{\mu}(\ell,\iota)+\mathfrak{S}_{\mu}(\ell,\jmath).\end{aligned} \tag{61}$$

Both sides of (61) are multiplied by

$$\frac{(\ell-\mathscr{o})(\jmath-\iota)}{\Gamma(\leftthreetimes)\Gamma(\rtimes)}\frac{\mathfrak{g}'((1-\upsilon)\mathscr{o}+\upsilon\ell)}{[\mathfrak{g}(\ell)-\mathfrak{g}\left((1-\upsilon)\mathscr{o}+\upsilon\ell\right)]^{1-\leftthreetimes}}\frac{\ltimes'((1-\mathscr{r})\iota+\mathscr{r}\jmath)}{[\ltimes(\jmath)-\ltimes((1-\mathscr{r})\iota+\mathscr{r}\jmath)]^{1-\beta}}$$

https://doi.org/10.3390/fractalfract10040228

and integrating the resulting inequality in relation to υ, r over $[0, 1] \times [0, 1]$, we get

$$\frac{(\ell-o)(\jmath-\imath)}{4\Gamma(\lambda)\Gamma(\varkappa)}(IA)\int_0^1\int_0^1\left[\begin{array}{c}\frac{\mathfrak{g}'((1-\upsilon)o+\upsilon\ell)}{[\mathfrak{g}(\ell)-\mathfrak{g}((1-\upsilon)o+\upsilon\ell)]^{1-\lambda}}\\ \frac{\ltimes'((1-r)\imath+r\jmath)}{[\ltimes(\jmath)-\ltimes((1-r)\imath+r\jmath)]^{1-\beta}}\\ \mathfrak{S}_\mu(\upsilon o+(1-\upsilon)\ell, r\imath+(1-r)\jmath)\end{array}\right]drd\upsilon$$

$$+\frac{(\ell-o)(\jmath-\imath)}{4\Gamma(\lambda)\Gamma(\varkappa)}(IA)\int_0^1\int_0^1\left[\begin{array}{c}\frac{\mathfrak{g}'((1-\upsilon)o+\upsilon\ell)}{[\mathfrak{g}(\ell)-\mathfrak{g}((1-\upsilon)o+\upsilon\ell)]^{1-\lambda}}\\ \frac{\ltimes'((1-r)\imath+r\jmath)}{[\ltimes(\jmath)-\ltimes((1-r)\imath+r\jmath)]^{1-\beta}}\\ \mathfrak{S}_\mu(\upsilon o+(1-\upsilon)\ell,\ (1-r)\imath+r\jmath)\end{array}\right]drd\upsilon$$

$$+\frac{(\ell-o)(\jmath-\imath)}{4\Gamma(\lambda)\Gamma(\varkappa)}(IA)\int_0^1\int_0^1\left[\begin{array}{c}\frac{\upsilon'((1-\upsilon)o+\upsilon\ell)}{[\mathfrak{g}(\ell)-\mathfrak{g}((1-\upsilon)o+\upsilon\ell)]^{1-\lambda}}\\ \frac{\ltimes'((1-r)\imath+r\jmath)}{[\ltimes(\jmath)-\ltimes((1-r)\imath+r\jmath)]^{1-\beta}}\\ \mathfrak{S}_\mu((1-\upsilon)o+\upsilon\ell,\ r\imath+(1-r)\jmath)\end{array}\right]drd\upsilon$$

$$+\frac{(\ell-o)(\jmath-\imath)}{4\Gamma(\lambda)\Gamma(\varkappa)}(IA)\int_0^1\int_0^1\left[\begin{array}{c}\frac{\mathfrak{g}'((1-\upsilon)o+\upsilon\ell)}{[\mathfrak{g}(\ell)-\mathfrak{g}((1-\upsilon)o+\upsilon\ell)]^{1-\lambda}}\\ \frac{\ltimes'((1-r)\imath+r\jmath)}{[\ltimes(\jmath)-\ltimes((1-r)\imath+r\jmath)]^{1-\beta}}\\ \mathfrak{S}_\mu((1-\upsilon)o+\upsilon\ell,\ (1-r)\imath+r\jmath)\end{array}\right]drd\upsilon$$

$$\leq_I \frac{(\ell-o)(\jmath-\imath)}{4\Gamma(\lambda)\Gamma(\varkappa)}\left[\mathfrak{S}_\mu(o,\imath)+\mathfrak{S}_\mu(o,\jmath)+\mathfrak{S}_\mu(\ell,\imath)+\mathfrak{S}_\mu(\ell,\jmath)\right]\times$$

$$(IA)\int_0^1\int_0^1\left[\frac{\mathfrak{g}'((1-\upsilon)o+\upsilon\ell)}{[\mathfrak{g}(\ell)-\mathfrak{g}((1-\upsilon)o+\upsilon\ell)]^{1-\lambda}}\ \frac{\ltimes'((1-r)\imath+r\jmath)}{[\ltimes(\jmath)-\ltimes((1-r)\imath+r\jmath)]^{1-\beta}}\right]drd\upsilon.$$

Then, we get

$$\mathbb{J}^{\lambda,\varkappa}_{o+,\imath+;\mathfrak{g},\ltimes}\mathfrak{X}_{3\mu}(\ell,\jmath)+\mathbb{J}^{\lambda,\varkappa}_{o+,\imath+;\mathfrak{g},\ltimes}\mathfrak{X}_{1\mu}(\ell,\jmath)+\mathbb{J}^{\lambda,\varkappa}_{o+,\imath+;\mathfrak{g},\ltimes}\mathfrak{X}_{2\mu}(\ell,\jmath)+\mathbb{J}^{\lambda,\varkappa}_{o+,\imath+;\mathfrak{g},\ltimes}\mathfrak{X}_{\mu}(\ell,\jmath)$$

$$\leq_I \mathfrak{S}_\mu(o,\imath)+\mathfrak{S}_\mu(o,\jmath)+\mathfrak{S}_\mu(\ell,\imath)+\mathfrak{S}_\mu(\ell,\jmath)\frac{[\mathfrak{g}(\ell)-\mathfrak{g}(o)]^{\lambda}[\ltimes(\jmath)-\ltimes(\imath)]^{\varkappa}}{\Gamma(\lambda+1)\Gamma(\varkappa+1)}$$

that is,

$$\frac{\Gamma(\lambda+1)\Gamma(\varkappa+1)}{[\mathfrak{g}(\ell)-\mathfrak{g}(o)]^{\lambda}[\ltimes(\jmath)-\ltimes(\imath)]^{\varkappa}}\mathbb{J}^{\lambda,\varkappa}_{o+,\imath+;\mathfrak{g},\ltimes}\mathfrak{X}_{\mu}(\ell,\jmath)\leq_I \mathfrak{S}_\mu(o,\imath)+\mathfrak{S}_\mu(o,\jmath)+\mathfrak{S}_\mu(\ell,\imath)+\mathfrak{S}_\mu(\ell,\jmath). \quad (62)$$

Similarly, both sides of (61) are multiplied by

$$\frac{(\ell-o)(\jmath-\imath)}{\Gamma(\lambda)\Gamma(\varkappa)}\ \frac{\mathfrak{g}'((1-\upsilon)o+\upsilon\ell)}{[\mathfrak{g}(\ell)-\mathfrak{g}((1-\upsilon)o+\upsilon\ell)]^{1-\lambda}}\ \frac{\ltimes'((1-r)\imath+r\jmath)}{[\ltimes((1-r)\imath+r\jmath)-\ltimes(\imath)]^{1-\beta}}$$

$$\frac{(\ell-o)(\jmath-\imath)}{\Gamma(\lambda)\Gamma(\varkappa)}\ \frac{\mathfrak{g}'((1-\upsilon)o+\upsilon\ell)}{[\mathfrak{g}((1-\upsilon)o+\upsilon\ell)-\mathfrak{g}(o)]^{1-\lambda}}\ \frac{\ltimes'((1-r)\imath+r\jmath)}{[\ltimes(\jmath)-\ltimes((1-r)\imath+r\jmath)]^{1-\beta}}$$

and

$$\frac{(\ell-o)(\jmath-\imath)}{\Gamma(\lambda)\Gamma(\varkappa)}\ \frac{\mathfrak{g}'((1-\upsilon)o+\upsilon\ell)}{[\mathfrak{g}((1-\upsilon)o+\upsilon\ell)-\mathfrak{g}(o)]^{1-\lambda}}\ \frac{\ltimes'((1-r)\imath+r\jmath)}{[\ltimes((1-r)\imath+r\jmath)-\ltimes(\imath)]^{1-\beta}}$$

and integrating the resulting inequalities in relation to υ, r over $[0, 1] \times [0, 1]$, we establish the following inequalities:

 https://doi.org/10.3390/fractalfract10040228

$$\frac{\Gamma(\measuredangle+1)\Gamma(\rtimes+1)}{[\mathfrak{g}(\ell)-\mathfrak{g}(o)]^{\measuredangle}[\ltimes(\jmath)-\ltimes(\imath)]^{\rtimes}}\mathbb{J}^{\measuredangle,\rtimes}_{o+,\jmath-;\mathfrak{g},\ltimes}\mathfrak{X}_\mu(\ell,\imath) \leq_I \mathfrak{S}_\mu(o,\imath)+\mathfrak{S}_\mu(o,\jmath)+\mathfrak{S}_\mu(\ell,\imath)+\mathfrak{S}_\mu(\ell,\jmath). \tag{63}$$

$$\frac{\Gamma(\measuredangle+1)\Gamma(\rtimes+1)}{[\mathfrak{g}(\ell)-\mathfrak{g}(o)]^{\measuredangle}[\ltimes(\jmath)-\ltimes(\imath)]^{\rtimes}}\mathbb{J}^{\measuredangle,\rtimes}_{\ell-,\imath+;\mathfrak{g},\ltimes}\mathfrak{X}_\mu(o,\jmath) \leq_I \mathfrak{S}_\mu(o,\imath)+\mathfrak{S}_\mu(o,\jmath)+\mathfrak{S}_\mu(\ell,\imath)+\mathfrak{S}_\mu(\ell,\jmath). \tag{64}$$

and

$$\frac{\Gamma(\measuredangle+1)\Gamma(\rtimes+1)}{[\mathfrak{g}(\ell)-\mathfrak{g}(o)]^{\measuredangle}[\ltimes(\jmath)-\ltimes(\imath)]^{\rtimes}}\mathbb{J}^{\measuredangle,\rtimes}_{\ell-,\jmath-;\mathfrak{g},\ltimes}\mathfrak{X}_\mu(o,\imath) \leq_I \mathfrak{S}_\mu(o,\imath)+\mathfrak{S}_\mu(o,\jmath)+\mathfrak{S}_\mu(\ell,\imath)+\mathfrak{S}_\mu(\ell,\jmath), \tag{65}$$

respectively.

By adding the inequalities (62) to (65), we have the following inequality.

$$\begin{aligned}\frac{\Gamma(\measuredangle+1)\Gamma(\rtimes+1)}{[\mathfrak{g}(\ell)-\mathfrak{g}(o)]^{\measuredangle}[\ltimes(\jmath)-\ltimes(\imath)]^{\rtimes}} \times \Big[\mathbb{J}^{\measuredangle,\rtimes}_{o+,\imath+;\mathfrak{g},\ltimes}\mathfrak{X}_\mu(\ell,\jmath)+\mathbb{J}^{\measuredangle,\rtimes}_{o+,\jmath-;\mathfrak{g},\ltimes}\mathfrak{X}_\mu(\ell,\imath)+\mathbb{J}^{\measuredangle,\rtimes}_{\ell-,\imath+;\mathfrak{g},\ltimes}\mathfrak{X}_\mu(o,\jmath)+\mathbb{J}^{\measuredangle,\rtimes}_{\ell-,\jmath-;\mathfrak{g},\ltimes}\mathfrak{X}_\mu(o,\imath)\Big] \\ \leq_I 4\big[\mathfrak{S}_\mu(o,\imath)+\mathfrak{S}_\mu(o,\jmath)+\mathfrak{S}_\mu(\ell,\imath)+\mathfrak{S}_\mu(\ell,\jmath)\big].\end{aligned} \tag{66}$$

If we divide both sides of inequality (66) by 16, then we have the second inequality in (54).

This completes the proof. □

Corollary 3. *Setting $\mathfrak{g}(v)=v$ and $\ltimes(r)=r$ in Theorem 4 yields the following inequalities for the Riemann–Liouville $F\cdot N\cdot V$-fractional double integrals:*

$$\begin{aligned}\tilde{\mathfrak{S}}\Big(\frac{o+\ell}{2},\frac{\imath+\jmath}{2}\Big) \leq_F \frac{\Gamma(\measuredangle+1)\Gamma(\rtimes+1)}{4\,(\ell-o)^{\measuredangle}(\jmath-\imath)^{\rtimes}} \odot \Big[\mathcal{J}^{\measuredangle,\rtimes}_{o+,\imath+}\tilde{\mathfrak{S}}(\ell,\jmath)\oplus\mathcal{J}^{\measuredangle,\rtimes}_{o+,\jmath-}\tilde{\mathfrak{S}}(\ell,\imath)\oplus\mathcal{J}^{\measuredangle,\rtimes}_{\ell-,\imath+}\tilde{\mathfrak{S}}(o,\jmath)\oplus\mathcal{J}^{\measuredangle,\rtimes}_{\ell-,\jmath-}\tilde{\mathfrak{S}}(o,\imath)\Big] \\ \leq_F \frac{\tilde{\mathfrak{S}}(o,\imath)\oplus\tilde{\mathfrak{S}}(o,\jmath)\oplus\tilde{\mathfrak{S}}(\ell,\imath)\oplus\tilde{\mathfrak{S}}(\ell,\jmath)}{4}.\end{aligned}$$

Corollary 4. *Assuming the conditions of Theorem 4 hold, setting $\mathfrak{g}(v)=\ln v$ and $\ltimes(r)=\ln r$ yields the following inequalities for the Hadamard $F\cdot N\cdot V$-fractional double integrals:*

$$\begin{aligned}\tilde{\mathfrak{S}}\Big(\frac{o+\ell}{2},\frac{\imath+\jmath}{2}\Big) \leq_F \frac{\Gamma(\measuredangle+1)\Gamma(\rtimes+1)}{16\,\big[\ln\frac{\ell}{o}\big]^{\measuredangle}\big[\ln\frac{\jmath}{\imath}\big]^{\rtimes}} \odot \Big[\mathfrak{J}^{\measuredangle,\rtimes}_{o+,\imath+}\tilde{\mathfrak{X}}(\ell,\jmath)\oplus\mathfrak{J}^{\measuredangle,\rtimes}_{o+,\jmath-}\tilde{\mathfrak{X}}(\ell,\imath)\oplus\mathfrak{J}^{\measuredangle,\rtimes}_{\ell-,\imath+}\tilde{\mathfrak{X}}(o,\jmath)\oplus\mathfrak{J}^{\measuredangle,\rtimes}_{\ell-,\jmath-}\tilde{\mathfrak{X}}(o,\imath)\Big] \\ \leq_F \frac{\tilde{\mathfrak{S}}(o,\imath)\oplus\tilde{\mathfrak{S}}(o,\jmath)\oplus\tilde{\mathfrak{S}}(\ell,\imath)\oplus\tilde{\mathfrak{S}}(\ell,\jmath)}{4}.\end{aligned}$$

Corollary 5. *Assuming the conditions of Theorem 4 hold, setting $\mathfrak{g}(v)=\frac{v^\rho}{\rho}$ and $\ltimes(r)=\frac{r^\sigma}{\sigma}$, $\rho,\sigma>0$ yields the following inequalities for the Hadamard $F\cdot N\cdot V$-Katugampola fractional double integrals:*

$$\begin{aligned}\tilde{\mathfrak{S}}\Big(\frac{o+\ell}{2},\frac{\imath+\jmath}{2}\Big) \leq_F \frac{\Gamma(\measuredangle+1)\Gamma(\rtimes+1)\rho^{\measuredangle}\sigma^{\rtimes}}{16\,[\ell^\rho-o^\rho]^{\measuredangle}[\jmath^\sigma-\imath^\sigma]^{\rtimes}} \odot \Big[{}^{\rho,\sigma}\mathbb{I}^{\measuredangle,\rtimes}_{o+,\imath+}\tilde{\mathfrak{X}}(\ell,\jmath)\oplus{}^{\rho,\sigma}\mathbb{I}^{\measuredangle,\rtimes}_{o+,\jmath-}\tilde{\mathfrak{X}}(\ell,\imath)\oplus{}^{\rho,\sigma}\mathbb{I}^{\measuredangle,\rtimes}_{\ell-,\imath+}\tilde{\mathfrak{X}}(o,\jmath)\oplus{}^{\rho,\sigma}\mathbb{I}^{\measuredangle,\rtimes}_{\ell-,\jmath-}\tilde{\mathfrak{X}}(o,\imath)\Big] \\ \leq_F \frac{\tilde{\mathfrak{S}}(o,\imath)\oplus\tilde{\mathfrak{S}}(o,\jmath)\oplus\tilde{\mathfrak{S}}(\ell,\imath)\oplus\tilde{\mathfrak{S}}(\ell,\jmath)}{4}.\end{aligned}$$

Theorem 5. *Let $\mathfrak{g}:[o,\ell]\to\mathbb{R}$ and $\ltimes:[\imath,\jmath]\to\mathbb{R}$ be positive increasing mappings on $(o,\ell]$ and $(\imath,\jmath]$ with continuous derivatives such that $\mathfrak{g}'(k)$ on (o,ℓ) and $\ltimes'(s)$ on $(\imath,\jmath)$, respectively. Let $\Delta=[o,\ell]\times[\imath,\jmath]$. If $\tilde{\mathfrak{S}}:\Delta\to\mathbb{F}_0^+$ is a $F\cdot N\cdot V$-coordinated convex mapping on Δ such that from μ-cuts here, we produce the collection of $I\cdot V$-mappings $\mathfrak{S}_\mu:\Delta\to\mathbb{R}_I^+$ described by*

 https://doi.org/10.3390/fractalfract10040228

$\left[\tilde{\mathfrak{S}}(\hbar, \jmath)\right]^{\mu} = \mathfrak{S}_{\mu}((\hbar, \jmath)) = \left[\underline{\mathfrak{S}}((\hbar, \jmath); \mu), \overline{\mathfrak{S}}((\hbar, \jmath); \mu)\right]$, *for all* $\mu \in [0, 1]$ *and* $(\hbar, \jmath) \in \Delta$, *then, for* $\curlywedge, \rtimes > 0$, *the following* $H \cdot H$*-type inequality holds:*

$$\begin{aligned}
\tilde{\mathfrak{S}}\left(\tfrac{o+\ell}{2}, \tfrac{\imath+\jmath}{2}\right) &\leq_F \frac{\Gamma(\curlywedge+1)}{8[\mathfrak{g}(\ell)-\mathfrak{g}(o)]^{\curlywedge}} \odot \left[\mathbb{J}^{\curlywedge}_{o+;\mathfrak{g}} \mathscr{H}\left(\ell, \tfrac{\imath+\jmath}{2}\right) \oplus \mathbb{J}^{\curlywedge}_{\ell-;\mathfrak{g}} \mathscr{H}\left(o, \tfrac{\imath+\jmath}{2}\right)\right] \\
&\oplus \frac{\Gamma(\rtimes+1)}{8[\ltimes(\jmath)-\ltimes(\imath)]^{\rtimes}} \odot \left[\mathbb{J}^{\rtimes}_{\imath+;\ltimes} \tilde{\mathfrak{D}}\left(\tfrac{o+\ell}{2}, \jmath\right) \oplus \mathbb{J}^{\rtimes}_{\jmath-;\ltimes} \tilde{\mathfrak{D}}\left(\tfrac{o+\ell}{2}, \imath\right)\right] \\
&\leq_F \frac{\Gamma(\curlywedge+1)\Gamma(\rtimes+1)}{16[\mathfrak{g}(\ell)-\mathfrak{g}(o)]^{\curlywedge}[\ltimes(\jmath)-\ltimes(\imath)]^{\rtimes}} \\
&\odot \left[\mathbb{J}^{\curlywedge,\rtimes}_{o+,\imath+;\mathfrak{g},\ltimes} \tilde{\mathfrak{X}}(\ell, \jmath) \oplus \mathbb{J}^{\curlywedge,\rtimes}_{o+,\jmath-;\mathfrak{g},\ltimes} \tilde{\mathfrak{X}}(\ell, \imath) \oplus \mathbb{J}^{\curlywedge,\rtimes}_{\ell-,\imath+;\mathfrak{g},\ltimes} \tilde{\mathfrak{X}}(o, \jmath) \oplus \mathbb{J}^{\curlywedge,\rtimes}_{\ell-,\jmath-;\mathfrak{g},\ltimes} \tilde{\mathfrak{X}}(o, \imath)\right] \\
&\leq_F \frac{\Gamma(\curlywedge+1)}{16[\mathfrak{g}(\ell)-\mathfrak{g}(o)]^{\curlywedge}} \odot \left[\mathbb{J}^{\curlywedge}_{o+;\mathfrak{g}} \mathscr{H}(\ell, \imath) \oplus \mathbb{J}^{\curlywedge}_{o+;\mathfrak{g}} \mathscr{H}(\ell, \jmath) \oplus \mathbb{J}^{\curlywedge}_{\ell-;\mathfrak{g}} \mathscr{H}(o, \imath) \oplus \mathbb{J}^{\curlywedge}_{\ell-;\mathfrak{g}} \mathscr{H}(o, \jmath)\right] \\
&\oplus \frac{\Gamma(\rtimes+1)}{16[\ltimes(\jmath)-\ltimes(\imath)]^{\rtimes}} \odot \left[\mathbb{J}^{\rtimes}_{\imath+;\ltimes} \tilde{\mathfrak{D}}(o, \jmath) \oplus \mathbb{J}^{\rtimes}_{\imath+;\ltimes} \tilde{\mathfrak{D}}(\ell, \jmath) \oplus \mathbb{J}^{\rtimes}_{\jmath-;\ltimes} \tilde{\mathfrak{D}}(o, \imath) \oplus \mathbb{J}^{\rtimes}_{\jmath-;\ltimes} \tilde{\mathfrak{D}}(\ell, \imath)\right] \\
&\leq_F \frac{\tilde{\mathfrak{S}}(o, \imath) \oplus \tilde{\mathfrak{S}}(o, \jmath) \oplus \tilde{\mathfrak{S}}(\ell, \imath) \oplus \tilde{\mathfrak{S}}(\ell, \jmath)}{4},
\end{aligned} \tag{67}$$

where

$$\tilde{\mathfrak{X}}1(\hbar, \jmath) = \tilde{\mathfrak{S}}(o + \ell - \hbar, \jmath),$$

$$\tilde{\mathfrak{X}}2(\hbar, \jmath) = \tilde{\mathfrak{S}}(\hbar, \imath + \jmath - \jmath),$$

$$\tilde{\mathfrak{X}}3(\hbar, \jmath) = \tilde{\mathfrak{S}}(o + \ell - \hbar, \imath + \jmath - \jmath),$$

$$\tilde{\mathfrak{D}}(\hbar, \jmath) = \tilde{\mathfrak{S}}(\hbar, \jmath) \oplus \tilde{\mathfrak{X}}2(\hbar, \jmath)$$

$$\mathscr{H}(\hbar, \jmath) = \tilde{\mathfrak{S}}(\hbar, \jmath) \oplus \tilde{\mathfrak{X}}1(\hbar, \jmath)$$

$$\tilde{\mathfrak{K}}(\hbar, \jmath) = \tilde{\mathfrak{X}}1(\hbar, \jmath) \oplus \tilde{\mathfrak{X}}3(\hbar, \jmath)$$

$$\mathscr{L}(\hbar, \jmath) = \tilde{\mathfrak{X}}2(\hbar, \jmath) \oplus \tilde{\mathfrak{X}}3(\hbar, \jmath)$$

$$\tilde{\mathfrak{X}}(\hbar, \jmath) = \tilde{\mathfrak{X}}1(\hbar, \jmath) \oplus \tilde{\mathfrak{X}}2(\hbar, \jmath) \oplus \tilde{\mathfrak{X}}3(\hbar, \jmath) \oplus \tilde{\mathfrak{S}}(\hbar, \jmath)$$

$$= \frac{\tilde{\mathfrak{D}}(\hbar, \jmath) \oplus \mathscr{H}(\hbar, \jmath) \oplus \tilde{\mathfrak{K}}(\hbar, \jmath) \oplus \mathscr{L}(\hbar, \jmath)}{2}$$

for $(\hbar, \jmath) \in [o, \ell] \times [\imath, \jmath]$. *where for all* μ*-cuts* $\in [0, 1]$, *we have* $\left[\tilde{\mathfrak{X}}1(\hbar, \jmath)\right]^{\mu} = \mathfrak{X}_{1\mu}(\hbar, \jmath)$, $\left[\tilde{\mathfrak{X}}2(\hbar, \jmath)\right]^{\mu} = \mathfrak{X}_{2\mu}(\hbar, \jmath)$, $\left[\tilde{\mathfrak{X}}3(\hbar, \jmath)\right]^{\mu} = \mathfrak{X}_{3\mu}(\hbar, \jmath)$, $[\tilde{\mathfrak{D}}(\hbar, \jmath)]^{\mu} = \mathfrak{D}_{\mu}(\hbar, \jmath)$, $[\mathscr{H}(\hbar, \jmath)]^{\mu} = \mathscr{H}_{\mu}(\hbar, \jmath)$, $\left[\tilde{\mathfrak{K}}(\hbar, \jmath)\right]^{\mu} = \mathfrak{K}_{\mu}(\hbar, \jmath)$, $[\mathscr{L}(\hbar, \jmath)]^{\mu} = \mathscr{L}_{\mu}(\hbar, \jmath)$ *and* $\left[\tilde{\mathfrak{X}}(\hbar, \jmath)\right]^{\mu} = \mathfrak{X}_{\mu}(\hbar, \jmath)$.

Proof. Since $\tilde{\mathfrak{S}}$ is a $F{\cdot}N \cdot V$-coordinated convex on Δ, if we define the mapping $h^1_{\hbar} : [\imath, \jmath] \to \mathbb{F}^+_0$, $h^1_{\hbar} = \tilde{\mathfrak{S}}(\hbar, \jmath)$, then $h^1_{\hbar}(\jmath)$ is convex for all $\hbar \in [o, \ell]$ and $\mathscr{H}^1_{\hbar}(\jmath) = h^1_{\hbar}(\jmath) \oplus \tilde{h^1_{\hbar}}(\jmath) = \tilde{\mathfrak{S}}(\hbar, \jmath) \oplus \tilde{\mathfrak{X}}_2(\hbar, \jmath) = \tilde{\mathfrak{D}}(\hbar, \jmath)$. If we apply the inequalities (22) for the convex mapping $h^1_{\hbar}(\jmath)$, then we have

$$h^1_{\hbar}\left(\frac{\imath+\jmath}{2}\right) \leq_F \frac{\Gamma(\rtimes+1)}{4[\ltimes(\jmath) - \ltimes(\imath)]^{\rtimes}} \odot \left[\mathbb{J}^{\rtimes}_{\imath+;\ltimes} \mathscr{H}^1_{\hbar}(\jmath) \oplus \mathbb{J}^{\rtimes}_{\jmath-;\ltimes} \mathscr{H}^1_{\hbar}(\imath)\right] \leq_F \frac{h^1_{\hbar}(\imath) \oplus h^1_{\hbar}(\jmath)}{2},$$

Then, for all μ-cuts $\in [0, 1]$, we have

https://doi.org/10.3390/fractalfract10040228

$$\mathfrak{S}_\mu(\hbar, \tfrac{\imath+\jmath}{2}) \leq_I \frac{\rtimes}{4[\ltimes(\jmath)-\ltimes(\imath)]^{\rtimes}}\left[(IA)\int_\imath^\jmath \frac{\ltimes'(s)}{[\ltimes(\jmath)-\ltimes(s)]^{1-\rtimes}}\mathfrak{D}_\mu(\hbar, s)ds+(IA)\int_\imath^\jmath \frac{\ltimes'(s)}{[\ltimes(s)-\ltimes(\imath)]^{1-\rtimes}}\mathfrak{D}_\mu(\hbar, s)ds\right] \leq_I \frac{\mathfrak{S}_\mu(\hbar,\imath)+\mathfrak{S}_\mu(\hbar,\jmath)}{2} \tag{68}$$

Both sides of (68) are multiplied by

$$\frac{\leftthreetimes}{[\mathfrak{g}(\ell)-\mathfrak{g}(o)]^{\leftthreetimes}}\frac{\mathfrak{g}'(\hbar)}{[\mathfrak{g}(\ell)-\mathfrak{g}(\hbar)]^{1-\leftthreetimes}}$$

and

$$\frac{\leftthreetimes}{[\mathfrak{g}(\ell)-\mathfrak{g}(o)]^{\leftthreetimes}}\frac{\mathfrak{g}'(\hbar)}{[\mathfrak{g}(\hbar)-\mathfrak{g}(o)]^{1-\leftthreetimes}}$$

then by integrating the obtained results in relation to x from o to ℓ, we get

$$\begin{aligned}&\frac{\Gamma(\leftthreetimes+1)}{[\mathfrak{g}(\ell)-\mathfrak{g}(o)]^{\leftthreetimes}}\mathbb{J}^{\leftthreetimes}_{o+;\mathfrak{g}}\mathfrak{S}_\mu(\ell, \tfrac{\imath+\jmath}{2})\\ &\leq_I \frac{\Gamma(\leftthreetimes+1)\Gamma(\rtimes+1)}{4[\mathfrak{g}(\ell)-\mathfrak{g}(o)]^{\leftthreetimes}[\ltimes(\jmath)-\ltimes(\imath)]^{\rtimes}}\left[\mathbb{J}^{\leftthreetimes,\rtimes}_{o+,\imath+;\mathfrak{g},\ltimes}\mathfrak{D}_\mu(\ell,\jmath)+\mathbb{J}^{\leftthreetimes,\rtimes}_{o+,\jmath-;\mathfrak{g},\ltimes}\mathfrak{D}_\mu(\ell,\imath)\right]\\ &\leq_I \frac{\Gamma(\leftthreetimes+1)}{2[\mathfrak{g}(\ell)-\mathfrak{g}(o)]^{\leftthreetimes}}\left[\mathbb{J}^{\leftthreetimes}_{o+;\mathfrak{g}}\mathfrak{S}_\mu(\ell,\imath)+\mathbb{J}^{\leftthreetimes}_{o+;\mathfrak{g}}\mathfrak{S}_\mu(\ell,\jmath)\right]\end{aligned} \tag{69}$$

and

$$\begin{aligned}&\frac{\Gamma(\leftthreetimes+1)}{[\mathfrak{g}(\ell)-\mathfrak{g}(o)]^{\leftthreetimes}}\mathbb{J}^{\leftthreetimes}_{\ell-;\mathfrak{g}}\mathfrak{S}_\mu(o, \tfrac{\imath+\jmath}{2})\\ &\leq_I \frac{\Gamma(\leftthreetimes+1)\Gamma(\rtimes+1)}{4[\mathfrak{g}(\ell)-\mathfrak{g}(o)]^{\leftthreetimes}[\ltimes(\jmath)-\ltimes(\imath)]^{\rtimes}}\left[\mathbb{J}^{\leftthreetimes,\rtimes}_{\ell-,\imath+;\mathfrak{g},\ltimes}\mathfrak{D}_\mu(o,\jmath)+\mathbb{J}^{\leftthreetimes,\rtimes}_{\ell-,\jmath-;\mathfrak{g},\ltimes}\mathfrak{D}_\mu(o,\imath)\right]\\ &\leq_I \frac{\Gamma(\leftthreetimes+1)}{2[\mathfrak{g}(\ell)-\mathfrak{g}(o)]^{\leftthreetimes}}\left[\mathbb{J}^{\leftthreetimes}_{\ell-;\mathfrak{g}}\mathfrak{S}_\mu(o,\imath)+\mathbb{J}^{\leftthreetimes}_{\ell-;\mathfrak{g}}\mathfrak{S}_\mu(o,\jmath)\right]\end{aligned} \tag{70}$$

respectively.

On the other hand, since $\tilde{\mathfrak{S}}$ is a coordinated convex on Δ, if we define the mapping $h^2_\hbar : [\imath,\jmath] \to \mathbb{F}^+_0$, $h^2_\hbar(s) = \tilde{\Xi}_1(\hbar, s)$, then $h^2_\hbar(s)$ is convex for all $\hbar \in [o,\ell]$ and $\tilde{\mathscr{H}}^2_\hbar(s) = h^2_\hbar(s) \oplus \tilde{h}^2_\hbar(s) = \tilde{\Xi}_1(\hbar, s) \oplus \tilde{\Xi}_3(\hbar, s) = \tilde{\mathfrak{K}}(\hbar, s)$. If we apply the inequalities (22) for the convex mapping $h^2_\hbar(s)$, then we have

$$h^2_\hbar(\frac{\imath+\jmath}{2}) \leq_F \frac{\Gamma(\rtimes+1)}{4[\ltimes(\jmath)-\ltimes(\imath)]^{\rtimes}} \odot \left[\mathbb{J}^{\rtimes}_{\imath+;\ltimes}\tilde{\mathscr{H}}^2_\hbar(\jmath) \oplus \mathbb{J}^{\rtimes}_{\jmath-;\ltimes}\tilde{\mathscr{H}}^2_\hbar(\imath)\right] \leq_F \frac{h^2_\hbar(\imath)\oplus h^2_\hbar(\jmath)}{2},$$

that is, for all μ-cuts $\in [0,1]$, we have

$$\begin{aligned}&\Xi_{1\mu}(\hbar, \frac{\imath+\jmath}{2})\\ &\leq_I \frac{\rtimes}{4[\ltimes(\jmath)-\ltimes(\imath)]^{\rtimes}} \odot \left[(IA)\int_\imath^\jmath \frac{\ltimes'(s)}{[\ltimes(\jmath)-\ltimes(s)]^{1-\rtimes}}\mathfrak{K}_\mu(\hbar,s)ds+(IA)\int_\imath^\jmath \frac{\ltimes'(s)}{[\ltimes(s)-\ltimes(\imath)]^{1-\rtimes}}\mathfrak{K}_\mu(\hbar,s)ds\right]\\ &\leq_I \frac{\Xi_{1\mu}(\hbar,\imath)+\Xi_{1\mu}(\hbar,\jmath)}{2}\end{aligned} \tag{71}$$

Similarly, both sides of (71) are multiplied by

$$\frac{\leftthreetimes}{[\mathfrak{g}(\ell)-\mathfrak{g}(o)]^{\leftthreetimes}}\frac{\mathfrak{g}'(\hbar)}{[\mathfrak{g}(\ell)-\mathfrak{g}(\hbar)]^{1-\leftthreetimes}}$$

and

$$\frac{\leftthreetimes}{[\mathfrak{g}(\ell)-\mathfrak{g}(o)]^{\leftthreetimes}}\frac{\mathfrak{g}'(\hbar)}{[\mathfrak{g}(\hbar)-\mathfrak{g}(o)]^{1-\leftthreetimes}}$$

https://doi.org/10.3390/fractalfract10040228

then by integrating the obtained results in relation to x from σ to ℓ, we get

$$\begin{aligned} &\frac{\Gamma(\lambda+1)}{[\mathfrak{g}(\ell)-\mathfrak{g}(\sigma)]^{\lambda}}\mathbb{J}^{\lambda}_{\sigma+;\mathfrak{g}}\Sigma_{1\mu}(\ell,\tfrac{\imath+\jmath}{2}) \\ \leq_I &\frac{\Gamma(\lambda+1)\Gamma(\varkappa+1)}{4[\mathfrak{g}(\ell)-\mathfrak{g}(\sigma)]^{\lambda}[\kappa(\jmath)-\kappa(\imath)]^{\varkappa}}\left[\mathbb{J}^{\lambda,\varkappa}_{\sigma+,\imath+;\mathfrak{g},\kappa}\mathfrak{K}_{\mu}(\ell,\jmath)+\mathbb{J}^{\lambda,\varkappa}_{\sigma+,\jmath-;\mathfrak{g},\kappa}\mathfrak{K}_{\mu}(\ell,\imath)\right] \\ \leq_I &\frac{\Gamma(\lambda+1)}{2[\mathfrak{g}(\ell)-\mathfrak{g}(\sigma)]^{\lambda}}\left[\mathbb{J}^{\lambda}_{\sigma+;\mathfrak{g}}\Sigma_{1\mu}(\ell,\imath)+\mathbb{J}^{\lambda}_{\sigma+;\mathfrak{g}}\Sigma_{1\mu}(\ell,\jmath)\right] \end{aligned} \quad (72)$$

and

$$\begin{aligned} &\frac{\Gamma(\lambda+1)}{[\mathfrak{g}(\ell)-\mathfrak{g}(\sigma)]^{\lambda}}\mathbb{J}^{\lambda}_{\ell-;\mathfrak{g}}\Sigma_{1\mu}(\sigma,\tfrac{\imath+\jmath}{2}) \\ \leq_I &\frac{\Gamma(\lambda+1)\Gamma(\varkappa+1)}{4[\mathfrak{g}(\ell)-\mathfrak{g}(\sigma)]^{\lambda}[\kappa(\jmath)-\kappa(\imath)]^{\varkappa}}\left[\mathbb{J}^{\lambda,\varkappa}_{\ell-,\imath+;\mathfrak{g},\kappa}\mathfrak{K}_{\mu}(\sigma,\jmath)+\mathbb{J}^{\lambda,\varkappa}_{\ell-,\jmath-;\mathfrak{g},\kappa}\mathfrak{K}_{\mu}(\sigma,\imath)\right] \\ \leq_I &\frac{\Gamma(\lambda+1)}{2[\mathfrak{g}(\ell)-\mathfrak{g}(\sigma)]^{\lambda}}\left[\mathbb{J}^{\lambda}_{\ell-;\mathfrak{g}}\Sigma_{1\mu}(\sigma,\imath)+\mathbb{J}^{\lambda}_{\ell-;\mathfrak{g}}\Sigma_{1\mu}(\sigma,\jmath)\right] \end{aligned} \quad (73)$$

respectively.

Moreover, if we define the mapping $h^1_{s}:[\sigma,\ell]\to\mathbb{F}^+_0$, $h^1_{s}(k)=\tilde{\mathfrak{S}}(k,s)$, then $h^1_{s}(k)$ is convex for all $s\in[\imath,\jmath]$ and $\tilde{\mathscr{H}}^1_{s}(k)=h^1_{s}(k)\oplus\tilde{h}^1_{s}(k)=\tilde{\mathfrak{S}}(k,s)\oplus\Sigma_{1\mu}(k,s)=\tilde{\mathscr{H}}(k,s)$. If we apply the inequalities (22) for the convex mapping $h^1_{s}(k)$, then we have

$$h^1_{s}(\frac{\sigma+\ell}{2})\leq_F\frac{\Gamma(\lambda+1)}{4[\mathfrak{g}(\ell)-\mathfrak{g}(\sigma)]^{\lambda}}\odot\left[\mathbb{J}^{\lambda}_{\jmath+;\mathfrak{g}}\tilde{\mathscr{H}}^1_{s}(\ell)\oplus\mathbb{J}^{\lambda}_{\ell-;\mathfrak{g}}\tilde{\mathscr{H}}^1_{s}(\sigma)\right]\leq_F\frac{h^1_{s}(\sigma)\oplus h^1_{s}(\ell)}{2},$$

For all μ-cuts $\in[0,1]$, we have

$$\begin{aligned} &\mathfrak{S}_{\mu}(\tfrac{\sigma+\ell}{2},s) \\ \leq_I &\frac{\lambda}{4[\mathfrak{g}(\ell)-\mathfrak{g}(\sigma)]^{\lambda}}\left[(IA)\int_{\sigma}^{\ell}\frac{\mathfrak{g}'(k)}{[\mathfrak{g}(\ell)-\mathfrak{g}(k)]^{1-\lambda}}\mathscr{H}_{\mu}(k,s)dk+(IA)\int_{\sigma}^{\ell}\frac{\mathfrak{g}'(k)}{[\mathfrak{g}(k)-\mathfrak{g}(\sigma)]^{1-\lambda}}\mathscr{H}_{\mu}(k,s)dk\right] \\ \leq_I &\frac{\mathfrak{S}_{\mu}(\sigma,s)+\mathfrak{S}_{\mu}(\ell,s)}{2} \end{aligned} \quad (74)$$

Similarly, both sides of (74) are multiplied by

$$\frac{\beta}{[\kappa(\jmath)-\kappa(\imath)]^{\beta}}\,\frac{\mathrm{g}'(s)}{[\kappa(\jmath)-\kappa(s)]^{1-\beta}}$$

and

$$\frac{\beta}{[\kappa(\jmath)-\kappa(\imath)]^{\beta}}\,\frac{\mathrm{g}'(s)}{[\kappa(s)-\kappa(\imath)]^{1-\beta}}$$

then integrating the established results in relation to y from $\imath$ to $\jmath$, we obtain the following inequalities:

$$\begin{aligned} &\frac{\Gamma(\varkappa+1)}{[\kappa(\jmath)-\kappa(\imath)]^{\varkappa}}\mathbb{J}^{\varkappa}_{\imath+;\kappa}\mathfrak{S}_{\mu}(\tfrac{\sigma+\ell}{2},\jmath) \\ \leq_I &\frac{\Gamma(\lambda+1)\Gamma(\varkappa+1)}{4[\mathfrak{g}(\ell)-\mathfrak{g}(\sigma)]^{\lambda}[\kappa(\jmath)-\kappa(\imath)]^{\varkappa}}\left[\mathbb{J}^{\lambda,\varkappa}_{\sigma+,\imath+;\mathfrak{g},\kappa}\mathscr{H}_{\mu}(\ell,\jmath)+\mathbb{J}^{\lambda,\varkappa}_{\sigma+,\jmath-;\mathfrak{g},\kappa}\mathscr{H}_{\mu}(\sigma,\jmath)\right] \\ \leq_I &\frac{\Gamma(\varkappa+1)}{2[\kappa(\jmath)-\kappa(\imath)]^{\varkappa}}\left[\mathbb{J}^{\varkappa}_{\imath+;\kappa}\mathfrak{S}_{\mu}(\sigma,\jmath)+\mathbb{J}^{\varkappa}_{\imath+;\kappa}\mathfrak{S}_{\mu}(\ell,\jmath)\right] \end{aligned} \quad (75)$$

and

$$\begin{aligned} &\frac{\Gamma(\varkappa+1)}{[\kappa(\jmath)-\kappa(\imath)]^{\varkappa}}\mathbb{J}^{\varkappa}_{\jmath-;\kappa}\mathfrak{S}_{\mu}(\tfrac{\sigma+\ell}{2},\imath) \\ \leq_I &\frac{\Gamma(\lambda+1)\Gamma(\varkappa+1)}{4[\mathfrak{g}(\ell)-\mathfrak{g}(\sigma)]^{\lambda}[\kappa(\jmath)-\kappa(\imath)]^{\varkappa}}\left[\mathbb{J}^{\lambda,\varkappa}_{\sigma+,\jmath-;\mathfrak{g},\kappa}\mathscr{H}_{\mu}(\ell,\imath)+\mathbb{J}^{\lambda,\varkappa}_{\ell-,\jmath-;\mathfrak{g},\kappa}\mathscr{H}_{\mu}(\sigma,\imath)\right] \\ \leq_I &\frac{\Gamma(\varkappa+1)}{2[\kappa(\jmath)-\kappa(\imath)]^{\varkappa}}\left[\mathbb{J}^{\varkappa}_{\jmath-;\kappa}\mathfrak{S}_{\mu}(\sigma,\imath)+\mathbb{J}^{\varkappa}_{\jmath-;\kappa}\mathfrak{S}_{\mu}(\ell,\imath)\right] \end{aligned} \quad (76)$$

respectively.

 https://doi.org/10.3390/fractalfract10040228

Furthermore, if we define the mapping $h_{\jmath}^2 : [\mathcal{o}, \ell] \to \mathbb{F}_0^+$, $h_{\jmath}^2(\hbar) = \tilde{\Delta}_2(\hbar, \jmath)$, then $h_{\jmath}^2(\hbar)$ is convex for all $\jmath \in [\imath, \jmath]$ and $\tilde{\mathscr{H}}_{\jmath}^2(\hbar) = h_{\jmath}^2(\hbar) \oplus \tilde{h_{\jmath}^2}(\hbar) = \tilde{\Delta}_2(\hbar, \jmath) \oplus \tilde{\Delta}_3(\hbar, \jmath) = \tilde{\mathscr{L}}(\hbar, \jmath)$. If we apply the inequalities (22) for the convex mapping $h_{\jmath}^2(\hbar)$, then we have

$$h_{\jmath}^2\left(\frac{\mathcal{o}+\ell}{2}\right) \leq_F \frac{\Gamma(\measuredangle+1)}{4[\mathfrak{g}(\ell)-\mathfrak{g}(\mathcal{o})]^{\measuredangle}} \odot \left[\mathbb{J}_{\mathcal{o}+;\mathfrak{g}}^{\measuredangle} \tilde{\mathscr{H}}_{\jmath}^2(\ell) \oplus \mathbb{J}_{\ell-;\mathfrak{g}}^{\measuredangle} \tilde{\mathscr{H}}_{\jmath}^2(\mathcal{o})\right] \leq_F \frac{h_{\jmath}^2(\mathcal{o}) \oplus h_{\jmath}^2(\ell)}{2},$$

for all μ-cuts $\in [0,1]$, we have

$$\begin{aligned} \Delta_{2\mu}\left(\tfrac{\mathcal{o}+\ell}{2}, \jmath\right) \leq_I \frac{\measuredangle}{4[\mathfrak{g}(\ell)-\mathfrak{g}(\mathcal{o})]^{\measuredangle}} &\left[(IA)\int_{\mathcal{o}}^{\ell} \frac{\mathfrak{g}'(\hbar)}{[\mathfrak{g}(\ell)-\mathfrak{g}(\hbar)]^{1-\measuredangle}} \mathscr{L}_{\mu}(\hbar, \jmath) d\hbar + (IA)\int_{\mathcal{o}}^{\ell} \frac{\mathfrak{g}'(\hbar)}{[\mathfrak{g}(\hbar)-\mathfrak{g}(\mathcal{o})]^{1-\measuredangle}} \mathscr{L}_{\mu}(\hbar, \jmath) d\hbar\right] \\ &\leq_I \frac{\Delta_{2\mu}(\mathcal{o},\jmath)+\Delta_{2\mu}(\ell,\jmath)}{2} \end{aligned} \tag{77}$$

Similarly, both sides of (77) are multiplied by

$$\frac{\beta}{[\ltimes(\jmath)-\ltimes(\imath)]^{\beta}} \frac{w'(\jmath)}{[\ltimes(\jmath)-\ltimes(\jmath)]^{1-\beta}}$$

and

$$\frac{\beta}{[\ltimes(\jmath)-\ltimes(\imath)]^{\beta}} \frac{w'(\jmath)}{[\ltimes(\jmath)-\ltimes(\imath)]^{1-\beta}}$$

then integrating the obtained results in relation to y from $\imath$ to $\jmath$, we obtain the following inequalities:

$$\begin{aligned} &\frac{\Gamma(\rtimes+1)}{[\ltimes(\jmath)-\ltimes(\imath)]^{\rtimes}} \mathbb{J}_{\imath+;\ltimes}^{\rtimes} \Delta_{2\mu}\left(\tfrac{\mathcal{o}+\ell}{2}, \jmath\right) \\ \leq_I &\frac{\Gamma(\measuredangle+1)\Gamma(\rtimes+1)}{4[\mathfrak{g}(\ell)-\mathfrak{g}(\mathcal{o})]^{\measuredangle}[\ltimes(\jmath)-\ltimes(\imath)]^{\rtimes}} \left[\mathbb{J}_{\mathcal{o}+,\imath+;\mathfrak{g},\ltimes}^{\measuredangle,\rtimes} \mathscr{L}_{\mu}(\ell, \jmath) + \mathbb{J}_{\ell-,\imath+;\mathfrak{g},\ltimes}^{\measuredangle,\rtimes} \mathscr{L}_{\mu}(\mathcal{o}, \jmath)\right] \\ \leq_I &\frac{\Gamma(\rtimes+1)}{2[\ltimes(\jmath)-\ltimes(\imath)]^{\rtimes}} \left[\mathbb{J}_{\imath+;\ltimes}^{\rtimes} \Delta_{2\mu}(\mathcal{o}, \jmath) + \mathbb{J}_{\imath+;\ltimes}^{\rtimes} \Delta_{2\mu}(\ell, \jmath)\right] \end{aligned} \tag{78}$$

and

$$\begin{aligned} &\frac{\Gamma(\rtimes+1)}{[\ltimes(\jmath)-\ltimes(\imath)]^{\rtimes}} \mathbb{J}_{\jmath-;\ltimes}^{\rtimes} \Delta_{2\mu}\left(\tfrac{\mathcal{o}+\ell}{2}, \imath\right) \\ \leq_I &\frac{\Gamma(\measuredangle+1)\Gamma(\rtimes+1)}{4[\mathfrak{g}(\ell)-\mathfrak{g}(\mathcal{o})]^{\measuredangle}[\ltimes(\jmath)-\ltimes(\imath)]^{\rtimes}} \left[\mathbb{J}_{\mathcal{o}+,\jmath-;\mathfrak{g},\ltimes}^{\measuredangle,\rtimes} \mathscr{L}_{\mu}(\ell, \imath) + \mathbb{J}_{\ell-,\jmath-;\mathfrak{g},\ltimes}^{\measuredangle,\rtimes} \mathscr{L}_{\mu}(\mathcal{o}, \imath)\right] \\ \leq_I &\frac{\Gamma(\rtimes+1)}{2[\ltimes(\jmath)-\ltimes(\imath)]^{\rtimes}} \left[\mathbb{J}_{\jmath-;\ltimes}^{\rtimes} \Delta_{2\mu}(\mathcal{o}, \imath) + \mathbb{J}_{\jmath-;\ltimes}^{\rtimes} \Delta_{2\mu}(\ell, \imath)\right] \end{aligned} \tag{79}$$

respectively.

Summing the inequalities (69), (70), (72), (73), (75), (76), (78), and (79), we have the following inequalities:

 https://doi.org/10.3390/fractalfract10040228

$$\frac{\Gamma(\lambda+1)}{[\mathfrak{g}(\ell)-\mathfrak{g}(o)]^{\lambda}}\begin{bmatrix}\mathbb{J}^{\lambda}_{o+;\mathfrak{g}}\mathfrak{S}_{\mu}(\ell,\frac{\imath+\jmath}{2})+\mathbb{J}^{\lambda}_{\ell-;\mathfrak{g}}\mathfrak{S}_{\mu}(o,\frac{\imath+\jmath}{2})\\+\mathbb{J}^{\lambda}_{o+;\mathfrak{g}}\mathfrak{X}_{1\mu}(\ell,\frac{\imath+\jmath}{2})+\mathbb{J}^{\lambda}_{\ell-;\mathfrak{g}}\mathfrak{X}_{1\mu}(o,\frac{\imath+\jmath}{2})\end{bmatrix}$$
$$+\frac{\Gamma(\rtimes+1)}{[\ltimes(\jmath)-\ltimes(\imath)]^{\rtimes}}\begin{bmatrix}\mathbb{J}^{\rtimes}_{\imath+;\ltimes}\mathfrak{S}_{\mu}(\frac{o+\ell}{2},\jmath)+\mathbb{J}^{\rtimes}_{\jmath-;\ltimes}\mathfrak{S}_{\mu}(\frac{o+\ell}{2},\imath)\\+\mathbb{J}^{\rtimes}_{\imath+;\ltimes}\mathfrak{X}_{2\mu}(\frac{o+\ell}{2},\jmath)+\mathbb{J}^{\rtimes}_{\jmath-;\ltimes}\mathfrak{X}_{2\mu}(\frac{o+\ell}{2},\imath)\end{bmatrix}$$
$$\leq_I \frac{\Gamma(\lambda+1)\Gamma(\rtimes+1)}{4[\mathfrak{g}(\ell)-\mathfrak{g}(o)]^{\lambda}[\ltimes(\jmath)-\ltimes(\imath)]^{\rtimes}}\times\begin{bmatrix}\mathbb{J}^{\lambda,\rtimes}_{o+,\imath+;\mathfrak{g},\ltimes}\mathfrak{D}_{\mu}(\ell,\jmath)+\mathbb{J}^{\lambda,\rtimes}_{o+,\jmath-;\mathfrak{g},\ltimes}\mathfrak{D}_{\mu}(\ell,\imath)+\mathbb{J}^{\lambda,\rtimes}_{\ell-,\imath+;\mathfrak{g},\ltimes}\mathfrak{D}_{\mu}(o,\jmath)+\mathbb{J}^{\lambda,\rtimes}_{\ell-,\jmath-;\mathfrak{g},\ltimes}\mathfrak{D}_{\mu}(o,\imath)\\+\mathbb{J}^{\lambda,\rtimes}_{o+,\imath+;\mathfrak{g},\ltimes}\mathfrak{K}_{\mu}(\ell,\jmath)+\mathbb{J}^{\lambda,\rtimes}_{o+,\jmath-;\mathfrak{g},\ltimes}\mathfrak{K}_{\mu}(\ell,\imath)+\mathbb{J}^{\lambda,\rtimes}_{\ell-,\imath+;\mathfrak{g},\ltimes}\mathfrak{K}_{\mu}(o,\jmath)+\mathbb{J}^{\lambda,\rtimes}_{\ell-,\jmath-;\mathfrak{g},\ltimes}\mathfrak{K}_{\mu}(o,\imath)\\+\mathbb{J}^{\lambda,\rtimes}_{o+,\imath+;\mathfrak{g},\ltimes}\mathscr{H}_{\mu}(\ell,\jmath)+\mathbb{J}^{\lambda,\rtimes}_{o+,\jmath-;\mathfrak{g},\ltimes}\mathscr{H}_{\mu}(o,\jmath)+\mathbb{J}^{\lambda,\rtimes}_{o+,\jmath-;\mathfrak{g},\ltimes}\mathscr{H}_{\mu}(\ell,\imath)+\mathbb{J}^{\lambda,\rtimes}_{\ell-,\jmath-;\mathfrak{g},\ltimes}\mathscr{H}_{\mu}(o,\imath)\\+\mathbb{J}^{\lambda,\rtimes}_{o+,\imath+;\mathfrak{g},\ltimes}\mathscr{L}_{\mu}(\ell,\jmath)+\mathbb{J}^{\lambda,\rtimes}_{o+,\jmath-;\mathfrak{g},\ltimes}\mathscr{L}_{\mu}(o,\jmath)+\mathbb{J}^{\lambda,\rtimes}_{o+,\jmath-;\mathfrak{g},\ltimes}\mathscr{L}_{\mu}(\ell,\imath)+\mathbb{J}^{\lambda,\rtimes}_{\ell-,\jmath-;\mathfrak{g},\ltimes}\mathscr{L}_{\mu}(o,\imath)\end{bmatrix}$$
$$\leq_I \frac{\Gamma(\lambda+1)}{2[\mathfrak{g}(\ell)-\mathfrak{g}(o)]^{\lambda}}\begin{bmatrix}\mathbb{J}^{\lambda}_{o+;\mathfrak{g}}\mathfrak{S}_{\mu}(\ell,\imath)+\mathbb{J}^{\lambda}_{o+;\mathfrak{g}}\mathfrak{S}_{\mu}(\ell,\jmath)+\mathbb{J}^{\lambda}_{\ell-;\mathfrak{g}}\mathfrak{S}_{\mu}(\ell,\imath)+\mathbb{J}^{\lambda}_{\ell-;\mathfrak{g}}\mathfrak{S}_{\mu}(\ell,\jmath)\\+\mathbb{J}^{\lambda}_{o+;\mathfrak{g}}\mathfrak{X}_{1\mu}(\ell,\imath)+\mathbb{J}^{\lambda}_{o+;\mathfrak{g}}\mathfrak{X}_{1\mu}(\ell,\jmath)+\mathbb{J}^{\lambda}_{\ell-;\mathfrak{g}}\mathfrak{X}_{1\mu}(o,\imath)+\mathbb{J}^{\lambda}_{\ell-;\mathfrak{g}}\mathfrak{X}_{1\mu}(o,\jmath)\end{bmatrix}$$
$$+\frac{\Gamma(\rtimes+1)}{[\ltimes(\jmath)-\ltimes(\imath)]^{\rtimes}}\begin{bmatrix}\mathbb{J}^{\rtimes}_{\imath+;\ltimes}\mathfrak{S}_{\mu}(o,\jmath)+\mathbb{J}^{\rtimes}_{\imath+;\ltimes}\mathfrak{S}_{\mu}(\ell,\jmath)+\mathbb{J}^{\rtimes}_{\jmath-;\ltimes}\mathfrak{S}_{\mu}(o,\imath)+\mathbb{J}^{\rtimes}_{\jmath-;\ltimes}\mathfrak{S}_{\mu}(\ell,\imath)\\+\mathbb{J}^{\rtimes}_{\imath+;\ltimes}\mathfrak{X}_{2\mu}(o,\jmath)+\mathbb{J}^{\rtimes}_{\imath+;\ltimes}\mathfrak{X}_{2\mu}(\ell,\jmath)+\mathbb{J}^{\rtimes}_{\jmath-;\ltimes}\mathfrak{X}_{2\mu}(o,\imath)+\mathbb{J}^{\rtimes}_{\jmath-;\ltimes}\mathfrak{X}_{2\mu}(l,\imath)\end{bmatrix}$$

That is, we have

$$\frac{\Gamma(\lambda+1)}{[\mathfrak{g}(\ell)-\mathfrak{g}(o)]^{\lambda}}\left[\mathbb{J}^{\lambda}_{o+;\mathfrak{g}}\mathscr{H}_{\mu}(\ell,\frac{\imath+\jmath}{2})+\mathbb{J}^{\lambda}_{\ell-;\mathfrak{g}}\mathscr{H}_{\mu}(o,\frac{\imath+\jmath}{2})\right]$$
$$+\frac{\Gamma(\rtimes+1)}{[\ltimes(\jmath)-\ltimes(\imath)]^{\rtimes}}\left[\mathbb{J}^{\rtimes}_{\imath+;\ltimes}\mathfrak{D}_{\mu}(\frac{o+\ell}{2},\jmath)+\mathbb{J}^{\rtimes}_{\jmath-;\ltimes}\mathfrak{D}_{\mu}(\frac{o+\ell}{2},\imath)\right]$$
$$\leq_I \frac{\Gamma(\lambda+1)\Gamma(\rtimes+1)}{2[\mathfrak{g}(\ell)-\mathfrak{g}(o)]^{\lambda}[\ltimes(\jmath)-\ltimes(\imath)]^{\rtimes}}\times\begin{bmatrix}\mathbb{J}^{\lambda,\rtimes}_{o+,\imath+;\mathfrak{g},\ltimes}\mathfrak{X}_{\mu}(\ell,\jmath)+\mathbb{J}^{\lambda,\rtimes}_{o+,\jmath-;\mathfrak{g},\ltimes}\mathfrak{X}_{\mu}(\ell,\imath)\\+\mathbb{J}^{\lambda,\rtimes}_{\ell-,\imath+;\mathfrak{g},\ltimes}\mathfrak{X}_{\mu}(o,\jmath)+\mathbb{J}^{\lambda,\rtimes}_{\ell-,\jmath-;\mathfrak{g},\ltimes}\mathfrak{X}_{\mu}(o,\imath)\end{bmatrix}$$
$$\leq_I \frac{\Gamma(\lambda+1)}{2[\mathfrak{g}(\ell)-\mathfrak{g}(o)]^{\lambda}}\left[\mathbb{J}^{\lambda}_{o+;\mathfrak{g}}\mathscr{H}_{\mu}(\ell,\imath)+\mathbb{J}^{\lambda}_{o+;\mathfrak{g}}\mathscr{H}_{\mu}(\ell,\jmath)+\mathbb{J}^{\lambda}_{\ell-;\mathfrak{g}}\mathscr{H}_{\mu}(o,\imath)+\mathbb{J}^{\lambda}_{\ell-;\mathfrak{g}}\mathscr{H}_{\mu}(o,\jmath)\right]$$
$$+2\frac{\Gamma(\rtimes+1)}{[\ltimes(\jmath)-\ltimes(\imath)]^{\rtimes}}\left[\mathbb{J}^{\rtimes}_{\imath+;\ltimes}\mathfrak{D}_{\mu}(o,\jmath)+\mathbb{J}^{\rtimes}_{\imath+;\ltimes}\mathfrak{D}_{\mu}(\ell,\jmath)+\mathbb{J}^{\rtimes}_{\jmath-;\ltimes}\mathfrak{D}_{\mu}(o,\imath)+\mathbb{J}^{\rtimes}_{\jmath-;\ltimes}\mathfrak{D}_{\mu}(\ell,\imath)\right]$$

which completes the proof of the second and third inequalities in (67). On the other hand, from the first inequality in (22), we have

$$\mathfrak{S}_{\mu}(\frac{o+\ell}{2})\leq_I \frac{\lambda}{4[\mathfrak{g}(\ell)-\mathfrak{g}(o)]^{\lambda}}\begin{bmatrix}\int_{o}^{\ell}\frac{\mathfrak{g}'(\hbar)}{[\mathfrak{g}(\ell)-\mathfrak{g}(\hbar)]^{\lambda}}\left[\mathfrak{S}_{\mu}(\hbar)+\mathfrak{S}_{\mu}(o+\ell-\hbar)\right]\jmath k\\+\int_{o}^{\ell}\frac{\mathfrak{g}'(\hbar)}{[\mathfrak{g}(\hbar)-\mathfrak{g}(o)]^{\lambda}}\left[\mathfrak{S}_{\mu}(\hbar)+\mathfrak{S}_{\mu}(o+\ell-\hbar)\right]\jmath k\end{bmatrix} \tag{80}$$

Since F is the $F{\cdot}N\cdot V$-coordinated convex on Δ, by using inequality (80), we obtain

$$\mathfrak{S}_{\mu}(\frac{o+\ell}{2},\frac{\imath+\jmath}{2})\leq_I \frac{\lambda}{4[\mathfrak{g}(\ell)-\mathfrak{g}(o)]^{\lambda}}\begin{bmatrix}(IA)\int_{o}^{\ell}\frac{\mathfrak{g}'(\hbar)}{[\mathfrak{g}(\ell)-\mathfrak{g}(\hbar)]^{\lambda}}\left[\mathfrak{S}_{\mu}(\hbar,\frac{\imath+\jmath}{2})+\mathfrak{S}_{\mu}(o+\ell-\hbar,\frac{\imath+\jmath}{2})\right]d\hbar\\+(IA)\int_{o}^{\ell}\frac{\mathfrak{g}'(\hbar)}{[\mathfrak{g}(\hbar)-\mathfrak{g}(o)]^{\lambda}}\left[\mathfrak{S}_{\mu}(\hbar,\frac{\imath+\jmath}{2})+\mathfrak{S}_{\mu}(o+\ell-\hbar,\frac{\imath+\jmath}{2})\right]d\hbar\end{bmatrix}$$
$$=\frac{\Gamma(\lambda+1)}{4[\mathfrak{g}(\ell)-\mathfrak{g}(o)]^{\lambda}}\left[\mathbb{J}^{\lambda}_{o+;\mathfrak{g}}\mathscr{H}_{\mu}(\ell,\frac{\imath+\jmath}{2})+\mathbb{J}^{\lambda}_{\ell-;\mathfrak{g}}\mathscr{H}_{\mu}(o,\frac{\imath+\jmath}{2})\right], \tag{81}$$

and similarly, we have

https://doi.org/10.3390/fractalfract10040228

$$\mathfrak{S}_\mu\left(\tfrac{o+\ell}{2},\tfrac{\imath+\jmath}{2}\right) \leq_I \frac{\rtimes}{4[\ltimes(\jmath)-\ltimes(\imath)]^{\rtimes}}\begin{bmatrix}(IA)\int_\imath^\jmath \frac{\ltimes'(s)}{[\ltimes(\jmath)-\ltimes(s)]^{\leftthreetimes}}\left[\mathfrak{S}_\mu(\tfrac{o+\ell}{2},s)+\mathfrak{S}_\mu(\tfrac{o+\ell}{2},\imath+\jmath-s)\right]ds\\ +(IA)\int_\imath^\jmath \frac{\ltimes'(s)}{[\ltimes(s)-\ltimes(\imath)]^{\leftthreetimes}}\left[\mathfrak{S}_\mu(\tfrac{o+\ell}{2},s)+\mathfrak{S}_\mu(\tfrac{o+\ell}{2},\imath+\jmath-s)\right]ds\end{bmatrix}$$
$$= \frac{\Gamma(\rtimes+1)}{4[\ltimes(\jmath)-\ltimes(\imath)]^{\rtimes}}\left[\mathbb{J}^{\rtimes}_{\imath+;\ltimes}\mathfrak{D}_\mu(\tfrac{o+\ell}{2},\jmath)+\mathbb{J}^{\rtimes}_{\jmath-;\ltimes}\mathfrak{D}_\mu(\tfrac{o+\ell}{2},\imath)\right] \tag{82}$$

Combining the inequalities (81) and (82), we obtain the first inequality in (67). From the second inequality in (22), we have

$$\frac{\leftthreetimes}{4[\mathfrak{g}(\ell)-\mathfrak{g}(o)]^{\leftthreetimes}}\begin{bmatrix}(IA)\int_o^\ell \frac{\mathfrak{g}'(\hbar)}{[\mathfrak{g}(\ell)-\mathfrak{g}(\hbar)]^{\leftthreetimes}}[\mathfrak{S}_\mu(\hbar)+\mathfrak{S}_\mu(o+\ell-\hbar)]d\hbar\\ +(IA)\int_o^\ell \frac{\mathfrak{g}'(\hbar)}{[\mathfrak{g}(\hbar)-\mathfrak{g}(o)]^{\leftthreetimes}}[\mathfrak{S}_\mu(\hbar)+\mathfrak{S}_\mu(o+\ell-\hbar)]d\hbar\end{bmatrix} \leq_I \frac{\mathfrak{S}_\mu(o)+\mathfrak{S}_\mu(\ell)}{2} \tag{83}$$

By using inequality (83), we obtain the following inequalities:

$$\frac{\Gamma(\leftthreetimes+1)}{4[\mathfrak{g}(\ell)-\mathfrak{g}(o)]^{\leftthreetimes}}\left[\mathbb{J}^{\leftthreetimes}_{o+;\mathfrak{g}}\mathscr{H}_\mu(\ell,\imath)+\mathbb{J}^{\leftthreetimes}_{\ell-;\mathfrak{g}}\mathscr{H}_\mu(o,\imath)\right] \leq_I \frac{\mathfrak{S}_\mu(o,\imath)+\mathfrak{S}_\mu(\ell,\imath)}{2} \tag{84}$$

$$\frac{\Gamma(\leftthreetimes+1)}{4[\mathfrak{g}(\ell)-\mathfrak{g}(o)]^{\leftthreetimes}}\left[\mathbb{J}^{\leftthreetimes}_{o+;\mathfrak{g}}\mathscr{H}_\mu(\ell,\jmath)+\mathbb{J}^{\leftthreetimes}_{\ell-;\mathfrak{g}}\mathscr{H}_\mu(o,\jmath)\right] \leq_I \frac{\mathfrak{S}_\mu(o,\jmath)+\mathfrak{S}_\mu(\ell,\jmath)}{2} \tag{85}$$

$$\frac{\Gamma(\rtimes+1))}{4[\ltimes(\jmath)-\ltimes(\imath)]^{\rtimes}}\left[\mathbb{J}^{\rtimes}_{\imath+;\ltimes}\mathfrak{D}_\mu(o,\jmath)+\mathbb{J}^{\rtimes}_{\jmath-;\ltimes}\mathfrak{D}_\mu(o,\imath)\right] \leq_I \frac{\mathfrak{S}_\mu(o,\imath)+\mathfrak{S}_\mu(o,\jmath)}{2} \tag{86}$$

and

$$\frac{\Gamma(\rtimes+1))}{4[\ltimes(\jmath)-\ltimes(\imath)]^{\rtimes}}\left[\mathbb{J}^{\rtimes}_{\imath+;\ltimes}\mathfrak{D}_\mu(\ell,\jmath)+\mathbb{J}^{\rtimes}_{\jmath-;\ltimes}\mathfrak{D}_\mu(\ell,\imath)\right] \leq_I \frac{\mathfrak{S}_\mu(\ell,\imath)+\mathfrak{S}_\mu(\ell,\jmath)}{2} \tag{87}$$

Combining the inequalities (84) to (87), we obtain the last inequality in (67). This completes the proof completely. □

Remark 4. *(i) Assuming the conditions of Theorem 5 hold, setting $\mathfrak{g}(v)=v$, $\ltimes(r)=r$ and $\mu=0$ yields the following inequalities for the Riemann–Liouville F·N · V-fractional double integrals:*

$$\begin{aligned}
&\mathfrak{S}\left(\tfrac{o+\ell}{2},\tfrac{\imath+\jmath}{2}\right)\\
&\leq_I \frac{\Gamma(\leftthreetimes+1)}{4(\ell-o)^{\leftthreetimes}}\left[\mathcal{J}^{\leftthreetimes}_{o+}\mathfrak{S}(\ell,\tfrac{\imath+\jmath}{2})+\mathcal{J}^{\leftthreetimes}_{\ell-}\mathfrak{S}(o,\tfrac{\imath+\jmath}{2})\right]\\
&\quad+\frac{\Gamma(\rtimes+1)}{4(\jmath-\imath)^{\rtimes}}\left[\mathcal{J}^{\rtimes}_{\imath+}\mathfrak{S}(\tfrac{o+\ell}{2},\jmath)+\mathcal{J}^{\rtimes}_{\jmath-}\mathfrak{S}(\tfrac{o+\ell}{2},\imath)\right]\\
&\leq_I \frac{\Gamma(\leftthreetimes+1)\Gamma(\rtimes+1)}{4(\ell-o)^{\leftthreetimes}(\jmath-\imath)^{\rtimes}}\begin{bmatrix}\mathcal{J}^{\leftthreetimes,\rtimes}_{o+,\imath+}\mathfrak{S}(\ell,\jmath)+\mathcal{J}^{\leftthreetimes,\rtimes}_{o+,\jmath-}\mathfrak{S}(\ell,\imath)\\ +\mathcal{J}^{\leftthreetimes,\rtimes}_{\ell-,\imath+}\mathfrak{S}(o,\jmath)+\mathcal{J}^{\leftthreetimes,\rtimes}_{\ell-,\jmath-}\mathfrak{S}(o,\imath)\end{bmatrix}\\
&\leq_I \frac{\Gamma(\leftthreetimes+1)}{8(\ell-o)^{\leftthreetimes}}\left[\mathcal{J}^{\leftthreetimes}_{o+}\mathfrak{S}(\ell,\imath)+\mathcal{J}^{\leftthreetimes}_{o+}\mathfrak{S}(\ell,\jmath)+\mathcal{J}^{\leftthreetimes}_{\ell-}\mathfrak{S}(o,\imath)+\mathcal{J}^{\leftthreetimes}_{\ell-}\mathfrak{S}(o,\jmath)\right]\\
&\quad+\frac{\Gamma(\rtimes+1)}{8(\jmath-\imath)^{\rtimes}}\left[\mathcal{J}^{\rtimes}_{\imath+}\mathfrak{S}(o,\jmath)+\mathcal{J}^{\rtimes}_{\jmath-}\mathfrak{S}(\ell,\jmath)+\mathcal{J}^{\rtimes}_{\imath+}\mathfrak{S}(o,\imath)+\mathcal{J}^{\rtimes}_{\jmath-}\mathfrak{S}(\ell,\imath)\right]\\
&\leq_I \frac{\mathfrak{S}(o,\imath)+\mathfrak{S}(o,\jmath)+\mathfrak{S}(\ell,\imath)+\mathfrak{S}(\ell,\jmath)}{4}.
\end{aligned}$$

which are proved by Budak et al. [17] *in a previous study.*

https://doi.org/10.3390/fractalfract10040228

(ii) Assuming the conditions of Theorem 5 hold, setting $\mathfrak{g}(v) = v, \ltimes(r) = r$, and $\mu = 0$ yields the following inequalities for the Riemann–Liouville F·N · V-fractional double integrals:

$$
\begin{aligned}
&\tilde{\mathfrak{S}}\left(\tfrac{o+\ell}{2}, \tfrac{\imath+\jmath}{2}\right) \\
\leq_F\ & \frac{\Gamma(\curlywedge+1)}{4(\ell-o)^{\curlywedge}} \odot \left[\mathcal{J}_{o+}^{\curlywedge}\tilde{\mathfrak{S}}\left(\ell, \tfrac{\imath+\jmath}{2}\right) \oplus \mathcal{J}_{\ell-}^{\curlywedge}\tilde{\mathfrak{S}}\left(o, \tfrac{\imath+\jmath}{2}\right)\right] \\
&\oplus \frac{\Gamma(\rtimes+1)}{4(\jmath-\imath)^{\rtimes}} \odot \left[\mathcal{J}_{\imath+}^{\rtimes}\tilde{\mathfrak{S}}\left(\tfrac{o+\ell}{2}, \jmath\right) \oplus \mathcal{J}_{\jmath-}^{\rtimes}\tilde{\mathfrak{S}}\left(\tfrac{o+\ell}{2}, \imath\right)\right] \\
\leq_F\ & \frac{\Gamma(\curlywedge+1)\Gamma(\rtimes+1)}{4(\ell-o)^{\curlywedge}(\jmath-\imath)^{\rtimes}} \odot \begin{bmatrix} \mathcal{J}_{o+,\imath+}^{\curlywedge,\rtimes}\tilde{\mathfrak{S}}(\ell,\jmath) \oplus \mathcal{J}_{o+,\jmath-}^{\curlywedge,\rtimes}\tilde{\mathfrak{S}}(\ell,\imath) \\ \oplus \mathcal{J}_{\ell-,\imath+}^{\curlywedge,\rtimes}\tilde{\mathfrak{S}}(o,\jmath) \oplus \mathcal{J}_{\ell-,\jmath-}^{\curlywedge,\rtimes}\tilde{\mathfrak{S}}(o,\imath) \end{bmatrix} \\
\leq_F\ & \frac{\Gamma(\curlywedge+1)}{8(\ell-o)^{\curlywedge}} \odot \left[\mathcal{J}_{o+}^{\curlywedge}\tilde{\mathfrak{S}}(\ell,\imath) \oplus \mathcal{J}_{o+}^{\curlywedge}\tilde{\mathfrak{S}}(\ell,\jmath) \oplus \mathcal{J}_{\ell-}^{\curlywedge}\tilde{\mathfrak{S}}(o,\imath) \oplus \mathcal{J}_{\ell-}^{\curlywedge}\tilde{\mathfrak{S}}(o,\jmath)\right] \\
&\oplus \frac{\Gamma(\rtimes+1)}{8(\jmath-\imath)^{\rtimes}} \odot \left[\mathcal{J}_{\imath+}^{\rtimes}\tilde{\mathfrak{S}}(o,\jmath) \oplus \mathcal{J}_{\jmath-}^{\rtimes}\tilde{\mathfrak{S}}(\ell,\jmath) \oplus \mathcal{J}_{\imath+}^{\rtimes}\tilde{\mathfrak{S}}(o,\imath) \oplus \mathcal{J}_{\jmath-}^{\rtimes}\tilde{\mathfrak{S}}(\ell,\imath)\right] \\
\leq_F\ & \frac{\tilde{\mathfrak{S}}(o,\imath)\oplus\tilde{\mathfrak{S}}(o,\jmath)\oplus\tilde{\mathfrak{S}}(\ell,\imath)\oplus\tilde{\mathfrak{S}}(\ell,\jmath)}{4}
\end{aligned}
$$

Corollary 6. *Setting $\mathfrak{g}(v) = \ln v$ and $\ltimes(r) = \ln r$ in Theorem 5 yields the following inequalities for the Hadamard F·N · V-fractional double integrals:*

$$
\begin{aligned}
\tilde{\mathfrak{S}}\left(\tfrac{o+\ell}{2}, \tfrac{\imath+\jmath}{2}\right) \leq_F\ & \frac{\Gamma(\curlywedge+1)}{8\left[\ln\frac{\ell}{o}\right]^{\curlywedge}} \odot \left[\mathfrak{J}_{o+}^{\curlywedge}\mathscr{H}\left(\ell, \tfrac{\imath+\jmath}{2}\right) \oplus \mathfrak{J}_{\ell-}^{\curlywedge}\mathscr{H}\left(o, \tfrac{\imath+\jmath}{2}\right)\right] \oplus \frac{\Gamma(\rtimes+1)}{8\left[\ln\frac{\jmath}{\imath}\right]^{\rtimes}} \odot \left[\mathfrak{J}_{\imath+}^{\rtimes}\tilde{\mathfrak{D}}\left(\tfrac{o+\ell}{2}, \jmath\right) \oplus \mathfrak{J}_{\jmath-}^{\rtimes}\tilde{\mathfrak{D}}\left(\tfrac{o+\ell}{2}, \imath\right)\right] \\
\leq_F\ & \frac{\Gamma(\curlywedge+1)\Gamma(\rtimes+1)}{16\left[\ln\frac{\ell}{o}\right]^{\curlywedge}\left[\ln\frac{\jmath}{\imath}\right]^{\rtimes}} \odot \left[\mathfrak{J}_{o+,\imath+}^{\curlywedge,\rtimes}\tilde{\mathfrak{X}}(\ell,\jmath) \oplus \mathfrak{J}_{o+,\jmath-}^{\curlywedge,\rtimes}\tilde{\mathfrak{X}}(\ell,\imath) \oplus \mathfrak{J}_{\ell-,\imath+}^{\curlywedge,\rtimes}\tilde{\mathfrak{X}}(o,\jmath) \oplus \mathfrak{J}_{\ell-,\jmath-}^{\curlywedge,\rtimes}\tilde{\mathfrak{X}}(o,\imath)\right] \\
\leq_F\ & \frac{\Gamma(\curlywedge+1)}{16\left[\ln\frac{\ell}{o}\right]^{\curlywedge}} \odot \left[\mathfrak{J}_{o+}^{\curlywedge}\mathscr{H}(\ell,\imath) \oplus \mathfrak{J}_{o+}^{\curlywedge}\mathscr{H}(\ell,\jmath) \oplus \mathfrak{J}_{\ell-}^{\curlywedge}\mathscr{H}(o,\imath) \oplus \mathfrak{J}_{\ell-}^{\curlywedge}\mathscr{H}(o,\jmath)\right] \\
&\oplus \frac{\Gamma(\rtimes+1)}{16\left[\ln\frac{\jmath}{\imath}\right]^{\rtimes}} \odot \left[\mathfrak{J}_{\imath+}^{\rtimes}\tilde{\mathfrak{D}}(o,\jmath) \oplus \mathfrak{J}_{\imath+}^{\rtimes}\tilde{\mathfrak{D}}(\ell,\jmath) \oplus \mathfrak{J}_{\jmath-}^{\rtimes}\tilde{\mathfrak{D}}(o,\imath) \oplus \mathfrak{J}_{\jmath-}^{\rtimes}\tilde{\mathfrak{D}}(\ell,\imath)\right] \\
\leq_F\ & \frac{\tilde{\mathfrak{S}}(o,\imath)\oplus\tilde{\mathfrak{S}}(o,\jmath)\oplus\tilde{\mathfrak{S}}(\ell,\imath)\oplus\tilde{\mathfrak{S}}(\ell,\jmath)}{4}
\end{aligned}
$$

Corollary 7. *Assuming the conditions of Theorem 5 hold, setting $\mathfrak{g}(v) = \frac{v^{\rho}}{\rho}$ and $\ltimes(r) = \frac{r^{\sigma}}{\sigma}$ yields the following inequalities for the F·N · V-Katugampola fractional double integrals:*

$$
\begin{aligned}
&\tilde{\mathfrak{S}}\left(\tfrac{o+\ell}{2}, \tfrac{\imath+\jmath}{2}\right) \\
\leq_F\ & \frac{\Gamma(\curlywedge+1)\rho^{\curlywedge}}{8\left[\ell^{\rho}-o^{\rho}\right]^{\curlywedge}} \odot \left[{}^{\rho}\mathbb{I}_{o+}^{\curlywedge}\mathscr{H}\left(\ell, \tfrac{\imath+\jmath}{2}\right) \oplus {}^{\rho}\mathbb{I}_{\ell-}^{\curlywedge}\mathscr{H}\left(o, \tfrac{\imath+\jmath}{2}\right)\right] \oplus \frac{\Gamma(\rtimes+1)\sigma^{\rtimes}}{8\left[\jmath^{\sigma}-\imath^{\sigma}\right]^{\rtimes}} \odot \left[{}^{\sigma}\mathbb{I}_{\imath+}^{\rtimes}\tilde{\mathfrak{D}}\left(\tfrac{o+\ell}{2}, \jmath\right) \oplus {}^{\sigma}\mathbb{I}_{\jmath-}^{\rtimes}\tilde{\mathfrak{D}}\left(\tfrac{o+\ell}{2}, \imath\right)\right] \\
\leq_F\ & \frac{\Gamma(\curlywedge+1)\Gamma(\rtimes+1)\rho^{\curlywedge}\sigma^{\rtimes}}{16\left[\ell^{\rho}-o^{\rho}\right]^{\curlywedge}\left[\jmath^{\sigma}-\imath^{\sigma}\right]^{\rtimes}} \odot \left[{}^{\rho,\sigma}\mathbb{I}_{o+,\imath+}^{\curlywedge,\rtimes}\tilde{\mathfrak{X}}(\ell,\jmath) \oplus {}^{\rho,\sigma}\mathbb{I}_{o+,\jmath-}^{\curlywedge,\rtimes}\tilde{\mathfrak{X}}(\ell,\imath) \oplus {}^{\rho,\sigma}\mathbb{I}_{\ell-,\imath+}^{\curlywedge,\rtimes}\tilde{\mathfrak{X}}(o,\jmath) \oplus {}^{\rho,\sigma}\mathbb{I}_{\ell-,\jmath-}^{\curlywedge,\rtimes}\tilde{\mathfrak{X}}(o,\imath)\right] \\
\leq_F\ & \frac{\Gamma(\curlywedge+1)\rho^{\curlywedge}\sigma^{\rtimes}}{16\left[\ell^{\rho}-o^{\rho}\right]^{\curlywedge}} \odot \left[{}^{\rho}\mathbb{I}_{o+}^{\curlywedge}\mathscr{H}(\ell,\imath) \oplus {}^{\rho}\mathbb{I}_{o+}^{\curlywedge}\mathscr{H}(\ell,\jmath) \oplus {}^{\rho}\mathbb{I}_{\ell-}^{\curlywedge}\mathscr{H}(o,\imath) \oplus {}^{\rho}\mathbb{I}_{\ell-}^{\curlywedge}\mathscr{H}(o,\jmath)\right] \\
&\oplus \frac{\Gamma(\rtimes+1)\rho^{\curlywedge}\sigma^{\rtimes}}{16\left[\jmath^{\sigma}-\imath^{\sigma}\right]^{\rtimes}} \odot \left[{}^{\sigma}\mathbb{I}_{\imath+}^{\rtimes}\tilde{\mathfrak{D}}(o,\jmath) \oplus {}^{\sigma}\mathbb{I}_{\imath+}^{\rtimes}\tilde{\mathfrak{D}}(\ell,\jmath) \oplus {}^{\sigma}\mathbb{I}_{\jmath-}^{\rtimes}\tilde{\mathfrak{D}}(o,\imath) \oplus {}^{\sigma}\mathbb{I}_{\jmath-}^{\rtimes}\tilde{\mathfrak{D}}(\ell,\imath)\right] \\
\leq_F\ & \frac{\tilde{\mathfrak{S}}(o,\imath)\oplus\tilde{\mathfrak{S}}(o,\jmath)\oplus\tilde{\mathfrak{S}}(\ell,\imath)\oplus\tilde{\mathfrak{S}}(\ell,\jmath)}{4}.
\end{aligned}
$$

5. Conclusions

In this work, we have developed several weighted $H \cdot H$-type inequalities within the framework of $F{\cdot}N \cdot V$-convex and $F{\cdot}N \cdot V$-coordinated convex mappings. By employing differentiable $F{\cdot}N \cdot V$-functions together with appropriate weighting schemes, we derived new inclusions that extend classical $H \cdot H$-inequalities to a more general fuzzy setting using different fuzzy fractional integrals. This approach provides a flexible and robust method for handling uncertainty and imprecision inherent in many real-world and mathematical problems. Furthermore, a number of meaningful special cases of the main results were examined, demonstrating that the established inequalities unify and generalize several well-known results involving Riemann–Liouville-type fractional integrals and loga-

https://doi.org/10.3390/fractalfract10040228

rithmic integral operators. These special cases highlight the effectiveness of generalized fractional integrals in the $F{\cdot}N \cdot V$-framework and illustrate the broad applicability of the obtained results.

The findings presented in this paper contribute to the ongoing development of fuzzy analysis and fractional inequality theory. Future research may focus on extending the proposed inclusions to other generalized notions of convexity, such as strongly convex, s-convex, or preinvex $F{\cdot}N \cdot V$-functions, as well as exploring additional classes of fractional operators. Such investigations may lead to further refinements and new applications of $H \cdot H$-type inequalities in fuzzy mathematics and related fields.

Author Contributions: Conceptualization, Y.S.; methodology, J.E.M.-D. and A.G.; software, Y.S., L.C. and A.G.; validation, Y.S. and A.A.; formal analysis, J.E.M.-D. and A.G.; investigation, J.E.M.-D.; resources, Y.S. and L.C.; data curation, Y.S. and L.C.; writing—original draft preparation, Y.S.; writing—review and editing, Y.S.; visualization, Y.S. and L.C.; supervision, A.A.; project administration, J.E.M.-D.; funding acquisition, Y.S. All authors have read and agreed to the published version of the manuscript.

Funding: This research was funded by the Deanship of Postgraduate Studies and Scientific Research at Majmaah University through the project number (R-2026-2435).

Data Availability Statement: All original contributions presented in this study are contained within the article. Further inquiries may be addressed to the corresponding author.

Acknowledgments: The author extends the appreciation to the Deanship of Postgraduate Studies and Scientific Research at Majmaah University for funding this research work through the project number (R-2026-2435). The authors also would like to express their sincere thanks the the referee for the useful comments and suggestion in preparing this manuscript.

Conflicts of Interest: The authors declare no conflicts of interest.

Abbreviations

The following abbreviations are used in this manuscript:

$F{\cdot}N$	Fuzzy-number
$F{\cdot}N \cdot V$	Fuzzy-number-valued
$H \cdot H$	Hermite–Hadamard
$I \cdot V$	Interval-valued

References

1. Dragomir, S.S.; Pearce, C.E.M. *Selected Topics on Hermite–Hadamard Inequalities and Applications*; RGMIA Monographs, Victoria University: Melbourne, Australia, 2000.
2. Pečarić, J.E.; Proschan, F.; Tong, Y.L. *Convex Functions, Partial Orderings and Statistical Applications*; Academic Press: Boston, MA, USA, 1992.
3. Chen, F. A note on Hermite–Hadamard inequalities for products of convex functions. *J. Appl. Math.* **2013**, *2013*, 935020. [CrossRef]
4. Pavić, Z. Improvements of the Hermite–Hadamard inequality. *J. Inequal. Appl.* **2015**, *2015*, 222. [CrossRef]
5. Moore, R.E. *Interval Analysis*; Prentice-Hall: Englewood Cliffs, NJ, USA, 1966.
6. Moore, R.E.; Kearfott, R.B.; Cloud, M.J. *Introduction to Interval Analysis*; SIAM: Philadelphia, PA, USA, 2009.
7. Alefeld, G.; Herzberger, J. *Introduction to Interval Computations*; Academic Press: New York, NY, USA, 1983.
8. Neumaier, A. *Interval Methods for Systems of Equations*; Cambridge University Press: Cambridge, UK, 1990.
9. Hansen, E.R.; Walster, G.W. *Global Optimization Using Interval Analysis*, 2nd ed.; CRC Press: Boca Raton, FL, USA, 2004.
10. Jaulin, L.; Kieffer, M.; Didrit, O.; Walter, E. *Applied Interval Analysis*; Springer: London, UK, 2001.
11. Kulisch, U.; Miranker, W. *Computer Arithmetic in Theory and Practice*; Academic Press: New York, NY, USA, 1981.
12. Kaucher, E. Interval analysis in the extended interval space IR. *Comput. Suppl.* **1980**, *2*, 33–49.
13. Sadowska, E. Hadamard inequality and a refinement of Jensen inequality for set-valued functions. *Results Math.* **1997**, *32*, 332–337. [CrossRef]

 https://doi.org/10.3390/fractalfract10040228

14. Jleli, M.; Samet, B. On Hermite–Hadamard type inequalities via fractional integrals of a function with respect to another function. *J. Nonlinear Sci. Appl.* **2016**, *9*, 1252–1260. [CrossRef]
15. Tunc, T. Hermite–Hadamard type inequalities for interval-valued fractional integrals with respect to another function. *Math. Slovaca* **2022**, *72*, 1501–1512. [CrossRef]
16. Zhao, D.; Ali, M.A.; Murtaza, G. On the Hermite–Hadamard inequalities for interval-valued coordinated convex functions. *Adv. Differ. Equ.* **2020**, *2020*, 570. [CrossRef]
17. Budak, H.; Agarwal, P. On Hermite–Hadamard-type inequalities for coordinated convex mappings utilizing generalized fractional integrals. In *Advanced Theory and Applications of Fractional Calculus*; Springer: Cham, Switzerland, 2018; pp. 227–249.
18. Lupulescu, V. Fractional calculus for interval-valued functions. *Fuzzy Sets Syst.* **2015**, *265*, 63–85. [CrossRef]
19. Budak, H.; Kara, H.; Ali, M.A.; Khan, S.; Chu, Y. Fractional Hermite–Hadamard-type inequalities for interval-valued coordinated convex functions. *Open Math.* **2021**, *19*, 1081–1097. [CrossRef]
20. Kara, H.; Ali, M.A.; Budak, H. Hermite–Hadamard-type inequalities for interval-valued coordinated convex functions involving generalized fractional integrals. *Math. Methods Appl. Sci.* **2021**, *44*, 104–123. [CrossRef]
21. Zadeh, L.A. Fuzzy sets. *Inf. Control* **1965**, *8*, 338–353. [CrossRef]
22. Diamond, P.; Kloeden, P.E. *Metric Spaces of Fuzzy Sets: Theory and Applications*; World Scientific: Singapore, 1994.
23. Rojas-Medar, M.A.; Jiménez-Gamero, M.D.; Chalco-Cano, Y.; Viera-Brandão, A.J. Fuzzy quasilinear spaces and applications. *Fuzzy Sets Syst.* **2005**, *152*, 173–190. [CrossRef]
24. Kaleva, O. Fuzzy differential equations. *Fuzzy Sets Syst.* **1987**, *24*, 301–317. [CrossRef]
25. Chalco-Cano, Y.; Román-Flores, H. On new solutions of fuzzy differential equations. *Chaos Solitons Fractals* **2008**, *38*, 112–119. [CrossRef]
26. Zhang, D.; Guo, C. Fuzzy integrals of set-valued mappings and fuzzy mappings. *Fuzzy Sets Syst.* **1995**, *75*, 237–241. [CrossRef]
27. Saeed, T.; Cătaş, A.; Khan, M.B.; Alshehri, A.M. Some new fractional inequalities for coordinated convexity over convex sets pertaining to fuzzy-number-valued settings governed by fractional integrals. *Fractal Fract.* **2023**, *7*, 856. [CrossRef]
28. Khan, M.B.; Mohammed, P.O.; Noor, M.A.; Abualnaja, K.M. Fuzzy integral inequalities on coordinates of convex fuzzy interval-valued functions. *Math. Biosci. Eng.* **2021**, *18*, 6552–6580. [CrossRef]
29. Osuna-Gómez, R.; Jiménez-Gamero, M.D.; Chalco-Cano, Y.; Rojas-Medar, M.A. Hadamard and Jensen inequalities for s-convex fuzzy processes. In *Soft Methodology and Random Information Systems*; Springer: Berlin/Heidelberg, Germany, 2004; pp. 645–652.
30. Khan, M.B.; Noor, M.A.; Abdeljawad, T.; Mousa, A.A.A.; Abdalla, B.; Alghamdi, S.M. LR-preinvex interval-valued functions and Riemann–Liouville fractional integral inequalities. *Fractal Fract.* **2021**, *5*, 243. [CrossRef]
31. Khan, M.B.; Srivastava, H.M.; Mohammed, P.O.; Guirao, J.L.; Jawa, T.M. Fuzzy-interval inequalities for generalized preinvex fuzzy interval-valued functions. *Math. Biosci. Eng.* **2022**, *19*, 812–835. [CrossRef]
32. Zabandan, G. An extension and refinement of Hermite–Hadamard inequality and related results. *Int. J. Nonlinear Anal. Appl.* **2020**, *11*, 379–390.
33. Sarıkaya, M.Z.; Kılıçer, D. On the extension of Hermite–Hadamard type inequalities for coordinated convex mappings. *Turk. J. Math.* **2021**, *45*, 2731–2745. [CrossRef]
34. Khan, M.B.; Mohammed, P.O.; Noor, M.A.; Hamed, Y.S. New Hermite–Hadamard inequalities in fuzzy-interval fractional calculus and related inequalities. *Symmetry* **2021**, *13*, 673. [CrossRef]

 https://doi.org/10.3390/fractalfract10040228

MDPI AG
Grosspeteranlage 5
4052 Basel
Switzerland
Tel.: +41 61 683 77 34

Fractal and Fractional Editorial Office
E-mail: fractalfract@mdpi.com
www.mdpi.com/journal/fractalfract

www.ingramcontent.com/pod-product-compliance
Lightning Source LLC
Chambersburg PA
CBHW040745250926
51850CB00007BB/1409
9783725878833